Handbook of Demonstrations and Activities in the Teaching of Psychology

Second Edition

Volume 3

Personality, Abnormal, Clinical-Counseling and Social

Edited by

Mark E. Ware
Creighton University

David E. Johnson
John Brown University

 LAWRENCE ERLBAUM ASSOCIATES, PUBLISHERS
2000   Mahwah, New Jersey   London

Lawrence Erlbaum Associates, Inc., Publishers
10 Industrial Avenue
Mahwah, New Jersey 07430

Library of Congress Cataloging-in-Publication Data

Handbook of demonstrations and activities in the teaching of psychology / edited by
Mark E. Ware, David E. Johnson.-- 2nd ed.
    p.   cm.
  Includes bibliographical references and index.
  Contents: v. 1. Introductory, statistics, research methods, and history – v. 2.
Physiological-comparative, perception, learning, cognitive, and developmental – v. 3.
Personality, abnormal, clinical-counseling, and social.
  ISBN 0-8058-3048-0 (set : alk. paper) –ISBN 0-8058-3045-6 (v. 1 : alk. paper) –
ISBN 0-8058-3046-4 (v. 2 : alk. paper) – ISBN 0-8058-3047-2 (v. 3 : alk. paper)
    1. Psychology–Study and teaching (Higher) 2. Psychology–Study and teaching–
Activity programs. 3. Psychology–Study and teaching–Simulation methods. 4.
Psychology–Study and teaching–Audio-visual methods. I. Ware, Mark E. II. Johnson,
David E., 1953-

BF77.H265 1999
150'.71'1–dc21
                                                                99-056223

Printed in the United States of America

10 9 8 7 6 5 4 3 2 1

Dedicated to

Charles L. Brewer

teacher, colleague, and friend

Table of Contents

4. Examining Miscellaneous Issues

Section III: Clinical-Counseling

1. Learning Concepts and Principles

2. Acquiring Skills - Undergraduate Students

3. Acquiring Skills - Graduate Students

4. Treating Fears

5. Advocating a Research Perspective

Section IV: Social

1. Focusing on Experimentation

2. Emphasizing Writing in Social Psychology

3. Illustrating Concepts in Social Perception and Social Cognition

4. Demonstrating Bias in Social Perception and Social Cognition

5. Teaching about Attitudes and Persuasion

6. Exploring about Aggression

Preface

In the preface to this book's first edition, we provided a brief historical context for publishing a collection of teaching demonstrations and activities. Before summarizing those remarks, we would like to point out that an additional motivation for producing a second edition was to document and celebrate the silver anniversary year (1998) of *Teaching of Psychology* (*ToP*), the official journal of the Society for the Teaching of Psychology (STP), Division Two of the American Psychological Association.

Since its inception in 1974, *ToP* has become increasingly respected as a journal devoted to improving teaching and learning at all educational levels. An article (Weimer, 1993) in *Change* featured three from among almost 50 pedagogical journals; *ToP* was one of those three. Readers, who are interested in a history of the journal, will find the founding editor's personal account (Daniel, 1992) both stimulating and informative.

The journal's history was preceded by almost a century of psychologists' interest in teaching. For example, G. Stanley Hall, one of modern psychology's promoters, devoted considerable attention to teaching-learning processes. Hall's (1905) analysis concluded that a goal of pedagogy was to "unfold all the powers of the individual to their maximal maturity and strength" (p. 375). In earlier writing about pedagogy, Hall (1881) commented that "reverence of knowledge for its own sake is superstitious. Ignorance is preferable to knowledge which does not affect life, and the object of discipline is to make it practical" (p. 321). Hall's comments predated more recent writing about active learning.

At the National Conference on Enhancing the Quality of Undergraduate Education in Psychology, one committee discussed the use of pedagogical techniques called active learning. The committee's observation (Mathie, 1993) that "there is too much information being offered to students and too little attention being paid to the strategies for learning, inquiry, and problem solving" (p. 184) seemed to reiterate and operationalize Hall's insight. Thus for over a century, psychologists have recognized that effective teaching and learning consist of developing and applying students' skills. Because effective teaching strategies are never out of vogue, the present book consists of a collection of tried and tested teaching demonstrations and activities.

ToP previously published all of the articles in this book. We reviewed articles published from 1985 through 1998, *ToP*'s silver anniversary year, and excluded from consideration over 100 excellent articles about teaching psychology that were not directly related to the 13 topics in this book. Examples of excluded topics are cross-cultural, sports, and industrial/organizational psychology, as well as psychological testing, human sexuality, psychology and the law, and writing across the curriculum.

We organized 291 articles, the same number as in the first edition, into three volumes. Overall, 56% of the articles did not appear in the first edition. Volume 1 consists of 97 articles about teaching strategies for courses that make up the core of most psychology curricula; introductory psychology, statistics, research methods, and history of psychology. Topical headings in Volumes 2 and 3 reflect the content and order of topics in many introductory psychology texts. Volume 2 consists of 99 articles about teaching physiological-comparative, perception, learning, cognitive, and developmental psychology. Volume 3 consists of 95 articles about teaching personality, abnormal, clinical-counseling, and social psychology. The percent of articles representing each of the 13 topical areas was about evenly distributed. Noteworthy exceptions were the topics of research methods (18%), social (18%), and developmental (13%)

In general, we assigned articles to the course names in which authors developed the demonstration or activity. A table at the end of each volume identifies the primary course in which readers might use each demonstration. For more than half of the articles, we also identified other (secondary) courses in which readers might use demonstrations. For almost 25% of the articles, we identified more than one additional course for using the activity.

A few months before this book was published, psychology educators met in a national forum called Psychology Partnership Project (P3) at James Madison University. In part, the P3's mission was to "identify, establish, and nurture partnerships [promoting] the teaching of psychology . . . ." Several discussion points (e.g., research, curriculum, faculty development, and instructional technology) bear directly on improving pedagogy. P3 participants and contributors to this book share a common commitment to fostering excellence in teaching. In recognition for that commitment, all royalties from the sale of this book will be paid directly to STP and earmarked for promoting the laudable activities of its Fund for Excellence

Mark E. Ware
David E. Johnson

References

Daniel, R. S. (1992). *Teaching of Psychology*, the journal. In A. E. Puente, J. R. Matthews, & C. L. Brewer (Eds.), *Teaching psychology in America: A history* (pp. 433-452). Washington, DC: American Psychological Association.

Hall, G. S. (1881). American and German methods of teaching. *The Harvard Register, 3,* 319-321.

Hall, G. S. (1905). What is pedagogy? *Pedagogical Seminary, 12,* 375-383.

Mathie, V. A. (with Beins, B., Benjamin, Jr., L. T., Ewing, M. M., Hall, C. C. I., Henderson, B., McAdam, D. W., & Smith, R. A.). (1993). Promoting active learning in psychology courses. In T. V. McGovern (Ed.). *Handbook for enhancing undergraduate education in psychology* (pp. 183-214). Washington, DC: American Psychological Association.

Weimer, M. (1993, November-December). The disciplinary journals on pedagogy. *Change,* 44-51.

SECTION I:
PERSONALITY

Discovering Students' Perspectives

Alvin Wang developed a 9-item implicit personality theory (IPT) scale to demonstrate the naive, lay beliefs students have regarding the construct of personality. Students completed the IPT Scale during Week 1 and Week 16 in a personality course. Comparison of Week 1 and Week 16 scores indicated that individual IPTs were resistant to change. Pedagogically, these results demonstrate the role of IPTs in the construction and validation of explicit personality theories. Also, class discussion on topics such as individual differences, attribution theory, self-serving bias, and personal constructs were enhanced when students' IPTs were made explicit.

Dana Anderson, Paul Rosenfeld, and Lori Cruikshank pointed out that despite its recent growth, implicit psychology is largely excluded from undergraduate personality textbooks. Students' preconceptions about personality likely bias their evaluation of formal personality theories and are generally ignored by personality instructors. The authors presented an exercise that required students to critique their preconceived beliefs about personality as if these beliefs constituted formal personality theories. Students rated the assignment as difficult but thought-provoking and valuable for the insight it gave them into the formal theories and their own beliefs.

With the goal of increasing students' awareness of their own implicit theories of personality, Marlowe Embree had them complete an 18-item questionnaire about various issues in personality. The instructor completed the questionnaire four times, each time taking the role of a prototypical figure in personality theory (Skinner, Freud, Rogers, and Glasser). In class, the instructor compared student responses to the prototypes and discussed the class's perspectives on the issues.

To make personality psychology personally involving, Dana Dunn developed an exercise based on imagoes, the characters that McAdams (1985, 1993) argued dominate life stories and personal myths. An imago is an idealized and personified self-concept we form in early or midadulthood. Broader than roles played in daily life, imagoes serve a unifying function: to make our stories and myths coherent. While keeping a journal, students identified individual myths and major life events, and then they wrote about the imagoes most frequently used to make sense out of their lives.

Jane Einhorn designed an activity in which students used their own experience to develop a distinction between self and personality; the author characterized the former as more central and the latter as more peripheral. The instructor had students identify their favorite color, song, flower, smell, scene, person, and food. She then instructed students to identify whether each item reflected self or personality. Almost all students identified the scene as a reflection of self and the other a reflection of personality. The instructor also had students discuss which answers their best friends had known and which they had not. The results led to some interesting revelations.

Exploring Theories

Marianne Miserandino designed an exercise to help students appreciate the extent of Sigmund Freud's influence on modern American culture. Students indicated their agreement or disagreement with 15 statements reflecting a traditional Freudian perspective. Statements and students' responses were the catalyst for a discussion of psychoanalytic principles and Freudian influence. Students in graduate and undergraduate psychology classes found the exercise to be thought provoking, helpful, and useful in making them aware of Freud's influence on American culture.

Gordon Bear described a humorous slip of the tongue incident that afforded a vivid introduction to personality theories. Interpretations consisted of classic Freudian thinking, a contemporary psychodynamic perspective, and two cognitive models that view the slip as unmotivated.

To facilitate the learning of theoretical principles associated with a psychoanalytic perspective on personality, Janet Carlson devised a board game called *Psychosexual Pursuit*. Student teams competed against each other to complete their psychosexual development while retaining considerable psychic energy to invest in adult concerns. The author described the rules governing play and special advantages of this learning experience. The article contains a reproduction of the game board.

Using a component of Kelly's theory of personal constructs, dichotomous templates, Mitchell Handelsman developed an exercise to increase the students' abstract and relational thinking skills. The instructor identified personality concepts (e.g., id, ego, superego) and asked students to construe them, that is to identify how two of the concepts were similar to each other and different from the third, using some important dimension. Working in small groups, students construed several sets of three or more concepts. The author pointed out that such an exercise encouraged students to familiarize themselves more thoroughly with definitions of terms because of the exercise's challenge.

To help them understand Maslow's construct of peak experiences, James Polyson directed students to write about their own experiences. An additional goal was to help students develop their writing skills. Although the author used this exercise in introductory psychology, it has direct application in personality classes. Student evaluations confirmed the activity was successful and pointed out some potential problems.

Richard Logan described how he used "Three Approaches to Psychotherapy" as a case study for interpreting each client's personality from various theoretical perspectives. The author reported that students sensed that they participated in a dialectical process involving competing approaches to personality.

Emphasizing Writing

Susan Mueller (née Susan Cloninger) described a method in which students wrote papers using different theories of personality to understand the published biography or autobiography of a real person. The instructor provided questions to guide discussion and written assignments that related text material to the term paper. According to the author, advantages of this method were its intrinsic interest to students, its breadth of scope within a liberal arts framework, and its effectiveness in fostering critical thinking and classroom discussion.

Janet Carlson's students wrote four short papers, each interpreting the personality of a fictional character from a comic strip or children's story by using a specific theoretical orientation; psychoanalytic, dispositional, phenomenological, and behavioral. The author discussed advantages of this technique as well as student evaluations.

Susan Beers developed an exercise in asking questions as preparation for writing essays. The goal of the exercise was to encourage students to analyze and evaluate personality theories. Students wrote questions that they discussed and classified according to Bloom's taxonomy. Twice during the term students chose questions to develop into essays and students discussed rough drafts of the essays in small groups. The proportion of evaluative questions that students wrote increased during the term. A questionnaire administered at the end of the term indicated that 90% of the students viewed the exercise positively.

1. DISCOVERING STUDENTS' PERSPECTIVES

Making Implicit Personality Theories Explicit: A Classroom Demonstration

Alvin Y. Wang
University of Central Florida

The concept of implicit personality theory (IPT) refers to the everyday unscientific belie& that people have concerning personality (Cloninger, 1993). IPTs allow people to form social inferences based on the limited amount of information they have about others as well as themselves (Bruner & Tagiuri, 1954; Schneider, 1973). With the ascendance of cognitive psychology in the 1960s, the notion of IPTs has been a topic of interest to cognitive-social researchers (Schneider, 1973). For instance, the notion of IPT is invoked to explain two ubiquitous phenomena: the general bias in judgments exhibited toward others (e.g., stereotyping and prejudice) and individual differences in person perception (e.g., impression formation). Also, recent reports indicate that people who possess static, rigid IPTs tend to make dispositional attributions regarding the actions of others. In contrast, people who hold fluid IPTs believe that traits are malleable and that individuals can change over time (Dweck, Hong, & Chiu, 1993).

Nevertheless, the study of IPTs is largely omitted from undergraduate courses on personality because of the traditional emphasis on explicit (i.e., formal) theories of personality (Anderson, Rosenfeld, & Cruikshank, 1994; Embree, 1986). Another reason for this unfortunate omission of IPT from class discussion is that lay preconceptions of personality tend to lack the scope, precision, and articulation of formal personality theories (Anderson et al., 1994; Embree, 1986). However, disregarding the role of IPTs obscures the fact that the construction and validation of explicit theories in the social sciences are not immune from IPTs. Indeed, "the concept of IPT implies that we bring preconceptions to the formal study of personality" (Cloninger, 1993, p. 20). In this view, students' understanding of explicit personality theories will benefit from an appreciation of the role of IPTs when examining explicit theories of personality. Pedagogically, an in-class demonstration of IPTs will also help students resolve the familiar ques tion, "How did this theorist (e.g., Freud) come up with the ideas for his/her theory?" Moreover, by making their own IPTs explicit, students can account for why they typically display a preference for one explicit theoretical perspective over another.

There have been previous attempts to investigate the IPTs of psychology students. Embree (1986) reported an in-class demonstration of IPTs with 10 American college students. However, because the ideas compared in his questionnaire were theoretically advanced, there was the "danger that students would be unable to respond meaningfully to the questionnaire before taking the class" (p.79). The consequence is that Embree's measure can not assess the IPTs of students until they are familiar with explicit theories of personality. One other attempt at assessing the IPTs of undergraduates involved Finnish college students (Kalliopuska, 1985). However, this study did not provide any description of the psychometric properties of the IPT instrument used.

This study had three goals. The primary purpose of this study was to develop a survey that demonstrates to psychology students the existence of their own IPTs. Because the primary goal of this IPT scale was pedagogical; brevity, clarity, and ease-of-scoring were crucial to the scale's development. A second objective of this study was to determine linkages between individual IPTs and student preferences for explicit theories of personality. The third purpose of the study was to assess the extent to which IPTs change as students learn various explicit theories of personality.

Method

The Course

Students enrolled in an upper-level Personality Theories class completed the IPT scale twice: during Week 1 and Week 16 of the semester. General Psychology was the only course prerequisite for enrollment and virtually all students were psychology majors. The mandatory reading assignments were from Cloninger (1993), and eight formal theories comprised the semester's discussion: psychoanalytic, analytical, interpersonal psychoanalysis, psychosocial, humanistic, behavioral, trait-type, and cognitive social theory. Complete data sets were obtained from 162 students (96 women and 66 men). The mean age of the participants was 22.3 years.

Course Purpose

The purpose of the course was to introduce students to the theories and research that form the basis of the psychological study of personality. The intent was to encourage students to evaluate critically each theoretical perspective rather than to adopt unconditionally the position of each theorist. Hence, the instructor discussed each theory in a balanced fashion by having students consider its strengths and weaknesses. The expectation was that by the end of the semester, students could form their own conclusions regarding the merits and limitations of each theory.

IPT Scale

The scale's language reflects the "folk wisdom" or "naive theories" that are the basis for people's IPTs. In a prior class on personality theories, I collected students' statements on their views of personality when the semester began. These statements formed the basis for the IPT scale reported here. Table 1 shows the final version of the nine-item IPT scale. Using a forced-choice format, students chose between the paired-belief statements ("a" or "b") for each of the items. For example, in item 1 students chose between: (a) I believe that "actions speak louder than words" or (b) If I want to get to know someone, I listen to what they have to say. Typically, students did not need more than 5 min to complete the IPT scale.

Theory Preference Scale

During the last class period (Week 16) students received an 8-item, Likert-type rating scale in which they rated the extent to which they agreed or disagreed with each of the theoretical perspectives discussed during the semester. Each of the eight theories discussed was rated along a 5-point Likert type scale from 0 (*strongly disagree*) to 4 (*strongly agree*). After they completed the theory preference scale, I gave the IPT scale a second time.[1]

Results

To demonstrate the existence of their IPTs, I examined student responses with respect to any preferences or biases they displayed toward items on the IPT scale. Table 2 shows the percentage of students choosing the "a" statements of the IPT scale items on Week 1 and Week 16. Inspection of the pattern of Week 1 data suggests some definite preferences (i.e., commonality) in students' IPTs prior to discussion of explicit theories of personality. That is, students generally believed in the distinctiveness of individuals (item 2b) and the importance of learning (item 5b). In addition, students tended to believe in the complexity of people (item 7a) and the existence of unconscious motives (item 6a).

To more fully understand the psychometric properties of the IPT scale, I analyzed Week 1 responses to determine the scale's factor structure (see Table 1) . The nine items exhibited acceptable commonality ratings with the other items (multiple $R^2 > .50$). A principal components factor analysis revealed four relatively unique factors that accounted for 65.2% of the total variance. Interpretation of the factors suggested that four dimensions of belief are the basis for students' responses to the IPT scale locus of control, nativism-empiricism, cognitive complexity, and humanism. This pattern of findings suggests that the IPT scale is a multifaceted instrument that probes a variety of theoretical dimensions. Because it is relatively broad in scope, it can be a useful pedagogical tool for revealing the diversity of students' lay beliefs regarding the construct of personality. Additionally, because items on the IPT scale exclude jargon or reference to explicit theories of personality, it can be administered to students who have not yet received any formal instruction in personality theory. In this way, student preference for particular IPTs can be shown in a way that circumvents the limitations of Embree's (1986) instrument.

Regarding the second issue under investigation, there was evidence that by Week 16, relations existed between students' IPTs and their preference for particular explicit theories of personality. Students' belief that "people are what they are" largely because of inborn characteristics (item 5a) was most highly correlated with a preference for trait-type theory, $r(150) = .30$, $p < .005$. The belief that the behavior of humans largely follows the same laws that govern the behavior of other animals (item 9a) correlated with a preference for behaviorism, $r(150) = .19$, $p < .02$. This pattern of results gives evidence for the construct validity of the IPT scale.

The third issue under investigation concerned the temporal stability of students' IPTs. The right column of Table 2 shows the percentage of responses that did not change after 16 weeks. This percentage was quite high: Across all items, an average of 77.9% of the responses ("a" or "b") did not change. From a psychometric standpoint, this degree of temporal consistency suggests that the IPT scale exhibits acceptable test-retest reliability.

Although I did not directly assess student impressions of the IPT scale, I gave a course evaluation to students at the end of the semester. One survey item asked students whether they agreed with the statement "the personality tests given in class were useful in helping me understand the reading material." A total of 94% of the students

---

[1]A legitimate question is whether responses to the theory preference scale may influence responses to the implicit personality theory (IPT) scale during Week 16. However, most Week 1 choices on the IPT scale (77.9%) remained unchanged by Week 16 (see Table 2). This high degree of test-retest reliability suggests that the effect of the theory preference scale on the IPT scale was minimal.

Table 1. Sorted and Rotated Factor Loadings of the Nine IPT Scale Items Using Student Responses From Week 1.

IPT Scale Item	Factor 1	Factor 2	Factor 3	Factor 4
1. (a) I believe that "actions speak louder than words." (b) If I want to get to know someone, I listen to what they have to say.	.79	.00	.00	.00
2. (a) I believe that psychological theory should emphasize the commonality of all people regardless of their backgrounds or upbringing. (b) I believe that psychological theory should emphasize the distinctiveness and uniqueness of all people—psychology should try to understand what makes individuals different from one another.	.69	.00	.00	.00
3. (a) I believe that people exist because of some "higher purpose." (b) There is no such thing as a "higher purpose," and even if there is, humans can never know what it might be.	.00	.69	.00	.00
4. (a) Ultimately, I believe that the study of personality should strive to be a highly quantifiable and objective science like physics or biology. (b) Ultimately, I believe that the study of personality should strive to be a highly intuitive and subjective discipline like art or music.	.00	−.67	.00	.00
5. (a) "People are what they are" largely because they are born with certain characteristics and tendencies. (b) "People are what they are" largely because of the learning and socialization they experience.	.00	.00	.83	.00
6. (a) Virtually all human behaviors, thoughts, and feelings are influenced by the unconscious. (b) There is no such thing as the unconscious—even if it does exist, it can not be studied by psychologists.	.00	.38	.66	.00
7. (a) People are extremely complex to understand, because at any time their actions are due to several different motives. (b) People are fairly simple to understand, because at any time their actions are due only to a few basic motives.	.00	.00	.00	.73
8. (a) I believe that an individual's personality is flexible and can change throughout life. (b) I believe that an individual's personality is rigid and does not change all that much.	.32	.00	−.27	.55
9. (a) The behavior of humans largely follows the same laws and principles that govern the behavior of other animals like dogs and cats. (b) The behavior of humans can not be reduced to the laws and principles that govern the behavior of other animals like dogs and cats.	−.32	.42	.00	.51

Note. IPT = implicit personality theory.

agreed or strongly agreed with this statement. Also, the instructor noted that some of the liveliest class discussions occurred when students provided rationales for their responses on the IPT scale.

Discussion

Despite the fact that IPTs can influence person perception, social inference, and interpersonal behavior, individuals are rarely "capable of analyzing these [i.e., IPTs] in detail and of actively dealing with them

Table 2. Percentage of "a" Responses Chosen During First and Last Weeks of the Semester and the Percentages of Students Whose IPT Scale Choices Did Not Change Across the Semester

IPT Scale Item	Week 1 (% Choosing "a")	Week 16 (% Choosing "a")	% Unchanged Responses
1	47.9	49.4	73.4
2	9.5	12.3	86.3
3	26.8	27.2	81.7
4	31.4	31.5	71.4
5	12.0	11.7	87.5
6	85.2	78.4	75.3
7	85.8	80.9	82.5
8	24.2	19.1	75.6
9	37.5	32.1	67.3

Note. IPT = implicit personality theory.

cognitively as the basis for [their] appraisals and decisions" (Kalliopuska, 1985, p. 1071). Therefore, I suggest that the IPT scale reported here be given at the beginning of the semester to make explicit the lay belief systems that operate on an implicit level. Pedagogically, this demonstration has at least two merits. First, in a relatively brief and face-valid manner, it encourages students to articulate and understand their preconceptions regarding personality. Second, sharing of students' diverse IPTs in class serves to stimulate discussion regarding the assumptions that form the basis for the construction and validation of explicit theories of personality. For instance, debating their responses on items 5 and 9 allows students to recognize that the positions of nativism and empiricism are theoretical assumptions and not facts. In turn, students should show a greater awareness that these assumptions can form the basis for an explicit (i.e., formal) approach to personality such as trait-type theory (nativism) and behaviorism (empiricism).

By giving the IPT scale again at the end of the semester, class discussion can center on the observation that most students do not readily change their IPTs, even after studying various formal theories of personality. This finding naturally prompts the question as to why IPTs are fairly resistant to change over time. Class discussion that incorporates the topics of self-serving bias and selective information seeking will allow students a means for resolving this issue. The instructor can also steer the discussion toward George Kelly's (1955) theory of personal constructs as well as attribution theory. For example, discussion of Kelly's notion of the choice corollary will allow students to understand individual differences across IPTs. Also, Kelly's belief that people try to find validation for their own personal constructs explains why students' IPTs tend to be stable, even after exposure to several explicit theories of personality.

Finally, insight into the role of IPTs can be a means for attaining closure by the end of the semester. Conceptual closure is encouraged by class discussions that challenge students to evaluate critically which formal theory they are most likely to endorse. For instance, students who prefer the trait-type approach may do so because it more closely matches their personal IPTs compared to other explicit theories of personality (Embree, 1986). In short, the "theories that will be most generally believed, besides offering us objects able to account for our sensible experience . . . [are] also those which appeal urgently to our aesthetic, emotional, and active needs" Cames, 1890/1983, p. 940)

References

Anderson, D. D., Rosenfeld, P., & Cruikshank, L (1994). An exercise for explicating and critiquing students' implicit personality theories. *Teaching of Psychology, 21*, 174-177.

Bruner, J. S., & Tagiuri, R. (1954). The perception of people. In G. Lindzey (Ed.), *Handbook of social psychology* (Vol. 2, pp. 634-654). Reading, MA: AddisonWesley.

Cloninger, S. (1993). *Theories of personality: Understanding persons*. Englewood Cliffs, NJ: Prentice Hall.

Dweck, C. S., Hong, Y., & Chiu, C. (1993). Implicit theories: Individual differences in the likelihood and meaning of dispositional inference. *Personality and Social Psychology Bulletin, 19*, 644 - 656.

Embree, M. C. (1986). Implicit personality theory in the classroom An integrative approach. *Teaching of Psychology, 13*, 78-80.

James, W. (1983). *The principles of psychology*. Cambridge, MA: Harvard University Press. (Original work published 1890)

Kalliopuska, M. (1985). Rationales for an implicit personality theory. *Psychological Reports, 57*, 1071-1076.

Kelly, G. A. (1955). *The psychology of personal constructs*. New York: Norton.

Schneider, D. J. (1973). Implicit personality theory: A review. *Psychological Bulletin, 79*, 294-309.

An Exercise for Explicating and Critiquing Students' Implicit Personality Theories

Dana D. Anderson
Pacific Lutheran University

Paul Rosenfeld
Navy Personnel Research and Development Center San Diego, CA

Lori Cruikshank
Pacific LutheranUniversity

Personality theorists have long studied lay beliefs about personality in part because all professional theorists are also lay theorists. As Monte (1977) indicated, "men and women who create personality theories have sovereign theories of their own. Consequently, some part of each theorist's comprehension of human character is always a reflection of . . . self-comprehension" (p. 171).

Bruner and Tagiuri (1954) introduced the concept of *implicit personality* theory to describe those commonsense but largely unarticulated beliefs held by laypersons regarding interrelations among personality traits. This formulation has broadened to the present-day notion of implicit psychology (Wegner & Vallacher, 1977), which includes laypersons' assumptions about traits, person perception, motivation, causal attribution, psychopathology and most other areas within personality psychology (Feshbach & Weiner, 1991). Despite growing emphasis on implicit psychology within the personality literature, we often ignore our students' preexisting beliefs when teaching them about personality. Furthermore, because implicit theories differ from formal personality theories in scope, precision, and articulation, implicit psychology is largely excluded from undergraduate personality textbooks, even though students' own implicit personality theories can color their perceptions of formal theories (Embree, 1986).

Our students' naive beliefs are not formal theories, but they perform many of the same functions that formal theories serve for personality psychologists (Heider, 1958). Therefore, we consider it vital to their understanding and fair evaluation of formal theories that students in personality courses be aware of their own presumptions about personality. Moreover, their implicit theories presumably underlie much of students' social behavior and may affect their memory and self-concept (Ross, 1989). Therefore, increasing students' ability to examine and explicate their own beliefs seems a worthwhile educational objective.

Exercise Format and Grading Criteria

We use an exercise that requires students to write and critique their own presumptions about personality as if these constituted formal theories. Students examine their theories through a term paper consisting of two drafts. The drafts are preceded by a paragraph, due the third week of class, that summarizes their theories' basic assumptions. This paragraph requires students who often procrastinate on anxiety provoking assignments to start working early on this one. The paragraph also gives us an opportunity to redirect students who have misunderstood this unusual assignment. In the first draft, due at midterm, students present their naive theory: its basic assumptions, structure, and implications. We return this draft with our written critique of the presentation. Students respond in their second draft by clarifying their theory and by conducting their own critique of the theory itself using the textbook's (e.g., Mischel, 1993) standards for evaluating formal personality theories.

Grading criteria for the paper are presented in the course syllabus and discussed in class. These criteria for the first draft include how clearly and coherently the student states the theory's assumptions and how explicitly the student draws the interrelations among these assumptions. Also considered are how coherently the student goes about drawing the theory's empirical and practical implications and how diligent the student is in comparing these to the existing personality research literature. Sample papers, one A and one B paper, are provided with the syllabus.

The second draft is graded according to how much it improves on the first draft in clarity, specificity, and coherence. The second draft's self-critique section is graded according to how skillfully students apply to their own theories the evaluative standards used by the text to continue formal theories. These standards include how coherent and logically consistent the theory is, how well it accounts for individual differences and commonalties in personality, how well it identifies the underlying causes of everyday behavior and provides standards for identifying healthy and pathological behavior, how testable the theory is, its potential utility for research, and how well it fits with the existing research record. In making good use of these evaluative standards, students' critique of their own theory must be clear, thorough, and fair. The grading criteria and evaluation standards we identify provide a structure for our feedback on the first draft. This structuring is helpful because the feedback required is extensive and time-consuming. We find this a worthwhile cost because students generally respond positively to the feedback, often completely revamping their final draft. The latter are usually longer than term papers we receive in other courses. Although the syllabus recommends 8 to 10 pages, second drafts average 15 pages, and one recent complex and well constructed theory was 40 pages. More important, these drafts are generally as much more thoughtful than the norm as they are more lengthy.

We have used this exercise with senior-, junior-, and, more recently, sophomore-level classes with enrollments ranging from 15 to 40. Our impression is that its particular benefits for younger students and non majors lie in increasing their awareness of their own preconceptions about personality and their appreciation of theory building's inherent difficulties. Older students and majors seem the most able to use the assignment to begin their own theory building. They also generally become more astute critics. Given the labor-intensive nature of the assignment, instructors with large sections, especially mixed service-course and major course sections, may wish to use the exercise as an honors assignment for upper level majors.

Potential Problems and Strategies for Solving Them

We have found the two-draft, feedback, and rewrite approach to be useful in teaching students to think and write critically (Baird & Anderson, 1990). This approach is demanding for faculty and students, but it seems especially appropriate for this assignment, because this task can be intellectually difficult and emotionally daunting. The assignment can be intimidating because it requires original theoretical work with which few students have experience. Another problem is that implicit theories are, by definition, largely outside one's awareness, so articulating them is inherently difficult (Bruner & Tagiuri, 1954). With reassurance that we recognize this difficulty and temper our evaluations accordingly, students can, in our experience, formulate and examine their own theories. Following Kelly (1955), we often tell students that a good starting point is to consider what questions they ask themselves when meeting a new acquaintance, because those questions often reflect important dimensions within their implicit theories. A related difficulty is, as Kelly (1955) noted, that one's implicit theory is intensely personal; it reveals much of one's own personality. Hence, students deserve additional reassurance that their confidentiality will be respected and that we are evaluating the quality of their critique, not grading the theory itself.

Besides reassurances, students require some structure to assist them in articulating their beliefs. The course syllabus and textbook provide several dimensions students can use to compare their beliefs to the assumptions held by formal personality theories. Using these dimensions avoids confusing students and provides them with an additional incentive for attending carefully to their textbook. The dimensions include whether a theory is deterministic versus voluntaristic, causal versus teleological, dispositional versus situational, ideograph versus nomothetic, and favorable to nature versus nurture. Other dimensions include the theory's emphasis on conscious versus unconscious processes, whether it posits hedonism versus other factors (e.g., natural selection) as the basic motivational force underlying personality, and its units of analysis (e.g., behaviors, situations, conflicts, and schemata).

Their reactions to the formal theories' assumptions can help students recognize their own positions on these dimensions. For instance, when confronting the situationalist position, our students are often surprised to discover the depth of their theories' commitment to dispositionalism. Many students are startled to find that they agree with Freud's emphases on hedonism when they viscerally reject his theory itself. Furthermore, recognizing such assumptions often makes students aware of the contradictions among their own assumptions. Often, for example, highly dispositional student theories are highly voluntaristic. Recognizing the apparent inconsistency and attempting its resolution can launch a good self-critique. Moreover, some excellent attempts at theory building have begun with a student's realization that teleology, determinism, and testability coexist somewhat uncomfortably within a single theory.

Likewise, self-critiques grow when students recognize, most often after our first-draft feedback, that large chunks of their theories are not integrated or even interconnected. Many times, for instance, their theories propose something like defense mechanisms without relating these to their theories' posited motivational processes or identifying those theoretical constructs that require or provide protection.

During this process, students often discover that they have adopted assumptions from formal theories they have studied. We want students in the syllabus that the theories they present must be truly their own implicit theories and not a hasty patchwork of other theorists' ideas, so students

ask if we consider such adoptions plagiarism. Ordinarily, the upshot of these discussions is that students realize they have modified the borrowed concepts to fit with other parts of their implicit theories or have failed to do so when their theories' logic dictated they should have. Either way, they have additional material for their self-critique and, usually, a heightened appreciation of how all theories rest on their predecessors' shoulders. Students whose first drafts show that they have borrowed too liberally and have provided too little of their own thinking can correct this problem on the second draft.

Implicit theories' assumptions, their strengths and weaknesses, also become clearer as students search for supporting empirical evidence. Often, students realize that the assumptions they have just arduously identified are contradicted by existing research. Our student dispositionalists, for instance, must grapple with a literature that supports the effects of situations complexly interacting with dispositions other than the particular ones endorsed by most student theories. The necessary links between a theory, its testable implications, and its practical applications seem clearer for students who have tested their own cherished beliefs against the research literature.

Through these strategies, the exercise aims to increase students' knowledge and understanding of the classic formal theories' basic structures and expand students' awareness of the personality research literature by making these structures and this literature personally and academically relevant to the students' appreciation of their own beliefs. The syllabus encourages students to follow the strategies, and the bulk of our feedback on their first drafts directs the students in tailoring these strategies to address the particular needs of their own papers. Good second drafts clarify the theories when possible but go on to acknowledge through the students' self-critiques the contradictions and other discovered weaknesses in their theories. Students often have difficulty at first accepting the notion that they will be rewarded for finding something wrong with their theories. They are reassured by reminders that they cannot lose if they examine their theory; they will find either strengths or weaknesses, and finding either strengths or weaknesses will provide material for a good self-critique section in the second draft.

Student Evaluations of the Exercise

We have collected survey data evaluating the exercise from students in two course sections. Using a 5-point scale ranging from *strongly disagree* (1) to *strongly agree* (5), students evaluated the exercise's effectiveness. Abbreviated versions of the survey statements, students' mean ratings, and standard deviations are presented in Table 1.

Students reported that the exercise met our first goal by increasing their understanding of the formal personality theories covered in the course. Most agreed that the exercise improved their grasp of the formal theories'

Table 1. Students' Endorsement of Statements on Personality Theory Paper Exercise

Statement	M	SD
Exercise improved understanding of formal theories' assumptions and logic	3.8	0.9
Improved appreciation of formal problems of theory construction	4.2	0.7
Improved appreciation of formal theories' handling of basic issues	4.0	0.6
Increased awareness of formal theories' internal contradictions	3.8	0.5
Increased awareness of formal theories' practical implications	3.7	0.8
Improved understanding of personality research's importance	3.7	0.8
Improved understanding of personality research's difficulties	4.3	0.6
Improved understanding of own theory's assumptions and logic	3.9	0.9
Increased awareness of own theory's internal contradictions	4.2	0.7
Increased awareness of own theory's practical implications	4.1	0.9
Increased awareness of own beliefs	4.0	1.0
Feedback on draft helped clarify own ideas	4.5	0.7
Feedback on draft clarified assignment requirements	4.3	1.0
Sample paper helped with draft	3.4	1.5
Feedback on paragraph helped with draft	3.5	1.3
Assignment was unusually difficult	2.6	1.2
Assignment was fair	4.2	1.1
Assignment requirements were clear	3.5	1.3
Assignment benefits justified work required	3.6	1.2
Liked basing paper on own ideas	3.8	1.4
Paper made me think	4.9	0.4
Improved quality of my critical thought	3.9	0.9
Continue using assignment	4.3	1.2

Note. N = 24. Subjects rated each statement on a 5-point scale ranging from *strongly disagree* (1) to *strongly agree* (5).

assumptions and logic (M = 3.8). It heightened their appreciation of how formal theories handled basic construction problems like operationalization (M = 4.2) and theoretical issues like voluntarism versus determinism (M = 3.8) and practical implications (M = 3.7). It also improved students' understanding of the importance (M = 3.7) and difficulty (M = 4.3) of research investigations of formal personality theories.

The exercise seemed equally effective in meeting our second goal of increasing students' awareness of the strengths and limitations of their own personality theories. They reported improved understanding of their own theories' assumptions and logic (M = 3.9), internal contradictions (M = 4.2), and practical implications (M = 4.1). Most students said that the paper heightened their awareness of their own beliefs (M = 4.0).

Students generally believed that the draft-redraft method helped them to overcome the assignment's difficulties. They strongly endorsed feedback from their first draft as useful in clarifying their own ideas (M = 4.5) and the instructor's expectations for the paper (M = 4.3). They showed less enthusiasm for the sample paper (M = 3.4) and feedback on their initial summary paragraph (M = 3.5). Students tended not to perceive the exercise as unusually difficult (M = 2.6), and they regarded it as fair (M = 4.2). Most students rated the exercise as clear in its requirements (M = 3.5), reported that the paper's benefits outweighed its difficulty (M = 3.6), and enjoyed the

unusual opportunity to base a term paper mainly on their own ideas (M = 3.8).

Students concluded that the assignment succeeded in its most important educational objective: It made them think (M = 4.9). They believed it succeeded in its more specific goal of improving the quality of their critical thought (M = 3.9) and strongly endorsed the continued use of the exercise in future personality courses (M = 4.3).

Over the years, students' remarks on course evaluation forms have generally supported the assignment. Students report recognizing how their preconceptions bias their evaluation of the formal theories covered in the course and acknowledge a fresh respect for formal theorists, even those whose views they reject, because they have directly experienced the technical difficulties of theory construction.

On the negative side, students express concerns about the weighting of the assignment; the combined summary paragraph and two drafts count for 50% of their grade. Vocal minorities of commenting students consider the assignment ambiguous or a distraction from their leading formal personality theories. We plan to continue surveying our students to see if they persist in viewing these difficulties as outweighed by the exercise's benefits.

Additional benefits of this exercise may exist. Cognitive psychologists contend that much of our knowledge is organized in schemata that facilitate information processing both about self and others. The self-concept is thought to be one of these schemata (Markus, 1977). Greenwald (1980) and others have contended that more self-relevant information is better remembered, and Kuiper and Rogers (1979) found that memory for other people's traits is facilitated when they are tied to a person's own self-concept. Thus, if the more formal theories are encoded with reference to the student's own beliefs, they should be better recalled by students completing this exercise.

Anecdotal support for this self-referencing effect was obtained when one of us ran into a former student nearly 10 years after she had been in one of the first classes that used this exercise. She remembered the class, particularly her theory (which the instructor had long since forgotten), and she still had a copy of it!

In addition to the cognitive benefits of self-reference, the assignment moves the student from passive consumer of personality theories to an active, producing, personality theorist. Benefits of active learning have been discussed (cf. Benjamin, 1991) but usually not in the context of personality courses.

We are impressed by the courage our students show in engaging this assignment even though it often requires them to abandon the safety of assuming either that their own beliefs are the only correct ones or that only "expert" theorists' ideas are valuable. By doing so, they must question their own construction of social reality and embark on the enterprise that is at the heart of our discipline. As Wegner and Vallacher (1977) suggested, "although even the most lofty scientific theories have their beginnings in the murky depths of the scientists' own common-sense implicit theories, they are eventually written down and must stand the test of scrutiny by other scientists" (p. 21). Our students' willingness to stand this test is truly gratifying.

References

Baird, B. N., & Anderson, D. D. (1990). Writing in psychology. *The Teaching Professor, 4*, 5-6.

Benjamin, L. T., Jr. (1991). Personalization and active learning in the large introductory psychology class. *Teaching of Psychology, 18*, 68-74.

Bruner, J. S., & Tagiuri, R. (1954). The perception of people. In G. Lindzey (Ed.*), Handbook of social psychology* (pp. 634-654). Cambridge, MA: Addison-Wesley.

Embree, M. C. (1986). Implicit personality in the classroom: An integrative approach. *Teaching of Psychology, 13*, 78-80.

Feshbach, S., & Weiner, B. (1991). *Personality* (3rd ed.). Lexington, MA: Heath.

Greenwald, A. G. (1980). The totalitarian ego: Fabrication and revision of personal history. *American Psychologist, 35*, 603-613.

Heider, F. (1958). *The psychology of interpersonal relations.* New York: Wiley.

Kelly, G. A. (1955). *The psychology of personal constructs.* New York: Norton.

Kuiper, N. A., & Rogers, T. B. (1979). Encoding of personal information: Self other differences. *Journal of Personality and Social Psychology, 37*, 499-514.

Markus, H. (1977). Self-schemata and the processing of information about the self. *Journal of Personality and Social Psychology, 35*, 63-78.

Mischel, W. (1993). *Introduction to personality* (5th ed.). New York: Harcourt Brace.

Monte, C. F. (1977). *Beneath the mask: An introduction to theories of personality.* New York: Praeger.

Ross, M. (1989). Relation of implicit theories to the construction of personal histories. *Psychological Review, 96*, 341-357.

Wegner, D. M., & Vallacher, R. R. (1977). *Implicit psychology: An introduction to social cognition.* New York: Oxford University Press.

Notes

1. Opinions expressed in this article are ours; they are not official, and do not represent the views of the U.S. Navy Department.
2. We thank Ruth L. Ault, Charles L. Brewer, and five anonymous reviewers for their comments. We also thank Debra Bobango, the self-referencing student referred to in the article, for her recollections and reflections on the exercise.
3. An earlier version of this article, based on preliminary survey results, was presented at the annual meeting of the Western Psychological Association, Portland, OR, May 1992.
4. Requests for a recent course syllabus should be sent to Dana D. Anderson, Department of Psychology, Pacific Lutheran University, Tacoma, WA 98447-0003.

Implicit Personality Theory in the Classroom: An Integrative Approach

Marlowe C. Embree
University of Wisconsin- Sheboygan County Center

The notion of implicit personality theory (Bruner & Tagiuri, 1954) has played an important role in social psychology. However, it is largely ignored in many undergraduate-level treatments of personality. Perhaps one reason for this apparent discrepancy is the fact that, traditionally, implicit personality theories are thought to be very different from formal theories of personality. The former are thought to consist largely of expectations about interrelationships between traits (e.g., the expectations that a kind person will also be generous). These expectations form the basis of a theory of personality in the sense that they generate predictions about what people are like. However, the expectations are implicit in that they are not acquired through formal instruction and are not necessarily accessible to conscious awareness and analysis. In contrast, formal theories of personality consist largely of statements about wider issues in personality (e.g., processes of personality development). The statements and predictions of formal personality theories are articulated in precise terms, unlike those of implicit personality theory. Then, too, formal theories of personality are learned in the classroom, rather than being generated empirically in the process of social inter action.

Thus, it is difficult to integrate the notion of implicit personality theory into a course in personality, because the manner in which formal personality theories are usually treated in the classroom does not lend itself well to a study of implicit personality theory. In teaching the Psychology of Personality course, I have attempted to treat the notion of implicit personality theory in a manner that encourages students to evaluate what they think about the issues raised in the study of the formal theories, by structuring the course around a consideration of ways in which formal theories differ (based largely on the analysis of Hall & Lindzey, 1970). The demonstration discussed in this article represents one way of making these issues explicit.

Method

Subjects

Subjects were 10 students (those present on the day of testing, of 12 enrolled) in the spring, 1984 Psychology of Personality class. Although a sample of this size is of question able value for research purposes, the results obtained were instructive and useful pedagogically.

Procedures

Students were asked to complete an 18-item Likert-type questionnaire. Each item consisted of a short statement about personality (e.g., "People frequently are not aware of the real reasons for their behavior"). Students were asked to rate the extent to which they agreed or disagreed with each item on a 7-point scale, high scores representing strong agreement .

As a basis for analyzing student responses, I completed the questionnaire four times, each time responding as if I were a key figure in the psychology of personality. The four individuals chosen, in an attempt to represent points of view prototypical of major theoretical orientations, were Skinner, Freud, Rogers, and William Glasser, the founder of reality therapy. This method enabled student responses to be compared with those of psychologists whose theories were presented in class. The

Table 1. Prototype Ratings and Mean Student Ratings of the Questionnaire

Item Number	S	F	R	G	M
1. Because each person is a unique individual, there is really no point in trying to fit everyone into a single "theory."	1	4	7	4	5.5
2. It's more important to be concerned with what people do, not why they do it, if one is concerned with helping them to change.	7	1	1	7	2.2
3. Understanding how people view their own lives is very important in coming to an adequate understanding of personality.	1	4	7	7	6.1
4. People (e.g., children) really do go through "stages"; the stages are real, not just a way of speaking about behavior.	1	7	4	4	5.1
5. People frequently are not aware of the real reasons for their behavior.	4	7	4	4	4.5
6. A person must make a deliberate, conscious choice to change, or she or he cannot be helped.	1	4	7	7	6.0
7. If I wanted to know something about a person, I'd find it much more useful to have a personal interview with her or him than to look at some objective personality test results.	1	7	7	7	5.2
8. A person is the product of her or his environment.	7	4	1	1	5.2
9. If one understands adults, she or he will have no trouble understanding children.	7	4	4	4	3.1
10. The focus of therapy or counseling should be to change outward behavior, not inward thoughts or feelings.	7	1	1	7	2.0
11. People are usually quite consistent from one situation to another.	1	4	4	4	4.4
12. What people choose or decide is an important determinant of what they do.	1	1	7	7	5.7
13. Understanding people's motives and goals is an important part of helping them to change.	1	4	7	7	5.9
14. Formal psychological tests provide a complete, overall picture of personality.	4	1	1	4	3.2
15. Early childhood experience largely determines adult personality.	1	7	1	1	4.9
16. The current environment largely shapes what a person is and does.	7	1	1	1	4.3
17. The same general laws or principles apply to all people.	7	4	1	4	3.0
18. The notion of the "unconscious mind" is a very useful one in attempting to help people to change.	1	7	4	1	4.4

Note. S = ratings for Skinner, F = ratings for Freud, R = ratings for Rogers, G = ratings for Glasser.

13

18 scale items, the four prototype ratings for each item, and the subjects' average ratings on the items are presented in Table 1.

Results

In order to assess student agreement with each of the four prototypes, "agreement scores" were calculated. Viewing each set of responses geometrically as a point in 18-dimensional space, a subject's agreement with a given prototype can be conceptualized in terms of the Euclidean distance between the two points (subject and prototype). From an extension of the Pythagorean theorem, this distance can be compared as follows:

1. Subtract the subject's score on each item from the prototype rating for that item, obtaining a difference score for each item.
2. Square each difference score.
3. Add them.
4. Take the square root of the sum.

To convert this distance to an index of agreement with the prototype, divide by MD (a number indicating the maximum possible distance between subject and prototype, as discussed later), subtract this value from 1, and multiply by 100. (MD differs for each prototype, being 24.372 for Skinner, 20.785 for Freud, 22.649 for Rogers, and 21.424 for Glasser.) The index of agreement can range from 0 (*minimal agreement with the prototype*) to 100 (*maximal agreement*). This technique, although less mathematically sophisticated, is somewhat akin to discriminate function analysis (Morrison, 1976).

Most students took a Rogerian point of view in the sense that eight of the students (80%) had a higher AR (agreement with Rogers) score than AS (agreement with Skinner), AF (agreement with Freud), or AG (agreement with Glasser) scores. The remaining two students could be classified as Freudian in orientation by the same criterion. Similarly, the mean AR score (56.7) was the highest of the four, followed by AF (49.3), AG (43.9), and AS (28.1). Looking at score ranges, one gets the impression that students took a dim view of behaviorism (AS scores ranged from 16 to 38), and they were fairly supportive of the other three positions (ranges from: 42-61 for AF, 48-67 for AR, and 31-62 for AG).

Another way in which these data can be analyzed is to look at the correlations between the scores. Two cautions are needed here. First, a sample size of 10 is inadequate for drawing firm conclusions from the correlation matrix. Second, because the scores are not statistically independent, to some extent a pattern of negative correlations between scores is unavoidable. Nonetheless, the pattern of correlations is interesting.

Given the fact that reality therapy was developed as an alternative to classical psychoanalysis (see Glasser, 1975), it is interesting to note that AG and AF scores are negatively correlated ($r = -.64$, $p < .05$). Conversely, AG and AR scores are positively correlated ($r = .66$, $p < .05$), a

relationship that may reflect the fact that Glasser and Rogers would probably agree on many of the issues covered by the questionnaire (but not necessarily on other issues, e.g., the extent to which therapy should be directive). No other correlations were significant.

Discussion

These results were presented to the students in class. Two general points were made: first, the class as a whole had some definite points of view concerning the formal theories discussed in class (favoring phenomenology and largely discounting behaviorism); second, there was some internal consistency in student responses (endorsing one view necessitated rejecting others).

It would be of interest to use this or a similar questionnaire as a before-after tool to see if student responses are substantially modified as a result of exposure to course material. Of course, there is the danger that students would be unable to respond meaningfully to the questionnaire before taking the class. However, the questionnaire items deliberately avoid formal terminology, possibly circumventing this problem.

Perhaps the major pedagogical advantage of the questionnaire is that it alerts the students to the fact that they do have opinions-sometimes very decided ones-about the very issues that have traditionally divided personality theorists. From a theoretical perspective, it is significant that implicit personality theory is often viewed in a relatively narrow sense (in terms of perceived interrelationships between traits rather than unarticulated abstract propositions about personality). Schneider (1973) notes that "there has been an emphasis on the dimensional aspect of trait similarities to the relative exclusion of questions concerning the content and dynamic qualities of implicit personality theory" (p. 307). This may account for the fact that implicit personality theory is not widely incorporated into the classroom teaching of the psychology of personality. This study is a small step toward integrating a broader view of implicit personality theory into the classroom presentation of formal theories of personality.

References

Bruner, J. S., & Tagiuri, R. (1954). The perception of people. In G Lindzey (Ed.), *Handbook of social psychology* (Vol. 2, pp. 634-654). Cambridge, MA: Addison-Wesley.

Glasser, W. (1975). *Reality therapy: A new approach to Psychiatry* New York: Harper & Row.

Hall, C. S., & Lindzey, G. (1970). *Theories of personality* (2nd ed.). New York: Wiley.

Morrison, D. F. (1976*). Multivariate statistical methods* (2nd ed.). New York: McGraw-Hill.

Schneider, D. J. (1973). Implicit personality theory: A review. *Psychological Bulletin, 79*, 294-309.

Identifying Imagoes: A Personality Exercise on Myth, Self, and Identity

Dana S. Dunn
Moravian College

Faculty often teach personality psychology by reviewing the four broad theoretical perspectives: the psychoanalytic, trait, cognitive-behavioral, and humanistic approaches. Alternatively, introductory personality sometimes focuses on great theorists and their ideas, a psychometric search for traits and consistency, debates between opposing views (e.g., free will vs. determinism), or exploration of developmental or biological themes. Although each of these approaches offers a means of understanding the psychology of individuals, they also share a limitation: None of them are very personally involving for students.

In contrast to these traditional approaches, biographical and autobiographical approaches to personality are intrinsically involving for students (e.g., Mueller, 1985). McAdams's (1993) narrative approach to personality emphasizes autobiography as well as social roles, culture, and individual construal processes in identity development. McAdams posited that we make sense out of our lives by essentially telling stories about ourselves to others and to ourselves. Stories define people, and McAdams believed that each person unconsciously weaves stories together to create a personal myth. This article describes a narrative exercise using *imagoes*— idealized self-representations that populate stories about the self—to explore McAdams's theory of personality development.

Personal Myth and Imagoes

Personal myths are central stories about the self that pull together parts of ourselves into a meaningful whole. Myths have a beginning, a middle, and an ending, and there is usually a clear plot and evidence of character development (here, our own). They can be partially cultural (e.g., comedic myths emphasize the chance to find happiness and avoid pain; tragic myths highlight life's absurdity) or more idiosyncratic. When we articulate personal myths, we convey an artful (if critical) statement about our personal development. Personal myths are part truth and part fabrication because we base them on memories, perceptions, and hoped-for futures. As McAdams (1993) put it, "We do not discover ourselves in myth; we *make ourselves* through myth" (p. 13).

A key component in personal myth is the *imago*. Imagoes are personified self-concepts that we form in early or midadulthood, such as the scholar, the breadwinner, the martyr, the rugged individualist, the caregiver, and the athlete. We can create imagoes consciously or unconsciously, and although they are broader than roles we play in daily life (e.g., spouse, student, or teacher), they serve a unifying function: to make our life stories and personal myths coherent (McAdams, 1993).

McAdams (1993) emphasized four key points about imagoes. First, imagoes are archetypal personalities, not real people, in our life stories. Second, imagoes comprise only one part of an individual's life story; they are characters, not the whole story. Third, imagoes may be positive or negative, and thus they can guide us toward what we wish to become or away from what we fear becoming. Finally, similar to the personal myths they populate, imagoes can be common yet unique: Two people may have a caregiver imago but interpret its meaning differently.

An Exercise on Myth, Self, and Identity

I developed an exercise for use in an introductory personality course; introductory psychology, statistics, and research methods are prerequisites. The exercise is worth 20% of the final course grade, and students complete it after the semester's midpoint. As a supplement to a personality text, we read the book *The Stories We Live By* (McAdams, 1993) during the first half of the semester.

Table 1. Questions for the Daily Myth, Self, and Identity Journal Entries

a.	Did any event today cause you to think about who you are as a person, your life, your personal goals, and so on? If so, describe the event and its relevance to you.
b.	Did any person today cause you to think about yourself, your role(s), your current place in life? If so, describe the person, and then why and how the person caused you to reflect on yourself. Does this person fulfill any important role(s) in your life? If so, explain the role(s); if not, why not?
c.	What did you think most about today? Why? Does this thought relate to your self? If so, how and why?
d.	Write one sentence that describes your role(s) today.

To begin the exercise, students must read chapter 10, wherein McAdams (1993) offered suggestions about how to explore personal myths. I modified McAdams's suggestions by adding a writing component. Specifically, students keep a daily journal for at least 2 weeks so they can answer questions about roles and write about personal goals and meaningful events in their lives. The questions that guide these daily journal entries appear in Table 1.

While keeping the journal, students continue to follow McAdams's (1993) narrative technique. They divide their lives into a series of "chapters" with titles (more than 2 but less than 9), write about 8 key events (peak and nadir experiences; a turning point; an earliest memory; important memories from childhood, adolescence, and adulthood; as well as a memory that stands out from the past), and describe several influential individuals and how each has affected their lives. Students also anticipate what their futures will be like, including their plans and dreams, and review areas of their lives that evoke stress, serve as challenges, and underscore fundamental beliefs and values.

Students then examine their journal entries and their answers to McAdams's (1993) autobiographical narrative questions in search of major themes, as well as recurring patterns or unusual or surprising issues. Any resulting themes, patterns, and issues are used to write a 5-page paper that summarizes a student's life myth and identifies his or her imagoes (the journal entries and the narrative answers are attached to it). This paper provides students with an opportunity to describe the roles their characteristic imagoes play in their life stories, to discuss their life myths, and to consider how these two resources relate to generativity. Generativity refers to one's self-legacy—the psychological gifts one creates and hopes to leave behind for succeeding generations (McAdams, 1993; also cf. Erikson, 1968). Finally, students are asked to indicate what, if anything, they learned about themselves from the exercise.

Instructor's Impressions and Student Reactions

I have used McAdams's (1993) book and the exercise with much success. Students are enthusiastic about writing auto. biographies, and their papers are insightful and often poignant. They take the exercise seriously, conscientiously addressing necessary points, editing out unduly repetitive ideas, and actively searching for themes and imagoes. I am pleased by the effort they put into their writing and moved by their experiences. The only difficulty I encounter is grading their lives and imagoes-not an easy feat, but a welcome one if I receive such quality work.

After completing the identity exercise, students evaluated it. In the spring of 1995, 23 students (9 men, 14 women) completed the evaluation forms (total enrollment was 26). Students rated (a) how much they liked the project overall on a 7-point scaled ranging from 1 (*did not like at all*) to 7 (*liked very much*) and (b) how much they learned about themselves on a 7-point scale ranging from 1 (*not much*) to 7 (*a great deal*) . On average, students liked the exercise ($M = 5.2$, $SD = 1.2$) and they learned a lot about themselves ($M = 5.2$, $SD = 1.2$) in the process.

Beyond this quantitative confirmation, students commented that the exercise vividly illustrated McAdams's (1993) theory of personality development. Many remarked that, although it was time consuming, keeping a daily journal was revelatory. They were appropriately critical, suggesting that parts of the exercise be made less restrictive. For example, several students suggested that journal entries be less directive, as the former approach encouraged redundancy. In reading their comments, I also discovered that, although traditional-age undergraduates may possess some imagoes, these students are only beginning to develop personal myths for their lives. In contrast, nontraditional students tend to have better developed myths and—not surprising, given broader life experience—a better sense of generativity.

An important caveat regarding the use of the exercise must be mentioned. Faculty and students need to be aware that any self-discovery exercise can be problematic if and when it raises uncomfortable issues about the self, one's family, and so on. Ethically speaking, students should not feel compelled to disclose such private information during the exercise, and they must be informed that their project grades will not suffer as a result. Similarly, teachers must publicly pledge to honor student privacy and, when necessary, assign a more traditional paper.

Conclusion

In my view, good pedagogy directs self-reflective enthusiasm and imagination into a worthy intellectual activity. Writing about imagoes to understand the place of myths and stories in the development of one's personality achieves this end.

References

Erikson, E. H. (1968). *Identity: Youth and crisis.* New York: Norton.

McAdams, D. P. (1985). The "imago" A key narrative component of identity. In P. Shaver (Ed.), *Review of personality and social psychology* (Vol. 6, pp. 115-141). Beverly Hills, CA Sage.

McAdams, D. P. (1993). *The stories we live by: Personal myths and the making of the self.* New York: Morrow.

Mueller, S. C. (1985). Persons in the personality course: Student papers based on biographies. *Teaching of Psychology, 12*, 74-78.

Notes

1. Portions of this article were presented at the Second Annual American Psychological Society Teaching Institute, June 1995, New York. Preparation of this article was partially sponsored by the Moravian College Faculty Development and Research Committee.

2. Sarah Dunn, Stacey Zaremba, Randolph A. Smith, and three reviewers provided valuable comments on an earlier version of this article.

3. 3. Requests for a detailed set of instructions for the exercises should be sent to Dana S. Dunn, Department of Psychology, Moravian College, 1200 Main Street, Bethlehem, PA 180184650; e-mail dunn@moravian.edu.

Teaching Personality: Discovering the Difference Between Self and Personality

Jane Einhorn
Union County College

In teaching a course in personality, it is often very difficult to convey to the students the key difference between the self and personality. The students' difficulties are mirrored by psychologists themselves, who also disagree about the distinction. My own conclusion is that the telling difference between the two concepts lies in the centrality of the characteristics. That is, the self presents itself as the central and (although growth is possible) practically immutable core, but the personality is more peripheral and fluctuating in its reaching out toward others.

My method of communicating this to students is by inductive, particularistic reasoning. In that way, I need not present them with a predigested distinction that they will readily forget. Instead, they were asked to draw out the difference between self and personality from their own experience. It was then easy to compare their several ways of looking at this for the class, and the principal difference of the centrality of the concepts could then be clearly seen. They were asked to write down their favorite color, song, flower, smell, scene, person, and food. After having completed the list, they were to go back and indicate for each choice whether it reflected their self or their personality.

I expected that of all seven terms, it would be "scene" that most reflected the self. This was true for most of my 25 students. A peaceful ocean scene was most frequently cited, as if in its peace and seclusion we are alone with our "selves."

According to the students, color is not always a reflection of our self because it sometimes is related to the way we relate to the world, as in our choice of color in clothing. Favorite food was selected as a key to personality rather than self. It expressed something about the individual. Favorite person seemed to reflect both personality and self, and the other items were evenly split between self and personality.

The stated purpose of this class exercise was to have each student discover the difference between self and personality, and it accomplished its purpose. Some of the students' definitions of self were, "true inner feelings," "my real sense of being," "me as an individual," "everything that is close and significant to me," "self is something that has been part of me as long as I can remember," "things that reflect an integral part of me," and the part of you that "doesn't change."

Personality, on the other hand, was designed as "something that changes with exposure," "aspects of my being . . . more directly influenced by my environment," "changes with time and moods," "how you act and what you reveal," "capable of change and more outward," "things a little further removed," and finally, "I don't have separate identity in my personality, I seem to try to fit the mold."

These definitions of self and personality were derived by the students after having compared those topics on which they answered "self" to those on which they answered "personality." As an additional step, the students were asked to go back to the list and indicate which answers their best friend knows about and which they don't know about. After appraising their own answers, I got such diverse responses as, on the one hand, "My personality can be picked up by an acquaintance, only your best friend knows the real you," and, on the other, "It seems that I have not even let my best friend in close enough to know my deepest thoughts."

It should be noted that the students' excitement in participating in this exercise was reflected in one student's statement upon discovering for herself the difference between self and personality: "This is all very exciting; I actually got goose pimples."

2. EXPLORING THEORIES

Freudian Principles in Everyday Life

Marianne Miserandino
Beaver College

Sigmund Freud was one of the great minds of the 19th century and one of the most influential theorists in the history of psychology. A testament to Freud's genius is that many of his theories, ideas, and terms have permeated European and American culture and are still evident 100 years later in modern America, for better or for worse (Torrey, 1992). But just as the proverbial fish is the last to know that the water is wet, it is often difficult for beginning psychology students to appreciate the genius of Freud when so much of his thought is already familiar to them.

A recent computer search of the Expanded Academic Index of bibliographic references and abstracts of more than 1,500 scholarly and general interest journals in the humanities, social sciences, general sciences, and current events from 1990 to 1993 led to references of psychoanalysis and culture, feminism, literature, motion pictures, philosophy, and religion. On the PsycLIT data base alone, between 1987 and 1993 Freud appeared in the title or abstract of more than 2,000 articles; the keyword *psychoanalytic* was used in more than 7,300 references. Beyond the obvious influences in literature and literary criticism, some of the more unusual references were psychosexual stages as reflected in the Masters of the Universe series of action figures (Ainslie, 1989); the family drama as reflected in the comic book characters Batman and Robin (Lang, 1990) and in the paintings of Mary Cassat (Zerbe, 1987); pre-oedipal issues in Ingmar Bergman's film *Cries and Whispers* (Brattemo, 1990), Alfred Hitchcock's film *The Man Who Knew Too Much* (McEwen, 1987), and in the films *The Shining* (Cocks, 1987) and *Back to the Future* (Bick, 1990).

Students' familiarity with Freudian concepts may make it even more difficult for instructors to present the heavily theoretical psychoanalytic perspective. Yet, in the last 7 years *Teaching of Psychology* has published only two articles related specifically to Freudian principles. In the most recent one, Carlson (1989) noted how the psychoanalytic perspective is perhaps the most difficult of all personality systems to present, and she described a demonstration to compensate for the dearth of available exercises. Her "Psychosexual Pursuit" is an engaging board game in which players must complete their psychic development around the game board before depleting their supply of psychic energy ($100). Highlights of the game include rolling dice (the higher the roll, the greater overindulgence during a given stage), buying the use of a defense mechanism, and rolling doubles to get out of the latency stage.

Davidson (1987) described a project for an undergraduate laboratory in personality assessment on the anal personality type. Based on lectures and readings on Freudian principles, students develop hypotheses about the relation among the three anal traits of frugality, orderliness, and obstinacy and the various domains of expression for each. Students then construct and validate a questionnaire to measure the anal personality and, in the process, increase their understanding of Freudian concepts and questionnaire design.

In addition to reviewing the basic principles of Freudian theory, the exercise described herein is designed to help students see the range and variety of Freud's influence in American thinking today. Students indicate the strength of their agreement or disagreement with 15 statements chosen to represent the breadth of Freudian concepts (see Table 1). Statements are worded so that a Freudian psychologist would strongly agree with 9 and strongly disagree with 6 of them. Statements cover Freud's general theory of psychosexual development (Statement 1), as well as individual stages: oral (Statement 6); anal (Statement 9); phallic, with the oedipal complex (Statements 4 and 8) and the oedipal fixation of penis envy (Statements 10 and 12); and genital (Statements 2, 11, and 14). Other statements tap Freud's notion of the death instinct as manifested by aggression (Statements 3 and 7), repression (Statement 5), dream symbolism (Statement 13), and parapraxes or Freudian slips (Statement 15). All statements were designed to illustrate principles assimilated by popular culture and typically covered in an introductory psychology or personality textbook.

Procedure

Students respond to each statement by choosing one of the following responses: *strongly disagree, disagree, neutral, agree,* or *strongly agree.* Each response receives a

Table 1. The 15 Freudian Principle Statements

[a]1. Events that occurred during childhood have no effect on one's personality in adulthood.

[a]2. Sexual adjustment is easy for most people.

3. Culture and society have evolved as ways to curb human beings' natural aggressiveness.

4. Little boys should not become too attached to their mothers.

5. It is possible to deliberately "forget" something too painful to remember.

6. People who chronically smoke, eat, or chew gum have some deep psychological problems.

[a]7. Competitive people are no more aggressive than noncompetitive people.

8. Fathers should remain somewhat aloof to their daughters.

[a]9. Toilet training is natural and not traumatic for most children.

10. The phallus is a symbol of power.

11. A man who dates a woman old enough to be his mother has problems.

12. There are some women who are best described as being "castrating bitches."

[a]13. Dreams merely replay events that occurred during the day and have no deep meaning.

14. There is something wrong with a woman who dates a man who is old enough to be her father.

[a]15. A student who wants to postpone an exam by saying "My grandmother lied . . . er, I mean died," should probably be allowed the postponement.

Note. Unless specified otherwise, these items are scored as follows: *strongly disagree* = 1, *disagree* = 2, *neutral* = 3, *agree* = 4, and *strongly agree* = 5. Add up the score for each question to yield a total score.
[a]These items are scored in reverse, *strongly disagree* = 5, *disagree* = 4, *neutral* = 3, *agree* = 2, and *strongly agree* = 1.

score of 1 through 5 representing the extent of concurrence with the Freudian perspective. Respondents with a Freudian perspective would strongly agree with 9 of the items and strongly disagree with 6 (marked with asterisks in Table 1). Their total score, summed across the 15 items, should be near the maximum score of 75. Respondents who agree with the marked items and disagree with the unmarked items (the non-Freudian position) would get minimal points per item and should have a total score near 15.

Results

Three professors used this exercise in four different introductory psychology classes, including one graduate seminar. Scores from 78 undergraduates in three classes ranged from 39 to 56 ($M = 47.6$, $SD = 4.3$). Individual scores for graduate students ($n = 12$) in a counseling program, who were taking an introductory course in psychology because their undergraduate degrees were not in psychology, were not available. The class agreed or strongly agreed with Freudian notions on an average of 6.5 of the statements. The student with the lowest score held a Freudian position for only 4 of the 15 questions, whereas the two highest scorers held Freudian positions for 12 questions.

Instructors in all of these classes used the exercise to introduce Freudian principles. Students then studied Freud's theories in more depth. One of the undergraduate instructors readministered the exercise to her class after they discussed Freud in class, thus using it as a test of attitude change after exposure to Freudian theories. Although the range of the 19 scores was greater on the posttest (41 to 61 compared to 41 to 56), the mean did not change significantly (pretest $M = 48.1$, $SD = 4.4$; posttest $M = 47.2$, $SD = 4.6$). The maximum attitude shift in both directions was 8 points.

Discussion

Discussion of students' responses should center on why they believe as they do. Where did they learn these ideas? What kind of evidence should be used to evaluate some of these statements? Would a person from another culture answer these questions differently? What other factors would affect people's responses? Were some of these statements true in the past but are not true now? If so, why? What has changed. Were students surprised that some of the statements are associated with Freudian theory? Why? Can students identify the Freudian concept? Can students explain the reasoning behind each question?

One of the basic tenets of Freud's theory is that humans are driven by life instincts (e.g., sex) and by death instincts (e.g., aggression). If anxiety or social constraints prevent direct expression of sexuality or aggression, these impulses will be expressed indirectly or unconsciously. Thus, dreams and parapraxes are two ways of studying unconscious wishes or impulses. Similarly, Freud believed that the aggressive drive is often sublimated into competition and achievement.

Furthermore, Freud proposed that individuals pass through a series of psychosexual stages during which id impulses of a sexual nature must find satisfaction in a socially acceptable way. Unresolved conflicts between id impulses and society's restrictions during childhood affect one's personal adjustment in adulthood. For example, people who chronically smoke, eat, or chew gum—oral-incorporative personalities—are said to have had trouble with feeding and weaning early in the oral stage. Similarly, problems concerning toilet training during the anal stage may lead to the development of anal-expulsive or anal-retentive personalities in adulthood. Problems during the genital stage are often manifested in an Oedipus complex and castration anxiety in men or in an Electra complex and penis envy in women. Because of penis envy, women fixated at this stage, according to Freud, symbolically castrate men through embarrassment, deception, and derogation.

The discussion can address a possible double standard of acceptable behavior for men and women on questions about fathers and daughters (Statement 8) versus mothers and sons (Statement 4) or of dating an older person

(Statements 11 and 14). Did anybody respond to these sets of statements differently? Why? What does this mean

Student Evaluations

Student reactions to this exercise were positive. Using a 7-point scale ranging from *not at all* (1) to *very* (7), with *neutral* (3) as the midpoint, the graduate class ($n = 14$) found it particularly thought provoking ($M = 6.1$, $SD = .86$) and a useful way to introduce Freudian principles ($M = 6.3$, $SD = .91$). They also reported that the exercise made them realize the extent of Freud's influence on American culture ($M = 6.1$, $SD = 1.14$) and gave them an appreciation for the range and variety of Freud's theories ($M = 5.7$, $SD = 1.07$). In the three undergraduate classes, 67% of the 79 introductory psychology students found the exercise to be somewhat to very thought provoking, and 50% to 60% found the exercise helpful in making them realize the range, variety, and extent of Freud's influence. Most students (54%) agreed that overall the project was very useful.

Undergraduate students' written comments on the evaluation echoed these results: "It was helpful because it made you think about everyday affairs and people you know. A good way to begin to help people to understand Freud." "I didn't know Freud believed so many things on so many subjects." "Interesting how you put his theories into questions and scenarios of today's world." "Freud's theories are interesting but he tended to be quite an extremist. It seems society, especially the media, believes in Freud's concepts." Finally, Freud would certainly applaud the insight of one of the counseling graduate students who said "more in-depth [discussion of the] connection between questions and answers would be interesting."

By turning basic principles of Freudian psychology into statements that reflect current American views and values, an interesting and entertaining demonstration was created. This exercise helped students learn the basics of Freudian psychology and appreciate Freud's genius. A similar demonstration could be created for other personality theorists, such as Carl Jung, Melanie Klein, Erik Erikson, Karen Horney, or B. F. Skinner. The design of such a questionnaire is left to readers and their students.

References

Ainslie, R. C. (1989). Master of the universe: Children's toys as reflections on contemporary psychoanalytic theory. *Journal of the American Academy of Psychoanalysis, 17*, 579-595.

Bick, I. J. (1990). Outatime: Recreationism and the adolescent experience in *Back to the future. Psychoanalytic Review, 77*, 587-608.

Brattemo, C. E. (1990). Reality transformed to dream: Some comments on Ingmar Bergman's film *Cries and whispers* and the collapse of language. *Scandinavian Psychoanalytic Review, 13*, 47-61.

Carlson, J. F. (1989). Psychosexual pursuit: Enhancing learning of theoretical psychoanalytic constructs. *Teaching of Psychology, 16*, 82-84.

Cocks, G. (1987). The hinting: Holocaust imagery in Kubrick's The shining. *Psychohistory Review, 16*, 115-136.

Davidson, W. B. (1987). Undergraduate lab project in personality assessment: Measurement of anal character. *Teaching of Psychology, 14*, 101-103.

Lang, R. (1990). Batman and Robin: A family romance. *American Imago, 47*, 293-319.

McEwen, D. (1987). Hitchcock: An analytic movie review. *Psychoanalytic Review, 74*, 401-409.

Torrey, E. F. (1992). *Freudian fraud: The malignant effect of Freud's theory on American thought and culture.* New York: HarperCollins.

Zerbe, K. J. (1987). Mother and child: A psycho-biographical portrait of Mary Casatt. *Psychoanalytic Review, 74*, 45-61.

Notes

I thank Patricia Scully and Lester Sdorow for pretesting this exercise at Beaver College, and I thank Ruth Ault and three anonymous reviewers for comments and suggestions on a draft of this article.

A Freudian Slip?

Gordon Bear
Ramapo College of New Jersey

A college freshman is telling his roommates an anecdote about George Washington Carver (1864-1943), the scientist who discovered hundreds of uses for the peanut. According to a biography the student had read, Carver used to say of himself, "When I was young, I was intensely curious about everything and prayed, 'Lord, teach me the mysteries of the universe,' but God replied, 'I'm sorry, George, those mysteries are reserved for me alone.' So [Carver continued], I changed my prayer to 'Lord, teach me the mysteries of the peanut,' and God answered, 'All right, George, that's more your size.' "

From the student's mouth, the second prayer emerges as "Lord, teach me the mysteries of the penis." Embarrassed, the student corrects himself and finishes the anecdote. His roommates chuckle, perhaps at the mistake, and change the subject. The student ponders another mystery: Where had that word *penis* come from? He had been thinking about Carver's humility, not about sex, but he was largely lacking in sexual experience, and none was easily forthcoming at his all-male school. Perhaps, then, that slip of his tongue enunciated an unconscious wish.

I offer this incident as a possible example of a Freudian slip (Freud, 1901/1960). The classic psychodynamic interpretation posits an anxiety-provoking sexual impulse, operating independently of the conscious line of thought, that took advantage of the similarity between *penis* and *peanut* to press past the forces of repression and momentarily capture control of the vocal mechanism.

After discussing Freud's theory of parapraxes, the instructor can cite more recent psychodynamic theorizing and research. Weiss's (1990) observations of psychoanalysis suggest that repressed material becomes overt not through sudden victory in a struggle against censorship but through intelligent planning that eventuates in unopposed action at a carefully chosen moment. Weiss's theory of "unconscious control" raises the possibility that the student unconsciously had intended for some time to introduce the topic of sexual experience and merely took advantage of an opportunity. In this interpretation, no mental conflict existed at the moment of the slip.

Cognitive psychology also recognizes the unconscious (Kihlstrom, 1987) and offers theories of parapraxes, from which one may construct interpretations of the slip as an unmotivated error. Motley's (1985) work suggests that extraneous sexual thoughts—not necessarily repressed, just operating in parallel with those to which the student was attending—caused activation to spread through associated items in the student's lexicon. The word *penis* was thus activated both by semantic associations to the sexual thoughts and by phonological association to the intended word *peanut*. Penis thereby became more strongly activated than *peanut* and reached the threshold for pronunciation first.

Norman's (1981) cognitive theory raises the possibility that the student was thinking ahead to speaking a word like *genus* or *Venus* (e.g., "Carver's crossbreeding produced new species within the genus of legumes"). In what Norman would call the faulty triggering of a schema for action, penis may have resulted from a simple mental combination of *peanut* and *genus*. (Heckhausen & Beckmann, 1990, offered an alternative to Norman's theory but do not consider slips of the tongue.)

The incident retold here has several pedagogical virtues. It is humorous and vivid and illustrates a larger lesson about the possibility of an unconscious mind. It allows a classic psychodynamic interpretation but also modem alternatives. Because it is amenable to those incompatible interpretations, it demonstrates a limitation of anecdotal evidence: inconclusiveness.

Moreover, it truly happened, as I can testify, for I was that embarrassed freshman in the fall of 1961.

References

Freud, S. (1960). The psychopathology of everyday life. In J. Strachey (Ed.), *The standard edition of the complete psychological works of Sigmund Freud* (Vol. 6). London: Hogarrh. (Original work published 1901)

Heckhausen, H., & Beckmann, J. (1990). Intentional actions and action slips. *Psychological Review, 97,* 36-48.

Kihlstrom, J. (1987). The cognitive unconscious. *Science, 237,* 1445-1452.

Motley, M. T. (1985). Slips of the tongue. *Scientific American, 253,* 116-127.

Norman, D. A. (1981). Categorization of action slips. *Psychological Review, 88,* 1-15.

Weiss, J. (1990). Unconscious mental functioning. *Scientific American, 262,* 103-109.

Psychosexual Pursuit: Enhancing Learning of Theoretical Psychoanalytic Constructs

Janet F. Carlson
Fairfield University

Courses in personality are taught in most undergraduate psychology programs. Course titles such as Theories of Personality document the substantial theoretical bases on which most such courses rely. Instructors who teach these theoretical classes are often confronted with the difficult task of vitalizing potentially dry material in an effort to sustain student interest and facilitate learning. The issue also faces textbook authors and publishers, as evidenced by the attempts of several authors to enliven the material with demonstrations (Liebert & Spiegler, 1987), exercises and experiments (Phares, 1988), or other mnemonic aids (Ewen, 1980). Although textbook selection and creative lectures may suffice to translate theoretical constructs into more hands-on learning experiences, this is not always the case

Perhaps more than the other major personality strategies (Liebert & Spiegler, 1987; Millon, 1973; Pervin, 1975 Scheier & Carver, 1988), the psychoanalytic perspective is particularly difficult to present as class activities or demonstrations. Note, for example, the treatment of this strategy in Liebert and Spiegler (1987). The other strategies discussed by these authors (e.g., dispositional, phenomenological, and behavioral) have as many as seven demonstrations of the theories or parts thereof. The psychoanalytic strategy, however, has but one. To offset this lack, I developed a game called Psychosexual Pursuit, the details of which are summarized in this article.

Overview

The game is suitable for up to 50 players. A team approach works well when enrollment is too high (e.g., more than 10 students) to permit individual play. Each player or team requires a game piece (coins or checkers work well), two dice, $100 of play money (small denominations), and a copy of the game board (reproduced as Figure 1). The object of the game is to complete one's psychosexual development and "finish" as an adult, while retaining as much psychic energy (play money) as possible. The four sides of the game board correspond to four stages of psychosexual development—oral, anal, phallic, and genital. There are substages for the oral and anal stages and a period of latency separates the phallic and genital stages, in keeping with traditional psychoanalytic theory (Cameron & Rychlak, 1985; Phares, 1988).

How to Play

The player places the game piece on the open triangle space preceding the six square spaces at each stage of development. One die is rolled to determine the square to which the game piece is moved. The player must then pay the indicated amount of libido, represented by the play money. The higher the roll, the greater the expenditure of psychic energy consumed by the resolution of the crucial conflict associated with the stage. A percentage system is used, so bankruptcy is unlikely, although anything is possible—as in real life. Bankruptcy, therefore, represents a highly maladaptive adjustment, such as one might observe in the psychotic individual (Vaillant, 1977). Very high rolls (5s or 6s) place the player at risk for fixation, and the player must decide whether to "gamble" by employing (i.e., buying) a defense or to pay 20% of the remaining assets. Upon choosing to buy and use a defense, a player returns the game piece to the appropriate starting triangle and rerolls one die to determine the mechanism's price ($1, 5%, or 10%). The second roll must be less than 5; otherwise, the player rolls until obtaining a 1, 2, 3, or 4. Although the defense must initially cost less than the 20% option, the player must pay the same fee at the starting point of each subsequent stage of development. This procedure is consistent with the psychoanalytic view that defenses require a continuing investment of psychic energy (Kendall & Norton-Ford, 1982), and that some defenses are more efficient and less costly than others (Vaillant, 1977).

Upon completing a given stage or substage, the player moves the game piece to the next open triangle at the subsequent developmental stage. Play then advances to the next player or team.

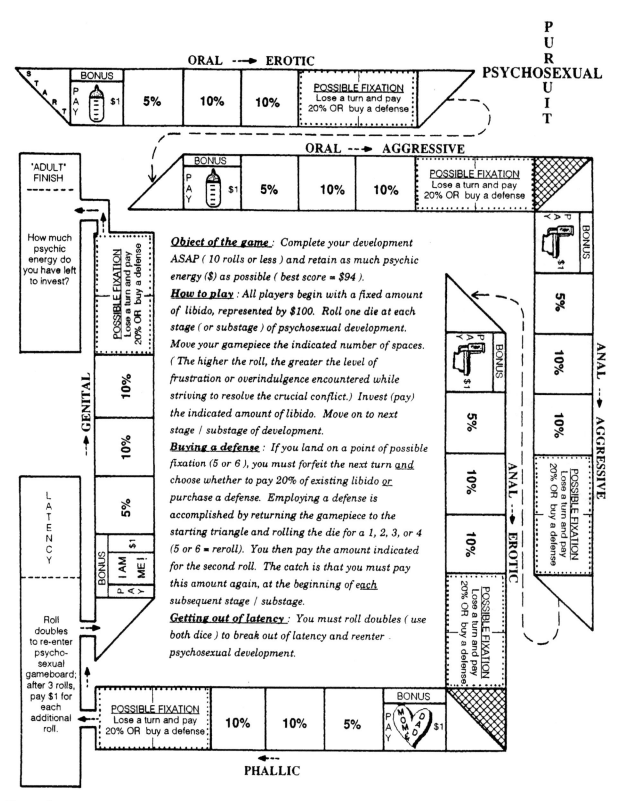

ORAL → EROTIC

| BONUS | PAY $1 | 5% | 10% | 10% | POSSIBLE FIXATION Lose a turn and pay 20% OR buy a defense |

P U R S U I T

PSYCHOSEXUAL

START

ORAL → AGGRESSIVE

| BONUS | PAY $1 | 5% | 10% | 10% | POSSIBLE FIXATION Lose a turn and pay 20% OR buy a defense |

'ADULT' FINISH

How much psychic energy do you have left to invest?

GENITAL

POSSIBLE FIXATION Lose a turn and pay 20% OR buy a defense

10%

10%

5%

BONUS — PAY I AM ME! $1

LATENCY

Roll doubles to re-enter psycho-sexual gameboard; after 3 rolls, pay $1 for each additional roll.

Object of the game : Complete your development ASAP (10 rolls or less) and retain as much psychic energy ($) as possible (best score = $94).

How to play : All players begin with a fixed amount of libido, represented by $100. Roll one die at each stage (or substage) of psychosexual development. Move your gamepiece the indicated number of spaces. (The higher the roll, the greater the level of frustration or overindulgence encountered while striving to resolve the crucial conflict.) Invest (pay) the indicated amount of libido. Move on to next stage / substage of development.

Buying a defense : If you land on a point of possible fixation (5 or 6), you must forfeit the next turn and choose whether to pay 20% of existing libido or purchase a defense. Employing a defense is accomplished by returning the gamepiece to the starting triangle and rolling the die for a 1, 2, 3, or 4 (5 or 6 = reroll). You then pay the amount indicated for the second roll. The catch is that you must pay this amount again, at the beginning of each subsequent stage / substage.

Getting out of latency : You must roll doubles (use both dice) to break out of latency and reenter psychosexual development.

BONUS PAY $1

5%

10%

ANAL → AGGRESSIVE

BONUS PAY $1

5%

10%

10%

ANAL → EROTIC

POSSIBLE FIXATION Lose a turn and pay 20% OR buy a defense

POSSIBLE FIXATION Lose a turn and pay 20% OR buy a defense

BONUS PAY MOM DAD ME $1

| POSSIBLE FIXATION Lose a turn and pay 20% OR buy a defense | 10% | 10% | 5% |

PHALLIC

Figure 1. The game board for Psychosexual Pursuit.

Latency corresponds to the period between the phallic and genital stages or roughly from Age 6 to Age 12 (Phares, 1988). During this time, the player is essentially suspended from psychosexual activity until rejoining the game as an adolescent by using both dice and rolling doubles. This procedure ensures that every player will spend at least some time in latency and will eventually reenter psychosexual development. If doubles do not turn up on three rolls, a player must pay $1 for each roll beyond the third. After traversing the genital stage, the player emerges as a young adult and tallies up the remaining assets to determine how much psychic energy is left to invest in the pursuits of adult life.

Advantages and Commentary

Perhaps the most compelling advantage of Psychosexual Pursuit as a teaching aid is its intrinsic appeal to students. It also uses materials that are readily available to most instructors, such as checkers, dice, and play money. More to the point, however, is the fact that students must rely on or learn several important psychoanalytic constructs in order to do well in the game. In reality, the students are likely to learn these things before playing the game. Knowing that they are about to play the game, they pay close attention to the instructor's explanation of the rules, which also constitute the basics of the psychoanalytic theory. The directions reviewed before the game begins include an explanation of possible outcomes, such as bankruptcy, and can be used to relate the procedures to theoretical constructs more directly. During the game, students must apply knowledge about the operations of defense mechanisms, the nature of libido as a fixed energy system, the benefits of adequate conflict resolution, the disadvantages of becoming fixated, as well as the names and sequence of the various stages and substages of psychosexual development. By experiencing the consequences of these processes, the students' learning and interest are increased. For these reasons, the game is popular and exciting for students in my class and serves as a valuable learning tool as well.

References

Cameron, N., & Rychlak, J. F. (1985). *Personality development and psychopathology: A dynamic approach* (2nd ed.). Boston: Houghton Mifflin.

Ewen, R. B. (1980). *An introduction to theories of personality*. New York: Academic.

Kendall, P. C., & Norton-Ford, J. D. (1982). *Clinical psychology: Scientific and professional dimensions*. New York: Wiley.

Liebert, R. M., & Spiegler, M. D. (1987). *Personality: Strategies and issues* (5th ed.). Chicago: Dorsey.

Millon, T. (Ed.). (1973). *Theories of psychopathology and personality* (2nd ed.). Philadelphia: Saunders.

Pervin, L. A. (1975*). Personality theory, assessment, and research* (2nd ed.). New York: Wiley.

Phares, E. J. (1988). *Introduction to personality* (2nd ed.). Glenview, IL: Scott Foresman.

Scheier, M. F., & Carver, C. S. (1988). *Perspectives on personality*. Needham Heights, MA: Allyn & Bacon.

Vaillant, G. E. (1977). Natural history of male psychological health: V. The relation of choice of ego mechanisms of defense to adult adjustment. *Archives of General Psychiatry, 33,* 535-545.

Note

I thank Kurt F. Geisinger for his careful reading of the manuscript and constructive comments.

Abstract and Relational Thinking via Personal Constructs

Mitchell M. Handelsman
University of Colorado at Denver

When concepts are taught in class, they are usually introduced with a definition and embellished with one or more examples. Often, however, the relationships among concepts are not pursued directly. Several problems result. First, students do not learn how to think abstractly and hence to relate concepts to each other. Second, students get concept definitions and examples confused. For example, they may define the superego as "when you feel guilty about having premarital sex." Third, students feel frustrated when they are asked to relate concepts on the test if they have not been shown how to do this during class periods.

The exercise described here is designed to address these concerns. It is based on Kelly's (1955) theory of personal constructs. Constructs, for Kelly, are dichotomous templates that people use to interpret and anticipate their experience. People abstract relevant features of events, objects, and people, and use these dimensions to "construe" similarities and differences among elements of experience. For example, the construct "tall versus short" can be used to appreciate the similarity, along that dimension, between Wilt Chamberlain and Ronald Reagan, and their difference from Willie Shoemaker.

In order to assess the idiosyncratic constructs people use, Kelly devised the Role Construct Repertory Test. The person taking the test is asked to construe sets of three significant people to determine how two are similar and different from the third along an important and relevant dimension. For example, an individual's mother and brother may be well-educated, but his or her father is not. The construct "educated versus not educated" may be an important tool in that person's hypothesizing about these people. This person can construe other significant persons with the same construct .

The adaptation of this approach for classroom use involves substituting important course concepts for people. For example, the concepts id, ego, and superego are written on the board. Students are then asked to construe them, that is, to state how two of the concepts are similar and different from the third along some important dimension. One such construct may be "innate versus acquired." The id would be construed as innate, while the superego and ego would be construed as forming after birth. Or, the id and superego could be construed as "not in touch with reality," in contrast to the ego, which would be construed under the opposite pole, "in contact with reality." Once these constructs are developed, they can be used to construe other concepts to be studied later. For example, the construct "active versus passive" may be used to relate the concept of "ego" as postulated by Freud, Hartmann, and White. Later, Jung's and Adler's conceptions of ego may be construed along the same dimension.

One effective way to use this technique is to have students work in groups to construe several sets of three (or more) concepts. In the course of discussion, students will first need to become familiar with the concepts involved—if they haven't already. They will actively seek definitions and examples of concepts from books, notes, and each other. They will then share ideas about important features to be abstracted and constructs to be applied. In short, they will be actively learning and using course material.

Although development of abstract thinking is the primary goal of the exercise, it could be that students will learn the content more effectively. Students may be more motivated to learn the concepts in this exercise because they are doing so as a means to an end (i.e., accurate construction), rather than as a sterile and arbitrary end in itself.

Rather than move from the concepts to the concrete level of examples, this exercise compels students to move up a level of abstraction to features that refer to the relationships among concepts. For example, in addition to seeing the ego and superego as independent concepts, the student can now see them as similar in their lack of independent energy (in contrast to the id), and as differing in their contact with reality. In introducing this exercise to students, it is useful to talk about different levels of abstraction, and to attack directly the differences among examples, definitions, and higher-order abstractions

Because Kelly's constructs imply contrast as well as similarity, students will have a new way to handle "compare and contrast" questions. They can do more than simply define each concept in turn. Although some students are able to answer such questions anyway, the present technique allows all students to learn—and practice—the skills involved.

The discrepancy between what is taught and what is tested can be reduced by having some test questions worded exactly as the exercise itself. Questions that tap students' ability to construe sets of concepts may also allow them to be more creative. The specific constructs used are less important than the skill of appropriately applying a construct to a group of concepts. Students may generate and correctly apply constructs that the instructor had not thought of. Consequently, students may not think that they have to read the instructor's mind in order to demonstrate mastery of material and skills.

At the extreme of allowing this skill to be content-free the author has asked the following question on tests "Choose three concepts we've studied, and tell me how two of them are similar and different from the third along some important dimension. Be creative." This allows students to demonstrate the skill they have learned at the same time as they demonstrate knowledge of course content. An added advantage is that it reduces the salience of the typical argument that students didn't excel on the test because the professor asked the wrong questions.

Rather than teach content and hope that students will somehow pick up abstract and relational thinking skills in an indirect fashion, this exercise facilitates the direct teaching of such skills. After the specific course content has been forgotten or become obsolete, students will be able to continue using the skills they have learned.

Reference

Kelly, G. A. (1955). *The psychology of personal constructs* (2 vols.). New York: Norton.

Students' Peak Experiences: A Written Exercise

James Polyson
University of Richmond

One of the methods Abraham Maslow (1962) used to understand what happens during a peak experience was to develop a composite picture of this phenomenon based on the written comments of college students. Maslow's procedure suggested the possibility of having undergraduate psychology students write essays about peak experiences they have had as a way of helping them understand the theoretical construct by relating it to meaningful events in their own lives. An additional goal of this exercise was to help students develop their writing skills.

The Written Assignment

After a brief lecture on peak experiences, students in three introductory psychology classes ($N = 122$) and one personality class ($N = 40$) were asked to describe a peak experience as vividly and accurately as possible. That is, they were to write an essay describing where they were at the time of the peak experience, what they were doing, how they felt during and after the experience, and what the experience meant to them then and now. Just as Maslow asked his psychology students over 20 years ago, the present students were asked to "think of the most wonderful experience of your life: the happiest moments, ecstatic moments, moments of rapture, perhaps from being in love, or from listening to music or suddenly 'being hit' by a book or painting, or from some creative moment" (1962, p. 67). They were referred to Maslow's characteristics of a peak experience, which had been covered in the lecture, but were reminded that one peak experience is not likely to involve all the physical, cognitive, and emotional characteristics of Maslow's "composite."

The maximum length of the paper was two typed pages. Three grading criteria were announced:

1. demonstrated ability to apply Maslow's theoretical construct while describing and explaining a personal experience;
2. adherence to requirements such as length, and turning it in on time;
3. quality of the writing: Students were given a handout summarizing some of the major criteria for good writing in psychology such as conciseness, clarity, smooth flow of ideas, spelling, and grammar. In grading papers, I made brief notations, to point out writing problems and strengths.

Students were told that the brief length would allow them to concentrate on the quality of their writing; therefore, content and style would be weighted equally in the grading procedure. They were also informed that after the papers were graded I would read aloud some excerpts from the best papers, unless the student requested that I not do so. Perhaps due to the personal nature of the exercise, 28 of the 162 participants (17%) requested that their papers be exempted from presentation. Students were also given the opportunity to choose an alternate assignment of similar length and difficulty, but no one pursued that option.

At the end of the semester, students completed an anonymous questionnaire assessing whether the assignment had been a worthwhile learning experience consistent with their personal goals for the course. An open-ended item inquired about any aspects) of the assignment the student liked and/or disliked most.

Student Evaluations

Student evaluations corroborated my subjective impression that this was a very successful activity. When asked "How worthwhile was this assignment?," 65% marked "quite worthwhile," and 33% marked "somewhat worthwhile." Only 2% indicated that the assignment was "not very worthwhile" and no one checked "totally worthless." The students were also nearly unanimous in their approval ratings on the item "How interesting was the assignment?" In addition, a vast majority (93%) of the students responded "yes" to the item "Was this assignment consistent with your personal goals for the course?" and 96% marked "yes" to the question "Should this assignment be repeated next semester?" Perhaps the key item on the questionnaire from an instructional standpoint was "Did this assignment facilitate your learning of Maslow's theories concerning peak experiences?" Ninety-five percent responded "yes." Chi-square tests suggest that the exercise was equally effective in both courses.

Discussion

The thoughtfulness and enthusiasm students showed during this assignment were impressive. Every student was able to write about a peak experience that demonstrated at least a few of the characteristics of Maslow's construct—the intrinsically good feelings; the total attentiveness in the here and now; the effortless functioning; the spontaneity and harmony with the environment; and/or the freedom from blocks, fears, and doubts. Most of the peak experiences had occurred during athletic, artistic, religious, or nature experiences, or during intimate moments with a friend or family member. There were a number of peak experiences in which the student achieved an important personal or collective goal. There were also peak experiences in which the student overcame some adversity or danger or helped someone in need.

In short, these essays presented a wide variety of happy, fulfilling experiences. That was a primary reason for the success of the exercise, according to students' comments. They enjoyed reminiscing about a joyful event and learning about others' happy experiences. Many students also liked the fact that the exercise involved creative expression in conjunction with scientific theory and they liked the opportunity to apply what they had learned. Several students remarked that this was the first time they had actually looked forward to writing a paper in college.

These written comments along with the questionnaire data show that writing about an important personal experience in order to understand a major theoretical construct was a very good learning experience. That is consistent with the finding by McKeachie, Lin, Moffett, and Daugherty (1978) that teaching is more effective when it allows students to express their own views and interests. Similarly, I found that this exercise enhanced my own interest in peak experiences. I became aware of how important these events are in the lives of my students, and I began to appreciate the richness of Maslow's construct. I decided to learn more about empirical research and practical applications involving peak experiences, especially in the field of sports psychology (e.g., Ravizza, 1977). And I truly enjoyed focusing on such an optimistic topic in courses that frequently emphasize psychopathology and human problems.

Despite the overall success of the assignment, students' comments pointed out a few potential problems. A few students found it embarrassing to hear feelings being discussed in the classroom, and there were a few suggestions that the writer's name should not be mentioned during the presentation. These concerns emphasize the need for sensitivity and respect when discussing students' peak experiences. Not giving the names is a reasonable option; however, it might detract from the learning experience if the authors were unable to answer questions or discuss the experience from their unique perspectives. Furthermore, identifying the authors seems consistent with the principle of taking responsibility for one's views and feelings. In my opinion, the option of not having one's paper presented in class is a sufficient precaution.

A few students did not like being graded on this paper, even though I emphasized that it was the paper and not the peak experience that was being graded (by definition the latter would receive an A+). And there were some complaints about the emphasis I placed on writing as a grading criterion. I believe that effective writing is an important component of this exercise. I am comfortable grading and providing feedback to students about their written communication and it appears that a growing number of psychology teachers feel likewise (Calhoun & Selby, 1979; Klugh, 1983; Spiegel, Cameron, Evans, & Nodine, 1980).

As with any good educational exercise, there were some students who found this one difficult. Apparently there was little difficulty in choosing a peak experience but, as several students noted, it was hard to write about feelings. In fact, that is what I liked best about the assignment: It encouraged students to integrate affect and intellect, consistent with Carl Rogers's (1969) views on the exploration of feelings as an integral part of academic learning. In that respect, it may be possible to generalize the present technique to other topics and courses.

References

Calhoun, L. G., & Selby, J. W. (1979). Writing in psychology: A separate course? *Teaching of Psychology, 6*, 232.

Klugh, H. E. (1983). Writing and speaking skills can be taught in psychology classes. *Teaching of Psychology, 10*, 170-171.

Maslow, A. H. (1962). *Toward a psychology of being.* Princeton, NJ: Van Nostrand.

McKeachie, W. J., Lin, Y. G., Moffett, M. M., & Daugherty, M. (1978). Effective teaching: Facilitative vs. directive style. *Teaching of Psychology, 5*, 193-194.

Ravizza, K. (1977). Peak experiences in sport. *Journal of Humanistic Psychology, 17*, 35-40.

Rogers, C. R. (1969). *Freedom to learn.* Columbus, OH: Charles E. Merrill.

Spiegel, T. A., Cameron, S. M., Evans, R., & Nodine, B. F. (1980). Integrating writing into the teaching of psychology: An alternative to Calhoun and Selby. *Teaching of Psychology, 7*, 242-243.

Note

An earlier draft of this paper was presented at the Division Two Activities Exchange at the 1984 APA Convention. I wish to acknowledge the chair of that program, Joseph J. Palladino, for his helpful comments on that draft. I also thank Darlene Burbage for her assistance in the preparation of this report.

Using a Film as a Personality Case Study

Richard D. Logan
Department of Human Development
University of Wisconsin-Green Bay

While taking a testing course in the 1960s, I learned how the Wechsler Adult Intelligence Scale can also serve as a diagnostic projective technique. Since then, I have tried to find psychological materials that can be used for purposes other than their original one. In particular, I am always looking for theoretically unbiased, case-study materials for students in my theories of personality course. The search is frustrating. For example, written case histories usually reflect the author's own theoretical inclination. Especially when they are used to illustrate different theoretical perspectives, such materials should not be biased toward or against any viewpoint.

The three-part film series, *Three Approaches to Psychotherapy* (Shostrom, 1965), features Carl Rogers, Fritz Perls, and Albert Ellis giving demonstrations of their respective approaches to therapy with an actual client. The film series apparently serves its purpose of introducing different approaches to psychotherapy, judging by its long use in counseling, therapy, and adjustment courses. The purpose of the three films is to illustrate different versions of the therapeutic process. However, over the course of the sessions, the client (Gloria) provides a great deal of information about her life and character that invites interpretation for another purpose. This information is not filtered through constructs of a case-study author, although Rogers, Perls, and Ellis do exert some constraining influence. Therefore, these films lend themselves to an assignment in which students are asked to make and support different theoretical interpretations of Gloria's personality.

I use the film series in my course on theories of personality, the textbook for which is Rychlak's (1981) *Introduction to Personality and Psychotherapy*. I show the segment with Rogers counseling Gloria as we begin studying Rogers's theory and after we study Freud, Adler, Jung, Sullivan, Dollard and Miller, and Skinner, in that order. I divide the class into six small groups. Each group views the film and interprets the client's personality or behavior from a particular theoretical perspective. Each group then describes for the class the significant themes its members observed from their assigned theoretical viewpoint. The suitability of the film for this exercise is borne out by the fact that students are able to present thorough interpretations from each perspective. The Freudian group sees a panoply of traits characteristic of an unresolved Oedipus complex; the Adlerians see a neurotic overstriving for perfection; the Jungians see a wrestling with the unconscious shadow complex and faces of the anima and animus; the Sullivanians see indications of a dissociated sexual/angry self; and the Dollard and Miller group sees a powerful approach-avoidance conflict surrounding sex, men, and father. I ask the Skinnerian group to observe the interaction between client and therapist; they usually make some interesting observations about how Rogers may be shaping Gloria's behavior—and vice versa—with various social reinforcers, such as smiling, nodding, and saying "mm-hmm." If time permits, I show the entire series, including Perls and Ellis as well as Rogers, and all three sessions become the material for personality interpretation.

Because the film series portrays realistic therapeutic sessions, students feel that they are participating in a dialectical process involving competing approaches to personality theory. The exercise also serves as preparation for the take-home final exam, which requires students to write several extensive theoretical interpretations of a lengthy case study. The exercise also helps to emphasize the important point that there is no one path to the truth in the field of personality theory.

References

Rychlak, J. F. (1981). *Introduction co personality and psychotherapy*. New York: Houghton-Mifflin.

Shostrom, E. L. (Producer and Director). (1965). *Three approaches to psychotherapy* [Film]. Santa Ana, CA: Psychological Films.

3. EMPHASIZING WRITING

Persons in the Personality Theory Course: Student Papers Based on Biographies

Susan C. Mueller
Russell Sage College

In teaching an upper-level undergraduate course in personality theory, I have wrestled with the discrepancy between the excitement I felt about theories and the insights they offered about myself and people in my life, on the one hand, and the much more abstract and lifeless version of the field that students seemed to be getting from the textbook. I tried to revitalize the course with supplementary readings, and although sometimes they worked and sometimes not, even the successes were too limited in scope to convey to students the transformation in understanding people, which I deemed the aim of studying personality theory. Of course, it is possible that my vision was not realistic for undergraduates in a first personality course; but I knew some of these students in other contexts and felt that they were capable of sharing more of my vision. The route must be at fault.

An experimental component was needed—an intellectual laboratory. Textbook abstractions are only a convenient summary of the concepts of a discipline whose value and truth cannot be established except in application. A variety of techniques exist for applying personality concepts to people, but I dismissed many of them as impractical or undesirable. The simplest technique would be self examination. After all, being a person oneself is an implicit course prerequisite, so that material is readily at hand. Introspective exercises and journals were a possibility—and I had used them with success in an elective course on "The Self." But such introspective devices are less suitable for a personality theory course, because many personality theories are centrally concerned with the issue of maladjustment, and self-diagnosis in the context of the classroom raises ethical dilemmas. What are we to do with the student who, rightly or wrongly, makes the self-diagnosis of, for example, an anally fixated, non-self-actualized neurotic? Teachers typically do not have the time or training to deal with the kinds of situations such assignments are likely to elicit.

An alternative, offered by many text writers, is to illustrate each theory with its originator's biography. Freud's oedipal conflict, Adler's conquest over rickets, and Skinner's disciplined life make fascinating topics for discussion. But this approach conveys the impression that a theory lacks consensual scientific validity. This intimation, repeated throughout the term, probably outlasts attempted antidotal lectures on experimental validation.

Another option is to require students to apply theories to standard case materials. One supplementary text available for this purpose is written by White, Riggs, and Gilbert (1976). While this approach avoids the worst pitfalls of the self-analysis and theorist biography methods, it risks the limitation that students may not readily relate to the particular biographical materials selected by the instructor. Without interest in the case materials themselves, the student experiences a dry academic exercise.

Another method, which I shall describe, retains the objective and integrative strengths of the case materials approach, yet avoids its tendency toward academic artificiality by giving students greater latitude to explore directions suggested by their own interests. My students write a term paper using various theories of personality to understand the biography (or autobiography) of a real person, living or dead. Theories become less abstract—tools for understanding, rather than dry conceptual schemes to be memorized. And because the target person is selected by the student, rather than assigned by the instructor, there is room for self-exploration in a manner less threatening, and less invasive of privacy, than straightforward self-analysis.

A wealth of material is available for this purpose, and the variety is enormous—from historical figures to current rock stars, from heroes and heroines to tragic and demagogic villains. In three class sections (from 1981 to 1983), 71 students have written on 58 different target persons. (See Table 1 for a summary of persons whom students have analyzed.) Though nearly all of my students at this women's college have been female, many (45%) have written about men.

The Assignment

Students are required to submit a term paper analyzing their selected target person, using concepts from a variety of theories presented in the course. The assignment has an explicit and focused aim of applying theoretical material to

Table 1. Persons Selected for Analysis by Students

Louisa May Alcott	Jill Kinmont
Lauren Bacall	G. Gordon Liddy
Elizabeth Blackwell	Anne Lindberg
Louise Bryant	Charles "Lucky" Luciano
Barbara Cartland	Helen Keller
Joan Crawford	John F. Kennedy
Salvador Dali	Henry Kissinger
Dorothy Day	Douglas MacArthur
Emily Dickinson (2)	Malcolm X
Babe Didrikson (2)	Margaret Mead
Walt Disney	Jim Morrison (2)
Eleanor of Aquitaine	Wolfgang Amadeus Mozart
Frances Farmer	Richard Nixon
Albert Fish	Lee Harvey Oswald
F. Scott Fitzgerald	Elvis Presley
Jane Fonda	James Earl Ray
Betty Ford	Carl Rogers
Anne Frank	Eleanor Roosevelt (7)
Sigmund Freud (2)	Franklin D. Roosevelt
Mahatma Gandhi	Lillian Roth
Judy Garland	Russell Sage
Kahlil Gibran	Edie Sedgwick
Barry Goldwater	B. F. Skinner
Patricia Hearst	Captain Slocum
Lillian Hellman	Elizabeth Cady Stanton
Katherine Hepburn	Harry Truman
Adolf Hitler (4)	Gloria Vanderbilt
Alice James	Maria Von Trapp
Janis Joplin	Shelley Winters

Note: Numbers in parentheses indicate number of students reporting on a given person (if more than one).

the understanding of specific individual lives. This concern with application, which I think of as highlighting "correspondence rules" for relating theory to observables, influences both the selection of material to be covered in lecture and the kinds of assignments made throughout the term. For example, in lecture, rather than simply explaining the concept of Freudian psychosexual stages and fixations, soldiers metaphor and all, I am compelled to describe traits commonly thought to be derived from various psychosexual stages. (The list provided by Engler, 1979, p. 55, is good for this purpose.)

I provide several directive questions throughout the term to facilitate the task of applying theories to biographies (see Table 2). Students write brief (one page) answers, and class discussions build on these interim reports. Because these reports constitute preliminary conceptualizations of sections of the term paper, students are obligated to work on the term paper throughout the course, and they receive feedback about their ideas from fellow students as well as from the instructor. This structure eases the student's burden at the end of the term and has substantially improved the papers submitted, compared with earlier terms in which no interim reports were required

The course is organized around five paradigms: the trait paradigm, the learning paradigm, the psychoanalytic paradigm, the sociocultural paradigm, and the existentialhumanistic paradigm. Each paradigm is introduced with a lecture describing and evaluating the perspective. The text I currently use is Hergenhahn's (1984) *An Introduction to Theories of Personality*, which provides students with a highly readable and concise description of each theory, thus freeing class time for supplementary topics and discussion. I do not follow the order of the text because the modified progression described here seems more appropriate for the course as it is constituted.

Trait Paradigm

The course begins with trait theory, both because the concept of individual differences is a central issue in personality theory, and because the trait approach is more descriptive and less dynamic than other material, making it easier (or students to apply without extensive background. I point out the historical logic of beginning here in honor of Allport's first personality course in this country. Students consider the relevance of this approach to the biographies they have selected by identifying two or three salient traits of their target persons, illustrating each trait with supportive details. Class discussion of the process of inferring traits as underlying dispositions from behavioral observations is enriched by the wealth of detail that students bring to the course from their diverse biographies.

Learning Paradigm

The next perspective, learning, follows logically since some of the behavioral observations considered by students in the trait perspective do not seem to them to be sufficient evidence to infer a general personality trait. Learning principles provide an alternative conceptual scheme, emphasizing current and environmental determinants. Social learning theory profits from a fairly thorough discussion of modeling, including reasons for the choice of a particular model.

Table 2. Questions Assigned for Brief Written and Oral Reports

1. *Trait Paradigm:* Identify one trait that characterizes the personality you are studying. Argue either side of the "generality-specificity" issue, that is, the trait is *general* and enduring, or it is *specific* to a particular set of environmental stimuli and reinforcements. Give details from the biography to support your point.

2. *Learning Paradigm:* Describe some aspect of the personality that has been influenced by environmental reinforcements or conditioning. Explain this influence, and speculate how the personality might have been different if the environment had been different.

3. *Psychoanalytic Paradigm:* Describe the unconscious conflicts and contents of the personality. Give supporting evidence.

4. *Sociocultural Paradigm:* Identify the one most significant other (e.g., mother, father, sibling) in the childhood experience of the personality that you are studying. Describe the effects of this relationship.

5. *Humanistic Paradigm:* Evaluate whether or not the personality you have investigated can be characterized as self-actualized. Give reasons.

Psychoanalytic Paradigm

The psychoanalytic perspective as it is portrayed in most personality theory texts offers much abstract theory but little systematic help at a level that enables undergraduates to relate these concepts to observable manifestations. As mentioned above, I supplement text material with descriptions of traits characteristic of oral, anal, and phallic personalities, in order to provide continuity with the trait approach previously covered, and to show the relevance of psychoanalytic theory to normal personality. The biographical method provides a ready opportunity for students to seek evidence of trauma at the appropriate psychosexual stage in order to explain the adult personality traits they have observed. Several kinds of additional supplementary presentations are helpful and can be used as time permits. Dream interpretation is generally a high-interest topic for students, and provides an opportunity to consider symbolism and the language of the unconscious. Frequently, though, students report that no dreams are discussed in the biographical material they are reading. When students report on persons in the arts—for example, van Gogh—or persons who are or seem to be psychotic, there is an opportunity to use these materials as illustrations of the effect of id processes on overt behavior. Other biographies provide ready evidence of sexual inhibition or sublimation.

Sociocultural Paradigm

In the next course unit, dealing with the sociocultural paradigm, students consider significant others in the childhood experience of the individual. This issue is one that students find easy to address, and one they frequently raise on their own, even when I have omitted this question. An alternative discussion could focus on the cultural context as it influences personality, an issue that sometimes emerges, particularly in biographies of 19th-century women, where students clearly see the culturally limited options available to their selected persons. Within this paradigm, Erikson's developmental theory (which I have been sometimes tempted to omit because it is covered in developmental courses) is greeted enthusiastically by students, whose papers effectively use this approach, perhaps because Erikson's naming of basic virtues is concrete and because the developmental perspective is well-suited to biographical material.

Humanistic Paradigm

Humanistic theories invite interpretations of whether or not the figure was self-actualized. The concept of "self-actualization" can be detailed with Maslow's (1971) oftquoted list of characteristics of self-actualized persons. But, because so few persons are self-actualized, a more thorough description of the earlier stages seems warranted.

The biographical data often suggest particular obstacles to selfactualization that emerge from the cultural context or the particular environment, and this is an insight that has implications beyond the academic assignment. Students may also consider whether, and how, persons are able to transcend potentially limiting environments. The question raised by Anderson (1975), whether "self-actualization" is a purely scientific judgment, or a value judgment, is readily understood by students grappling with the task of judging whether their target person is self-actualized. (Student decisions sometimes surprise me; always, the discussion is lively.) This experience of separating the issue "Do I like the person?" from the question, "How psychologically developed is this person?" is also a potentially important learning experience for real life.

Discussion

Significant amounts of history can be learned through biographical selections, and this helps break down the artificial walls created in academia among various disciplines. Students readily see that a particular trait manifestation must be considered in an historical context. They readily acknowledge the effects of economic depression, war, and cultural values as they attempt to understand their chosen target person.

I do not formally discuss in class the thesis that target persons are chosen for various psychologically determined reasons. That seems to me to violate the trust created by the assignment, taken (as it generally is) at face value. But clearly target persons are not chosen at random, as insightful students occasionally proclaim with excitement.

Because each student is an "expert" on the biography selected for intensive investigation, the passivity that is fostered by the model of teaching in which the teacher is the expert (cf. Mann et al., 1970) is avoided. Students have an opportunity to truly be the one in the room who knows the most about a particular topic, a strength similar to Aronson's (1978) concept of the jigsaw classroom, which encourages a climate of mutual respect. Brilliant scholars and mediocre students alike can contribute to the unusual community effort to glean interesting tidbits about "real people"—that Adolf Hitler was a vegetarian and a chocolate freak, that Joan Crawford cleaned what her maids overlooked, and so forth. The instructor is also a learner in this process. I have learned much from students about popular heroes and heroines, as well as traditional literary and historical figures, and the excitement that comes from mutual learning and teaching has energized all of us.

There is an important difference between the expertise a student feels through this assignment and the inflated overconfidence of a pedant. In my experience, students are humble in their interpretations and do not consider themselves to be expert personality analysts, either in this course or beyond. Perhaps the underlying theme of the course, that all theories have some merit but also significant shortfalls—a theme frequently repeated by allusion to the metaphor of several blind men each confronting part of an elephant—offers some protection. In addition, the incompleteness of any particular viewpoint is emphasized by the requirement that projects be comprehensive, including all perspectives. To some measure, humility may emerge naturally from the inevitable complexity of the task, in which biographical materials offer much of interest that defies definitive explanation by any theory, particularly when several biographies with similar apparent causes produce divergent outcomes.

The same complexity that protects from overconfidence, however, introduces another danger. The comprehensibility and applicability of theories may be too readily taken as evidence of the theory's validity (although lack of class consensus about which theories are useful mitigates this risk). A thorough discussion of scientific validation through empirical research seems particularly needed as protection against this danger. Perhaps an ambitious class could even frame hypotheses (or obtain them from lecture or research) based on various theories, and then test them, using their selected biographies as a database. (That might make a creative final exam question!) Obvious methodological difficulties would have to be acknowledged, but the exercise would be a way of stressing empirical validation, not simply comprehensibility, as a test of a theory's value.

One of the main benefits of this exercise is that it encourages students to talk about people, helping to restore the "person" to the field (cf. Carlson, 1971). It seems to me that this is a major strength of the personality theory course, as opposed to a course in personality research. The assignment is one that can be discussed with others outside the class—other students, parents (whether highly educated or not)—and thus it confirms an image of education as an enterprise that develops persons, rather than simply filling them with some foreign matter called knowledge. Although the course as I teach it maintains a rather traditional format, rather than a structurally innovative one (cf. Rogers, 1969), it does encourage students to spend much time and effort examining material of their own selection, and provides a forum for interchange of ideas with other learners. Most importantly, the major aim of a course in personality theory—to learn to view people with an educated vision—is extensively practiced throughout the term.

References

Anderson, W. (1975). The self-actualization of Richard M. Nixon. *Journal of Humanistic Psychology, 15*, 27-34.

Aronson, E. (1978). *The jigsaw classroom.* Beverly Hills, CA: Sage.

Carlson, R. (1971). Where is the person in personality research? *Psychological Bulletin, 75*, 203-219.

Engler, B. (1979). *Personality theories: An introduction.* Boston: Houghton Mifflin.

Hergenhahn, B. R. (1984). *An introduction to theories of personality* (2nd ed.). Englewood Cliffs, NJ: Prentice-Hall.

Mann, R., Arnold, S. M. Binder, J. L., Cytrynbaum, S., Newman, B. M., Ringwald, B. E., Ringwald, J. W., & Rosenwein, R. (1970). *The college classroom: Conflict, change, and learning.* New York: Wiley.

Maslow, A. M. (1971). *The farther reaches of human nature.* New York: Viking.

Rogers, C. R. (1969). *Freedom to learn: A view of what education might become.* Columbus, OH: Merrill.

White, R. W., Riggs, M. M., & Gilbert, D. C. (1976). *Case workbook in personality.* Prospect Heights, IL: Waveland Press.

From Metropolis to Never-neverland: Analyzing Fictional Characters in a Personality Theory Course

Janet F. Carlson
Graduate School of Education and Allied Professions
Fairfield University

In structuring an entry-level graduate course in personality, I believe it important to provide fairly complete, balanced coverage of a range of theories. This approach exposes students to the broad conceptual strategies that constitute the field as well as to individual theorists within these perspectives. Several textbooks are organized by four or five such perspectives (e.g., Carver & Scheier, 1988; Liebert & Spiegler, 1990; Ryckman, 1989), making the task of providing balanced exposure somewhat easier.

Many students enter the course with a favorite theoretical perspective. Vyse (1990) noted that senior psychology majors and those who have completed courses in personality or abnormal psychology were "most likely to have adopted a theory" (p. 227), as 59% of the respondents in his study reported having done so. The entry-level graduate students who are the subjects of this article are similar to the psychology majors sampled by Vyse. They have chosen psychology as their academic focus and have had some coursework in related areas. Thus, it is not surprising that many of them declare theoretical preferences early in the course. Developing a particular orientation may be helpful in some areas of practice, but students in a course in personality theory are not yet deeply involved in service delivery. They should consider alternative theories to broaden their own horizons or, at least, to develop an appreciation of theories favored by professionals who may not share their perspective. Thus, although textbooks offer broad coverage of personality theories, many students appear to need encouragement and direct experience with other theories to get out of their psychoanalytic, humanistic, behavioral, or other theoretical ruts.

To provide an experiential component to the personality theory course, Mueller (1985) assigned a term paper that applied one theory of personality to published biographies of real people. Mueller noted that this assignment made the theories less abstract. Logan (1988) described the use of a well-known, though somewhat dated, film series, *Three Approaches to Psychotherapy* (Shostrom, 1965), as a case study illustration of a variety of perspectives on personality. Similarly, Polyson (1983) suggested studying a television character's behavior as an effective method of increasing the relevance of the personality course's content.

Although these techniques have merit, they are limited in several ways. A single paper, such as Mueller (1985) and Polyson (1983) assigned on a biographical or television character, does not push the theoretically entrenched student beyond the comfort of the preferred orientation. The biographical assignment relies on secondhand accounts of an individual's life, unless the selected person has written an autobiography. Polyson's assignment is also limited by its dependence on a relatively brief portion of a character's behavior. Shostrom's (1965) film series illustrates the differences in therapeutic approaches stemming from theoretical differences, but observing the film does not require students to apply theoretical principles actively.

To address these shortcomings, I require a series of four papers, in each of which students analyze a character's behavior over time according to a specific theoretical orientation. The technique allows students to use firsthand information without eliciting the undesirable aspects of conducting a self-examination (Mueller, 1985) or an analysis of a family member or friend.

At the beginning of the semester, students select a fictional character from a comic strip or a well-known children's story as the subject. They are advised to select a character based primarily on their familiarity with and liking for the character, as they will spend considerable time analyzing the character's personality according to each of the four theoretical orientations covered in the course: psychoanalytic, dispositional, phenomenological, and behavioral. Without citing examples, I inform students that they may select people or animals who may be superheroes (e.g., Batman, Spiderman, and Superman), fictional but realistic characters (e.g., Tom Sawyer), fantasy figures (e.g., Alice-in-Wonderland, Peter Pan, Pinnochio, and Winnie-the-Pooh), or comic strip characters (e.g., Calvin, Cathy, Dagwood, Garfield, and Snoopy). Two or 3 weeks into the semester, I ask for confirmation of each student's character to be sure the characters are appropriate. Characters should appear in print, and the source should provide enough information for a credible analysis. Characters who say or do very little (e.g., Woodstock from the comic strip *Peanuts*) are difficult to use. Although the choice of character is left as open as possible, 1 do require that students choose characters with whom I am already familiar. Otherwise, evaluating the papers becomes difficult and prohibitively time consuming.

Students may apply a specific theory from the family of theories under study, or they may use concepts common to all the members of a particular orientation. The five- to seven-page papers are due at the end of each unit of lectures and readings on each orientation.

Students have been quite creative in their approaches to the assignment, both in selecting characters and in choosing a topic. Some have written excerpts from hypothetical therapy or testing sessions with the character. One student applied the dispositional perspective to Dagwood Bumstead, assembling a CIA dossier to assess his appropriateness for a job involving extensive travel and international espionage.

Evaluation

To evaluate the activity, I mailed a survey to all students who completed the course the previous semester. Directions indicated that the survey was intended to provide feedback to the instructor about the personality course and that respondents should not put their names on the forms. Preaddressed and prestamped envelopes were provided. Two follow-up letters were sent about 4 and 8 weeks after the first mailing. One survey was returned undelivered; of the remaining 18 surveys, 13 (72%) were completed and returned.

The survey included 10 questions that asked students to endorse or rank their preference for components of the course. Students rated these items on a 5-point scale ranging from *not at all helpful* (1) to *very substantially helpful* (5). On the two questions specifically addressing the papers, 10 respondents (77%) indicated that the assignments helped them quite a bit or very substantially in understanding the strategies covered in the course, and 11 (85%) indicated that the assignments helped them quite a bit or very substantially in developing a more comprehensive appreciation of the approaches used to conceptualize personality. In response to a question asking them to endorse those aspects of the course that had helped broaden their perspectives on personality, 12 (92%) students indicated that the papers had contributed to this development, and half of these respondents ranked the papers as the "single most important influence."

In addition, two open-ended questions asked about the best feature of the course and course improvements. In response, 6 (46%) listed the paper assignments as the best feature. Although no one suggested elimination of the

papers or major modifications to the assignment, suggested improvements included requiring fewer assignments, grading less strictly, doing a sample character analysis as a class activity, and incorporating historical figures as potential subjects.

In previous classes, informal feedback indicated that students found the assignment appealing, as it provided an interesting challenge that contained elements of choice and creativity. The variety of characters has kept me interested and challenged as well. Students have said such things as, "This is the best way to teach this course" and "It's a lot of work, but you really do learn the material." Students also indicated that other components of the course were important in their learning. One survey item listed eight aspects of the course, and students indicated which ones contributed to their learning. All respondents checked three or more items. Thus, although the assignment contributes substantially to broadening students' understanding, it is just one component of a successful course.

Advantages

One advantage of this technique is that the experience begins early in the semester and extends throughout the course. Students apply knowledge of personality theories several times, and they must be fluent in more than one theory in order to do well in the course. Furthermore, students directly encounter the strengths and limitations of each perspective. For example, many students create fictitious therapy sessions to illustrate how a therapist with a given orientation would view the character's personality. Students discover this format works well for some orientations (e.g., psychoanalytic) but not for others (e.g., trait approaches).

Each paper requires a fairly complete analysis of the character's personality. Because I am familiar with the characters, I can readily note when some salient feature of a personality is overlooked. The focus of each paper shifts with the emphasis of the particular perspective under review. For example, for the psychoanalytic perspective the papers invariably center on intrapsychic events, whereas many of the behavioral papers emphasize observed actions. The assignment permits a deeper exploration of single theorists if the student is so inclined. Most students, however, have not found it necessary to go beyond the textbook, supplementary readings from a list I provide, and class lectures

Limitations

If students are to profit from the feedback, it must be specific and returned promptly. I generally provide detailed written comments within 1 week for a class of about 20 students. Beyond this modest number, it may be difficult to give such timely feedback. The feedback should include how well the student applied the theory to the character and how well the character's behaviors illustrate this application. A modification of the technique may be feasible for larger classes, such as creating a single term paper with four subsections corresponding to each of the conceptual strategies covered in the course or altering the length of each paper.

References

Carver, C. S., & Scheier, M. F..(1988). *Perspectives on personality*. Needham Heights, MA: Allyn & Bacon.

Liebert, R. M., & Spiegler, M. D. (1990). *Personality: Strategies and issues* (6th ed.). Chicago: Dorsey Press.

Logan, R. D. (1988). Using a film as a personality case study. *Teaching of Psychology, 15*, 103-104.

Mueller, S. C. (1985). Persons in the personality theory course: Student papers based on biographies. *Teaching of Psychology, 12,* 74-78.

Polyson, J. A. (1983). Student essays about TV characters: A tool for understanding personality theories. *Teaching of Psychology, 10*, 103-105.

Ryckman, R. M. (1989). *Theories of personality* (4th ed.). Belmont, CA: Brooks/Cole.

Shostrom, E. L. (Producer & Director). (1965). *Three approaches to psychotherapy* [Film]. Santa Ana, CA: Psychological Films.

Vyse, S. A. (1990). Adopting a viewpoint: Psychology majors and psychological theory. *Teaching of Psychology, 17,* 227-230.

Note

I thank Kurt F. Geisinger for his advice on the evaluation procedures

Questioning and Peer Collaboration as Techniques for Thinking and Writing About Personality

Susan E. Beers
Sweet Briar College

One of the first decisions teachers of personality make is which of the many theories should be covered in a course. However, most of us would be sorely disappointed if, at the end of the term, students had only memorized the handful of theories we had chosen. The value of studying personality theories lies in the comparison and evaluation of alternative viewpoints, not in memorizing them. Because such reasoning involves complex skills, many students require support as they approach course material. I have attempted to offer such support by integrating questioning and the writing of essays into my course in personality.

Although many teachers encourage students to raise questions, question asking is not often formally taught. In the typical classroom, it is the teacher who asks the questions and the students who respond (see Dillon, 1984). Although a good deal of research has been conducted on the types of questions teachers ask and the types of responses questions elicit from students (e.g., Carin & Sund, 1971; Groisser, 1964; Sanders, 1966; Wilen, 1984), little work has been done on ways to help students themselves raise interesting questions. This is a pity as creative work invariably involves exploring the parameters of a question (Csikszentmihalyi & Getzels, 1970; Moore, 1985).

A variety of schemes have been proposed for understanding questioning (cf. Christenbury & Kelly, 1983). This exercise, and some others (e.g., Carin & Sund, 1971; Hunkins, 1976), relied on Bloom's (1956) taxonomy of educational objectives. Bloom's taxonomy includes six cognitive objectives: knowledge, comprehension, application, analysis, synthesis, and evaluation. Awareness of the taxonomy, it is argued, helps students raise thoughtful questions by making them familiar with the various levels at which questions may be asked.

Creative thinking may begin with a question and is often sustained through the act of writing. Current literature on the writing process emphasizes that writing does more than simply record thought. Writing is a powerful tool for learning: for discovering and developing one's thoughts as well as communicating them to others (Elbow, 1981; Flower & Hayes, 1981; Newell, 1984).

As interest in the writing process has increased, a variety of strategies for integrating writing with other classroom activities have emerged. One of the more popular is peer group collaboration, in which groups of students assist each other as they engage in writing projects. Although peer collaboration may not always be an effective substitute for teacher commentary (Newkirk, 1984), it does have the advantage of providing students with a known, rather than ambiguous, audience for their writing, and it encourages students to focus on the essentially communicative aspects of the writing process (George, 1984).

In the spring of 1984 I attempted to support students' efforts in thinking and writing by making question asking and peer collaboration in writing central activities in my course in personality. The exercise was designed to serve three purposes: to encourage students to raise questions, to help students become aware of different levels of questioning, and to encourage students to see writing as an integral part of the inquiry process. The course enrolled 28 students, most of whom were sophomore or junior psychology majors.

Description of the Exercise

Students were assigned to write three questions derived from class discussion, readings, or their independent thinking each week of the term, except for those weeks that essays were due or exams were taken. Each week, copies of all the questions were made available to each student.

During the first week, students received little guidance concerning the nature of the questions that might be written. They were simply told to write questions that would be appropriate for a good essay exam. Copies of that week's questions were returned to the students with a handout (Stano, 1984) listing Bloom's taxonomy and key words that might be found in questions in each of Bloom's six categories. Two key words for each category were as

Table 1. Proportion of Questions Classified at Each Level of Bloom's Taxonomy

Cognitive Level	Week 1	Week 2	Week 4	Week 9
Knowledge	.00	.00	.02	.05
Comprehension	.45	.31	.26	.45
Application	.00	.14	.00	.00
Analysis	.33	.33	.26	.19
Synthesis	.05	.05	.07	.02
Evaluation	.05	.12	.28	.22
Unclassifiable	.12	.05	.12	.07

Table 2. Student Ratings of the Usefulness of the Question Asking and Essay Writing Exercise

Component	Usefulness						
	1	2	3	4	5	6	7
Writing Questions	.05	.11	.05	.11	.16	.37	.16
Categorizing Questions	.05	.00	.10	.25	.25	.15	.20
Copies of Questions	.00	.05	.10	.05	.30	.25	.25
Discussion of Drafts	.06	.06	.00	.00	.28	.28	.33
Overall Utility	.00	.00	.10	.00	.25	.35	.30

Note. Based on a 7-point scale ranging from *not at all useful* (1) to *very useful* (7).

follows: knowledge—*state, list;* comprehension—*explain, identify*; application—*apply, demonstrate*; analysis—*compare, differentiate*; synthesis—*create, hypothesize*; evaluation—*judge, revise.*

Each student was assigned two questions (at random, without replacement) to classify according to the taxonomy. Class discussion focused on the utility of the taxonomy and the function of various types of questions. Students were quick to note that questions at the level of knowledge and comprehension might be appropriate when material was new or difficult to understand. They seemed to appreciate, however, that questions at the higher levels were more interesting. Students were encouraged to consider the questions that they had written and try to write questions one step higher in the taxonomy for the subsequent week.

Questions were categorized by the students four times during the course of the term. Their questions also served as the foci for lectures and were included on the exams.

The writing of three- to five-page essays served as the culminating activity for the question-asking exercise. Twice the class was divided into small groups to "look for interesting essay topics" in the questions that had been written for that week. Class discussion focused on what makes an essay topic interesting, and how one might begin to organizes says addressing the questions that the groups had chosen.

The essays also were discussed. Students chose topics and then brought copies of rough drafts of their essays to class. In that class meeting, students worked in small groups to read and discuss each other's work. The essays were to be revised on the basis of these discussions before being submitted to the instructor.

The process of question writing, categorization, discussion of rough drafts, and revision was repeated as students wrote a second essay. Participation in the question writing activities accounted for 15% of a student's grade, as did each of the essays. The remaining 55% of the grade was determined by the student's performance on two in-class exams and a take-home final.

Evaluation

The proportion of questions classified in each of Bloom's categories during the four times students engaged in the classification exercise is presented in Table 1. These data should be interpreted with caution. Although questions were often discussed in class, no formal attempt was made to assess the reliability of their categorization. To the extent that the data may be trusted, they indicate that students wrote more questions at the evaluation level as the term progressed. Questions at the level of comprehension decreased early in the term, but may have increased later in the term.

At the end of the term students completed a questionnaire to rate the utility of each component of the exercise and the exercise as a whole. The proportion of students rating each component at each point of a 7-point scale ranging from *not at all useful* (1) to *very useful* (7) is presented in Table 2. Students' written comments were also solicited.

Table 2 indicates that the majority of students rated writing and categorizing questions as above average in usefulness (69% and 60%, respectively). However, a sizable minority rated these components as average or below average in usefulness. In the written comments, several students mentioned that they found writing questions useful because it encouraged them to keep up with the reading. Others mentioned that, over time, writing questions became routine. Although some students may have become bored with writing questions, 80% indicated that they found having copies of others' questions above average in usefulness.

It is my impression that the question-writing and categorization tasks had a number of positive effects. Question writing made for a livelier class than might have occurred otherwise. The majority of students clearly had at least skimmed the readings prior to class, and were "primed" to attend and to participate in discussion. In their written evaluations, several students categorized the class as a whole using Bloom's taxonomy, and one student mentioned that she categorized exam questions in another course before answering them. Although I have no way of knowing how many students transferred their knowledge of questioning from this course to others, it does seem that the categorization task helped at least some students to think about the nature of knowledge and learning more explicitly than they had previously.

Although I would not eliminate writing or categorizing questions from this exercise in the future, I am concerned about the students who found the exercise, over time, tedious. In the future, tedium might be reduced if fewer than three questions were required each week. Fewer questions would also allow time for more questions to be explicitly addressed in class meetings.

As indicated in Table 2, 89% of the students found the small group discussions of rough drafts to be above average in utility. The quality of their writing was probably facilitated by this component of the exercise, as it ensured that rough drafts would be written at least 2 weeks before an essay was due, increasing the probability of revision. Importantly, involvement in the writing of others seemed to increase students' interest in both course content and writing. Several students mentioned that they wished there had been the opportunity to read others' essays after they had been revised. Although students write essays or longer papers in all courses I teach, never before have students indicated an interest in learning from the writing of their peers.

Overall, 90% of the students indicated that this exercise was above average in utility. I also believe that, on the whole, the exercise was a success. Although I was a bit disappointed that the level of student questions did not consistently increase as the term progressed, it seemed most important to encourage students to become sensitive to questioning at a level appropriate to their understanding of specific course material. I think that this goal was accomplished.

In addition, reading students' questions allowed me to plan classes that would both interest and inform students. Although it was a bit disconcerting to be told often that I "wasn't needed" as I dropped in on the small discussion groups, it was delightful to see students actively engaged in writing and talking with each other about course material. And, most important, I read few dull essays. Rather, I read essays on "George Kelly's Unconscious Desire to be Sigmund Freud," "A Defense of Radical Behaviorism," and "Similarities Where One Least Expects Them: Freud and Rogers." Many were essays that made me think in new ways about theories I have taught for 10 years.

Moore argues that "the productive question is more important and often a greater achievement than the solution" (1985, p. 85). The exercise described here did not ensure that only productive questions would be raised, but it did encourage students to seek out interesting questions. Although the exercise seems particularly well suited to the topic of personality, it could be adapted to other courses that require students to address complex theoretical material.

References

Bloom, B. S., Jr. (1956). *Taxonomy of educational objectives: Handbook I. The cognitive domain.* New York: D. McKay.

Carin, A. A., & Sund, R. B. (1971). *Developing questioning techniques: A self-concept approach.* Columbus, OH: Charles E. Merrill.

Christenbury, L., & Kelly, P. P. (1983). *Questioning: A path to critical thinking.* Urbana, IL: National Council of Teachers of English.

Csikszentmihalyi, M., & Getzels, J. W. (1970). Concern for discovery: An attitudinal component of creative production. *Journal of Personality, 38,* 91-105.

Dillon, J. T. (1984). Research on questioning and discussion. *Educational Leadership, 42,* 50-56.

Elbow, P. (1981*). Writing with power.* New York: Oxford University Press.

Flower, L., & Hayes, J. R. (1981). Plans that guide the composing process. In C. H. Frederiksen & J. F. Dominic (Eds.), *Writing: The nature, development, and teaching of written communication: Vol. 2. Writing: Process, development and communication* (pp. 39-58). Hillsdale, NJ: Lawrence Erlbaum Associates, Inc.

George, D. (1984). Working with peer groups in the composition classroom. *College Composition and Communication, 35,* 320-326.

Groisser, P. (1964). *How to use the fine art of questioning.* Englewood Cliffs, NJ: Prentice-Hall.

Hunkins, F. P. (1976). *Involving students in questioning.* Boston: Allyn & Bacon.

Moore, M. T. (1985). The relationship between the originality of essays and variables in the problem-discovery process. *Research in the Teaching of English, 19,* 84-95.

Newell, G. E. (1984). Learning from writing in two content areas: A case study/protocol analysis. *Research in the Teaching of English, 18,* 265-287.

Newkirk, T. (1984). Direction and misdirection in peer response. *College Composition and Communication, 35,* 305-311.

Sanders, N. M. (1966). *Classroom questions: What kinds?* New York Harper & Row.

Stano, S. S. (1984). *Critical chinking handout.* Unpublished manuscript, Catholic Schools Office, Diocese of Erie, Erie, PA.

Wilen, W. W. (1984). Implications of research on questioning for the teacher educator. *Journal of Research and Development in Education, 17,* 31-35.

Notes

1. The preparation of this paper was funded by a Cabell Faculty Enrichment Grant.
2. I thank the students in Psychology 218 (Spring, 1984) for their enthusiasm and support.

SECTION II:
ABNORMAL

Developing Simulations

Three computerized case simulations, originally developed for graduate training, were used as adjuncts in Matthew Lambert and Gerard Lenthall's undergraduate courses in Abnormal Psychology and Counseling Theories. The simulations presented clients with agoraphobia, chronic headache pain, and bulimia. Students took a therapist's role and assessed, diagnosed, and treated the simulated clients. The experience allowed them to practice many course-related concepts.

In Frederic Rabinowitz's abnormal psychology class, three student volunteers played the role of an accused serial killer, and the instructor played the part of a court-appointed clinician to role-play conditions that might encourage the manifestation of a multiple personality. The exercise used methods similar to the interviewing procedures and context of the Hillside Strangler murder case, and students acknowledged the presence of more than one personality. The author discussed the ethical considerations of using this procedure.

Timothy Osberg, in class and without warning, began a monologue that illustrated the disordered thought and speech of a schizophrenic. The monologue contained examples of the common disturbances in the content and form of thought characteristic of schizophrenia. After the monologue the instructor thoroughly debriefed the students. Both introductory and abnormal psychology classes found the demonstration engaging and useful.

Using Case Studies

Mary Procidano required her students to write a case-study reaction paper and a research proposal in an abnormal psychology course. Students chose the case-study from a list generated by the instructor and used selected journal articles as models for developing the research proposal. Students valued the research proposal because it provided an opportunity to be creative; they valued the case-study method because it gave an opportunity to read an interesting book.

David Perkins described an assignment in which students organized, prepared, and revised a case study of abnormal behavior using a single theoretical perspective. Students chose persons of historical significance as their subjects. The assignment provided an excellent opportunity to integrate psychology with other liberal arts disciplines and received very positive evaluations.

Teaching Abnormal Psychology Through the Arts and Literature

Joan Chrisler gave students a writing assignment based on the main character of a novel, an autobiography, or a biography about mental illness. Students described the character's symptoms and the treatment and provided a diagnosis and treatment plan. The assignment promoted critical thinking and empathy for the mentally ill.

Dana Anderson developed a teaching exercise for an undergraduate abnormal psychology course to strengthen students' critical-thinking abilities. Students completed a term paper critiquing a book that questioned conventional wisdom in the field. The article listed several books representing a variety of unconventional perspectives. Students completed the paper in stages during which they read the book, took a position on the book's topic, and wrote two drafts of the paper. The exercise increased students' historical perspective and sensitized them to controversial issues. The exercise also required students to engage in an active dialogue with their instructor about an issue raised by the book.

Joan Chrisler assigned her students the task of writing a poem about the experience of mental illness. The instructions for the assignment were open-ended (i.e., students could write poems in any form). The author presented several examples of low and high quality poems along with tips for grading. Writing poetry promoted creative thinking and empathy for the mentally ill.

Michael Fleming, Ralph Piedmont, and Michael Hiam described a course entitled Psychology and Film: Images of Madness, which a psychologist and a film historian taught. Feature films constituted the major elements of instruction. The films allowed students to investigate the relationship between art and psychology and the effects of the film medium on perceptions and attitudes. The authors listed the themes and films that they used.

Examining Miscellaneous Issues

Forrest Scogin and Henry Rickard provided the opportunity for students to fulfill a component of an abnormal psychology course by doing volunteer work in a hospital setting. Students spent 25 hr in their assigned facility. The program operated for many years, and student reactions were quite positive. The program supplemented the traditional course offerings and provided a service for the university and mental health facilities. The authors included guidelines for implementing and managing a volunteer program.

This article described a class activity using the Revised Facts on Suicide Quiz that focused on myths and misinformation about suicide. Richard Hubbard and John McIntosh administered the quiz to their students after lectures about depression. Subsequently, the authors discussed the results in class. The activity can take from 55 to 75 min but can be modified for shorter or longer time periods. The article also contained references to support correct answers.

An adaptation of the television game show, Jeopardy, helped overcome some of the discomfort of studying for the final exam in Carolin Keutzer's abnormal psychology class. The game increased student interaction, encouraged the application of information, and added a light touch to a subject students sometimes find distressing.

Stephen Wurst and Karen Wolford described several activities that helped nondisabled students gain a better understanding about learning disabilities, physical disabilities, and emotional disorders. The instructors developed simulations and lists of speakers who were appropriate for both abnormal and perception classes. Students reported increased empathy toward persons with disabilities as a result of the activities.

In abnormal psychology courses, Stuart Keeley, Rahan Ali, and Tracey Gebing trained students in several techniques for asking questions that supported critical thinking. Evidence collected at the end of the courses suggested that students had learned to make significantly more evaluative questions

1. DEVELOPING SIMULATIONS

Using Computerized Case Simulations in Undergraduate Psychology Courses

Matthew E. Lambert
Department of Psychiatry
University of Missouri-Columbia at the
Missouri Institute of Psychiatry

Gerard Lenthall
Keene State College

Computer simulations for use in teaching undergraduate psychology courses have steadily increased over the past several years (Castellan, 1983). Among the programs that have found a receptive audience in under-graduate instructors are those simulating psychological experiments (e.g., Anderson, 1982; Castellan, 1983; Eamon, 1980; Eamon & Butler, 1985; Grant, 1983; King, King, & Williamson, 1984) and social research methodology (Fazio & Backler, 1983).

Despite the apparently successful use of simulations in research methodology-oriented courses, few simulations have been developed for other undergraduate psychology courses. Simulations for Abnormal Psychology or other specialized courses, such as Counseling Theories, could facilitate student understanding of course material. Simulations could also expose students to various aspects of psychology not available through textbooks; such exposure might affect a student's decision to pursue a psychologically related career.

This article describes three computerized simulations used in undergraduate Abnormal Psychology and Counseling Theories courses.

Therapy Case Simulations

The three computerized simulations were variations on a case simulation developed for graduate-level behavior therapy training and described by Lambert (1987a, 1987b). The cases, named *Mr. Howard*, *Mr. Kopf*, and *Ms. Barnes*, reflected problems of agoraphobia, chronic headache pain, and bulimia, respectively. These are relatively common problems seen in mental health facilities and often discussed in students' course materials. The goal of each simulation was for students to take on a therapist's role, diagnose, and then treat the simulated client using various psychological tools provided in the simulations. Those tools included psychological tests, consultations and referrals to other health professionals, interviews, and specialized behavioral assessments and treatments. Approximately 50 to 60 pieces of information could be gathered by using the various tools during the simulation process.

Content for each simulation was selected by reviewing the behavioral literature published between 1980 and 1987 for each of the problem behaviors simulated. Behavioral assessments were selected if at least two research studies used them as either initial screening or outcome measures. Similarly, treatments were selected if they had been found to have had some efficacy in at least one treatment study. Assessments and treatments that previous research had demonstrated to be ineffective or inefficient were also included. Such options provide students the opportunity to explore the types of case information generated by inappropriate assessment or treatment strategies. When the research literature was inconclusive about the validity of an assessment or treatment approach, I made decisions based on my previous experience working with the simulated problems. Traditional psychological tests were also included so that students could see how the information elicited with these instruments differed from the more specialized behavioral techniques.

The simulations were programmed to run on any IBM or compatible personal computer equipped with a graphics adapter card and operating under PC/MS DOS Version 2.1 or later. The simulations could be enhanced by the use of a color monitor and a printer. Although not necessary for simulation use, a printer is desirable so that students may receive hard copies of the simulation summaries and personal records of their performance with the simulations. Each simulation takes approximately 45 to 60 min to complete.

Using the Simulations

Individual students sit in front of a microcomputer and proceed through the simulation, entering responses on the keyboard and receiving information from the computer screen. When starting the programs, users are presented an on-line orientation to the simulation task, describing their role in completing the simulations. After entering demographic data, to be stored by the computer along with simulation performance data, students are provided a statement of the client's presenting problem and told that the client is waiting to be seen. The following presenting problem statement appears at the start of the agoraphobia (Mr. Howard) simulation:

> Mr. Howard was referred to the mental health center because of increased feelings of tension and restlessness which are interfering with his ability to work. This tension and restlessness has been getting worse over the last 4 to 5 months. Mr. Howard is now in the waiting room ready to see you for his first appointment.

After the presenting problem statement, a menu (see Table 1) appears on the screen. Students choose various diagnostic assessment or treatment categories from the menu by pressing the keyboard number associated with that option. Selecting one of the main menu options leads to a submenu from which specific techniques may be chosen. After selecting a specific assessment or treatment from the submenu, the student is presented with a summary of the method's use and its outcome for that simulated client. Users may then select other assessments or treatments in the same category or branch directly to another assessment or treatment option. This branching strategy provides a more accurate reflection of an actual therapeutic process.

As an example of these procedures, selecting the Gather Assessment Information option from the main menu leads to a submenu (see Table 2) listing specific assessment areas available to the student. Similarly, selecting the Cognitive Behavior Assessment submenu option is followed by another menu listing specific cognitive assessment strategies. Choosing one of the specific assessment strategies is then followed by a description of the assessment technique, such as the description presented next for the cognitive assess-met strategy of Self-Monitoring Level of Anxiety Over a 24-Hr Period.

Table 1. Main Menu Options for the Agoraphobia Simulation

1. Examine intake information
2. Gather assessment information
3. Conduct treatment
4. Consult with another health professional
5. Refer to another health professional

Table 2. Assessment Submenu Options for the Agoraphobia Simulation

1. Clinical behavioral interview
2. Psychophysiological behavior assessment
3. Cognitive behavior assessment
4. Motoric behavior assessment
5. Psychological testing
6. Behavioral inventories
7. Review *DSM-III* diagnostic criteria

> Mr. Howard is asked to subjectively rate his level of anxiety at 1-hr intervals for a 24-hr period beginning at 7:00 a.m. on a Monday until 7:00 a.m. the following day. He is to use a 10-point scale for the ratings, with 1 being *not anxious* and 10 being *as anxious as he could be.*

After reading the description, the student is offered options of following through with the assessment and viewing the results, selecting other assessments, conducting treatment, or consulting/referring to other health professionals. Multiple branching paths programmed into the simulations enable students to move directly from one assessment strategy to another at any time. The procedure for selecting and implementing treatments is also structured in this way.

Students proceed through the simulations in this manner, selecting assessments and treatments, trying them out, and observing the results. Because of the multiple branching possibilities, no one assessment and treatment pattern is necessary to elicit successful case resolution. Students may explore as few or as many menu options as they desire in working through the case. The larger the number of menu options selected, the more opportunities students have to observe the range of behaviors that can be affected by having psychological problems.

On the other hand, students may also gain an understanding of how clients respond when treatment is drawn out due to the use of inappropriate or inefficient assessments and treatments. The simulations are programmed to recognize if the cumulative real-time duration of assessment and treatment strategies would exceed 6 months without significant change in the client's symptoms. Upon this recognition, the computer flags certain client statements for presentation to the student following completion of any further treatment approaches. The statements presented next, which could follow selection of an excessive number of assessment or treatment options, were taken from the agoraphobia simulation:

> Mr. Howard still reports not being able to go back to work for more than a day or two at a time. He informs you that he is in danger of losing his job if he can't return to work on a regular basis soon. He makes this statement to you: "How much longer will I have to suffer with this?"

> Mr. Howard returns for his next session stating he suffered an "anxiety attack" while at the store with his wife. The people running the store thought he was ill and wanted to call an ambulance for him. He states, "this isn't working

either, I want you to do something that's going to help me, not make me worse."

From this flagging component, students should come to understand that providing psychological treatment involves a balance between collecting sufficient information to understand a problem and providing efficient treatment to alleviate it.

Use in Undergraduate Courses

Two simulations, Mr. Howard and Mr. Kopf, were used with an Abnormal Psychology class ($N = 27$) during the fall semester of 1986. Seven students completed the Mr. Howard simulation and 20 students completed the Mr. Kopf simulation. The third simulation, Ms. Barnes, was used by 16 students in a Counseling Theories course during the spring semester of 1987.

Students in both courses were informed that completing one of the simulations was a course requirement, yet their performance would not be graded. They were told to view the simulation exercise as a learning experience to facilitate understanding the course material. Each student was required to write a one-page reaction paper upon completion of the simulation exercise.

Before working with the simulations, all students were given an orientation to microcomputer use by the faculty supervisor of the computer laboratory. Orientation sessions were given during regular class times and consisted of instruction in starting the computers and loading the simulation software. Students were also given an instruction sheet describing the simulation start-up process and were informed that a computer lab consultant would be available to assist them with any problems.

Because of high demand for computer use and a limited number of microcomputers, one microcomputer was reserved for several days during which students were to sign up for a simulation session outside of regular class time. Thirty-min sessions were established for the Abnormal Psychology students, but the class had difficulty completing the simulations in the allotted time. Therefore, the time period was expanded to 60 min for the Counseling Theories students.

Students' Reactions

The students' reaction papers indicated that they generally viewed the simulation exercise as a positive learning experience that should be continued and possibly expanded. The majority of students reported that the exercise helped them understand how material learned during the course is actually used when working with real people. However, many students indicated that the simulation exercise demonstrated limitations in their knowledge of psychology. This lack of knowledge led some students to view their simulation performance negatively.

Many students included statements supporting the use of microcomputers as teaching tools. Several students who stated that they were initially anxious about using a computer reported that the simulation exercise reduced their anxiety. It is uncertain if this perceived anxiety reduction generalized to other computer-related tasks.

Conclusions and Implications

Undoubtedly, student reactions to the simulations reflected a favorable "novelty effect"—all agreed that the simulations were an interesting change of pace. In addition, many students were pleasantly surprised to find that they enjoyed working with the computer. Those positive reactions are notable, but what appears especially relevant is that the majority found using the simulations to be a valuable learning experience.

Many students find it difficult to master abstract concepts, inherent in Abnormal Psychology and Counseling Theories, unless they have concrete examples, which such simulations provide. At the same time, the simulations acted as a motivator for learning the methods and strategies necessary to integrate course material. Moreover, the simulations not only spurred the students to make decisions, thus actively applying their knowledge, but in several instances, the process of doing so increased their knowledge. Having to make repeated decisions in a task such as this quickly elucidates unknown areas of ignorance. The simulations' detailed descriptions and explanations of assessment and treatment methods were a decided asset, filling in those areas that many students chose to explore. This advantage was most likely underutilized, however, because students only had access to the simulations once during the semester. An arrangement allowing the students to control when and for how long they use the simulations can probably facilitate learning even more.

Two caveats to further use of these simulations in undergraduate settings must be remembered; both are based on the original intended use with graduate-level education. First, because the simulations provide a context for increased student involvement and because younger students lack a coherent professional identity, some students may overreact to what they perceive as a poor (or good) performance. Instructors may need to provide some advance inoculation here. They should emphasize that the simulations are used only as supplements to the course and that a perceived good or poor performance implies neither good nor poor therapeutic skills.

Second, the simulations represent a very distinct theoretical perspective. Students may embrace the theoretical model portrayed in the simulations merely on the basis of its presentation via a computer. Accepting information as factual simply because it was presented by a computer has been a concern stemming from the use of other psychologically related software (Sampson, 1986). If courses are based on a generalist model seeking to make students aware of a range of theoretical orientations, efforts should be made to represent the programs as just one of several approaches to treating the problems portrayed.

Despite these potential concerns, the use of computer case simulations in undergraduate psychology courses offers significant potential. An ideal situation is one that includes computer simulations as part of a reasonably priced instructional package consisting of text, study guide, and material-oriented, computerized case simulations. Such a package could provide students with both theoretical and applied materials. With this package, students could get a "hands-on" feel for psychology.

References

Anderson, D. E. (1982). Computer simulations in the psychology laboratory. *Simulation & Games, 13,* 13-36.

Castellan, N. J. (1983). Strategies for instructional computing. *Behavior Research Methods & Instrumentation, 15,* 270-279.

Eamon, D. B. (1980). LABSIM: A data-driven simulation program for instruction in research design & statistics. *Behavior Research Methods & Instrumentation, 12,* 160-164.

Eamon, D. B., & Butler, D. L. (1985). Instructional programs for psychology: A review and analysis. *Behavior Research Methods, Instruments, & Computers, 17,* 345-351.

Fazio, R. H., & Backler, M. H. (1983). Computer lessons for a social psychology research methods course. *Behavior Research Methods & Instrumentation, 15,* 135-137.

Grant, M. J. (1983). Using computer simulation to teach attitude surveying. *Behavior Research Methods & Instrumentation, 15,* 574-576.

King, A. R., King, B. F., & Williamson, D. A. (1984). Computerized simulation of psychological research. *Journal of Computer Based Instruction, 11,* 121-124.

Lambert, M. E. (1987a). A computer simulation for behavior therapy training. *Journal of Behavior Therapy & Experimental Psychiatry, 18,* 245-248.

Lambert, M. E. (1987b). MR. HOWARD: A behavior therapy simulation. *The Behavior Therapist, 10,* 139-140.

Sampson, J. P., Jr. (1986). The use of computer-assisted instruction in support of psychotherapeutic processes. *Computers in Human Behavior, 2,* 1-19.

Note

A package of four (an additional case, Ms. Mayne [cocaine abuse], has been completed) simulations, software documentation materials, and related research materials are available on loan from the author to professionals wishing to use them in teaching graduate and undergraduate psychology courses. The programs are also available to researchers wishing to evaluate their usefulness in training mental health professionals. Information about how to construct and evaluate similar computerized case simulations may also be obtained from the author.

Creating the Multiple Personality: An Experiential Demonstration for an Undergraduate Abnormal Psychology Class

Fredric E. Rabinowitz
University of Redlands

The multiple personality disorder has been recognized by the American Psychiatric Association (1987) and defined as a dissociative disorder that involves the existence within the individual of two or more distinct personalities, each of which is dominant at a particular time. The personality that is dominant at any particular time determines the individual's behavior. Each personality is complex and integrated with its own unique behavior patterns and social relationships.

It has been suggested that a disproportionate number of multiple personality cases have been diagnosed by a small group of clinicians (Spanos, Weekes, & Bertrand,

1985). Although only 13 cases were reported from 1934 to 1971 (Rosenbaum, 1980), the number of reported cases in psychiatric journals has increased exponentially since 1971, with some clinicians claiming to have seen 50 or more of these individuals (Allison, 1974; Bliss, 1980, 1984; Kluft, 1982). Although some investigator's (e.g., Allison & Schwartz, 1980) believe that earlier cases had been misdiagnosed as schizophrenia or other personality disorders, others suggest that the increase in cases reported may be due to secondary gains achieved by playing the role of a multiple personality patient (Spanos et al., 1985, Thigpen & Cleckley, 1984) .

The multiple personality phenomenon has been explained by psychodynamic theorists as well as social psychologists. The psychodynamic perspective suggests that individuals manifesting this disorder have experienced some severe childhood trauma that has resulted in an unconscious splitting defense mechanism to protect the ego from disintegration. When combined with psychological stressors in adulthood, this childhood predisposition toward splitting may result in an individual manifesting two or more distinct personalities, which have little knowledge of each other (Gruenewald, 1984; Herzog, 1984).

In contrast, the social psychological perspective suggests that individuals learn to enact the role of the multiple personality patient based on the widespread information about this disorder found in books and movies about multiple personality (Spanos et al., 1985; Sutcliff & Jones, 1962; Thigpen & Cleckley, 1984). The motivation to take on the multiple personality role may be rooted in a desire to avoid responsibility for ego-dystonic activities and to gain positive attention from the psychiatric community, which tends to perceive multiple personality cases as more interesting than most other disorders (Thigpen & Cleckley, 1984).

Sutcliff and Jones (1962) suggested that many manifestations of multiple personality occur following hypnotic procedures. Hypnosis is popularly believed to help tap into unconscious parts of the personality (Frankel, 1976), but it has also been described as a legitimate social context to allow for imagination and role demands to be manifested (Sarbin, 1976). A clinician who uses hypnotic procedures may actually legitimize the manifestation of a multiple personality by suggesting that another personality emerge and speak in the hypnotic state. During the trial of Kenneth Bianchi, the Hillside Strangler, hypnotic procedures were used to see if a hidden personality that knew about the murders existed (Schwarz, 1981). Bianchi described another identity that had actually committed the murders of several women in California.

Spanos et al. (1985) showed that individuals subjected to the same interviewing techniques and context as Bianchi would also manifest a multiple personality. Using these researchers' methodology, it was hypothesized that students asked to play the role of an accused murderer, subtly cued by an authority figure (e. g., the teacher),

would show symptoms of the multiple personality disorder without advance knowledge of these symptoms.

The following demonstration was designed to show students: (a) the diagnostic characteristics of the multiple personality and how to distinguish it from other disorders, (b) how demand characteristics and contextual variables affect responses to the clinical interview, (c) the role of the courtroom psychiatrist in the legal system, and (d) how various theoretical models explain the existence of the multiple personality.

Procedure

The 27 students in the Abnormal Psychology course were asked to respond to an original questionnaire, the Imagination Potential Scale, at the beginning of the 90-min class. This questionnaire was designed after the Harvard Group Scale for Hypnotic Susceptibility (Shor & Orne, 1963) and based on data suggesting that a vivid imagination and deep involvement in the arts, reading, or religion are good indicators of suggestibility (Hilgard, 1965). Three individuals, chosen from those who scored highest on the scale, were asked if they would take part in a classroom experiment. They were told that they did not have to participate and could withdraw if they were not comfortable with the procedures. After securing their permission, I took the three individuals outside the classroom and read them the following instructions based on the Spanos et al. (1985) study:

You are to play the role of an accused murderer, Harry (Betty) Michaels. He (she) has been accused of killing three women: Ann, Louise, and Mary (three men Andy, Larry, and Marty). Despite much evidence of guilt, a "not guilty" plea has been entered. The court has ordered a psychiatric evaluation. You will be asked to participate in a simulated psychiatric interview. You should play the role of Harry (Betty) throughout the interview, and use any knowledge you have about criminals and any information you can pick up from the setting to give a convincing performance. If I suggest the use of hypnosis, go along with role playing being hypnotized as well.

Each subject was brought into the classroom individually while the others waited in the hall, out of earshot of the class. The teacher identified himself as the court-appointed psychiatrist and asked the student to sit across from him. He requested the following information:

Tell my why you are here.
Tell me about Ann (Andy), Louise (Larry), and Mary (Marty).
Tell me about your childhood.
Tell me about your relationship with your parents. Tell me about your girlfriends (boyfriends).

Following the answers to these questions, the teacher/psychiatrist says:

I believe it will be possible to find out more information under hypnosis. Is that O.K.? You will be hypnotized by

53

the following procedure. Focus on the end of my pen; as I lower it to the floor, your eyes will become heavy and close. You will then be hypnotized.

After following these procedures, the subject will follow the suggestion to close his or her eyes. The next statements by the teacher/psychiatrist are directly from the Bianchi transcripts (Schwarz, 1981, pp. 139-143):

> I've talked a bit to Harry (Betty) but I think that perhaps there might be another part of Harry (Betty) that I haven't talked to, another part that maybe feels somewhat differently from the part I talked to. I would like to communicate with that other part. When the different part is present, please raise your right hand.
>
> Would you talk to me, part, by saying "I'm here?"
> Part, are you the same thing as Harry (Betty) or are you different in any way?

The subject should respond to the questions and continue by answering the following:

> Who are you?
> Tell me about yourself.
> Do you have a name I can call you?
> Tell me about yourself,_____
> What do you do?
> Tell me about Ann (Andy), Louise (Larry), and Mary (Marty).
> Tell me about Harry (Betty). What is he (she) like?
> When I count to 10 you will awaken from the hypnosis.
> What do you remember from the hypnosis?

Results

The procedure was repeated for each subject as the class watched. At the end of the three performances, the three subjects were brought to the front of the room to be debriefed by the instructor and to answer questions from the class. The typical questions from the observers tended to focus on whether the subjects were really hypnotized and why they had described another personality during the interview.

All subjects acknowledged a second personality with another name. Although they initially denied guilt, they each admitted committing the crime when playing the part of the other personality. In each case, the second personality was described in diametrically opposed terms to the first (i.e., if Betty was nice and good, then Sarah was mean. and vengeful). One of the subjects could not remember the name of her alternative personality when questioned following the demonstration. During the debriefing, which involved discussion about role playing and hypnotic suggestibility, the subjects agreed among each other that they were playing the role of being hypnotized and that the alternative personalities that emerged seemed to be easy explanations for their supposed deviant behavior.

The debriefing and question and answer session provided a lead-in to a discussion of multiple personality

phenomena from various viewpoints. These included a definition of the disorder and its differential diagnosis, the specifics of the Bianchi case from which the demonstration was taken, theories about the etiology of multiple personality and its increased prevalence in recent years, the role of psychiatric and legal intervention, and clinical treatment considerations.

The results of this classroom demonstration coincided with those of Spanos et al. (1985). They found that when compared to a group of subjects exposed to less manipulative instructions and a no-hypnosis control group, the Bianchi treatment group subjects were more likely to choose a different name when asked about their other personality (81%), were likely to admit guilt of the crime when speaking as the second personality (61%), and were likely to have some amnesia of the hypnotic episode (61%).

Discussion

This demonstration suggests that the multiple personality can be created in the classroom situation; however, there are ethical and theoretical limitations to be considered. Because the instructor is using highly suggestive directions, it is possible that the subjects may actually become hypnotized during the demonstration. Knowledge of hypnotic procedures and trance states is highly recommended when performing this demonstration (e.g., Shor, 1969). Debriefing after the procedure should include information about the nature of hypnosis and suggestibility (e.g., Barber, 1972) as well as the role of demand characteristics and contextual cues (e.g., Orne, 1962).

It should also be emphasized that the Bianchi case appeared to be an example of a known sociopath manipulating the symptomatology of the multiple personality for secondary gain in his legal proceedings. Many researchers and clinicians believe that the multiple personality exists as a legitimate disorder and differentiate it from psychotic disorders, personality disorders, and malingering (e.g., Meyer & Osborne, 1987). Therefore, a discussion of various theoretical perspectives following the demonstration is essential to ensure that students do not assume that all multiple personality cases are always under the control of the identified individual, the result of creative imagination, or based on suggestive instructions from an authority figure.

References

Allison, R. B. (1974). A new treatment approach for multiple personalities. *American Journal of Chemical Hypnosis, 17,* 15-32.

Allison, R. B., & Schwartz, T. (1980). *Minds in many pieces: The making of a very special doctor.* New York: Rawson, Wade.

American Psychiatric Association. (1987). *Diagnostic and statistical manual of mental disorders* (3rd ed., rev.). Washington, DC: Author.

Barber, T. (1972). *LSD, marihuana, yoga, and hypnosis.* Chicago: Aldine .

Bliss, E. L. (1980). Multiple personalities: A report of 14 cases with implications for schizophrenia and hysteria. *Archives of General Psychiatry, 37,* 1388-1397.

Bliss, E. L. (1984). A symptom profile of patients with multiple personalities, including MMPI results. *Journal of Nervous and Mental Disease, 171,* 197-202.

Frankel, F. (1976). *Hypnosis: Trance as a coping mechanism.* New York: Plenum.

Gruenewald, D. (1984). On the nature of multiple personality: Comparisons with hypnosis. *International Journal of Clinical and Experimental Hypnosis, 32,* 170-190.

Herzog, A. (1984). On multiple personality: Comments on diagnosis, etiology, and treatment. *International Journal of Clinical and Experimental Hypnosis, 32,* 210-221.

Hilgard, E. (1965). *Hypnotic susceptibility.* New York: Harcourt, Brace & World.

Kluft, R. P. (1982). Varieties of hypnotic interventions in the treatment of multiple personality. *American Journal of Clinical Hypnosis, 24,* 230-240.

Meyer, R. G., & Osbome, Y. H. (1987). *Case studies in abnormal behavior.* Boston: Allyn & Bacon.

Orne, M. (1962). On the social psychology of the psychological experiment: With particular reference to demand characteristics and their implications. *American Psychologist, 17,* 776-783.

Rosenbaum, M. (1980). The role of the term schizophrenia in the decline of diagnoses of multiple personality. *Archives of General Psychiatry, 37,* 1383-1385.

Sarbin, T. (1976). Hypnosis as role enactment. In P. Sheehan & C. Perry (Eds.), *Methodologies of hypnosis* (pp. 123-152). New York: Wiley.

Schwarz, J. R. (1981). *The hillside strangler: A murderer's mind.* New York: New American Library.

Shor, R. (1969). Three dimensions of hypnotic depth. In C. Tart (Ed.), *Altered states of consciousness* (pp. 251-261). New York: Wiley.

Shor, R., & Orne, E. (1963). Norms on the Harvard Group Scale for Hypnotic Susceptibility, Form *A. International Journal of Clinical and Experimental Hypnosis, 11,* 39-48.

Spanos, N. P., Weekes, J. R., & Bertrand, L. D. (1985). Multiple personality: A social psychological perspective. *Journal of Abnormal Psychology, 94,* 362-376.

Sutcliff, J. P., & Jones, J. (1962). Personal identity, multiple personality, and hypnosis. *International Journal of Clinical and Experimental Hypnosis, 10,* 231-269.

Thigpen, C. H., & Cleckley, H. M. (1984). On the incidence of multiple personality disorder. *International Journal of Clinical and Experimental Hypnosis, 32,* 63-66.

Note

Requests for the Imagination Potential Scale, should be sent to Frederic E. Rabinowitz, Department of Psychology, University of Redlands, Redlands, CA 92373-0999.

The Disordered Monologue: A Classroom Demonstration of the Symptoms of Schizophrenia

Timothy M. Osberg
Niagara University

One of the challenges in teaching students about schizophrenia is to provide vivid descriptions of its symptoms. Recent films depicting case examples of people with schizophrenia have helped. For example, *Madness* (a segment from PBS's *The Brain* series) and *Into Madness*

(from HBO's *America Undercover* series) contain some compelling case examples of this disorder. A more powerful demonstration of the bizarre symptoms experienced by people with schizophrenia would be for the instructor to model the typical outward presentation of schizophrenia to the class. This article describes a classroom demonstration that simulates a verbal encounter with a person experiencing symptoms of schizophrenia. My goal was to achieve a portrayal that was sensitive and accurate.

Procedure

Modeling schizophrenia does not require an instructor to learn all the bizarre behavioral nuances that may accompany it. Demonstrating the bizarre quality of language and thought that might be observed in a person with schizophrenia suffices. Before discussing schizophrenia and without any prior warning, I launch into the following monologue:

Okay class, we've finished our discussion of mood disorders. Before I go on I'd like to tell you about some personal experiences I've been having lately. You see I've [pause] been involved in highly abstract [pause] type of contract [pause] which I might try to distract [pause] from your gaze [pause] if it were a new craze [pause] but the sun god has put me into it [pause] the planet of the lost star [pause] is before you now [pause] and so you'd better not try to be as if you were one with him [pause] because no one is one with him [pause] any one who tries to be one with him [pause] always fails because one and one makes three [pause] and that is the word for thee [pause] which must be like the tiger after his prey [pause] and the zommon is not common [pause] it is a zommon's zommon. [pause] But really class, [holding your head and pausing] what do you think about what I'm thinking about right now? You can hear my thoughts can't you? I'm thinking I'm crazy and I know you [point to a student] put that thought in my mind. You put that thought there! Or could it be that the dentist did as I thought? She did! I thought she put that radio transmitter into my brain when I had the novocaine! She's making me think this way and she's stealing my thoughts!

You can read the monologue to students, but practicing it several times before class gives it a more spontaneous quality. Your affect during the monologue can also influence its impact. Persons with schizophrenia often show either inappropriate affect (e.g., laughing when talking about tragic things) or blunted affect (i.e., displaying no emotion at all). I suggest caution in how you modulate your affect during the monologue. Some instructors with a flair for the dramatic might want to heighten its impact by displaying the silly affect of the person with the disorganized subtype of schizophrenia. However, this runs the risk of offending students who may have a friend or family member who suffers from schizophrenia.

After the monologue and after students collect themselves (reactions range from laughter to incredulity), I explain that the speech was meant to demonstrate the language of a person with schizophrenia. I ask students to give their reactions to my speech. I ask them what they were thinking and if they felt uncomfortable. The answers

to these questions prompt a discussion of how people with schizophrenia might feel about the way others react to them. The schizophrenic person might be sensitive to and hurt by the reactions of others. Other issues can also be examined. To what extent do the bizarre and seemingly meaningless ideas expressed have idiosyncratic meaning for the person? Might some of the delusions represent the person's primitive attempts to explain the symptoms he or she is beginning to experience? The monologue also helps to debunk the common misconception that schizophrenia means multiple personality.

While discussing the text's material on schizophrenia, I refer to the monologue because it contains simple examples of the more common disturbances in the content and form of thought as spelled out in the *DSM-III-R* (American Psychiatric Association, 1987). Disturbances in the form of thought include *loose associations* (jumping from topic to unrelated topic), *neologisms* (creating new words), *perseveration* (repeatedly returning to the same topic), and *clanging* (rhyming and punning). Disorders of thought content include *thought broadcasting* (believing others can hear one's thoughts), *thought insertion* (feeling people are inserting thoughts into one's mind*), thought withdrawal* (believing someone is removing one's thoughts), and *delusions of being controlled* (by some external force). Examples of these phenomena in the monologue include:

Clanging—abstract/contract/distract; gaze/craze;
  makes three and that is the word for thee
preservation—no one is one. . . and any one who tries
  to be one . . . fails because one and one
neologism—zommon
loose association—included throughout
thought broadcasting—You can hear my thoughts
  can't you?
thought insertion—You put that thought there!
thought withdrawal—she's stealing my thoughts
delusions of being controlled—she put a radio
  transmitter in my brain

I reproduce the foregoing list as an overhead (the monologue itself can also be reproduced as an overhead and presented before this) and review each example as I discuss the common symptoms of schizophrenia described in the *DSM-III-R*.

Evaluation

On the four occasions I have used this demonstration, the students have been very engaged by it. Their reactions are enthusiastic and generate lively discussion. Students evaluated the demonstration after I used it in an abnormal psychology class ($N = 27$). An open-ended question asked students to describe their thoughts as I spoke the monologue. Also, students rated the demonstration on a scale ranging from *not very useful* (1) to *very useful* (4) and indicated their recommendations concerning whether I should use the demonstration in future classes on a scale marked *No, Maybe, and Yes, definitely.*

Students' open-ended comments included: "I was confused"; "I thought you were crazy"; "It made me nervous"; "I couldn't understand what was going on. I looked around to see everyone else's reactions"; "I would have felt uncomfortable if someone I met on the street talked like that instead of a classroom professor"; and "I thought for [a schizophrenic] to do this must take some higher thought processes—the way he rhymed, etc." In light of some of these comments, one reviewer of this article pointed out the possibility that a student with a friend or family member diagnosed as schizophrenic might react strongly to the demonstration. However, to date no student has been upset after the demonstration. To the contrary, on one occasion, a student with a family member diagnosed as schizophrenic approached me after class to praise the demonstration. She confided that the demonstration and discussion had helped her gain a better understanding of her relative's disorder. Nevertheless, you might want to prepare yourself to handle any concerns raised by students during or after class by assembling referral information for a local mental health clinic or mental health organization.

The mean rating of the usefulness of the demonstration was 3.7 ($SD = .49$), indicating that students thought it had considerable merit. In addition, 100%

indicated Yes, definitely in response to my question about whether I should use the demonstration in future classes. Thus, students consider the monologue an engaging and useful demonstration. It takes only 10 to 15 min, including discussion, and offers an alternative to lengthy video portrayals or field trips for introductory psychology or abnormal psychology classes.

References

American Psychiatric Association. (1987). *Diagnostic and statistical manual of mental disorders* (3rd ed., rev.) Washington, DC: American Psychiatric Association.

Raymond, A., & Raymond, S. (Producers), & Raymond, S. (Director). (1989). *Into madness* [Film]. AR/SR Productions (HBO Presentation).

Sage, D. L., Jr. (Producer, Director). (1984). *Brain*, Part 7: Madness [Film]. New York: WNET.

Note

I thank Charles L. Brewer and three anonymous reviewers for their helpful comments on an earlier version of this article.

2. USING CASE STUDIES

Students' Evaluation of Writing Assignments in an Abnormal Psychology Course

Mary E. Procidano
Fordham University

Motivated by the writing-across-the-curriculum (WAC) movement, psychology professors have integrated a variety of writing assignments into their courses. However, there is little consensus regarding the relative value of different writing assignments, appropriate components of assignments, or criteria used to evaluate assignment effectiveness. I investigated the effectiveness of two types of writing assignments in an abnormal psychology course. Both assignments had reading and revision components, and their relative effectiveness was assessed by students' appraisal of the assignments' usefulness.

This project was guided by the assumption that assignments should reflect important themes or methods in a discipline. In abnormal psychology, for example, two salient and complementary approaches to collecting and interpreting data are idiographic and nomothetic. The idiographic approach, typified by case studies, is useful to explicate rare phenomena or procedures or to raise etiological hypotheses. In contrast, the nomothetic approach, typified by controlled empirical research, is used to generate general inferences about diagnostic or other groups (e.g., Davison & Neale, 1986). This project integrated both of these approaches into a writing assignment.

Blevins-Knabe (1987) suggested some appropriate outcome criteria for writing assignments by recommending that writing experiences should ameliorate students' writing deficiencies and promote their involvement with course material. These criteria were used in evaluating the writing assignments described here.

The extent to which educational goals are achieved might be influenced by students' characteristics. For instance, more able students or those with more experience in a discipline may respond differently to some assignments than their less able or less experienced counterparts. However, the role of student characteristics has been neglected in the study of writing assignment outcomes.

Components of Assignments

Some perspectives are available in the current literature regarding assignment components that might improve students' writing skills. For instance, some authors have commented that the WAC movement has not attended adequately to students' serious difficulties in reading comprehension and higher order reasoning (e.g., Chamberlain & Burrough, 1985). In psychology, these limitations are evident when students accept the findings of empirical research in an unquestioning way (Anisfeld, 1987), skim research articles, or avoid the detail of method and results sections (Chamberlain & Burrough, 1985). Therefore, each assignment in this project included a reading component.

Descriptions of the WAC movement also have emphasized that good writing is a process and that feedback and revision should be integrated into writing assignments (e.g., Snodgrass, 1985). However, Mallonee and Breihen (1985) found that professors' written feedback is often used not for such educative purposes, but solely to justify the assigned grades. Sommers (1982) found that professors' written comments on students' papers were often characterized by "hostility and mean spiritedness" (pp. 148-149); such comments do not help students to revise papers or stimulate their motivation. My assignments incorporated reading, feedback, and revision. I provided constructive written feedback on the first drafts and allowed students to revise their papers.

This Study

This project evaluated case-study and research-proposal writing assignments in an abnormal psychology course. The assignments incorporated reading and feedback/revision components. The specific research questions were: Was it useful to require second drafts? What was the relative effectiveness of the two types of assignments? What role did student characteristics play in the obtained results? What was the nature of students' additional comments?

Method

Participants

The participants were 26 (19 women, 7 men) undergraduates (7 sophomores, 10 juniors, 9 seniors) enrolled in my abnormal psychology course. The class enrollment was 30 however, 2 students were not available for the assessment because they were exempt from the final exam, and 2 chose not to participate. Twenty-two students were psychology majors; the others were majoring in pre-med., sociology, and modem languages. All students had completed a prerequisite introductory psychology course. The number of previous psychology courses taken ranged from 1 to 10 (median = 3.5).

Procedure

For the case-study writing assignment, students read one book of their own choosing from a list of seven (Axline, 1969; Bruch, 1979; Clarke & Wardman, 1985; Freud, 1963; Levine, 1982; Sheehan, 1983; Vine, 1982). The books were chosen to reflect a range of disorders and etiological/ theoretical perspectives. Based on information from the text and lectures, students presented their opinions about what they believed to be important issues in five-page reaction papers. One 50-min class period was devoted to explaining the purpose and nature of the paper, and ad hoc questions were entertained later.

For the research-proposal writing assignment, students wrote original research proposals, adhering to the guidelines of the *Publication Manual of the American Psychological Association* (American Psychological Association [APA], 1983). Fourteen published articles pertaining to a range of disorders were placed on library reserve for students to use as models. One class period was devoted to explaining the purpose and nature of the assignment and reviewing APA style. In addition, students were required to schedule individual appointments in which we discussed their topics and research designs; additional questions were entertained during and after class on an ad hoc basis.

Detailed written feedback was provided on the first drafts of both assignments. The feedback covered organization of the papers, clarity, correctness of the presentation, logic, research design, and grammatical points. Revisions were required on either or both papers if As were not achieved. (Each paper could be revised only once.) Moderately strict grading criteria were used. Each original draft counted for 10% of the final course grade, and each revision counted 5%, so that the writing assignments accounted for 30% of the final grade.

A graduate student administered the evaluation questionnaire after the final exam. The directions on the questionnaire indicated that it was intended to provide feedback to the instructor about the writing assignments. Students were directed to be honest in their answers and not to put their names on the forms. The first set of questions asked for background information (gender, year in school, and major). Students also were asked to indicate their grade point averages (GPAs) and the number of psychology courses taken previously as global indices of ability and prior experience, respectively. Then parallel sets of questions for each of the writing assignments were provided. Students rated the evaluative items on a 5-point scale ranging from *very useless and irrelevant* (1) to *very useful and relevant* (5).

The items were:

> Overall, I found the assignment:
> In terms of developing my writing skills, the assignment was:
> In terms of developing my interest in psychology, the assignment was:
> Overall, the comments provided on my first draft were:
> For the purpose of revising my paper, the comments provided on my first draft were:
> In terms of developing my writing skills, requiring a second draft of this paper was:
> In terms of developing my interest in psychology, requiring a second draft of this paper was:

In addition, open-ended questions asked students to indicate what they liked most and least about each assignment. Responses were categorized and frequencies tabulated.

Results

The first set of analyses compared the relative usefulness of first and second drafts and of the case study versus research proposal. With one exception, the mean usefulness ratings ranged from 4.00 to 4.65 (i. e., between *somewhat useful and relevant* and *very useful and relevant*). Students evaluated the first and second drafts about equally. The one exception pertained to the case-study revision, which was judged to be less effective in developing interest in psychology, $t(17) = 4.57$, $p < .001$. (Two-tailed tests were used for all comparisons. The degrees of freedom term in analyses pertaining to revisions is smaller than that in other analyses, because students not required to revise papers could mark "not applicable" to questions about revisions.)

When case-study paper ratings were compared to research proposal ratings to assess the relative effectiveness of the two assignments, the one significant difference indicated that students perceived the research proposal to be more useful than the case study for developing their interest in psychology, $t(25) = 2.67$, $p = .01$.

Next, the roles of students' ability and prior experience were examined. GPA was related to some of the outcome criteria, including usefulness of the case study overall, $r(22) = .36$, $p = .04$, and with respect to developing students' interest in psychology, $r(22) = .48$, $p = .009$, and to usefulness of the research proposal with respect to developing writing skills, $r(22) = .53$, $p = .004$. The number of previous psychology courses was related to ratings of the usefulness of written comments provided on the first draft of the case study, $r(17) = .45$, $p = .03$, and marginally to the case study's usefulness in terms of developing writing skills $r(23) = .29$, $p = .08$.

Finally, responses to the open-ended questions concerning what students liked most and least about the two assignments were categorized. Every student identified at least one positive aspect of the case-study assignment. The two most frequently reported responses were "learning about the subject matter" (14) and "reading the book" (11). Negative responses were less prevalent. For the research proposal, 19 students reported that they liked the challenge of "being creative" (11) and "designing [their] own experiment[s]" (8).

Discussion

Although students' ratings were generally favorable regarding both assignments and their revisions, the research proposal was more successful. Students found it more useful than the case study in developing their interest in psychology. Most of them enjoyed the opportunity to be creative by designing their own experiments. Requiring a second draft of the proposal also had demonstrable value.

Students may have perceived the nomothetic approach, and therefore the proposal, as more important than the idiographic approach in abnormal psychology. Such a perception is consistent with the emphasis in the lectures and textbook (Davison & Neale, 1986) as well as with the philosophy of the psychology department in which the course was offered (i.e., majors are required to complete four research methods courses, including two semesters of statistics and research design and two of experimental psychology).

In contrast to the research proposal, the case-study paper may have seemed like a mere "writing exercise." In fact, the most positively evaluated aspect of the case-study assignment (learning about the subject, reading the book) seems attributable to the reading component of the assignment, rather than to writing. Rewriting the case study was rated the least useful assignment. Perhaps this relatively low evaluation is attributable to the nature of the comments that were provided on the first draft, which may have lacked sufficient specificity to be helpful in rewriting. The most frequent problem that students had in writing the case-study paper was in relying heavily on presenting summaries of events in the books, rather than developing their own schemas of important issues and elaborating their own reactions.

Some of the most meaningful outcome criteria appear to have been influenced by students' ability (as reflected by GPA). More able students may be inclined to perceive assignments as more valuable.

This study was limited because it relied solely on students' opinions as outcome criteria. Future research should evaluate the effectiveness of these assignments in improving students' writing skills and comprehension. It also should be noted that the procedure used in this project was time-consuming and may be difficult to implement in large classes. Students did not need substantial prior experience with psychology to benefit from these assignments. Thus, the research proposal/revision combination appears to be generalizable to other types of psychology classes.

This exploratory study demonstrated the potential utility of writing assignments, particularly research proposals and revisions. The value of such assignments seems to depend on communicating to students a clear rationale for the value of writing skills and on integrating important aspects of a discipline into the assignments.

References

American Psychological Association. (1983). *Publication manual of the American Psychological Association* (3rd ed.). Washington, DC: Author.

Anisfeld, M. (1987). A course to develop competence in critical reading of empirical research in psychology. *Teaching of Psychology, 14*, 224-227.

Axline, V. (1969). *Dibs in search of self.* New York: Ballantine.

Blevins-Knabe, B. (1987). Writing to learn while learning to write. *Teaching of Psychology, 14*, 239-241.

Bruch, H. (1979). *The golden cage: The enigma of anorexia nervosa.* New York: Vintage.

Chamberlain, K., & Burrough, S. (1985). Techniques for teaching critical reading. *Teaching of Psychology, 12*, 213-215.

Clarke, J. C., & Wardman, W. (1985). *Agoraphobia: A clinical and personal account.* Elmsford, NY: Pergamon.

Davison, G. C., & Neale, J. M. (1986). *Abnormal psychology: An experimental clinical approach* (4th ed.). New York: Wiley.

Freud, S. (1963). *Dora: An analysis of a case of hysteria.* New York: Macmillan.

Levine, A. G. (1982*). Love Canal: Science, politics, and people.* Lexington, MA: Lexington Books.

Mallonee, B. C., & Breihen, J. R. (1985). Responding to students' drafts: Interdisciplinary consensus. *College Composition and Communication, 36*, 213-230.

Sheehan, S. (1983). *Is there no place on earth for me?* New York: Vintage.

Snodgrass, S. E. (1985). Writing as a tool for teaching social psychology. *Teaching of Psychology, 12*, 91-94.

Sommers, N. (1982). Responding to student writing. *College Composition and Communication, 33*, 148-156.

Vine, P. (1982). *Families in pain.* New York: Pantheon.

Notes

1. This research was supported by a Fordham College-Mellon Foundation Faculty Development Grant.

2. I thank Joseph Palladino, James Eison, Jane Halonen, and Barbara Nodine for their helpful conceptual suggestions and the anonymous reviewers for their valuable comments on an earlier draft of this article. Colleen Golden and Elisabeth Hennessey

A Case-Study Assignment to Teach Theoretical Perspectives in Abnormal Psychology

David V. Perkins
Ball State University

Theoretical perspectives, or paradigms (Kuhn, 1970), have received increased attention in psychology courses at all levels over the past 20 years. This trend has been especially prominent in undergraduate courses in abnormal psychology (Sarason, 1983), for which most of the texts are organized explicitly in terms of theoretical perspectives (e.g., biological, psychodynamic, behavioral, cognitive, and humanistic). A key lesson of this approach is that data enlarge and shape our understanding of theories, which act as lenses, focusing our attention on certain types of empirical relations. However, it is difficult for many undergraduate students to appreciate the pervasive reciprocal influence of theory and data without an active, sustained effort.

A case-study assignment promotes active, self-directed learning by requiring students to teach themselves and the instructor about psychopathology and about relevant theoretical perspectives. Chrisler (1990) described an assignment in which the student selects a case from a predetermined list and then writes a paper summarizing the character's symptoms, diagnosis, and treatment. This article describes an alternative procedure that more explicitly emphasizes the role of theoretical perspectives in abnormal psychology.

Case-Study Assignment

An assignment I have required in Abnormal Psychology for the past 10 years involves the preparation and revision of a 10-page paper that examines an individual's life and behavior from a single theoretical perspective. Students are required to choose a figure from history, literature, the arts or current events and must submit this choice for approval early in the term.

A representative list of about 150 individuals examined in previous papers is provided for illustration; however, students are encouraged to select an individual not on this list. Acceptable cases are those for which sufficient objective information about the individual's overt behavior patterns and circumstances (e.g., family living conditions, major life events, and milestones) is readily available. Fictional as well as real individuals are acceptable, and useful examples are Ernest Hemingway, Vincent Van Gogh, Betty Ford, Ivan Desinovitch, Holden Caulfield, Norman Bates, Theodore Bundy, and Marilyn Monroe. Although students rarely submit them, unacceptable cases would include a person known only to the student (e.g., a parent or friend), minor characters in literature, or other persons for whom little reliable information exists.

The 10 pages include three sections: (a) 2 to 3 pages summarizing the individual's behavior (details are presented in theory-free language, but are chosen primarily for their relevance to the given theoretical perspective), ending with a diagnosis using all five axes of the Diagnostic and Statistical Manual of Mental Disorders (3rd ed., rev. [*DSM-III-R*]; American Psychiatric Association, 1987); (b) 4 to 5 pages explaining the individual's behavior, using specific concepts from the chosen perspective (e.g., specific defense mechanisms, faulty cognitions, stigma, and social rejection); and (c) 2 to 3 pages outlining a hypothetical treatment regime based on the given perspective (e.g., psychoanalysis, systematic desensitization, or phenothiazines), including some prediction about the likely success or failure of this treatment.

One or more biographies of the individual are the primary sources most students use in summarizing the factual details. Most students also cite at least one source (e.g., the course text) for information about the theoretical perspective they use. Students are cautioned that a diagnosis stated or implied by an author or biographer may or may not be consistent with contemporary practice (i.e., *DSM-III-R*) and that they are responsible for providing a valid, defensible diagnosis. The student's grade is based primarily on the accuracy, precision, and detail evident in applying the perspective to an analysis and treatment of abnormal behavior. The most frequent shortcoming is an etiological analysis that is insufficiently specific and detailed or includes concepts from more than one theoretical perspective.

This assignment is difficult for some students to do well. Therefore, I require students to submit both a rough draft and a revised final paper (only the latter is graded). It is also important to encourage steady work on this assignment throughout the course. In fact, the assignment may not be feasible in summer sessions or other intensive terms, although under these conditions I have had success substituting oral presentations of cases for written papers.

A few differences between this approach and that of Chrisler (1990) are worth noting. For example, instead of choosing from a predetermined list, each student takes full responsibility for finding a case to study, and the cases my students select tend not to be the classics (e.g., Dibs and Sybil) found on Chrisler's (1990) list. Chrisler seemed to focus more on the nature of therapy provided to the individual than on etiological explanation, whereas I reverse this emphasis. Finally, to provide for sufficient conceptual depth in a paper of 10 pages, my students are permitted to use only one theoretical perspective to structure the analysis, and the same perspective must be used in outlining the hypothetical treatment regime.

Discussion

This assignment is useful for a variety of reasons. It is helpful in evaluating a student's ability to think about behavior from an explicit theoretical perspective (i.e., as psychologists do) and to communicate these thoughts in writing. In addition, preparing a case study helps students see that any single perspective in psychology is incomplete and oversimplified (Mueller, 1985) and that a given perspective should be judged in terms of how useful it is, rather than whether it is true or false. Students also recognize that the usefulness of a given theory can be limited to a specific purpose. Psychoanalysis, for example, may produce interesting, heuristic insights into the origins of a case of obsessive compulsive anxiety disorder, yet be of little value in facilitating the most effective treatment; on the other hand, a behavioral analysis of etiology in the same case may seem pedestrian, but lead to a relatively efficient and effective intervention.

This assignment also demonstrates the advantages and pitfalls of the case study as a method of research in abnormal psychology. For example, concrete illustrations of important psychological principles can be found in almost any interesting life, and the details of a particular case will sometimes stimulate further thinking by the student. As scientists, however, students also recognize the absence of systematic experimental controls in their case studies and how retrospectively fitting an imperfect theory to complex behavioral facts may bias the final conclusions.

A case-study assignment addresses the significant interest some students have in applying concepts from abnormal psychology to specific individuals. The diversity of individuals selected for study and the novelty of some cases that are presented convince me of the personal meaningfulness of this experience for most students. The almost unlimited number of potential cases provides an opportunity for undergraduate students to integrate abnormal psychology with material from literature, history, fine arts, or other fields, thus promoting a liberal education (Mueller, 1985; Williams & Kolupke, 1986).

Finally, from the instructor's vantage point, the high degree of structure makes this assignment relatively easy to grade objectively, even with a large class. Invariably, a few students perform much better on this assignment than they do on exams, and many students have told me that this case study assignment was the single best element of the course.

References

American Psychiatric Association. (1987). *Diagnostic and statistical manual of mental disorders* (3rd ed., rev.). Washington, DC: Author.

Chrisler, J. C. (1990). Novels as case-study materials for psychology students. *Teaching of Psychology, 17,* 55-57.

Kuhn, T. S. (1970). *The structure of scientific revolutions* (2nd ed.). Chicago: University of Chicago Press.

Mueller, S. C. (1985). Persons in the personality theory course: Student papers based on biographies. *Teaching of Psychology, 12,* 74-78.

Sarason, I. G. (1983). Contemporary abnormal psychology: Developments and issues. In C. J. Scheirer & A. M. Rogers (Eds.), *G. Stanley Hall Lecture Series* (Vol. 3, pp. 75-115). Washington, DC: American Psychological Association.

Williams, K. G., & Kolupke, J. (1986). Psychology and literature: An interdisciplinary approach to the liberal curriculum. *Teaching of Psychology, 13,* 59-61.

Notes

1. I thank Chris Lovejoy and two anonymous reviewers for helpful comments on earlier drafts of this article.
2. Requests for a complete handout describing this assignment, including an illustrative list of cases analyzed, should be sent to David V. Perkins, Department of Psychological Science, Ball State University, Muncie, IN 47306.

3. TEACHING ABNORMAL PSYCHOLOGY THROUGH THE ARTS AND LITERATURE

Novels as Case-Study Materials for Psychology Students

Joan C. Chrisler
Connecticut College

Goals often expressed by professors include improving their students' ability to write clearly, to think critically, and to apply these skills to their lives outside the classroom. Because "thinkers and writers become better thinkers and writers by thinking and writing" (Eble, 1976, p. 92), it is clear that frequent short writing assignments requiring students to present their own opinions and analyses will do more to develop students' skills than will the traditional end of term paper. The most effective assignments will be those without answers readily obtainable from published sources.

A good way to encourage the application of thinking and writing skills to daily life is to base assignments on the types of activities students are likely to engage in outside the classroom (e.g., reading novels). Several writers (Bennett, 1985; Williams & Kolupke, 1986; Zeren & Schultz, 1988) have suggested team teaching psychology and literature as a way of improving writing, critical thinking, and perceived relevance of psychological theory and research. These courses generally apply the major theories of personality and motivation to the interpretation of literary works and can be taught as one course with the two instructors alternately presenting material (Williams & Kolupke, 1986) or as the coordinated teaching of introductory psychology and basic composition courses (Bennett, 1985; Zeren & Schultz, 1988). This article describes an assignment for psychology students based on a literary work.

Writing Assignment

Students are given a list of novels, biographies, and autobiographies (see Table 1) describing cases of schizophrenia, depression, multiple personality, personality disorders, and organic brain syndromes. Many of these books have been made into films which the students have seen. I prefer that they choose a book with which they are not familiar so that they approach the character with an open mind, rather than through the film director's point of view. Students are to read their book and prepare a 5- to 10-page paper about the main character.

Table 1. Suggested Readings for a Case-Study Assignment

Axline, V. (1976). *Dibs in search of self.* New York: Ballantine.

Barnes, M., & Berke, J. (1972). *Mary Barnes: Two accounts of a journey through madness.* New York: Harcourt.

Gordon, B. (1980). *I'm dancing as fast as I can.* New York: Bantam.

Greene, H. (1964). *I never promised you a rose garden.* New York: New American Library.

Guest, J. (1982). *Ordinary people.* New York: Ballantine.

Hodgkins, E. (1964). *Episode: A report on an accident inside my skull.* New York: Atheneum.

Kesey, K. (1975). *One flew over the cuckoo's nest.* New York: New American Library.

Keyes, D. (1982). *The minds of Billy Milligan.* New York: Bantam.

Levonkron, S. (1978). *The best little girl in the world.* Chicago: Contemporary Books.

Mee, C. (1978). *Seizure.* New York: Evans.

Naylor, P. (1977). *Crazy love.* New York: Morrow.

Neufeld, J. (1970). *Lisa bright and dark.* New York: New American Library.

Plath, S. (1975). *The bell jar.* New York: Bantam.

Rebeta-Burditt, J. (1986). *The cracker factory.* New York: Bantam.

Reed, D. (1976). *Anna.* New York: Basic Books.

Rubin, T. (1986). *Jordi.* Mattituck, NY: Amereon.

Rubin, T. (1986). *Lisa and David.* Mattituck, NY: Amereon.

Schatzman, M. (1973). *Soul murder: Persecution in the family.* New York: Random House.

Schreiber, F. (1974). *Sybil.* New York: Warner.

Sechehaye, M. (1985). *Autobiography of a schizophrenic girl.* New York: New American Library.

Sheehan, S. (1983). *Is there no place on earth for me?* New York: Random House.

Thigpen, T., & Cleckley, H. M. (1985). *The three faces of Eve.* Augusta, GA: Cleckley-Thigpen.

Vonnegut, K. (1975). *The Eden express.* New York: Bantam.

Wexler, S. (1970). *The story of Sandy.* New York: American Library.

Wolf, E. (1969). *Aftershock.* New York: Putnam.

The students are cautioned that this paper is not to be a typical book report and that they are not to summarize the plot. Rather, they should adopt the perspective of a psychotherapist and prepare a case study of the book's main character. The students' task is to describe and discuss the character's behavior; specifically, they must address the following questions: (a) What are the character's symptoms? (b) Into which *DSM-III* category does the character fit and why? (c) What type of therapeutic treatment did the character receive? (d) What treatment would you recommend if you were the therapist? (e) Which theory of mental illness best explains the development of the character's symptoms?

Discussion

The answers to the questions are not as obvious as they may seem. For example, although most of the books give the main character's diagnosis, some of the older books use categories that are no longer in the *DSM-III* or that have been renamed. This situation forces the students to compare their list of symptoms to the textbook or directly to the *DSM-III* to find the category that best fits the character. Sometimes students disagree with the diagnosis given to the character by the book's author. Points are awarded for a good argument in favor of the student's choice of diagnosis, and I try to avoid suggesting that there is one right answer in every case.

The therapeutic treatments the characters receive are so varied that this is perhaps the most interesting section for the students to write about. The older books describe treatment techniques that are no longer in use (e.g., hydrotherapy or wrapping patients in cold, wet sheets and tying them to their beds) or that have been recognized as inappropriate or ineffective for particular types of illness (e.g., psychoanalysis for acute schizophrenics). This gives students the opportunity to object to the treatments and to argue in favor of other approaches. Students will gain a better understanding of therapy in action as they read about the character's experiences. Characters in these books take medications of various kinds and receive electroconvulsive and insulin shock treatments. They participate in individual, group, and family therapy with therapists who use psychodynamic, cognitive, behavioral, and humanistic techniques. Students are usually good at identifying which therapy the character receives.

The last question—which theory of mental illness best explains the development of the character's symptoms?—is the most difficult to answer and instructors may decide not to assign it to lower level classes. Less sophisticated and less able students regularly assume that the perspective given by the book's author is the best one and adopt it without question. It is disheartening to read paper after paper stating that psychoanalytic theory best explains the development of schizophrenia as students disregard biochemical and genetic evidence in their up-to-date textbooks and adopt the opinion of an author of a novel or biography written 20 or 30 years ago. Return of the papers is always followed by a discussion of the fact that the books' authors have constructed cases that fit their points of view and the fact that the student authors must do the same.

All books on the list are interesting and well written; most have been best sellers, and students enjoy reading them. Paperback editions of most of the books are widely available in bookstores; the older, out-of-print books can be found in most public libraries. The books give students a better idea of what it is like to experience mental illness than do textbook descriptions of symptoms. Reading about the characters seems to promote empathy for the mentally ill as much as writing about them promotes critical thinking.

This is a versatile assignment; I have used it in both Introductory Psychology and Abnormal Psychology classes with students from the community college level to the university level. Upper division students usually write more sophisticated papers than lower division students do, but all complete the assignment and benefit from it. Because of the number of possible characters and the variety of approaches one can take to describe them, I never tire of reading these papers and am surprised at how often I, too, learn something from this assignment.

References

Bennett, S. M. (1985). Coordinated teaching of psychology and composition: A valuable strategy for students and instructors. *Teaching of Psychology, 12,* 26-27.

Eble, K. E. (1976). *The craft of teaching: A guide to mastering the professor's art.* San Francisco: Jossey-Bass.

Williams, K. G., & Kolupke, J. (1986). Psychology and literature: An interdisciplinary approach to the liberal curriculum. *Teaching of Psychology, 13,* 59-61 .

Zeren, A. S., & Schultz, N. L. (1988, March). *Classifying the character of Esther Greenwood.* Paper presented at the conference on the Teaching of Undergraduate Psychology, Farmingdale, NY.

Questioning the Conventional Wisdom and Critiquing Unconventional Perspectives in Abnormal Psychology: A Written Exercise

Dana D. Anderson
Pacific Lutheran University

As Perkins (1991) noted, undergraduate abnormal psychology courses increasingly emphasize theoretical perspectives, usually the biological, psychodynamic, behavioral, cognitive, and humanistic viewpoints. It is important for students in such courses to understand these perspectives and to recognize, as Perkins's students did after completing a case study of abnormal behavior from a single theoretical perspective, that no one perspective constitutes an adequate account for all human deviance. Nevertheless, the risk remains that students will conclude that these usual five viewpoints exhaust the theoretical possibilities and that they constitute an adequate account for deviance. This risk seems exacerbated by the organization of most abnormal texts. The conventional five viewpoints are generally well integrated within the text, reappearing in each chapter to account for each category of disorder. Less conventional views are usually relegated :o a single, early chapter and subsequently ignored.

Ironically, the chapter in which unconventional views are isolated is often the same chapter in which historical views are segregated. Costin (1982) noted that the latter type of segregation characterizes psychology tests and encourages students in their common misperception: The truth has always been and will always be whatever we currently hold it to be. Such text organization can deprive students of the historical awareness fundamental to critical thought. Furthermore, this organization avoids genuine engagement with some of the most controversial and sensitive ideas in the field. Costin (1985) suggested that genuine engagement with challenging ideas and an integrated historical perspective are necessary to our teaching if we are to meet our basic educational objective of training our students' intellects.

One exercise I use to counter these risks in my abnormal psychology course is a term paper assignment for which students must read and critique a book that takes an unconventional perspective on abnormal behavior. The list of books I use is attached to the course syllabus. It includes works from the antipsychiatry movement (e.g., Laing, 1967, 1969) and libertarian critiques of the mental health movement (e.g., Szasz, 1961, 1970) as well as Marxist (e.g., Brown, 1973; Foucault, 1965) and feminist (e.g., Chesler, 1972; Ehrenreich & English, 1978) critiques of mental health professional practices. Labeling theory (e.g., Goffman, 1961; Scheff, 1984) is represented as is role theory (e.g., Sarbin, 1969; Sarbin & Allen, 1968). I include critiques by nonpsychologists of psychological testing (e.g., Gould, 1981; Green, 1981) as well as more general critiques of the social impact of psychology and its ideas (e.g., Gross, 1978, Wallach & Wallach, 1983). Works on the history of the mentally ill and their treatment (e.g., Porter, 1987; Valenstein, 1986) round out the list. The university library has copies of the books, and most are also available in paperback. Most of these works either document the history of the field of abnormal psychology or themselves influenced the field's history.

I instruct students to select one major theme from the book and to review critically the author's argument. Criteria for the review include the soundness of the author's reasoning, the quality of empirical evidence the author marshals to support the theme, and how well the author accounts for opposing points of view and rival interpretations of the evidence. Students must conclude their papers with a well defined and well supported position of their own on the theme critiqued. The position must be supported by both logical and empirical evidence, and it must be soundly reasoned and consistent with at least the research presented in class and the course text. I assist students in using these criteria because students are typically unfamiliar with them. Although Abnormal Psychology is a junior-level course for psychology majors, many nonmajors enroll and introductory psychology is the sole prerequisite. Therefore, I spend the first day of class reviewing common research design flaws and logical fallacies.

Students select a book and theme by the third week of the semester. They then submit an opening paragraph stating their selections and outlining their preliminary evaluation of the author's argument. The early deadline discourages procrastination and allows corrective feedback for those students (few but inevitable) who are, despite instructions writing a book report. The recommended length of the paper is 5 to 10 pages. The paper is completed in two drafts: one at midterm and one, incorporating response to my feedback, at semester's end. The first draft counts 20% of the course grade and the second draft counts 25%. This heavy contribution emphasizes the importance of students' critical thinking to course objectives. Grading, particularly on the first draft, takes into account students' typically low levels of logical and methodological sophistication. Grading emphasizes improvement beyond this baseline in the second draft. This draft-redraft approach is generally an effective way of teaching students to write (Baird & Anderson, 1990). The exercise creates a semester-long dialogue with each student. Such dialogue is vital for students to learn to communicate their thoughts effectively, and active involvement of students who must take a stand on an issue increases the quality of students' critical skills (Benjamin, 1991; Costin, 1985; Ferguson, 1986; Gorman, Law, & Lindegren, 1981).

In feedback to students, I address how closely their first draft matches the criteria for the paper and suggest areas for improvement. Almost always, improvement includes placing the work within its proper historical context and inferring its relevance to contemporary concerns in the field. Despite my emphasis throughout the course on using a historical perspective, students rarely do so in their first drafts. For example, they often fail to realize that Szasz's (1961, 1970) works contributed to increased restrictiveness in involuntary commitment laws; they denigrate his critique of commitment procedures as outdated or as too idealistic to be practical. Students have difficulty understanding, in the abstract, what a historical perspective is. Most seem to require feedback on the particular relevance of history for their own paper's concern in order to appreciate the general benefits of a historical perspective. They do respond to the feedback; second drafts are better written and more historically informed. For example, students who, in their first drafts, dismiss as irrelevant Valenstein's (1986) criticisms of psychosurgery on the grounds that such surgery is rare today come to recognize by their second drafts the cautionary implications of his critique for other, more contemporary treatment. Several of these students recognized in their drafts that AIDS is as desperate a contemporary problem as schizophrenia was in the 1940s and came to understand the currency of Valenstein's point that desperate problems encourage desperate, sometimes irresponsible, solutions. They viewed current medical and social responses to AIDS patients from a fresh, chastened viewpoint.

Besides being more historically informed, second drafts are generally better written, clearer, and more grammatical than initial drafts. Second drafts are better reasoned, showing fewer logical fallacies and internal contradictions, than first drafts. Assumptions are more clearly recognized as such; inferences are drawn with more awareness and care; and standards for judgments are articulated and defended where they were originally simple prejudices, left implicit or forwarded as self-evidently unimpeachable.

Student feedback generally supports the effectiveness of this exercise. Among 67 students completing three course sections during the past 4 years, the mean rating for the exercise on a scale ranging from *unsatisfactory* (1) to *exceptional quality, top 2%* (7) was 5.4. Student comments indicated they disliked the difficulty of the exercise and found it stressful but believed the exercise made them more reflective in their approach to deviance, clarified their ideas, and improved their critical abilities. Students were especially positive about the midterm feedback and the opportunity to respond in their second drafts.

This exercise requires students to confront with skepticism all the existing wisdom concerning human deviance. Such confrontation strengthens their critical abilities and provides the historical foundation on which they may someday construct new wisdom's of their own (Cole, 1982; Zachry, 1985).

References

Baird, B. N., & Anderson, D. D. (1990). Writing in psychology. *The Teaching Professor, 4,* 5-6.

Benjamin, L. T., Jr. (1991). Personalization and active learning in the large introductory psychology class. *Teaching of Psychology, 15,* 68-14.

Brown, P. (Ed.). (1973). *Radical psychology.* New York: Harper & Row.

Chesler, P. (1972). *Women & madness.* New York: Doubleday.

Cole, D. L. (1982). Psychology as a liberating art. *Teaching of Psychology, 9,* 23-26.

Costin, F. (1982). Some thoughts on general education and the teaching of undergraduate psychology. *Teaching of Psychology, 9,* 26-28.

Costin, F. (1985). Courage in the classroom. *Teaching of Psychology, 12,* 125-128.

Ehrenreich, B., & English, D. (1978). *For her own good: 150 years of the experts' advice on women.* Garden City, NY: Anchor.

Ferguson, N. B. L. (1986). Encouraging responsibility, active participation, and critical thinking in general psychology students. *Teaching of Psychology, 13,* 217-218.

Foucault, M. (1965). *Madness and civilization: A history of insanity in the age of reason.* New York: Random House.

Goffman, E. (1961). *Asylums: Essays on the social situation of mental patients and other inmates.* Garden City, NY: Doubleday.

Gorman, M. E., Law, A., & Lindegren, T. (1981). Making students take a stand: Active learning in introductory psychology. *Teaching of Psychology, 8,* 164-166.

Gould, S. J. (1981). *The mismeasure of man.* New York: Norton.

Green, P. (1981). *The pursuit of inequality.* New York: Pantheon.

Gross, M. L. (1978). *The psychological society.* New York: Simon & Schuster.

Laing, R. D. (1967). T*he politics of experience.* New York: Pantheon.

Laing, R. D. (1969). *The divided self.* New York: Pantheon.

Perkins, D. V. (1991). A case-study assignment to teach theoretical perspectives in abnormal psychology. *Teaching of Psychology, 18,* 97-99.

Porter, R. (1987). *A social history of madness: The world through the eyes of the insane.* New York: Dutton.

Sarbin, T. R. (1969). The scientific status of the mental illness metaphor. In S. C. Plog & R. B. Edgerton (Eds.), *Changing perspectives in mental illness* (pp. 9-31). New York: Holt, Rinehart & Winston.

Sarbin, T. R., & Allen, V. L. (1968). Role theory. In G. Lindzey & E. Aronson (Eds. *), The handbook of social psychology* (Vol. 1, 2nd ed., pp. 488-567). Cambridge, MA: Addison-Wesley.

Scheff, T. J. (1984). *Being mentally ill: A sociological theory* (2nd ed.). New York: Aldine.

Szasz, T. S. (1961). *The myth of mental illness.* New York: Harper & Row.

Szasz, T. S. (1970). *The manufacture of madness: A comparative study of the Inquisition and the mental health movement.* New York: Harper & Row.

Valenstein, E. S. (1986). *Great and desperate cures.* New York: Basic Books.

Wallach, M. A., & Wallach, L. (1983*). Psychology's sanction for selfishness: The error of egoism in theory and therapy.* San Francisco: Freeman.

Zachry, W. H. (1985). How I kicked the lecture habit: Inquiry teaching in psychology. *Teaching of Psychology, 12,* 129-131.

Note

Requests for copies of the reading list should be sent to Dana D. Anderson, Department of Psychology, Pacific Lutheran University, Tacoma, WA 98447-0003.

Exploring Mental Illness Through a Poetry-Writing Assignment

Joan C. Chrisler
Connecticut College

Encouraging creative thinking and enhancing writing skills are important goals of teachers at all levels. In recent years, *Teaching of Psychology* has published numerous articles on how to incorporate writing assignments into psychology courses (e.g., Beers, 1985; Bennett, 1985; Klugh, 1983; Nodine, 1990). This article illustrates an atypical and challenging writing assignment for courses in introductory or abnormal psychology.

The aim of this assignment is to increase students' understanding of mental illness and their empathy toward the mentally ill. Popular culture frequently presents the mentally ill as objects of humor or derision; textbooks, with their dry language and reliance on the medical model, are more likely to portray the mentally ill as collections of symptoms than as people. The idea for this assignment arose as I was trying to think of a way to encourage students to identify with those who have psychological problems. I wanted a short writing assignment that would encourage students to reflect on what it might be like to experience mental illness. Poetry, with its emotional base, vivid imagery, and often fragmented language, seemed ideal.

Writing Assignment

Students are told 2 weeks before the assignment is due that they are to write a poem about the experience of mental illness. The format, length, and topic are left entirely up to them. They may choose to be concrete or abstract, serious or humorous, or personal or theoretical, and they may describe the experience using first- or third-person pronouns. The poems need not be written in a rhyming format. Anything goes !

The class generally seems shocked when they are told about the assignment, but after being assured that they will be judged primarily on content, rather than format or poetic language, they rise to the challenge. Because length is unimportant, one can count on receiving several haiku. Someone will always hand in "Roses are red; violets are blue. I'm schizophrenic and so am I." (This response is given a failing grade because, besides its lack of originality, it describes multiple personality and not schizophrenia.) However, most students take the assignment seriously and turn in work that shows that they have thought long and carefully about their topics. Most work is creative and interesting; some poems are so beautifully written that I refer them to the college literary magazine.

Students have responded to the assignment with varying degrees of enthusiasm. One student wrote about his negative emotional reaction to the assignment and titled it "Poemaphobia." (I gave him an A.) Many have told me that once they got over their amazement at being asked to write a poem for a psychology class they found the task to be both challenging and fun.

To earn an A, a poem must convey an excellent understanding (or be an excellent description) of anxiety, depression, psychosis, or some particular disorder (e.g., avoidant personality disorder). A B is given to a poem that conveys a good understanding or description of the experience of mental illness. Some latitude is available for the evaluation of writing ability. For example, an adequate description of avoidant personality would earn a grade of B; an adequate description that is also well written (e.g., the poem's lines contain the appropriate number of syllables for its rhyme scheme, and the poet's choice of words is good) would earn a B+. Oddly, despite the subjectivity involved in evaluating an assignment of this type, no students have ever complained about their grades.

For the past 2 years (after obtaining permission from the students—some give permission only if their work remains anonymous), I have posted the best work on a bulletin board in the psychology building. Much to the poets' delight, the display attracted students and faculty from all over campus.

I have used this assignment in three classes during the last few years and have been pleased with the results. I believe that the time students spend thinking about particular aspects of mental illness in preparation for this assignment results in better understanding and increased empathy for the mentally ill.

This is a versatile assignment for introductory and abnormal psychology classes. With a little ingenuity, it can be adapted for use in other courses. For example, students might write a poem about being elderly for a developmental psychology course, about the experience of chronic or terminal illness in a health psychology course, or about being the object of prejudice in a social psychology course. Readers are invited to try this assignment and judge its value for their classes.

References

Beers, S. E. (1985). Use of a portfolio writing assignment in a course on developmental psychology. *Teaching of Psychology, 12,* 94-96.

Bennett, S. M. (1985). Coordinated teaching of psychology and composition A valuable strategy for students and instructors. *Teaching of Psychology, 12,* 26-27.

Klugh, H. E. (1983). Writing and speaking skills can be taught in psychology classes. *Teaching of Psychology, 10,* 170-171.

Nodine, B. F. (Ed.). (1990). Psychologists teach writing [Special issue]. *Teaching of Psychology, 17*(1).

Note

An earlier version of this article was presented at the annual meeting of the American Psychological Association, Boston, August 1990.

Images of Madness: Feature Films in Teaching Psychology

Michael Z. Fleming
Ralph L. Piedmont
C. Michael Hiam
Boston University

Educational films of under 60 min are widely accepted and appreciated by psychology instructors and students. Feature films (90 to 110 min) have not been used as frequently as educational films, although some instructors have employed such films with apparent success. Kinney (1975) found that the full-length commercial film, *The Wild Child* (1970), was rated very favorably by students in comparison to educational films on developmental psychology. Dorris and Ducey (1978) and Nissim-Sabat (1979) related their successes in teaching psychology courses that use feature films as an integral part of the instruction.

Feature films, even from the pre-1920s silent days, are particularly suitable for handling intimate psychological subjects. These films can offer students a unique opportunity to see realistic manifestations of psychiatric disorders, apply models of psychopathology, and suggest modes of treatment. Through the subtleties of editing and the juxtaposition of sound and image, a good feature film can also afford students a "firsthand" perspective on madness that is not easily imparted by lectures or textbooks.

The value of feature films in psychology courses, however, does not end with their power to render a convincing depiction of madness. Such films can also make students aware of an important interaction between art and psychology. This interaction involves the cinema's ability to reflect and affect popular perceptions of madness and treatment. *One Flew Over the Cuckoo's Nest* (1975), for example, perpetuated certain stereotypes about mental illness but created a national furor over the use of electroconvulsive therapy. A brief historical overview of film portrayals of madness will reveal to students that these popular perceptions, like psychiatric nosology itself, have changed over time.

Since 1979, Michael Z. Fleming (the first author) has been co-teaching an interdisciplinary undergraduate course, Psychology and Film: Images of Madness, with a film historian at Boston University. The average enrollment of 80 students is drawn about equally from the College of Liberal Arts and the College of Communications. The psychology faculty liked the idea of an interdisciplinary course, but thought that it should not count as one of seven courses required for the psychology major.

The course uses a series of modem and classic feature films to introduce students to the interaction between psychiatric and cinematic disciplines. We attempted to document the students' understanding of this dialectic process.

Course Format

The course is taught in 15 class sessions that meet for 4 hr once a week. The two instructors lecture at the beginning of class, a film is then screened, and class discussion follows. Class discussion after the film takes the following form:

1. Initially, students are encouraged to talk about how the film affected them, focusing on their subjective, affective responses. The film's power to present wrenching emotional struggles needs first to be reacted to on a feeling level, and students are encouraged to voice their feelings without worrying about grounding them in logic.

2. The second phase of discussion is to take the students' stated feelings and connect them to the specific visual and auditory stimuli in the film that elicited such feelings. Analysis concentrates on a careful process of consensual validation of what was actually shown as opposed to what we believe we saw (e. g., the specific images in the alcoholic hallucinosis in *The Lost Weekend*, 1948).

3. The final phase of discussion links the readings and lectures to the film. For example, readings and lecture material on posttraumatic stress disorder are linked to the major and seemingly minor stressors presented *in The Deer Hunter* (1978) and the characterological flaws of the three friends who go to war.

Much of the lecture material is centered on the various diagnostic categories from the American Psychiatric Association's *Mental Disorders: Diagnostic and Statistical Manual* (lst ed. [*DSM*], 1952) and *the Diagnostic and Statistical Manual of Mental Disorders* (2nd ed. [*DSM-II*],

3rd ed. [*DSM-III*], and 3rd ed. rev. [*DSM-III-R*], 1968, 1980, and 1987, respectively). Handouts are given on specific diagnostic categories from the edition of the *DSM* in effect when the film was released. (The *DSM* is presented as the official scientific description of psychopathology of a period.) The presentation is supplemented by brief excerpts from the *DSMs*, which are distributed at the beginning of class and include a short summary statement of the psychopathological entity presented in the film. The lectures emphasize the "scientific views" of a period and the historical context in which psychopathology must be placed. The succinctness of the *DSM* is especially helpful for those who are not psychology majors.

The film's interaction with the psychiatric community is documented by discussions of period psychiatric literature. Student discussion is encouraged and, because of students' enthusiasm, frequently lasts beyond the scheduled end of class. A budget of $1,500 covers the rental cost of the 12 films. Although there is a text for the course (Fleming & Manvell, 1985), students are expected to read outside sources on the topics discussed in class (see appendix). Grading is based on two 10-page papers and a midterm exam. Students are asked to choose from a series of paper topics on the cause-and-effect relation between a thematic motif in film and psychiatry. After selecting a topic, students are encouraged to meet with the instructor to formulate a specific question and to plan an appropriate method for investigating it. The instructor suggests pertinent references during these discussions.

Themes of Madness and Films Selected

The changing perceptions of madness are investigated by screening two feature films separated by at least 20 years. To be selected for the course, the film must have been popular and have generated literary criticism. Popularity is assessed by looking at the films' gross earnings published in *Variety* magazine. Films selected have also enjoyed coverage in the popular and academic press, and students are encouraged to use literary indexes to research this aspect.

The course has been offered 12 times; some of the film themes and representative films that have been incorporated are:

1. The family and madness: *Now, Voyager* (1942) and *Ordinary People* (1979).
2. Institutionalization of the mad: *The Snake Pit* (1948) and *One Flew Over the Cuckoo's Nest* (1975).
3. Possession as madness: *Dr. Jekyll and Mr. Hyde* (1931) and *The Exorcist* (1973).
4. Murder and madness: *White Heat* (1949) and *Halloween* (1976).
5. War and madness: *Twelve O'Clock High* (1949) and *The Deer Hunter* (1978).
6. Drugs and madness: *The Lost Weekend* (1948) and *The Rose* (1979).

7. Paranoia and madness: *Rope* (1948) and *Invasion of the Body Snatchers* (1978).
8. Sanity as madness, madness as sanity: *You Can't Take It With You* (1938) and *King of Hearts* (1966).
9. The psychiatrist and madness: *Spellbound* (1945) and *Face to Face* (1975).

The following analysis of *The Lost Weekend* is an example of the substantive issues that can be illustrated by film. When we present the film, we first set the historical context by describing the cinematic presentation of alcoholism before the release of *The Lost Weekend*. Previous film treatments lead into popular and clinical views of alcoholism and the evolution of these views as they affected and then came to be affected by *The Lost Weekend*. Students seldom appreciate the fact that Alcoholics Anonymous (AA) is a relatively recent movement which had to, and still has to, fight for the acceptance of alcoholism as a disease. The popular view that dominated the depiction of alcoholics in films up to 1945 was that of an anonymous, indigent derelict. The limited attention of the psychiatric community to alcoholism emphasized biological treatments with greatest interest given to the rest and isolation of such patients. Alcohol was ostensibly a weakness of the poor, and those who were not indigent and suffered from it were hurried away to sanitariums that treated those who needed a "rest."

Discussion of the film raises many points: (a) Students erroneously come to think of contemporary views as "enlightened" and as always existing or certainly existing since 1900. An exploration of the relatively recent advent of AA is, therefore, eye-opening and allows for discussion of the role of self-help groups in substance abuse. (b) The film serves as an introduction to the social and economic forces that influence diagnoses in terms of the perception that only the poor were alcoholics. (c) Biological psychiatry versus social psychiatry and the social political forces that influence the dominance of either a nature or nurture etiology are raised in discussion of the film. Students are encouraged to read the period professional and lay literature associated with the film. Although *The Lost Weekend* supports a social etiology for the protagonist's alcoholism, it avoids the issue of repressed homosexuality stressed in the popular book on which the screenplay is based. (d) The film graphically portrays both substance use disorders (maladaptive behavior that surrounds the taking of the drug) and substance-induced disorders as dramatically depicted in the formication hallucinations of delirium tremens.

Those who teach a course on film and mental illness have a number of formats from which to choose. Two of the most obvious are: (a) using specific films to portray particular abnormal states that reflect the *DSM-III-R* criteria, or (b) using film as both reflector and effector and doing so from a historical perspective. Using both to some degree is also possible.

Changes in Students' Knowledge and Opinions

Students in a recent class completed a 10-item questionnaire that focused on knowledge of mental illness and depiction of illness in the cinema. Students rated each question on a scale ranging from *very little* (1) to *very much* (5). The questionnaire was distributed to 35 students (23 women, 12 men) on the last day of class. These students were representative of those who have taken the course over the years. There were an almost equal number of communications, psychology, and other liberal arts majors. Questions were designed to determine if students believed their knowledge increased as a result of the course.

When asked how much they knew about the study of people with mental illness and the depiction of the mentally ill in the film media, students responded strongly in the affirmative (Ms = 3.8 and 3.9, respectively). Films were seen as providing very accurate depictions of posttraumatic stress syndromes (M = 4.1), substance abuse (M = 4.0), antisocial behaviors (M = 3.9), and depressive disorders (M = 3.7). However, less well reflected in film were eating (M = 2.7) and sexual (M = 3.3) disorders. When asked the extent to which film influences individuals' perceptions of the mentally ill, students believed that the perceptions of the general public (M = 4.1), family members (M = 3.8), and nonmental health professionals (M = 3.6) were shaped by such images. Psychiatrists (M = 2.9) and the respondents themselves (M = 3.4), however, were rated as being less influenced by film.

University course evaluation forms were completed by all students (N = 35). Students felt that: (a) there were many opportunities for questions and discussion (M = 4.5), (b) the amount of work for the course was moderate (M = 3.3), and (c) the assigned readings were clear (M = 3.0) . Students considered the course germane to their education and careers (M = 3.9) and one they would definitely recommend to other students (M = 4.5). Overall, this course had a positive impact on the students. Not only was it effective in engaging the students in thought-provoking discussions and encounters, it was also a useful didactic vehicle for conveying a wide range of psychological information.

Conclusion

Courses like Psychology and Film: Images of Madness can help students who are going into mental health or communications fields to realize how each of their respective disciplines interacts with the other. Such courses can increase students' knowledge of psychopathology and their appreciation for how feature films influence our thinking about mental illness. From the students' perspective, the course provided information that they can take with them into their future careers in communication and psychology.

References

American Psychiatric Association (1952). *Mental disorders: Diagnostic and statistical manual* (lst ed.). Washington, DC: Author.

American Psychiatric Association. *(1968). Diagnostic and statistical manual of mental disorders* (2nd ed.). Washington, DC: Author.

American Psychiatric Association. (1980) . *Diagnostic and statistical manual of mental disorders* (3rd ed.) Washington, DC: Author.

American Psychiatric Association. (1987). *Diagnostic and statistical manual of mental disorders* (3rd ed., rev.). Washington, DC: Author.

Dorris, W., & Ducey, R. (1978). Social psychology and sex roles in films. *Teaching of Psychology, 5,* 168-169.

Fleming, M., & Manvell, R. (1985). *Images of madness: The portrayal of insanity in the feature film.* Cranbury, NH: Associated University Presses.

Kinney, D. K. (1975). Cinema thrillers: Reviews of films highly rated by psychology students. *Teaching of Psychology, 2,* 183-186.

Nissim-Sabat, D. (1979). The teaching of abnormal psychology through the cinema. *Teaching of Psychology, 6,* 121-123.

Note

Requests for an extended bibliography should be sent to Michael Z. Fleming, Department of Psychology, Boston University, 64 Cummington Street, Boston, MA 02215.

Appendix: Selected Bibliography on Film and Madness

A. General references

Fleming, M., & Manvell, R. (1985). *Images of madness: The portrayal of insanity in the feature film.* Cranbury, NH: Associated University Presses.

Munsterberg, H. (1970). *The photoplay: A psychological study.* New York: Dover.

Schneider, I. (1977). Images of the mind: Psychiatry in the commercial film. *American Journal of Psychiatry, 134,* 613–620.

Schneider, I. (1987). The theory and practice of movie psychiatry. *American Journal of Psychiatry, 144,* 996–1002.

B. Thematic references

1. Drugs and madness

Bacon, S. D. (1949). Current notes: A student of the problems of alcoholism views "The lost weekend." *Quarterly Journal of Studies on Alcoholism, 8,* 402–405.

Brower, D. (1948). An opinion poll on reactions to "The lost weekend." *Quarterly Journal of Studies on Alcoholism, 10,* 594–598.

2. War and madness

Grinker, R., & Spiegel, J. (1945). *Men under stress.* Philadelphia: Blakiston.

Renner, J. A. (1973). The changing patterns of psychiatric problems in Vietnam. *Comprehensive Psychiatry, 14*(2), 169–173.

Smith, J. (1973). Between Vermont and violence: Film portraits of Vietnam veterans. *Film Quarterly Studies, 26,* 24–33.

4. EXAMINING MISCELLANEOUS ISSUES

A Volunteer Program for Abnormal Psychology Students: Eighteen Years and Still Going Strong

Forrest Scogin
Henry C. Rickard
University of Alabama

Abnormal Psychology is one of the most popular undergraduate psychology courses, and many students would undoubtedly report that it is one of the most interesting. Readings, lectures, and discussion are the usual fare, and the subject matter is amply suited for such instruction. At the University of Alabama, however, traditional abnormal psychology coursework has been augmented with volunteer work. This experiential component has been operating for 18 years, and merits attention for its longevity and its favorable reception by students. Similar programs in child development courses (e.g., Fox Lopuch, & Fisher, 1984; Moffett, 1975; Stollak, 1975) and undergraduate internships (e.g., Shiverick, 1977) have been described, though apparently none are identical to the University of Alabama program. We would like to share the rationale and procedures for this program, as well as student feedback, so that other instructors may consider implementation.

Abnormal Psychology is an upper-level course. The two sections typically enroll between 80 and 100 students. A wide variety of majors take the course, with a preponderance of health-related majors enrolled (e.g., nursing, occupational therapy, and social work). Almost all of the students indicate that they have never worked or volunteered in a psychiatric setting, and a number of students enroll in the course primarily for the volunteer opportunity. Word of mouth and periodic media exposure in the student newspaper make prospective enrollees aware of this opportunity.

At the program's inception, Henry Rickard (the second author), impressed by the enthusiasm of a few students who had functioned as volunteers at the local state hospital, proposed making that experience available to all members of abnormal psychology classes. The department chair and the dean of Arts and Sciences supported the concept, and the innovation was launched in the fall of 1968. Fortunately, the major state psychiatric facility was located adjacent to the campus, and a large Veterans Administration neuro psychiatric hospital was nearby. The VA Hospital, in particular, had a well developed volunteer program that provided a ready vehicle through which students could receive orientation, legal protection, and general supervision. Consequently, the first class of 30 students was assigned to that facility for the semester. Approximately 25 hr of in hospital experience was required. The occasional student who chose not to work in the hospital, because of personal concerns or time limitations, wrote a term paper or completed some other equivalent class assignment. Approximately 93% of the 30 students participating in the pilot program considered the experience worthwhile and advocated that it should be continued as part of abnormal psychology coursework.

The program has continued through a succession of instructors and mental health volunteer services coordinators. We estimate that over the years, more than 3,000 students have volunteered time, provided a valuable service to many patients, and enriched their educational experience. No major negative incidents (e.g., student injury or patient abuse) have occurred during this time, which suggests that potential concerns about negative outcomes are based on low-probability occurrences.

Full cooperation of mental health agencies is imperative for a successful volunteer program. First and foremost, agencies must be willing to have volunteers serve their facilities. Further, the volunteer services staff or contact person at the cooperating agency must be willing to take responsibility for placement, training, and record-keeping, otherwise the program will require inordinate faculty time. Fortunately, in our experience the volunteer services staffs of the two large psychiatric facilities have been willing to donate a considerable amount of time to such administrative tasks. In an early semester class session, representatives of the two major facilities present information pertinent to the volunteer experience. This session also serves as an orientation that includes issues of confidentiality, appropriate dress and decorum, and patient rights.

Shortly after this presentation, students are informed of their volunteer assignments. An on-site supervisor is assigned for each placement by the volunteer services coordinator, and students are given designated hours of attendance. Our students function more as companions to patients than as therapists, and accordingly, volunteer work has included transporting patients through the hospitals, assisting in recreational activities, leading educational classes, and most frequently, simply socializing. We believe that our students, as a group, may be superior volunteers in that they are bright, capable, and have a better than average background in psychology.

The minimum required hours of volunteer work have fluctuated over the years, but lately we have required about 20 hr per semester. Almost all of the students are able to meet this minimum requirement. The hours accumulated by the student are recorded by the volunteer services director and sent to the instructor at the end of the semester. Student progress is informally monitored by soliciting reports of interesting occurrences during their recent visits. More formal monitoring of progress by weekly conferences or written materials requires too much time in classes of 50 to 70 students. In institutions with smaller enrollments, such monitoring may be feasible, and undoubtedly would contribute to a richer learning experience. Students having difficulties with patients, staff, or the course requirements are encouraged to meet individually with the instructor. The only other requirement for the volunteer component of the course is a brief, typewritten narrative of the student's experiences as a volunteer. This paper is an effort to facilitate some closure on the student's exposure to psychopathology and the mental health delivery system. The assignment also allows the student to provide the instructor with informal feedback about the adequacy and relevance of the volunteer program.

Initially, students express some concerns about working in an inpatient psychiatric facility, and some discussion related to these concerns is advised before their first visits. Themes of personal safety, observer discomfort, contagious infection, and overidentification with patients have all been broached. A brief discussion of volunteer experiences precedes most classroom lectures during the semester, and serves to set an informal and interactive tone for the material to follow. Unfortunately, it is often hard for the academic material presented in class to compete with the sometimes mysterious, tragicomic, and fantastic behavior of long-term psychiatric inpatients. However, it is this sort of competition that is profitable.

Integration of lectures and readings with volunteer experiences is accomplished by continued discussion of students' reactions to their work during class time. We have observed that students are typically very attentive when their peers are discussing what has recently occurred at their volunteer site. Lectures on specific clinical problems and techniques are augmented by student descriptions of real-life observations of the syndromes and interventions. For example, presentation of symptoms of schizophrenia is greatly embellished by encouraging students to recount neologisms or clang associations they have heard patients produce.

There are several potentially negative aspects to the volunteer experience for both students and instructors. For

a variety of personal and logistical reasons, some students are unable to become involved in the volunteer program, therefore, alternative experiences must be arranged. In the past several years this alternative has consisted of preparing book reviews of biographical and autobiographical accounts of psychopathology. Students are discouraged from electing this option and few do.

Another potential negative aspect of volunteer work is the occasional student who experiences psychological conflict. For some, sustained contact with disturbed children and adults is distressing to the point of interfering with their own functioning. In a class of approximately 60, an average of about 1 student will report such experiences to the instructor. One effort to minimize such negative reactions is to inform students that they will undoubtedly experience some naturally occurring discomfort in psychiatric settings. This is presented in the guise of the "medical student's syndrome," whereby identification with symptoms is a part of the learning process. Students are also encouraged to speak with the instructor if the volunteer work becomes problematic. As noted earlier, very few students find this necessary.

Before launching a volunteer program, the department or instructor should consult the university attorney to clarify individual and institutional liability. Likewise, the mental health facility must be willing to assume liability for volunteers. In this connection, we suggest that instructors refrain from advising ways in which students might best interact with patients. This is tempting in that students will often discuss problematic patient situations in class and will want guidance as to the most effective way to help (or not hurt) patients. Our practice has been to refer students to their facility supervisor for suggestions on how best to interact with their particular patient(s), including the processes of initiating and terminating the relationships.

We began a systematic evaluation of the volunteer experience in the spring semester of 1986. We devised a questionnaire, based in part on the instrument developed by Fox, Lopuch, and Fisher (1984), to assess students' reactions to the volunteer work. We also obtained demographic information about the students. The results of this questionnaire are presented in Table 1.

Eighty-four students completed the questionnaire. Seventy-five percent of the respondents were women (which was the approximate percentage of women in the total class), with an average age of 22.0 years. Seventy percent of the respondents were psychology majors or minors, with an average of 74.0 credit hours completed. Eighty-two percent of the students had no previous experience doing volunteer work in a mental health setting. To reduce evaluation apprehension, students completed the questionnaire anonymously and were informed that the results had no bearing on their grades.

The results of the survey suggest that students had a very positive overall reaction to the volunteer experience, became quite personally involved in the work, and reported a meaningful positive change in their attitudes

Table 1. Means and Standard Deviations of Student Responses to a Volunteer Questionnaire

Question	M	SD
1. Please rate your overall reaction to the Abnormal Psychology volunteer experience.	7.79	1.58
2. How personally involved in the volunteer experience did you become?	7.29	1.70
3. Have your attitudes about psychiatric patients/mental health care changed as a result of your volunteer experience?	7.24	2.49
4. To what extent did the volunteer experience increase your knowledge of abnormal psychology?	6.98	2.33
5. To what extent did the volunteer experience increase your motivation to study and understand material presented in the text and lectures?	6.73	2.37

Question	Positive/ Yes	Negative/ No
6. If there was a change in your attitudes, has this change been toward a more positive or more negative perception of psychiatric patients/mental health care?	91%	9%
7. Do you plan to continue your volunteer work after the semester ends?	29%	71%

Note. Eighty-four students completed the questionnaire. Questions 1 through 5 were fully-anchored, 11-point (0–10) Likert-type scales with higher values representing more positive responses.

toward psychiatric patients and mental health care. A somewhat less positive impact on academic knowledge and motivation was reported. Interestingly, students generally did not intend to continue their volunteer work after the semester, despite their positive reactions. This disinclination to continue may be attributable to a number of factors, including graduation, summer vacation, employment, or simple disinterest. More clearly, it suggests that most students would not have sought out volunteer work in a mental health facility were it not a course requirement. However, the 29% of the students indicating an interest in continuation represents approximately 900 possible volunteers over the course of 18 years. The potential positive impact of these persons on patient care and the community's perception of psychiatric treatment is enormous.

Another benefit of the volunteer program has been the decision or discovery by several students that a career in mental health or a related field is what they wish to pursue. Such sentiments have been revealed in the narratives students have written at the end of the semester. Conversely, some students have discovered that a career in mental health is not what they want to pursue. Whatever the case may be, exposure to the mental health care system is valuable "career guidance" for many of our students. In the students' written narratives of their volunteer experiences, the majority of the comments are positive. For example, one student commented, "It was a learning experience I will never forget," and another reported that "The volunteer work provided me with more insight into the material." Particularly gratifying were comments such as "I've not only found that I can work with people in mental institutions, but also that I have learned much and grown as a person by going there," and "Throughout my volunteer experiences, I felt I was making a difference." A few students did offer negative comments. For example, one reported straightforwardly that "I honestly did not enjoy my volunteer work" and another commented "I guess I felt like I was wasting my time." Among those who reported generally positive experiences, a frequent theme was the desire to exert greater beneficial effects on patients whom they contacted. For example, one student commented "The work frustrated me a little, because my goal would always be to get those people out of there, and with many of them, it is just impossible."

Implementation of a volunteer experience in abnormal psychology admittedly requires substantial planning and consultation. However, once the program is in place, our experience has been that little additional work is required. Thus, the initial efforts are rewarded by a continuing reciprocal service for the academic and mental health facilities. Students gain invaluable personal and professional experience, while the facilities experience an infusion of enthusiasm, intelligence, and welcome naivete.

References

Fox, R. A., Lopuch, W. R., & Fisher, E. (1984). Using volunteer work to teach undergraduates about exceptional children. *Teaching of Psychology, 11,* 113-115.

Moffert, P. S. (1975). Inner-city field work in learning disabilities. *Teaching of Psychology, 2,* 119-122.

Shiverick, D. D. (1977). A full-time clinical practicum for undergraduates. *Teaching of Psychology, 4,* 188-190.

Stollak, G. E. (1975). Sensitivity to children: Helping undergraduates acquire child care giving and mental health skills. *Teaching of Psychology, 2,* 8-11.

Note

We thank the volunteer staffs of Bryce Hospital and the Veterans Administration. Without their cooperation the program described here would have been impossible.

Integrating Suicidology Into Abnormal Psychology Classes: The Revised Facts on Suicide Quiz

Richard W. Hubbard
John L. McIntosh
Indiana University at South Bend

An informal review of standard textbooks and course syllabi in abnormal psychology reveals that although suicide is often mentioned, the degree of coverage is at best uneven. Suicide is an important topic for inclusion in abnormal psychology curricula for the following reasons:

1. There are more than 30,000 suicides annually, which ranks suicide eighth among the leading causes of death in the U.S. (National Center for Health Statistics [NCHSI, 1992). Because a self-inflicted death occurs every 17 min, suicide represents an important area for prevention and intervention in the field of psychology.

2. Discussions of suicide can provide important illustrations of core concepts in abnormal psychology, such as depression, helplessness/hopelessness, cognitive distortions, and problems associated with alcoholism.

3. Suicide (especially among youth and the elderly) has received much media attention, and students are increasingly interested in the topic. One reason for this interest may be its personal relevance to some college students. Studies indicate that perhaps 40% to 50% of college students have suicidal thoughts and as many as 15% may have actually attempted suicide at some time (Slimak, 1990, p. 11). Student risk of suicide is estimated at about half that of nonstudents the same age (Schwartz, 1990). The overall suicide rate for those aged 15 to 24 is presently 13 per 100,000 population (NCHS, 1992). In addition, if conservative general estimates are applied, at least 1 of every 80 college students is the survivor of a loved one's suicide (McIntosh, 1989).

The Facts on Suicide Quiz

The original Facts on Suicide Quiz (FOS; McIntosh, Hubbard, & Santos, 1985) was developed as a research instrument to identify levels of knowledge and misconceptions about suicide. The original FOS consisted of 32 true-false items. Subsequently, 5 of the original questions were eliminated, 13 items that were predominantly demographic in nature were rewritten as multiple-choice questions, and 9 new items were added (Questions 15, 20, 29, and 31 to 36 in Table 1). The modified quiz has a pool of 36 items: 18 true false items focus on clinical issues and 18 multiple-choice questions assess primarily demographic information. The true-false and multiple-choice questions may be used singly or in combination; they are of sufficient length and include enough breadth of concepts for good pretest and posttest measurement as well. The authors recommended that instructors select at least half the items if they choose to create their own version. The items of the Revised Facts on Suicide Quiz (RFOS) appear in Table 1 (McIntosh, Kelly, & Arnett, 1992).

The RFOS has been a useful educational tool in our undergraduate abnormal psychology class. We typically use it in conjunction with lectures on depression or a full presentation on suicide. We accompany the quiz with a discussion of the clues or warning signs that would assist students in identifying those who might be depressed or suicidal (see, e.g., Shneidman, 1965). We also provide a list of the available resources for suicide prevention, intervention, and treatment both locally and on campus (see, e.g., Evans & Farberow, 1988, pp. 64-66). It is important to note that the topic of suicide can provoke strong emotions from prior attempts and friends and families of suicide completes.

We acknowledge this fact at the onset and include resources for support and counseling among the list of local agencies.

We usually employ the RFOS in our abnormal psychology classes after a general lecture on depression, often by referring to a suicide that has been heavily reported in the media (e.g., celebrity suicides, such as Freddie Prinze or Marilyn Monroe, or the pact suicide of four high school students from New Jersey several years ago). After students have completed the quiz, either they are given an answer key and a discussion ensues or, when time permits, the instructor reviews each item and polls how many students answered items incorrectly.

Table 1. Revised Facts on Suicide Quiz

Circle the answer you feel is most correct for each question.

"T" (true), "F" (false), or "?" (don't know)

T F ? 1. People who talk about suicide rarely commit suicide. [73%]

T F ? 2. The tendency toward suicide is not genetically (i.e., biologically) inherited and passed on from one generation to another. [46%]

T F ? 3. The suicidal person neither wants to die nor is fully intent on dying. [38%]

T F ? 4. If assessed by a psychiatrist, everyone who commits suicide would be diagnosed as depressed. [57%]

T F ? 5. If you ask someone directly "Do you feel like killing yourself?," it will likely lead that person to make a suicide attempt. [95%]

T F ? 6. A suicidal person will always be suicidal and entertain thoughts of suicide. [76%]

T F ? 7. Suicide rarely happens without warning. [63%]

T F ? 8. A person who commits suicide is mentally ill. [70%]

T F ? 9. A time of high suicide risk in depression is at the time when the person begins to improve. [47%]

T F ? 10. Nothing can be done to stop people from making the attempt once they have made up their minds to kill themselves. [92%]

T F ? 11. Motives and causes of suicide are readily established. [58%]

T F ? 12. A person who has made a past suicide attempt is more likely to attempt suicide again than someone who has never attempted. [80%]

T F ? 13. Suicide is among the top 10 causes of death in the U.S. [83%]

T F ? 14. Most people who attempt suicide fail to kill themselves. [74%]

T F ? 15. Those who attempt suicide do so only to manipulate others and attract attention to themselves. [64%]

T F ? 16. Oppressive weather (e.g., rain) has been found to be very closely related to suicidal behavior. [26%]

T F ? 17. There is a strong correlation between alcoholism and suicide. [68%]

T F ? 18. Suicide seems unrelated to moon phases. [49%]

19. What percentage of suicides leaves a suicide note? [40%]
    a. 15–25%   b. 40–50%   c. 65–75%

20. Suicide rates for the U.S. as a whole are ____ for the young. [8%]
    a. lower than   b. higher than   c. the same as

21. With respect to sex differences in suicide **attempts**: [65%]
    a. Males and females attempt at similar levels.
    b. Females attempt more often than males.
    c. Males attempt more often than females.

22. Suicide rates among the young are ____ those for the old. [7%]
    a. lower than   b. higher than   c. the same as

(continued)

Table 1. (*Continued*)

23. Men kill themselves in numbers ____ those for women. [67%]
    a. similar to   b. higher than   c. lower than

24. Suicide rates for the young since the 1950s have: [97%]
    a. increased   b. decreased   c. changed little

25. The **most** common method employed to kill oneself in the U.S. is: [28%]
    a. hanging   b. firearms   c. drugs and poison

26. The season of **highest** suicide risk is: [11%]
    a. winter   b. fall   c. spring

27. The day of the week on which **most** suicides occur is: [60%]
    a. Monday   b. Wednesday   c. Saturday

28. Suicide rates for non-whites are ____ those for Whites. [35%]
    a. higher than   b. similar to   c. lower than

29. Which marital status category has the **lowest** rates of suicide? [59%]
    a. married   b. widowed   c. single, never married

30. The ethnic/racial group with the **highest** suicide rate is: [15%]
    a. Whites   b. Blacks   c. Native Americans

31. The risk of death by suicide for a person who has attempted suicide in the past is ____ that for someone who has never attempted. [80%]
    a. lower than   b. similar to   c. higher than

32. Compared to other Western nations, the U.S. suicide rate is: [21%]
    a. among the highest   b. moderate   c. among the lowest

33. The most common method in **attempted** suicide is: [63%]
    a. firearms   b. drugs and poisons   c. cutting one's wrists

34. On the average, when young people make suicide attempts, they are ____ to die compared to elderly persons. [41%]
    a. less likely   b. just as likely   c. more likely

35. As a cause of death, suicide ranks ____ for the young when compared to the nation as a whole. [86%]
    a. the same   b. higher   c. lower

36. The region of the U.S. with the highest suicide rates is: [36%]
    a. east   b. midwest   c. west

Note. Answer key: true items—2, 3, 7, 9, 12, 13, 14, 17, and 18; false items—1, 4, 5, 6, 8, 10, 11, 15, and 16. Items for which the correct answer is "a": 19, 22, 24, 27, 29, and 34. Items for which the correct answer is "b": 21, 23, 25, 32, 33, and 35. Items for which the correct answer is "c": 20, 26, 28, 30, 31, and 36. For easier scoring in classroom settings, Questions 1 to 18 might be rearranged to alternate true and false items. Similarly, Items 19 to 36 may be rearranged to alternate a, b, and c answers. The percentages in brackets following each question refer to the proportion of 331 undergraduates enrolled in general psychology who correctly answered the item.

In addition to using the RFOS in undergraduate abnormal psychology courses, we have also found it appropriate within the context of a lecture to undergraduates in a course on preventative community mental health and occasionally in other psychology courses (e.g., general psychology or psychology of aging). The RFOS (or FOS) has also been used as a pretest and posttest for in-service presentations for health care professionals (see McIntosh et al., 1985, for details and results) and crisis intervention trainees, as well as a discussion icebreaker with high school students and community groups. The quiz stimulates a great deal of discussion as it is scored immediately, and students have also indicated that it functions well as a handout or study guide for examinations.

Major benefits of the quiz have been that (a) it provides an organized structure for instruction in a field where research is scattered across several disciplines (e.g., psychiatry, psychology, sociology, nursing, public health, and social work), (b) it promotes discussion as students encounter their misconceptions regarding the topic, (c) the varied formats (true-false, multiple-choice) allow the material to be used in standard exams (d) it covers a lot of material in a meaningful and interesting way, and (e) it includes questions that identify gaps in basic knowledge and misconceptions about the psychological processes associated with suicide.

Preliminary reliability and validity tests of the FOS have been conducted (McIntosh et al., 1992). These data suggest good psychometric qualities for each format. Factor analysis to determine specific clusters of questions

Table 2. References Supporting the Answers of the RFOS

References	Items
Arana & Hyman (1989), p. 83; Kety (1990), p. 132	2
Buda & Tsuang (1990), pp. 27–28, 28–30	4, 17
Diekstra (1990), p. 540	32
Evans & Farberow (1988), pp. 120, 119, 244, 21, 254, 22, 244, 22	5, 10, 12, 14, 19, 21, 31, 33
Maltsberger (1991), p. 295	6
McIntosh (1991), pp. 61; 60–61; 58; 60; 65; 65; 65; 59; 63–65; 59–60; 63; 66–67	20, 22, 23, 24, 25, 26, 27, 28, 29, 30, 36
NCHS (1992), pp. 20, 20–21	13, 35
Pokorny (1968), pp. 57–58, 64–65, 71, 62, 66–70, 70–71	1, 8, 9, 11, 16, 18
Shneidman (1985), pp. 135, 143–144, 124–129	3, 7, 15
Shneidman & Farberow (1961/1970), p. 208	34

(e. g., demographics, causes, signs, and clinical aspects) is underway. Unpublished data for 331 undergraduates enrolled in general psychology resulted in a mean score on the RFOS of 19.8 (SD = 2.7), or 55% correct for the 36 items, comparable to mean scores on the FOS of 59.1% (McIntosh et al., 1985). As in the study of the FOS, the RFOS performance was higher for the predominantly clinical items (M = 11.6, SD = 2.0; 64.4%) that comprised Questions 1 to 18, as compared to the largely demographic multiple-choice items (M = 8.2, SD = 1.7; 45.6%). However, note that the two categories of items represent different question formats (true-false vs. multiple-choice); the probability of answering a question correctly by chance differs as well. Therefore actual performance differences are minimal and not directly comparable. Performance by these 331 undergraduates (see Table 1) showed accurate knowledge about some items (e. g. 5, 10, 24, 35) and incorrect information about others (e.g. 16, 20, 22, 25, 26, 30, 32). These findings regarding specific items were almost identical to those for the FOS.

Reference Guide for Answer Key

Full justification for each answer on the quiz is beyond the scope of this article. However, at least one source for each question is provided in Table 2. Further information for building a lecture around the questions and justifying the answers may be found in several core texts and articles (e.g., Evans & Farberow, 1988; McIntosh, 1985; Pokorny, 1968; Shneidman, 1985). Instructors should note that some of the answers are based on recent demographic data that will, of course, change over time. Although the quiz may need to be updated as new statistical trends in suicide become apparent the need for this should be minimal, as the questions cover what appear to be stable relationships observed over the last several decades.

Questions in our classes that are frequently missed or that create much student interest include Items 2, 7, 8, 10,

15, 16, 19, 22, 26, and 30. Discussion usually focuses on explanations for high rates among the elderly and Native Americans, increases among the young, and theories related to motivations for suicide. Students also inquire about the influence of rock music Lyrics and drug use on suicide rates and on "copy cat" or contagion observed in some high schools. Our class discussions always include social, cultural, and biological considerations, as well as psychological issues related to suicide. As discussions close, students are reminded that better outreach, assessment, and treatment are needed to reduce suicide rates and that eliminating myths about suicide can contribute to this goal.

References

Arana, G. W., & Hyman, S. (1989). Biological contributions to suicide. In D. Jacobs & H. N. Brown (Eds.), *Suicide: Understanding and responding: Harvard Medical School perspectives* (pp. 73-86). Madison, CT: International Universities Press.

Buda, M., & Tsuang, M. T. (1990). The epidemiology of suicide: Implications for clinical practice. In S. J. Blumenthal & D. J. Kupfer (Eds.), *Suicide over the life cycle: Risk factors, assessment, and treatment of suicidal patients* (pp. 17-37). Washington, DC: American Psychiatric Press.

Diekstra, R. F. W. (1990). An intentional perspective on the epidemiology and prevention of suicide. In S. J. Blumenthal & D. J. Kupfer (Eds.), *Suicide over the life cycle: Risk factors, assessment, and treatment of suicidal patients* (pp. 533-569). Washington, DC: American Psychiatric Press.

Evans, G., & Farberow, N. L. (1988). *The encyclopedia of suicide.* New York: Facts on File.

Kety, S. S. (1990). Genetic factors in suicide: Family, twin, and adoption studies. In S. J. Blumenthal & D. J. Kupfer (Eds.), *Suicide over the life cycle: Risk factors, assessment, and treatment of suicidal patients* (pp. 127-133). Washington, DC: American Psychiatric Press.

Maltsberger, J. T. (1991). The prevention of suicide in adults. In A. A. Leenaars (Ed.), *Life-span perspectives of suicide: Time-lines in the suicide process* (pp. 295-307). New York: Plenum.

McIntosh, J. L. (1985). *Research on suicide: A bibliography.* Westport, CT: Greenwood.

McIntosh, J. L. (1989, Spring). How many survivors of suicide are there ? *Surviving Suicide,* pp. 1, 4.

McIntosh, J. L. (1991). Epidemiology of suicide in the United States. In A. A. Leenaars (Ed.), *Life-span perspectives of suicide: Time-lines in the suicide process* (pp. 55-69). New York: Plenum.

McIntosh, J. L., Hubbard, R. W., & Santos, J. F. (1985). Suicide facts and myths: A study of prevalence. *Death Studies, 9,* 267-281.

McIntosh, J. L., Kelly, L., & Arnett, E. (1992). *The Revised Faction Suicide Quiz: Reliability and validity tests*. Unpublished manuscript, Indiana University at South Bend, Department of Psychology.

National Center for Health Statistics. (1992). Advance report of final mortality statistics, 1989. *NCHS Monthly Vital Statistics Report, 40*(8, Suppl. 2).

Pokorny, A. D. (1968). Myths about suicide. In H. L. P. Resnik (Ed.), *Suicidal behaviors: Diagnosis and management* (pp. 57-72). Boston: Little, Brown.

Schwartz, A. J. (1990). The epidemiology of suicide among students at colleges and universities in the United States. In L. C. Whitaker & R. E. Slimak (Eds.), *College student suicide* (pp. 25-44). New York: Haworth.

Shneidman, E. S. (1965). Preventing suicide. *Amencan Journal of Nursing, 65*(5), 111-116.

Shneidman, E. S. (1985). *Definition of suicide*. New York: Wiley.

Shneidman, E. S., & Farberow, N. L. (1970). Attempted and completed suicide. In E. S. Shneidman, N. L. Farberow, & R. E. Litman (Eds.*), The psychology of suicide* (pp. 199-225). New York: Science House. (Original work published 1961)

Slimak, R. E. (1990). Suicide and the American college and university: A review of the literature. In L. C. Whitaker & R. E. Slimak (Eds.), *College student suicide* (pp. 5-24). New York: Haworth.

Jeopardy© in Abnormal Psychology

Carolin S. Keutzer
University of Oregon

Abnormal psychology is an intrinsically interesting course, but at times a light touch is needed to compensate for the immersion in the more depressing topics. Using games in this class increases student interaction; encourages application of information to another arena, supplementing rote memorization; and militates against acquiring the proverbial "medical school syndrome." Games have been used in other psychology courses where they provided useful organization of the material for students (research methods; Gibson, 1991), enhanced learning of complex concepts (theories of personality; Carlson, 1989), and even provided comic relief from the anxiety-provoking task of preparing for the final exam (physiological psychology; Ackil, 1986). A favorite game with my students is the Jeopardy game.

This game is an adaptation of the television quiz show in which contestants select a category and give a response in the form of a question to the answer that comes up in the chosen category. Diagnostic "families" make excellent category topics. One set of six categories may include the following disorders: anxiety, dissociative, somatoform, psychosexual, personality, and mood. Five responses in order of increasing difficulty (as judged by the instructor or the game maker) are prepared for each category; their selection with the correct question is scored either 100,

200, 300, 400, or 500 points. For example, a 200-point answer may be, "a mood disorder involving mild, persistent depression over an extended period of time," and the correct question is "What is dysthymia?" If the category is continued to the 300-point level, the answer may be, "the period of time the symptoms must have been present to warrant the diagnosis of major depressive syndrome," and the correct question is "What is 6 months?"

If a player's response is correct, the player receives the points. If the player's response is incorrect, the player forfeits the point value. If the teacher indicates that the response to an answer is incorrect, then the first of the other players to signal has the opportunity to ask the question. That player responds and either wins or loses the same number of points. The player who asks the correct question chooses the next category and point value. If no player asks the correct question, the teacher reads the correct question aloud. The player who selected the previous category and point value then makes the next selection.

You can divide a class into three to six teams and designate a captain for each team. Extra people can be scorekeepers. Begin the game by having each captain roll a die. The player with the highest number goes first by choosing a category and the level of difficulty. Team leaders may each be given a small bell or clicker, or they may just raise their hands. The first one to signal the desire to respond is called on. Team members may whisper the correct response to their captains either before or after the captain has signaled.

The game continues until either a time limit or a point limit is reached. I use a time limit so that other tasks can be scheduled for the day. I often use this game at the beginning of the class period to provide stimulation for a later discussion and to get the students actively involved and enthusiastic about the subject. Twenty min seems about the optimal time to spend on the activity. Less time does not allow for the momentum to build and the class to become fully engaged; more time does not seem warranted for the benefits generated. A scorekeeper can keep score on the chalkboard so that the teacher and the students can follow the progress of each team.

There are many ways to vary the game. In a class of over 150 students, you may want to have 3 or 4 contestants and the rest act as the audience. Those in the audience may make a note of items that need clarification or further discussion. Members of the audience can also be called on when none of the contestants elects to respond or responds incorrectly. I have also used the game informally in a large class of 360 students as a warm-up during the first 5 or 6 min of class by asking students to raise their hands to give the correct question. Table 1 lists sample items for the dissociative disorder category.

In small classes where all members participate, I sometimes give prizes in the form of a bonus point on the next exam to the members of the winning team. In larger classes (100 to 300 students), bonus points for the top individual scores can be awarded. However, the game has an intrinsic appeal to most students and external incentives are not necessary.

Table 1. Jeopardy Answers and Questions: Dissociative Disorders

100 points	Answer: Traveling amnesia Question: What is a psychogenic fugue?
200 points	Answer: A type of amnesia in which all events during a circumscribed period of time are blocked out. Question: What is localized amnesia?
300 points	Answer: A type of disorder most often associated with early childhood abuse. Question: What is multiple personality disorder?
400 points	Answer: A disorder dominated by a feeling of unreality and of estrangement from the self, body, or surroundings. Question: What is depersonalization disorder?
500 points	Answer: The type of accompanying amnesia in a true multiple personality. Question: What is asymmetrical? (Material learned by the primary personality is remembered by all of the secondary personalities, but material learned by a secondary personality is not known to the other secondary personalities or to the primary personality.)

At the end of each term, students evaluate the course on 15 items, such as "How satisfied were you with the teacher's knowledge of the subject?" and "Did the instructor use class time efficiently?" In addition, two optional, open-ended questions ask "What aspects of the course did you find valuable and would like to see retained or expanded?" and "What aspects of the course do you feel need improvement ?" My last course had 144 students; 127 of them completed the survey. Of the students (n = 71) who wrote comments to the open-ended questions, none mentioned Jeopardy as something about the course that needed improvement. However, 23 of the 71 (32%) specifically mentioned the Jeopardy game as something valuable to be retained. My impression is that students greatly appreciate the opportunity to learn and have fun at the same time.

Although this game as described was devised for abnormal psychology, it can be adapted to suit almost any psychology course. I used a version of it in my theories of personality course once as a study aid for the midterm. The categories were famous theorists (e.g., Freud, Jung, Horney, and Adler), and the answers covered various concepts associated with each theorist. I allowed individuals to raise their hands to respond to the answer. The student who accumulated the most points had 1 point added to her midterm score (which turned out to be the highest score in the class before the addition). Gibson (1991) used the Jeopardy game in his research methods course, with categories ranging from general topics, such as the scientific method, to specific topics, such as reliability. My experience echoed his in that the game "stimulated enthusiasm for the topic and helped students identify where to focus their study for the exam" (p. 177).

References

Ackil, J. E. (1986). PhysioPursuit A trivia-type game for the classroom. *Teaching of Psychology, 13*, 91.

Carlson, J. F. (1989). Psychosexual pursuit: Enhancing learning of theoretical psychoanalytic constructs. *Teaching of Psychology, 16*, 82-84.

Gibson, B. (1991). Research methods Jeopardy: A tool for involving students and organizing the study session. *Teaching of Psychology, 18*, 176-177.

Note

Requests for the set of six categories for the Jeopardy game should be sent to Carolin S. Keutzer, Department of Psychology, University of Oregon, Eugene OR 97403-1227.

Integrating Disability Awareness Into Psychology Courses: Applications in Abnormal Psychology and Perception

Stephen A. Wurst
Karen Wolford
State University of New York-College at Oswego

The mandate for higher education to provide education to students "otherwise qualified" who have learning disabilities, emotional problems, and other handicaps was outlined in Section 504 of the Rehabilitation Act of 1973 (Scott, 1990). Accordingly, instructors and nondisabled students should understand the concepts of learning disability and emotional disorder and know the unique needs of people affected by these conditions. This need for understanding is especially important because the number of disabled students attending college has steadily risen. Hippolitus (1987) estimated that 18,300 students with learning disabilities were admitted to colleges in 1985, and another 7% to 20% will experience some type of emotional disorder during their college career.

Increasing disability awareness of nondisabled students and faculty is also vital due to the prevalent stigma of disability. The stigma of mental illness is more prominent and documented (O'Grady,1988), but the stigma of being physically disabled is also widespread (e.g., Fichten & Amsel, 1988). Burgo (1992) stated that the attitudinal barriers that society holds toward the disabled are far more insidious than structural barriers.

On our campus, the Committee of Services for Students with Disabilities and the Dean of Students Office attempt to heighten awareness through a 2-day Disability Awareness Program. Three major components of the program are as follows: (a) Nondisabled faculty and students can "adopt" a disability for the day, (b) faculty are encouraged to provide classroom activities that increase awareness, and (c) speakers are scheduled to address these issues. Such disability simulations have been used successfully not only in colleges and graduate schools (Glazzard, 1979) but also in high schools (Hallenback & McMaster, 1991) and elementary schools (T. W. Jones, Sowell, J. K. Jones, & Butler, 1981).

Three Program Components

We describe in this article how we incorporated the three components in abnormal psychology and perception courses. We also specify possible discussion topics to be used after each event.

Disability Simulation

Nondisabled individuals could select a visual impairment that simulated macular degeneration (using light-filtered glasses from the Eye Research Institute of Boston that block the central area of the visual field), a hearing deficit (using Flents Model No. 241 sound-reducing earplugs), a motor disability (using a wheelchair, using crutches, or wearing splints on the fingers of their dominant hand), or a psychological disability (not talking for the day). Participants received any equipment they needed for the simulation in the morning and then conducted their daily activities while simulating the disability. At the end of the day, participants returned the equipment and were asked to complete a questionnaire about their experiences. At a reception afterward, the nondisabled students could interact socially with students with disabilities.

In the abnormal psychology course, participants discussed the stigmatizing process (E. Jones et al., 1984), using their experiences as examples. The discussion in the perception course focused on two rationales for studying perception. The first is that senses tend to be taken for granted. Participants related the general difficulties they encountered and acknowledged the importance of preserving their senses by avoiding high-risk behavior that may result in injuries to the sensory organs. The second rationale is that perception is fundamental to psychology (e.g., Goldstein, 1990). To show the role perception plays in learning and memory, students itemized their difficulties during classes in which they simulated the disability, and they noted the relation between perception and emotion (e.g., Zimbardo, Andersen, & Kabat, 1981).

Classroom Activities

Three activities were used in two abnormal psychology sections (*n*s = 40 and 90) to introduce the topic of childhood disorders and learning disabilities, such as dyslexia and dysgraphia. One activity included projecting overhead transparencies backward while students attempted to take notes. The second activity instructed students not to say any word containing the letter e (to simulate expressive language disorders). The third activity was a mirror-tracing demonstration (using a Lafayette Instruments Mirror Tracer Model No. 31010) to approximate a learning disorder. Two volunteers attempted to draw a line within the boundaries of a maze while looking at their hand and the maze in a mirror, which reverses the image. Volunteers described the frustration of performing the task.

These activities were intended to give students insight into the emotional aspect of the disorder, rather than the exact experience. The instructor explained how students with learning disabilities face this kind of struggle continuously and how individual differences in learning styles occur in students with and without disabilities. The controversies in dyslexia research (e.g., Solan, Sutija, Ficarra, & Wurst, 1990; Vellutino, 1987) can then be fully described.

Speakers

A third important, although not novel, technique to increase students' awareness is to use speakers who can help students empathize with people with disabilities and understand different disorders. In abnormal psychology, effective speakers have been a person with bipolar disorder and another whose relative committed suicide despite professional treatment. Students can write a reaction paper after hearing the speakers.

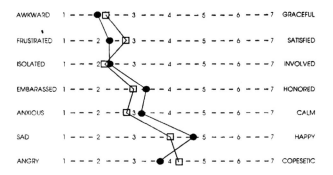

Figure 1. Mean ratings on the semantic differential scales as a function of type of disability simulated (filled circles indicated visual; open squares indicate auditory).

Evaluation of the Simulation Activity

From the perception class of 24 students, 18 (11 women, 7 men) students volunteered to participate in exchange for class credit. Twelve students simulated an auditory disability, and 6 simulated a visual disability. The 6 students who did not participate cited scheduling conflicts as the reason.

Students who adopted a disability completed a two-section questionnaire about their experiences. One part was a semantic differential probing the participants' emotional experience during the simulation. Results are presented in Figure 1. For presentation purposes, the positive emotions are listed on the left side of the graph, and the negative emotions are listed on the right (Sommer & Sommer, 1991).

Visual and auditory participants responded similarly and mostly in the negative direction. The strongest negative reactions were for *awkward* and *isolated*, followed by *frustrated* and *anxious*. Somewhat surprising, the *happy-sad* and the *copesetic-angry* scales were not as intense as the other reactions.

The second part of the questionnaire asked 10 openended questions concerning the participants' experiences and their attitudes. Four of these questions are relevant to this article. Did participants see people with disabilities differently after simulating their disability? Participants mentioned the challenges of routine tasks that nondisabled people take for granted (*n* = 11), emotional empathy with people with disabilities (*n*= 7), and the mental and physical strength of people with disabilities (*n* = 2).

Did participants view nondisabled people differently? Participants noted how nondisabled people act toward people with disabilities (*n* = 9), such as being "distant," "judgmental," "not as friendly," and "ignoring." Participants also wrote how "lucky" nondisabled people are (*n* = 3). Such responses support our major goals to have students (a) empathize with people with disabilities, (b) understand the stigma associated with disability, and (c) not to take their senses for granted.

How would the participants change their interactions with people with disabilities? Students said they would be "more sensitive" or "more patient" with people with disabilities (*n* = 7), they would speak louder to hearing-impaired people (*n* = 3), they would offer assistance more (*n* = 3), and they would be more respectful (*n* = 2). One student said the exercise would not change her interactions much because she already respected and interacted with people with disabilities.

How did the simulated disability affect participants' ability to function in class? Not surprising, all auditory disability participants mentioned that they had to listen more closely to the instructor, whereas visual disability participants cited their difficulties in seeing the overheads and chalkboard and in writing notes. Two auditory disability participants mentioned that they became less attentive and had more daydreams; two others reported being distracted by ambient sounds, especially when the class divided into small discussion groups. These results should prompt teachers to be more sensitive to the needs of students with disabilities.

Conclusions

These activities have been used successfully in teaching abnormal psychology and perception. They can also be used in other psychology courses, such as introductory and developmental psychology. Faculty interested in these activities may contact their office that serves students with disabilities to develop demonstrations for the entire college community. We recommend that college curricula address issues concerning the rights and needs of the differently abled in a variety of classroom and extracurricular settings to ensure all members of our society the rights and acceptance they deserve. After structural and attitudinal barriers are eliminated, people with disabilities can flourish and contribute more fully to society and to everyone's self-awareness.

References

Burgo, I. (1992, Spring). Opening doors to dignity. *Villanova Magazine*, pp. 2-7.

Fichten, C., & Amsel, R. (1988). Thoughts concerning interaction between college students who have a disability and their nondisabled peers. *Rehabilitation Counseling Bulletin, 32*, 22-40.

Glazzard, P. (1979). Simulation of handicaps as a teaching strategy for preservice and inservice training. *TEACHING Exceptional Children, 11*, 101-104.

Goldstein, E. B. (1990). *Sensation and perception.* Belmont, CA: Wadsworth.

Hallenbeck, M. J., & McMaster, D. (1991). Disability simulation for regular education students. *TEACHING Excepnonal Children, 23*, 12-15.

Hippolitus, P. (1987) . *College freshmen with disabilities preparing for employment* Washington, DC: President's Committee on Employment of the Handicapped.

Jones, E., Farina, A., Hastorf, A., Markus, H., Miller, D., & Scott, R. (1984). *Social stigma: The psychology of marked relationships.* New York: Freeman.

Jones, T. W., Sowell, V. M., Jones, J. K., & Butler, L. G. (1981). Changing children's perceptions of handicapped people. *Exceptional Children, 47*, 365-368.

O'Grady, T. (1988). Community psychiatry: A changing locus of rejection? *Perspectives in Biology and Medicine, 31*, 324-340.

Scott, S. S. (1990). Coming to terms with the "otherwise qualified" student with a learning disability. *Journal of Learning Disabilities, 23*, 398-405.

Solan, H., Sutija, V., Ficarra, A., & Wurst, S. A. (1990). Binocular advantage and visual processing in dyslexic and control children as measured by visual evoked potentials. *Optometry and Vision Science, 67*, 105-110.

Sommer, B., & Sommer, R. (1991). *A practical guide to behavioral research: Tools and techniques.* New York: Oxford University Press.

Vellutino, F. R. (1987). Dyslexia. *Scientific American, 256*(3), 34 41.

Zimbardo, P. G., Andersen, S. M., & Kabat, L. G. (1981). Induced hearing deficit generates experimental paranoia. *Science, 212*, 1529-1531.

Note

We thank the SUNY-Oswego Learning Enhancement Office, Committee for Services to Students with Disabilities, and the Dean of Students Office, especially Inez Alfors and Kathy Evans. We also thank Monica Everett for her assistance with the literature review, and Barbara Walters, Kevin Wallace, Ruth Ault, and three anonymous reviewers for their helpful comments.

Beyond the Sponge Model: Encouraging Students' Questioning Skills in Abnormal Psychology

Stuart M. Keeley
Rahan Ali
Tracy Gebing
Bowling Green State University

Isidor I. Rabi was a nuclear physicist who won the Nobel Prize in 1944 for his work on atomic nuclei. When someone asked him how he grew up to be a physicist, he told this story:

> When all his friends growing up in Brooklyn came home from school their mothers asked them, "So, what did you learn today?" But not his mother. When he came home his mother asked, "Izzy, did you ask a good question today?" (Barell, 1995, p.5)

We believe that many teachers of undergraduate psychology courses want their students to make enduring learning changes and want them to know how to think about psychological ideas, rather than simply what to think. An important component of this goal is to have students approach psychological ideas as active thinkers and learners (Meyers & Jones, 1993) and not merely as fact absorbers. Active learning requires students to embrace the process of asking good questions. Students with a strong questioning disposition mark up their books with questions. They also question lecturers and newspaper essays. When students perform these tasks, they make their own meanings, rather than simply reproduce others' thoughts.

However, educators have given scant attention to student questioning (Hunkins, 1966, 1995). According to Neil Postman, a long-time critic of American education:

> Everything we know has its origin in questions. Questions, we might say, are the principal intellectual instruments available to human beings. Then how is it possible that no more than one in one hundred students has ever been exposed to an extended and systematic study of the art and science of question-asking? How come Alan Bloom did not mention this, or E. D. Hirsh, Jr., or so many others who have written books on how to improve our schools? Did they simply fail to notice that the principal intellectual instrument available to human beings is not examined in school? (Postman,1995, p. 173)

Our purpose is to stimulate the development of classroom procedures that emphasize student questioning by sharing an important component of a recently taught class. It is our intent that using such procedures can help teachers actively respond to Postman's (1995) original concern. In addition, we present a preliminary evaluation of this approach on student question asking behavior.

We believe that it is desirable to decrease an "answers–by–the–experts" emphasis and increase a "questions–by–the–students" emphasis in many classrooms. This approach is consistent with the ideas of contemporary writers who encourage greater emphasis on active learning and critical thinking while facilitating student questioning as an essential teaching goal in the college classroom (Halpern & Nummedal, 1995; Meyers & Jones, 1993).

How might a questioning emphasis affect classroom learning? A shift to questioning has the potential to benefit the learning process. For example, Beers (1986) used Bloom's (1956) taxonomy to help train students in a personality course to ask high cognitive level questions; she followed a process of student question writing, student categorization of questions, discussion of rough drafts stimulated by the questions, and revision. Over the course of the term, her students increased the percentage of questions classified as evaluation, a high-level thinking activity considered to be an essential component of critical thinking (King, 1995; Paul, 1993).

King (1994) presented data to support the value of a guided student-questioning approach that emphasizes *higher order thinking* (HOT). She described HOT questions as those that cannot be answered by the factual material in the book or by the teacher's lectures. They require the student to think, rather than remember or look up. King guided students in becoming good HOT questioners by presenting them with question stems for generating questions based on the higher levels of Bloom's (1956) taxonomy of thinking—application, analysis and evaluation. For example, there were stems to generate application (How could ___ be used to ___ ?), develop examples (What is a new example of ___ ?), analyze relations (How does___ affect ___?), and other skills (King, 1995). She has found that such questioning techniques improve lecture comprehension and elicit inferences, explanations, and other high-level thinking (King, 1990, 1991a, 1991b) .

Gray (1993) provided another promising approach to student generated questioning, which he described as an immersion approach to critical thinking. He wanted students to "define their task as thinking about ideas in psychology, not simply learning (which to students often means memorizing) psychology" (p. 68). His approach emphasized HOT and incorporated several question-generating procedures. One procedure was to make the course's implicit questions explicit by having the students infer and write the questions that the course's readings and lectures were trying to answer. We believe that this is an important procedure because it helps to heighten students' awareness that answers imply questions—they do not stop a conversation (see Meyer, 1994).

Another procedure Gray (1993) mentioned was to require students to devise their own questions on each reading assignment—questions that the reading stimulated but did not answer. He gave students a handout that described the kinds of questions that might come to mind while reading a passage of text—such as questions about the evidence or logic behind some claim, the exact meaning of a murky concept, or possible implications of an idea or research finding. Students jotted down such questions as they read. After finishing the chapter, they selected five of their questions and elaborated on each in a paragraph that explained the question clearly, showed its linkage to some information in the chapter, and showed some of the students' own thought behind or about the questions.

The student-as-questioner approach we discuss includes some of the ideas of King (1990, 1991a, 1991b, 1994, 1995) and Gray (1993) but also differs in emphasis as well as breadth of student question taxonomies. First, we see the process of generating higher order questions as having primary educational benefit in itself, regardless of how much it improves comprehension or recall of classroom ideas (although we do believe that it can make such improvements). To ask questions, students must interact with the material more deeply, in a way that requires more active thinking. Also, knowing how to ask good questions provides the possibility of cultivating a natural disposition to ask questions. Second, like Beers (1986), we are particularly interested in students asking questions that help them evaluate what they read. In many classes, teachers infrequently ask students to thoroughly evaluate course material (Ellner & Bames, 1983). Yet, only when this type of interaction with the material occurs do students actively construct personal meaning from it. By habitually asking evaluation questions, students are no longer solely dependent on experts for their knowledge base. Our approach adds an explicit critical thinking taxonomy to facilitate evaluative activity.

With those values as context, we describe an approach to training questioning in the classroom and share an exploratory evaluation of that training.

Method

Participants

Students in one summer and one fall undergraduate abnormal psychology class served as participants. The summer class consisted of 27 students (16 seniors and 11 juniors) and met 4 days a week for 6 weeks. The fall class met twice a week for 15 weeks and consisted of 80 students (35 sophomores, 24 juniors, and 21 seniors). Despite the large class size, the instructor maintained an active learning, inquiry-oriented approach. Both classes were made up of diverse majors, with 5 students in the summer class and 11 students in the fall class majoring in psychology.

Teaching Procedures

Both classes required extensive readings in two texts: *Abnormal Psychology* (Oltmanns & Emery, 1995) and *Asking the Right Questions in Abnormal Psychology* (Keeley, 1995). The Oltmanns and Emery text is like many abnormal psychology texts in its comprehensive, fact-oriented coverage of abnormal psychology topics. The Keeley text emphasizes critical thinking questioning of empirical material in abnormal psychology. It first presents a model of critical thinking and a set of critical thinking questions. It then models critical questioning for the reader by presenting in-depth descriptions of widely cited studies in the field, followed by a critical evaluation of them. In both classes, reading assignments from the two books were intermixed. Students usually read a chapter from the Oltmanns and Emery text and then a chapter from the Keeley text.

From the first day of class, beginning with the syllabus, the instructor encouraged students to go beyond the "sponge" (memory-emphasis) model and designed all activities to encourage active learning. A major component of this emphasis was frequent student question-generating assignments. During the first few weeks of the classes, the instructor introduced various kinds of questions to students and required them to generate questions as part of the assignments. Three general question categories were (a) questions making questions implicit in the text explicit, (b) critical thinking evaluation questions, and (c) HOT questions.

For each new reading assignment, students submitted three to six questions based on their reading. The earliest assignments (about three) required students to write the major questions they believed their readings addressed. Next, the instructor introduced them to HOT question stems through a modified list of King's (1991b) question stems, with each stem illustrated by a question related to abnormal psychology. Some sample stems included the following: "What does the author mean by . . . ?" "What perspective is reflected by . . . ?" and "What assumptions are made when she argues . . . ?"

The instructor used these stems as guides to question-generating writing exercises, in which students wrote a specied number of HOT questions. As the semester progressed, the instructor introduced students to the critical thinking questions stressed in Keeley (1995) and had them add these to their list of HOT questions. The following are some of the sample questions: "What does the author mean by biopsychosocial model?" "What perspective is reflected by Breuer's interpretation of Anna O's problems ?" And "how good is the evidence that bipolar disorders are inherited?" Thus, as the semester progressed students had more prompts to question asking and had to generate questions using cues from both their HOT list and from their critical thinking text.

Students submitted their questions at the end of each class. The instructor used a grading system of star, check plus, check, and check minus; later coding these grades as 2,1,0 or -1; summing; and converting them to a letter grade. The instructor then included this grade as part of students' overall writing exercises grade, which accounted for 30% of their class grade. An additional instruction that improved the quality of questions and also made grading easier was the requirement that students provide enough context for the question that the instructor was able to determine the student's basis for asking it. Context could refer to reading or lecture material that stimulated the question, to events in other classes, to events in their lives, or to other relevant background information. For example, the instructor encouraged questions like the following: "On pages 184 and 185, your text discusses cognitive therapy and interpersonal therapy. Which of these two approaches do you believe would be most helpful in the case study that we discussed in class? Why?" Thus, throughout the semester, the instructor gave students frequent feedback on their written questions as he attempted to shape good question-asking behavior.

The course incorporated student-generated questions in a variety of ways. Sometimes the instructor collected and graded them, assuming that the process of generating the questions itself was useful because it required giving in-depth thought to the material prior to class. At other times, in the summer class, students met in small groups (usually three students) to share their questions and choose a couple of questions for later presentation as a stimulant to discussion. In the large fall class, the instructor would sometimes select several questions from among those submitted to discuss in class. At other times, he would randomly call on students to share a question as a means to stimulate class discussion.

Evaluation

To assess student questioning directly, we gave students pretest and posttest tasks in asking questions of written material. The pretest task occurred at the beginning (second class meeting) of the courses. The instructor informed students that the course would emphasize student question asking, and as an introduction, they were going to perform an initial questioning exercise to provide a preliminary measure of their question-asking ability. Although initially the instructor did not mention whether he would grade the task, he later informed students that he would not. Students read a brief passage, preceded by the following instructions:

Please read the attached article. What questions come to mind? Write down any questions you think are important to ask, having read this article. Begin each question on a separate line. Feel free to refer back to the article as you generate as many questions as you can. Be sure you are only writing questions, and not simply phrases or statements. What you write must be something you would put a question mark after. You will have 15 minutes. Do not move on to Part 2 until you are instructed to do so.

Students read a 260-word passage discussing an outcome study comparing treatments for depression. The passage described a study in which 250 depressed patients were randomly assigned to one of four treatments: imipramine, a drug placebo pill, interpersonal therapy, or cognitive-behavioral therapy. The passage provided recovery rates for each condition and ended with conclusions about treatments for depression. The passage was typical of many encapsulations of research findings found in psychology textbooks: A conclusion was made, with a brief description of an experiment or study supporting that conclusion. The passage provided little detail of the methodology and did not define important terms. The instructor encouraged students to write as many questions about the passage as possible. He did not tell students that there would be a similar task at the end of the course. At the end (penultimate class meeting) of the courses, the instructor gave students the posttest, which featured the same passage as in the pretest. Time between pretest and posttest spanned 5 weeks in the first course and 14 weeks in the second. The instructor treated the posttest as the students' final writing exercise grade.

The second and third authors rated pretest and posttest protocols of all students from both courses while blind to time of testing. The raters counted a response as a question if it clearly asked something (as opposed to declarative, thinking aloud comments). They scored each nonredundant question as one point. Following identification and point assignment, they categorized all questions as one of the following: clear evaluative, ambiguous-evaluative, implication/curiosity, or deficient. The raters randomly selected 30 of 108 total protocols for scoring and categorization by both. Agreement between the two for scoring was 94% with a kappa coefficient of .86, and for categorization was 87% with a kappa coefficient of .77. The categories were as follows:

1. Clear-evaluative questions unambiguously suggested the student was evaluating the information. They included questions that sought to clarify ambiguous terms, evaluate the evidence, or request information to directly help judge the worth of a claim or argument. The following were examples: "What were the criteria for measuring depression?" "How reliable are their measures?" And "what do the researchers mean by 'clinical management'?"

2. Implications/curiosity questions were consistent with the goals of the course but were not evaluative. Often these questions asked about implications from the information, tried to connect that information with other ideas, or stimulated further exploration of the topic. The following were examples: "What does the success rate of the drug treatment say about the cause of depression?" And "why were the treatments less effective for the milder forms of depression?" These and clear-evaluative questions were the most desirable question categories, given the course training in questioning.

3. Ambiguous-evaluative questions suggested the possibility of evaluation but were too ambiguous for the rater to determine whether the student was truly using that question to evaluate the information. An example of such a question was "Who were the therapists?" The student may have asked this to evaluate the credibility of the study; that is, learning more about the therapists could directly help evaluate the generalizability of the results. However, whether the student had this purpose when asking the question was unclear.

4. Deficient questions were those that raters considered irrelevant, confusing, or redundant. For example, some students wrote questions that were difficult to understand due to grammar or usage or that were confusing others wrote questions that were already clearly answered in the test passage.

We tabulated the overall number of questions students offered as well as the number of questions within each category. We conducted pretest to posttest analyses for each class separately; results for the 5-week and 15-week classes were similar, thus we combined responses from both classes for a total of 108 student pretests and posttests. The means and standard deviations appear in Table 1. The most striking finding is the significant increase in total and in clear-evaluative questions. The number of clear-evaluative questions more than doubled from pretest to posttest, accounting for most of the increase in total questions. The means in the other three categories, although changing significantly, changed little in terms of absolute value. The percentage of all questions that were clear-evaluative increased from 54.5% to 69.5%, an increase that seems understandable and desirable because the test essay was a write-up of a flawed research

Table 1. Mean Number of Student-Generated Questions By Category

Type of Questions	Pretest		Posttest		
	M	SD	M	SD	$t(107)$
Clear-evaluative	4.36	2.85	9.32	3.87	13.20**
Ambiguous-evaluative	0.45	0.84	0.96	1.18	4.29**
Implications/curiosity	2.77	2.27	2.09	2.00	−2.66*
Deficient	0.72	1.30	1.32	1.44	3.20*
Total	8.00	3.20	13.41	4.89	12.63**

*$p < .01$. **$p < .001$.

study. The decrease in implications/curiosity questions is somewhat perplexing and disappointing. One explanation is that the research study summary had a stronger "pull" for evaluative questions than for implications/curiosity questions once one read the Keeley (1995) text and became accustomed to asking evaluative questions of research reports. Also, the higher rate of implications/curiosity questions during pretest may reflect the fact that participants early in the semester were not yet very sensitive to evaluative questions and turned to other possibilities as a result of running out of evaluative questions to ask. It would be desirable in future research to use diverse kinds of essays for pretests and posttests.

The level of deficient questions was very low in both testings, and the significant increase over time seems to reflect the fact that many more total questions were asked at posttest, which increased the likelihood of more deficient questions. This interpretation is supported by the fact that the percentage of all questions judged to be deficient changed little, increasing from 9.0% to 9.8% from pretest to posttest. The overall results are consistent with the goals of the training of question asking in class and support the view that students can learn to ask higher order questions, especially valuation level questions.

Discussion

Our experience with these two classes has been encouraging. It seems that there is much promise to a classroom atmosphere that strongly encourages question asking by specifically training students how to ask questions and giving them ample practice in doing so. We believe that students in the two courses indeed became better question-askers over the course of the semester. First, it was clear from grading their submitted question assignments that they improved their questioning over time. Although some questioners were clearly more sophisticated than others, most students in both classes were consistently receiving at least a check plus by the end of the semester. Secondly, the pretest versus posttest results support the idea that students had learned how to ask evaluation questions. They asked significantly more evaluative questions, and their questions were more focused. Although such findings are encouraging, they must be interpreted with caution because of the absence of a control group that repeated the testing but received no training in questioning.

Two important considerations for teachers deciding whether to implement the questions-by-the student approach are implementation time and size of class. Our experience has been that the instructor must use about three 15 to 30 min segments of class time over the course of the semester to provide and explain question-generating guidelines. Also, the smaller the class the more optimal the approach because providing written feedback on questions is time consuming, and the approach interfaces very well with the use of small group discussions. However, despite time demand obstacles, we believe that teachers of larger classes can consider adopting a modified approach that requires students to frequently generate questions but minimizes written teacher feedback. Random collection of student questions, for example, is one possible modification.

We believe that when students perceive themselves as questioners rather than as fact-collectors, they will become more personally invested in the ongoing learning activity. They can stop being sponges for information that others deem important and instead become active critical and creative thinkers, constructing their own knowledge and having a much better sense of what they do and do not know. Our focus is consistent with contemporary views that knowledge claims result from an active, constructive process among knowledge makers, rather than from passively observing things as they are.

Unfortunately, we did not collect systematic data concerning students' reactions to a heavy question-asking emphasis. Such data are needed in future research. Many students informally expressed on teacher evaluation forms that the frequent question generating made them pay more attention as they studied and forced them to think more deeply about the material. For example, some students made the following comments: "The class helped me improve my thinking and studying skills." "The questions were helpful in further understanding the material." And "thinking of questions forced me to understand the material, and not just memorize and spit it out." A significant number of students-although still a minority-clearly preferred being sponge learners throughout the terre and thus continued to feel frustrated. For example, students commented, "HOT questions were too time-consuming." "It was difficult to get the reading done and think of questions." And "the class was a lot of work-I think I prefer being a sponge." We suspect that there will always be a core group of such resistors to an active learning, question-oriented approach (see Keeley, Shemberg, Cowell, & Zinnbauer, 1995) until the educational system makes a greater change to active learning than presently exists.

We believe that when students consistently generate questions about ideas, teachers have already achieved an important goal: active involvement with the material and familiarity with a learning tool that is potentially useful both in and out of the classroom. Even if students cannot answer their own questions, asking good questions can move them forward in the conversation of ideas in which they are involved. Thus, we believe an approach that encourages higher order student questioning is a promising approach because of both its impact on learning (thinking) in the classroom and its potential to generate long-tersn habits of HOT about abnormal psychology as well as other disciplines. We want our students to respond to the question, "Do you have any questions?" with a resounding, "Yes, we have lots of good questions!" We must look to future research to tell us whether training in questioning similar to that described here can produce the long term habit of asking such questions.

References

Barell, J. (1995). *Teaching for thoughtfulness* (2nd ed.). White Plains, NY: Longman.

Beers, S. E. (1986). Questioning and peer collaboration as techniques for thinking and writing about personality. *Teaching of Psychology, 13*, 75-77.

Bloom, B. S. (Ed.). (1956). *Taxonomy of educational objectives: The classification of educational goals.* New York: Longmans, Green.

Ellner, C. L., & Barnes, C. P. (1983). *Studies of college teaching.* Washington, DC: Lexington.

Gray, P. (1993). Engaging students' intellects: The immersion approach to critical thinking in psychology instruction. *Teaching of Psychology, 20,* 68-74.

Halpern, D. F., & Nummedal, S. G. (Eds.). (1995). Psychologists teach critical thinking [Special issue]. *Teaching of Psychology, 22*(1).

Hunkins, F. P. (1976). *Involving students in questioning.* Boston: Allyn & Bacon.

Hunkins, F. P. (1995). *Teaching thinking through effective questioning* (2nd ed.). Norwood, MA: Christopher-Gordon.

Keeley, S. M. (1995) *Asking the right questions in abnormal psychology.* Englewood Cliffs, NJ: Prentice-Hall.

Keeley, S. M., Shemberg, K. M., Cowell, B., & Zinabauer, B. (1995). Coping with student resistance to critical thinking: What the psychotherapy literature tells us. *College Teaching, 43,* 140-145.

King, A. (1990). Enhancing peer interaction and learning in the classroom through reciprocal questioning. *American Education Research Journal, 27,* 664-687.

King, A. (1991a). Effects of training in strategic questioning on children's problem-solving performance. *Journal of Educational Psychology, 83,* 307-317.

King, A. (1991b). Improving lecture comprehension: Effects of a metacognitive strategy. *Applied Cognitive Psychology, 5,* 331-346.

King, A. (1994). Inquiry as a tool in critical thinking. In D. F. Halpern (Ed.), *Changing college classrooms: New teaching and learning strategies for an increasingly complex world* (pp. 13-38). San Francisco: Jossey-Bass.

King, A. (1995). Inquiring minds really do want to know: Using questioning to teach critical thinking. *Teaching of Psychology, 22,* 13-17.

Meyer, M. (1994). *Rhetoric, language, and reason.* University Park: Pennsylvania State University Press.

Meyers, C., & Jones, T. B. (1993). *Promoting active learning.* San Francisco: Jossey-Bass.

Oltmanns, T. F., & Emery, R. E. (1995). *Abnormal psychology.* Englewood Cliffs, NJ: Prentice-Hall.

Paul, R. (1993). *Critical thinking: How to prepare students for a rapidly changing world* (3rd ed.). Rohnert Park, CA: Sonoma Stare University, Center for Critical Thinking and Moral Critique.

Postman, N. (1995). *The end of education: Redefining the value of school.* New York: Knopf.

Note

Send requests for lists of questions or question stems to Stuart Keeley, Department of Psychology, Bowling Green State University, Bowling Green, OH 43403; e-mail: skeeley @bgnet.bgsu.edu.

SECTION III
CLINICAL-COUNSELING

Learning Concepts and Principles

Students learned to analyze behaviors as examples of psychological defense using an interactive computerized teaching program that Roger Bibace, David Marcus, Debra Thomason, and Anne Litt developed. Students read a short paragraph describing a fictional situation illustrating a defensive behavior. Behaviors were analyzed in terms of actor-action-object propositions. The transformations in these three terms generated psychological defenses such as projection and reaction formation. Students' satisfaction with the program and their subsequent performance in identifying defense mechanisms indicated that the program helped to develop analytic skills.

To demonstrate the potential influence of two Adlerian principles—earliest recollections and birth order—on personality, Les Parrott developed two exercises. In one exercise, students recorded and studied their earliest recollections. In another exercise, students discussed their position in their family constellation. Students in undergraduate and graduate introductory counseling courses rated both exercises highly; undergraduates valued the birth order exercise more, but graduate students valued the earliest recollections exercise more.

Acquiring Skills-Undergraduate Students

For the interviewing component of an undergraduate clinical psychology course, Kristi Lane trained undergraduate theater majors as clients. The actor created the character of a client after reading appropriate case studies. The instructor assisted by providing feedback, helping to create client history, background, and personality characteristics, and by monitoring the degree of pathology that the actor portrayed. The author concluded that the actors added a realistic component to the course.

To give students experience in an assessment interview, Bernard Balleweg developed The Interviewing Team. The team consisted of several students who interviewed the instructor who role-played a client. Each student on the team collected one type of information (e.g., behavioral or somatic symptoms). A debriefing session followed the interview in which students developed hypotheses for the causes of the clients problems.

John Suler used Eliza, a widely known computer program that reacts to the user by simulating the responses of a psychotherapist, as a teaching aid in undergraduate clinical psychology courses. The author pointed out that students' interaction with the program could enhance their

understanding of interviewing and psychotherapy, the contrasts between clinical interactions controlled by humans and computers, and the role computers may play in the mental health field. The author also discussed methods for conducting the exercise, for integrating the program into the course syllabus, and for evaluating the exercise's impact on students.

During an intensive 5-week period of studying and practicing empathic-listening skills, senior undergraduates in Peter Fernald's externship engaged in 14 different learning activities, after which they completed a course assignment designed to assess their empathic-listening skills. The students rated both the learning activities and the empathic-listening assignment very favorably.

Gary Goldstein summarized a collaborative learning project for an upper-level undergraduate counseling course. Groups of students designed and presented a workshop on a therapeutic intervention for a specific patient population. Each student also wrote a paper on an individually selected topic. The article described examples of students' workshops, reactions to and evaluations of the assignment, and grading procedures. The author concluded that the assignment provided a model for the kind of collaborative work students may encounter in advanced study.

Acquiring Skills–Graduate Students

Kathryn Rickard and Robert Titley described an interviewing game used in a graduate-level, interviewing skills course. The goal of the game was to teach basic components of the interview process such as comfort with the interview, microcounseling skills, hypothesis generation, and hypothesis testing. The instructor played the part of a client and was interviewed by two teams of students. The article explained the students' role in the game and the game's procedure. Students gave favorable ratings to and positive feedback about the game.

To teach interviewing skills to first-year graduate students, John Sommers-Flanagan and John Means developed a four component exercise. First, the instructors told students that they should neither ask nor answer questions during their first two interviews. Second, students evaluated, orally and in writing, their own behavior during the interview. Third, peers, instructors, and analogue clients provided students with feedback regarding their interviewing skills and interpersonal styles. Fourth, the instructors evaluated the effects of the interview on the analogue clients because the graduate students acquired students from an introductory psychology research pool.

Danna Anderson, Colleen Gundersen, Daniel Banken, Jonathan Halvorson, and Denise Schmutte described two exercises using undergraduates to act as role-play clients for graduate counselor-trainees. The first exercise involved mock counseling sessions; the second was a mock case conference. The authors graded graduates on their counseling and case-conceptualization skills. The exercises seemed to be educationally beneficial and may have helped decrease undergraduates' negative stereotyping of persons with psychological problems.

Andrea Weiss designed a method to teach verbal helping skills to undergraduate and graduate students who did not have access to clinical populations. Students used open-ended interviews with volunteers as the primary training device; role-playing simulations and programmed instruction complemented this experience.

Treating Fears

Dolores Hughes demonstrated the behavioral technique of participant modeling by introducing a snake into the classroom. Students expressed their level of fear of the snake and, through a series of progressive steps, approached and handled the snake. Several students in the moderate and high fear conditions eventually handled the snake. This activity could be used in a wide range of courses such as introductory, abnormal, or behavior modification.

Timothy Lawson and Michael Reardon described a technique for demonstrating in vivo systematic desensitization in an engaging, humorous, and informative manner. The technique involved role playing the treatment of a student who ostensibly has a phobia of chalkboard erasers, which explained why he or she always sat at the back of the room. Students enjoyed the demonstration and believed it enhanced their understanding of systematic desensitization.

Advocating a Research Perspective

Timothy Osberg summarized a checklist of guidelines he used to teach students the basics of psychotherapy outcome research in several courses (e.g., abnormal, clinical, and even introductory psychology). The checklist is research-based and draws on techniques employed in recent representative psychotherapy outcome research studies. The author suggested several variations in the pedagogical use of the checklist. Student evaluations supported the usefulness of the checklist as a teaching tool.

Students applied abstract research concepts to a concrete analogue of therapy evaluation using Richard Viken's classroom demonstration. Students rated their food consumption and mood before and after an absurd pseudotreatment. The instructor used the data to demonstrate that absolutely useless treatments may initially appear to be highly effective and that careful attention to research design is necessary for appropriate therapy evaluation. Student evaluations indicated that this experiment helped them understand and remember important issues in therapy outcome research.

1. LEARNING CONCEPTS AND PRINCIPLES

Teaching Psychological Defenses: An Interactive Computerized Program

Roger Bibace
David Marcus
Debra Thomason
E. Anne Litt
Clark University

Students can learn to analyze behaviors as examples of psychological defense through the use of an interactive computerized teaching program. Our review of the literature in this area revealed a paucity of material for teaching students to distinguish among various defense mechanisms.

Although it is important to acknowledge that there are theoretical differences and vagueness about the defenses, our intention is neither to introduce a new theory of the defense mechanisms, nor to endorse a particular theory as the "correct" one. For pedagogical purposes, we chose the approach developed by Suppes and Warren (1975). This conceptualization of defense was well suited for a computerized teaching program because, as an attempt to present a mathematical model of the defense mechanisms, it is a relatively clear and objective analytic system. Therefore, this approach can be easily adapted to a stepwise analysis of defensive behavior. Other theorists have presented formal models of defense mechanisms (Holland, 1973), but these other algorithms were not as easily translated into computerized instruction. The Suppes and Warren approach is unique in that it articulates defensive behavior in terms of easily recognizable components.

Conceptual Framework

Central to Suppes and Warren's (1975) conceptualization of the defense mechanisms is the assumption that the contents of the unconscious consist of propositions that take the form of actor-action-object. This proposition takes the schematic form of Self + A + X, where A represents the action and X represents the object. A defense is a change in one or more of the three terms that make up the unconscious proposition in order for the proposition to become conscious. The defense mechanisms can then be generated by simply enumerating the various transformations that can be performed, singly and in combination, on each term in the proposition.

Suppes and Warren specified eight elementary transformations, thus generating eight basic defense mechanisms. The actor can be transformed from self as actor to other as actor (projection), and the propositional form that this takes is Other + A + X. The transformation from other as actor to self as actor (identification) is also possible. Suppes and Warren list four possible transformations of the action; for example, when an action is changed to its opposite, the defense is reaction formation (Self + Opp A + X). Finally, the object can be replaced with another object (displacement), and the propositional form this takes is Self + A + Y. A special case of this transformation occurs when the new object is the self (turning against the self), or Self + A + Self. Suppes and Warren also provided an exhaustive list of what they considered to be the remaining 36 defenses. For example, if the actor is transformed from self as actor to other as actor and the action is changed to its opposite, the defense would be a complex one, projection and reaction formation (Other + Opp A + X). Although the reification of some of these concepts is a potential danger in this approach, we found it useful for pedagogical purposes. In our program we used Suppes and Warren's tripartite representation of the defenses to have the learner analyze situations in which defensive behavior was exhibited and break them down into the three components: actor, action, and object. (Suppes and Warren should not be held responsible for our application of their framework. We are grateful for the contribution of their original ideas as presented in their article.)

Use of the Program

The program requires that the student first read a short paragraph describing a fictional situation in which a defensive behavior is enacted. The student is then asked a series of questions: Who is the actor? What is the action? Who or what is the object? Students are also provided with a glossary of the terms used in the program. Given the limited vocabulary of this program, the glossary aided students in choosing the proper synonym. If students answer any of these questions incorrectly, they are informed that the answer is incorrect and are given two more opportunities to respond. Unlike personalized system of instruction (PSI) books, a computer can inform students that their answer is wrong without immediately providing the correct response. After three attempts, the student is provided with the answer and proceeds to the next question. Following each question, the description of the situation is repeated along with a summary of the previous answers. Once the actor, action, and object are identified, the student is asked: Has the actor changed, and if so how? Has the action changed, and if so how? Has the object changed, and if so how? The correct answers to the last three questions combine to form the propositional statement of the defense. Finally, students are asked to name the defense represented by the propositional statement.

A total of 32 examples were used. After students successfully completed the first 16 examples, we assumed that they had internalized the analytic process by which the categorization was achieved. Therefore, students were given the opportunity to name the defense without having the computer go through the first seven questions. If the student incorrectly identified the defense, the program was designed to return to the seven preliminary questions.

The operation of the program may best be illustrated by a concrete example. What follows is extracted directly from the program:

It was early in the morning and Mr. and Mrs. Johnson clearly were not getting along. Mr. Johnson dealt his parting blow as he was on his way out the door for work, leaving Mrs. Johnson no chance to vent her fury at his cutting remark. She muttered a few curses under her breath, and resigned herself to returning to the preparation of her kids' lunches. Moments later, while slicing vegetables, she cut right into her finger with the knife.

In this example, Mrs. Johnson (the actor) momentarily hates (the action) Mr. Johnson (the object). Neither the actor (Mrs. Johnson) nor the action (Mrs. Johnson's fury) have changed; however, the object is changed from Mr. Johnson to the self (" . . . her fury at his cutting remark . . . she cut right into her finger with the knife."). The propositional form, in this case of turning against the self, would be Self + A + Self.

Table 1 outlines the defenses and their propositional forms that we used in this program.

Results and Evaluation

Although this program has proven useful in a number of different contexts (e.g., the training of residents in family medicine, clinical psychology graduate students, and advanced undergraduates), it was initially designed for an undergraduate course titled, Psychoanalytic Interpretation of Behavior. In this course students were exposed to a traditional method of teaching defense mechanisms (cf. Brenner, 1955; Menninger, 1947) during lecture periods. In addition, students were required to attend two 3-hr discussion groups using the computerized teaching program, which was their only exposure to our adaptation of Suppes and Warren's (1975) formal model. Our evaluation of the teaching program included a comparison of students' ability to identify defense mechanisms on an exam using the two different approaches as well as students' subjective comments on the program's merit.

Table 1. The Defenses and Their Propositional Forms

Mechanism	Number of Transformations	Propositional Form
Projection	1	Other + A + X
Identification	1	Self* + A + X[a]
Reaction formation	1	Self + Opp A + X
Intellectualization	1	Self + Intell A + X
Isolation	1	Self + Split A + X[b]
Repression	1	Self + Denial A (internal) + X[b]
Denial	1	Self + Denial A (external) + X[b]
Turning against the self	1	Self + A + Self
Displacement	1	Self + A + Y
Identification and reaction formation	2	Self* + Opp A + X
Projection and reaction formation	2	Other + Opp A + X
Projection and displacement	2	Other + A + Y
Reaction formation and displacement	2	Self + Opp A + Y
Intellectualization and displacement	2	Self + Intell A + Y
Projection, displacement, and reaction formation	3	Other + Opp A + Y

[a] self* = other as actor — self as actor.
[b] These are the modifications we introduced into Suppes and Warren's original list of the defenses.

Quantitative Analysis

It was not possible to measure the pedagogic value of the computer program because all of the students were exposed to both methods of analyzing defense mechanisms. However, we were able to assess the efficacy of the Suppes and Warren schema for identifying defenses by designing the midterm exam to permit a comparison of this method with the traditional approach. The exam included four essay questions that required students to identify the defense mechanisms described in a short vignette. Two of these questions dealt with an analysis using the traditional approach; the other two involved analysis using the Suppes and Warren model. The two questions involving the traditional approach required students to articulate the id, ego, and superego components of the behavior in identifying the defense mechanism. The two questions involving the Suppes and Warren model explicitly asked for each of the analytic steps (e.g., Who is the actor? What is the action?) which led to an identification of the defense. In order to get credit for naming the defense, students were required to follow the analytic sequence. Thus, students had to follow the Suppes and Warren schema in order for their responses to be scored as correct in our experimental design. No student introduced the traditional categories when analyzing these two examples.

A Wilcoxon matched-pairs signed-ranks test indicated that the number of correctly identified defenses was significantly greater when the Suppes and Warren model was utilized, $T (N = 52) = 276$, $p < .001$. It is possible that some students used the Suppes and Warren model on all four exam questions, but it is highly unlikely that they could have used the traditional approach to analyze the Suppes and Warren model questions. However, even the former possibility is counterindicated by the data. If students had only used the Suppes and Warren model, there should have been no difference between their performance on the two types of questions.

Qualitative Analysis

When students were asked to compare the traditional and computer methods, their responses were fairly consistent. Although two students believed that the traditional method was easier to understand, most students thought that the computer method was simpler and clearer. On the other hand, many students believed that the traditional method allowed for greater creativity and intuition, and for a holistic appraisal of the person's defensive behavior. A number of students commented that the two approaches were complementary; a combination of the computer and the traditional approach optimally facilitated the process of learning these interpretive methods. Furthermore, when students were asked whether the programmed instruction was useful enough to be continued, they unanimously agreed that it was.

Conclusion

From our analyses, it appears that our program is a useful pedagogical tool. The quantitative analysis indicated that the Suppes and Warren model is an effective way to teach students about psychological defense mechanisms. Further, students' qualitative responses favored the computer as a useful instructional tool: Students believed that the program aided their ability to identify defensive behaviors, and their belief was supported by the quantitative analyses performed. Students overwhelmingly favored the use of the program, despite the additional 6 hr of classwork it entailed. Given the ambiguity of traditional methods of analysis, communication about defense mechanisms may be facilitated by the use of this analytic method.

References

Brenner, C. (1955). *An elementary textbook of psycho-analysis.* New York: International Universities Press.

Holland, N. (1973). Defense, displacement and the ego's algebra. *The International Journal of Psycho-Analysis, 54,* 247-257.

Menninger, K. (1947). *The human mind.* New York: Knopf.

Suppes, P., & Warren, H. (1975). On the generation and classification of defence mechanisms. *The International Journal of PsychoAnalysis, 56,* 405-414.

Notes

1. We thank Leonard Cirillo for his critical reading of the manuscript and Lisa Budzek for her help with the student evaluations.
2. The computer program described here is disk-based and requires 64K of memory. Versions of the program are available for the Digital Rainbow 100 Personal Computer, Apple IIe, and IBM PC. Copies of the program are available on request from Roger Bibace, Department of Psychology, Clark University, Worcester, MA 01610.

Earliest Recollections and Birth Order:
Two Adlerian Exercises

Les Parrott
Seattle Pacific University

Adler holds an important place in psychology. He influenced neo-Freudians like Horney and Fromm as well as more modem theorists like Rogers and Ellis (Corsini & Wedding, 1989). Adler shifted the Freudian emphasis on the libido to the ego's striving for power and developed a personality model, a theory of psychopathology, the inferiority complex concept, and the foundation of a treatment method.

For Adler, individuals respond in ways that reflect neither genetic endowment nor social environment. Rather, persons are responsible and respond to their social field in adaptive, creative ways. Adler (1959) also contended that each individual strives toward an ideal that becomes apparent early in life and runs as a major theme throughout one's lifetime.

Surprisingly, Adler's influence often goes unnoticed. Ellenberger (1970) said "it would not be easy to find another author from which so much has been borrowed from all sides without acknowledgment than Adler" (p. 645). Wilder, in his introduction to *Essays in Individual Psychology* (Adler & Deutsch, 1959) wrote, "most observations and ideas of Alfred Adler have subtly and quietly permeated modem psychological thinking to such a degree that the proper question is not whether one is Adlerian but how much of an Adlerian one is" (p. xv).

Teaching Adler's principles can be challenging because of this apparent denial of his work (Ellenberger, 1970). The task, however, is further complicated by the basic misinformation about Adler's theory in many introductory textbooks. In a study of 12 basic propositions of individual psychology in introductory psychology textbooks, Silverman and Corsini (1984) concluded that Adler's work has been marred by either neglect or distortion.

Exercises that demonstrate Adler's principles should facilitate students' learning. Polyson (1983) found that students are more active in the learning process if personality theories are made relevant to their personal interests. Many studies support the advantages of active learning opportunities that allow students hands-on and "minds-on" experiences (e.g., Benjamin, 1991; Wittrock, 1984). The National Institute of Education's 1984 report,

Involvement in Learning: Realizing the Potential of American Higher Education, identified active learning as the top priority in American higher education today. This article describes and evaluates two such exercises.

The Earliest Recollection Exercise

As homework, which takes 15 to 30 min, students write out their earliest memory. What they believe happened is important, not whether it actually did happen. I encourage students to describe the memory in detail and to draw a picture of it. To reduce potential socially desirable outcomes, I give no other instructions. For example, a student might invent a memory that is designed for a more desirable interpretation.

Later in class, I introduce Adler's concept of early recollections. Adler (1959) considered early recollections "the most trustworthy way of exploring personality" (p. 97) because they often encapsulate a person's life theme or script (i.e., fictional goals). Freud believed the past determines the future, whereas Adler believed that the present determines the past. In other words, it makes no difference whether the early event actually happened; a belief that an event happened will influence a person's present condition. Adler (1958) wrote:

> There are no "chance memories." Out of the incalculable number of impressions which meet an individual, he chooses to remember only those which he feels, however darkly, to have a bearing on his situation . . . so that he will meet the future with an already tested style of action. (p. 73)

Thus, if people live their lives believing that others are always trying to humiliate them, the memories they are likely to recall are interpreted as humiliating experiences. I also provide several examples from my life.

Next, students process their early recollections from an Adlerian perspective to discover what the early recollections say about their personalities. Students are asked to finish three sentences: (a) Men are . . . , (b) Women are . . . . and (c) Life is . . . . They are to complete these sentences with only the information they have from their early recollections. I say, "If all you knew about life was what is in your early recollection, how would you complete these sentences?" I then discuss how these sentences could represent the values students introjected into their personalities and the light these sentences shed on their life themes-what Adler called life-style. Students are encouraged to examine the emergence of these themes in their personalities, especially during periods of personal stress. Adler (1959) saw these patterns becoming especially manifested in moments of anxiety and crisis.

Next, students consider 10 questions to examine their early recollections in light of Adler's theory: (a) Who is present in your early recollection?—mom, dad, siblings, friends, strangers; (b) Who is not present?; (c) How are different people portrayed?—basic thoughts and feelings; (d) What is the world like?—friendly, hostile, cooperative, exciting; (e) What is your role or behavior?—helping, passive, sick, dependent; (f) What is the outcome of your behavior?—success, punishment; (g) What is your primary social attitude?—I or we; (h) What is your dominant emotion?—happy, worried, fearful, guilty, proud; (i) What is your primary motive?—to help, to gain attention, to exert power; and (j) What are the underlying themes, expressed as a single sentence?—for example, I need to rescue people. Some students may share their earliest recollections with classmates as part of a general discussion focusing on how earliest recollections seem to influence personality.

The Birth Order Exercise

This 20-min exercise examines the effects of birth order on personality. I introduce Adler's concept within the broader context of family influences on personality. Adler said that the most important influence on a person is one's mother. She "provides the greatest experience of love the child will ever have" (Adler, 1964, p. 130). One's father is theorized to be the second greatest influence on personality. The third influence comes from one's family constellation or birth order. Adlerian psychologists use this third influence as a diagnostic indicator and maintain that birth order contributes greatly to the formation of one's personality and to personality differences among siblings (Adler, 1958; Ansbacher & Ansbacher, 1956; Forer, 1977).

Adler pointed to many differences between the first born and the last born, between an only child and a child with many siblings, and so on. Adler (1959) commented that the first born "must share the attention of his mother and father with a rival. [First borns] feel deeply the arrival of another child; and their sense of deprivation [molds] their whole style of life" (p. 144). Because the happiest time of life was before the birth of the new child, oldest children often "are admirers of the past and pessimistic over the future" (p. 157).

Middle born children are raised in a world in which the mother divides her attention among the siblings. Middle borns are stimulated, or perhaps provoked, to match the older child's exploits. "He behaves as if he were in a race, as if someone were a step or two in front and he had to hurry to get ahead of him. He is under full steam all the time" (Adler, 1959, p. 148).

In a large family, each succeeding child "dethrones" the previously born one, but the youngest is never removed from the "most pampered" position. "A spoiled child can never be independent. He loses courage to succeed by his own effort" (Adler, 1959, p. 151). Because youngest children have many pace-setting models, they may be driven to desire success in everything. Because universal accomplishment is unlikely, they may be driven to discouragement (also see Adler, 1937).

Before I explain the details of specific birth orders, however, students form groups with others who are in their same birth position: first borns, middle borns, and last borns. Only borns can comprise a fourth group or join the first borns. One member in each group takes notes to record the process. First, persons in the group state their feelings about being in that birth order position. Next, students discuss three questions: (a) How would you be different in another position?, (b) How would you be different if you were the other sex in your same position?, and (c) How does your position continue to affect you today?

Next, the whole class discusses their experiences. I facilitate the discussion by asking students about their feelings toward the other positions, whether they now have a better understanding of their siblings' positions, and how birth order theory might influence their future parenting. Students usually find comfort in identifying with classmates of the same birth order and share similar feelings toward siblings in other positions. They also often express a new sense of empathy for their siblings. I follow this discussion with a brief lecture on the specific characteristics of the birth order positions.

Evaluation of the Exercises

I evaluated the effectiveness of these exercises in two undergraduate introductory counseling classes and two graduate introductory counseling classes. During each course, the two exercises were completed in the same class period, which lasted approximately 2 hr. At the beginning of the next class period, students completed an anonymous evaluation of the exercises, rating them on a scale ranging from *of no value* (1) to *extremely valuable* (10). Data from 3 undergraduates and 1 graduate student were discarded because of the absence of a response. Final sample sizes were 47 undergraduates and 38 graduate students.

Tests of mean differences indicated that undergraduates ($M = 8.4$) valued the birth order exercise significantly more than graduates ($M = 7.1$), $t(83) = 2.36$, $p < .05$. In contrast, graduates ($M = 8.2$) valued the earliest recollection exercise significantly more than did undergraduates ($M = 6.8$), $t(83) = 2.50$, $p < .05$).

Conclusion

These exercises demonstrate two major concepts important in counseling courses that cover Adlerian psychotherapy. Both exercises were rated highly; however, undergraduates rated the birth order exercise as more valuable than did graduates, and graduates valued the earliest recollection exercise more. A possible explanation for this difference is that graduate students could perceive the birth order concept as less sophisticated than early recollection theory. As one graduate student put it, "Birth order is just too simplistic. . . [early recollections] carry more substance." Undergraduates may favor birth order more because it seems to provide better defined categories and the early recollection exercise seems to require a less defensive examination of one's personal history.

In either case, students rated both exercises highly. Through an informal survey at the end of the course, I noticed an increase in the number of students who evaluate Adler's theory favorably in comparison to other counseling theories. These exercises may increase students' appreciation for Adler's theory, and according to Mellor (1987), personality theories that are evaluated as interesting and relevant are significantly associated with high recall. Whether or not my students evaluate Adler's theory positively, most of them view the two exercises worthwhile for actively demonstrating Adler's principles.

References

Adler, A. (1937). Position in family constellation influences life style. *International Journal of individual Psychology, 3,* 211-227.

Adler, A. (1958). *What life should mean to you.* New York: Capricorn.

Adler, A. (1959). *The practice and theory of individual psychology.* Totowa, NJ: Littlefield Adams.

Adler, A. (1964). *Problems of neurosis.* New York: Harper & Row.

Adler, A., & Deutsch, D. (1959). *Essays in individual psychology.* New York: Grove.

Ansbacher, H. L., & Ansbacher, R. (Eds.). (1956). *The individual psychology of Alfred Adler* New York: Basic Books.

Benjamin, L. T., Jr. (1991). Personalization and active learning in the large introductory psychology class. *Teaching of Psychology, 18,* 68-74.

Corsini, R. J., & Wedding, D. (1989). *Current psychotherapies* (4th ed.). Itasca, IL: Peacock.

Ellenberger, H. (1970). *The discovery of the unconscious: The history and evolution of dynamic psychiatry.* New York: Basic Books.

Forer, L. (1977). Bibliography of birth order literature in the '70s. *Journal of Individual Psychology, 33,* 122-141.

Mellor, S. (1987). Evaluation and perceived recall of personality theories by undergraduate students. *Perceptual and Motor Skills, 65,* 879-883.

National Institute of Education. (1984*). Involvement in learning: Realizing the potential of American higher education.* Washington, DC: U.S. Department of Education.

Polyson, J. A. (1983). Student essays about TV characters: A tool for understanding personality theories. *Teaching of Psychology, 10,* 103-105.

Silverman, N. N., & Corsini, R. J. (1984). Is it true what they say about Adler's individual psychology? *Teaching of Psychology, 11,* 188-189.

Wittrock, M. C. (1984). Learning as a generative process. *Educational Psychologist, 11,* 87-95 .

2. ACQUIRING SKILLS–UNDERGRADUATE STUDENTS

Using Actors as "Clients" for an Interviewing Simulation in an Undergraduate Clinical Psychology Course

Kristi Lane
Winona State University

Finding "clients" is frequently a problem for instructors teaching an interviewing component of a clinical psychology course. Instructors in graduate programs are more likely to have access to new psychiatric inpatients who need intake interviews and can be used to train interviewing skills (Boice, Andrasik, & Simmons, 1984). Weiss (1986) noted that it is often difficult to find a clinical population for beginning students to interview. The problem of finding "clients" is most readily met by having trainees play the role. This practice presents the advantage of available clients but has the disadvantage of both client and interviewer knowing the techniques and purpose of the interview. The client may unknowingly assist the interviewer by giving answers that anticipate the interview procedure. Another solution to the client problem is to use subjects from the introductory psychology research pool who sign up to participate in a study called interviewing experiences (Sommers-Flanagan & Means, 1987). This practice was reported to be satisfactory, but the authors cautioned that emotional disturbances appeared in 15% to 25% of their introductory psychology clients. In response to this concern, Sommers-Flanagan and Means provided their graduate students with names of referral agencies and trained them to help make appointments at local agencies. Another potential problem results from ethical responsibilities if a serious personal problem and/or pathology (e.g., suicide ideation, chemical dependency, and relationship issues) is revealed. All these problems can be avoided by using a different source of clients. This article describes the unusual procedure of hiring and training theatre majors to portray clients.

The actors are undergraduate theatre majors who have had experience in improvisation. They are paid minimum wage from departmental funds. There is one actor for every 4 students, for a class size of 16 students. The instructor provides the actors with case-study dialogues (White, Riggs, & Gilbert, 1976) and case-study reports (Oltmanns, Neale, & Davison, 1986). The case studies are selected for an emphasis on adjustment disorders, anxiety disorders, mild or transitional depression, and identity issues. Major pathology is excluded from the case-study

material because it is difficult to role-play and the students are inexperienced undergraduates. Each actor develops four clients with different presenting problems by using the case-study information and individual creativity.

The interviewing section is 40% of the class and lasts for 4 weeks of the academic quarter. In the first week, the class is taught the basic attending skills and listening sequence (Ivey, 1983). The actors do not participate in class because they are developing their clients and crosschecking that development with the instructor. The most frequent directives to the actors at this point are to reduce the pathology of the clients, to add background information and history, and to develop areas of normal functioning. Students practice the component skills by role playing in their groups. Ivey's (1983) sequence suggested short practice sessions of one skill at a time. I try to reduce the likelihood of student self-disclosure during roleplays by using a scenario in which the students have no personal experience and must improvise the role of a spouse coming to a therapist to discuss dissatisfaction with the marriage.

The actors participate as clients in Weeks 2 through 4. Students are aware of the function of the actors from the course syllabus and are excited about having a "real client." The actors rotate among the four student groups. This procedure works well because there are 4 hr of class each week, four student groups, and four actors. The actor spends 1 hr per week with each group. The hour is divided into 15-min sections so that each student has the opportunity to interview for 10 min while the other three students serve as observers who provide feedback to the interviewer for 5 min. When the next student becomes interviewer, the actor can either change clients or continue the role-play for up to two interviews. The students benefit from this rotation, by experiencing four actors and a minimum of eight role-plays, which provides opportunities to respond to varied problems and clients. This training element is readily available from the actor clients.

The actors are clients for the 10-min tape-recorded interview completed out of class at the end of Week 2. The clinical situation of responding to a new client is simulated by the instructor assigning actor clients for each interview.

After students critique their tape recordings, they meet with the instructor to evaluate the interview.

During Weeks 3 and 4, the class hour has an initial period of 10 min in which the instructor discusses interviewing techniques (e.g., focusing on client problem and developing influencing skills) and provides general feedback based on observation of groups. Each group experiences two role-plays in each of the 4 class hours. The role-plays are 20 min long and focus on obtaining more extensive client information. The actor must continue to add depth to the character by developing the client's presenting problem such as describing the course and duration of symptoms, frequency of occurrence, and conditions under which the problem occurs. The most difficult acting task is for the actor to overcome the temptation to provide a monologue whenever the interviewer is silent. Actors have indicated that silence in improvisation needs to be filled, and they must fill it.

Each student interviewer is videotaped twice in an interview session with an actor client. After the first videotape, the students break into small groups to view and critique each member's videotape. The instructor meets with each group to review the tape, the critiques, and to provide evaluative comments. The second (and final) videotape measures the student's mastery of the interview skills and ability to critique those skills. The instructor meets with the actors to assist in deciding which role-plays to use in the final videotape. Students cannot request a specific actor, but they can request a specific "problem" to be role-played. The rare special requests usually involve particular interest in topics such as chemical dependency in women, stress due to disability from work injury, and abusive relationships. These are unique role-plays and more specialized than the actors would typically use. The practice simulates clinical settings that specialize in certain types of problems. The student completes an extensive critique of the interview session, including a written summary of client background and history of problem development. The instructor is present at the final videotape and later views the videotape while analyzing the student critique. The instructor meets with the student to provide evaluation of skill development during the interviewing segment of the course.

Videotapes are made available for the actors to view at the end of the course. Actors want to see their performance as a client. Final videotapes appeal to actors because they are produced professionally in the campus television studio. This experience serves as preparation and practice for the actors' career goals. In the past 3 years, actors' feedback to the instructor indicates this acting job is a positive experience and many want to participate the following year. Two actors began the client role in their second year of school and returned to this acting job until graduation. They listed it on their resume as paid acting experience. I invite acting students who have had experience with roles in school plays that are adaptable to the client role. The positive aspects of the experience go beyond the theatrical benefits. Acting students have reported learning about the counseling process, and several have said they were helped by being a client because they included their real problems in the role-play. Actors and students seem to benefit from the experience.

References

Boice, R., Andrasik, F., & Simmons, W. L. (1984). Teaching interviewing skills: A procedural account of measuring students' progress. *Teaching of Psychology, 11,* 110-111.

Ivey, A. E. (1983). *International interviewing and counseling.* Monterey, CA: Brooks/Cole.

Oltmanns, T. F., Neale, J. M., & Davison, G. C. (1986). *Case studies in abnormal psychology* (2nd ed.). New York: Wiley.

Sommers-Flanagan, J., & Means, J. R. (1987). Thou shalt not ask questions: An approach to teaching interviewing skills. *Teaching of Psychology, 14,* 164-166.

Weiss, A. R. (1986). Teaching counseling and psychotherapy skills without access to a clinical population: The short interview method. *Teaching of Psychology, 13,* 145-147.

White, R. W., Riggs, M. M., & Gilbert, D. C. (1976). *Case workbook in personality.* Prospect Heights, IL: Waveland.

The Interviewing Team: An Exercise for Teaching Assessment and Conceptualization Skills

Bernard J. Balleweg
Lycoming College

Mental health professionals have developed a variety of training programs to teach interviewing skills to counselors (e.g., Carkhuff, 1987; Ivey, 1988; Okun, 1987). Such programs generally stress basic interviewing skills, such as empathic listening and effective questioning. A few training programs (e.g., Cormier & Cormier, 1985; Egan, 1986) go beyond these basic techniques and teach assessment and conceptualization skills. Assessment consists of gathering information about the key symptoms of a client's presenting problems; conceptualization involves integrating the information to develop hypotheses about the nature and etiology of the client's problem (Cormier & Cormier, 1985). Assessment and conceptualization are vital for treatment planning, and inadequate assessment has been identified as a major contributor to negative outcomes in psychotherapy (Hadley & Strupp, 1976).

Despite the importance of assessment and conceptualization, there are few methods for teaching these skills. Instead, articles on teaching techniques typically focus on more basic interviewing skills (e.g., France, 1984; Weiss, 1986). The absence of good teaching strategies is unfortunate because it is difficult to teach students how to interview effectively and to integrate the resulting information into meaningful conceptual frameworks. The instructor who tries to teach assessment and conceptualization skills through role-playing must overcome several problems. First, students are often overwhelmed with the number of variables they must assess; their anxiety may cause them to omit significant pieces of assessment information. Second, students have difficulty role-playing authentic clients (Weiss, 1986), which limits the quality of the learning experience for the "therapist." Finally, role-plays conducted in pairs or triads provide immediate feedback to only two or three students at a time, while others may be making similar mistakes.

To overcome these obstacles, I developed an exercise called the interviewing team that involves students working as a team and interviewing me as I role-play a client. The goals of the exercise are: (a) to develop assessment interviewing skills through authentic role-playing and immediate feedback, and (b) to teach students to use their knowledge of counseling theory and abnormal behavior to conceptualize client problems.

Preparation

Student Preparation

Before the interviewing team is assembled, the students attend lectures and complete reading assignments that cover the assessment and conceptualization process. Cormier and Cormier's (1985) multidimensional, cognitive-behavioral assessment model is used because students grasp it relatively quickly. The following dimensions of the client's presenting problem are studied: behavior, affect, cognitions, somatic functioning, contextual factors, interpersonal factors, and antecedents and consequences that might trigger or maintain the client's problems. After teaching students the Cormier and Cormier model, I role-play an entire assessment interview, using a student volunteer as a client, and discuss my case conceptualization.

Instructor Preparation

To enhance authenticity, I portray former clients from my practice, protecting confidentiality by altering all identifying information and combining features of several cases. Instructors who do not have access to a clinical population could role-play a client from a case study book (e.g., Oltmanns, Neale, & Davison, 1986) after securing the authors' permission.

Portrayals of serious depression are particularly useful for this exercise because depression frequently includes clear behavioral, somatic, cognitive, and affective symptoms. In addition, a wide variety of problems that frequently accompany or precipitate depression (e.g., substance abuse, illnesses, eating disorders, and personality disorders) are introduced to increase the complexity of the case. Before the exercise begins, students are given basic demographic data about the client and are informed that client information has been altered to protect confidentiality.

Implementation

Conducting Role-Play Segments

The 10 students who are selected as members of the interviewing team are told that they are to work together to interview the instructor who portrays a client. Their goal is to assess all relevant dimensions of the client's presenting problems and to develop a conceptualization that includes hypotheses about the etiology of the problems as well as tentative ideas regarding treatment strategies.

Each team member is then assigned one of the following tasks: (a) starting the interview; (b) assessing the affective, behavioral, somatic, cognitive, contextual, or relational problem dimensions; (c) identifying antecedents and consequences; (d) inquiring about prior attempts at problem resolution; and (e) determining the client's strengths and resources.

The first student begins the interview and proceeds for 5 to 10 min. The instructor then stops the interview, gives feedback about the student's interviewing technique, and encourages immediate feedback from the class. The instructor then asks the interviewer to share initial hypotheses about the nature, severity, and etiology of the client's presenting problems. For example, the instructor might ask the student to evaluate the intensity of the client's depression and to discuss how cognitive-behavioral theory could explain the origin of the depression. This type of questioning is a crucial part of the exercise because it challenges students to: (a) integrate initial information and impressions, (b) apply their knowledge of counseling theory and abnormal behavior, and (c) formulate hypotheses to guide subsequent inquiries. Although the person who is role-playing the therapist has the opportunity to answer these questions first, all members of the team are encouraged to offer their observations and hypotheses. This team effort reduces performance pressure on each individual and helps build class cohesion.

The sequence of interviewing, receiving feedback, and questioning is repeated for each of the 10 role-play segments. Team members are repeatedly challenged to revise preliminary hypotheses to accommodate new information.

Switching Therapists

The decision to switch from one therapist to another is partially dictated by time, because role-play segments must average 5 to 10 min in order to complete the interview within a 2-hr class period and still allow time between

segments for feedback and discussion. To demonstrate how to obtain assessment information without disrupting the natural interview flow, I try to make transitions coincide with major shifts in content by the client.

On occasion, I make a transition to another therapist if the current therapist reaches an impasse and becomes anxious in searching for what to say next. Before the student's anxiety becomes counterproductive, I ask team members to recommend possible directions to proceed with the interview, and I encourage the student to try one of those directions. If the student quickly reaches another impasse, I shift to another student.

Concluding the Exercise

Throughout the exercise, students are encouraged to take notes on information relevant to their assessment area. When all role-play segments are completed, students are asked to review their notes and summarize the information obtained in their assessment area. The instructor helps the team discuss this information and use it to revise earlier hypotheses, identify areas that need further evaluation, and develop tentative treatment strategies.

Advantages and Disadvantages

The interviewing team exercise has several advantages as a method for teaching assessment and conceptualization skills: (a) it reduces student anxiety by dividing assessment responsibilities among team members, (b) it enhances the quality and authenticity of the role-play because the instructor role-plays the client, (c) it provides opportunities for immediate feedback, (d) it alerts the student about the necessity for reformulation and revision of hypotheses as more information is obtained, (e) it challenges students to apply their knowledge of psychological theory and psychopathology, (f) it helps build class cohesion, and (g) it provides students with the opportunity to observe and learn from each other.

Nevertheless, some drawbacks to the interviewing team approach need to be considered before it is implemented. This approach is difficult to use effectively in groups exceeding 10 students because larger groups lead to lengthy interviews, thus disengaging some members from the process. (A group with fewer students works well because the instructor can assign several tasks to one or more students.) Instructors of large classes can circumvent this problem by dividing the class into groups of 10 or fewer students and using specially trained students to play the role of the client and provide feedback as the interview unfolds. France (1984) successfully used peer trainers in an interviewing techniques course, and a similar process could be followed here. In addition, this exercise does not give individual students extensive practice in conducting assessment interviews and developing case conceptualizations. For additional practice, students can role-play full-length assessment interviews in pairs during subsequent class sessions or as homework assignments. Several students have told me that the interviewing team exercise significantly reduced their anxiety and gave them "a sense of direction" during later role-plays in pairs.

Applications

The interviewing team approach was developed for a senior-level, undergraduate, counseling techniques course and could be used in similar undergraduate courses on interviewing skills and counseling methods. At the undergraduate level, the goal of the exercise should be to introduce students to the assessment and conceptualization process. An introduction is important because it shows students that mental health professionals must combine interviewing techniques with knowledge of psychological theory and abnormal behavior to conceptualize and treat client problems. If undergraduates are not introduced to the conceptualization process, they may falsely assume that they are qualified to work with clients after acquiring basic interviewing skills. An introduction to the conceptualization process also does not quality undergraduates to work as professionals; consequently, they should be cautioned about the limitations of their expertise following training.

This exercise could be adapted for teaching assessment and conceptualization skills at the graduate level. For example, the instructor could require the team to include additional types of assessment information, such as life history data, a mental status exam, and a diagnosis. The instructor could also incorporate other theoretical perspectives. For example, within a psychoanalytic framework, students could be assigned various roles, such as noting characteristic defense mechanisms and identifying unconscious conflicts. The interviewing team offers the instructor a systematic approach to teaching assessment and conceptualization skills that maximizes class participation and immediate instructor feedback and can be used in graduate or undergraduate courses.

References

Carkhuff, R. R. (1987). *The art of helping VI*. Amherst, MA: Human Resources Development Press.

Cormier, W. H., & Cormier, L. S. (1985). *Interviewing skills for helpers: Fundamental skills and cognitive behavioral interventions*. Monterey, CA: Brooks/Cole.

Egan, G. (1986). *The skilled helper: A systematic approach to effective helping*. Monterey, CA: Brooks/Cole.

France, K. (1984). Peer trainers in an interviewing techniques course. *Teaching of Psychology, 11,* 171-173.

Hadley, S. W., & Strupp, H. H. (1976). Contemporary views of negative effects in psychotherapy. *Archives of General Psychiatry, 33,* 1291-1302.

Ivey, A. E. (1988). *Intentional interviewing and counseltng: Facilitating client development*. Pacific Grove, CA: Brooks/Cole.

Okun, B. F. (1987). *Effective helping: Interviewing and counseling techniques*. Monterey, CA: Brooks/Cole.

Oltmanns, T. F., Neale, J. M., & Davison, G. C. (1986). *Case studies in abnormal psychology*. New York: Wiley.

Weiss, A. R. (1986). Teaching counseling and psychotherapy skills without access to a clinical population: The short interview method. *Teaching of Psychology, 13,* 145- 147.

Notes

1. An earlier version of this article was presented at the annual meeting of the American Psychological Association, New Orleans, LA, August 1989.
2. I thank Joseph Palladino and three anonymous reviewers for their comments on an earlier draft of this article.

Computer-Simulated Psychotherapy as an Aid in Teaching Clinical Psychology

John R. Suler
Rider College

In the 1960s, researchers at the Massachusetts Institute of Technology pioneered the development of an interactive computer program, which simulates the actions of a psychotherapist, now widely known as Eliza. In reaction to the user's questions and statements, the program's responses imitate the therapeutic techniques of reflection, focusing, clarification, and open-ended inquiry. Although these programs were never intended to serve as "real" psychotherapy, they can be useful heuristic tools for understanding the psychotherapeutic process. I have used a version of Eliza adapted for IBM microcomputers as a teaching aid in an undergraduate clinical psychology course. Students' interaction with Eliza provides them with an intensive, individualized learning experience that can highlight important concepts about interviewing, psychotherapy, and clinical psychology. It can also enhance their understanding of the role computers may play in clinical activities.

Method of the Exercise

Instructions for the exercise and for operating the Eliza program are described in a handout and discussed in class. On their own time, students interact with Eliza for approximately 45 min. The instructions emphasize that during this time they honestly present a personal problem and persist in seeking help, despite any inadequacies or therapeutic mistakes they perceive in the program. After this period of seriously engaging Eliza in a therapeutic interaction, the students are instructed to "experiment" with the program, perhaps even "trick" it into responding with erroneous or nonsensical statements—and by doing so, gain insight into how the program works.

After the students completed the exercise, we discussed it in class and they prepared a paper in which they analyzed their interaction with Eliza. The following themes were emphasized: (a) their personal reactions to Eliza, including their perceptions of it as their "therapist," their thoughts and feelings about Eliza, whether or not they felt helped; (b) an evaluation of Eliza's therapeutic techniques and effectiveness, how the program seems to work, its strengths and weaknesses; (c) an analysis of the advantages and disadvantages of computers in psychoanalytic, behavioral, and humanistic therapies, and the types of problems and clients for which computers might be helpful; and (d) other possible applications in the field of mental health for computer programs that interact with clients.

Evaluation of the Exercise

After discussing the exercise and handing in their papers, one class ($N = 19$, 12 women, 7 men, M age = 21) answered a questionnaire consisting of rating scale items that assessed their reactions to the project. Their responses (see Table 1) indicated that the exercise had a substantial impact on them. A large majority agreed that the exercise was a valuable learning experience, and that it should be retained as part of the course. Ninety percent agreed that they better understood what is important for psychotherapy to be effective, and, in particular, what is important in the relationship between the therapist and client. These responses seemed to be related to the students' unanimous agreement that they had learned about the advantages and disadvantages of a computer conducting psychotherapy. In class and in their papers students covered important issues about human versus computerized therapy, such as (a) the role of empathy, warmth, identification, and "real" relationships in psychotherapy; (b) whether computers could be more objective and nonjudgmental; (c) whether fears about selfdisclosure, expressing emotions, and confidentiality would be greater with humans or computers; and (d) the cognitive and perceptual advantages of computers vis-a-vis humans, including breadth and efficiency of memory, language abilities, and access to visual and auditory information from the client.

The exercise was useful in highlighting important themes about the major theories of psychotherapy. The students unanimously agreed that they better understood the advantages and disadvantages of a computer

Table 1. Percentage of Students Expressing Agreement and Disagreement With Questionnaire Items About Interacting With Eliza

Item	Agree	Cannot Say	Disagree
Was a valuable learning experience	80	10	10
Helped me with my problem	31	0	69
Learned something about myself	48	21	31
Future students should have this opportunity	95	5	0
Better understand what it would be like to be in therapy	43	14	43
Better understand what is important for therapy to be effective	90	5	5
Better understand what is important in client/therapist relationship	90	0	10
Learned about pros and cons of computerized psychotherapy	100	0	0
Better understand how computer programs are designed to interact with people	31	38	31
Learned about my own thoughts and feelings about psychotherapy	64	5	31
Better understand pros and cons of computerized psychoanalytic therapy	100	0	0
Better understand pros and cons of computerized behavior therapy	43	31	26
Better understand use of computers in mental health field	74	21	5

Note. N = 19. Agree = students responding "strongly agree" and "agree"; Disagree = students responding "strongly disagree" and "disagree."

conducting psychoanalytic therapy. We discussed such issues as the effectiveness of computers for creating the atmosphere of ambiguity and neutrality recommended by classical theory, transference reactions to computers, whether computers have countertransference, collecting data for interpretations, and computers as "selfobjects" in terms of contemporary theory. It was often necessary to clarify what computers nowadays can and cannot do, and to speculate about the computers of the future. The students also contrasted computerized therapy with humanistic therapies that emphasize "authentic" relationships. Although we discussed the applications of computers in behavior therapy (their use in behavioral assessments; shaping interpersonal, behavioral, and cognitive skills; conducting such procedures as systematic desensitization), not all students agreed that working with Eliza helped them better understand the role of computers in behavioral treatment. This result may have been due to the fact that Eliza takes an "insight" approach, or that we had not yet completed the section on behavior therapy in the course syllabus.

Nevertheless, most students did agree that they better understood how computers might be used in the mental health field. We discussed the cost-effectiveness of computers, their application according to different types of psychopathology; and their use for structured interviews, diagnostic assessments, and psychological testing. There was no consensus about whether they better understood how computer programs are designed to interact with people. This may be attributed to the wide differences in the students' previous exposure to computer programming.

The students' personal reactions to Eliza varied greatly. They were divided on whether they thought working with Eliza gave them a sense of what it would be like to be in therapy and whether they learned anything about themselves. As compared to the students who agreed, twice as many disagreed that Eliza had helped them with their problem. In class the students readily described their impressions of the program's deficiencies

as a psychotherapist. However, twice as many students agreed as disagreed that they had learned about their own personal thoughts and feelings about psychotherapy. Therefore, Eliza generally does not supply students with an accurate experiential understanding of what therapy is like; nor does it resolve their problems. It was not intended to. But it can be used as a stimulus to help them explore their thoughts and feelings about psychotherapy.

The results suggest that methods for improving the exercise may include: (a) providing guidelines that maximize each student's ability to apply previous knowledge of computers and computer programming; (b) including readings about computers in clinical activities; and (c) adding other interactive computer programs that illustrate methods in structured. interviewing, psychological testing, and behavioral treatments.

Software and Its Availability

There is a wide variety of software that may be used as teaching aids in clinical psychology courses. Programs that administer, score, and interpret psychological tests are available for standardized personality assessment inventories, including the Myers-Briggs Type Indicator, 16 Personality Factor Test, the Minnesota Multiphasic Personality Inventory, and the California Personality Inventory. Programs are also available for the Adjective Checklist and the Adaptive Behavior Scale. For conducting structured clinical interviews, there is software for intake evaluations and mental status exams (which involve assessments of presenting complaint, symptoms, current situation, cognitive and emotional characteristics) and programs for taking a history of social, psychological, and developmental functioning (e.g., family relations, occupation, education, and social relationships). Software for assessing specific problem areas includes eating disorder inventories, health problem checklists, test anxiety scales, stress evaluations, and alcohol assessment.

More general assessment programs include personal problem checklists that assess the number, type, and hierarchy of personal problems.

Catalogs that describe these programs are available from various psychological resource services including: The Psychological Corporation, San Antonio, TX; Publishers Test Service, Monterey, CA; Projected Learning Programs, Chico, CA; Western Psychological Services, Los Angeles; Consulting Psychologists Press, Palo Alto, CA; Psychological Assessment Resources, Odessa, FL; Multi-Health Systems, Lynbrook, NY.

The Eliza program is widely available from local user groups, and often can be found in the software packages of college and university mainframe systems. Eliza diskettes are also available from various computer resource services (e.g., Pan World International, North Brunswick, NJ; Projected Learning Programs, Chico, CA). Versions of Eliza seem to differ only in slight modifications of the breadth and variety of responses the program offers to the user's statements and questions. Versions sold by services that market Eliza as a computer "game" may include modifications of the program that detract from its potential as a serious educational exercise. For more information about the history and descendants of Eliza, as well as other information about computer applications in clinical psychology, see Schwartz (1984).

Reference

Schwartz, M. D. (Ed.). (1984). *Using computers in clinical practice: Psychotherapy and mental health applications.* New York: Haworth.

Teaching Students to Listen Empathically

Peter S. Fernald
University of New Hampshire

Most psychotherapists and counselors regard empathy as a necessary condition for facilitating patient growth and change (Anthony, 1977; Carkhuff, 1972; Gelso & Fretz, 1992), and some even suggest that it is the most essential condition (Kohut, 1984; Margules, 1984; Rogers, 1957). Hence, students beginning their externships at a health service agency should be trained in this very important skill.

This article describes the empathic listening assignment (ELA), which teaches and assesses empathic-listening skills to undergraduates, as well as 14 learning activities that prepare students for the ELA. The students were senior psychology majors enrolled in an externship. The course involves a supervised practicum experience in one of several mental health or rehabilitation agencies: drug and alcohol abuse clients, A Safe Place, hospice, community mental health clinics, a local psychiatric hospital, and guidance/counseling programs in local schools. The students work 1 or 2 full days per week at their agencies for four or eight academic credits, respectively.

In addition to agency supervision, the course instructor also provides supervision through a weekly 3-hr seminar. One of the goals of the seminar is to help students acquire fundamental counseling skills, particularly the skill of empathic listening (Rogers, 1951, 1961). Instruction during the first four seminar meetings aims primarily at preparing students to complete the ELA.

Procedure

The course has more assigned work in the first 5 weeks than later on, including an all-day class meeting at the end of the fourth week.

Learning Activities

The first four seminar meetings focus intensively on 14 activities, listed in Table 1, that assist the externs in

118

Table 1. Means and Standard Deviations of the Externs' Ratings of the 14 Learning Activities

Item	M	SD
1. Reading Axline's (1964) *Dibs: In Search of Self.*	5.39	1.10
2. Listening to an audiotape of yourself in dialogue.	6.36	0.89
3. Observing agency staff members work with clients.	5.29	1.79
4. Class discussions of empathy, unconditional positive regard, and congruence.	5.79	0.94
5. Watching the filmed interview of Carl Rogers.	5.57	1.40
6. Driving your car through the carwash.[a]	1.57	1.55
7. Practicing empathic-listening skills on friends and others.	5.93	.96
8. Reading Rogers's (1951) chapters 2 and 3 in *Client-Centered Therapy.*	5.21	1.08
9. Practicing your empathic-listening skills with other externs at the all-day meeting.	5.93	1.53
10. Playing videogames.[a]	1.00	0.00
11. Practicing your listening skills with clients/patients at your externship agency.	6.21	1.08
12. Reading Rogers's (1980a) chapter.	4.64	1.54
13. Observing negative models (i.e., others who clearly do not demonstrate empathic-listening skills).	5.93	1.03
14. Experiencing for yourself what it feels like to be really listened to nonjudgmentally.	5.71	1.39
15. Understanding that empathic listening is not a technique, but rather it is a way of being in relationship to another human being.	6.50	0.50
16. Observing your instructor use empathic-listening skills in class.	6.36	0.61

[a]Filler items.

learning fundamental principles of person-centered counseling. The reading assignments include chapters 2 and 3 in Rogers (1951), Axline (1964), and Rogers (1980a), which describe in detail the three major characteristics (empathy, unconditional positive regard, and genuineness) of the personcentered counselor.

To facilitate students' learning, empathic listening is divided into component skills, and the students practice these skills in counselor/counselee pairs. The counselee is instructed to talk for a few minutes on any topic of his or her choice; for students desiring more structure, the instructor provides a list of 20 topics. In one such activity, the counselor is instructed to reflect (mirror back) content only; in another activity, the counselor is to reflect only feelings. These activities allow the externs to focus on just one aspect of empathic listening at a time.

Lest students believe that the person-centered approach is primarily a set of partistic technical skills, a more holistic learning activity emphasizes that empathic listening is, at its best, an I-Thou encounter (Rogers, 1961). With this orientation in mind, the counselor is instructed simply to "walk in the counselee's cognitive/emotional shoes."

Instruction through modeling is also included. The externs listen to an audiotape in which Rogers counsels a young man named Mike. The instructor turns off the tape from time to time, immediately after Mike has spoken, and asks the externs, "What would you say now, assuming you were Carl Rogers?" Students discuss their various

responses; then, the tape is started again, so the students hear exactly what Rogers in fact said. The same procedure is used with a two-part film and interview, *The Right to be Desperate* (Rogers, 1980c) and *On Hurt and Anger* (Rogers, 1980b), in which Rogers counsels a young man in remission from cancer.

The all-day class typically occurs at the instructor's home on a Saturday or Sunday. It includes two 3-hr meetings and 1 hr for a meal. This day provides a comfortable nonacademic setting in which the students have more opportunities to practice their person-centered counseling skills and become better acquainted with one another.

Empathic-Listening Assignment

During the first 4 weeks of the course, students are encouraged to practice empathic listening in all their daily interpersonal situations. Then, each student solicits a volunteer not in the seminar who is willing to assist the student in carrying out the ELA. The student clearly explains that the purpose of the assignment is not to provide psychological assistance but to assess the student's listening skills. Students obtain permission to both audio record and transcribe the recording, and they specify that they will remove or change all identifying features so that the instructor, who sees only the altered transcript, will not be able to identify the volunteer.

Students type a four- to five-page transcribed excerpt from the recording and then analyze and evaluate their listening skills in a three- to four-page paper. They specify both positive and negative aspects of their empathic-listening skills and suggest alternative statements they could have made.

Evaluation

At the fifth class meeting, a seminar group ($n = 15$) completed two questionnaires, 16 items relating to the learning activities that prepared them for the ELA (see Table 1) and 12 items pertaining directly to the ELA (see Table 2). On a scale ranging from *poor* (1) to *excellent* (7), students rated the educational value of the learning activities. Items on the ELA questionnaire were rated *very strongly disagree* (1) to *very strongly agree* (7). The ELA questionnaire included Item 13 which requests a brief qualitative statement about the ELA. Two other seminar groups (ns = 19 and 14) also completed the ELA questionnaire. Items 6 and 10 of the learning activities questionnaire and Items 4 and 8 of the ELA questionnaire were control/filler items de-signed to minimize a positive halo response set and encourage students' close attention.

Results

Mean ratings of the learning activities generally were very high, although the ratings for the assigned readings

Table 2. Means and Standard Deviations for the Externs' Ratings on the 12 ELA Questionnaire Items

Item	M	SD
1. The ELA was very challenging.	5.91	1.06
2. The ELA required that I understand and think carefully and critically about Rogers's person-centered approach.	6.40	0.80
3. Completing the ELA was a lot of work.	5.96	1.21
4. The best way to complete the ELA successfully is to make frequent use of Freudian interpretation.[a]	1.45	0.77
5. Having completed the ELA, I have much greater respect for Rogers's person-centered approach.	5.70	1.06
6. I learned a great deal from the ELA.	5.85	1.27
7. The ELA was one of the most valuable course assignments I have had at this university.	4.94	1.22
8. Conducting the ELA requires participation of *three* people.[a]	1.87	1.28
9. The ELA helped me improve my listening skills.	5.94	1.15
10. I strongly recommend that the ELA be included in future offerings of this course.	6.50	1.02
11. My empathic-listening skills improved significantly over the first 5 weeks of the semester.	6.20	0.91
12. Learning about empathic listening has significantly influenced the way I view my relationships with others.	5.73	1.29

[a]Filler items.

were only moderately high (Table 1). Ratings for Items 6 and 10, the control items, were appropriately low.

Analysis of variance revealed no significant differences between the three seminar groups on their ratings of the ELA, so the data were combined. Mean ratings on 7 of the 10 relevant items were 5.70 or higher (Table 2). Item 7 (most valuable course assignment at the university) received the lowest ratings. As expected, ratings on Items 4 and 8, the control items, were low. Most of the students' qualitative responses also were highly positive.

Discussion

Students' ratings of the 14 learning activities were very positive. The ratings suggest that the students improved their empathic-listening skills by observing models (Rogers on film, the instructor in the seminar, and staff members at their externship agencies) using empathic-listening skills, by listening to themselves on audiotape, by practicing their listening skills with one another, and through class discussion. Students' very high endorsement of Item 15 is noteworthy because much class discussion related to the observation that empathic listening involves primarily a way of being rather than technique. Although the assigned readings were rated positively, the students regarded them as generally less helpful than the other activities.

The externs' ratings of the ELA were very favorable. They regarded the ELA as a challenging task requiring careful and critical thought about the person-centered approach. They also indicated that (a) the ELA required much effort; (b) they learned a lot from the assignment, especially with regard to improving their listening skills and gaining greater respect for the person-centered approach; and (c) their learning about empathic listening significantly influenced the way they perceived their relationships with others. They recommended that the assignment be included in future offerings of the course. These findings suggest that the ELA is an effective instructional method.

A caveat, however, is in order. The findings are based on self-report. A more rigorous test would involve pre- and postinstruction testing with expert judges evaluating the externs' empathic-listening skills (Carkhuff, 1969, 1972; Carkhuff & Anthony, 1979).

In their qualitative responses, many students indicated surprise and even astonishment over how the ELA forced them to acknowledge their poor listening skills. As one student put it, "I thought the ELA would be a breeze. How difficult could listening be? WRONG! ! Upon reviewing the interview, I observed how some of my responses had a completely adverse effect." After commenting on how the ELA clearly demonstrated the difference between empathic listening and everyday conversations, another student said, "Even when you think you are listening, you aren't really, and the ELA really pointed this out." Such remarks suggest that recording and transcribing the interview elicits substantial motivation for paying more attention to their listening skills and trying to improve them. Note that after more than 50 years as a practicing psychotherapist, Rogers (1980d) commented, "I still regard this [listening to one's recorded sessions] as the one best way of learning to improve oneself as a therapist" (p. 138).

A few students indicated that, while conducting their interview, they experienced anxiety over knowing that their listening skills, or lack of them, were being recorded. Many of the students, contrarily, commented on how the opportunity to acknowledge and correct their listening errors in the analysis section of the ELA helped them feel at ease.

Many students have brief introductions to Rogers's person-centered approach in previous courses. They begin the externship believing it is a naively simple and ineffective counseling technique. The ELA emphasizes that empathic listening is neither simple nor easy and that it is based on a particular counseling theory. One student noted, "Once I had read my transcript of the interview, I realized how little I knew about person-centered theory. I saw how difficult it was to incorporate Rogers' principles into practice."

One limitation of the ELA is that the written transcript does not include important nonverbal cues (e.g., speed and intensity of vocalization, interruptions, and length of pauses). One student suggested that the instructor listen to the audiotape, and another suggested that the interviews be videotaped. These procedures would provide more feedback and, hence, a more powerful learning experience for the students, but they would be very time-consuming for the instructor. An important feature of the ELA is its efficiency. For the instructor reasonably well versed in the person-centered approach, reading, evaluating, and grading most ELAs is relatively quick and simple.

One consideration, however, complicates the evaluation process. Students' empathic-listening skills are not all that is demonstrated in the ELA. Amount of empathy is also a function of the counselee, and some counselees are easier to empathize with than others (Moos & MacIntosh, 1970). Instructors evaluating listening skills on the ELA, therefore, should try to take into account uncontrolled factors that facilitate or compromise the level of empathy demonstrated.

Many students said that learning about empathic listening significantly affected their personal lives. They indicated that they were both more effective in listening to others and more discerning of whether others were listening to them. Many students reported that their enhanced listening skills significantly improved their relationships with a friend, family member, or significant other.

Verbal communication involves primarily four modes: reading, writing, speaking, and listening. Academic curricula emphasize reading and writing; much less emphasis is given to speaking and listening. Actually, taking lecture notes and being held responsible on exams for information spoken by professors requires effective listening skills. The emphasis there, however, is exclusively on knowledge, facts, and information, not on understanding the cognitive/affection communication of a fellow human being. From the latter perspective, the ELA offers students a unique opportunity to acquire an important and underrated communicative skill that gets little attention in today's curricula.

References

Anthony, W. A. (1977). Psychological rehabilitation: A concept in need of a method. *American Psychologist, 32,* 358-362.

Axline, V. (1964). *Dibs: In search of self.* New York: Ballantine.

Carkhuff, R. R. (1969*). Helping and human relations: Selection and training* (Vol. 1). New York: Holt, Rinehart & Winston.

Carkhuff, R. R. (1972*). The art of helping.* Amherst, MA: Human Resource Development Press.

Carkhuff, R. R., & Anthony, W. A. (1979). *The skills of helping.* Amherst, MA: Human Resource Development Press.

Gelso. C. J., & Fretz, B. R. (1992). *Counseling psychology.* New York: Harcourt Brace.

Kohut, H. (1984). *How does analysis cure?* Chicago: University of Chicago Press.

Margules, A. (1984). Toward empathy: The uses of wonder. *American Journal of Psychiatry, 141,* 1025-1033.

Moos, R. H., & MacIntosh, S. (1970). Multivariate study of the patient-therapist system: A replication and extension. *Journal of Consulting and Clinical Psychology, 35,* 298-307.

Rogers, C. R. (1951). *Client-centered therapy.* Boston: Houghton Mifflin.

Rogers, C. R. (1957). The necessary and sufficient conditions of therapeutic personality change. *Journal of Consulting Psychology, 21,* 95-103.

Rogers, C. R. (1961). *On becoming a person.* Boston: Houghton Mifflin.

Rogers, C. R. (1980a). Client-centered psychotherapy. In H. I. Kaplan, B. J. Sadock, & A. M. Freedman (Eds.), *Comprehensive textbook in psychiatry* (Vol. 3, pp. 2153-2168). Baltimore: Williams & Wilkins.

Rogers, C. R. (1980b) *On hurt and anger* [Film]. Alexandria, VA: American Association for Counseling and Development.

Rogers, C. R. (1980c). *The right to be desperate* [Film]. Alexandria, VA: American Association for Counseling and Development.

Rogers, C. R. (1980d). *A way of being.* Boston: Houghton Mifflin.

Notes

1. A detailed description of the course may be obtained from the author.
2. Audiocassette recordings of Carl Rogers conducting personcentered counseling sessions with many different clients can be obtained from the Center for Studies of the Person, 1125 Torrey Pines Road, La Jolla, CA 92037.
3. I thank Kathy Bauman, Susan Kanor, Becky Regeth, Sande Webster, and Carol Williams for their critical readings of the article and editorial assistance.

Using a Group Workshop to Encourage Collaborative Learning in an Undergraduate Counseling Course

Gary S. Goldstein
University of New Hampshire at Manchester

Term paper assignments rarely encourage students to collaborate with each other. Instead, students usually write their papers individually and have little opportunity to share with each other what they have learned. Such assignments are quite different from the work of most psychologists, whose research and professional efforts are characterized by collaboration with and feedback from colleagues.

Some educators have recognized the importance of using collaborative assignments in the classroom. Magin (1982) used collaborative strategies successfully with engineering students, and Welds (1986) noted how her use of such strategies led to greater student self-direction in a semester-at-sea program. Dettmer (1986) argued that adult learners can make important contributions to collaborative assignments because of their extensive and varied backgrounds. Dunn and Toedter (1991) suggested that collaborative projects provide students with a model of peer review that they are likely to encounter in their professional lives. They also stated that such assignments sharpen students; awareness of the diversity of research interests and approaches in psychology as well as provide the opportunity for emotional support in the form of their peers' interest and understanding. In addition, collaborative assignments can nudge passive students out of their dependency on authority as the sole source of knowledge by combining individual research with peer teaching and learning. Working in a group can heighten students' sense of responsibility for their learning and expose them to a variety of perspectives on the topic at hand. Working on a group project throughout the semester can also help students critique their own work, allowing them to refine their writing in light of the feedback they receive from their peers.

Description of Assignment

For the past three semesters, I have used a collaborative learning project in my undergraduate, upper level counseling course. The students were all psychology majors, and about half were adult learners (i. e., 25 years or older, working part-or full-time, and supporting fam-ilies). The central focus of the course was on the major schools of psychotherapy—classical and contemporary psychoanalytic, cognitive-behavioral, and humanistic approaches. The assignment asked students to choose a research topic that reflected a different focus, namely, working with specific patient populations. The project consisted of two parts: an individual research paper and a group workshop presented to the class. Although students worked on the projects as a group, each member was required to complete an individual paper based on a topic from his or her workshop. For example, one group's workshop examined the area of victimization; individual papers from that group focused on rape victims, battered spouses, sexually abused children, and battered homosexual couples.

Each time I taught the course, there were three or four groups comprised of four or five students each. Group formation was constrained by students finding other class members with a shared interest. I facilitated this process by using 45 min early in the semester to brainstorm ideas for workshop topics and to help students find commonalities among their interests. Although I never had a problem, the instructor should be prepared to create groups if students cannot.

Each group's task was to design and present a workshop that involved active participation by the class. Although some didactic presentation was allowed, workshop members were required to involve the class, using experiential exercises, role-playing, video, or personality inventories. The workshops lasted for 1 hr, with an additional 30 min for feedback and discussion from the class.

Students were responsible for arranging group meetings outside of class to develop workshops, discuss ideas for their papers, and read rough drafts of each other's papers. Groups also met twice during class for about 1 hr to allow for further planning. During these sessions, I met with the different groups to discuss their workshops. Each group then summarized in about 10 min its project for the class and received feedback from class members in a brainstorming session. Also, I met with each group for about 1 hr outside of class to discuss their ideas, and I met individually with students, as needed, to review their papers.

Examples of Workshops

The workshops generated spontaneous discussions and allowed the students to examine issues more personally than may have otherwise occurred. For example, in one workshop, students created videotapes of themselves role-playing suicidal patients, asked the class to respond to them, and then analyzed these responses. This workshop resulted in students confronting their fears about working with suicidal patients in a more personal way than would have likely occurred in a typical class discussion. Another group role played victimized patients in a therapy group. Class members then anonymously (through writing) shared their own experiences of victimization (sexual, physical, and emotional abuse) which the workshop leaders related to their earlier role-play. A third group asked the class to keep "eating diaries" and to reenact the typical dinner situation of their childhood. This group then integrated these data into a discussion of eating disorders. A fourth group asked the class to role-play a sixth-grade classroom in which members of the workshop group played the parts of children with different disorders (e.g., conduct disorder and attention deficit disorder).

Ethical and Practical Concerns

Ethical issues can arise as a result of giving this assignment because students often confront personally disturbing material. Several precautionary steps can be taken to minimize potential problems. First, it is important to create an atmosphere of trust in the class by designing several exercises that give students the opportunity to personalize the class content and to respond to each other with empathy and support. Second, students affected emotionally by a specific topic should have the opportunity to consider how they feel about openly participating in the workshop. If a student's discomfort level had appeared particularly high, I would have considered referring that student to an appropriate professional. Workshop summaries given during the brainstorming sessions gave students a good idea of what would be expected of them by the other groups. Third, I encouraged students to discuss with me any hesitation they had about participating in a workshop, both at the beginning of the semester and during brainstorming sessions, and emphasized that participation was not mandatory if they felt uncomfortable about it. In three semesters, no student has exercised this option. Quite the contrary, students opened up during the workshops and disclosed personal experiences, thus enriching the presentations.

The assignment is time consuming because the instructor may need to allow class time for group meetings and workshop presentations. Therefore, I would not use

this assignment with more than five groups. The first time I gave the assignment students agreed to schedule brainstorming sessions and to present their workshops immediately after the 3-hr class; thus, time was not a major concern. We agreed on this meeting time by consensus after a discussion during the first class. Because the course met once a week at night, finding this common time was easy, and there were no scheduling conflicts with other classes. Some students, however complained that the extra hour conflicted with family responsibilities. Therefore, in subsequent semesters, I added 1 hr per week (which we used about five times) to the course's meeting time, designated solely for workshop preparation and presentations. Faculty at my campus can add this extra time to their classes without increasing the number of credit hours for the course. However, students know when they register for the course that they will sometimes need to adjust their schedule around this extra hour, which provides a formal meeting time for all students in the class.

Group projects present the potential for some students not to share equally in the workload or for some students to dominate the process. Requiring an individual research paper can mitigate these problems. Also, each student's involvement can be monitored by meeting with the groups on a regular basis. I asked students to take responsibility for dealing with these possible problems by first trying to resolve the issue among themselves. If this approach did not lead to a successful resolution, the students were asked to involve me. The unequal sharing of work created some difficulty for one group, but I was not informed of it until after the semester ended. In the future, I will collect anonymous feedback throughout the semester so that I can intervene at the appropriate time.

Evaluating Student Performance

Twenty-five percent of the students' final course grade was based on their written paper, and 5% was based on participation in the group workshop. Students could earn one of two grades for the workshop—an A if they participated in its design and presentation or an F if they did not participate. Furthermore, not participating in the workshop carried the additional penalty of automatic failure on the written paper.[1] Essentially, then, students earned an A for the workshop by participating in its design and presentation. I did not grade the quality of the workshop. Thus, I did not use grades as an incentive for student performance on the workshop. Instead, I depended on the students' interest in the topic and commitment to the course, peer pressure, and my encouragement when meet-ing with each group. All students participated in the work-shop, and grades on the papers ranged between B

---

[1]If students choose not to participate is a workshop, they will not suffer this penalty. Instead, they will be required to write the paper and outline their ideas for a workshop. Thirty percent of these students' final grades will be based on their paper.

and A—slightly higher than what students receive on the assignment without the workshop. Although I believe this grading system was successful, it may not be appropriate for less motivated students in lower level courses with less general interest in counseling.

Student Feedback on the Assignment

Although students have voiced some objections to the workshops, their reactions have been mostly positive. The course has had a total enrollment of 51 students during the past three semesters. Of these 51 students, 31 specifically mentioned the course project on end-of-semester anonymous course evaluations. Of these 31 students, 4 reported concern that the project required excessive work, 6 reported that the project produced scheduling problems, 3 reported difficulty working with other group members, 5 wished the project had counted more toward their final grade, and 23 reported positive feelings about the project. These numbers add up to more than 31 because some students wrote more than one comment. Sample responses included: "The workshop was most interesting as we had the opportunity to work collectively on a project"; "I felt the workshop was an effective example of learning group dynamics and management of therapeutic technique presented in class"; "I feel it was important to work with others and get their perspectives. I wish other classes required group collaborations"; and "I learned about the necessity of taking into consideration the different backgrounds, different priorities, and different points of views of others."

Students in one section of the course (n = 16) also rated items evaluating the project on a scale ranging from *strongly disagree* (1) to *strongly agree* (7). The items and their mean ratings were as follows:

"Working with my workshop group helped me learn about my topic" (M = 6.12).
"I found that listening to the other groups' workshop was a useful learning experience" (M = 6.5).
"Working on the group project was interesting" (M = 6.53).
"I would recommend using this group project again for the course" (M = 6.33).

Four of the 16 students wrote comments about the project on this instrument. Three students gave positive comments, and 1 reported that the project produced scheduling problems.

Overall, I concluded that the assignment was successful. I was impressed by the students' level of commitment and by the quality of their work. Workshop presentations were creative and generated exciting classroom discussions. Collegiality of the groups appeared to carry over into classroom discussion on a regular basis. Individual papers were, for the most part, outstanding and more original than typical term papers I have read. More important, the assignment provided a powerful collaborative model for the kind of work students may encounter in advanced study. It also added a unique dimension to the class by allowing students to personalize issues like suicide and abuse and enriched their learning by giving them perspective on how these issues relate to themselves and others.

References

Dettmer, P. (1986). Characteristics and needs of adult learners in gifted inservice and staff development. *Gifted Child Quarterly, 30,* 131-134.

Dunn, D. S., & Toedter, L. J. (1991). The collaborative honors project in psychology: Enhancing student and faculty development. *Teaching of Psychology, 18,* 178-180.

Magin, D. S. (1982). Collaborative peer learning in the laboratory. *Studies in Higher Education, 7,* 105-117.

Welds, K. (1986). Experiential education journal to develop self direction and authority. *Innovative Higher Education, 10,* 128-133.

Note

I gratefully acknowledge the assistance of Charles L. Brewer and three anonymous reviewers for their comments on a draft of this article.

3. ACQUIRING SKILLS–GRADUATE STUDENTS

The Hypothesis-Testing Game: A Training Tool for the Graduate Interviewing Skills Course

Kathryn M. Richard
Robert W. Titley
Colorado State University

Instructors of graduate-level introductory interviewing courses recognize a variety of training goals. Instilling subjective comfort with the interviewing process is an important elementary goal; fostering student's incorporation of basic microcounseling skills is another goal for many instructors (Ivey, Ivey, & Simec-Downing, 1987). Role playing and practice interviews provide excellent channels for training in these basic areas. However, according to the Ivey et al. "skills hierarchy" notion, higher level training goals include the development of the ability to conceptualize client problems and to use a hypothesis-generating and hypothesis-testing approach. These goals are more abstract than primary skills and, therefore, somewhat more difficult to present to the beginning graduate student. The assessment and rehearsal of skills at this level are also particularly problematic for another reason. Final grades or qualitative evaluations in interviewing courses taken early in training are often important criteria for evaluating performance and progress and for predicting subsequent success in the program. Because students are aware of such contingencies, they are often anxious and inhibited in their attempts to acquire skills and perform them, especially in the presence of instructors or supervisors.

This article describes a team game used in a graduate level interviewing course at Colorado State University. The game is designed to develop hypothesis-generation, hypothesis-testing, and conceptualization-building skills in what has proven to be a relatively nonthreatening atmosphere. The game, when used early in the course, can also serve to identify strengths and deficits in individual students. At the end of the course, it can be useful to help students measure their progress.

Guidelines and Rules for the Game

The instructor should introduce and explain the game in a way that fosters a comfortable, noncompetitive climate. An ideal number of players is 8 to 12 students. Materials needed include a stopwatch, two different colored strips of construction paper cut into 20 to 30 ticket-sized "markers," paper and pencil for each student, and preferably a long conference table so that players may sit on opposite sides of the table with timers and judges at either end.

The instructor role-plays a well conceptualized, hypothetical clinical case. Students interview the "client" in order to obtain information about the case and test the hypotheses generated as the game progresses. Diagnoses that have worked particularly well have been fairly standard and common ones such as personality disorders, phobias, depression, and adjustment disorders. Because the skills needed to deal with client resistance, avoidance, or passive aggressivity are not usually present at this stage, these characteristics should not be part of the instructor's client role.

Students volunteer to fulfill the following roles for the game: Team A members, Team B members, recording referees, and timing referees. Team A members (3 to 4 students) interview the client and record, in written format, hypotheses associated with questions asked of the client. They also challenge the questions asked by the opposing team. Team B members have identical responsibilities. Recording referees (1 or 2 students) act as judges and award points to the teams for questioning, hypothesis testing, appropriate challenges, and responses to challenges. They confer with the timing referees on their scoring of the teams and record the points accumulated. The timing referees (1 or 2 other students) also act as judges, but only in a consultation capacity to the recording referees; in cases of disagreement, the opinions of the recording referees are final. The primary duty of the timing referees is to monitor the information-gathering phases and interrupt the team members with a verbal command or electric buzzer when their allotted times are up.

Procedure

One and one half hours should be allotted for the game. Each team is allocated four 3-min segments for interviewing the client, with the teams alternating in sequence. During these 3-min segments, teams generate

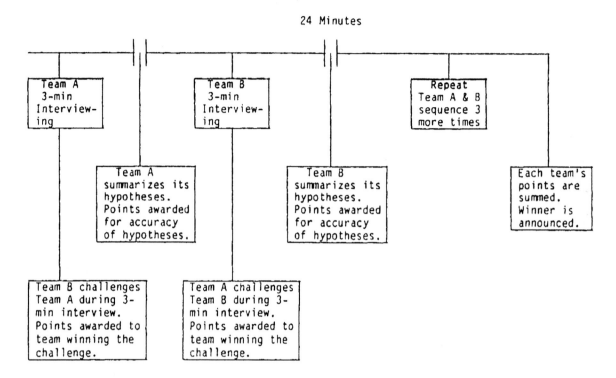

Figure 1. Procedural flow chart for hypothesis-testing game.

and evaluate hypotheses with the client. A total of 24 min of interviewing is conducted in this manner.

Students are told that the goals for interviewing are to gather information, use microcounseling skills when appropriate, follow up on relevant information, disregard irrelevant data, generate and test hypotheses, and maintain positive regard and rapport with the client. A student with a question or lead is encouraged to pursue and verbalize it at any time during the 3-min segment. Students are encouraged to make the introspective experience of dealing with clients more overt and explicit by using this deliberate, verbal form of evaluating the interviewing process. (Of course, such frequent interruptions during actual therapy would detract from the process.) There is no designated order or time limit for team members when interviewing. Members of the opposing team are encouraged to indicate a challenge by throwing markers onto the table at any time during the 3-min segment. Challenges are based on the challenger's belief that a crucial lead was bypassed, on the belief that a questioner is pursuing a "wrong track," or whenever there is a perceived problem with the interviewer's microcounseling skills.[1]

The timing referee records elapsed interview time prior to the challenge. When the challenge and response

are completed, the referee restarts the game and indicates the amount of time remaining. Following each challenge and before interviewing resumes, the recording and timing referees confer and points are awarded. After the 3-min challenge segment, the opposing team is allowed a 3-min interview, and the game proceeds as just described.

The Awarding of Points

Referees award points to teams as follows: After each segment of the game (each team's 3-min interview), the interviewing team evaluates the evidence for and against

their hypotheses during a private team discussion. Then they present this evidence and their lines of reasoning, summarizing two hypotheses that the team believes might best be pursued during subsequent interviewing. Teams are now allowed to challenge or interact with one another during this period. Referees evaluate the interviewing team's presentation and award points on a 10-point scale. A score of 1 indicates the referee's impressions that: (a) the proposed hypotheses/questioning would lead nowhere; (b) the team is off target with its thinking and questioning; or (c) hypotheses (deemed relevant based on existing evidence) were disregarded during the interview or presentation phase. A score of 10 indicates superior team decision making in these areas.

When a challenger marker is thrown, 1 point is awarded to the challenging team in order to encourage active involvement. If the challenging team wins the

[1]Information on procedure for referee's evaluations of challenges may be obtained by writing to Kathryn M. Rickard, Department of Psychology, Colorado State University, Fort Collins, CO 80523.

challenge, 5 additional points are added. When the interviewing team is challenged and wins the challenge, 6 points are awarded to that team. In the spirit of encouraging risk taking, if the interviewing team is challenged and loses the challenge, no points are subtracted from the interviewing team's score. However, the challenging team receives 6 points for a successful challenge. The team that throws the most markers by the end of the game receives an additional 10 points. Again, this procedure encourages active participation during the game.

Following the 24 min of interviewing, referees total each team's points and announce the winner. An instructor made trophy or an inexpensive prize is awarded to the winning team. (See Figure 1 for a flow chart for the game.)

Evaluation and Discussion

Students consistently rate the game toward the favorable end of a scale ranging from *not very helpful* (1) to *extremely helpful* (5), with a recent mean rating of 4.93 ($N = 17$). Open-ended questions on evaluation forms elicited responses such as: "Not only was the game enjoyable, but it was lighthearted enough to allow us to develop and present our ongoing conceptualization of the case in a nonthreatening environment." Students have expressed no negative reactions to the game.

It appears that the game addresses and achieves a number of goals for the introductory interviewing course. Students benefit not only through direct and vicarious feedback, but through the group process of deciding which information may or may not be relevant to the case. An additional indirect benefit is the icebreaking aspect of the game and subsequent disinhibition in students; even less vocal students participate.

Although this exercise does not provide a simulation of an actual clinical interview (e.g., multiple interviewers, possible interruption of interview flow), it appears to be an effective vehicle for introducing hypothesis-generating and decision-making techniques. This training tool should be used, of course, in conjunction with other training methods that compensate for these shortcomings and only as a part of a more comprehensive training format.

Reference

Ivey, A., Ivey, M., & Simec-Downing, L. (1987). *Counseling and psychotherapy.* Englewood Cliffs, NJ: Prentice-Hall.

Thou Shalt Not Ask Questions: An Approach to Teaching Interviewing Skills

John Sommers-Flanagan
John R. Means
University of Montana

Students enrolled in our Interviewing and Case History Techniques course are usually just beginning graduate school and have diverse backgrounds and experiences. Therefore, the first phase of the course consists of 2 weeks of teaching and learning. During this phase, students are oriented to the many categories of interviewer responses, depending on the goal of the interview or the interviewer's theoretical orientation, and are informed of the usual effects of each type of response on the interviewee. Students learn categories ranging from client-centered approaches (e.g., minimal nonverbal "encouragers" and reflection of content/feeling) to more directive responses (e.g., reassurance or advice). These categories are drawn from the work of Benjamin (1974) and Cormier and Cormier (1985). In addition, students are taught how to use questions and are required to complete several structured interviews toward the end of the course. For the most part, however, the four components of the course emphasized in this article occur during the 3 to 4 weeks following the teaching phase and before the students' experiences with structured interviewing.

The "No Questions Asked" Approach

The first component of the course is designed to help students become more client-centered and less directive in their initial interviews. They are required to complete 50-min interviews, record them using audio or video equipment, and present them to the class for feedback. The first two interviews must be completed without asking or answering any questions; the students rely exclusively on the less directive techniques of paraphrasing, reflection of feelings, and summary to "get their subject to talk." The purpose of having students rely on nondirective techniques during their first interviews is to assist them in developing good listening skills before learning more directive techniques. In this regard, Strupp and Binder (1984) stated: "Frequently underestimated is the degree to which the therapist's presence and empathic listening constitute the most powerful source of help and support one human being can provide another" (p. 41).

As the first interviews approach, the level of anxiety in class usually rises a bit, and a few students ask questions such as "What exactly is the goal of this first interview?" or "I'm not really sure what we're supposed to be focusing on?" We typically respond with "The goal of the interview is to listen and to communicate to your subject that you have listened, and no more than that" or "You are to focus on what your subject is saying and feeling." Other methods for decreasing students' anxiety include (a) giving them opportunities to practice the interviewing techniques during inclass role plays and (b) allowing them to view a videotape of the instructor conducting the type of interview that is required of them (i.e., a nondirective interview with an introductory psychology student volunteer). One of the most formidable obstacles to the development of good listening skills in these first-year graduate students is their tendency to believe that they need to "do" something for their clients. They are repeatedly assured that the best thing they can do is listen and stay out of the way so that the client can talk more freely (Strupp & Binder, 1984). Clinicians of varied theoretical views have acknowledged the importance of good listening skills as a foundation on which more directive or interpretive techniques may be built (Cormier & Cormier, 1985; Goldfried & Davison, 1976; Strupp & Binder, 1984).

A final point about the first component of this course should also be mentioned. Students are informed that the use of questions in an interview is, contrary to popular belief, not an essential tool of the skilled interviewer (Benjamin, 1974). Sometimes when interviewers use questions during interviews, they do so because of their own needs or agendas (e.g., excessive reliance on questions may represent an interviewer's need for structure and control or a desire to focus on a specific topic, which may or may not be relevant to the client). This particular orientation is provided to help students explore how specific interventions may be manifestations of their own personal or professional needs. Thus, the first interviewing commandment for these students becomes "Thou shalt not ask questions." We assure them that there is a time and place for questions, but the first two required interviews are not the appropriate time or place.

Self-Reflection and Self-Correction

In the second component of the course, students evaluate their own work. They transcribe at least five interactions between themselves and their analogue clients and mention "improved" or "corrected" responses that might have been more effective. They are encouraged to develop several alternative responses and to speculate on how the analogue client might have responded to them. This process often produces the kind of self-reflection that may help beginning students become more effective interviewers. It also helps students gain some distance from their own work and thus become capable of a more objective evaluation of their interviews. For example, many students have reported that, in the process of listening to their interview and transcribing the interactions, they discovered that they could have improved their techniques in many areas. For students who have inadvertently asked questions or otherwise directed their subjects too explicitly, this process provides an opportunity to demonstrate that they have the knowledge necessary to conduct a good nondirective interview.

Feedback

The third component of the course involves extensive feedback from classroom peers, instructors, and analogue clients. In addition to the self-evaluation mentioned earlier, each student receives feedback from other members of the class. It is important to establish a strong level of trust within the group of students to enable them to accept and use the feedback with openness and comfort. The interviews are usually somewhat threatening for most students; therefore, we work on how to give supportive and corrective feedback primarily through instruction and modeling. For example, we recommend that students always try to give some form of positive feedback to individuals who are presenting their work to the class. In addition, the instructors openly acknowledge their own mistakes and weaknesses when presenting their material.

An additional unique aspect of the course is that each student gets copies of rating scales filled out by analogue clients whom they interviewed. These scales include a modified version of the semantic differential (Osgood, Suci, & Tannenbaum, 1957) and a combination of the client personal reaction form (Ashby, Ford, Guerney, &

Guerney, 1957; Greenberg, 1969) and the helping relationship questionnaire (Luborsky, 1984). As a result, students learn the extent to which analogue clients perceived the interview as effective, warm, insightful, and positive. Although this aspect of the course often provides the most candid commentary, students are generally enthusiastic about such feedback.

Because students are likely to receive both positive and negative reviews of their performance from the analogue clients, we suggest three steps to facilitate this process. First, instructors should discuss the potential meaning of positive and negative responses from the analogue clients. For example, some clients report that the interview experience was helpful but negative or cold but effective. Discussing the possibility of such feedback can prepare students to cope with negative or inconsistent reviews of their performance. Second, it is often best if students are allowed to examine the feedback individually at first. Third, students should be encouraged to discuss the nature of their feedback with their peers in the classroom.

Obtaining Analogue Clients

It is often difficult or impossible to obtain a clinical population for beginning students to interview (Weiss, 1986). To alleviate the problem, we use subjects from the introductory psychology research pool as analogue clients. Obtaining subjects from the research pool requires several steps. First, approval of the university's human subjects review committee must be obtained. Second, subjects sign up to participate in a study that we call "interviewing experiences." Third, when students gather in a large group for the first screening session, they are informed of the requirements of the project. We emphasize that the interviewers are learning new skills, that the students will be asked to talk openly for about 50 min (preferably about issues of personal concern), and that their cooperation and feedback are highly valued to help the interviewers become more skilled. Fourth, all subjects are informed of the audiotape or videotape requirement and are asked to sign a release that permits graduate students in the interviewing course to have access to the tapes. Subjects are told that what they say to the interviewer will be confidential in the sense that only instructors and students from the interviewing course will have access to the tapes. Fifth, subjects are encouraged to relax, to enjoy the interview experience, and to view it as an opportunity to have someone listen closely to them for nearly an hour. Sixth, subjects' telephone numbers are obtained so that the interviewers may call them to schedule appointments. Finally, subjects are asked to return for a postinterview assessment meeting (from 1 to 2 weeks after their interview) to complete questionnaires that evaluate their reactions to the interview and receive credit for their participation. (Such activities could be completed immediately after the interview.)

From the outset, the faculty supervisor's telephone and office numbers are given to the subjects in case they have complaints about any aspect of their treatment. Not one of the more than 250 undergraduate students who have participated in this procedure has refused to participate or to sign the audio/video release. Moreover, we have yet to receive a formal or anonymous complaint about our procedure.

One note of caution may be helpful for others who use this procedure: Our research subjects have displayed emotional disturbances more frequently than we expected. Approximately 15% to 25% of the subjects who have been interviewed have reported symptoms of psychopathology such as depression, suicide ideation, anorexia, bulimia, alcohol/drug abuse, sexual abuse, generalized anxiety, and marital/interpersonal conflicts. Therefore, we provide interviewers with a list of referral sources ranging from a battered women's shelter to various clinics that offer psychological services. In addition, we present lectures on crisis management before the interviews begin. Graduate students also are told how to assist subjects in making appointments with local agencies.

There are several advantages of using the introductory psychology subject pool for obtaining analogue clients. First, it resolves our previous problem of a shortage of subject volunteers; therefore, graduate students may obtain analogue clinical experience. Second, various scales and questionnaires are now administered to analogue clients before and after they are interviewed. This research emphasis provides graduate students with important feedback about their impact on the subjects. In addition, the questionnaire information is gradually becoming a source of data concerning the effect of the interview experience on the subjects' attitudes toward psychology (e.g., how much more or less likely they would be to pursue psychotherapy, how positive they view psychology as a profession, etc.). Given the current interest in treatment-acceptability research and accountability in psychotherapy, such objective measures of the analogue clients' reactions to the interview are highly desirable (Strupp, Hadley, & Gomes-Schwartz, 1977). Third, introductory psychology students have an interview experience from which they can, to some extent, formulate more realistic attitudes toward psychotherapy and psychotherapists. In fact, a number of analogue clients usually request formal psychotherapy after their positive experience of being interviewed by a graduate student.

However, there are some distinct disadvantages of using introductory psychology students as analogue clients. For example, preinterview and postinterview sessions with students must be conducted by the instructor or a teaching assistant to administer the questionnaires, to orient the students about what to expect during the interviews, and to debrief them afterward. Scoring the scales and questionnaires is also time consuming. Nevertheless, we are more than satisfied with the benefits of this approach and recommend it to others.

References

Ashby, J., Ford, D., Guerney, B., & Guerney, L. (1957). Effects on clients of a reflective and a leading type of psychotherapy. *Psychological Monographs, 71*(24, Whole No. 453).

Benjamin, A. (1974). *The helping interview* (2nd ed.). Boston: Houghton Mifflin.

Cormier, W. H., & Cormier, L. S. (1985). *Interviewing strategies for helpers* (2nd ed.). Monterey, CA: Brooks/Cole.

Goldfried, M. R., & Davison, G. C. (1976). *Clinical behavior therapy.* New York: Holt, Rinehart & Winston.

Greenberg, R. P. (1969). Effects of presession information on perception of the therapist and receptivity to influence in a psychotherapy analogue. *Journal of Consulting and Clinical Psychology, 33,* 425-429.

Luborsky, L. (1984). *Principles of psychoanalytic psychotherapy: A manual of supportive/expressive treatment.* New York: Basic Books.

Osgood, C. E., Souci, G. J., & Tannenbaum, P. H. (1957). *The measurement of meaning.* Urbana: University of Illinois Press.

Strupp, H. H., & Binder, J. (1984). *Psychotherapy in a new key: A guide to time-limited dynamic psychotherapy.* New York: Basic Books.

Strupp, H. H., Hadley, S. W., & Gomes-Schwartz, B. (1977). *Psychotherapy for better or worse: An analysis of the problem of negative effects.* New York: Aronson.

Weiss, A. R. (1986). Teaching counseling and psychotherapy skills without access to a clinical population The short interview method. *Teaching of Psychology, 13,* 145-147.

Note

The authors thank Joseph J Palladino and three anonymous reviewers for their helpful comments on earlier drafts of this article.

Undergraduate Role Players as "Clients" for Graduate Counseling Students

Dana D. Anderson
Colleen Buren Gundersen
Daniel M. Banken
Jonathan V. Halvorson
Denise Schmutte
Pacific Lutheran University

Following Rogers (1957), most faculty who teach graduate counseling methods courses probably consider empathy a vital skill for their counselor—trainees to learn. In defining *empathy*, Gladstein (1983) and Goldstein and Michaels (1985) emphasized as basic to the empathic response the ability to take on another's role. Playing the counselor role in role play is, of course, a standard training technique for graduate students. Truax and Carkhuff (1967) concluded that the less common practice of taking on the client role can increase graduate trainees' empathy for future clients.

We believe that undergraduates can also gain in empathy if they role play persons seeking counseling. As anyone who has taught an undergraduate abnormal psychology course can attest, negative stereotypes toward people who seek mental health intervention persist (Farina, Holland, & Ring, 1966; Farina & Ring, 1965; Goffman, 1963; Nunally, 1961; Sarbin & Mancuso, 1970). Replacing such stereotypes with acceptance is an avowed goal of several popular abnormal psychology undergraduate texts (e.g., Mahoney, 1980; Sarason & Sarason, 1984). Because empathy can be an antidote to stereotyping (Katz, 1963), undergraduates who take on the client role can come to see that people who need counseling as fellow humans and individuals rather than as alien stereotypes.

We devised two exercises using undergraduates as roleplay "clients" for graduate counseling students to increase undergraduates' acceptance of persons with psychological problems. These exercises also solve the common practical problem of finding clients for beginning trainees (Lane, 1988).

Exercises

Both exercises take advantage of undergraduate abnormal psychology courses taught during the same semester as our graduate counseling methods and psychopathology courses. Consequently, our undergraduates are learning about the wide range of human psychological problems while our graduate students are learning to assess and intervene with such problems.

We describe the exercises to the undergraduates during their class meetings. Participation by undergraduates is optional, and they receive no course credit. The exercises require acting ability, self-confidence, and personal stability. Because these qualities are not ordinarily academic requirements in undergraduate abnormal psychology courses, awarding academic credit would unfairly penalize class members who lack them. Because these qualities are necessary for counselor-trainees, the graduate students' participation is mandatory and graded.

The first exercise is used with the counseling methods trainees and involves mock counseling sessions. Before the sessions, we provide each undergraduate participant with a brief description of the personality and problem of the client to be role played. Descriptions, averaging two single-spaced, typed pages in length, provide sufficient information about the client to ensure clinical accuracy while allowing improvisation so that students create their own versions of the client. Standard instructions encourage role players to relax and to use personal experience in the role if they feel comfortable doing so. We have depicted problems ranging from mild anxiety through moderate posttraumatic stress disorder to suicidal depression.

The undergraduate and a member of the graduate counseling methods class meet outside class for one mock session at the beginning of the semester and one at the end. Students videotape their sessions. Postsession, the graduate instructor views the tapes to evaluate the quality of and improvement in the graduate student's performance. The instructor also interviews all students and conveys the evaluation and the undergraduate's feedback to each counselor-trainee during the interview. Undergraduates' impressions, although instructive, do not weight in trainees' grades.

The second exercise is a simulated case conference for the graduate psychopathology course. As part of their regular coursework, undergraduate abnormal psychology students create a fictional case history for a character with one of the psychological problems covered in the course. Those who participate in the second exercise role play their case history character during a class meeting of the graduate psychopathology course. As in actual case conferences, the graduate class as a group interviews the client "presented" by the graduate instructor to arrive at a conceptualization of the client's problem. The instructor then critiques graduates' conceptualizations. Consistent with the first exercise, the instructor handles the role-play client's instructions and feedback to the class.

Benefits

The exercises benefit both graduates and undergraduates. Graduates have the rare opportunity to hear how their efforts appear from the client's perspective. Furthermore, trainees find that undergraduates, because they do not fear retaliation for challenging performances or feedback, make more instructive roleplay partners than do fellow graduate students.

We hoped that the exercises would benefit undergraduates by increasing their academic and empathic understanding of psychological problems. We recently interviewed 10 of our undergraduate role players (about half of those who had participated) after their course ended. The undergraduate role players generally agreed that the exercises, particularly the second one, increased their academic knowledge of abnormal psychology and of counseling and interview techniques.

All interviewed undergraduates said that they developed empathy for their role-play characters. One, seeming to speak for the majority, described beginning the exercise from a detached observer's viewpoint but increasingly seeing the situation through the client's eyes as the exercise progressed. All interviewees remarked further that they could not divorce their own personalities and experiences from those of their characters and acknowledged drawing on their own difficulties when enacting the characters. Two students reported experiencing, during role play, heightened emotion like that of their characters. These experiences seem to reflect the role-taking, identification, and affective aspects of empathy, which Gladstein (1983) listed as common elements in attempts to define the concept.

Conclusions

If conducted with some safeguards, these exercises can provide educational benefits for graduates and undergraduates. Emotional symptoms are prominent in client roles, and heightened experience of symptoms is a potential risk for undergraduate role players. Excessive empathy (i.e., too great an identification with the client's problems) may be so threatening to the student that the client is defensively rejected (Hoffman, 1981), defeating the purpose of the exercise. Thus, the exercise requires informed consent and advance screening of volunteers. Private role rehearsal with the instructor beforehand helps in assessing a student's ability to withstand the stresses of the role and to enact it credibly.

Abnormal psychology courses are typically among the most popular of undergraduate offerings in psychology, attracting large numbers of majors and nonmajors. They offer us a prime opportunity to alter negative and stereotypic public attitudes toward those who seek psychological services. We hope these exercises will assist instructors whose course objectives include improving students' attitudes toward persons with psychological problems. We believe the exercises are a useful response to Rogers's (1983) general call that educators teach empathy in the classroom as an intrinsically valuable life skill.

References

Farina, A., Holland, C. H., & Ring, K. (1966). The role of stigma and set in interpersonal interaction. *Journal of Abnormal Psychology, 71*, 421-428.

Farina, A., & Ring, K. (1965). The influence of perceived mental illness on interpersonal relations. *Journal of Abnormal Psychology, 70*, 47-51.

Gladstein, G. A. (1983). Understanding empathy: Integrating counseling, developmental, and social psychology perspectives. *Journal of Counseling Psychology, 30*, 467-482.

Goffman, E. (1963). *Stigma: Notes on the management of a spoiled identity.* Englewood Cliffs, NJ: Prentice-Hall.

Goldstein, A. P., & Michaels, G. Y. (1985). *Empathy: Development, training, and consequences.* Hillsdale, NJ: Lawrence Erlbaum Associates, Inc.

Hoffman, M. L. (1981). Is altruism part of human nature? *Journal of Personality and Social Psychology, 40*, 121-137.

Katz, R. L. (1963). *Empathy: Its nature and uses.* New York: Free Press.

Lane, K. (1988). Using actors as "clients" for an interviewing simulation in an undergraduate clinical psychology course. *Teaching of Psychology, 15*, 162-164.

Mahoney, M. J. (1980). *Abnormal psychology: Perspectives on human variance.* San Francisco: Harper & Row.

Nunally, J. C. (1961). *Popular conceptions of mental health.* New York: Holt, Rinehart & Winston.

Rogers, C. R (1957). The necessary and sufficient conditions of therapeutic personality change. *Journal of Consulting Psychology, 21*, 95-103.

Rogers, C. R. (1983). *Freedom to learn.* Columbus, OH: Merrill.

Sarason, I. G., & Sarason, B. R. (1984). *Abnormal psychology: The problem of maladaptive behavior* (4th ed.). Englewood Cliffs, NJ: Prentice-Hall.

Sarbin, T. R., & Mancuso, J. D. (1970). Failure of a moral enterprise: Attitudes of the public toward mental illness. *Journal of Consulting and Clinical Psychology, 35*, 159-173.

Truax, C. B., & Carkhuff, R. R. (1967). *Toward effective counseling and psychotherapy.* Chicago: Aldine.

Notes

1. Anderson and Schmutte, the instructors for the courses described, express their gratitude to our Pacific Lutheran University undergraduate students who graciously consented to discuss their experiences in interviews with their fellow students, Gundersen, Banken, and Halvorson. Thanks especially to Brent Baldree, Sandra Bird, Jacob Matthew, Matt Orme, Amber Rogers, Lisa Sigurdson, Scott Squires, Cheryl Walker, and Laura Williamson.

2. Denise Schmutte is now at Children Services, Everett, WA.

Teaching Counseling and Psychotherapy Skills Without Access to a Clinical Population: The Short Interview Method

Andrea R. Weiss
Drexel Urliversity

Teaching helping and listening skills to psychology students is best accomplished by having them counsel with real people. However, in many educational settings, particularly those without doctoral training programs in counseling or clinical psychology that maintain their own clinics, clinical populations willing to be counseled are not available. Therefore, the counseling or psychotherapy instructor is forced to explore other alternatives for teaching basic helping skills. One alternative is to ask students to find their own counselees. When I first began to teach counseling psychology I resorted to this approach, which was productive for some students. These students managed to find strangers, or relative strangers, to counsel and did useful and helpful work with them. For example, students worked with friends of friends, or friends of relatives, or casual acquaintances from the dormitory or neighborhood. However, it was difficult for most students to find people who were appropriate, that is, individuals over the age of 18 who were nor friends or relatives of the counselor-in-training who wanted to talk for a limited period of time about an important but not serious personal problem with someone who had virtually no counseling experience.

An alternative for providing a counseling experience without using real clients is to have the students counsel each other in role-playing situations. These are often called *simulated counseling experiences.* (Allowing students to do "real" peer counseling with one another is not appropriate because group discussions of the counseling sessions would violate the principles of confidentiality and the welfare of the consumer.) These simulated counseling exercises have been useful training strategies, as they have enabled students to practice new skills in a supportive atmosphere and receive immediate feedback from classmates on their skill mastery. However, there is a general feeling of artificiality about these exercises, because they lend themselves best to practicing one helping skill at a time and because the counselees are usually playing the role of someone else or feeling some way that is not genuine at the moment.

A second alternative is to use a programmed instruction package, such as the one by Evans, Hearn,

Uklemann, and Ivey (1984) in which students choose, from among several alternatives, a counselor comment or question that best represents a particular kind of interviewing skill or one that will be most facilitative to the depicted client. The Evans et al. (1984) book has much to offer. The programmed exercises allow the students more practice with each skill than they can get in any one real-life counseling session, the alternatives are excellent models of well-phrased therapeutic interventions, and the text includes discussion, which can be obtained immediately following the student's choice, of why each counselor intervention was appropriate or not for the given situation. However, there are limitations to programmed instruction as a substitute for an actual counseling experience. First, students are not required to generate their own comments or questions, but merely to recognize which of those already given is most appropriate. Second, it is not obvious that there is any transfer from this kind of experience to a real-life counseling or psychotherapy experience.

Procedure

After 4 years of teaching counseling and psychotherapy without regular access to clients for my students, I have developed an approach that incorporates both the roleplaying technique and programmed instruction as complements to the primary clinical experience of conducting a series of short interviews. Specifically, as a homework assignment, students are asked to interview someone (anyone at all, and on tape) for not more than 5 or 10 min, in an attempt to answer an assigned open-ended question. Students accomplish this task by using the attending and listening skills they are practicing in classroom role-playing exercises and in their programmed instruction books. They are then required to transcribe the interviews completely and to label the microskills they have used according to the Ivey and Authier categories (Ivey & Simek-Downing 1980). The transcription and labeling are crucial components of the assignment, as they permit the student and the teacher to do a microskill-based analysis of the effectiveness of the interview.

In a 10-week term the students are required to complete five of these interviews. At the beginning of the term, students receive a handout that includes the directions for doing and transcribing the five interviews. The handout also contains the five questions they will be asking and the due date for each assignment. Scheduling an interview question every 2 weeks has worked well. During the first week between assignments, I read and write comments on the most recently completed interview. The students then receive my feedback and have a full week to do their next interviews. Students are not permitted to turn in the interviews in bulk. The third interview is recorded on videotape, and the class spends 2 to 4 hr (one or two class periods) watching these videotapes and providing feedback about each student's nonverbal and verbal interviewing behavior. For example, students are asked to comment on each other's posture, body position, and facial expressions, and each other's usage of the various attending and influencing skills. They observe that particular interviews seem richer than others, and are encouraged to try to understand why. Are certain helping skills facilitative, or is it the interviewer's flexibility in using different microskills?

The other four interviews are recorded on audiotape. We generally listen to portions of these interviews in class so that the students receive feedback and suggestions from their classmates in addition to the feedback they obtain on their written transcriptions of the interviews. The interview questions become progressively more challenging and/or personal as the term progresses, but all are selected with the primary goal of facilitating discussion that is stimulating, rich in personal meaning, and open-ended. In addition, because of my phenomenological/existential orientation I tend to assign questions that encourage the interviewees and interviewers to examine their values and their meaning constructs. The interview questions for undergraduate students are as follows:

Interview 1. How has the women's movement affected you?
Interview 2. If you won $1,000,000 in the lottery, what would you change about the way you live your life?
Interview 3. How might you be different if you were a male (female)?
Interview 4. How would you live your life differently if you knew you would live forever?
Interview 5. What role does adventure (or beauty, or friendship) play in your life?

Because our psychology graduate students are committed to the helping professions, their assigned questions include several that they may be likely to ask on practicum placements or in their jobs. Questions 4 and 5 have been included for this purpose. The interview questions for graduate students are as follows:

Interview 1. How has the threat of nuclear war affected your life?
Interview 2. How would you live your life differently if you knew you would live forever?
Interview 3. What role does friendship play in your life?
Interview 4. What are the things about yourself that you like most?
Interview 5. If you could relive any part of your life, what would you change?

The value of these interview assignments, in comparison with role-playing exercises or programmed instruction, lies in their closer approximation to a real-life counseling or psychotherapy experience. Students doing interviews are talking to people who are being themselves rather than playing roles, and they are forced to generate their own helpful questions and comments rather than rely on someone else's ideas. However, it is important to stress that interviews are not substitutes for role playing and programmed instruction experiences. During the early part of the term when the students are learning the various attending and listening skills from lectures and their textbook, they also complete, as homework, the Evans et al. (1984) programmed instruction exercises illustrating these skills. In addition, we spend portions of many class periods practicing the microskills through role playing.

Students split up into pairs and take turns interviewing each other with the aid of a particular skill. For example, students who have taken the counselor role might be asked to spend 5 min using open questions to interview students who have taken the counselee role. Students who have taken the role of counselee will either adopt a psychological problem for the duration of the exercise or use a relatively minor personal problem that they feel comfortable sharing. When members of a pair have had a turn at each role, they repeat the exercise using closed questions. When that task has been completed, and student partners have given each other feedback on their performances as interviewers, the entire class discusses their experience with the two kinds of questions. During the next class period student pairs might practice using the skills of paraphrasing and directives, and compare effects of these approaches. This kind of focused practice is essential preparation for the outside-of-classroom interviewing assignments, because the students, in order to conduct productive interviews, need to know the relative advantages of the various skills.

An additional benefit of this interviewing approach is increased self-awareness for some students. Students are advised to prepare for their interviews by trying to answer the interview questions themselves. Because the questions are somewhat provocative, this preparatory exercise encourages self-examination and thinking about feelings, and in some students leads to expanded self-knowledge. Students have, for example, learned some things about their values, life goals, and personalities by trying to answer the question, "How would you live your life differently if you knew you would live forever?" Some have realized how important physical health and spending their lifetimes with family members are to them. Others have realized how important time pressure is in their accomplishments. It has occurred to them that without the pressure of finite deadlines they might drift through life and accomplish little. Struggling with the question, "How has the threat of nuclear war affected your life?," has led some students to realize more clearly that they were, in fact, being psychologically affected by this threat. The question, "How has the women's movement affected you?," has had some very interesting outcomes. Students too young to remember the heyday of the feminist movement often "rediscover" that change in sex role expectations has occurred and has affected their lives, and students interviewing students who are more chauvinistic in their outlook learn what it means to try to keep one's values of one's counseling work.

Students who have enrolled in one of the counseling courses are initially surprised to receive the interviewing assignments, some because it is more "hands-on" work than they have ever encountered in a course and others because they expected to do "real" counseling. Many also complain about the time-consuming transcription process. However, the undergraduate and graduate students almost universally evaluate these interviewing assignments as among their most useful learning experiences. The importance of detailed feedback from the instructor cannot be overemphasized. Although the microskills labeling does help the students to do a productive analysis of the effectiveness of their work, the instructor's comments add to their understanding and, perhaps of most importance, provide the positive reinforcement, encouragement, and goal setting necessary for continued progress.

References

Evans, D. R., Hearn, M. T., Uklemann, M. R., & Ivey, A. E. (1984). *Essential interviewing: A programmed approach to effective communication* (2nd ed.). Monterey, CA: Brooks/Cole.

Ivey, A. E., & Simek-Downing, L. (1980). *Counseling and psychotherapy: Skills, theories, and practice.* Englewood Cliffs, NJ: Prentice-Hall.

4. TREATING FEARS

Participant Modeling as a Classroom Activity

Dolores Hughes
Iona College

Participant modeling is a behavioral technique in which the therapist models approach and coping responses, encouraging and guiding the client to take a progressively active role in interacting with anxiety-provoking stimuli. Its major goals are the extinction of avoidance responses and the conditioning of appropriate approach responses. This technique has also been called *contact desensitization, demonstration plus participation,* and *guided participation* (Redd, Porterfield, & Andersen, 1979).

Many studies have demonstrated the effectiveness of participant modeling in the treatment of fears and phobias (e.g., Bandura, Adams, & Beyer, 1976; Bandura, Blanchard, & Ritter, 1969; Ritter, 1969). The classic study of modeling for this purpose used young adults whose fear of snakes was severe enough to restrict some of their everyday activities (Bandura et al., 1969). Although all subjects in three treatment groups showed improvement in comparison with a control group, the subjects who imitated the behavior of a live model with guided participation demonstrated the most improvement. Several subsequent studies have demonstrated that this type of participant modeling is the most effective method of reducing snake phobias (e.g., Bandura et al., 1976).

Bandura (1977) suggested that participant modeling is effective because it provides individuals with experiences that enhance their perceptions of self-efficacy. Efficacy expectations are governed by information from a variety of sources. The most reliable source of information derives from performance accomplishments. Because participant modeling requires these accomplishments, it is particularly effective for inducing behavioral, affective, and attitudinal changes (Bandura, Adams, Hardy, & Howells, 1980).

The following activity was designed to: (a) demonstrate participant modeling as a technique for reducing fear and avoidance of nonpoisonous snakes, (b) illustrate the concept of self-efficacy, (c) illustrate some of the problems encountered when evaluating the effectiveness of therapeutic techniques, (d) actively engage students in the learning process, and (e) encourage critical thinking.

Procedure

This activity was conducted in the context of a unit on behavior therapies in my Introductory Psychology course. Approximately 1 week before the activity, students completed a questionnaire about their fear of nonpoisonous snakes. I told them that an expert in wildlife biology, James Rod of the National Audubon Society, would be visiting class to help with this activity.

He began the activity with a brief lecture about the biology of snakes and their ecological importance. He answered several questions about snakes before uncovering an aquarium containing a red rat snake, *Elapse quota,* commonly known as a corn snake. He removed the snake and handled it with obvious competence and a complete lack of fear.

Students were invited to hold the snake, and some always did so. I then selected students, based on their scores on the fear questionnaire, who were moderately afraid. I requested, but did not insist, that they try to do some or all of the following steps in sequence as the expert held the snake: (a) approach the snake within a radius of 6 ft, (b) gradually approach the snake more and more closely, (c) lightly touch its tail, (d) lightly touch the middle of its body, (e) touch the middle of its body more firmly, and (f) help the expert hold the snake. Then, students were asked to hold the snake by themselves.

Each of these steps was done slowly for each moderately afraid student with encouragement and reassurance from the expert, other students, and me. Students were asked to report what they were feeling as they went through these steps. Finally, I asked students who had scored high on the fear questionnaire if they were willing to do some or all of these steps, and some were always willing to try.

Students' Evaluations

Evaluations were obtained from 406 students in 14 sections of my Introductory Psychology course from 1976 to 1988. Class sizes ranged from approximately 20 to 40 students.

Using a 5-point scale, students were asked two questions: (a) How interesting was the activity? (1 = *not at all*, 5 = *extremely interesting*), and (b) How helpful was the activity for understanding the technique of participant modeling? (1 = *not at all*, 5 = *extremely helpful*). Combining all sections, the mean rating for interest was 4.33, and the mean rating for helpful was 4.21.

Discussion

The students' evaluations and comments were very favorable. Many students stayed after class to talk with the expert and touch or hold the snake. I am always struck by the combination of fear and fascination that students exhibit toward snakes.

Many students said they never believed they could touch or hold any snake. They seemed very proud that they were able to approach the snake and actually touch or hold it. Some students later reported that they had told their parents and friends about being able to touch or hold the snake. All of the students' comments were consistent with Bandura's (1984, 1986) concept of self-efficacy or sense of mastery, which has been emphasized as a component of all effective therapeutic techniques.

This activity is very interesting and helpful to students. It provides an excellent introduction to behavior therapies and introduces students to the difficulties involved in identifying the specific factors that are effective in therapeutic techniques. It also encourages students to think critically.

I ask students to think of the factors that were part of this activity. They usually report: (a) characteristics of the snake, such as size and color; (b) characteristics of the expert model and the peer models; (c) encouragement and reassurance from the expert model, other students, and me; (d) motivation to cooperate; and (e) participation in front of a classroom of peers. They understand that we did not isolate which factors may have been most strongly influencing behavior, and we did not use a control group. It is possible that all, some, one, or none of the factors were effective, and there may have been unidentified variables operating.

Students should realize that those who participated were probably not phobic. These students, therefore, were not representative of clients who enter treatment for phobias. This limitation leads to a discussion of the problem of treatment analogues (e.g., Bernstein & Paul, 1971; Borkovec & Nau, 1972). Much of our knowledge about the effectiveness of behavioral approaches for reducing anxiety derives from college students who volunteer for studies; they may not be typical of clients who share some specific problem.

Furthermore, we do not know if students' attitudes and behaviors will be permanently changed and will transfer to situations outside of the classroom. Some of the

students who participated expressed doubts about touching a snake in other circumstances. These doubts lead to a discussion about the obstacles encountered in measuring the observable and permanent effects of any therapy.

I have always included an expert model as well as peer models, but the activity may be effective without the expert model. When modeling is used in the treatment of phobias, a distinction is often made between coping and mastery models. Coping models initially exhibit fearful performances and gradually become increasingly competent as modeling proceeds. Mastery models, in contrast, exhibit fearless performances from the beginning. Kazdin (1974) and Meichenbaum (1972) suggested that coping models may be more effective than mastery models. Coping models can, however, be ineffective. Geer and Turteltaub (1967), for example, found that models who demonstrated nonfearful behaviors toward snakes improved subjects' attitudes toward snakes. In contrast, fearful models did not produce attitudinal changes.

In my activity, some students served as coping models, and other students, who were not afraid of snakes, served as mastery models. If instructors prefer to include an expert model, and I do recommend using one, they may ask faculty or students in biology departments for help. Or they may check with pet stores, zoos, nature centers, and environmental organizations. Staff members of nature centers will probably help, because they want to educate people about wildlife.

The need to educate people about wildlife and help them overcome their fears of wildlife, especially snakes, was cogently addressed by Morgan & Gramann (1989). They successfully used a variety of behavioral techniques, including participant modeling, to help students change their attitudes toward snakes.

My experience suggests that people who are knowledgeable about snakes are eager to help others overcome their fears of snakes. They want people to appreciate that nonpoisonous snakes are harmless and ecologically important. I also discovered that some of my students have positive attitudes toward snakes before this activity.

This activity or modifications of it should be useful in courses such as abnormal psychology, behavior modification, learning, or research methods. It lends itself to a variety of modifications and applications that can engage students in the learning process. Students understand that participant modeling can be used in a variety of anxiety provoking situations. The concept of participant modeling and its broad applications are easy for students to understand and appreciate. Students find this activity interesting, helpful, and enjoyable.

References

Bandura, A. (1977). Self-efficacy: Toward a unifying theory of behavioral change. *Psychological Review, 84*, 191-215.

Bandura, A. (1984). Recycling misconceptions of perceived self-efficacy. *Cognitive Therapy and Research, 8*, 231-255.

Bandura, A. (1986). *Social foundations of thought and action: A social cognitive theory.* Englewood Cliffs, NJ: Prentice-Hall.

Bandura, A., Adams, N. E., & Beyer, J. (1976). Cognitive processes mediating behavioral change. *Journal of Personality and Social Psychology, 35*, 125-139.

Bandura, A., Adams, N. E., Hardy, A. B., & Howells, G. N. (1980). Tests of the generality of self-efficacy theory. *Cognitive Therapy and Research, 4*, 39-66.

Bandura, A., Blanchard, E. B., & Ritter, B. (1969). Relative efficacy of desensitization and modeling approaches for inducing behavioral, affective, and attitudinal changes. *Journal of Personality and Social Psychology, 13*, 173-199.

Bernstein, D. A., & Paul, G. L. (1971). Some comments on therapy analogue research with small animal "phobias." *Journal of Behavior Therapy and Experimental Psychiatry, 2*, 225-237.

Borkovec, T. D., & Nau, S. D. (1972). Credibility of analogue therapy rationales. *Journal of Behavior Therapy and Experimental Psychiatry, 3*, 257-260.

Geer, J. H., & Turteltaub, A. (1967). Fear reduction following observation of a model. *Journal of Personality and Social Psychology, 6*, 327-331.

Kazdin, A. E. (1974). Covert modeling, model similarity, and reduction of avoidance behavior. *Behavior Therapy, 5*, 325-340.

Meichenbaum, D. H. (1972). Examination of model characteristics in reducing avoidance behavior. *Journal of Behavior Therapy and Experimental Psychiatry, 3*, 225-227.

Morgan, J. M., & Gramann, J. H. (1989). Predicting effectiveness of wildlife education programs: A study of students' attitudes and knowledge toward snakes. *Wildlife Society Bulletin, 17*, 501-509.

Redd, W. H., Porterfield, A. T., & Andersen, B. L. (1979). *Behavior modification: Behavioral approaches to human problems.* New York: Random House.

Ritter, B. (1969). Treatment of acrophobia with contact desensitization. *Behaviour Research and Therapy, 7*, 41-45.

Note

I thank my husband, James P. Rod, who is a wildlife biologist employed by the National Audubon Society, for generously volunteering to serve as my expert model.

A Humorous Demonstration of In Vivo Systematic Desensitization: The Case of Eraser Phobia

Timothy J. Lawson
Michael Redrawn
College of Mount St. Joseph

Systematic desensitization (SD) is a common topic covered in general, abnormal, and clinical or counseling psychology courses. Developed by Wolpe (1958), SD involves associating a relaxed state with graduated exposure to anxiety-provoking stimuli. SD typically involves three steps. During the first step, the therapist teaches the client to relax, creating a response that is incompatible with anxiety. For the second step, the therapist and client work together to create an anxiety hierarchy, ordering anxiety-provoking stimuli from lowest to highest (related to a common fear dimension, such as proximity to a snake). The therapist ensures that there is not a large difference in anxiety ratings between any two adjacent hierarchy items. For the third step, the therapist (starting at the bottom of the hierarchy) guides the progressive association of each hierarchy item with relaxation, until the client is able to remain relaxed in response to each item. The therapist may accomplish this association by asking the client to imagine hierarchy items (traditional SD) or by actually presenting the feared items (in vivo SD). Therapists sometimes combine traditional SD and in vivo SD, using the former technique first.

Although Balch (1983) acknowledged the need for more creative ways of teaching therapeutic techniques, few authors have discussed methods for teaching SD. Sprecher and Worthington (1982) tried having general psychology students experience SD for seven 30 min sessions. However, they concluded that this teaching method was too lengthy and produced few therapeutic benefits.

We present a technique for demonstrating in vivo SD in an engaging, humorous, and informative manner that uses relatively little class time. Our technique involves brief role playing similar to that recommended by Balch (1983) for teaching client-centered therapy (see also Low, 1996).

Nature of the Demonstration

The second author, Michael, conducted the demonstration in three sections of general psychology. Prior to the demonstration, he explained the three steps of SD (see the first paragraph for a similar explanation). He explained that he would demonstrate the technique with a student who was ostensibly currently in therapy with him because of a phobia of chalkboard erasers. Before the beginning of the class period, the course instructor had selected a student who always sat at the back of the room and quietly asked the student to play along with the demonstration.

To start the demonstration, Michael explained that the student always sat at the back of the room because of a phobia of chalkboard erasers. He stated that he had already taught progressive relaxation to the student, worked with the student to develop an anxiety hierarchy, and desensitized the student to a photograph of a chalkboard eraser. Michael then showed the class the photograph and moved it toward the student to show that the student had indeed been desensitized to it.

Then, Michael explained that he planned to desensitize the student to items higher in the anxiety hierarchy. He took a caged eraser out of his briefcase and showed it to the student. The toy metal cage was slightly larger than the eraser and was locked with a small toy padlock. As Michael moved closer to the student with the caged eraser, the student acted anxious and Michael asked the student to take some deep breaths and to invoke the relaxation training.

Once the student was relaxed, Michael removed the eraser from the cage and showed it to the student until the student became relaxed once again. He moved the uncaged eraser closer and closer to the student until, finally, the student could touch the eraser without becoming overly anxious. At each step, Michael asked if the student was feeling anxious and progressed only after the student reported low anxiety. Michael then ended the demonstration and explained that the student did not really have an eraser phobia, but that the procedure he demonstrated was similar to that used with real phobias. He also noted that SD usually takes more than one session (10-12 sessions may be more typical).

Evaluation of the Demonstration

At the end of the class sessions in which Michael performed the demonstration, the instructors gave students a questionnaire for evaluation. We asked students to rate, on a scale ranging from 1 (*strongly disagree*) to 5 (*strongly agree*), the extent to which they agreed with the statements, "This demonstration increased my understanding of how systematic desensitization is used to treat phobias," and "I enjoyed watching this demonstration." The questionnaire also contained space for students to provide additional comments. Fifty-nine students provided ratings, but one was excluded from statistical analyses because the ratings and comments were not consistent with each other, suggesting the student misunderstood the rating scales. Students indicated a high level of agreement with the former ($M = 4.41$, $SD = .75$) and the latter ($M = 4.40$, $SD = .86$) statements.

Fifty-six students provided open-ended comments, and they were overwhelmingly positive. Typical comments included: "It was funny . . . showed, in detail, the steps used to desensitize a person," "it was a creative way to teach something and made it very interesting to learn," "funny and explained to me what systematic desensitization was in terms that I could really understand," "Words don't describe it as well as the demonstration," and "entertaining way to facilitate learning." Only 4 students had negative comments, all of which indicated that they thought the demonstration was "silly," or it could have involved better acting on the part of the student.

Conclusions

We have found this demonstration to be an easy, engaging, and humorous way to teach students about SD. Although fictitious, eraser phobia is consistent with actual phobias in that it focuses on a frequently encountered object and causes avoidance of the feared object (i.e., by sitting in the back of the room). The demonstration provides students with a live example of a therapeutic technique, yet it does not require the amount of time involved in the technique discussed by Sprecher and Worthington (1982) . Moreover, students appreciate the fact that it is entertaining and that it goes beyond what they would get from the text or a typical lecture.

Although this demonstration has proved valuable for our purposes, variations on it may better suit particular courses or instructor preferences. For a course in counseling, for example, the instructor may give a longer demonstration by presenting the complete anxiety hierarchy along with a detailed description of how it was developed and by having the student actor report subjective units of discomfort at each hierarchy step. Another way to provide students with more detail may be to use the demonstration to spur a discussion about the advantages and disadvantages of traditional versus in vivo SD or about the essential components of SD (see Spiegler & Guevremont, 1993). Instructors may also want to select the student actor prior to the day of the demonstration to coach the student on how to play the role of an SD client.

Although we emphasize to students that SD is more complex than the demonstration, instructors may also want to warn students that what they have learned from the demonstration does not qualify them to conduct therapy with others. Finally, instructors may also point out that conducting therapy with one's student would create a multiple relationship that would violate the ethical principles of the American Psychological Association.

References

Balch, W. R. (1983). The use of role playing in a classroom demonstration of client-centered therapy. *Teaching of Psychology, 10,* 173-174.

Low, K. G. (1996). Teaching an undergraduate seminar in psychotherapy. *Teaching of Psychology, 23,* 110-112.

Spiegler, M. D., & Guevremont, D. C. (1993). *Contemporary behavior therapy* (2nd ed.). Monterey, CA: Brooks/Cole.

Sprecher, P. L., & Worthington, E. L., Jr. (1982). Systematic desensitization for test anxiety as an adjunct to general psychology. *Teaching of Psychology, 9,* 232-233.

Wolpe, J. (1958). *Psychotherapy by reciprocal inhibition.* Stanford, CA: Stanford University Press.

Note

We thank Randolph A. Smith and the anonymous reviewers for their helpful comments.

5. ADVOCATING A RESEARCH PERSPECTIVE

Teaching Psychotherapy Outcome Research Methodology Using a Research-Based Checklist

Timothy M. Osberg
Niagara University

In recent years, the practice of psychotherapy has come under fire (Coughlin, 1995) . Managed care has held psychologists and other mental health professionals more accountable for providing evidence of the effectiveness of their techniques. Some managed care insurers refuse to pay for treatments in the absence of proof of their efficacy. Partially in response to this pressure, an effort to develop a database of empirically validated treatments has begun (Chambless et al., 1996; Task Force on Promotion and Dissemination of Psychological Procedures, 1995). The goals of this effort include better informing both the lay public and practicing clinicians about recent strides in developing and validating effective psychotherapeutic techniques for a wide range of problems. Furthermore, a recent issue of *American Psychologist* (VandenBos, 1996) included articles debating the direction future psychotherapy outcome research studies should take.

In light of these recent events, providing our students with a basic understanding of the principles of psychotherapy outcome research methodology is now more important than ever. Some scientist-practitioners have suggested that a weakening of the bridge between science and practice has led many practitioners to ignore research findings and utilize untried techniques (Coughlin, 1995). My goal was to develop a teaching technique that would effficiently summarize methodological issues in psychotherapy outcome research and reaffirm the important connection between research and practice in the minds of students.

Despite its central place within clinical psychology, few teaching techniques relevant to psychotherapy outcome research have appeared. A search I conducted revealed a single published report (Viken, 1992) that only partially covers the issues raised here. Viken's demonstration cleverly illustrated the use of an instructor-designed "pseudotreatment" to identify pitfalls of therapy outcome studies, particularly regression effects. This article provides an additional tool for informing students about this important area of clinical research.

The Checklist

I developed a checklist of guidelines for a well-designed psychotherapy outcome study. I compiled the guidelines after reviewing the common methodological strategies employed in 16 psychotherapy outcome studies published in the *Journal of Consulting and Clinical Psychology* (see Appendix). I chose this journal because it is considered a leading outlet for the publication of psychotherapy outcome studies. The selected articles include assessments of a variety of different treatments addressing a range of problems. I use the checklist as an organizational tool for introducing and discussing the topic of psychotherapy outcome research in several undergraduate classes including abnormal psychology, clinical psychology, and even introductory psychology. In addition, the list would be relevant within the undergraduate research methodology course and numerous graduate courses and practical. Although my use of the checklist varies from course to course, I generally present it on an overhead transparency after my introductory lecture on psychotherapy and presentations on various therapy approaches. I discuss the checklist in the context of the importance of empirically validating the techniques therapists employ in psychotherapy and address the special methodological problems in doing so.

The checklist consists of eight questions students should pose concerning any given study. What follows is a more detailed description of the checklist that can be incorporated into a corresponding lecture.

1. **What type of control group is used**? Control groups can vary from untreated waiting-list controls to more sophisticated minimal contact controls. The latter type of control group member attends a near-equivalent number of sessions and provides a control for the possibility that gains in the treated group are due to such nonspecific factors as attention and the opportunity to talk about one s problems. Consistent with ethical

guidelines, researchers provide treatment to the untreated groups at the end of the study or sooner.

2. **Do participants' expectancies vary between the control and treatment groups, or between treatment groups?** In studies comparing a control group to a treatment group or several treatment groups, researchers recognize the need to assess participants expectancies for change prior to the beginning of the study. Assessing expectancies for change is particularly important in studies comparing the efficacy of more than one treatment. If participants in one treatment group have more confidence in the treatment they receive, this could be a confound for any subsequent advantage they may show over other treatment groups at the completion of the study. Researchers often use pretreatment expectancies as a covariate in data analyses.

3. **Is treatment fidelity or integrity assessed?** This concept involves an assessment of the extent to which researchers adequately operationalize the treatment under study. Therapists adhere to extensive treatment manuals to provide the treatment in a standardized manner. Obviously, a null finding for a given treatment is meaningless if the researchers did not provide it in the proper way. Researchers often videotape a random sampling of therapy sessions and employ expert raters to judge the effectiveness of the implementation of the therapy.

4. **How long was the therapy program?** This question relates to treatment fidelity. Length of treatment ranged from 8 to 16 weeks ($M = 12.2$ weeks) in the studies reviewed.

5. **Were participants adequately diagnosed prior to the treatment?** Initial diagnosis of participants should include a multimethod approach. Various assessment methodologies include self-report measures of symptomatology, structured interviews, behavioral observation, and ratings by clinicians. Researchers should calculate indexes of interrater agreement for the latter measures (e.g., Cohen's Kappa).

6. **Were treatment gains evaluated over time?** Researchers typically assess participants on the dependent measures of interest at several intervals including pretreatment, immediately posttreatment, and at one or more follow-up periods (e.g., 3 months, 6 months, 1 year, etc.). Pretreatment assessment allows a determination of whether participants, indeed, carry the appropriate diagnosis and enables the researcher to block treatment and control participants on such dimensions as severity of disorder and various demographic measures. Follow-up assessments allow researchers to evaluate the durability of treatment gains.

7. **Are the results analyzed both in terms of statistical significance and clinical significance?** Common statistical analysis techniques include the calculation of Group (treatment group or groups vs. controls) × Time (pre-, post-, and follow-up assessments) analyses of variance or multivariate analyses of variance when using several related dependent measures in the assessment. Researchers determine the effectiveness of treatment by comparing each treated group to the untreated controls. By comparing treatment group means against each other, researchers evaluate the relative effectiveness of treatments. These kinds of comparisons are called *outcome analyses*. Such analyses focus on the statistical significance of group mean differences. Moreover, recent studies have begun to include comparisons of final treatment group means against norms on the various dependent measures derived from a "normal" sample of participants who were not a part of the treatment aspect of the study. This type of *normative analysis* evaluates the efficacy of the treatment in returning participants to a normal level of functioning. For example, a statistically significant reduction of 10 points in depression scores for a group of treated patients, leaving their mean score nearly identical to a group of nondepressed controls, is evidence of a clinically significant reduction in scores as well.

8. **Is the importance of treatment modality considered?** Some studies provide group treatment whereas some administer individual treatment. Researchers should examine the differential efficacy of format. For example, a therapy shown to be effective when provided individually may not be as effective in group format.

Evaluation and Suggested Uses

Students ($n = 12$) in my senior advanced topics course (focusing on psychotherapy outcome research) completed the checklist after reading most of the 16 psychotherapy outcome studies used to develop the checklist. They responded anonymously to questions (rated on a Likert scale ranging from 1 [*strongly disagree*] to 4 [*strongly agree*]) concerning the checklist's completeness, its usefulness in outlining key issues in psychotherapy outcome research, and whether the checklist had enhanced their understanding of the articles they had read. The means and standard deviations for rated completeness, usefulness, and enhancement of understanding were 3.17 ($SD = .39$), 3.58 ($SD = .52$), and 3.50 ($SD = .52$), respectively.

In addition to the appropriateness of presenting and discussing the psychotherapy outcome checklist in a variety of both undergraduate and graduate courses, it may also be beneficial to the professional in the field as a set of guidelines for evaluating studies relevant to practice. An additional use of the checklist is to have students apply it to media reports of treatment studies, including both psychological and medical reports as well as product evaluations. This use fits with the work of others who have developed techniques for encouraging students to apply principles of good research to media reports (e.g., Connor-Greene, 1993; Rider, 1992). Aside from simply using the checklist in a lecture-discussion format, several variations are possible. Students could be assigned one (or more) of the outcome studies listed in the Appendix (or a more recent study) and asked to evaluate it in light of the checklist as a writing assignment. The checklist would also form a good structure for essay exam or take-home assignments in clinically relevant courses. Another variation would be to have students generate their own checklists prior to introducing this one. This activity would highlight methodological issues in psychotherapy outcome research the student may not have thought co address.

A further elaboration on the use of the checklist would be to have students read Seligman's (1995) article outlining the virtues of larger scale survey research approaches such as *Consumer Reports'* ("Mental Health," 1995) reader survey of the effectiveness of psychotherapy. This assignment would provide a basis for a class discussion of the comparative advantages and disadvantages of the traditional experimental approach to outcome research and such survey approaches. Instructors could also assign additional readings from the recent special issue of *American Psychologist* (VandenBos, 1996) debating the relative merits of experimental versus survey methods for conducting therapy outcome studies (e.g., Jacobson & Christensen, 1996) and connecting outcome research to policy issues (e.g., Barlow, 1996; Newman & Tejeda, 1996).

In summary, the use of the checklist is an efficient way to highlight the special methodological problems of psychotherapy outcome research. Students find it helpful in summarizing the key issues in this type of research and report that it enhances their understanding of psychotherapy outcome research studies. The checklist's brevity enables its use in a variety of courses. Finally, the checklist serves to highlight the need to empirically validate treatments in the scientist-practitioner tradition.

References

Barlow, D. H. (1996). Health care policy, psychotherapy research, and the future of psychotherapy. *American Psychologist, 51,* 1050-1058.

Chambless, D. L., Sanderson, W. C., Shoham, V., Johnson, S. B., Pope, K. S., Crits-Cristoph, P., Baker, M., Johnson, B., Woody, S. R., Sue, S., Beutler, L, Williams, D. A., & McCurry, S. (1996). An update on empirically validated therapies. *The Clinical Psychologist, 49,* 5-18.

Connor-Greene, P. A. (1993). From the laboratory to the headlines: Teaching critical evaluation of press reports of research. *Teaching of Psychology, 20,* 167-169.

Coughlin, E. K. (1995, August 4). Psychotherapy besieged. *The Chronicle of Higher Education,* pp. A7, A12.

Jacobson, N. S., & Christensen, A. (1996). Studying the effectiveness of psychotherapy: How well can clinical trials do the job? *American Psychologist, 51,* 1031-1039.

Mental health: Does therapy help? (1995, November). *Consumer Reports, 60,* 734-739.

Newman, F. L., & Tejeda, M. J. (1996). The need for research that is designed to support decisions in the delivery of mental health services. *American Psychologist, 51,* 1040-1049.

Rider, E. A. (1992). Understanding and applying psychology through use of news clippings. *Teaching of Psychology, 19,* 161-163.

Seligman, M. E. P. (1995). The effectiveness of psychotherapy: The *Consumer Reports* study. *American Psychologist, 50,* 965-974.

Task Force on Promotion and Dissemination of Psychological Procedures, Division of Clinical Psychology, American Psychological Association. (1995). Training in and dissemination of empirically validated psychological treatments: Report and recommendations. *The Clinical Psychologist, 48,* 3-24.

VandenBos, G. R. (Ed.). (1996). Outcome assessment of psychotherapy [Special issue]. *American Psychologist, 51*(10).

Viken, R. J. (1992). Therapy evaluation: Using an absurd pseudotreatment to demonstrate research issues. *Teaching of Psychology, 19,* 108-110.

Appendix
Studies Reviewed in Developing Guidelines

Beck, J. G., Stanley, M. A., Baldwin, L. E., Deagle, E. A., III, & Averill, P. M. (1994). Comparison of cognitive therapy and relaxation training for panic disorder. *Journal of Consulting and Clinical Psychology, 62,* 818-826.

Borduin, C. M., Mann, B. J., Cone, L. T., Henggeler, S. W., Fucci, B. R., Blaske, D. M., & Williams, R. A. (1995). Multisystemic treatment of serious juvenile offenders: Long-term prevention of criminality and violence. *Journal of Consulting and Clinical Psychology, 63,* 569-578.

Ehlers, A., Stangier, U., & Geiler, U. (1995). Treatment of atopic dermatitis: A comparison of psychological and dermatological approaches to relapse prevention. *Journal of Consulting and Clinical Psychology, 63,* 624-635.

Fortmann, S. P., & Killen, J. D. (1995). Nicotine gum and self-help behavioral treatment for smoking relapse prevention: Results from a trial using population-based recruitment. *Journal of Consulting and Clinical Psychology*, *63*, 460-468.

Greene B., & Blanchard, E. B. (1994). Cognitive therapy for irritable bowel syndrome. *Journal of Consulting and Clinical Psychology, 62*, 576-582.

Jamison, C., & Scogin, F. (1995). The outcome of cognitive bibliotherapy with depressed adults. *Journal of Consulting and Clinical Psychology, 63*, 644-650.

Jeffery, R. W., Wing, R. R., Thorson, C., Burton, L. R., Raether, C., Harvey, J., & Mullen, M. (1993). Strengthening behavioral interventions for weight loss: A randomized trial of food provision and monetary incentives. *Journal of Consulting and Clinical Psychology, 61*, 1038-1045.

Kendall, P. C. (1994). Treating anxiety disorders in children: Results of a randomized clinical trial. *Journal of Consulting and Clinical Psychology, 62*, 100-110.

Laberge, B., Gauthier, J. G., Cote, G., Plamondon, J., & Cormier, H. J. (1993). Cognitive-behavioral therapy of panic disorder with secondary major depression: A preliminary investigation. *Journal of Consulting and Clinical Psychology, 61*, 1028-1037.

Lochman, J. E., Coie, J. D., Underwood, M. K., & Terry, R. (1993). Effectiveness of a social relations intervention program for aggressive and nonaggressive, rejected children. *Journal of Consulting and Clinical Psychology, 61*, 1053-1058.

Monti, P. M., Rohsenow, D. J., Rubonis, A. V., Niaura, R. S., Sirota, A. D., Colby, S. M., Goddard, P., & Abrams, D. B. (1993). Cue exposure with coping skills treatment for male alcoholics: A preliminary

investigation. *Journal of Consulting and Clinical Psychology, 61*, 1011-1019.

Rosen, J. C., Reiter, J., & Orosan, P. (1995). Cognitive-behavioral body image therapy for body dysmorphic disorder. *Journal of Consulting and Clinical Psychology, 63*, 263-269.

Stephens, R. S., Roffman, R. A., & Simpson, E. E. (1994). Treating adult marijuana dependence: A test of the relapse model. *Journal of Consulting and Clinical Psychology, 62*, 92-99.

Stolberg, A. L., & Mahler, J. (1994). Enhancing treatment gains in a school-based intervention for children of divorce through skill training, parental involvement, and transfer procedures. *Journal of Consulting and Clinical Psychology, 62*, 147-156.

Turner, S. M., Beidel, D. C., & Jacob, R. G. (1994). Social phobia: A comparison of behavior therapy and atenolol. *Journal of Consulting and Clinical Psychology, 62*, 350-358.

Wadden, T. A., Foster, G. D., & Letizia, K. A. (1994). One-year behavioral treatment of obesity: Comparison of moderate and severe caloric restriction and the effects of weight maintenance therapy. *Journal of Consulting and Clinical Psychology, 62*, 165-171.

Note

I thank the editor and three anonymous reviewers for their helpful comments on an earlier draft of this article.

Therapy Evaluation: Using an Absurd Pseudotreatment to Demonstrate Research Issues

Richard J. Viken
Indiana University

Instructors of abnormal psychology, clinical psychology, and psychotherapy courses face a special problem in conveying course material. Research-based information must compete with inaccurate but skillfully packaged information from the media and from commercial interests that market fad treatments in the form

of books, audiotapes, individual therapy, and various technologies. There are effective, validated techniques for behavior change (Garfield & Bergin, 1986), but students also face an array of unsubstantiated interventions that purport to be effective for depression, low self-esteem, procrastination, social anxiety, fatigue, smoking, and weight loss. Support for the efficacy of these approaches often comes from the testimony of developers, therapists, and former clients or from an appeal to common sense. Personal testimony and common sense do not provide a valid basis for therapy evaluation, and the efficacy of psychological interventions cannot be established without systematic research (Garfield & Bergin, 1986; McFall, in press; Smith, 1980).

Most textbooks for clinical courses include discussions of appropriate research strategies. In the face of a daily barrage of misinformation, however, the memorization of abstract principles of research design is unlikely to have a lasting impact on student judgment. It is important to find effective methods for conveying research information, because a class in abnormal psychology or psychotherapy is often our only opportunity to teach undergraduates how to be informed consumers in the psychological marketplace.

In most areas of psychology, abstract principles can be taught through laboratory demonstrations that provide concrete illustrations of basic psychological principles. However, it is difficult to construct demonstrations of critical thinking and research principles in clinical psychology, and only a few such techniques (e.g., Rabinowitz, 1989; Ward & Grasha, 1986) have been reported. This article describes a demonstration designed to provide students with a classroom experience in one important area of clinical psychology: therapy outcome evaluation.

The Demonstration

Students are informed that the class will engage in a demonstration of issues important in therapy evaluation. They are told that the demonstration will (a) be based on an absurd pseudotreatment invented by the instructor and pseudosymptoms that are really just normal variations in behavior, and (b) illustrate issues found in evaluation of real treatments for real problems.

Most instructors of clinical courses will already have discussed what students should do if they become concerned about symptoms or problems that are presented in the course. Although students have never reported concerns arising from this demonstration, please take this precaution. Students are free to participate or not, and they keep their own data, turning them in anonymously at the end of the demonstration. I have conducted this demonstration in four classes and have found that over 95% of the students participate.

On the first day of the demonstration, participating students make self-ratings of: (a) their mood in the last 24 hr, ranging from *happiest they have ever been* (100) *to saddest thew have ever been* (1), with 50 representing *average mood*; and (b) their food consumption during the last 24 hr ranging from *most food ever consumed in 24 hours (100)* to *no food consumed* (1), with 50 representing *average food consumption*.

The treatment is administered in the next class period. I use a treatment that I call "Norwegian acupuncture" (a reference to my ethnic background), in which students press their left elbows with their right forefingers and solemnly repeat the words *Det er ikke gull alt som glimrer* (All that glitters is not gold). Instructors should modify the title and the treatment to enhance personal interest for themselves or their students. Any manifestly ridiculous treatment will do. To maintain the integrity of the "experimental design," there is no discussion at this point.

One week after the first ratings (a few days after the treatment), students rate their posttreatment food consumption and mood, recording them on the same paper used in the pretreatment ratings. I collect the anonymous food and mood ratings and select for analysis the pretreatment scores composing the bottom 10% of the mood ratings and the top and bottom 10% of the food ratings. These extreme pretreatment scores are paired with the posttreatment scores for the same people. Then, we have groups defined by the lowest pretreatment mood scores as well as the lowest and highest pretreatment food scores. A typical plot of the mean pretreatment and posttreatment scores for the three groups is presented in Figure 1.

The figure illustrates the substantial changes in food and mood ratings for these groups following treatment by Norwegian acupuncture. The sad people get happier, the overeaters eat less, and the undereaters eat more. In each of four classes, the changes from Time 1 to Time 2 in the low-mood, low-food, and high-food groups were statistically significant as judged by paired t tests. Absolute change scores for the group means have ranged from 14 to 30. Means and variances of the population (i.e., the class) generally did not differ significantly from Time 1 to Time 2, allowing evaluation of absolute change effects. On one occasion, the population mean for mood was significantly higher at Time 2. Under these circumstances, the data can be mean corrected, allowing evaluation of regression effects relative to the Time 1 and Time 2 means.

In a class discussion, the Norwegian acupuncture treatment is evaluated using the standard criteria of effectiveness—generalizability, cost, side effects, acceptability to client, and ease of maintaining compliance. We establish that an effective treatment should make sad people happier. It should make the people who are eating too much eat less and the people who are eating too little eat more. Using the figure, I demonstrate that my treatment is associated with all of these changes. Thus, we have a treatment that is effective, inexpensive, fast, has no negative side effects, and generalizes to at least two problem areas (in fact, to any symptom that varies week by week). It even has opposite but correct therapeutic effects for two extreme eating patterns. What do students make of these findings? Do they believe in this treatment? What could have gone wrong with our evaluation?

Students want to disprove Norwegian acupuncture because it is absurd and because they are certain that it could not have affected the class in the manner suggested by the figure. At this point, they begin to recall (or reinvent) standard research design issues. Hypotheses that are eventually rejected include placebo effects (it is important to use a very silly treatment), demand, maturation or other general trends, differential dropout, experimenter bias, and external events. The remaining possibility is a regression effect. Regression effects are a persistent source of errors in clinical judgment by researchers, practitioners, and consumers (Campbell & Stanley, 1963; Dawes, 1986; Kahneman & Tversky, 1973).

Avoiding any statistical treatment of the regression phenomenon, I point out that mood and food consumption fluctuate over time, and I draw a vaguely sinusoidal pattern on the board to illustrate. Students readily recognize that if they choose an extreme point, such as very sad mood, nearly all of the later points will be less extreme. The same fluctuations are characteristic of most of the symptoms for which people seek help from fad treatments. Because people are most likely to seek help when they are at a negative extreme, they will, on average, tend to feel better after the therapy. For this reason, absolutely useless treatments will often be judged to be beneficial by patients, therapists, and researchers using simple pre-post designs.

Students can now return to the abstract principles of research design that they learned in their text and use them to design a study (they usually choose a waiting list or placebo control) to prove that Norwegian acupuncture has no effect. The focus of the remaining discussion is on the reasons why common sense, pre-post designs, or testimony by therapists and patients are never sufficient to establish the efficacy of psychological interventions.

Evaluation

One month after the demonstration, students (N = 84) were asked to respond to the following statements on a scale ranging from *strongly agree* (1) to *strongly disagree* (5): (a) I learned more about the problems of therapy evaluation from the class demonstration than I did from reading about them or hearing a lecture about them (*M* = 1.3), and (b) I remember more about the problems of therapy evaluation from the class demonstration than I do from the readings or lectures (*M* = 1.7). On the same scale, students were asked whether the class demonstration was useful (*M* = 1.8), enjoyable (*M* = 2.0), interesting (*M* = 1.9), or a waste of time (*M* = 4.3). More informally, the utility of the demonstration has been reflected in the fact that students often use this example in discussing the conclusions of studies covered later in the semester. A few students also bring in examples of therapies described in the popular press for which regression effects or other confounds represent the most parsimonious explanation for therapeutic "success."

References

Campbell, D. T., & Stanley, S. C. (1963). *Experimental and quasiexpenmental designs for research.* Chicago: Rand McNally.

Dawes, R. M. (1986). Representative thinking in clinical judgment. *Clinical Psychology Review, 6,* 425-441.

Garfield, S. L., & Bergin, A. E. (Eds.). (1986). *Handbook of psychotherapy and behavior change* (3rd ed.). New York: Wiley.

Kahneman, D., & Tversky, A. (1973). On the psychology of prediction. *Psychological Review, 80,* 237-251.

McFall, R. M. (in press). Manifesto for a science of clinical psychology. *The Clinical Psychologist.*

Rabinowitz, F. E. (1989). Creating the multiple personality: An experiential demonstration for an undergraduate abnormal psychology class. *Teaching of Psychology, 16,* 69-71.

Smith, M. L. (1980). Integrating studies of psychotherapy outcomes. *New Directions for Methodology of Social and Behavioral Science, 5,* 47-60.

Ward, R. A., & Grasha, A. F. (1986). Using astrology to teach research methods to introductory psychology students. *Teaching of Psychology, 13,* 143-145.

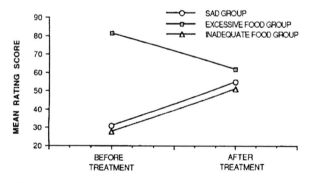

Figure 1. Change in mood and food ratings following treatment.

SECTION IV:
SOCIAL

Focusing on Experimentation

Sandra Carpenter helped students examine societal trends in stereotyping by engaging them in a content analysis research project. Students identified a research problem, then collected data from sources such as music videos and magazines. This process enabled students to learn a variety of methodological concepts without the requirement of sophisticated technology. It also sensitized them to the ways that the media portray ethnic and minority groups.

Neil Lutsky devised a research paradigm for use in undergraduate laboratory experiments in social psychology. Students compared the responses of control subjects on a survey question to those of experimental subjects who had been exposed to contrived responses of another person to the same question. This methodology allowed the students to extend the scope of their studies to topics such as social comparison, impression management, and self-persuasion.

Daniel Wann asked groups of students in an undergraduate social psychology class to select two interesting experiments and develop a dramatic script to describe the research. Students located the props necessary to implement the experiment and performed the play for the class. Students enjoyed the exercise and believed it enhanced their learning and interest in psychological research.

Diane Symbaluk and Judy Cameron used a replication of Asch's (1946) and Kelley's (1950) classic studies on impression formation to help students learn about the process of conducting research. The technique involved the students in all aspects of research including collecting data and data analysis.

In the Laboratory in Social Psychology course, David Sattler, Sudie Back, and Harriet Pollitt asked students to design and implement an exit survey of graduating psychology majors. Students learned many aspects of survey research including choice of topics to measure, item wording, administration procedures, and data analysis. The activity also benefited the department in its development of an exit survey for graduating seniors.

Emphasizing Writing and Literature

Sara Snodgrass described several ways she facilitated students' writing in an introductory social psychology course. Students kept a journal, wrote analyses of published articles, implemented an observational study, and wrote a formal research report. The techniques

described in this article can be applied to any course in psychology.

In a journal writing activity, Stuart Miller asked students to apply social psychological concepts to specific experiences in their lives. Evidence suggested that students gained significant self-knowledge as a result of the exercise.

Don Osborn used the utopian novel, *Erewhon*, to illustrate a variety of social psychological concepts and to enhance the liberal arts value of his social psychology course. The novel afforded numerous examples of social psychological concepts such as attribution theory, interpersonal attraction, and the motivation for consistency between actions and attitudes. The author gave several helpful tips to instructors who might wish to adopt a similar strategy.

Illustrating Concepts in Social Perception and Social Cognition

Juli Eflin and Mary Kite gave students a series of premises and conclusions on index cards and asked them to construct an Inference to the Best Explanation (IBE), a type of inductive reasoning. Students constructed the IBEs by combining the premises and conclusions that each possessed on the index cards. This activity improved students' scientific reasoning by focusing attention on the causal, explanatory nature of psychological theories.

Francis McAndrew asked students to grade exam papers of fictitious students. The patterns of responses on the "exams" reflected either an ascending or descending level of performance. Students expressed a significant primacy effect in the way they evaluated the intelligence and performance of the test taker. The exercise facilitated discussion of key issues related to experimental design and attribution theory.

Michael White and Debra Lilly presented Kelley's (1973) covariation attribution model by showing students videotaped behavior rather than the more traditional written descriptions. The videotape contained sets of sequentially presented behavioral situations that led students to analyze behavior using Kelley's model. Students easily made the appropriate attributions and applied them to everyday situations.

Donelson Forsyth and Katherine Wibberly developed an effective demonstration of the self-reference effect, which occurs when individuals show superior memory for information that pertains to their self-schemas. Students evaluated whether or not each adjective in an orally presented list was self-descriptive. After a delay, they attempted to recall all the adjectives from the list. Memory for self-referent terms was superior to memory for terms that were not self-referent. The authors suggested that the exercise offered an effective demonstration of schematic processing under normal classroom conditions and confirmed predictions derived from depth-of-processing and schema-based memory models of social cognition.

Su Boatright-Horowitz developed a demonstration of Nuttin's (1985) *name letter effect* for use in the classroom. Students organized themselves into pairs with one "experimenter" and one "subject." Experimenters measured the subjects' preferences for letters of the alphabet, some of which were contained in the subjects' name. Results indicated that subjects showed a preference for letters contained in their names which replicates the *name letter effect*.

In order to demonstrate the over justification effect, Harry Hom gave students descriptions of Lepper, Greene, and Nisbett's (1973) research and asked them to predict the outcome of the various conditions. Students predicted the outcome of the conditions quite poorly and this promoted discussion of these counterintuitive effects.

Joy Berrenberg demonstrated several impression formation principles by asking students to bring photographs of an acquaintance to class, having other students relate their first impressions of the persons in the photos, and assessing the accuracy of those impressions. The exercise gave students an opportunity to examine their own impression-formation processes. This activity can illustrate other processes such as the origins of implicit personality theories, person prototypes, and the accuracy of first impressions.

Robin Lashley asked her students to complete a simple personality inventory about their instructor. The student responses served as discussion points that illustrated several social psychological concepts such as stereotypes, impression formation, actor-observer bias, and implicit personality theory.

Demonstrating Bias in Social Perception and Social Cognition

Mary Kite outlined three activities that demonstrated common perceptual errors described in the social psychological literature; the actor-observer effect, the false consensus bias, and priming effects. These activities produced reliable and robust results and demonstrated how cognitive shortcuts can result in inaccurate judgments.

To demonstrate the social desirability bias in survey research, Randall Gordon administered a questionnaire to students to assess their oral hygiene practices. The method used to reduce subjects' response bias involved a manipulation of the questionnaire's instructions. Both instructions asked subjects to respond but not to sign their names. The modified instructions also contained information such as the assurance of anonymity, the need for accurate information, and the role of the subject as a

contributor of valuable information. The results of the two forms of questionnaires differed as a function of instructions.

George Demakis used the Simpson criminal trial as a vehicle to demonstrate the hindsight bias. Some students made pre-verdict predictions about the outcome of the trial and others made post-verdict judgments of what they would have predicted before the verdict. Students exhibited considerable hindsight bias. Demakis suggested that this technique could be used for a wide variety of events (e.g., athletic contests and elections).

C. R. Snyder demonstrated the unique invulnerability effect in a simple demonstration in which students were told the average longevity for persons in the U.S. and then asked to predict their own age of death. In two classes, students overestimated their age of death by nine years, even though the second class had been informed that the demonstration would show their sense of unique invulnerability.

Dana Dunn asked students in a social psychology class to list their strengths and weaknesses. The exercise generated a self-serving attributional bias, that is, students' self-descriptions revealed a bias toward reporting positive attributes. The instructor used this bias to guide a discussion about motivational and cognitive processes in attribution.

James Friedrich designed a simple demonstration of the self-serving bias by asking students to rate either the likelihood that they would rate themselves as better than average or that the average person would do so. Consistent with the self-serving bias, students rated themselves to be less likely to rate themselves above average if, in fact, they were not. This effect existed even though the self-serving bias had been thoroughly explained to the students prior to the demonstration.

Teaching about Attitudes and Persuasion

David Carkenord and Joseph Bullington induced cognitive dissonance in students by pointing out inconsistencies between their behaviors and attitudes. The procedure assessed students attitudes on four issues (e.g., world hunger) after which they publicly proclaimed their adherence to the expressed attitudes. Students believed the experience enhanced their understanding of cognitive dissonance and provided selfinsight.

To help students identify major persuasion techniques employed in advertisements, Vivian Makosky used several activities that required students to locate and analyze prototypical examples. Students collected the advertisements according to four different variations developed by the author.

D. W. Rajecki asked students to rate the desirability of a snack that was progressively contaminated by contact with human residues (the instructor's coffee cup and a comb). Repeated measurements showed progressive contamination. The students' ratings revealed quick and statistically reliable shifts from accepting (liking) to rejecting (disliking) the snack. The author listed several courses that could benefit from this demonstration including research methods, learning, and motivation.

Exploring Aggression

To introduce the concept of aggression, Ludy Benjamin gave descriptions of several incidents (e.g., a spider eats a fly or a girl kicks a wastebasket) to students and asked them to determine if the incidents constituted aggression. The activity generated discussion about the definition of aggression and related issues of causation and control. It also provided a context for discussion about disagreements among psychologists on the operationalization of variables.

Dana Dunn's students read the 1932 "Why War?" correspondence between Albert Einstein and Sigmund Freud and composed letters responding to the letter. This assignment allowed students to explore several perspectives about the origins and functions of human aggression. The author described additional variations for the exercise.

William Davidson gave his social psychology students a list of 12 aggression instigators and asked them to find scenes of violence in movies that illustrated the effects of these instigators. Students attempted to find a scene that included the maximum number of instigators. The student who found the scene with the most instigators received bonus points on the exam that covered aggression.

David Rainey devised a simple method to demonstrate a gender difference in the acceptance of aggressive behavior during sport competition. Students read descriptions of behaviors from six sport competition situations and judged those behaviors as acceptable or unacceptable. Men endorsed significantly more aggressive acts than did women. The author examined several significant issues to guide classroom discussion.

Examining Group Processes

Blaine Peden, Allen Keniston, and David Burke gave students direct experience with the tensions that exist between outcomes based on individual versus collective decision-making. Based upon two different protocols, students chose to receive bonus points on their exams. One protocol required them to choose between one sure point or the possibility of a randomly determined zero to eight points; the second protocol required students to make a choice that was linked to the choices made by the entire class. The experience helped students learn more about psychology and scientific values; it also provided personal insight into their own decision-making strategies.

Janet Larsen used two classroom demonstrations based on the prisoner's dilemma to illustrate elements of decision making. The demonstrations required minimal preparation and allowed the entire class to participate. In one demonstration, students asked for $1.00 or 10¢, with the proviso that, if more than 20% of the class asked for $1.00, no one got anything. The second demonstration involved students in an iterated prisoner's dilemma game. The scores earned by students reflected their strategies to behave either cooperatively or competitively.

Helen Harton, Laura Green, Craig Jackson, and Bibb Latané designed an activity that demonstrated several group dynamics principles. Students discussed their answers to a short multiple choice quiz with their neighbors and then answered them again. The discussion consistently led to outcomes predicted by social impact theory.

Marianne Miserandino devised a classroom activity in which students surveyed peers' attitudes toward a target behavior and variations of it. Responses for each question were compiled and graphed. Results illustrated the group's approval and disapproval of the target behavior, the strength of the approval or disapproval, the ideal behavior, and the range of tolerable behavior. The activity increased students' understanding and appreciation of survey research and the power of a peer-group norm.

Teaching about Spatial and Nonverbal Behavior

In a demonstration of the regulatory nature of personal space, Bryan Gibson, Paul Harris, and Carol Werner asked students to note the behavior of a partner who was asked to relate a personally intimate experience (e.g., describe your first kiss or most embarrassing moment). Although participants were not required to follow through on the instructions to relate the personal event, they displayed many behaviors that characterized attempts to regulate intimacy with their partner (e.g., lack of eye contact, and turning or moving away from the partner). The demonstration allowed students to see that personal space is one of several interacting nonverbal cues people use to regulate intimacy.

Students in Richard Ferraro's introductory psychology class designed and implemented simple field experiments to test hypotheses about personal space violations. The exercise culminated in classroom presentations of the results and submission of APA style manuscripts describing the experimental procedures. Students believed the exercise was more valuable than lectures on the same topics.

James Grosch and John Sparrow demonstrated lie detection, a topic that most students find fascinating, using an inexpensive, highly portable galvanic skin response monitor. The demonstration, which took only 10 min per student, stimulated discussion about various methods used to detect deception. The authors concluded that students in a wide variety of courses such as perception, physiological, and industrial/organizational psychology could benefit from this exercise.

Donna Desforges and Thomas Lee designed an activity that allowed students to experience the difference between cues from perceived and actual deception. Students viewed classmates telling the truth and lying and then judged their truthfulness. Students' judgments indicated that deception detection was accurate less than 50% of the time. Instructors used this outcome to stimulate discussion about the difference between perceived and actual cues of deception.

Mark Costanzo and Dane Archer used The Interpersonal Perception Task, consisting of a videotape of 30 brief scenes, to illustrate the complexity of verbal and nonverbal cues. Viewers answered questions about the people in the videos by decoding the verbal and nonverbal cues in the scenes. Using this technique, the instructors highlighted the subtlety and complexity of communication cues, taught about specific cues to accuracy, demonstrated the relative importance of communication channels, and helped students understand the process of interpretation.

Examining Stereotypes of Gender and Race

Randall Gordon developed a demonstration to introduce the concept of stereotypes and their measurement. The demonstration relied on a diagnostic ratio measure of stereotypes developed in previous research. The author outlined the results of the demonstration along with suggestions for discussing several stereotype formation concepts.

Susan Goldstein taught students a lesson about stereotyping by attaching labels with specific traits to their foreheads and asking them to interact with one another. The one restriction was that they treat each other according to the traits. After a period of interaction, students attempted to guess the trait attached to their foreheads and discussed the relevance of the exercise to concepts in social perception.

Hilary Lips turned to science fiction novels as a vehicle to promote critical thinking about gender roles. Students read novels such as Ursula K. LeGuin's *The Left Hand of Darkness* and Marge Piercy's *Woman at the Edge of Time*. Significant classroom discussion related the content of the novel with current societal norms and students were encouraged to speculate about how the "alternative" worlds would affect our conceptions of such concepts as family and marriage.

In several classes, Melinda Jones projected slides of advertisements from current magazines and from magazines published in the 1950s. The classes analyzed the gender bias in the advertisements using criteria from previous research. The advertisements showed significant gender stereotyping. This exercise is suitable for a variety of classes in addition to social psychology (e.g., psychology of women, introductory, or consumer psychology).

To understand the content and function of gender stereotypes, Mary Crawford asked students to read a typical Harlequin-style romance novel. Students then wrote a paper analyzing the novel's approach to femininity, masculinity, love, and relationships. Students also attempted to explain why women write and read novels of this genre. Later, students used their graded papers as resources for a class discussion.

Michelle Hebl designed an elegant demonstration of sex bias in leader selection by asking students in mixed-sex groups (two men, two women) to choose a leader. Some groups expected to engage in a task-oriented competitive activity while other expected to engage in a social cooperative activity. Task oriented groups that stressed competition overwhelmingly selected men as leaders, but social cooperative groups selected men and women equally. The activity led to discussion about the causes and consequences of gender stereotyping.

Harriette Richard's students learned about the development of racial identity by analyzing characters in literature or film with one of two formal models of racial identity. Students wrote short papers outlining their analyses and gave 10 min oral presentations to the class. Overall, students believed that the project provided important insights into the development of racial identity.

Sandra Lawrence engaged students in an exercise in which they constructed mobiles from materials provided by the instructor. Some groups of students received elaborate packets of raw materials while others received packets with meager amounts of raw materials. Students in both groups realized the potential effects of "privilege" on performance and emotional reactions as reflected in their written conclusions at the end of the activity.

Thomas Ford, Robert Grossman, and Elizabeth Jordan used a case study of an African-American student in a predominately White institution as a vehicle for discussion about unintentional racism. Class discussions centered around definitions of racism and concepts such as the fundamental attribution error were introduced. The instructors also presented tips for moderating discussions of racism and data that suggested this technique increases student awareness of subtle racism.

Integrating Social Psychology and Personality

Melinda Jones helped students gain an appreciation for the impact of dispositions on social behavior. Students completed the Self-Monitoring Scale, viewed several advertisements, and rated the effectiveness of each advertisement. The activity illustrated that high self-monitors tended to be more responsive to advertisements that appealed to the image of a product, whereas low self-monitors tended to be more responsive to advertisements that make claims about the quality of a product.

Miri Goldstein's students accessed the personal home pages of social psychologists on the World Wide Web and formed Implicit Personality Theories (IPTs) based on the information contained on the pages. They also designed their own home pages and speculated about the possible

IPTs conveyed by their pages. The exercise proved to be an excellent way to relate IPT to impression formation.

Jeffry Simpson developed a way to demonstrate the interaction between personality dispositions and a significant social behavior. Students completed and scored a self-monitoring scale and a dating survey. The instructor provided instructions for classifying the students (e.g., high vs. low self-monitors and exclusive vs. multiple daters). Results revealed that self-monitoring orientation was meaningfully related to commitment in dating relationships. Specifically, high self-monitors tended to adopt an uncommitted orientation to dating relationships, whereas low self-monitors tended to adopt a committed one.

Examining Miscellaneous Issues

Richard Sherman promoted active learning and application of social psychology by assigning students several World Wide Web (Web) assignments. In one assignment, he introduced the topics of attitudes and persuasion by having students access the Web pages of political parties and candidates and identify or evaluate the persuasion principles used on those pages.

David Dodd deindividuated students by asking them to list the things they would do if assured that they would not be caught or held responsible for their actions. The majority of the responses fell into antisocial and nonnormative categories. The activity helped students understand the concept of deindividuation in a personally relevant manner. An interesting sidelight to this article was that the author found no response differences between prison and campus classes.

1. FOCUSING ON EXPERIMENTATION

Content Analysis Project for Research Novices

Sandra Carpenter
The University of Alabama, Huntsville

How are young African American men portrayed in rap videos ? One of my African American students, using content analysis, found aggression and materialism to be the most prevalent characteristics portrayed. In a social psychology course, I assign a content analysis research project to document stereotypes portrayed in the media. This project requires no sophisticated technology, but teaches novices, through iterative feedback, to do psychological research. In content analysis, a researcher examines artifacts (e.g., words, visual images, the use of color) for the occurrence of particular categories or events. For example, to determine attitudes and conceptualizations of lesbians, students could analyze televised and textual materials, rather than using the more typical survey approach that is fraught with problems due to nonprobability sampling, small sample sizes, poorly constructed questions, and time invested in data gathering. Similar to other psychological research designs, systematic observation and clearly operationalized variables are of integral importance. Unlike other research designs, the content analysis methodology allows students to test societal-level hypotheses without collecting or analyzing massive amounts of data. For example, the media tend to reflect certain trends in the culture (e.g., attitudes toward and representations of certain groups), then portray these as representations of "truth" (Merriam & Makower, 1988). Students in my course test the hypothesis that societal stereotypes of a group coincide with the ways in which the media portrays members of the group. Students first perform a literature search to identify a socially held stereotype, then ascertain whether the stereotype characteristics can be found at a higher rate than nonstereotypic characteristics in the media.

Most students have neither encountered nor used content analysis prior to their experiences in my course. Therefore, I discuss content analysis methodology many times during the course of the semester, and students undertake this project in four stages. At each stage, students submit written documents, which I return with feedback prior to their undertaking the next stage of the project. I show current students excellent products generated by previous students (in my course, I use the poster format for project presentation). This display provides a schema for students' thinking about their own projects, in terms of both procedure and product. I refer students who want additional information about content analysis methodology to Krippendorff (1980). In the description that follows, I focus on the components of a content analysis that differ from the typical study in which persons are the unit of analysis. I have designed the project to help students develop particular research skills through the completion of certain tasks. The stages of this project, along with the associated tasks and research skills, are delineated in Table 1.

Table 1. Content Analysis Project: Tasks and Research Skills Associated With Each Stage

Stage	Task	Research Skill
1	Literature search	Identify research problem
	Hypothesis generation	Specify predicted relationships
2	Medium selection	Identify sampling of the medium
	Coding category development	Specify definitions of characteristics
	Unit of analysis selection	Indicate sampling structure of the medium
3	Data collection specification	Delineate procedure for observation
	Coding sheet design	Develop matrix for frequency counts
	Data analysis proposal	Indicate data summaries and comparisons
4	Limitations description	Provide external validity assessment
	Implications–speculation	Derive possible outcomes from data pattern

Project Stages

Students' first tasks are to locate a journal article on stereotypes in the media and to generate a specific hypothesis that they can realistically test. I stress that connection of the analysis to theoretical, empirical, or applied issues is essential (Holsti, 1969). I evaluate Stage 1 products in terms of the relevance of the hypothesis to the journal article (which is attached to the hypothesis) and of the clarity and specificity of the hypothesis.

In Stage 2, students design a method to test the hypothesis, supplying specific information about the proposed medium, details about the sample, and a description of the procedure to collect data. Students may use any printed or recorded medium for analysis. For example, students interested in gender stereotypes may analyze sexuality in the portrayals of women and men in music videos. Students interested in portrayals of African Americans or Asians may document the incidence and characterizations of members of these groups in children's textbooks.

When describing the medium they will use, students indicate what they will analyze: how many television commercials, what time of day, which television channel. Prior to this stage, we discuss various sampling techniques in class. Students initially define the universe of materials that they could analyze, then describe and justify the procedure they will use to sample from that universe (e.g., random, accidental, representative, influential). I urge students to choose their sample carefully and to acquire a sufficiently large sample.

Students also generate the coding categories they will use in the content analysis. Prior to this task, we discuss, in class, the types of categories that may best test the hypothesis. Categories must reflect the purpose of the study and be mutually exclusive (Holsti, 1969). As an example, one student expected the media would portray women as more passive and men as more aggressive. She developed a specific set of rules for determining the presence of these characteristics in magazine advertisements.

Students must also indicate the unit of analysis they plan to use. Holsti (1969) referred to this element of material analyzed as the "recording unit." Is a particular woman in a music video passive if she exhibits one passive behavior, or should all her passive behaviors be counted? Is the entire video classified as aggressive if one aggressive action occurs? In some cases, the context also needs to be recorded. Would a smile be interpreted similarly in the context of an unexpected meeting with a previous lover as it would be in the context of watching another person ridiculed? Students sometimes modify the details of their hypotheses at this stage to better match the actual methodology they decide to undertake.

In Stage 3, students delineate their proposal for data collection and summary. Students often show me their coding sheets to obtain feedback about the practicality for use during data collection as well as ease of transfer for data analysis. If the medium is movies or television, I suggest that students use videotape, in case they miss something the first time. During class, we discuss the advantages of having multiple coders for interobserver reliability purposes. I urge, but do not require, students to elicit the cooperation of a volunteer research partner for categorization. Students must describe the data analysis they plan to use before collecting the data—to best match collection, coding, and analysis. Many students have no statistical training, so they typically calculate descriptive statistics. Students with more training may opt to utilize inferential statistics. Students represent their data either in graphic or table format. I spend time during class indicating how and when to use each type of descriptive

statistic and pictorial representation (e.g., bar graphs rather than line graphs for categorical variables).

In Stage 4, students address theoretical issues of external validity. They critique their methodology and state implications of the results. Critiques could include references to the sample used (e.g., only certain magazines of certain years), the coding criteria, and the choice for measurement of the hypothetical constructs. When stating implications of the study, students discuss what the obtained stereotypic portrayals indicate about cultural representations of the groups being studied and what consequences these portrayals may have on the medium's consumers.

Student Response to the Project

Students' open-ended, spontaneous comments indicate positive responses to the project. "Doing the [content analysis] poster was more enjoyable than writing a paper—a good experience," "I appreciated the fact that the parts were turned in separately for your comments instead of all at once," "The project was good because it was both educational and fun. I feel that is much easier to internalize ideas when we have some kind of positive hands-on experience."

In addition, I designed the project to develop particular skills. Students from two social psychology classes ($N = 32$) evaluated the content analysis project using a 5 point, Likert-type scale, ranging from 1 (*strongly disagree*) to 5 (*strongly agree*). I interpreted ratings of 4 or 5 on this scale (i.e., *agree* or *strongly agree*), in response to the statement "This project significantly developed my research skills" (for example), as agreement that significant development had occurred. The percentages of students who agreed that significant development had occurred were: knowledge development, 88%; analytic skill development, 91%; research skill development, 91%; and organizational skill development, 82%. Students also rated whether the project was a good measure of these skills. I anticipated that these ratings would be lower than those already cited; students may perceive few assessments to be good measures of their skills. However, it is valuable to know whether students perceive an evaluative measure to be valid. Again, I interpreted ratings of 4 or 5 (i.e., *agree* or *strongly agree*) as indicating agreement that the project provided good measures of students' skills. Percentages of students who perceived the content analysis to be a good evaluation tool were: measure of analytic skill, 81%; measure of research skill, 78%; and measure of organizational skill, 88%. Thus, the majority of students valued the project in terms of both skill development and evaluation.

Conclusions

As noted previously, students in my course present their research using a poster format, although a content analysis also lends itself to written or oral presentation. This content analysis project is equally effective in a 6-week summer course and a more traditional 14-week semester. The step-wise structure of the project allows for successful completion of each stage of the project in even a restricted time span. Successful completion of each stage virtually ensures a successful final product, such that a persistent student is rewarded (i.e., a good paper, a high grade). An additional pedagogical advantage of the content analysis project is that it is unlikely to overlap with observational projects assigned in other psychology courses (e.g., coding children's play behavior in developmental psychology). However, the content analysis may also be relevant to other psychology courses—analysis of formal versus informal conversations (psycholinguistics course), analysis of language used by schizophrenics (abnormal psychology course), or idiographic analysis of personal constructs used in letters (personality course). Thus, psychology faculty may tailor the content analysis project to fit their own instructional needs. Furthermore, those who teach cross-listed or interdisciplinary courses, in which such a level of analysis is appropriate or necessary, may find a content analysis to be a valuable research tool for students to acquire.

References

Holsti, O. R (1969). *Content analysis for the social sciences and humanities.* Reading, MA: Addison Wesley.

Krippendorff, K. (1980). *Content analysis: An introduction to its methodology.* Beverly Hills, CA: Sage.

Merriam, J. E., & Makower, J., (1988). *Trend watching: How the media create trends and how to be the first to uncover them.* New York: AMACOM.

A Scheme and Variations for Studies of Social Influence in an Experimental Social Psychology Laboratory

Neil Lutsky
Carleton College

How may undergraduates learn more about the significance and complexities of social influence? One means is to have students design and complete experimental studies based on a method that reliably demonstrates social influence. In this article, I review such a research paradigm for student experiments on social influence in a social psychology laboratory course.

The General Design of the Laboratory

The laboratory introduces the literatures, findings, logic, and methods of experimental social psychology by actively involving students in the planning, execution, and evaluation of research. The laboratory's approach is similar to Chamberlain's (1988). For each of four topics addressed (social influence, person perception, cognitive dissonance, and helping behavior), students discuss an assigned target article, identify factors that may have affected the research outcome reported in the article, generate possible explanations for the results, and consider how issues and ideas they have raised could be explored in research using a method similar to that presented in the target article. I guide this discussion and comment on why particular designs may be more or less tractable and meet or fail to meet the ethical standards that govern research at the college, but I allow the group rather free rein to settle

165

on an issue of common interest and to design a related experiment.

During the remainder of the 3-hr laboratory session, the students draft the materials and specify the procedures for the study. I have obtained the prior approval of Carleton's Biosafety and Research Ethics Committee for the general study and ensure that the specific adaptation of the method falls within the bounds of what has been approved. After class, I prepare final instructions and research materials, which the students pick up and use to complete their data collection before a specified laboratory meeting. At that meeting, we analyze the project data and discuss results. Each student later submits a short research paper in APA format or poster for each project, and these are graded individually.

A Survey Paradigm for Experiments on Social Influence

The target article assigned for the laboratory on social influence is White (1975). White reported a series of field experiments on the effect of varying magnitudes of discrepancy between others' opinions and the subjects' likely private ones on subjects' public responses. He compared the uncontaminated survey responses of control subjects to the replies of experimental subjects responding to a survey question (e.g., "How many hours per week do you think you would be willing to donate to tutoring?") after others had apparently given their opinions. White designed the others' responses to differ from the subjects' presumed opinions in particular ways of interest (e.g., he varied the means and variability's of the set of influence judgments) and documented substantial effects on stated opinions in all of the influence conditions he created.

Social psychologists have long used methods similar to White's (1975) to demonstrate social influence (e.g., Moore, 1921). All substitute what King and Ziegler (1975) called a "paper-stooge" for confederates in social influence research (e.g., Asch, 1955). (King & Ziegler actually proposed a paper-stooge version of the classic Asch experiment for laboratory courses.) The paper-stooge paradigm that White developed offers a particularly accessible and adaptable foundation for undergraduate work.

Using White's (1975) method, my class created two forms of a survey sheet containing identical instructions and 20 response lines. The instructions posed the following survey question: "How much should you be expected to spend on all of your textbooks for three courses during an average term at Carleton?" On half of the survey forms, all 20 response lines were blank; on the other half, 8 of the lines were filled in with handwritten names and with answers selected to be deviant from local norms (as previously determined in the laboratory). Members of the laboratory course each recruited a set number of potential respondents in the field and randomly assigned them to the

experimental (social influence) or control survey conditions.

The results of two studies demonstrate that the paradigm produces robust influence effects. In one, 16 subjects exposed to paper-stooge textbook expense figures averaging $180.00 gave a mean response of $145.94. This differed significantly from the control (i.e., uninfluenced) mean response of $99.69, $t(30) = 3.59$, $p < .01$. In a second study when 16 respondents were exposed to bogus responses averaging $80.00, their average response was $82.20. This differed significantly from the control result of $105.00 for this project, $t(54) = 3.01$, $p < .01$. Thus, socially influenced judgments obtained using these methods varied from uninfluenced ones in a high or low direction as a function of the locus of a social anchor.

Variations on a Scheme: Student Uses of the Social Influence Paradigm

My students have readily adapted White's (1975) basic paradigm to explore a variety of issues. A brief review of some examples illustrates the breadth of purposes that the basic paradigm can serve.

Several groups have explored the significance of the survey question, doubting that social influence would extend to more important matters. One group learned that the Financial Aid Office at the college was interested in student opinions on textbook expenses, which figured into students' financial aid packages. The class informed respondents that their opinions would be shared with the Financial Aid Office; opinions of subjects in the control group were shared with that office. Even with this indication of the importance of survey responses, respondents showed substantial social influence effects.

Another laboratory group developed a question with moral meaning. Their survey included a background statement providing arguments for and against euthanasia and asked respondents to indicate what chance of recovery, from 0% to 100%, they would recommend that a hypothetical patient's life support systems be discontinued. Social influence using an anchor mean of 50% resulted in a significantly looser recovery criterion of 35.9% compared to the mean uninfluenced response of 20.1%.

One laboratory section investigated the classic idea that influence is attenuated when the judgment to be given is more objectively grounded (Festinger, 1954). This class compared responses to the textbook expense opinion question to a factual version of that question: "How much did you spend on all of your textbooks for your three courses this term at Carleton?" The class documented massive social influence on the opinion question but no social influence on the factual one.

Students have read the posters prepared from previous social influence projects and have often built new designs on the findings and ideas of their peers. Some groups have explored possible accounts for influence effects, including the role of conformity pressure (Asch, 1955), social comparison (Festinger, 1954), self-persuasion (Petty & Cacioppo, 1981), peripheral persuasion (Petty & Cacioppo, 1981), impression management (Goffman, 1955), and project methodology. One class asked whether social influence was due to the social character of the frame of reference or to the cognitive anchor provided by the paper-stooges' responses (e.g., Tversky & Kahneman, 1974). To answer this, the class devised a cognitive anchor condition in which respondents indicated whether they should be expected to spend more or' less than $180.00 on texts and then to specify how much more or less than $180.00 they should be expected to spend. Other subjects were exposed to a social anchor condition in which $180.00 equaled the paper-stooge mean. Although the mean response in the cognitive anchor condition was significantly different from the uninfluenced responses, the social anchor produced stronger effects.

Evaluation and Discussion

Student course evaluations indicate high satisfaction with the social influence laboratory. Students rated the value and interest of the four projects conducted in the laboratory using a scale ranging from *not at all* (1) to *extremely* (7), and the rating of the social influence project ($M = 6.0$, $SD = .69$) exceeded that for the other three laboratories, which were also rated positively.

I believe students are impressed with the effects they reliably obtain with the social influence paradigm and with their own ability to develop and execute an informative experiment. The laboratory on social influence demonstrates how human behavior may be altered by the actions of others, a phenomenon of keen interest to students and of central import to the discipline (e.g., Allport, 1985; Paicheler, 1988; Turner, 1991). Moreover, White's (1975) paradigm for the study of social influence is one that students can easily understand and use. In addition, my students generally have little difficulty with the simple statistical analyses (usually *t* or *F* tests) the project requires. These potential challenges are of special concern to the many students in my laboratory who have not taken data analysis and methodology courses.

A primary virtue of White's (1975) paradigm is that it is so open to diverse applications. A student laboratory group could examine individual differences in influenceability (e.g., Rhodes & Wood, 1992) by assessing subject variables in the scheme presented. Another group could vary the subjects' perceived similarity to the members of the paperstooge reference group (e.g., Festinger, 1954). Other groups could construct appropriate paper-stooge manipulations to study magnitude of discrepancy effects (White, 1975) or the role of a dissenter on a group's social influence (e.g., Asch, 1955; Milgram,

1974). The paradigm is a rich and productive way to involve students as active and thoughtful researchers in social psychology. I highly recommend it.

References

Allport, G. W. (1985). The historical background of social psychology. In G. Lindzey & E. Aronson (Eds.), *The handbook of social psychology: Vol. 1. Theory and method* (pp. 1-46). New York: Random House.

Asch, S. E. (1955). Opinions and social pressure. *Scientific American, 193,* 31-35.

Chamberlain, K. (1988). Devising relevant and topical undergraduate laboratory projects: The core article approach. *Teaching of Psychology, 15,* 207-208.

Festinger, L. (1954). A theory of social comparison processes. *Human Relations, 7,* 117- 140.

Goffman, E. (1955). On face-work: An analysis of ritual elements in social interaction. *Psychiatry, 18,* 213-231.

King, M., & Ziegler, M. (1975). *Research projects in social psychology.* Monterey, CA: Brooks/Cole.

Milgram, S. (1974). *Obedience to authority: An experimental view.* New York: Harper & Row.

Moore, H. T. (1921). The comparative influence of majority and expert opinion. *American Journal of Psychology, 32,* 16-20.

Paicheler, G. (1988). *The psychology of social influence.* Cambridge, England: Cambridge University Press.

Petty, R. E., & Cacioppo, J. T. (1981). *Attitudes and persuasion: Classic and contemporary approaches.* Dubuque, IA: Brown.

Rhodes, N., & Wood, W. (1992). Self-esteem and intelligence affect influenceability: The mediating role of message reception. *Psychological Bulletin, 111,* 156-171.

Tversky, A., & Kahneman, D. (1974). Judgment under uncertainty: Heuristics and biases. *Science, 185,* 1124-1131.

Turner, J. C. (1991). *Social influence.* Pacific Grove, CA: Brooks/Cole.

White, G. M. (1975). Contextual determinants of opinion judgments. *Journal of Personality and Social Psychology, 32,* 1047-1054.

Note

An earlier version of this article was presented at the annual meeting of the American Psychological Association, Washington, DC, August 1992.

Performing Experiments in Undergraduate Social Psychology Classes

Daniel L. Wann
Murray State University

Research has consistently demonstrated that learning is substantially facilitated by techniques that actively involve the students (Older, 1979). For example, Kixmiller, Wann, Grover, and Davis (1988) asked students to learn the details of a journal article in one of three ways. Some students simply read the article and studied its contents, others made a presentation about the article from a third-person point of view, and the rest made a presentation from a first-person viewpoint (i.e., students presented the article as if they were the experimenter). A later recognition test revealed that subjects in the first-person condition performed better than those in the third-person condition, who performed better than subjects who learned the material in a traditional manner.

Similar methods designed to increase student involvement have been popular in psychology courses. For example, students can play the roles of patients, volunteers, hospital staff, and therapists to simulate a mental hospital or clinical experience (Balch, 1983; Schofield & Klein, 1975). Toner (1978) asked students in an adolescent psychology class to write plays dealing with issues discussed in their textbook, and students in introductory psychology have role-played the various parts of a neuron (Hamilton & Knox, 1985).

This article describes a role-playing technique that I used in a junior-level social psychology class. Comprehension of research and its methodology is vital to understanding social psychology. To facilitate such understanding, I required students to develop and perform dramatic plays covering research articles on social psychological phenomena.

Method

Undergraduate students ($N = 25$) in a junior-level social psychology class participated in this project. On the first day of class, students were informed that they would be required to perform two different psychological experiments. They were responsible for (a) acquiring a copy of the article, (b) using the article to write a script, and (c) developing the props necessary to perform the play. Instructions stressed accuracy and attention to detail, as these factors would weigh heavily in my grading of the exercise. For example, if the article stated that subjects were tested while facing a mirror, then students acting as subjects were to complete the materials in a similar setting. However, because research articles are not always explicit in describing the behaviors of experimenters and subjects, some poetic license was allowed. Students could ignore the gender of the participants and experimenters, unless it was vital to understanding the play (although it may be wise to inform students that gender can have dramatic effects that researchers are often unable to predict). Students would play the roles of experimenters, confederates, and subjects, and the plays were to be approximately 10 min long.

Students formed five groups of four to six individuals, and each group was given a reference list of 12 social psychological experiments. The list included classic studies, such as Milgram's (1963) research on obedience. I briefly described the focus and results of each experiment and indicated when each play would be performed. The groups then were allowed to discuss the research. Each group selected two experiments with the restrictions that its two plays could not be performed on the same day and that two groups could not select the same experiment.

At the end of the semester, students were asked to evaluate the exercise. The evaluation form contained items designed to assess students' impressions concerning the construction and performance of their own plays and their reactions to watching the performances of the other groups.

Results

Students' responses to the items assessing their reactions to performing the plays made it readily apparent that this exercise was informative and enjoyable. Eighty-eight percent of the students stated that the exercise was highly enjoyable, and 100% stated that the exercise should be used in other courses. In addition, 92% of the students perceived the exercise as an effective learning tool, and 88% said that it greatly increased their understanding of and interest in psychological research. Responses to items assessing students' attitudes toward viewing the plays also indicated the effectiveness of this technique. All students stated that they enjoyed watching the other plays, and 92% thought that viewing the plays greatly facilitated their understanding of and interest in the research. Finally, 96% reported that watching the other plays gave them a greater understanding of the various methodologies used in social psychological research.

Discussion

The evaluations suggest that this exercise was an interesting, enjoyable, and effective teaching technique. In fact, several students have asked other faculty members to use this exercise in other classes. This project can be altered to fit a wide variety of psychology courses. For example, plays dealing with experiments in animal learning (e.g., operant research or latent learning) could easily be written. Other courses that could effectively incorporate this exercise include developmental (e.g., attachment research) and cognitive psychology (e.g., memory research on eyewitness testimony) .

Finally, instructors may wish to videotape the performances. Those that are especially effective in demonstrating the research could be shown to lower division courses, such as introductory psychology. Describing complicated research in a lecture is often difficult. Viewing a simulation of the research would probably increase understanding of and interest in psychological research.

References

Balch, W. R. (1983). The use of role-playing in a classroom demonstration of client-centered therapy. *Teaching of Psychology, 10,* 173-174.

Hamilton, S. B., & Knox, T. A. (1985). The colossal neuron: Acting out physiological psychology. *Teaching of Psychology, 12,* 153-156.

Kixmiller, J. S., Wann, D. L., Grover, C. A., & Davis, S. F. (1988). Effect of elaboration levels on content comprehension. *Bulletin of the Psychonomic Society, 26,* 32-33.

Milgram, S. (1963). Behavioral study of obedience. *Journal of Abnormal and Social Psychology, 67,* 371-378.

Older, J. (1979). Improving the introductory psychology course. *Teaching of Psychology, 6,* 75-77.

Schofield, L. J., Jr., & Klein, M. J. (1975). Simulation of the mental hospital experience. *Teaching of Psychology, 2,* 132- 134.

Toner, I. J. (1978). A "dramatic" approach to the teaching of adolescent psychology. *Teaching of Psychology, 5,* 218-219.

Notes

1. Preparation of this article was supported by a Murray State University College of Humanistic Studies Innovative Approaches to Teaching Grant.

2. I thank Michael A. Hamlet for his assistance on this project and three anonymous reviewers for their insightful comments on an earlier draft of this article.

3. Requests for a list of articles used in the class project should be sent to Daniel L. Wann, Department of Psychology, Murray State University, Murray, KY 42071-3305 or to A18611F@MSUMUSIC via bitnet.

The Warm-Cold Study: A Classroom Demonstration of Impression Formation

Diane G. Symbaluk
Department of Social Sciences
Grant MacEwan College

Judy Cameron
Department of Educational Psychology
University of Alberta

Although students often emerge from a research methods course with a good grounding in the principles and logic of research, some have difficulty planning, conducting, and writing their own studies. One way to make the transition from formal knowledge to application less difficult is to have students conduct research in the classroom. The warm-cold procedure we describe in this article gives students hands-on experience in experimental design. The experiment is an excellent demonstration of how minimal information about an individual influences people's overall impressions of that individual. The study requires little preparation, produces robust findings, and can be conducted in one or two class periods. What follows is a brief description of Asch's (1946) and Kelley's (1950) original research on the topic, an outline of how to conduct the warm-cold study, and suggestions for modifying this technique.

Original Research

In a pioneering study on impression formation, Asch (1946) read a list of adjectives to his students that purportedly described a real person. One group of students heard the individual described as "intelligent, skillful, industrious, warm, determined, practical, and cautious." A second group heard the same description except that the word cold replaced warm. After hearing the list, students wrote a brief sketch describing the type of person to whom such traits would apply. Finally, from a list of bipolar adjective pairs, students chose the traits they thought best characterized the individual. Asch found that the two groups' overall impressions were strikingly different. Students who had heard the adjective warm described the individual far more positively than those exposed to cold background information.

Kelley (1950) demonstrated that the effects of the warm-cold variable extended to impressions of a real person. Students who received the warm descriptor described a "guest lecturer" more favorably than those who read cold background information. The work of Asch (1946) and Kelley initiated much research in the area of person perception (for an overview of the field, see Brown, 1986).

Procedures for Conducting the Warm-Cold Study

Audiotape Preparation

In our class demonstrations, students listened to an audiotape of two confederates posing as a psychologist and a client. To prepare the audiotape, record a 10-min conversation between two individuals. Obtain written consent from the confederates to use the tape for a class project. Use three to five pictures taken from magazines that depict people in a variety of settings (e.g., a couple on a beach, a homeless person sleeping under a bridge, etc.). The psychologist (first confederate) asks the client (second confederate) to answer three questions about each picture: "What do you see in the picture? What do you think the people in the photographs are feeling? And what will happen next?" The client should try to answer each question with as much detail as possible. In our demonstrations, a man played the role of the psychologist, and a woman served as the client.

Introducing the Study

Disguise the true purpose of the experiment by informing students that they will participate in a study on

170

personality assessment in which they will rate the personality of someone undergoing therapy. Inform students they will hear an audiotape of a male psychologist administering a Thematic Apperception Test (TAT) to a female client. Tell students that, in the TAT, the client views pictures and discusses them, thus revealing to the psychologist certain aspects of her personality.

Conducting the Experiment

Before playing the tape, tell students that they will receive a brief description of the client. Shufffle the information sheets prior to the class to ensure random assignment to conditions. Give one third of the students background information describing the client as warm, another third information describing the client as cold, and the remaining participants information that omits the words warm or cold. The warm, cold, and neutral descriptions serve as the independent variable. Our descriptions were:

> The persons you are about to hear are a male psychologist and a female client who is a graduate student at York University. The student was born in Toronto and graduated from Carleton University. People who know her describe her as an industrious person who is warm (cold), practical, and determined.

After students listen to the tape, ask them to write a brief description of the client's personality. Then, announce that, to get an additional and perhaps more objective measure of the woman's personality, students will complete a semantic differential scale.

Give the semantic differential scale to each student. The scale consists of 20 bipolar adjective pairs (unsociable-sociable, uncertain-self–assured, unintelligent-intelligent, irritable-good-natured, boring-interesting, repellent-attractive, intolerant-tolerant, insincere-sincere, cruel-kind, discourteous-courteous, cold-warm, selfish-unselfish, foolish-wise, dishonest-honest, violent-gentle, aimless-motivated, humorless-witty, unpleasant-pleasant, weak-strong, passive-active), each scored on a continuum from 1 (*negative*) to 7 (*positive*). Students' written descriptions of the client and their ratings on the scale constitute the dependent measures. You can include a suspicion check regarding the plausibility of the deception by asking participants to indicate what they believe to be the purpose of the study.

After collecting the assessments, debrief students on the true purpose of the study. The debriefing provides a clever lead-in to a discussion of ethical issues and the need for deception in some experimental research. Spend the remainder of class time discussing the importance of this research, identifying the central research question (Does prior information bias impressions of a target individual?), and describing the independent and dependent measures. Provide students with Asch's (1946) and Kelley's (1950)

original articles; review these studies in the next class period and discuss other relevant literature on impression formation (e.g., Brown, 1986; Landy & Sigall, 1974; Nisbett & Wilson, 1977; Paulhus & Bruce, 1992; Widmeyer & Loy, 1988).

Data Analysis

Use students' written descriptions of the woman's personality to determine whether a difference in one stimulus trait (warm, cold, control) produces contrasting impressions. Analyze students' descriptions of the client by listing words, themes, items, and phrases that appear to differ across conditions. When we conducted the study, participants in the cold condition tended to use words such as "unimaginative," "unemotional," "sad," "distant," and "guarded" whereas the warm group described the same woman as "optimistic," "pleasant," "calm," "happy," and "caring."

For ratings on the semantic differential scale, note that "warm-cold" appears as one of the 20 adjective pairs; use this item as a manipulation check to determine whether participants actually read the background information. To obtain the overall impression score for each student, omit the warm-cold item and sum the remaining 19 circled ratings (overall scores range from 19 to 133). Conduct an analysis of variance on the difference among the means of the three conditions. Finally, determine whether anyone guessed the true purpose of the experiment, and explain that this individual's data may be biased. Exclude any suspicious participants' data from the analysis.

Discussing the Findings

To conclude the demonstration, draw out the implications of the findings, discuss limitations, and provide students with guidelines for writing a research report based on the results. In each of the seven times we used this demonstration, we found a significant main effect of background information on participants' ratings for the overall impression of the client. Students in the warm condition gave significantly higher impression ratings than participants in the control group and the cold condition, which usually did not differ. The implications of this finding are of particular importance to those who make important decisions about others based on limited information.

Conclusions

The purpose of this article was to outline a technique for teaching experimental design. There are several alternative procedures that work well with this study. If the class is small, an instructor can omit the control condition and use the warm and cold descriptors only. Instructors may wish to include different adjective descriptors (e.g., kind-cruel, sociable-unsociable) in an attempt to determine which traits have the greatest impact on impression formation. Other modifications to the study could include substituting the psychological attribute (warm-cold) with characteristics such as ethnicity, political perspective, feminist position, educational attainment, professional standing, or socioeconomic status.

When we conducted the study, the audiotape presented a psychologist and a client. Alternatively, an instructor may present a videotaped social interaction between a researcher and participant or have a guest speaker talk to a group of students. In general, students are surprised to find that their judgments of others are affected by previous descriptions. This is a highly replicable finding that can be used to challenge basic assumptions and, in doing so, intrigue students in a variety of disciplines.

References

Asch, S. E. (1946). Forming impressions of personality. *Journal of Abnormal and Social Psychology, 41,* 258-290.

Brown, R (1986). *Social psychology* (2nd ed.). New York: Free Press.

Kelley, H. H. (1950). The warm-cold variable in first impressions of persons. *Journal of Personality 18,* 431-439.

Landy, D., & Sigall, H. (1974). Beauty is talent Task evaluation as a function of the performer's physical attractiveness. *Journal of Personality and Social Psychology, 29,* 299-304.

Nisbett, R. E., & Wilson, T. D. (1977). The halo effect Evidence for unconscious alteration of judgments. *Journal of Personality and Social Psychology, 35,* 250-256.

Paulhus, D. L., & Bruce, M. N. (1992). The effects of acquaintanceship on the validity of personality impressions: A longitudinal study. *Journal of Personality and Social Psychology, 63,* 816-824.

Widmeyer, W. N., & Loy, J. W. (1988). When you're hot, you're hot! Warm-cold effects in first impressions of persons and teaching effectiveness. *Journal of Educational Psychology, 60,* 89-99.

Note

The demonstration outlined in this article was based on an idea first developed by James C. Moore, Department of Sociology, York University and W David Pierce, Department of Sociology, University of Alberta.

An Exit Survey Project for a Social Psychology Laboratory

David N. Sattler
Sudie Back
Harriet Pollitt
College of Charleston

One of the challenges of teaching a laboratory in social psychology course is to generate interest in and enthusiasm for research. Students may find research more meaningful when they participate in active-learning exercises that integrate methodology with interesting phenomena and have responsibility for designing and conducting a research project (cf. Cooper, 1995). Camac and Camac (1993) found that students enjoy learning about reliability and validity when they design and assess a sensation-seeking questionnaire of their own making. Lutsky (1993) found that students' interest in research increases when they plan, execute and evaluate experiments on social influence. These exercises demonstrate the value of teaching science as science is practiced (cf. Lutsky, 1986; Zachry, 1985).

This article describes a project that teaches the complexities of survey research by actively involving students in planning and conducting an exit survey. Exit surveys ask graduating seniors to assess a department's strengths and weaknesses in instruction, curricula, advising, research opportunities, and other areas (Doll & Jacobs, 1988; Giacalone & Duhon, 1991). The project is unusual because the topic is relevant to students, and their survey may assist the faculty in generating items and topics for an official departmental exit survey. These features may increase students' interest in research, promote a sense of responsibility, and allow students to study a practical problem.

The goals of the course are introducing the methods of social psychological research, designing and conducting three research projects (observation, survey, and experiment), writing three reports in APA format, generating interest in research, and improving critical-thinking skills. The exit survey project accomplishes most of the course goals. As students design experiments, the instructor emphasizes important methodological concepts (e.g., validity and reliability) and ethical issues. Students learn to identify and correct flaws in the design (e.g., threats to internal validity), analyze their data with computer statistical packages (e.g., SPSS), and critically evaluate research.

The one-credit hour course enrolls a maximum of 14 students per section. The prerequisites are courses in introductory psychology, statistics, and research methods, and the prerequisite is a social psychology course. Two or three sections are taught each semester.

Method

The following schedule describes the survey research topics and the corresponding class activities. It is appropriate for a lab that meets 2 to 3 hr per week. The exit survey project occupies the middle 6 weeks of the 16-week course. The class activities generally followed Campbell and Katona's (1965) recommendations for planning and conducting a survey (also see Judd, Smith, & Kidder, 1991). These involve stating the general and specific objectives, identifying the population and sample, developing and administering the questionnaire, analyzing the data, and reporting the findings.

Week 1

The lectures provided an overview of survey research including the advantages and disadvantages of surveys, the relations among research, theory, and application, types of samples (e.g., probability and nonprobability samples), and sampling strategies. Outside of class, each student generated a list of potential survey research topics.

Week 2

Students presented and discussed their lists of survey research topics for 1 hr. Then, the majority of students voted to design and conduct an exit survey to assess graduating seniors' impressions of the department. An instructor could assign the topic or limit students' choices of topics, but students appear to take greater responsibility for and interest in a project of their choosing. Students considered various issues and decided to include the following five categories: academic advising and professors, psychology courses, extracurricular activities, library, and miscellaneous. Next, the students selected the population; sample, and sampling strategy. The lectures covered Issues of questionnaire design, effective wording of questions (e.g., leading and double-barreled questions and clarity), reliability, and validity.

Week 3

In class, students worked in groups of 2 or 3 persons each and wrote 10 items for each of two categories for 1½ hr. Students in each group presented their items to the class, and the instructor made constructive comments focusing on item wording and social desirability. Students revised the questions and wrote new ones. Sample items included: "How helpful was your adviser in answering questions about your career plans?," "How satisfied are you with the number of psychology journals at the college library?," and "Would you recommend the psychology major to someone at the college?" Participants used a scale ranging from *not at all* (1) to *very much* (5) to answer the 30 items on the survey. Other questions asked for demographic information, overall grade point average (GPA), psychology GPA, and post graduation plans. The instructor typed the final form of the survey. The lectures covered test-retest reliability, interrater reliability, item sequencing, filler items, Likert scales, and anchor points.

Week 4

Students developed the survey administration procedures for ½ hr and wrote a consent form. The lectures covered ethical issues in research, survey administration, confounding variables, and experimenter bias. Two three-person groups administered the survey to 41 senior psychology majors who completed the survey in their lab classes. The survey was anonymous and took 5 min. Students were debriefed and thanked for participating. The human subjects review was conducted in accordance with the College Institutional Review Board criteria.

Weeks 5 to 6

In class, the instructor helped students code and analyze the data. The students wrote an SPSS command file and data file. The lectures covered statistical procedures (e.g., correlation, analysis of variance, and factor analysis) and effective report writing using APA style. Each student submitted a final copy of a research report in APA format the following week.

Evaluation and Discussion

Nine months after the course ended, two independent study students administered a nine-item questionnaire asking the lab students to assess the project. Because we did not ask students to evaluate the project at the end of the course, they were asked to reflect on the effectiveness of the project. We contacted 10 of the 14 students, who answered the items on a scale ranging from *not at all* (1) to *very much* (5).

Students believed that the project increased their understanding of (a) conducting survey research ($M = 4.50$, $SD = .75$), (b) questionnaire construction ($M = 4.50$, $SD = .54$), (c) questionnaire administration ($M = 4.00$, $SD = .93$), and (d) reliability and validity ($M = 3.75$, $SD = 1.10$). They also indicated that the project enhanced their (a) critical thinking skills ($M = 3.75$, $SD = .99$), (b) interest in and enthusiasm for research ($M = 3.75$, $SD = 1.30$), (c) sense of responsibility for the project ($M = 4.13$, $SD = .99$), and (d) knowledge of APA style ($M = 4.13$, $SD = 1.10$). Overall, students rated the project positively ($M = 4.13$, $SD = .84$).

Students appreciated learning to design and conduct a methodologically sound study. They applied critical-thinking skills and liked being responsible for the project. Student feedback suggested that the project helped achieve the course goals. One limitation to the findings is the small sample size.

Exit surveys can provide valuable information to departments because graduating seniors have experiences and perspectives about the department that are not assessed in traditional ways (e.g., standardized course evaluations). The lab students presented their survey to the department committee responsible for developing an official exit survey. A few questions asking about psychology courses and extracurricular activities were either revised and included on the department survey or used to generate new questions. Thus, department exit surveys may be enhanced by students' contributions.

References

Camac, C. R., & Camac, M. K. (1993). A laboratory project in scale design: Teaching reliability and validity. *Teaching of Psychology, 20,* 102-104.

Campbell, A. A., & Katona, G. (1965). The sample survey: A technique for social science research. In L. Festinger & K. Katz (Eds.), *Research methods in the behavioral sciences* (pp. 15-55). New York: Dryden.

Cooper, J. L. (1995). Cooperative learning and critical thinking. *Teaching of Psychology, 22,* 7-9.

Doll, P. A., & Jacobs, K. W. (1988). The exit interview for graduating seniors. *Teaching of Psychology, 15,* 213-214.

Giacalone, R. A., & Duhon, D. (1991). Assessing intended employee behavior in exit interviews. *Journal of Psychology, 125,* 83-90.

Judd, C. M., Smith, E. R., & Kidder, L. H. (1991). *Research methods in social relations* (6th ed.). Orlando, FL: Holt, Rinehart & Winston.

Lutsky, N. (1986). Undergraduate research experience through the analysis of data sets in psychology courses. *Teaching of Psychology, 13,* 119-122.

Lutsky, N. (1993). A scheme and variations for studies of social influence in an experimental social psychology laboratory. *Teaching of Psychology, 20,* 105-107.

Zachry, W. H. (1985). How I kicked the lecture habit: Inquiry teaching in psychology. *Teaching of Psychology, 12,* 129-131.

Note

We gratefully acknowledge the College of Charleston Laboratory in Social Psychology students who participated in the project. We thank Elizabeth Thompson, Christie Allen, Robin Bowers, Ruth L. Ault, and three anonymous reviewers for their helpful comments on an earlier draft.

2. EMPHASIZING WRITING AND LITERATURE

Writing as a Tool for Teaching Social Psychology

Sara E. Snodgrass
Skidmore College

In the typical psychology course, students write examinations and term papers in which writing is used almost exclusively as a tool for the evaluation of their learning. In recent years, the process of writing has been suggested as a useful tool, not just for evaluation, but also for learning (e.g., Emig, 1977; Flower, 1981; Irmscher, 1979). The process of writing can be used as a problem-solving tool and as a tool for producing creative and analytical thinking. In addition, Calhoun and Selby (1979) and Costin (1982) have expressed concern over the lack of basic communication and writing skills often found in college undergraduates. Boice (1982), Klugh (1983), Spiegel, Cameron, Evans, and Nodine (1980), among others, have addressed this issue by suggesting that the teaching of writing skills be incorporated into the regular psychology curriculum.

I have integrated writing into my introductory course in social psychology in several ways, primarily for the purpose of giving the students a tool for learning the material, secondarily for the purpose of helping them with their writing skills, and finally for the purpose of evaluation. Writing as a process is integrated into the Introductory Social Psychology course in several ways: (a) the students are required to keep a course log in which they write their reactions to the readings, class films, and demonstrations, ideas for papers and projects, and other "free" writing; (b) the students write two short analyses of journal articles, through which they learn how to find psychological literature in the library and learn ways to approach reading and analyzing journal articles; (c) each student plans and implements an observational study of some social psychological phenomenon. This project incorporates writing throughout the project's process.

Course Log

The course log serves several different functions. First, it stimulates class discussions. Students are frequently asked to write in their logs for 5-10 minutes in class following a film or a class demonstration, freely writing their feelings about and reactions to what they have just experienced. The ensuing class discussion is always lively, with most students participating. The writing

process provides each of them with something to contribute, and their own personal thoughts have already established an element of respect by being written. Spiegel et al. (1980) also report finding that students participate more readily in class discussions after writing for 5-10 minutes.

Second, the logs serve as a workbook as the students read the text. Many of the students choose to follow my suggestion to write out their thoughts about the textbook readings. This provides a means of summarizing the material, giving their own reactions, applying the content to their own lives, and is an excellent source for review for examinations. The first time I used the logs, I collected them and looked over them at the end of the semester to evaluate the technique (rather than to evaluate the students). I found that the students who made the best grades on tests were the ones who used the logs more extensively (taking notes from readings, writing anecdotes that came to mind as they read, etc.). Of course, I could not tell whether the use of the logs helped improve grades on tests, or if students who tend to do well on tests are also the students who will take more notes and do their assignments more conscientiously. Since that first time, I have not looked at the logs. I believe that the students are motivated to use them as they see fit without having to be "checked," and that checking them is likely to decrease their intrinsic motivation and their free expression.

Third, many class demonstrations incorporate writing in the logs. For example, when we study self-perception, we begin by writing 10 answers to the question "Who am I?" in the logs. When studying impression formation, the students describe their first impressions of someone they met at the beginning of the school year and then describe their current impressions, discussing why their impression may have changed. This is written in the logs, not to be turned in, but as "free" writing. When we discuss attitude change and persuasion, the students write what they would say to a good friend to persuade that person not to drive home from a party after heavy drinking. This stimulates discussion on styles of persuasion. Many other class activities incorporate writing in the logs. This procedure makes the material more relevant to their own lives and forces them to think about the material as they write. Hettich (1976, 1980) and Anderson (1982) also report success with the use of autobiographical journal entries as a means of processing class material.

Fourth, when we begin talking about final projects for the course, in which students are to observe unobtrusively some social behavior and collect data to analyze and report, they begin by brainstorming in their logs. The brainstorming is guided; they have to be taught how to brainstorm (i.e., I hand out a "Brainstorming Guide" with questions to guide them as they brainstorm in their logs). I found that after using this method of brainstorming in their logs, very few individual conferences were requested for help in choosing a topic for the projects.

The log is applicable to any content area and any size class. Perhaps in other content areas there are not such obvious assignments for the logs as the everyday social experiences that were used here, but to have the students write their understanding of some portion of a lecture that was particularly complex or particularly important would produce questions that might not surface without the writing process, and would also solidify the material in the students' minds. The use of class logs is one writing technique that is not limited to smaller classes. In fact, through writing in logs, the students in large classes are given the opportunity to react to the material and to express themselves even when class discussion is limited.

Graded Writing Assignments

The students are required to turn in five writing assignments throughout the semester; each of these assignments builds on the previous one. Each paper is returned with ample feedback about style, format, references, and citations, as well as content. This feedback is then used to improve the next paper. The first two assignments require students to analyze journal articles, learning to use psychological literature. The last three assignment comprise the final project, in which they design an unobtrusive observational study, collect data, and write a formal research report.

The primary purposes of these assignments are to give the students a tool with which to think about the class material and to teach them to use methods of scientific inquiry. These assignments teach them to use the psychological literature to pursue their own interests and questions, and to experience the difference between systematic observation of social phenomena and the casual observations we make every day. In other words, students learn how scientific inquiry works and actually experience the process themselves. Cole (1982) addressed this issue when he wrote ". . . teaching the methods of psychology is more valuable to the student than the teaching of whatever psychologists 'know' about human behavior at a given point in time . . . . Content changes. It is the modes of inquiry that offer the surest road to the coping skills [necessary for career advancement in today's job market]" (p. 25).

Analyses of Journal Articles

The first assignment asks students to find and read one of five specified journal articles and to write a 5-page summary and analysis of the article. The assignment is completely described in a handout, giving them questions to consider as they analyze the article, what audience they should direct their writing toward, and the grading criteria. In addition, they are given guides for reading and summarizing journal articles.

The second assignment asks them to choose a topic from class, to find three articles in the library on the topic, and to write a 5-7 page paper summarizing the articles and analyzing their relevance to each other, their relevance to social psychology, and their relevance to life outside the laboratory. These assignments are used to teach the students about social psychological literature, where to find it, how to read it, how to research a specific topic, how to analyze it, and how to write in a psychological format (including citations and references). Again, a complete description of the assignment is handed out, including questions to consider while analyzing the articles, the audience they should direct their writing style toward, and grading criteria. In addition I give them a guide to finding literature in psychology and a guide to doing references in psychology.

The last three assignments comprise the final project and are the (a) proposal, (b) introduction and methods, and (c) complete research report with abstract and references.

Final Project

This is the students' favorite part of the course. Each student chooses a social psychological phenomenon of interest and designs an unobtrusive observational study to examine the phenomenon. Students think of a hypothesis, research the literature, collect data, and write a formal research report in APA style. Writing is used throughout the project, beginning with brainstorming in the logs. Students turn in a short proposal in which they describe their idea, give a rationale for choosing it, and their initial ideas for how they might collect data. After the proposal is approved, they do a brief literature search on the topic and write a more formal paper, which is similar in format to the introduction and method sections of APA research articles. Feedback on this paper is used in improving their designs and methods of data collection and in improving the introduction and method sections for their final papers. The final project report is due at the end of the semester. This paper is written in formal APA style, including an abstract and references. Because the writing is done in steps, through the proposal and the literature review and methods, the final papers are much easier for the students to write, and the products they turn in are significantly better than when they are merely told to "write a term paper." Extensive handouts are prepared to lead the students through the project. They are given an overall description of the entire project, the brainstorming guide, a description of what I want in the proposal, a thorough description of the introduction and method sections with a step-by-step guide to preparing them, and a guide to the format of the completed report.

The students (predominantly sophomores) get very excited about this project, and course evaluations reveal that this is one of the best parts of the course in their opinions. They often comment that, even though the project is one of the most challenging things they have done, it did not seem so overwhelming a task as typical term papers or final projects because they were led through it step-by-step and were given feedback throughout. Also, the due dates of the three parts prevent them from leaving it all until the end of the semester.

From the teacher's viewpoint, I am extremely pleased with the improved quality of the final papers I receive now, as compared to when my assignment was to "write a term paper" or to "do a research project." The papers are much more carefully written, more reflective of their knowledge of social psychology, and more interesting to read. The students' grades on their final projects are much better as a result of feedback on smaller portions of them.

The graded assignments are also applicable to other areas of psychology. Obviously the analysis of published research articles is appropriate in all areas, but the final project can also be used in developmental psychology by having students collect data through observation of younger siblings or children in a nursery school; in cognition and perception by doing small experiments on roommates and friends; and, with a little creativity, in other areas as well.

Second Thoughts

Although I am firmly convinced that incorporating writing throughout the course as part of the process of learning is very successful, I admit that there are some negative aspects. The feedback on each assignment is tremendously time-consuming. In order for this to work as intended, each paper must have ample feedback about writing skills, style, content, format, and so on, so that the student can correct as many problems in the next paper as possible. Initially, creating all the guides and handouts took an inordinate amount of time, but I now know it was worth it. The papers I receive are much more interesting to read, are almost always the type of paper I intended, and are much better written, more thoughtful, and more reflective of students' understanding of social psychological concepts than before.

The first class in which I used these assignments had 30 students. I was exhausted at the end of the semester, but very satisfied with the class. The following semester I had 60 students enrolled in two sections of the class (apparently all the writing did not scare the students away). In an attempt at self-preservation, I decided to cut the number of writing assignments on which I had to give such detailed feedback by giving the students a grading option. Those who wanted an A for the course had to make an A average and do the final project with the three writing assignments to be turned in (proposal, introduction, and methods, which included journal article analysis, and final research report). Those who wanted a B had to make a B average or above and had to do a library paper (a slightly enlarged version of assignment #2 described above under "Analyses of Journal Articles"). Those satisfied with a C or less could get by with taking the three tests, and doing no writing other than test questions. My plan was that I would get only the best students doing the more extensive writing assignments. My plan failed. Initially, 78% of the students chose option A, to do the final project. After the proposal assignment, I encouraged several of them to take their topics and do library papers instead, and over time several more dropped the research project. I finished with 64% of the class doing the extensive writing assignments. Half of these students made B or C for the course and knew that they had no chance for an A, yet chose to do the project anyway. Apparently, students are not as prone to take the easy way out as we may have believed. I think that this failure of my plan to ease my workload provides strong evidence that using writing as a tool in the process of learning social psychology is appealing to students, and that the improved papers, test grades, and class participation are evidence that it works. However, the use of the graded assignments as described here would not be feasible for large classes (70+) without teaching assistants to help read and provide feedback on the papers. As is true of so many of the better methods of teaching, those that involve extensive feedback are dependent on a small to moderate student-teacher ratio.

Students learn much more about psychology by using these writing techniques. They are actively involved in the material, and writing forces them to think about it and to relate it to their own lives. Examinations are better because the students have actively worked with the material. They leave the course not only knowing much of the content of psychology, but feeling confident that they can use the psychological literature in the future, having great respect for research as a result of their own studies, knowing how to write a psychological paper, and having increased confidence in their own abilities to think analytically about psychological concepts.

References

Anderson, W. P. (1982). The use of journals in a human sexuality course. *Teaching of Psychology, 9,* 105-107.

Boice, R. (1982). Teaching of writing in psychology: A review of sources. *Teaching of Psychology, 9,* 143-147.

Calhoun, L. G., & Selby, J. W. (1979). Writing in psychology: A separate course? *Teaching of Psychology, 6,* 232.

Cole, D. L. (1982). Psychology as a liberating art. *Teaching of Psychology, 9*, 23-26.

Costin, F. (1982). Some thoughts on general education and the teaching of undergraduate psychology. *Teaching of Psychology, 9*, 26-28.

Emig, J. (1977, May). Writing as a mode of learning. *College Composition and Communication, 28*, 122-128.

Flower, L. (1981). *Problem-solving strategies for writing.* New York: Harcourt Brace Jovanovich.

Hettich, P. (1976). The journal: An autobiographical approach to learning. *Teaching of Psychology, 3*, 60-63.

Hettich, P. (1980). The journal revisited. *Teaching of Psychology, 7*, 105-106.

Irmscher, W. F. (1979, October). Writing as a way of learning and developing. *College Composition and Communication, 30*, 240-241.

Klugh, H. E. (1983). Writing and speaking skills can be taught in psychology classes. *Teaching of Psychology, 10*, 170-171.

Spiegel, T. A., Cameron, S. M., Evans, R., & Nodine, B. F. (1980). Integrating writing into the teaching of psychology: An alternative to Calhoun and Selby. *Teaching of Psychology, 7*, 242-243.

Notes

1. An extended version of this paper was presented at the annual convention of the American Psychological Association, August, 1984, Toronto, Ontario, Canada.
2. Copies of all assignments and guides are available from the author.

Self-Knowledge as an Outcome of Application Journal Keeping in Social Psychology

Stuart Miller
Towson State University

I (Miller, 1993) had students in an undergraduate course in social psychology keep journals that described the application of concepts from that course to their daily social experiences. I (Miller, 1994) found that these journals could facilitate the learning of social psychological principles and provide evidence of psychosocial growth in students during the semester. Thus, a content analysis of the journal entries revealed various cognitive, emotional, and behavioral changes concerning the self, others, and broader social issues.

Among other things, students acquired increased knowledge of the self as a result of the self-reflective process stimulated by this form of journal keeping. Forty-seven percent of the journal entries in the course contained descriptions of some new piece of information that students learned about their behavior or experiences (Miller, 1994). Journal entries generated by students in one of the sections I reported were subjected to a qualitative analysis to determine the type of self knowledge students obtained by relating social psychological concepts to personal social experiences.

Method

In Spring 1992, 26 students at Towson State University took a junior-level course in social psychology in which several representative topics were covered in depth. Students learned about social cognition, diversity, relationships, prosocial behavior, and social influence.

Students were prepared for the journal assignment by practicing the application of social psychological concepts and theories in small classroom groups. For example,

180

students were given several real-world examples of the operation of a particular principle before being asked to share their own examples with group members. The groups reported their examples to the class and received feedback on their work. If necessary, students were asked to repeat this exercise to improve their application skills. For the journals, students were asked to engage in a similar process by (a) selecting any concept from the topics covered in the course, (b) describing an experience from their daily lives that involved the operation of this concept, and (c) showing specifically how the experience and the course concept were related. Students were required to make at least one application journal entry per week.

Of the 403 entries turned in by the class, 207 of them (an average of 8.0 per student) provided evidence of *self-knowledge*, defined as the acquisition of new insights (from courserelevant material) about the nature, determinants, or consequences of one's thoughts, feelings, or actions (Miller, 1994). Journal entries were examined further by classifying them according to type of knowledge. The aspects of the self that students described in their entries fell into three categories: thoughts (cognitive), feelings (emotional), and actions (behavioral). In addition, students applied the following four cognitive operations to these components of the self: (a) They attached learned social psychological labels to their experiences, (b) they engaged in explanation by discovering antecedents of their experiences, (c) they made inferences about the consequences of their experiences, and (d) they engaged in a self-assessment of their strengths and weaknesses.

Thus, a 3 × 4 system of classification, yielding 12 forms of self-knowledge, was used to describe the journal entries. Students labeled, explained, educed consequences of, or self assessed their thoughts, feelings, or actions.

Results

Using the classification system developed for this study, a frequency count was made of the forms of self-knowledge students gained through applied learning of the course material. This count indicated that students primarily acquired information about their actions. Of the 207 journal entries analyzed, 47% were devoted to this category. To a lesser extent, students learned about their thoughts (32%) and feelings (21%). The most frequently occurring cognitive operation was explaining (50%). The other cognitive operations were used much less often: educing consequences (26%) labeling (14%), and self-assessing (10%). A combination of he two classifications (i.e., aspect of the self and cognitive operation) revealed that students primarily learned how to explain (24%) and educe consequences about (14%) their actions and to explain their thoughts (14%) and feeling 12%). Other categories of self-knowledge occurred with frequency of less than 10%.

Students acquired most of their self-knowledge by applying concepts from four of the topics covered in the course: social, cognition, relationships, diversity, and prosocial behavior. Of the 207 entries, 31%, 30%, 21%, and 15% came from these areas, respectively. Only 3% of the entries concerned social influence, a topic shortened due to time limitations at the end of the semester.

Most of the entries that involved attaching new labels to behavior and experience came from attributional phenomena (e.g., self-serving bias) covered in the social cognition area (57%). Students learned to evaluate their social skills and categorize their feelings of love and liking in the relationship area, accounting for most of the self-assessment entries (90%) entries involving the knowledge of either the antecedents oz he consequences of behavior and experience were distributed across the areas of social cognition (30%), diversity (25%) relationships (24 %), and prosocial behavior (19%).

Discussion

Application journal keeping allows students to integrate course learning with personal experience, a process that pro. notes self-knowledge. A content analysis of journal entries permits instructors to determine what students learn about .course material and about the self through this application process .

In my study, 12 different forms of self-knowledge, acquired through keeping application journals in a social psychology course, were identified. Students used four different cognitive operations (labeling, explaining, educing consequences, and self-assessing) to understand each of three different aspects of the self (thoughts, feelings, and actions).

Acquiring a clearer understanding of the self is an important component of psychosocial development in college students, for which investigators such as Pace (1990) and Terenzini, Theophilidies, and Lorang (1984) have reported progress in national studies of student personal development. Keeping application journals in social psychology may be a valuable educational experience that facilitates self-knowledge. As students apply psychological concepts to their personal experiences, they acquire a new language to describe and evaluate the self and achieve insights about the antecedents and consequences of their experience of the self. The analysis of journal entries also provides a method of assessing this form of student affective growth.

References

Miller, S. (1993). The social environmental autobiographical portfolio. In W. Oxman & M. Weinstein (Eds.), *Critical thinking as an educational ideal: Proceedings of the 1992 Fifth Annual*

Conference of the Institute for Critical Thinking (pp. 387-393). Montclair, NJ: Montclair State College.

Miller, S. (1994, June). *A course-embedded approach to assessing affective outcomes.* Paper presented at the Ninth Annual American Association of Higher Education Conference on Assessment and Quality, Washington, DC.

Pace, C. (1990). *The undergraduates: A report of their activities and progress in college in the 1980s.* Los Angeles: University of California, Center for the Study of Evaluation.

Terenzini, P., Theophilidies, C., & Lorang, W. (1984). Influences on students' perceptions of their personal development during the first three years of college. *Research in Higher Education, 55,* 621-636.

Note

I (Miller, 1993,1994) collected the journal entries on which this study was based. These earlier studies concerned the use of student journals for assessing higher order thinking and affective outcomes.

Samuel Butler's *Erewhon* as Social Psychology

Don R. Osborn
Bellarmine College

One of the challenges in teaching social psychology at a liberal arts college is finding a good supplementary reader to demonstrate that social psychology principles are also found in other disciplines. One of the best ways to connect psychology to a wider pattern of human experience is through literature (Grant, 1987). Gorman (1984) showed how the imaginative use of Vonnegut's (1975) *The Eden Express* enlivened an introductory psychology course. 1 similarly report the successful use of Samuel Butler's (1872/1983) novel *Erewhon*. It effectively illustrates at least five social psychological principles through the plot and interplay of characters.

In his afterward to the Signet edition, writer Kingley Amis called *Erewhon* "the first modern Utopian romance." It is played out in an imaginary land created by Samuel Butler as a basis for his attacks on "modern" life and thought. The protagonist, Higgs, is a sheep farmer in an unnamed British colony in 1868. He is the first outsider to traverse an impassable mountain range and discover *Erewhon*—a land populated by natives whose beliefs provide the basis for using this book in a social psychology course.

Five of the notable social psychological issues that *Erewhon* addresses are discussed here.

1. The importance of physical attractiveness in interpersonal attraction. The Erewhonians are described as robust and beautiful people, always glowing with good health and taking pride in their appearance. One's character is reflected by physical appearance to the extent that an Erewhonian may ask another more physically attractive friend to pose for his or her statue. One of the major factors in Higgs's positive reception and treatment by the Erewhonians was his superlative overall appearance and his rare light complexion. This theme anticipates the findings of classic interpersonal attraction research (e.g., Walster, Aronson, Abrahams, & Rottman, 1966), which demonstrated how judgments of others are influenced by physical attractiveness. Later, when Higgs falls into disfavor with the king, critical newspaper articles impugn his attractiveness on the grounds that a fair complexion is common in Higgs's homeland. This criticism anticipates Jellison and Zeisset's (1969) work, which confirms the rarity-enhances-attractiveness view. They found that an attractive feature has a greater positive effect on attractiveness judgments when it is rare than when it is common.

2. The human tendency to want others to agree with our ideas and values. Explicitly, this drive for interpersonal agreement occurs in various asides throughout the book as Higgs explains his behaviors and feelings. For example, as he is adjusting to the unusual Erewhonian view that treats crime as an illness, Higgs must accede to the government's desire for him to be the house guest of a convicted

embezzler. Higgs characterizes this situation as showing "a greater perversity of mental vision than I had been yet prepared for. And this made me wretched; for I cannot bear having much to do with people who think differently from myself" (Butler, 1872/1983, p. 93). The Erewhonians themselves hold "A man's business is to think as his neighbors do, for heaven help him if he thinks good what they count bad" (p. 189). These and other incidents provide excellent examples of the importance of similarity in several areas of social psychological research. Byrne (1971) showed that similarity is one of the most important determinants of interpersonal attraction. Concepts from balance theory (Heider, 1946) have been fruitful in understanding attitude organization and change.

3. <u>The tendency to have our values and behaviors congruent.</u> Use of the drive for logical-affective consistency in attitudes to modify attitudes and/or behavior has been demonstrated by McGuire's (1981) work on the *Socratic effect*. McGuire showed that forcing people to logically justify the relation among their beliefs, attitudes, and behaviors can lead to change beyond the effect of a particular persuasive message. One of the historical developments in *Erewhon* was a political movement that outlawed meat eating. The citizens either had to become vegetarians or outlaws. The basis for the success of this Erewhonian movement was an application of the Socratic effect. The Socratic effect was used by first establishing the rights of animals as a philosophical value, thus causing Erewhon to go through a period of compulsory vegetarianism. Then this animal right-to-life viewpoint was extended to vegetables, and Erewhonians were logically (though temporarily) forced to live on a diet of rotten vegetables, without dairy products or eggs. This sequence shows, in a powerful and memorable way, how the need for cognitive and behavioral consistency can be used to change people's attitudes and behaviors.

4. <u>The importance of values in understanding human action.</u> The Fishbein model of attitudes fits nicely here (Fishbein & Ajzen, 1975). Fishbein posited that "normative beliefs" are elements in attitudes that are defined as our beliefs about what other people think we should do. The importance of others' evaluations was represented in Victorian times by Mrs. Grundy, a character in Morton's (1926) *Speed the Plough*. This character personified Victorian concepts of propriety and came to symbolize the powerful social controlling effect of conventional proprieties. Butler satirized this human tendency by anagramatically converting *Grundy* to a very popular god, *Ydgrun*, in Erewhon's polytheistic society. In addition to personifying and demonstrating Fishbein's concept of normative belief, the Ydgrunites (followers of Ydgrun) provide a fine example of Kohlberg's Level 3 moralizing. Kohlberg and Kramer (1969) identified six stages of moral development differentiated by the basis for judging an act moral. The Level 3 basis is the opinions of others.

In Erewhon, wealth is regarded as one of the best measures of social value, along with physical attractiveness. Rich people in Erewhon are so admired for their contributions to society that they are not taxed at all. This point is useful in discussing recent political belief systems. The reduction of tax rates for higher income Americans in the last major federal tax legislation shows this same positive attitude toward the rich in our society.

5. <u>The importance of causal attributional schemas in determining our attitudes toward others, proper social behavior, and proper social policy.</u> The Erewhonians deal with the problem of holding people responsible for their actions by maintaining that each person chose to be born. The Erewhonians believe there is a "World of the Unborn" wherein disembodied souls live; by choosing to be born, they become newborn babies. Newborn Erewhonians are required to sign a "Birth Formulae." This legal document asserts that they came into the world of their own free will, they imposed their existence on their unfortunate parents, and they take all responsibility for their lives on their own shoulders. This concept of preexistence seems initially quite odd to the typical student, but it is a view that is also Mormon dogma and characteristic of many New Age religious views (MacLaine, 1983). The similarity of these contemporary religious beliefs to the Erewhonian view provides a bridge for the students when discussing the implications of preexistence for attributional schemas.

The most fascinating attributional twist in Erewhon is that sick people are treated like criminals (fined and imprisoned), whereas criminals are treated like sick people (attended and cured by "straighteners" who prescribe floggings, bread and water diets, and other painful treatments). This reversal of our society's usual attributional schema and the implications of this reversal significantly add to the students' appreciation of the importance of attributional judgments in human behavior. The "Just World" hypothesis is exemplified by the Erewhonians because it is the basis for the law-of the land. In the chapter, "Some Erewhonian Trials," the case of a man accused of having pulmonary consumption is discussed. This crime was punished by a life sentence of hard labor. As a general principle of Erewhonian justice, a judge lecturing a prisoner says, "You have suffered a great loss. Nature attaches a great penalty to such offenses, and human law must emphasize the decree of nature" (Butler, 1872/1983, p. 113).

These are the major points I found useful in enriching my class. The evaluation data reported in Table 1 show the success of this supplementary reader.

The data are combined from two semesters of classes: 19 students enrolled in fall 1986 and 18 in fall 1987. In the fall 1986 class, I assigned *Erewhon* as a supplementary text, included questions on the weekly quizzes, and pointed out some applications in lecture. I did not spend any significant class time on it. In fall 1987, I had small-group discussion sections every month of the semester. The students' task was to generate social psychological examples from *Erewhon*. Because there were no significant differences between classes in average ratings

Table 1. Student Evaluation of Erewhon as a Supplementary Text

Item	M	SD
1. *Erewhon* added to the liberal arts value of the class[a]	2.89	.93
2. How valuable was *Erewhon* in demonstrating:[b]		
A. importance of physical attractiveness?	2.49	1.38
B. human tendency to want agreement with our own ideas and values?	2.30	.85
C. drive to have values and behavior congruent?	2.76	1.19
D. importance of values in understanding human actions?	2.65	1.11
E. overall importance of causal attributions?	2.46	.90
F. importance of attributions in the crime and illness issue?	2.33	1.07
G. attributions and the world of the unborn and the birth formulae?[c]	3.00	1.27

Note. $N = 37$.
[a]Item 1: The response scale ranged from *very strongly agree* (1) to *very strongly disagree* (7). [b]Item 2: The response scale ranged from *very valuable* (1) to *totally useless* (7). [c]For this item, ratings by the two classes were significantly different, $p < .05$.

(except for Item 2G) the data were combined from both semesters in the table. The student evaluations suggest that *Erewhon* can be used successfully, even when the instructor does not spend class time on discussion groups.

For Item 2G, the fall 1986 class rating ($M = 2.58$) was significantly more positive toward this topic than the fall 1987 class ($M = 3.44$), $t(35) = 2.18$, $p < .05$. Although the reason for this difference is unclear, students in 1987 may have been more negative because they attended a campus event that strongly endorsed views opposed to Erewhonian beliefs. The Erewhonians make sharp distinctions between the value of different lives, whereas the "seamless garment" concept, discussed at the event, is a Catholic view that emphasizes the equal value of all human life.

There are many other relevant and fascinating issues in *Erewhon*. One student noted that the story supported the idea of social adaptability. Higgs easily and readily adapted to the strange Erewhonian belief system. Instead of missing a social engagement for illness, he knew to excuse himself with an expression such as "to have the socks," which is a way of saying the urge to shoplift was so great the missing guest had to stay home. This example fits the rule-role model (Goffman, 1959) of human behavior. This theory suggests that human actions should be interpreted as dramatic performances designed to produce certain effects in others. The example is also a good discussion starter on the "natural attitude" as elucidated by the phenomenologist Schutz (1932/1964), and ethnomethodologist Garfinkel (1967). This theory maintains that people are socialized to believe a culturally determined set of commonsense agreements concerning the nature of the world. The natural attitude is adopted when people accept these social conventions for reality and do not question their validity. For example, the natural attitude in the Middle Ages was that the earth is flat and the center of the universe. Sexism, racism, ageism, and speciesism are all current issues that provide good material for a discussion of the natural attitude.

Another major thematic example is Darwin's theory of evolution, which had a strong and profound personal impact on Butler (1872/1983). Five chapters deal with evolution as applied to organisms and machines. Within this topic, one organizing principle used by Butler is intelligence, which is shown to be a more complicated issue than the single number-IQ people think. Discussions of Gardner's (1983) work would be enriched by Butler's arguments. In the chapter, "The Book of the Machines," Butler made some startlingly accurate predictions about the course of machine evolution, specifically his prediction of computer developments. His speculations on essential issues in judgments of adaptive behavior, personhood, and what is distinctively human are relevant to discussions of evolutionary theory, artificial intelligence, and cognitive psychology.

Psychology instructors looking for a different type of supplementary text could profit from reading *Erewhon*. It contains many incidents that can add a valuable literary dimension to general, developmental, social, and other psychology courses.

References

Butler, S. (1983). *Erewhon*. New York: Penguin Books. (Original work published 1872)

Byrne, D. (1971). The *attraction paradigm*. New York: Academic.

Fishbein, M., & Ajzen, I. (1975). *Belief, attitude, intention, and behavior: An introduction to theory and research.* Reading, MA: Addison-Wesley.

Gardner, H. (1983). *Frames of mind*. New York: Basic Books.

Garfinkel, H. (1967). *Studies in ethnomethodology*. Englewood Cliffs, NJ: Prentice-Hall.

Goffman, E. (1959). The presentation of self in everyday life. Garden City, NY: Doybleday.

Gorman, M.E. (1984). Using *The Eden Express* to teach introductory psychology. *Teaching of Psychology, 11*, 39-40.

Grant, L. (1987). Psychology and literature: A survey of courses. *Teaching of Psychology, 14*, 86-88.

Heider, F. (1946). Attitudes and cognitive organization. *Journal of Psychology, 21*, 107-112.

Jellison, J., & Zeisset, P. (1969). Attraction as a function of the commonality and desirability of a trait shared with another. *Journal of Personality and Social Psychology, 11*, 115-120.

Kohlberg, L., & Kramer, R. (1969). Continuities and discontinuities in childhood and adult moral development. *Developmental Psychology, 12*, 93-120.

MacLaine, S. (1983). *Out on a limb*. New York: Bantam Books.

McGuire, W. (1981). The probabilogical model of cognitive structure and attitude change. In R. E. Petty, T. M. Ostrom, & T. C. Brock (Eds.), *Cognitive responses in persuasion* (pp. 291-308). Hillsdale, NJ: Lawrence Erlbaum Associates, Inc.

Morton, T. (1926). *Speed the plough.* London: Oxford University Press.

Schutz, A. (1964). The dimensions of the social world. In A. Brodersen (Ed.; T. Luckmann, Trans.*), Alfred Schutz: Collected papers II, Studies in social theory* (pp. 20-63). The Hague: Nijhoff. (Original work published 1932)

Vonnegut, M. (1975). The *Eden express.* New York: Bantam Books.

Walster (Hatfield), E., Aronson, V., Abrahams, D., & Rottman, L. (1966). Importance of physical attractiveness in dating behavior. *Journal of Personality and Social Psychology, 4,* 508-516.

Note

I thank Joseph Palladino and three anonymous reviewers for their helpful comments.

3. ILLUSTRATING CONCEPTS IN SOCIAL PERCEPTION AND SOCIAL COGNITION

Teaching Scientific Reasoning Through Attribution Theory

Juli T. Eflin
Department of Philosophy
Ball State University

Mary E. Kite
Ball State University

Students' poor reasoning ability has been discussed at length in *Teaching of Psychology* (e.g., Gray, 1993, Rickabaugh, 1993), and many suggestions for reforming psychology classes rightly focus on critical reasoning as the needed remedy. The special issue on critical thinking (Halpern & Nummedal, 1995) has several common themes for improving the reasoning ability of psychology students: (a) use of cooperative learning, (b) explicit emphasis on problem solving procedures; (c) effectiveness of verbalizing methods and strategies; and (d) importance of metacognition, which is the ability to choose appropriate cognitive strategies deliberately for a given problem or situation. Teaching critical reasoning is intended to move students from copying down and memorizing results to understanding the reasoning that leads to results. What becomes central is the reasoning processes that will remain valuable through theory change and in nondiscipline-specific settings.

Angelo (1995) defined *critical reasoning* as "the intentional application of rational, higher order thinking skills such as analysis, synthesis, problem recognition and problem solving, inference and evaluation" (p. 6). The activity we describe is consistent with the goals of teaching critical reasoning; yet it focuses more specifically on teaching scientific reasoning, addressing the narrower concern of finding causes. That is, students are invited to think about and discuss the nature of making causal inferences and to evaluate those inferences based on standard-reasoning criteria.

An understanding of scientific reasoning can be increased by embedding the teaching of scientific reasoning in the content of psychology courses (Nisbett, 1993). We use a cooperative-learning activity to illustrate how psychologists use one particular form of scientific reasoning to make causal claims: Inference to the Best Explanation (IBE). Many types of inductive reasoning are special cases of IBE, so it is widely applicable, general, and powerful (Lipton, 1991). Essentially, an IBE involves identifying premises (the phenomena to be explained), generating possible hypotheses to account for the phenomena, and then weighing the merits of these hypotheses according to specific criteria. Whether the phenomena are based on everyday observations or data collection, the connection between IBEs and the scientific method of psychology can be seen. Psychological explanations provide an account of the causes sufficient to produce some observed behavior. As noted, this concern with causes is one distinguishing feature of scientific reasoning. Teaching about explanatory reasoning aims to improve students' understanding of the scientific method.

Table 1. Commonsense Example of Inference to the Best Explanation

Phenomena to be explained (premises):
  A banner across the room has a stylized elephant and "Welcome New Members" printed on it.
  Everyone in the room is between 18 and 30 years old.
  The room is in the student center.
  Some of the people in the room are wearing "Dole '96" buttons.
  There are free pamphlets titled "The History of the Republican Party."
  Everyone is smiling and friendly.
  No one is wearing black leather or has green hair.
Explanation (conclusion):
  You are at a meeting of Young Republicans.

Steps in Teaching IBE

The two steps we use to increase students' understanding of scientific reasoning are lecturing about IBE, including illustrating IBE with a commonsense example, and applying the concept to a psychological theory. For the latter step, we developed an interactive exercise for applying IBE to correspondent inference theory (Jones & Davis, 1965).

Lecture: General Form of IBE

In a 15-min lecture, we highlight the separation of the phenomena to be explained from the hypothesis that does the explaining. To begin, we simply draw an arrow on the board from the phrase "phenomena to be explained" to the phrase "causal hypothesis." The phenomena to be explained are the premises of the inductive argument, and the causal hypothesis is the conclusion (Herrnstein, Nickerson, de Sanchez, & Swets, 1986). We begin with an engaging, commonsense example (see Table 1).

What explains the collection of phenomena in this example is the (probable) fact that one is at a meeting of Young Republicans. Such a conclusion makes sense of the phenomena because it ties them together, showing how the statements fit into a comprehensible whole. What is important is getting students to realize that, by reaching this conclusion, they are making an inference from some facts to an explanation for those facts. But students must also realize that not just any explanation will do; explanations can be ranked according to evaluative criteria such as the three that follow.

Consistency is one criterion. The hypothesis offered as an explanation cannot be inconsistent with any of the evidence. *Quality of evidence* is a second criterion. If the evidence is selective, for example, the hypothesis is undermined. Consider again the example in Table 1. "You are at a meeting of Young Republicans" may not be the best explanation if some evidence has been omitted. If, for example, there are pamphlets from other political parties, there is also a donkey on the banner, and there are buttons for other candidates, then a better explanation would be "You are at a campus political clubs rally."

A third criterion, *coherence*, is important because a good explanation unifies and systematizes phenomena. When phenomena fit together as a whole, they form a comprehensible system. Students grasp the basic notion of coherence easily, but refinement requires discussing what undermines coherence: anomalies and ad hoc hypotheses. An anomaly is a new phenomenon that is part of the phenomena to be explained; the explanation should account for it, yet fails to do so. Ad hoc additions save the hypothesis by accounting for the anomaly but the cost is a reduction of coherence.

Applying IBE to Psychological Theories

The commonsense example is engaging and enables students to understand the structure of an explanatory argument. It does not, however, show the power of an IBE for reaching causal claims. This can be accomplished in the second step by applying the abstract form of IBE to correspondent inference theory (Jones & Davis, 1965). This theory concerns the process by which observers infer that personal characteristics (dispositions) account for an actor's actions. According to the theory, observers make the decision by considering both the action and the alliterative actions available to the actor. Observers narrow possible causes by considering the correspondence, or the clarity and directness, of the relation between the disposition and the behavior. Acts are high in correspondence when the observer concludes that the best explanation for the action was the actor's disposition. In this case, other possible causes, such as social desirability or situation effects, are ruled out.

The abstract form of IBE can be rewritten for correspondent inference theory by drawing an arrow from "witnessed behavior" to "causal explanation." Examples easily illustrate the way correspondent inference theory makes use of IBE to make causal inferences (see Table 2). In the first example, Sam's interest in money accounts for the seemingly incongruous behavior of taking a low-status job in a crime-ridden neighborhood of a city that he hates. Sam's love of money causes him to take the job. In the second example, Becky's refusal to give money to the mugger can best be explained by the conclusion that Becky has courage.

Students recognize the causal nature of these inferences and easily see that a disposition held by an actor not only explains witnessed behavior but is causally responsible for it. Furthermore, students make the right attribution if they are looking for an explanation that is also a cause. Correspondent inference theory makes sense if students see it as an explanatory framework.

The exercise. We generate arguments, each composed of five to seven statements, for this activity. Most arguments are consistent with correspondent inference theory (see Table 2 for examples), but we also include general examples similar to the one in Table 1. For each argument, one of the statements is the explanation for the behaviors or events and the rest are the phenomena to be explained. Each statement is written on a separate 5 × 8 in. index card. The cards are then randomly distributed, one card per student. The number of arguments used depends on the number of students in each class because each student receives one card.

We simply tell students to sort out the arguments by finding other people whose statements seem to fit with their own. Pandemonium ensues. With the background of the lecture, however, students are able to use heuristics

Table 2. Examples of Inference to the Best Explanation Based on Correspondent Inference Theory

Example 1:
  Phenomena to be explained:
    Sam hates Philadelphia.
    Sam hates winters.
    Sam accepts a job in Philadelphia.
    The job is low status.
    The job is in a crime-ridden neighborhood.
    The job pays $100,000 per year.
  Explained by:
    Sam is interested in money.
Example 2:
  Phenomena to be explained:
    Becky refuses to give money to a mugger.
    The mugger is shabbily dressed.
    The mugger verbally threatens Becky.
    The mugger has a gun.
    No one is nearby.
  Explained by:
    Becky is brave.

such as shouting "Who has a card about Sam?" to sort the arguments quickly. Occasionally, a student has trouble determining in which argument his or her statement belongs. In this case, we give hints. Once a group of students believes it has an entire IBE, group members write it on the chalkboard. The pandemonium lasts about 5 min; the entire process takes about 15 min.

After the IBEs are placed on the board, we ask students to describe their rationale. As students suggest reasons for accepting one particular statement as the conclusion, we link their suggestions to the previous lecture material for evaluating explanatory hypotheses. We also highlight how attribution theory is a specific example of an IBE.

Finally, we spend about 20 min discussing argument strength by soliciting students' evaluation of alternative conclusions. They examine the premises from an argument to see whether those alternatives would make good causal inferences. For example, by considering why "Becky is frugal" is not a good explanation in the mugger example, students learn how to apply criteria to evaluate explanations as good, better, and best. They also generate alternative conclusions that were not included in the original argument. "Becky is foolhardy" or "Becky does not mind dying for a few dollars" may be as reasonable as "Becky is brave" for explaining her behavior. This gives instructors the opportunity to discuss the problem of multiple causation and the difficulty in making causal claims for human behavior. Thus, students begin to learn that psychological theories are tools to analyze behavior, not merely information to be memorized for a test. The arguments used in the exercise provide a concrete framework for discussing psychology's complexities.

We have conducted this classroom exercise with introductory psychology students and social psychology students, but with course-specific examples the activity could be used in other content areas as well. Examples

Table 3. Student Evaluation of Activity

	M	SD
1. I found this classroom activity to be enjoyable.	3.88	.90
2. This exercise increased my understanding of the way in which humans make inferences about behavior.	4.04	.74
3. Scientific reasoning is not that different from common-sense reasoning.	3.50	.94
4. I understand concepts better when they are presented in lecture form rather than as a classroom exercise.	2.15	.85
5. Participating in this exercise has increased my interest in studying the way people think.	3.56	.89
6. Scientific reasoning is easy to understand.	3.48	.80
7. I would never want a career that required scientific reasoning of this form.	2.00	.84
8. Psychological principles are established through scientific reasoning.	4.13	.74
9. I learn more when activities such as this one are used as supplements to lecture.	4.23	.88
10. Although I usually enjoy classroom activities, I did not enjoy this one.	1.56	.80

Note. Higher numbers (maximum = 5.0) indicate more positive reactions to the item except for Items 4, 7, and 10. For these items, lower numbers indicate more positive reactions. *N* = 52.

typically used for a class can be restated to fit the activity, and instructors can adjust the difficulty to fit the level of the class being taught. For lower division courses, examples for which any alternative hypothesis is poor are most appropriate. In upper division courses, contrarily, instructors could consider arguments that vary in difficulty, with some hypotheses requiring considerable analysis to distinguish the best alternative. Instructors can highlight the nature of psychology and the care that must be taken before a causal claim can be made.

Examples and procedures need to be modified for a particular teaching environment. Nonetheless, there are some general guidelines for constructing examples. First, the optimal number of statements per argument is five to seven. Too many statements result in too many students in a group. Conversely, with too few statements, the class is too fragmented. Second, the statements should be worded carefully using the same sentence structure for premises and conclusion. By keeping a consistent voice (active or passive) and person (first or third), the statements do not inadvertently cue the conclusion. Third, different themes should be used for different arguments to help students find other members of their group.

As designed, the activity works well for classes of 15 to 40 students. In smaller classes, it may be more appropriate for all the students to work on each example, discussing them straight from the cards laid out on a table. Some ingenuity would have to be employed to modify this exercise for very large lecture classes. One option may be to display the phenomena on an overhead projector and ask for possible explanations. The alternatives can then be considered in light of the evaluative criteria.

Evaluation of the Activity

Participants

Participants (*N* = 52) were students from two sections of a junior-level social psychology class. All students (*N* = 66) in those sections who attended class heard the lecture and participated in the activity. Students could, however, choose to evaluate the activity in exchange for extra credit. Although all students volunteered, they also had to attend the lecture, participate in the activity, and complete all materials to receive credit. The 14 who did not meet these requirements were given an alternative extra-credit assignment.

Assessment Instruments

Pretest. To evaluate students' reasoning ability, we asked participants to read a series of statements from a general argument on evolution. This argument contained five premises and one conclusion, presented in a random order. Students marked each statement as either a premise or a conclusion and then wrote their reasons for labeling the conclusion as such. Nonpsychology examples were used to test for skills transfer to out-of-class settings.

Posttest. At posttest, students reevaluated the pretest argument. They also used the same procedure to evaluate a new argument on continental glaciation that had eight premises and one conclusion.

Survey. Ten items assessed students' perceptions of the activity and its purpose (see Table 3). Assessments were based on 5-point rating scales ranging from 1 (*strongly disagree*) to 5 (*strongly agree*).

Procedure

To evaluate the effectiveness of the learning activity, we used a nonequivalent control group design. Students in both sections of social psychology were pretested on their reasoning ability. Both groups of students then heard a lecture on attribution theory given by the course instructor. The following class day, students in one section, who were randomly determined to be the control group, completed a posttest of reasoning ability, followed by the reasoning activity. Students in the other section (experimental group) participated in the reasoning activity and then completed the posttest. Finally, both groups evaluated the activity using the items reported in Table 3.

Results

Number of premises correctly labeled for the evolution example was analyzed using a 2 (control, experimental group) × 2 (pretest, posttest) mixed analysis of variance (ANOVA). The significant Group × Test interaction, $F(1, 49) = 4.71$, p < .05, indicated that scores for the experimental group (pretest $M = 2.84$, posttest $M = 3.68$) improved more than did the scores for the control group (pretest $M = 2.46$, posttest $M = 2.42$).

An independent groups *t* test compared the number of correctly labeled premises for the continental glaciation example by group. Results showed that the experimental group ($M = 6.36$) correctly labeled more premises than did the control group ($M = 3.12$), $t(49) = 4.59$, p < .001.

Mean ratings and standard deviations for each item on the evaluation survey are reported in Table 3. Results showed that students were positive about the classroom activity; all means are significantly more positive than the neutral value of the scale, $ts(51) > 3.80$, ps < .01. The small standard deviations suggest agreement in student assessment. The results are particularly encouraging because visiting instructors implemented the exercise, and students had to adjust to the change in faculty. One may expect even more positive assessments if the exercise is conducted by the course instructor.

Discussion

This activity involved using correspondent inference theory (Jones & Davis, 1965) to demonstrate how the general argument form of IBE underlies psychological theory. This exercise has impact because it leads students to verbalize reasoning strategies and evaluative criteria, both with other students and with faculty (Astin, 1992; McKeachie, 1988). Once students understand this general reasoning form, they can more readily transfer the reasoning skill from one theory to another or modify it to suit specific theories. Due to the generality of the concepts covered, the exercise can be easily adapted for other psychological theories. Kelley's (1967) ANOVA model, for example, also assumes that observers make an inference to the best explanation by considering the distinctiveness, consistency, and consensus of behavior. Observers then conclude that the act is best accounted for either by something about the actor (internal attribution) or by something situational (external to the actor). To demonstrate this process, instructors can construct a set of cards with information about the distinctiveness, consensus, and consistency of the action (phenomena to be explained) and the causal attribution (explanation).

IBE applies to other psychological theories as well. Discussing theories of emotion, for example, can deepen and enrich students' understanding of causal and explanatory inferences. The theories of Cannon (1927), Lange and James (1922), and Schachter and Singer (1962) are all candidates for an IBE. Each suggested an explanation for emotions based on a proposed causal structure. Consider the Cannon hypothesis that emotions are explained directly by events that serve as stimuli. These same events also cause various physiological reactions, but the physiological reactions themselves do not play either an explanatory or causal role in emotional phenomena.

Similarly, the James-Lange theory proposed that the immediate or proximate cause of emotion is physiological reactions. Experiences that people label as emotions are explained by changes taking place within their bodies. Events (i.e., stimuli) are the cause and explanation of physiological reactions, but they are not the direct cause of emotion. Finally, Schachter and Singer (1962) hypothesized that cognitive assessment of external events (stimuli), along with sensing internal arousal, explains emotions. According to these authors, people ascribe emotions to themselves only by assessing the stimuli and noting their internal arousal. This argument, too, takes the form of an IBE. All three theories are attempts to explain the same phenomena. To decide among them, hypotheses must be generated and tested to see which is borne out. In this way, the evaluative criteria, especially consistency, can be reapplied.

We have used attribution theory and theories of emotion to demonstrate how knowledge of general-reasoning forms can be applied to psychological theories. Yet, the breadth of this reasoning form cannot be overstated. Virtually anytime psychologists draw cause-and-effect conclusions, they have made inferences to the best explanation. Instructors, then, can use this exercise in any course that emphasizes such causal conclusions. One must merely construct sets of cards with premises and conclusions that fit the theory or concept being discussed. In fact, instructors can best enhance scientific reasoning by teaching about IBEs at the beginning of their course and returning to it at relevant points throughout that course (Kuhn, 1993; McMillan, 1990).

The flexibility of this teaching exercise makes it a handy tool. Students gain a framework for understanding the causal, explanatory nature of psychological theories; instructors can use it to reinforce scientific reasoning throughout the term.

References

Angelo, T. A. (1995). Classroom assessment for critical thinking. *Teaching of Psychology 22*, 6-7.

Astin, A. W. (1992). *What matters in college? Four critical years*. San Francisco: Jossey-Bass.

Cannon, W. B. (1927). The James-Lange theory of emotions: A critical examination and an alternative theory. *American Journal of Psychology*, 39, 106-124.

Gray, P. (1993). Engaging students' intellects: The immersion approach to critical thinking in psychology instruction. *Teaching of Psychology, 20*, 68-74.

Halpem, D. F., & Nummedal, S. G. (Eds.). (1995). Psychologists teach critical thinking [Special issue]. *Teaching of Psychology, 22*(1).

Hemastein, R. J., Nickerson, R. S., de Sanchez, M., & Swets, J. A. (1986). Teaching thinking skills. *American Psychologist, 41*, 1279-1289.

Jones, E. E., & Davis, K. E. (1965). A theory of correspondent inferences: From acts to dispositions. In L. Berkowitz (Ed.) *Advances in experimental social psychology* (Vol. 2, pp. 219-266). New York: Academic.

Kelley, H. H. (1967). Attribution theory in social psychology. In D. Levine (Ed.), *Nebraska symposium on motivation* (Vol. 15, pp. 192-240). Lincoln: University of Nebraska Press.

Kuhn, D. (1993). Science as argument: Implications for teaching and learning scientific thinking. *Science Education, 77*, 319-337.

Lange, C. G., & James, W. J. (1922). The *emotions*. Baltimore: Waverly.

Lipton, P. (1991). *Inference to the best explanation*. London: Routledge.

McKeachie, W. (1988). Teaching thinking. *Update*, 2, 1.

McMillan, J. A. (1990). Enhancing college students' critical thinking: A review of studies. In K. St. Pierre, M. Riordan, & D. Riordan (Eds.), *Research in instructional effectiveness* (pp. 137-162). Harrisonburg, VA: Center for Research in Accounting Education.

Nisbett, R. E. (1993). *Rules for reasoning*. Hillsdale, NJ: Lawrence Erlbaum Associates, Inc.

Rickabaugh, C. A. (1993). The psychology portfolio: Promoting writing and critical thinking about psychology. *Teaching of Psychology, 20*, 170-172.

Schachter, S., & Singer, J. E. (1962). Cognitive, social, and physiological determinants of emotional states. *Psychological Review, 69*, 379-399.

Note

We thank Bemard E. Whitley, Jr., for allowing us to conduct the exercise in his social psychology class and the students in that class who volunteered to participate. We also thank Teresa Cox for assisting with data analyses.

A Classroom Demonstration of the Primacy Effect in the Attribution of Ability

Francis T. McAndrew
Knox College

One of the most active areas of research in social psychology today is the study of how individuals make judgments about the causes underlying the behavior of other people. This diverse area of investigation is loosely grouped under the label of "attribution theory." Given its current dominance in the field, most courses in social psychology and many introductory courses devote a large amount of time to exploring the various attribution theories and attributional phenomena that research has uncovered. As is the case with any psychological process, students gain a deeper appreciation of the dynamics of attribution if they are put in a situation where they see these processes at work in themselves and realize that what is being described is not simply some abstract textbook curiosity but something that they do every day. It can be especially valuable for students to become aware of some of the biases that seem to be built into the way they process information about other people.

A topic that is particularly well suited to classroom demonstrations of attributional processes is the question of how we make judgments about the ability of others. This question has advantages for the teacher. First, it is intrinsically interesting to students in that attributions based on performance in athletic events, job interviews, and the classroom ultimately come down to some conclusion about the stimulus person's "ability." Second, attributional situations relevant to ability can be full of very concrete, quantifiable information (such as the number of points scored on a test), allowing precise manipulation of the stimuli presented to the students.

One peculiar bias that commonly occurs when making attributions about ability is referred to as the "primacy effect." This phenomenon refers to the tendency for an observer's judgment to be influenced more strongly by the early information about a stimulus person than by information that comes later. A number of studies (e.g., Jones, Rock, Shaver, Goethals, & Ward, 1968; McAndrew, 1981; Newtson & Rindner, 1979) have demonstrated that subjects almost completely disregard late information when making judgments about the ability of others, as long as the task in question does not involve an ability that is thought to improve with practice (Larkin, D'Eredita, Dempsey, McClure, & Pepe, 1983). Newtson and Rindner (1979) proposed that the primacy effect occurs because individuals cease to process information effectively when they reach a point of subjectively sufficient information for making an attribution. For example, these studies have repeatedly found that a person who does well in the early stages of a problem-solving task is perceived as more intelligent than a person who does well in the later stages. In addition, the early achiever is judged as having performed better and is expected to perform better than the late achiever on subsequent tasks. All of these attributions occur even though the objectively measured performance of the two stimulus persons is exactly the same.

Because the primacy effect involves both the evaluation of others and the processing of information, it may be covered in courses on cognitive, social, industrial/organizational, or introductory psychology. A highly effective classroom demonstration of this primacy effect is based on a procedure developed by McAndrew (1981), and it can be made very flexible with some modifications suggested by Watson, deBortali-Tregerthan, and Frank (1984).

Procedure

In the demonstration, students will correct the answer sheets from a multiple-choice test taken by two hypothetical students. The teacher must first decide whether a between-subjects or a within-subjects demonstration is more suitable. Using a between-subjects design, each student will correct only one answer sheet from one hypothetical student. In the within-subjects design, each student will receive two different answer sheets from two different hypothetical students. In either case, the teacher prepares two different sets of answer sheets. One set shows an "ascending" pattern of success whereby the hypothetical student begins by getting most of the questions wrong, but late in the test begins to improve. The "descending" pattern is the reverse of this; the student starts out doing well, after which performance deteriorates. If a between-subjects design is used, one half of the class receives the ascending pattern and the other half receives the descending pattern. In the within-subjects design, each student receives one copy of each pattern. The between-subjects design is more efficient for very large classes and can be used to demonstrate the process of random assignment and the logic behind comparing randomly assigned groups. On the other hand, Watson et al. (1984) have pointed out that the demonstration may be more meaningful if the students experience the primacy effect firsthand by serving as their own controls, and that dividing small classes in half can result in very small groups. For these reasons, the demonstration will be described hereafter as a within-subjects design, keeping in mind that it can easily be changed to a between-subjects procedure when circumstances call for it.

Materials

Each student will receive two multiple-choice answer sheets, one marked "Person #1" and the other marked "Person #2." Each answer sheet will appear to be a completed set of 30 items. Each item consists of five alternatives (lettered "a" through "e"), one of which is circled. Each answer sheet is followed by a second attached page containing the following three questions:

1. Out of the 30 problems, how many would you estimate that this student answered correctly?
2. If this person were to complete the test, taking the next set of 30 problems (the test has 60 problems), how many would you estimate that the person would get correct?
3. On the scale below, circle the "X" that best reflects your estimate of this student's general intelligence.

Unintelligent X X X X X X X X X Intelligent

Instructions to Students

The multiple-choice test should be described to students as the first 30 items of a 60-item test of mental ability. It will be more involving for the students if they believe that they are grading a *real* test taken by a *real* student. Details about the nature of the test questions, purpose of the test, and where the test takers were from can be added to make it more interesting and realistic without affecting the outcome of the demonstration. The entire demonstration should be described as an attempt to find out how well people can form impressions about others based on nothing but a test performance.

Half of the class is assigned to correct Person # 1's test first the other half corrects Person #2's test. As the teacher reads through the list of "correct" responses, students put a check mark beside each wrong answer. As soon as the list of 30 items is finished, students complete the three questions on the second page of the questionnaire without referring back to the answer sheet. This procedure is then repeated for the second hypothetical student.

Answer Key

For the ascending pattern of success, the answers (in order) for the 30 items on the stimulus person's answer sheet should be: a,a,d,c,e,d,c,c,b,e,a,c,d,a, b,b,e,b,b,c,d, b,a,d,e,c,d,c,b,a. For the descending pattern, the answers should be: a,c,c,b,d,d,b,b,c,d,b,a,c,a, b,b,e,a,e,d, c,c,b,c,e,b,b,d,c,a. The "correct" answers read out loud by the teacher for the 30 items should be: a,c,c,b,a,d,b, b,a,e,a,a,c,a,a,e,b,b,d,c,a,a,d,e,a,d,c,b,a. Using these patterns, the number of "correct" answers will be 15 out of 30 (50%) for both the ascending and descending patterns of performance. The "ascending" stimulus person gets 5 correct answers on the first 15 items and 10 correct answers on the second 15. The "descending" person gets 10 correct out of the first 15 items and 5 correct on the second 15.

Concluding Remarks

Most students (experience suggests that 80% is not an unreasonable number to expect) will show a very strong primacy effect by estimating that the "descending" performer did significantly better than the "ascending" performer, by judging the intelligence of the descending performer as being higher, and by predicting that the descending performer will do better in the future. The effect is robust enough that a comparison of the group means using a *t* test will usually be significant, even with relatively small groups. However, it is usually easier for the teacher and more impressive for the students to note the high percentage of the class that fell prey to the primacy effect, and to put the raw data on the board so that differences in judgments made about the two stimulus persons are convincingly obvious. Many students will be so surprised to hear that the scores were the same in both cases that they will insist on counting the answers on the answer sheets to verify the fact. Discussing these results leads easily into a more general discussion of how we make judgments about others, the importance of first impressions, and other issues that are at the heart of attribution theory. The demonstration can be as useful as a springboard for discussion as it is for its purely didactic purpose. In addition, this exercise can be used to teach something about methodology rather than attribution theory; it is ideally suited to illustrate the trade-offs involved when deciding between within-subjects and between-subjects designs.

For example, in statistics and research methods classes students can be shown that the variability in each group can be (and should be!) the same even though the central tendencies are different, and that as group size increases, smaller differences between the means take on greater significance. It will also be clear that when deciding whether to use between-subjects or within-subjects designs, an experimenter will have to anticipate how the change in degrees of freedom will be balanced by other gains or losses in the experiment as a whole. The instructor might also point out that there are many different ways of interpreting any set of data. In this case, you may compare the mean scores from each stimulus person, examine the percentages of subjects giving higher ratings to one stimulus person versus the other, or simply compare the number of students who showed the primacy effect to the number who did not. Obviously, with a little ingenuity, many statistical/design issues can be introduced through this demonstration.

In summary, the exercise described here is easy, effective, and flexible; it is well suited for small discussion-oriented classes as well as the large lecture hall.

References

Jones, E. E., Rock, L., Shaver, K. L., Goethals, G. R., & Ward, L. M. (1968). Pattern of performance and ability attribution: An unexpected primacy effect. *Journal of Personality and Social Psychology, 10,* 317-340.

Larkin, J., D'Eredita, T., Dempsey, S., McClure, J., & Pepe, M. (1983, April). *Hope for late bloomers: Another look at the primacy effect in ability attribution.* Paper presented at the meeting of the Eastern Psychological Association, Philadelphia, PA.

McAndrew, F. T. (1981). Pattern of performance and attributions of ability and gender. *Personality and Social Psychology Bulletin, 7,* 583-587.

Newtson, D., & Rindner, R. J. (1979). Variation in behavior perception and ability attribution. *Journal of Personality and Social Psychology, 37,* 1847-1858.

Watson, D. L., deBortali-Tregerthan, G., & Frank, J. (1984). *Instructor's manual to accompany "Social psychology: Science and application."* Glenview, IL: Scott, Foresman.

Teaching Attribution Theory With a Videotaped Illustration

Michael J. White
Debra L. Lilly
Ball State University

Concept learning is an important teaching objective. Exclusive classroom focus on concepts, however, may create a sense of irrelevance and boredom in students. This is especially true if concepts are not tied to actual situations or otherwise illustrated. Apart from increasing student interest, vivid, real-life illustrations serve to define and emphasize meaningful relationships among concepts. And as meaning increases, so will retention (Anderson, 1985).

Social psychology's attribution theories embody an especially complex set of concepts. This loose collection of ideas attempts to explain how persons cognitively interpret (i. e., attribute) the cause, implications, and context of their own and others' behavior (e.g., Heider, 1958; Jones & Davis, 1965; Kelley, 1973; Weiner, 1979). One strategy used to teach attribution theory encourages students' self-awareness of how they use attribution processes to explain the behavior of their friends and acquaintances (McAndrew, 1985). Although this approach is commendable, we have tried another. Specifically, a series of behavioral situations have been illustrated on an instructional videotape. Students who view the videotape are led systematically (indeed they are compelled) to arrive at attributions for the behavior shown on the tape. For several reasons, Kelley's (1973) covariation attribution model is the focus of these situations. The reasons are: (a) It is a highly complex theory or model, (b) students consistently have difficulty understanding its concepts, and (c) the nature of the theory lends itself to systematic visual representation.

The videotape was shot in our university's television production studio. The premise of the videotaped situations is taken from an example used by McArthur (1972) and involves persons at a dance. The question posed to viewers is, "Why did the woman have her feet stepped on by her partner?" Is it because she is clumsy, because her partner is clumsy, or because of some unique combination of events? These attributional questions force viewers to extract and analyze information presented using the analytical framework proposed by Kelley (1973). Three sets of scenes are presented on the tape. Only the first set of scenes is discussed in detail.

The tape begins with a graphic representation of Kelley's (1973) attribution cube, which illustrates the three referents available for social perceivers to observe. These referents include: (a) persons, (b) persons over time, and (c) entities (i.e., people with whom the referent persons interact or events in which the referent persons participate). The tape then continues with persons dancing at a "dance class." The camera focuses on one couple. On four separate occasions, the viewer sees the male partner (Bob) step on the female partner's (Kim's) foot. A sentence appears on the screen: "Bob almost always steps on Kim's foot when they dance." This particular combination of events illustrates a condition of high consistency (i.e., Bob is consistent over time when interacting with Kim, the entity).

The next series of scenes appears. In them, Bob dances with Jane, Betty, and Michelle. He steps on no one's feet. The fourth scene shows Bob dancing with Kim. Bob trips over Kim's foot again. The sentence appears: "Bob almost never steps on anyone else's feet when they dance." This combination of events illustrates high distinctiveness (i.e., Bob reacts in a distinctive way to Kim, the entity).

Four more scenes follow. In the first three, Jim, George, and Alan dance with Kim. None of them trips over her foot. The fourth scene shows Bob stepping on Kim's foot again. This is emphasized with the sentence: "Hardly anyone else steps on Kim's feet when they dance." Low consensus has been illustrated; other persons do not interact with the entity, Kim, in the same fashion as Bob, the person of interest.

Finally, viewers are asked the question, "Why did Bob trip on Kim's feet?" They are given three possible answers: (a) Bob is clumsy (i. e., an attribution to a disposition of his), (b) Kim is clumsy (i.e., an attribution to an external cause from Bob's standpoint), and (c) it is due to some unique pattern of interaction between them (i.e., a joint explanation). Answer c is correct in this case. Viewers are also asked how certain they are concerning the cause. Under the conditions shown (i.e., high consistency, high distinctiveness, and low consensus), attributions are made with confidence according to Kelley's model. As noted earlier, 2 other combinations of 12 scenes each are shown in order to illustrate different combinations of behaviors and attributional possibilities.

It is also important for students to learn how persons deviate from Kelley's (1973) normative model. Accordingly, the tape is accompanied by a lecture and readings that describe the wide range of biases and errors in the attribution process (Fiske & Taylor, 1984; Lau & Russell, 1980; Storms, 1973). As Gayné (1966) suggested, these additional activities help the students to understand the principles underlying attribution processes.

Class discussion centers around the implications of the concepts, the operation of the concepts in the videotape, and the generalizations that students made to their own experiences. After the discussion, students are reminded that their attributions offer only possible explanations for the behaviors observed. Alternative perspectives, including those by Dweck and Licht (1980), Jones and Davis (1965), and Weiner (1982), are then introduced and discussed.

Informal observation suggests that this approach is highly effective. Students are animated while watching the videotape and easily draw the "appropriate" attributional conclusions. Their attention is directed to the ease and naturalness with which they make their attributions. any so doing, they experience one of the important premises of the theory: People are "naive scientists" who spontaneously use covariation in social information to make inferences about puzzling behaviors. Furthermore, the concepts of the theory are no longer abstract and removed, but are linked to their own thinking and perception.

References

Anderson, J. R. (1985). *Cognitive psychology and its implications*. New York: Freeman.

Dweck, C. S., & Licht, B. G. (1980). Learned helplessness and intellectual achievement. In J. Garber & M. E. P. Seligman (Eds.), *Human helplessness: Theory and applications* (pp. 197-221). New York: Academic.

Fiske, S. T., & Taylor, S. E. (1984). *Social cognition*. Reading, MA: Addison-Wesley.

Gayné, R. M. (1966). The learning of principles. In H. J. Klausmeier & C. W. Harns (Eds.), *Analysis of concept learning* (pp. 81-95) . New York: Academic.

Heider, F. (1958). *The psychology of interpersonal relations*. New York: Wiley.

Jones, E. E., & Davis, K. E. (1965). From acts to dispositions: The attribution process in person perception. In L. Berkowirz (Ed.), *Advances in experimental social psychology* (Vol. 2, pp. 218-266). New York Academic.

Kelley, H. H. (1973). The processes of causal ambition. *American Psychologist, 28,* 107-128.

Lau, R. R., & Russell, D. (1980). Attributions in sports pages. *Journal of Personality and Social Psychology, 39,* 29-38.

McAndrew, F. T. (1985). A classroom demonstration of the primacy effect in the attribution of ability. *Teaching of Psychology, 12,* 209-211.

McArthur, L. Z. (1972). The how and what of why: Some determinants and consequences of causal attribution. *Journal of Personality and Social Psychology, 22,* 171-193.

Storms, M. D. (1973). Videotape and the attribution process. Reviewing actors' and observers' point of view. *Journal of Personality and Social Psychology, 27,* 166- 175.

Weiner, B. (1979). A theory of motivation for some classroom experience. *Journal of Educational Psychology, 71,* 3-25.

Weiner, B. (1982). The emotional consequences of causal attributions. In M. S. Clark & S. T. Fiske (Eds.) *Affect and cognition: The 17th annual Carnegie symposium on cognition* (pp. 185-209). Hillsdale, NJ: Lawrence Erlbaum Associates, Inc.

Notes

1. We thank Joe Pacino for his assistance in producing the videotape.
2. Persons interested in obtaining a copy of the videotape should contact the Office of Research, Ball State University, Muncie, IN 47306.

The Self-Reference Effect: Demonstrating Schematic Processing in the Classroom

Donelson R. Forsyth
Katherine Hsu Wibberly
Virginia Commonwealth University

Schemas have emerged as central theoretical constructs in contemporary analyses of interpersonal perception. Drawing on studies of the reconstructive nature of memory, schema theory assumes that information about the social world is organized within a system of cognitive associations. These networks consist of memory nodes pertaining to specific schema-relevant concepts and pathways that link these nodes to one another (Kihlstrom et al., 1988). *Person schemas*, for example, summarize one's intuitive understanding of other people, including their typical behaviors, traits, and goals. *Self-schemas* organize perceptions of one's own qualities, and *stereotypes* describe the typical characteristics of people in various social groups. *Event schemas*, or scripts, define and structure one's perceptions of social situations (Fiske & Taylor, 1991).

We could not encode, store, or retrieve social information if we did not possess schemas. Students, however, sometimes have difficulty recognizing the impact of schemas on social perception and cognition. Researchers have documented a number of schematic-processing effects, but these effects are often so subtle that relatively sensitive measures are required to detect them. Moreover, even though the effects of schematic processing are ubiquitous, individuals have no access to these cognitive processes; perceivers cannot monitor their use of schemas when encoding and retrieving information (Nisbett & Wilson, 1977). Behaviorally oriented students tend to question the need to posit these cognitive constructs.

Given the centrality of the schema concept in social and cognitive psychology and students' difficulties in grasping this complex construct, we developed a classroom demonstration of schema-based processing. The demonstration takes advantage of the self-reference effect: the tendency for individuals to show superior memory for information that pertains to their self-schemas. When individuals are asked to describe their political beliefs, those who possess well defined self-schemas pertaining to politics can describe their beliefs in much more detail than individuals who are aschematic with regard to politics

(Fiske, Lau, & Smith, 1990). People who adopt a feminine gender identity (feminine schematics) require less time when they are asked to rate their feminine attributes rather than their masculine attributes. Masculine schematics show the reverse tendency, and individuals who are aschematic on both masculinity and femininity respond with equal rapidity and confidence to both types of attributes (Markus, Crane, Bernstein, & Siladi, 1982). Also, when individuals are exposed to a long string of adjectives, they can recall more of the self-referent adjectives compared to the nonrelevant adjectives (Rogers, Kuiper, & Kirker, 1977).

We used an incidental memory procedure to demonstrate the self-reference effect. Students were asked to indicate which of a number of adjectives read aloud were selfdescriptive. Next the students were, without previous warning, asked to recall as many of the adjectives as they could. Students then reviewed their list of recalled adjectives and indicated whether or not each recalled adjective had been previously rated as self-referent or non referent. The self reference effect was demonstrated if the percentage of self referent items recalled exceeded the percentage of nonreferent items recalled.

Method

Undergraduate (16 women and 14 men) and graduate (23 women and 5 men) students enrolled in Social Psychology participated in the study. At the beginning of the exercise, each participant numbered a blank sheet of paper from 1 to 20. The instructor, who was a man, then read a list of 18 adjectives aloud after telling the students to circle the number corresponding to the adjective if they felt it was selfdescriptive. If, for example, students thought that Item 6, "loyal," described them, then they would circle the number 6 on their sheet of paper. The items were drawn from Tzuriel (1984) and included the following: forceful, quiet, generous, dominant, tender, loyal, independent, compassionate, adaptable, courageous, cheerful, secretive, principled, romantic, responsible, dynamic, forgiving, and careful.

When the self-rating task was completed, the instructor talked about miscellaneous class matters for 1 min. He then told the subjects to list, in any order, all of the adjectives they could remember. When students finished the incidental recall task, the instructor distributed the list of items. The students counted and recorded the total number of adjectives they circled during the self-rating task, the number of self-referent words recalled, and the number of nonreferent words recalled. Then they calculated the percentage of self referent adjectives recalled and the percentage of nonreferent adjectives recalled. Percentages were used to take into account the varying number of self-referent words initially identified by subjects. If, for example, a subject felt that 12 of the 18 items were self-referent, then by chance alone his or her recall list would include more self-referent items. Evidence of self-reference, in this procedure, requires that the percentage of self-referent items recalled exceeds the percentage of nonreferent items recalled.

Results

Analysis of students' responses suggests that the demonstration effectively documented the self-reference effect. Subjects recalled only an average of 42.5% of the nonreferent words compared to 56.0% of the self-referent terms. A 2 x 2 (Sex x Type of Adjective [self-referent vs. nonreferent]) mixed analysis of variance yielded only a main effect for type of adjective, $F(1, 56) = 13.82$, $p < .001$.

Discussion

The procedures used in this demonstration, although rudimentary, are sufficiently sensitive to document the self reference effect: Subjects' memory for self-referent items was superior to their memory for items that were not self referent. The procedure is also a practical one. Because it does not require individual testing sessions or reaction time assessment, it can be used during class with a large group of students.

The demonstration also facilitates the analysis of several methodological and theoretical issues concerning schematic processing of information. Initially, students maintained that their incidental recall scores were shaped primarily by the vividness of the trait terms. Attention-getting trait terms, they contended, were better remembered than more pallid terms. The exercise, however, convincingly demonstrated to them the impact of their self-schemas because more memorable words were also more self-descriptive words. The discussion also proved useful in illustrating research design and data analysis. Some students, for example, failed to correct for initial frequencies of self-descriptive terms when they first explored the effect. Students often recalled more self-referent words than nonreferent words, but this difference cannot be interpreted until scores are adjusted to reflect the number of items initially selected as self-referent.

The demonstration also facilitated the analysis of depth of-processing and schema-based memory models of social cognition (Klein, Loftus, & Burton, 1989). First, depth-of processing theory maintains that self-referent information is processed at a deeper level than nonreferent information. If, for example, the students were asked "Does the word have more than two syllables?," they could respond without processing the word very deeply. Such shallow processing would not lead to particularly durable memories. In contrast, self referent encoding requires much deeper processing (Klein & Kihlstrom, 1986). Second, schema theories suggest that the more elaborate the schema that will hold the incoming information, the better our ability to recall that information. Self-schemas may be the most complex and intricate associative networks in our memory system, so self-referent information is particularly memorable. Both of these theories could be demonstrated in the classroom by varying the initial question posed to subjects. Although some students could answer the question "Does the word describe you?," others could be asked "Does the word have more than two syllables" or "Does the word describe your psychology teacher?" (Bellezza, 1984).

Depending on interest, the exercise could also be used to explore the cognitive consequences of gender identity. Because the adjectives used fall into three categories—masculine, feminine, and neutral—students' self-ratings reflect their sex-role orientation. Masculine individuals, for example, should circle more of the items that reflect masculine qualities (e.g., dominant and independent), whereas feminine individuals should circle more of the items that reflect feminine qualities (e.g., tender and compassionate). Recall scores, too, can be reexamined to explore memory biases. Individuals who incorporated masculinity into their self-concepts should recall more masculine than feminine words, whereas feminine schematics should remember more feminine adjectives than masculine ones (Markus et al., 1982).

References

Bellezza, F. S. (1984). The self as a mnemonic device: The role of internal cues. *Journal of Personality and Social Psychology, 47,* 506-516.

Fiske, S. T., Lau, R. R., & Smith, R. A. (1990). On the varieties and utilities of political expertise. *Social Cognition, 8,* 31-48.

Fiske, S. T., & Taylor, S. E. (1991). *Social cognition* (2nd ed.). New York: McGraw-Hill.

Kihlstrom, J. F., Cantor, N., Albright, J. S., Chew, B. R, Klein, S. B., & Niedenthal, P. M. (1988). Information processing and the study of the self. In L. Berkowitz

(Ed.), *Advances in experimental social psychology* (Vol. 17, pp. 2-48). New York: Academic.

Klein, S. B., & Kihlstrom, J. F. (1986). Elaboration, organization, and the self-reference effect in memory. *Journal of Experimental Psychology: General, 115*, 26-38.

Klein, S. B., Loftus, J., & Burton, H. A. (1989). Two self reference effects: The importance of distinguishing between self-descriptiveness judgments and autobiographical retrieval in self-referent encoding. *Journal of Personality and Social Psychology, 56*, 853-865.

Markus, H., Crane, M., Bernstein, S., & Siladi, M. (1982). Self schemas and gender. *Journal of Personality and Social Psychology, 42*, 38-50.

Nisbett, R. E., & Wilson, T. D. (1977). Telling more than we can know: Verbal reports on mental processes. *Psychological Review, 84*, 231-259.

Rogers, T. B., Kuiper, N. A., & Kirker, W. S. (1977). Self reference and the encoding of personal information. *Journal of Personality and Social Psychology, 35*, 677-688.

Tzuriel, D. (1984). Sex role typing and ego identity in Israeli, oriental, and western adolescents. *Journal of Personality and Social Psychology, 46*, 440-457.

A Classroom Demonstration of Nuttin's (1985) Ownership Effect: The Letters of My Own First Name

Su L. Boatright-Horowitz
University of Rhode Island

Numerous studies have demonstrated that events or objects associated with oneself are preferred relative to similar events or objects unrelated to the self (e.g., Beggan, 1992; Irwin & Gebhard, 1946). Although the underlying mechanisms are unknown, humans universally perceive the world in a self-enhancing fashion, a proclivity suggested by some researchers to be automatic and reflexive (e.g., Nuttin, 1985; Paulhus, Graf, & Van Selst, 1989; Zajonc, 1980; see also Taylor, 1989, for a discussion of the influence of awareness on positive illusions). This unconscious preference for self may be reliably demonstrated in preference tests for first and surname letters (the name letter effect; e.g., Nuttin, 1985) and appears to be independent of culture and language (Nuttin, 1987). Furthermore, research conducted so that each letter served as its own control within a large population of subjects (Nuttin, 1987) still resulted in significant name letter preferences, demonstrating that the phenomenon was not a mere exposure effect (Zajonc, 1968). Additional research suggested that preferences for name letters cannot be understood in terms of a mastery pleasure effect (Hoorens, Nuttin, Herman, & Pavakanun, 1990), because stronger preferences were associated with first learned languages than those learned later in life. Thus, the name letter effect appears to be a robust phenomenon in which positive affective responses result from name ownership. The aim of this study was to modify and replicate Nuttin's (1985, 1987) procedures for use in a classroom setting.

Method

Subjects

Participants were 50 undergraduates enrolled in a social psychology course at the University of Rhode Island. All students in attendance for a course lecture on self-esteem were requested to participate.

Procedure

After a brief (about 5 min) review of material discussed in the previous lecture, students were asked to participate in an experiment. They were requested to organize themselves into pairs and to change their seats if necessary to sit next to their partner. After some encouragement, this step was accomplished, and the pairs of students were asked to "introduce themselves to each other and to chat for a few minutes." (These brief instructions placed no special emphasis on the exchange or remembrance of names so that subject expectancy effects would be minimized, and the brevity of the instructions helped ensure that introductions would be carried out.) All students appeared to comply, and many pairs of students were observed to be laughing and talking. These conversations were allowed to continue for about 1 to 2 min, then each pair was asked to decide who was to be the experimenter and who was to be the subject in the upcoming study. Because Nuttin's (1985) ownership effect was briefly mentioned in the course textbook, students were asked to make this decision based on their relative familiarity with the assigned readings so that the role of subject would be played by the more naive individual. Students serving as subjects were then asked to leave the classroom and wait just outside the closed door.

The experimenters moved to the side of the classroom farthest from the door so that the instructions they received could not be heard by the students outside. These students were then asked to derive a list of letters beginning with the letters forming the first name of their subjects. They were also told to select an equal number of letters not contained in the first name of their subject and to match, if possible, the numbers of vowels and consonants. (If time permits, these procedures can be modified to take into account the relative frequency of letters in English or other languages as students derive lists of nonname comparison letters; see Nuttin, 1987, p. 389) If a subject's name contained too many vowels to permit matching, an appropriate number of consonants could be selected. If a name contained duplicate letters, students were told to treat each duplication as a single letter. All selected letters were then arranged in a pseudo-random fashion and written on a sheet of paper in preparation for testing. Experimenters were instructed to ask subjects to rate their liking of each letter on the list using a 5-point scale ranging from *like a little* (1) to *like a lot* (5). They were also asked to conduct the test as quickly as possible "without giving their subjects a chance to think about what they were doing" and to hold the sheets of paper so that their subjects could not view the full list. Finally, experimenters were asked to record the subjects' answers to permit later analysis of the group results. Instructions to the experimenters did not reveal the specific hypothesis for this experiment, although the experimenters undoubtedly knew that subjects could be expected to respond differentially to name and "nonname" letters. However, the request that researchers conduct the test rapidly served an additional function of minimizing possible experimenter bias effects.

After returning to their seats, experimenters required 2 or 3 min more to derive their lists. When everyone was ready, the subjects reentered the classroom and testing began for each pair of students. A scan of the classroom

revealed that the experimenters were carefully following instructions and were holding their sheets of paper so that subjects could not read the lists of letters. Once testing was underway, the instructor began drawing a chart on the chalkboard to illustrate a later portion of the lecture, but the drawing could also serve to mislead subjects about the purpose of the experiment. After testing was completed, students were requested to calculate the total rating score for the letters in each subject's name and the total rating score for letters not contained in the subject's name. Upon hearing this, many of the students serving as subjects groaned or otherwise indicated surprise about the goal of the experiment. Scores were written on the chalkboard as the experimenters called out the relevant information. A scan of the data suggested that the demonstration was successful. More experimenters reported a higher total score for subjects' name letters than for nonname letters.

Results and Discussion

There were 25 sets of total rating scores for the class. (I requested that experimenters use total rating scores because they could be easily and quickly calculated by students.) For 64% of the subjects tested, the total rating of preference for the letters in the subjects' own names was greater than their total rating of preference for the letters not contained in their names. Twelve percent of the subjects rated their preference for the letters of their names as equal to their preference for letters not in their names, and the remaining 24% indicated a preference for letters not contained in their own names. Data were analyzed using a sign test for correlated samples so that the number of letters on each list (and the number of letters per name) would not directly influence the results. Subsequent analyses revealed that a significant number of these subjects preferred the letters of their own names when compared to a matched list of letters not contained in their names ($z = 1.80$, $p < .05$; directional test; see Seigel, 1956, for a discussion of nonparametric statistical tests).

Nuttin's (1985, 1987) name letter effect is a powerful phenomenon that can be reliably demonstrated in a teaching situation to illustrate self-enhancement or systematic preferences that are not normally accessible to conscious awareness. This classroom demonstration is particularly useful because it requires that students question the validity of verbal reports as a means of assessing the bases of personal preferences (see Nisbett & Wilson, 1977, for full discussion). My personal observations suggest that, without an experiential-learning component to class discussions, these ideas can be counterintuitive for many undergraduates.

References

Beggan, J. K. (1992). On the social nature of nonsocial perception: The mere ownership effect. *Journal of Personality and Social Psychology, 62,* 229-237.

Hoorens, V., Nuttin, J. M., Jr., Herman, I. E., & Pavakanun, U. (1990). Mastery pleasure versus mere ownership: A quasi-experimental cross-cultural and cross-alphabetical test of the name letter effect. *European Journal of Social Psychology, 20*, 181-205.

Irwin, F. W., & Gebhard, M. E. (1946). Studies in object-preferences: The effect of ownership and other social influences. *American Journal of Psychology, 59*, 633-651.

Nisbett, R. E., & Wilson, T. D. (1977). Telling more than we can know: Verbal reports on mental processes. *Psychological Review, 84*, 231-259.

Nuttin, J. M., Jr. (1985). Narcissism beyond Gestalt and awareness: The name letter effect. *European Journal of Social Psychology, 15*, 353-361.

Nuttin, J. M., Jr. (1987). Affective consequences of mere ownership: The name letter effect in twelve European languages. *European Journal of Social Psychology, 17*, 381 402.

Paulhus, D. L., Graf, P., & Van Selst, M. (1989). Attentional load increases the positivity of self-presentation. *Social Cognition, 7*, 389-400.

Siegel, S. (1956). *Nonparametric statistics for the behavioral sciences.* New York: McGraw-Hill.

Taylor, S. E. (1989). Illusions in perspective. In S. E. Taylor (Ed.) *Positive illusions: Create self-deception and the healthy mind* (pp. 227-246). New York: Basic Books.

Zajonc, R. B. (1968). Attitudinal effects of mere exposure. *Journal of Personality and Social Psychology, 9*, 1-27.

Zajonc, R. B. (1980). Feeling and thinking: Preferences need no inferences. *American Psychologist, 35*, 151-175.

Note

I thank Jerry Cohen for our many discussions of the name letter effect and for our continued collaboration investigating this phenomenon

Can You Predict the Overjustification Effect?

Harry L. Hom, Jr.
Southwest Missouri State University

Much research has been devoted to the interesting and puzzling phenomenon known as the *overjustification effect* (Lepper, Greene, & Nisbett, 1973). This effect was noted when an individual's subsequent intrinsic motivation to perform an attractive activity is undermined by the presence of a salient, extrinsic reward to perform the activity initially. Extensive empirical work supported the effect in both children and adults for rewards and other forms of extrinsic incentives (Deci & Ryan, 1985; Lepper & Gilovich, 1981). Many researchers (e. g., Lepper & Greene, 1978) considered the effect counterintuitive.

One of the more widely accepted explanations of the overjustification effect is based on attribution and self-perception theory (Bem, 1972; Kelly, 1972). When presented with an extrinsic reward for engaging in an activity, individuals are thought to attribute their behavior to the reward and discount their intrinsic interest in the activity. Persons who have two plausible explanations for their behavior will emphasize the external one ("I'm doing it for the reward") at the expense of the internal attribution ("I like it"). If the external inducement offers an incentive that seems inappropriately large, individuals may conclude that the activity is only worth doing for the reward. When discounting occurs, the individual's subsequent intrinsic interest in the activity is undermined.

However, when college students in psychology classes learn about the overjustification effect and its theoretical explanation, they are not surprised and often say, "Everyone knows that" or "I knew it all along." These statements could be explained by several theoretical perspectives, including achievement motivation and hindsight bias. For several years, I have questioned why the overjustification effect would be unexpected to psychologists but not to students. Studies in which students tried to predict research outcomes revealed that they did not, in fact, "know it all along" (Hom & Riche, 1988). In this article, I describe a classroom activity designed to lead students to develop an appreciation of the hidden nature of the overjustification effect. In addition, I introduced students to (a) the limitations of commonsense views of human behavior, (b) information about the use of rewards at home and school, and (c) a discussion of intrinsic and extrinsic motivation.

Description of the Activity

After a short discussion about whether preschool children liked to draw and receive recognition in the form of "good player" badges and honor roll boards, I asked students to imagine that we were conducting the experiment at one of our local preschool centers. I told them to pay close attention so they could make predictions before knowing the actual outcome of an experiment. Then I gave them the following synopsis of Lepper et al.'s (1973) research.

Only preschoolers showing high interest in drawing during free playtime were selected for the research. The children were tested individually and assigned randomly to one of three conditions. In the expected reward condition, children were shown a good player badge and told that if they did a good job of drawing, they could earn a good player badge and have their names put on the school honor roll board. All children in this condition got the expected awards. In the unexpected reward condition, children were asked to draw without any mention of the awards. Unexpectedly, at the end of drawing, all of these children were given the awards. Finally, in the control condition, children were asked simply to draw without promise or presentation of the awards. After this task, children were observed back in their classroom during free playtime, and the amount of time spent drawing was recorded.

After presenting the various conditions, I had the students list the similarities and differences among the three conditions for reward expected and reward received. Then students predicted how much time they thought the children from each condition would draw during the later free-play period. I drew bar graphs of their time predictions on the chalkboard, and then the class voted for one of them. Depending on the level of discussion I encouraged, this exercise took from 20 to 75 min.

The correct prediction is that children from the expected reward condition should later draw less than children from either the control condition or the unexpected reward condition, with no significant differences between the latter two conditions. After I provided students with the correct experimental results, they were receptive to a discussion of the overjustification hypothesis as well as other theoretical accounts of the phenomenon (e.g., Deci & Ryan, 1985).

Evaluation of the Exercise

The need for this exercise is demonstrated in three ways. First, students' time predictions were inaccurate. Second, students' reactions to the exercise were positive. Third, students' performance on test items was good.

Data on students' specific time predictions for the expected reward, unexpected reward, and control conditions were available from two Child Psychology classes. Students typically generated three to five predictions. Although their predicted outcomes were diverse, their hypothesized results did not correspond to the overjustification effect. The most popular incorrect prediction was that both expected and unexpected rewards would be more effective than the control condition. Usually, students were uncertain about the relative merits of expected and unexpected rewards. Not one student generated the correct prediction in these two classes.

These classroom data did not support the notion that students were knowledgeable about the overjustification effect. Our previous research involving 13 studies using 349 subjects (Hom & Riche, 1988) similarly indicated that students were unlikely to predict the overjustification effect; only 1% of the subjects did so.

Students in three undergraduate Child psychology classes ($N = 77$) completed an evaluation questionnaire in the class period after the exercise. On a scale ranging from *not much* (1) to *a great deal* (5), they indicated that they enjoyed the exercise ($M = 3.8$), it was better than other class activities ($M = 3.9$), it aided their understanding of the overjustification effect ($M = 4.1$), it was appropriate for class time ($M = 3.8$), and it was worthwhile ($M = 3.9$) overall.

Two multiple-choice questions concerning the concept of overjustification presented in the exercise were included on the final examination. The percentage of correct responses by 115 students for these two questions was 49.6% and 53.9%. Because only 77 (67%) students had been in class for the overjustification exercise, the test scores may represent a higher level of comprehension than the absolute values indicate.

When the exercise was part of a guest lecture, students in an Educational Psychology class ($N = 19$) also evaluated this activity positively on the 5-point scale mentioned earlier; all evaluation items averaged at least 4.2. In addition, these students took a 10-item pop quiz. Multiple-choice items concerned the overjustification effect, its theoretical explanation, and other relevant research related to intrinsic and extrinsic motivation. Student performance ranged from 60% to 100% ($M = 81.6\%$).

Since 1975, my colleagues and I have used this activity extensively with class sizes from 30 to 50 students, and I have used it in talks to community organizations. The overjustification activity has been successful in challenging students to question their beliefs about rewards when they are asked to make predictions about age groups ranging from preschoolers to college students. Students seldom predict the overjustification effect, but they participate in a positive and enthusiastic fashion. They enjoy this technique even though it shows them that they did not know it all along.

References

Bem, D. J. (1972). Self-perception theory. In L. Berkowitz (Ed.), *Advances In experimental social psychology* (Vol 6, pp. 1-62). New York: Academic.

Deci, E. L., & Ryan, R. M. (1985). *Intrinsic motivation and self determination in human behavior.* New York: Plenum.

Hom, H. L., Jr., & Riche, J. (1988, August). *Failure of individuals to predict the detrimental reward effect.* Paper presented at the annual meeting of the American Psychological Association, Atlanta.

Kelly, H. H. (1972). *Causal schemata and the attribution process.* New York: General Learning Press.

Lepper, M. R., & Gilovich, T. (1981). The multiple functions of reward: A social-developmental perspective. In S. S. Brehm, S. M. Kassin, & F. X. Gibbons (Eds.), *Developmental social psychology: Theory and research* (pp. 1-31) . New York: Oxford University Press.

Lepper, M. R., & Greene, D. (1978). Overjustification research and beyond: Toward a means-ends analysis of intrinsic and extrinsic motivation. In M. R. Lepper & D. Greene (Eds.), *The hidden costs of reward* (pp. 109-148). Hillsdale, NJ: Lawrence Erlbaum Associates, Inc.

Lepper, M. R., Greene, D., & Nisbett, R. E. (1973). Undermining children's interest with extrinsic reward: A test of the "overjustification" hypothesis. *Journal of Personality and Social Psychology, 28,* 129-137.

Note

I thank Arden Miller, Donn Kaiser, and Susan Hom for their comments on an earlier draft of this article.

A Classroom Exercise in Impression Formation

Joy L. Berrenberg
University of Colorado at Denver

The process of impression formation has been the focus of theory and research in social psychology for several decades. The topic is covered in a variety of courses, including introductory psychology, personality, social psychology, industrial/organizational psychology, and human relations. The exercise described in this article provides students with a vivid and concrete demonstration of their own impression-formation strategies.

Impression formation is concerned, in part, with the way in which we make initial judgments about others. Although these judgments are based on limited information, we depend on them to help shape expectations concerning subsequent social interactions (Levinger, 1983).

The process of forming first impressions is frequently introduced to students through a lecture on implicit personality theories (Bruner & Taguiri, 1954) and/or person prototypes (Cantor & Mischel, 1977). The central assumption of these positions is that people possess cognitive categories, which they use to judge and sort new acquaintances. More specifically, an implicit personality theory is thought to be a naive assumption that certain human characteristics are correlated. Thus, when we identify a particular trait in someone, we consult our personal theories for other characteristics that go along with that trait. For example, if a man is described as tall, we might assume that he is also dark and handsome.

In a similar vein, person prototypes consist of internal descriptions of standard types of people. We compare and match each new acquaintance to our prototypes. Once matched, we assume that the individual possesses all of the characteristics of the prototype. This process occurs frequently with first names. We meet a woman named Jane and feel an immediate fondness for her because we retrieve memories of our beloved Aunt Jane.

First impressions are usually formed without any direct evidence that the target person possesses the ascribed traits thus, they are subject to considerable error (Norman, 1963). Such unverified impressions are relatively resistant to subsequent disconfirming evidence (Snyder, Tanke, & Berscheid, 1977).

Students frequently verbalize the unfairness of "judging a book by its cover." Clearly, many of them feel personally exempt from using impression-formation strategies. This exercise is an effective demonstration of the ubiquity of personal impression-formation strategies. It also generates data (e.g., an impression-agreement score) that can be used to stimulate class discussion.

Method

Part 1

Early in the course, students are asked to submit a clear, standard size photograph of someone 18 years or older whom they know fairly well. The only restriction is that the photo be in good taste (i.e., not lewd or bizarre in dress or pose). Students answer a series of questions about the person in their photograph to the best of their ability. There is a multitude of demographic and personality questions that can be used in this exercise. Some good ones include: (a) What is the person's occupation? (b) What is the person's favorite sport/hobby/activity? (c) What is the person's favorite type of music? (d) How shy/outgoing is the person on a scale of 1 to 10? (e) How liberal/conservative is the person on a scale from 1 to 10? (f) How warm/cold is the person on a scale from 1 to 10? Note that the potential for obtaining objective answers is decreased for questions that involve personality attributions. To maintain anonymity but allow for identification, students write their own birth date on the back of the photograph and on the completed questionnaire.

Part 2

Several weeks later, in conjunction with a lecture on impression formation, students are asked to form groups of four to six persons. Three or four photos (without matching answer sheets) are distributed to each group. It is important to establish that no one in a particular group is familiar with any of that group's photographs. Working individually at first, group members examine the photographs one at a time, form an impression, and then respond to the selected questions. It may be desirable to have students rate the confidence they have in their judgments. After completing this task, the groups discuss their answers. They are asked to assess the similarity of their impressions for each photograph by counting the number of same or similar answers on each question. In addition, they discuss and write down the cues (e.g., age, clothing, hairstyle) used in forming their own impressions. This phase of the exercise usually produces considerable enthusiasm as students share their implicit personality theories and person prototypes.

Part 3

After about 20 min, the groups are given the answer keys corresponding to their photographs. They compare their questionnaire responses to the answers provided by the acquaintance and assess their agreement by counting the number of matched or near-matched answers.

Results

The exercise generates several useful bits of data. First, a social consensus score can be computed by converting the group agreement scores into percentages. Typically, groups show low-to-moderate agreement (i.e., 20% to 30% of their responses are the same). Second, a rank-ordered list of cues used in impression formation can be obtained by counting the number of times a cue was used. Clothing is usually ranked first, followed by age, context/activity, facial attractiveness, and physical build. Finally, agreement scores can be derived by converting the number of corresponding answers to a percentage figure. In a recent demonstration with 58 introductory psychology students, 62% answered two or fewer questions correctly out of six questions.

Concluding Remarks

A class discussion follows the presentation of results; several topics can be covered. One topic focuses on the ease with which we form impressions of strangers and the confidence we feel in ascribing traits on the basis of limited information. Another possibility is to examine the social consensus figure and use it as a springboard for discussing the stereotypes and person prototypes that are shared by a culture.

The agreement data often provide students with direct evidence of the errors in their own judgment processes. The identification of these errors can lead to a discussion of why we continue to rely on our impression-formation strategies even when we know they can be incorrect.

Finally, the list of rank-ordered cues encourages students to examine their own implicit personality theories and person prototypes. Students can be encouraged to explain the origin of these structures in operant and classical conditioning terms.

This exercise has never failed to create interest and lively discussion. A recent course evaluation showed that 72% of the students ($N = 58$) found it to be an "extremely valuable" or "quite valuable" learning experience, 86% said that it was the "most enjoyable" or "one of the most enjoyable" class exercises they had ever done, and 80% recommended that it "definitely" be used in future classes.

The exercise can be modified to fit different situations. For example, the group component can be eliminated, with the entire exercise being completed on an individual basis. If there is concern about the ethics of using photographs without the subjects' written consent, it is possible to obtain photos and written consent from students in one class for use in other classes. An advantage of this latter approach is that it overcomes the limitation of relying on secondhand answers to the questions. In the former method, the personal information (particularly any personality attributions) provided by the acquaintance may itself be subject to impression-formation processes. Those desiring more rigor may control the amount of information provided in the photographs by asking for "head-only" or "full-body" poses.

Occasionally, the constraints of time or class size do not permit the collection of photographs from students. When this occurs, it is possible to use pictures from magazines or yearbooks. Although this format precludes the assessment of agreement, it does prompt a good general discussion of impression-formation processes. In sum, this exercise provides a concrete demonstration of our capacity for forming first impressions on the basis of limited information.

References

Bruner, J. S., & Taguiri, R. (1954). The perception of people. In G. Lindzey (Ed.), *Handbook of social psychology* (Vol. 2, pp. 634-654). Reading, MA: Addison-Wesley.

Cantor, N., & Mischel, W. (1977). Traits as prototypes: Effects on recognition memory. *Journal of Personality and Social Psychology, 35,* 38-48.

Levinger, G. (1983). Development and change. In H. H. Kelley, E. Berscheid, A. Christensen, S. H. Harvey, T. L. Huston, G. Levinger, E. McClintock, L. A. Peplau, & D. R. Peterson (Eds.), *Close relationships* (pp. 315-359). San Francisco: Freeman.

Norman, W. T. (1963). Toward an adequate taxonomy of personality attributes: Replicated factor structure in peer nomination personality ratings. *Journal of Abnormal and Social Psychology, 66,* 574-583.

Snyder, M., Tanke, E. D., & Berscheid, E. (1977). Social perception and interpersonal behavior: On the self-fulfilling nature of social stereotypes. *Journal of Personality and Social Psychology, 35,* 656-666.

Using Students' Perceptions of Their Instructor to Illustrate Principles of Person Perception

Robin L. Lashley
Kent State University

The term *person perception* is used to refer to the various cognitive processes by which individuals interpret their own and others' behavior. This is an important topic in social psychology, and often receives coverage in adjustment personality, applied, and introductory courses as well.

An effective technique for demonstrating the nature of person perception, and especially the many perceptual and memorial biases to which it is susceptible, is to have students respond to a simple personality inventory designed to assess their perceptions of their instructor. This exercise is most effective if used several weeks into the semester and shortly before the topic of person perception is introduced: long enough for students to have formed stable impressions of the instructor but not so long that they have too much information on which to base their judgments. The inventory consists of two sections. The first contains a number of multiple-choice questions that require the students to make judgments regarding the instructor's identifying characteristics (e.g., age and marital status), preferences (e.g., favorite kind of music, favorite color, ideal vacation, and hobbies), and background (e.g., number of siblings and state of origin). The second section contains a list of 20 personality traits (see Anderson, 1968, or a thesaurus) to which the student responds "yes" (this word describes my instructor), "no" (this word does not describe my instructor), or "it depends" (it depends on the situation my instructor is in).

To assure anonymity, students are instructed to make two copies of their ratings. They retain one copy; the other is collected and used to prepare a tabular summary, which is distributed when person perception is discussed in class. After sharing the "true" (i.e., self-perceived) answers, the instructor can use the data to illustrate numerous principles of person perception, including the following.

1. Agreements between the instructor's and the students' judgments serve as instances of successful person perception (Hastorf, Schneider, & Poleflka, 1970). Many of these reflect inferences that are readily made by noting the instructor's physical appearance (e.g., a wedding ring to infer marital status and facial wrinkles to infer age), or consistent behavior (e.g., degree of eye contact both in and out of class to infer confidence and choice of clothing to infer favorite color).

2. Students' responses to Section 1 items often reveal strongly stereotyped thinking (Miller, 1982). College students have had ample experience to develop definite expectations about those who choose teaching as a profession. This "teacher stereotype" is strengthened each time they selectively note confirming instances and discount discrepant evidence. My students expect the typical teacher to be a married, conservative, introverted intellectual who prefers dark colors, sedentary hobbies, and structured vacations.

Other common stereotypes often surface as well. Many (often erroneous) judgments are made on the basis of the instructor's age, gender, and physical attractiveness.

3. The importance of first impressions (Asch, 1946) is easily demonstrated. In justifying their perceptions of the instructor, students often demonstrate greater use of events that occurred early in the semester. The students' impressions may have been determined even before the course began (i.e., by the instructor's "reputation" around campus). The instructor can point out how subsequent behavior may be selectively perceived and recalled to confirm the initial impression.

4. Responses to Section 2 items demonstrate the actorobserver difference in person perception. The actor (instructor) tends to explain his or her own behavior in terms of the situation; observers (students) tend to explain that same behavior in terms of the actor's dispositions Jones & Nisbett, 1971). Therefore, the frequency of "it depends" responses by the instructor usually exceeds that of the students. The *fundamental attribution error*, the tendency for observers to underestimate situational factors and to overestimate dispositional factors when explaining an actor's behavior (Ross, 1977), can also be discussed. Students readily substantiate their "yes" or "no" responses with recalled instances of the instructor's classroom behavior, despite the fact that these observations are highly situationally constrained.

5. Any trait in Section 2 for which there is a discrepancy between the instructor's judgment and the majority of the students' judgment can be used to discuss the validity of self perceptions versus others' perceptions. If the instructor's perception is more favorable than the students', a self serving bias (Shavit & Shouval, 1980) may be operating. That is, the students may be focusing on behaviors that the instructor has discounted in an effort to maintain a positive self-concept.

6. Throughout the discussion, students will have discovered many of their own implicit beliefs about people and behavior: beliefs about which traits are correlated; beliefs about the causes of behavior; beliefs about traits that characterize persons of a particular age, gender, or occupation. In short, they will have become aware of the *implicit personality theories* (Schneider, 1973) by which they attempt to explain and predict instances of behavior.

Students generally enjoy this exercise and derive several benefits from it: They acquire a better understanding of person perception, they come to appreciate the relevance of this process to their own social interactions, and they get to know their instructor better in the process!

References

Anderson, N. H. (1968). Likableness of 555 personality trait words. *Journal of Personality and Social Psychology, 9,* 272-279.

Asch, S. E. (1946). Forming impressions of personality. *Journal of Abnormal and Social Psychology, 41,* 258-290.

Hastorf, A. H., Schneider, D. J., & Polefka, J. (1970). *Person perception.* Reading, MA: Addison-Wesley.

Jones, E. E., & Nisbett, R. E. (1971). *The actor and the observer: Divergent perceptions of the causes of behavior.* Morristown, NJ: General Learning Press.

Miller, A. G. (Ed.). (1982). *In the eye of the beholder: Contemporary issues in stereotyping.* New York: Praeger.

Ross, L. (1977). The intuitive psychologist and his shortcomings: Distortions in the attribution process. In L. Berkowitz (Ed.), *Advances in experimental social psychology* (Vol. 10, pp. 174-221). New York: Academic.

Schneider, D. J. (1973). Implicit personality theory: A review. *Psychological Bulletin, 79,* 294-309.

Shavit, H., & Shouval, R. (1980). Self-esteem and cognitive consistency effects on self-other evaluation. *Journal of Experimental Social Psychology, 16,* 417-425.

Notes

1. I thank Wayne Weiten and two anonymous reviewers for their helpful comments on an earlier draft of this article.

2. Portions of this article were presented at the Ninth Annual National Institute on the Teaching of Psychology sponsored by the University of Illinois at Urbana-Champaign at Clearwater Beach, FL, January 1987.

3. Requests for copies of the personality inventory should be sent to Robin L. Lashley, Department of Psychology, Kent State University, Tuscarawas Campus, New Philadelphia, OH 44663.

4. DEMONSTRATING BIAS IN SOCIAL PERCEPTION AND SOCIAL COGNITION

Observer Biases in the Classroom

Mary E. Kite
Ball State University

Although humans are remarkably efficient information processors, efficiency and accuracy do not always go hand in hand. By rapidly interpreting their world, people can easily and inadvertently err. Myers (1990) labeled this process "illusory thinking" (p. 131) and suggested that such biases can have profound social consequences. Making people aware of such biases may decrease their vulnerability to these errors (Nisbett & Ross, 1980).

Studies of observer biases document the consistency with which we draw incorrect conclusions; however, sometimes the sheer number of such biases, as presented in textbooks, limits their impact on students. Other activities demonstrate perceptual biases, such as the primacy effect in social judgments (Lasswell, Ruch, Gorfein, & Warren, 1981; Watson, 1987a), the fundamental attribution error (Watson, 1987b), and the self-serving attributional bias (Dunn 1989). This article describes other activities that illustrate the actor-observer effect, the false consensus bias, and priming effects. My goal is to show how efficient information processing can result in inaccurate perceptions—topics relevant to introductory, social, personality, and cognitive psychology courses.

The Actor-Observer Effect

Method

This demonstration is derived from Study 3 of Nisbett, Caputo, Legant, and Marecek (1973), which clearly demonstrated the actor-observer effect: People attribute their own behavior to situational factors and others' behavior to consistent traits. The activity takes about 15 min and introduces the topic of observer biases. Students use a list of 20 polar trait terms twice (see Table 1) . First, they rate a famous television personality (e.g., Dan Rather, Barbara Walters) by checking whether that person possesses a trait (or its polar opposite) or whether they believe the person's behavior depends on the situation. Second, they make the same ratings for themselves.

Students report the number of traits (or their opposites) and the number of "depends on the situation" responses checked for themselves and for the famous person. I record these responses in columns on the

chalkboard and compute four mean scores. Although it is necessary to report only the mean number of traits, students grasp the concept more easily when presented with the means for the trait ratings and the means for the "depends on situation" ratings. The first pair of means highlights the belief that others' traits are more consistent than their own, whereas the second pair of means highlights the belief that their own traits ale more variable than others'. In lower level courses, I do not discuss how to analyze these means statistically; however, a *t* test comparing the students' self-ratings to their ratings of the television personality should reveal the expected significant differences.

Results and Discussion

Five social psychology classes produced results that consistently replicated those of Nisbett et al. (1973). Students from one class checked a mean of 16.4 consistent traits for Barbara Walters and a mean of 12.0 consistent traits for themselves. To reinforce the reliability of this bias, I report that Nisbett et al. (1973) found a mean of 15.1 traits checked for Walter Cronkite and a mean of 11.9 checked for myself. Nisbett et al.'s (1973) data for best friend ($M = 14.2$) and acquaintance ($M = 13.4$) show that the better one knows people, the more likely one is to believe that their behavior depends on the situation rather than their dispositions.

After the demonstration, at least one student notes that he or she did not engage in the actor-observer bias. I use this opportunity to discuss how mean scores apply to groups of people but do not necessarily predict every individual's behavior. This issue is, of course, relevant to most psychological research, and students who understand this distinction enhance their ability to focus on general patterns of results.

The False Consensus Bias

Method

The false consensus bias describes a tendency to overestimate the degree to which others share one's opinions, even extreme ones (e.g., Ross, Greene, & House,

Table 1. Polar Trait Terms Used to Demonstrate the Actor–Observer Effect

Serious	Lighthearted
Subjective	Analytic
Future oriented	Present oriented
Energetic	Relaxed
Unassuming	Self-assertive
Lenient	Firm
Reserved	Emotionally expressive
Dignified	Casual
Realistic	Idealistic
Intense	Calm
Skeptical	Trusting
Quiet	Talkative
Cultivated	Natural
Sensitive	Tough-minded
Steady	Flexible
Self-sufficient	Sociable
Dominant	Submissive
Cautious	Bold
Uninhibited	Self-controlled
Conscientious	Happy-go-lucky

1977). This effect can be demonstrated in less than 5 min. Ask the class to suggest an opinion topic (e.g., I like Madonna; George Bush is a good President) and then note their level of agreement with the statement on a scale ranging from *strongly disagree* (1) to *strongly agree* (5). Then ask students to estimate the percentage of people in the class that share their opinion. Pigott and Leone (1990) suggested a similar procedure, using a yes-no format.

Results and Discussion

A show of hands provides the number of people selecting each response, and I record that number on the board. After I compute the percentage of students choosing each option, students indicate again by a show of hands whether they overestimated the number of people in agreement with them. In three social psychology classes, at least 60% of the students believed that others agree with them. Ross et al. (1977, Study 1) reported agreement rates ranging from 50% to 75%.

Mullen et al.'s (1985) meta-analytic study of the false consensus bias suggests possible topics for class discussion. First, this bias is quite general across reference groups (e.g., friends vs. college students in general) and issues (e.g., preferred type of bread or preferred presidential candidate). However, the strongest false consensus effects emerge with factual information or political expectations (e.g., outcome of presidential elections or future use of nuclear weapons), and the weakest effects occur with personal issues (e.g., donating blood or having difficulty making friends). Second, the effect may reflect people's tendency to overestimate the probability of events easily brought to mind (e.g., the availability heuristic; Tversky & Kahneman, 1973). Students are easily engaged in discussion of whether these ideas explain their tendency to exhibit this bias. Likewise, they typically recognize the social costs and benefits of a false consensus for both individuals and society. Finally, as Pigott and Leone (1990) suggested, students can debate whether having others agree with us makes our opinions "correct."

Priming Effects

Method

Activating, or priming, a category increases the likelihood that people will evaluate the stimulus person in those terms. Stated another way, recently used words or ideas influence the interpretation of new information (e.g., Bargh & Pietromonaco, 1982; Higgins, Rholes, & Jones, 1977). To demonstrate this effect, I have modified the "Donald" studies (Wyer & Srull, 1981). This activity requires some advance preparation and about 15 min from each of two class periods, but it also makes vivid a procedure and outcome that is difficult to visualize. The activity involves the unrelated experiment technique, wherein students believe they are completing two studies together merely to save time (e.g., Durso & Mellgren, 1989). The first experiment purportedly examines how people build sentences. I distribute two sets of word groups on colored paper. One colored paper contains

Table 2. List of Neutral, Hostile, and Kind Sentences for Priming Activity

Neutral	Hostile	Kind
walks dog he far	leg break arm his	child he helps friend
she clothes wears buys	hit boy dog she	girl buys gift boy
write you letter I	hate me I you	mother rocks him child
tall is man short	burns boy child girl	believe you me help
picture takes job she	kick chair she desk	house toy he builds
goes went out man	you bites dog boy	father fixes toy makes
slow he ran fast	me hurt you I	love him her you
job I do found	cat child you scratch	boy shares food eats
reads boy book you	man bird shoots boy	flowers picks she gives
map you read book	you beat I me	man cookies bakes bread
I watch him call	breaks glass he window	she makes friends has
I you bread eat	throws book he chair	man hugs child woman
rides fast drives she	you loud yell scream	hand package he holds
I call you me	kills he man bug	boy reads you book
women knew man boy	I you boy kick	cat girl pets dog

Table 3. Ambiguous Donald Story From Wyer and Srull (1981)

I ran into my old friend Donald the other day, and I decided to go over and visit him, since by coincidence we took our vacations at the same time. Soon after I arrived, a salesman knocked at the door, but Donald refused to let him enter. He also told me that he was refusing to pay his rent until the landlord repaints his apartment. We talked for awhile, had lunch, then went out for a ride. We used my car, since Donald's car had broken down that morning, and he told the garage mechanic that he would have to go somewhere else if he couldn't fix his car that same day. We went to the park for about an hour and then stopped at a hardware store. I was sort of preoccupied, but Donald bought some small gadget, and then I heard him demand his money back from the sales clerk. I couldn't find what I was looking for, so we left and walked a few blocks to another store. The Red Cross had set up a stand by the door and asked us to donate blood. Donald lied by saying he had diabetes and therefore could not give blood. It's funny that I hadn't noticed it before, but when we got to the store, we found that it had gone out of business. It was getting kind of late, so I took Donald to pick up his car and we agreed to meet again as soon as possible.

words that form "kind" sentences, whereas the other contains words that form "hostile" sentences; both word groups are intermixed with neutral word groups (see Table 2). The students' task is to construct three-word sentences from each series of four words.

While students complete the first task, I distribute the questionnaire for what they believe is the second study. Because I need to know whether students initially formed kind or hostile sentences, those with one color paper receive a questionnaire labeled A and those with the other color receive a questionnaire labeled B. This questionnaire is actually identical for both groups and contains an ambiguous story about "Donald" (see Table 3) followed by a series of questions about his characteristics: friendly, likable, kind, considerate, and thoughtful, assessed on scales ranging from *not at all* (1) to *very much* (7). Distributing the second questionnaire in this manner does not seem to arouse suspicion because it appears to save class time and students are busy constructing sentences. Students now complete the second experiment on person perception by reading the story and making anonymous evaluations of Donald. If priming is effective, students who created hostile sentences should rate Donald as less likable than students who created kind sentences .

Results

To save time, I collect the students' questionnaires and, before the next class, compute mean ratings for each question and for the sum of the five ratings. Before presenting the outcome during the next meeting, I return the questionnaires because students often forget what they completed. Although the results for two social psychology classes have not produced statistically significant differences, the means were in the predicted direction and serve to demonstrate the concept of priming. For one class, the hostility primed group reported a mean liking score of 2.5 and the kindness primed group reported a mean liking score of 2.9, with higher numbers indicating greater liking. Discussion focuses on the pervasiveness of priming effects (which are apparently not mediated by individual

differences; Devine, 1989) and their implications for everyday life (e.g., advertising, watching violent movies, offering help in emergencies). Furthermore, I inform students that priming effects are more likely when additional time has passed between the activation of the category and the evaluation of the stimulus person (e.g. Higgins et al., 1977). The short time frame of this demonstration may explain why our effects are weaker than those in the published literature. Teachers might also note that priming studies are an excellent representation of the relation between social and cognitive psychology.

Discussion

These three activities illustrate how our beliefs and experiences influence our perceptions of others. Moreover, discussions of these activities can focus on the bases for such biases and their impact on everyday life. Students report that active participation helps them understand and remember these effects.

One discussion opportunity explores how efficient information processing sometimes has undesirable consequences, such as when the media capitalize on our perceptual biases to influence our preference for political candidates or a certain brand of toothpaste. Students might also consider whether prejudice is rooted in these biases. Does prejudice stem from our beliefs about the consistent traits of entire social groups? Is it perpetuated by our belief that everyone agrees with us about what those traits are? Does merely activating the social category influence our judgments of individual members of those social groups?

I have also used our views on the Soviet Union to explore how our perceptions can change but the process by which we draw those conclusions does not. We may, for example, have a more positive attitude toward the Soviets but still be likely to think their characteristics are consistent and that others share our beliefs.

Funder (1987) noted that perceptual errors are a "hot topic" (p. 75) and fun, as the number of teaching activities focused on such errors attests. These observations, however, preface a critical questioning of whether such perceptual processes represent mistakes with real-life consequences. Sophisticated students will find food for thought in Funder's criticisms and even beginners can consider whether judgments made in a laboratory setting have relevance to everyday social perception (see also Hogan, DeSoto, & Solano, 1977).

These activities are useful for units on person perception, and parallels can be drawn among the three kinds of biases. Any of the three activities, however, can stand alone and engender discussion about how human error affects our interpretation of others' characteristics and behavior.

References

Bargh, S. A., & Pietromonaco, P. (1982). Automatic information processing and social perception: The influence of trait information presented outside of conscious awareness on impression formation. *Journal of Personality and Social Psychology, 40*, 750-760.

Devine, P. G. (1989). Stereotypes and prejudice: Their automatic and controlled components. *Journal of Personality and Social Psychology, 56*, 5-18.

Dunn, D. S. (1989). Demonstrating a self serving bias. *Teaching of Psychology, 16*, 21-22.

Durso, F. T., & Mellgren, R. L. (1989). *Thinking about research: Methods and tactics of the behavioral scientist.* St. Paul: West.

Funder, D. C. (1987). Errors and mistakes: Evaluating the accuracy of social judgment. *Psychological Bulletin, 101*, 75-90.

Higgins, E. T., Rholes, C. R., & Jones, C. R. (1977). Category accessibility and impression formation. *Journal of Experimental Social Psychology, 13*, 141-154.

Hogan, R., DeSoto, C. B., & Solano, C. (1977). Traits, tests, and personality research. *American Psychologist, 32*, 255-264.

Lasswell, M. E., Ruch, F. L., Gorfein, D. S., & Warren, N. (1981). Person perception. In L. T. Benjamin, Jr., & K. D. Lowman (Eds.), *Activities handbook for the teaching of psychology* (Vol. 1, pp. 185-187). Washington, DC: American Psychological Association.

Mullen, B., Atkins, J. L., Champion, D. S., Edwards, C., Hardy, D., Story, J. E., & Vanderklok, M. (1985). The false consensus effect: A meta-analysis of 115 hypothesis tests. *Journal of Experimental Social Psychology, 21*, 262-283.

Myers, D. G. (1990). *Social psychology* (3rd ed.). New York: McGraw-Hill.

Nisbett, R. E., Caputo, C., Legant, P., & Marecek, J. (1973). Behavior as seen by the actor and as seen by the observer. *Journal of Personality and Social Psychology, 27*, 154-164.

Nisbett, R. E., & Ross, L. (1980). *Human inference: Strategies and shortcomings of social judgment.* Englewood Cliffs, NJ: Prentice Hall.

Pigott, M., & Leone, C. (1990). *Instructor's manual to accompany Brehm and Kassin's social psychology.* Boston: Houghton Mifflin.

Ross, L., Greene, D., & House, P. (1977). The "false consensus effect": An egocentric bias in social perception and attribution processes. *Journal of Experimental Social Psychology, 13*, 279-301.

Tversky, A., & Kahneman, D. (1973). Availability: A heuristic for judging frequency and probability. *Cognitive Psychology, 5*, 207-232.

Watson, D. L. (1987a). The primacy effect in social judgments. In V. P. Makosky, L. G. Whittemore, & A. M. Rogers (Eds.), *Activities handbook for the teaching of psychology* (Vol. 2, pp. 132-134). Washington, DC: American Psychological Association.

Watson, D. L. (1987b). The fundamental attribution error. In V. P. Makosky, L. G. Whittemore, & A. M. Rogers (Eds.), *Activities handbook for the teaching of psychology* (Vol. 2, pp. 135-137). Washington, DC: American Psychological Association.

Wyer, R. S., & Srull, T. K. (1981). Category accessibility: Some theoretical and empirical issues concerning the processing of social stimulus information. In E. T. Higgins, C. P. Herman, & M. P. Zanna (Eds.), *Social cognition: The Ontario symposium* (Vol. 1, pp. 161-196). Hillsdale, NJ: Lawrence Erlbaum Associates, Inc.

Note

I thank Saul Kassin who suggested replicating the Nisbett et al. (1973) experiment in the classroom and Bernard Whitley, Jr. for comments on a draft of this article.

Social Desirability Bias: A Demonstration and Technique for Its Reduction

Randall A. Gordon
Western Carolina University

The problems of over reporting socially desirable behaviors and underreporting socially undesirable behaviors have received wide attention in surveys of research literature (Cahalan, 1968; Hyman, 1944; Parry & Crossley, 1950). Many techniques have been developed to reduce this type of response bias on questionnaires, most of which involve modifying the manner in which the questions are asked (Sudman & Bradburn, 1982). Some techniques have involved reducing the degree to which the question is viewed as threatening by the respondent. For example, the overstatement of socially desirable behavior has been reduced by beginning a question with "Did you happen to . . .?" and by asking about behavior during a circumscribed time period as opposed to beginning the question with "Do you ever . . .?" (Bradburn & Sudman, 1979).

While pilot-testing a questionnaire to assess attitudes and behaviors regarding oral hygiene among college students, it became evident that the reported frequencies of behaviors such as dental checkups and tooth brushing were higher than the average for the general population (U.S. National Center for Health Statistics, 1974, 1979). These differences may have been partially due to increased awareness of the importance of dental hygiene, but they were large enough to suggest that some over reporting might have taken place. To examine the possibility that subjects were over reporting their frequency of dental hygiene behavior, a technique was devised that focused on highlighting the role of the respondent as a contributor of important information.

Before the questionnaire was administered, subjects were verbally given additional information concerning the purpose of the questions and the importance of honesty and accuracy in their self-reports. The confidentiality and anonymity of their responses were also emphasized, along with the important contribution that their responses would provide. Subjects who received these modified instructions reported substantially lower rates of dental checkups and other dental health care behavior than previous subjects who had only been informed of the anonymity of their responses.

The effect of the instructional manipulation led to the development of a simple classroom demonstration of social desirability bias in survey research. The demonstration reveals the effect of instructional sets on questionnaire responses and leads to discussion of possible reasons for underreporting and over reporting on questionnaires, in addition to other related issues in survey research (e.g., acquiescent response style and representativeness in sampling). The following is a description of a systematic assessment of the effect of such an appeal on reducing social desirability bias.

Method

Two forms of the questionnaire were developed; they were identical, except for the instructions. Both forms had the title "Dental Hygiene Behaviors" at the top, and the standard format included the following instructions:

> Over the last several years, psychologists have started to work in conjunction with dentists in order to help improve this area of health care. We would appreciate your an. answering the following questions regarding dental hygiene behaviors. Please do not write your name on this sheet. Thank you for your participation.

The modified instructions read as follows:

> Over the last several years, psychologists have started to work in conjunction with dentists in order to help improve this area of health care. One of the *most important* tasks in this area of research (behavioral dentistry) is to collect *accurate information* on the frequency of various dental hygiene behaviors. Therefore, we would appreciate your answering the following questions as *honestly* and *accurately* as possible. Please do not write your name on this sheet. We are not interested in individual responses, just the behaviors of people in general. Thank you for your participation.

Both forms of the questionnaire requested the respondent's age and sex and answers to the following questions:

1. Do you have regular dental checkups? If so, how often and why? If not, why not?

2. How often do you brush your teeth? Why?
3. Do you floss your teeth? If so, how often and why? If not, why not?

Forty-eight students (24 men and 24 women) enrolled in undergraduate courses in social psychology were randomly assigned to receive either the standard or modified form of the questionnaire. Students were given 15 min to complete the questionnaires. The forms were then returned facedown to the instructor. The purpose of the demonstration and a summary of the results were presented to students during the following class meeting.

Results

Given the directional nature of the experimental hypothesis (that the modified instructions on the questionnaire would reduce the frequency of reported behaviors), all statistical tests were one-tailed. An assessment of the three major items revealed significant differences between the groups in the predicted direction.

Responses to the item "Do you have regular checkups?" were coded in the following manner: no = 0 and yes = 1. A significantly greater percentage of subjects who received the standard format responded affirmatively to this question (96%) than subjects who received the modified instructions (71%), $t(46) = 2.41$, $p < .01$. Subjects who received the standard instructions also reported brushing their teeth more times a day ($M = 2.63$) than did the group that received the modified instructions ($M = 2.19$), $t(46) = 1.92$, $p < .03$.

A difference approaching significance was found between the groups on the item that asked subjects if they floss their teeth. Responses were coded in the same manner used for the checkup question. The results revealed a trend in the predicted direction. Subjects who received the standard format answered affirmatively more often (79%) than subjects who received the modified format (58%), $t(46) = 1.56$, $p < .06$.

The results suggest that having regular dental checkups and brushing regularly may be considered to be more socially desirable behaviors than flossing one's teeth. Given the much smaller segment of the population that flosses regularly, subjects may have felt less pressure to overstate the frequency of this behavior. It should be noted that the majority of responses to the follow-up portion of the flossing question ("If not, why not?") produced responses that indicated a lack of knowledge regarding the purpose of flossing, the benefits, and the amount of time that it takes.

The degree to which random assignment produced experimental equivalence was partially assessed by examining the average age and sex ratios of respondents in the two groups. Random assignment produced groups with identical sex ratios (12 men and 12 women in each group) and relatively similar average ages: M (standard format) = 21.33 years and M (modified format) = 21.58 years.

Although the modified instructions significantly reduced the tendency to over report socially desirable behavior, it is possible that these instructions did not alleviate the problem entirely. A comparison of the mean number of tooth brushings per day by the modified instruction group in this study ($M = 2.19$) and the mean response to this question from a national health survey ($M = 1.60$) revealed a relatively large difference (U.S. National Center for Health Statistics, 1974). As previously suggested, this finding may represent a real difference between the frequency of tooth brushing in the general population and among college students.

Discussion

To prepare material for lecture and discussion, additional information on the prevalence of social desirability bias and procedures that have been used to reduce it can be found in Sudman and Bradburn (1982). This book devoted a chapter to the problem of social desirability and described techniques for its reduction. A more recent review is provided by Nederhof (1985). This review was written from a self-presentational perspective that regards social desirability as the result of self- and other-deception. The article examined the relevant research literature and described seven methods that have been used to prevent or reduce social desirability bias.

The problem of social desirability remains as a source of error in much survey research, and this type of demonstration alerts students to this potential problem. To lead into a discussion of the results, students should first be told that there were two forms of the questionnaire that varied only in the content of the instructions. Some students may already be aware of this through discussion with classmates. Hypotheses regarding the purpose of the modified instructions should now be discussed. Students who participated in the demonstration were surprised to find out that the modified instructions could create the observed differences between groups.

After revealing the extent to which experimental equivalence has been attained, a discussion of possible reasons for the observed effect of the modified instructions can be conducted. This discussion might focus on whether students believe that social desirability bias on questionnaires is due to a desire to appear "good" to others or to oneself.

As Cahalan (1968) suggested, in a reevaluation of a major survey that examined social desirability, subjects may over report socially desirable behaviors in order to protect their self-image. If a desire to appear good in one's own eyes is the cause of over reporting, then appearing socially desirable to others may be of little concern; a focus on anonymity may have a minimal effect on reducing such bias. It is possible that the manipulation used in the demonstration reduced the over reporting of behavior by focusing students on the contribution they were making to others (e.g., the scientific community), thereby reducing the need to appear "good" to themselves. It is clear that a variety of approaches must be used collectively in order to reduce this response bias to tolerable levels.

The use of dental hygiene behavior as the topic of the questionnaire was due to a personal interest in this form of behavior. The demonstration could easily be modified to focus on other forms of socially desirable behavior such as wearing seat belts or the amount of time spent studying. This type of demonstration could also be used in a variety of courses. It would be appropriate for classes in tests and measurement, research methodology, and other courses that focus on attitude measurement and survey research.

To summarize, the results support the hypothesis that more accurate responses can be obtained by stressing the following: the importance of the information being provided by subjects, the importance of honest and accurate self-reports, and the anonymity of subjects' responses. As a classroom demonstration, the exercise can be used to illustrate a potential source of bias in survey research. It may also be used to demonstrate the technique of random assignment and the relative degree of experimental equivalence that it provides.

References

Bradburn, N. M., & Sudman, S. (1979). *Improving interview method and questionnaire design: Response effects to threatening questions in survey research.* San Francisco, CA: Jossey-Bass.

Cahalan, D. (1968). Correlates of response accuracy in the Denver validity study. *Public Opinion Quarterly, 32,* 607-621.

Hyman, H. H. (1944). Do they tell the truth? *Public Opinion Quarterly, 8,* 557-559.

Nederhof, A. J. (1985). Methods of coping with social desirability bias: A review. *European Journal of Social Psychology, 15,* 263-280.

Parry, H. J., & Crossley, H. M. (1950). Validity of responses to survey questions. *Public Opinion Quarterly, 14,* 61-80

Sudman, S., & Bradburn, N. M. (1982). *Asking questions.* San Francisco, CA: Jossey-Bass.

U.S. National Center for Health Statistics. (1974*). Diet and dental health, a study of relationships: United States, 1971-1974* (Data from the National Health Survey, Series 11, No. 225). Washington, DC: Government Printing Office.

U.S. National Center for Health Statistics. (1979*). Dental visits volume and interval since last visit: United States, 1978-1979* (Data from the National Health Survey, Series 10, No. 138). Washington, DC: Government Printing Office.

Note

I thank two anonymous reviewers for their helpful comments and suggestions on an earlier version of this article.

Hindsight Bias and the Simpson Trial: Use in Introductory Psychology

George J. Demakis
Elmhurst College

In introductory psychology, providing a rationale for psychology as the scientific study of behavior is critical. Many students enter their first psychology course with "folk" theories of behavior, and they see psychology as simply intuitive and commonsensical. To help students appreciate the need for the scientific method in the study of behavior, teachers can discuss cognitive biases, such as the overconfidence phenomenon, the confirmation bias, and the hindsight bias (Myers, 1995; Wood, 1984). The focus of this article is how to demonstrate the hindsight bias in the classroom and how it illustrates critical points about psychological science.

The *hindsight bias* is a tendency to exaggerate one's ability to have foreseen the outcome of an event, after learning the outcome. More simply, on learning the outcome of an event, individuals may claim that they "knew it all along." For instance, Leary (1982) had participants estimate prior to or after an election the percentage of votes candidates would receive. Consistent with a hindsight bias, ratings made after the election were more accurate than ratings made before the election. Similarly, more accurate hindsight versus foresight judgments have been observed with the outcome of football games, medical diagnoses, and legal decisions (Hawkins & Hastie, 1990). Such events, with discrete outcomes, provide an excellent opportunity to illustrate the hindsight bias.

The recent adjudication in the Simpson criminal trial also provided an excellent opportunity to illustrate the hindsight bias and to provide an active-learning experience about cognitive biases. In October 1995, Simpson was found not guilty of murdering Nicole Brown Simpson and Ronald Goldman. Consistent with the hindsight bias, I predicted that participants who estimated the outcome of the trial postverdict would be more accurate (i.e., more likely to indicate that Simpson was not guilty) than participants who made preverdict judgments.

Method

Participants

Three classes of introductory psychology students participated ($N = 66$). One class ($n = 24$) made preverdict predictions regarding the outcome of the Simpson trial, and two classes ($n = 42$) made postverdict predictions about what they would have predicted the outcome to have been. Age and sex characteristics of the groups were equivalent. Sixty-five (98%) participants were White and 1 (2%) was Native American.

Procedures

One week prior to the Simpson verdict, the pretrial group predicted the outcome of the trial (guilty, not guilty, or hung jury). One month after the verdict, I requested that the postverdict group to "think back before the jury reached a verdict . . . [and] recall what you would have predicted the outcome to have been."

Results and Discussion

There was a significant difference between pre- and postverdict predictions $\chi^2(2, N = 66) = 9.38, p < .009$. Participants who made posttrial ratings were more likely to predict a not guilty verdict (57% vs. 25%) and less likely to predict a hung jury verdict (14% vs. 46%) than

participants who made pretrial predictions. There was no change in predictions about guilty verdicts (29%). These data indicate the presence of the hindsight bias.

In introductory psychology, I focus first on the possible motivational and cognitive mechanisms by which the hindsight bias might operate and then on how notions of psychology as common sense might be fostered. Motivationally, the hindsight bias may operate because individuals desire to present themselves in a positive fashion (Hawkins & Hastie, 1990). One can easily think of many social and personal pressures to claim that one "knew it all along" (see Taylor & Brown, 1988). Cognitively, the tendency for individuals to automatically incorporate new information into their knowledge base makes delineation of old and new information difficult (Fischhoff, 1975). Once new information is incorporated, individuals are likely to overestimate how much they knew in advance. In addition to the Simpson findings, several examples can illustrate this phenomenon (Wood, 1984). For example, jurors may be unable to ignore information even when instructed to do so by a judge, because once this information is incorporated into their knowledge base, they may perceive that they knew it all along. In all, after a discussion of the mechanisms by which the hindsight bias may operate, I discuss how reasoning about behavior might be affected.

The hindsight bias may lead students to view research findings, particularly those in social and personality psychology, as commonsensical. I suggest that commonsensical or "folk" approaches to psychology are simply the use of the hindsight bias to make retrospective "explanations" about behavior (Stanovich, 1992). Specifically, I discuss many commonly used and occasionally contradictory proverbs and clichés used to explain behavior (e.g., "Birds of a feather flock together" vs. "Opposites attract"). I indicate that these proverbs are typically invoked only after a behavior has occurred and that, with their wide applicability, any behavior may be "explainable." At this juncture, students typically perceive the difficulty in relying on intuitive approaches to understanding behavior and are receptive to the need for the scientific method in psychology. Issues important for scientific analysis (e.g., empiricism, falsifiability) may be presented here, followed by specific discussion of research methods in psychology.

According to students, this demonstration assisted comprehension of the hindsight bias and the larger issue of the scientific method in psychology. Similar demonstrations can be conducted with other events that have a discrete outcome (e.g., athletic events and elections). As in this demonstration, I recommend use of participantsfrom different classes to make pre- and postevent predictions. Other attempts to demonstrate this bias have failed when participants from the same class made both pre and postevent predictions. This failure is not surprising because participants are likely to recall a single prediction and to respond similarly later. Although this issue may be circumvented by having participants make predictions about multiple events, I have found that the most effective demonstration of this bias is to have different classes make pre- and postevent predictions.

References

Fischhoff, B. (1975). Hindsight≠foresight: The effect of outcome knowledge on judgment under uncertainty. *Journal of Experimental Psychology: Human Perception and Performance, 1*, 288-299.

Hawkins, S., & Hastie, R. (1990). Hindsight: Biased judgments of past events after the outcomes are known. *Psychological Bulletin, 107*, 311-327.

Leary, M. (1982). Hindsight distortion and the 1980 presidential election. *Personality and Social Psychology Bulletin, 8*, 257-263.

Myers, D. (1995). *Psychology* (4th ed.). New York: Worth.

Stanovich, K. (1992). *How to think straight about psychology* (3rd ed.) . New York: HarperCollins.

Taylor, S., & Brown, J. (1988). Illusion and well-being: A social psychological perspective on mental health. *Psychological Bulletin, 103*, 193-210.

Wood, G. (1984). Research methodology: A decision-making perspective. In A. Rogers & C. Scheirer (Eds.), *The G. Stanley Hall lecture series* (Vol. 4, pp. 189-217). Washington, DC: American Psychological Association.

Note

I thank Jane Jegerski for helpful comments on earlier drafts of this article.

Unique Invulnerability: A Classroom Demonstration in Estimating Personal Mortality

C. R. Snyder
University of Kansas-Lawrence

In various social and clinical psychology courses, readings sometimes touch on the propensity of people to positively bias self-referential information. Such illusions often are adaptive and help the person to negotiate reality with beneficial results (Snyder & Higgins, 1988; Taylor & Brown, 1988, 1994). One such bias is to distort information so that negative human outcomes are less likely to happen to us than to other people. This psychologically protective process is called *unique invulnerability* (Perloff, 1987; Snyder & Fromkin, 1980). Unlike other positive illusions, however, persons with unique invulnerability illusions may encounter difficulties when they do not take the necessary precautions against potential harm (Weinstein & Klein, 1996). Because I have a lecture in my graduate course dealing with illusions, I am interested in presenting this topic in a stimulating fashion. What follows is a description of a unique invulnerability demonstration that I have used.

Study 1

Method

Participants. Twenty-six graduate students (3 men and 23 women) from various doctoral programs at the University of Kansas took Social Psychology—Theory, Research, and Clinical Applications in the spring of 1995.

Materials and procedure. The reading, to be completed prior to the fourth class period, was the chapter entitled "Accuracy and Bias in Self-Knowledge" by Brown (1991). At the beginning of this class lecture on self-biases, the students in attendance (25 out of 26) participated in an exercise. I began by informing the class that the actuarially predicted age of death for U.S. citizens (men and women together) is 75 years (National Center for Health Statistics, 1992). After delivering this information, I asked students to write down (anonymously) their

219

estimated ages of death and their gender on a blank slip of paper. Once these estimates were handed in, a student read aloud each estimated age of death, and I drew a dot on a transparency showing ages (from low to high) in a vertical array. While I entered the ages of death on the transparency, a class member calculated the means.

Results

As I drew the individual ages of death on the transparency, the class increasingly became aware that they had displayed unique invulnerability. The estimated average age of death for the 25 class members was 84.32 years (range = 60-93, SD = 8.35), which differed significantly from the age 75 actuarial comparison, $t(24)$ = 5.58, p < .001. The averages for the men (n = 3, M = 91.33) and women (n = 22, M = 83.36) did not differ significantly.

Study 2

Because of the robustness of unique invulnerability among some students even after a discussion of the demonstration, I tried to lessen the phenomenon in the same class taught the next year. A major reason for lessening unique invulnerability is that thoughts of invulnerability can result in people taking unnecessary chances with unfortunate consequences.

Method

Participants. Twenty graduate students took the course in the spring of 1996, with 17 (4 men and 13 women) attending on demonstration day.

Materials and procedure. I announced on the first day of class that a demonstration of unique invulnerability would occur later in the class; moreover, at the beginning of the particular class period on self-illusions, I noted that a demonstration of unique invulnerability would occur in that lecture. The readings were the same as in Study 1, as were the other procedures, except for the aforementioned additional comments about the occurrence of the unique invulnerability demonstration.

Results

As with Study 1, class members began to make comments as the dots on the transparency showed their high age of death estimates. Next, I announced the averages. The average age of death for the 17 class

members was 84.00 years (range = 68-100, SD = 8.01), differing significantly from the age 75 actuarial comparison, $t(16)$ = 4.63, p < .001. The averages for the men (M = 80.75) and women (M = 85.00) did not differ significantly.

General Discussion

The topic of unique invulnerability is a highly charged one as judged by these two classroom experiences. After the Study 1 demonstration, most class members were impressed with how this demonstration made the unique invulnerability phenomenon hit home. However, about one third of the class disagreed strongly, with their basic rebuttal being that they really were going to live well into their 80s and 90s. They remained "true believers" in their unique invulnerability, and the other class members slowly dissected their arguments as to why they maintained that they were going to live longer. I intervened at times to point out that we all have illusions and that some of them can be adaptive.

The liveliness of the debate was enhanced for students in Study 2 as compared to students in Study 1. Again, I intervened so as to moderate the discussion. A few people who said they would live well into their 90s came up to me at the break to make sure that I understood the special reasons that applied to their longevity.

At the end of the class periods in Study 1 and Study 2, there was a small number of people who seemed quite staunch in their perceived unique invulnerability (even after the demonstration). This reaction was reminiscent of real-life observations (Festinger, Riecken, & Schachter, 1965) of a group who prophesied that visitors from outer space were coming to pick them up. Each time the predicted extraterrestrial pickup time came and went without any sight of the space voyagers, the core strong believers became more entrenched in their beliefs. What is noteworthy in this second demonstration (Study 2) is that information highlighting the unique invulnerability illusion did not dampen the enthusiasm of some students about their projected longevity. In the degree to which they live their lives accordingly and do not take precautions about matters that can lead to an early death, such students are putting themselves in harm's way. Although students may have some longevity advantages related to their education and cognitive abilities, those among us who mentor them need to do our best to see that they remain around as long as possible. Anything that we can do to make them appropriately cautious means that we will have these valuable citizens around longer. Relatedly, a critical part of this exercise is to ask students what they think can be done to help people to recognize and lessen the potentially harmful illusions in their lives.

These results replicate other recent classroom-demonstration findings in which students maintain self-serving positive illusions in spite of knowing about the relevant research (Friedrich, 1996). Together with these findings, it appears that such demonstrations clearly produce active learning experiences. In conducting such exercises, the instructor must take care to avoid appearing immune from such positive biases. In fact, I routinely tell my classes that I have many of the illusions that we are discussing. Equally important, however, instructors should help students to find ways of abandoning biases, such as unique invulnerability, especially when such biases increase the potential for harm in students' lives.

References

Brown, J. D. (1991). Accuracy and bias in self-knowledge. In C. R. Snyder & D. R. Forsyth (Eds.), *Handbook of social and clinical psychology: The health perspective* (pp. 158-178). Elmsford, NY: Pergamon.

Festinger, L., Riecken, H. W., & Schachter, S. (1965). *When prophecy fails*. Minneapolis: University of Minnesota Press.

Friedrich, J. (1996) . On seeing oneself as less self-serving than others: The ultimate self-serving bias? *Teaching of Psychology, 23*, 107-109.

National Center for Health Statistics. (1992). *Vital statistics of the United States: Vol. II. Section 6 life tables*. Washington, DC: Public Health Services.

Perloff, L. (1987). Social comparison and illusions of unique invulnerability to negative life events. In C. R. Snyder & C. E. Ford (Eds.), *Coping with negative life events: Clinical and social psychological perspectives* (pp. 217-242). New York: Plenum.

Snyder, C. R., & Fromkin, H. L. (1980). *Uniqueness: The human pursuit of difference*. New York: Plenum.

Snyder, C. R., & Higgins, R. L. (1988). Excuses: Their effective role in the negotiation of reality. *Psychological Bulletin, 104*, 23-35.

Taylor, S. E., & Brown, J. D. (1988). Illusion and well-being: A social psychological perspective on mental health. *Psychological Bulletin, 103*, 193-210.

Taylor, S. E., & Brown, J. D. (1994) . Positive illusions and well-being revisited: Separating fact from fiction. *Psychological Bulletin, 116*, 21-27.

Weinstein, N. D., & Klein, W. M. (1996). Unrealistic optimism: Present and future. *Journal of Social and Clinical Psychology, 15*, 1-7.

Notes

1. I thank the students in the spring 1995 and 1996 semesters of Psychology 777: Social Psychology—Theory, Research, and Clinical Applications for their willingness to wrangle with the self-biases that, in one form of another, visit all of us. Special gratitude also is expressed to Beth Dinoff for her input on this article.

2. Requests for a full-sized copy of the transparency used for the exercise should be sent to C. R. Snyder, 305 Fraser Hall, Graduate Training Program in Clinical Psychology, Department of Psychology, University of Kansas, Lawrence, KA 66045-2462; e-mail: crsnyder @kuhub.cc.ukans.edu.

Demonstrating a Self-Serving Bias

Dana S. Dunn
Moravian College

The presentation and discussion of particular attributional biases in introductory social psychology courses frequently engage student interest. Students readily recognize the overuse and abuse of dispositional attributions, for example, through the "fundamental attribution error" (L. Ross, 1977). I noticed, however, that self-serving attributional biases are not as readily recognized by students. As first time readers in social psychology, students seem to take note of their inferential failings when making attributions about others, but may be less likely to do so when making attributions about themselves. Self-serving or "hedonic" biases should be intrinsically interesting because they raise issues involving individual information processing as well as motivations to enhance self-esteem.

When attention is drawn to them, the differing roles for success and failure attributions seem obvious and familiar: Students accept personal credit for high scores on exams, for example, but are reluctant to accept responsibility for failing performances. Yet the recognition that such self-serving biases may extend beyond the internal-external dimension of success and failure often escapes students. My impression is that students frequently fail to consider other ways in which they seek to portray themselves in a favorable light. To broaden the understanding of self-serving attributions and to place them firmly in the realm of students' experience, I used a simple, in-class demonstration that both captures their interest and illustrates the impact of self-serving attributions.

I used two approaches. One method involves having students anonymously list what they consider to be their individual "strengths" and "weaknesses." I do not reveal the purpose of the exercise but, as I pass out a one-page questionnaire, I inform the students that the psychology of the self will be one of the topics discussed during the next class. The questionnaire simply asks students to first write down what they believe are their personal strengths and then list their weaknesses. I emphasize that anonymity must be maintained and remind students not to put their names on the questionnaires.

After collecting their lists, I promise to report the results in the next class. I tabulate the number of strengths and weaknesses, recording the mean for each category. Not surprisingly, students tend to report almost twice as many positive as negative attributes about themselves. In addition to eliciting a number of sheepish grins, the presentation of results usually prompts a discussion concerning the processes underlying self-serving biases. Do we tend to list more positive than negative self-descriptions due to some motivational bias such as self-esteem maintenance? Or, is our information processing the origin of the bias? Perhaps we recall more easily those situations in which we displayed positive rather than negative traits. Further, this differential recall may confirm existing expectations about ourselves; we simply spend more time thinking about our perceived positive attributes. The discussion allows me to introduce the egocentric bias (i.e., people overestimate their contributions to a jointly produced outcome, M. Ross & Sicoly, 1979). This may be another instance of differential recall influencing self-attribution.

In an alternative exercise, I have students verbalize their strengths and weaknesses during class. I write a heading for strengths on one half of a chalkboard and weaknesses on the other, while asking the class members to think about themselves in these terms. Student participation in this version of the exercise is voluntary; only those students who indicate a willingness to offer self-descriptions are called on. Instructors should be extremely cautious not to embarrass students by requiring them to participate in an exercise involving self-disclosure.

After students' responses are recorded on the chalkboard, I note that the number of strengths outweighs the weaknesses. Then, I turn exclusively to the weaknesses list, discussing each item individually. Usually, several (if

not most) of the weaknesses show another example of self-enhancement. For example, "lazy" can be deemed a relatively negative trait, but descriptions like "too trusting," "workaholic," and "sensitive" still maintain some positive connotations. Indeed, many of the weaknesses students offer resemble the negative-yet-still-positive traits they might use to describe themselves to a prospective employer during an interview. I point out that because these descriptions were collected in a public setting, some self-presentational concerns were probably operating. The discussion of self-presentational issues allows for a careful consideration of how presenting ourselves to observers may differ from the manner in which we reflect on our perceived self-images. A motivation toward modesty may have a role in the former situation; however, an informational bias better accounts for the latter situation. I discuss the aforementioned role of differential recall in emphasizing the positive rather than the negative aspects of our characters.

Regardless of which method I use, after considering the results in some detail, I try to guide class discussion toward the implications of self-serving biases. Are these biases adaptive or troublesome for our views of ourselves? When do they cease to aid us and, instead, become a potentially dysfunctional aspect of the attribution process? In response to these questions, students frequently raise the issue of individual differences, pointing out that extremes exist: Some people are truly narcissistic; others tend toward self-disparagement.

Students seem to enjoy this exercise because it makes discussing inferential bias and attribution theory more personal. It also presents a novel way of thinking about the self, one that offers some explanation for our tendency to see ourselves favorably. Comments of several students indicate that it is something of a revelation to discover that such self-reflection is susceptible to error and open to doubt.

Additional demonstrations of self-serving biases are included in Wood (1984). These exercises may lead students to scrutinize thoughts about themselves a bit more and to broaden their appreciation for potential bias in self-perception.

References

Ross, L. (1977). The intuitive psychologist and his shortcomings: Distortions in the attribution process. In L. Berkowitz (Ed.), *Advances in experimental social psychology* (Vol. 10, pp. 173-220). New York: Academic.

Ross, M., & Sicoly, F. (1979). Egocentric biases in availability and attribution. *Journal of Personality and Social Psychology, 37,* 322-336.

Wood, G. (1984). Research methodology: A decision-making perspective. In A. M. Rogers & C. J. Scheirer (Eds.), *The G. Stanley Hall lecture series* (Vol. 4, pp. 189-217). Washington, DC: American Psychological Association.

On Seeing Oneself as Less Self-Serving Than Others: The Ultimate Self-Serving Bias?

James Friedrich
Willamette University

Research has shown that, in a wide range of contexts and on a variety of measures, people exhibit what has been termed a *self-serving bias* in judgment. For example, we tend to attribute our successes to internal causes and our failures to external forces, overestimate our likelihood of engaging in socially desirable behaviors, misremember our behavior in self-enhancing ways, overestimate the accuracy of our judgments, show unrealistic levels of optimism about experiencing positive events and avoiding negative events in our future, overestimate the degree to which others share our views and opinions, and underestimate the degree to which others share our skills and positive attributes (see Myers, 1990, for a review).

Another way we exhibit this self-serving bias is by seeing ourselves as being better than average on many socially desirable dimensions—a phenomenon sometimes referred to as the *Lake Wobegon effect* after Garrison Keillor's fictitious town where all the children are above average. Although some people necessarily are average on any given quality, not everyone can be. I once read the results of a faculty survey conducted as part of an accreditation self-study in which 100% of the faculty rated their teaching performance as better than the average performance at the institution. This notion is illustrated more formally in a study reported by Myers (1990), based on data collected by the College Entrance Examination Board. Over 800,000 students taking the Scholastic Aptitude Test (SAT) were asked to indicate how they felt they compared to others their own age in terms of several abilities. For leadership ability, 70% rated themselves above average, and only 2% rated themselves below average. For the ability to get along with others, 60% rated themselves in the top 10%, and 0% rated themselves below average—results that may explain why nearly every student who has spoken to me about a roommate conflict has reported the same difficulty (their roommate's poor skills in getting along with others).

Experimental work has also demonstrated that we generally perceive our own behavior to be fairer and more moral than the behavior of others. Interestingly, however, this same work has shown similar self-enhancing perceptions to be weak or absent for the socially desirable dimension of intelligence (Allison, Messick, & Goethals, 1989; Van Lange, 1991). This and other research (e.g., Dunning, Meyerowitz, & Holzberg, 1989) indicates that self-enhancement in judgments of relative standing seems to be greatest on dimensions that are not only socially desirable but also ambiguous (open to idiosyncratic definition by the respondent), more controllable (and thus more self-revealing), and less easily verified or objectively scaled.

Several of the examples already noted—teaching performance, leadership ability, and skill at getting along with others—fit this description. Another quality that falls into this domain is self-servingness itself. The tendency to be self-serving in one's judgments is likely to be perceived as an undesirable quality that we may expect to be exhibited less strongly in ourselves than in other people. The tendency to be modest (or at least accurate) in one's self-assessments represents the desirable pole of this dimension, complete with the value overtones associated with humility and lack of conceit. Moreover, misperceptions of one's own self-servingness would be difficult to define, quantify, and verify objectively. Finally, self-serving judgment is likely to be perceived as a largely voluntary, controllable quality (although researchers in the area argue that the truth of the matter is quite the opposite).

In a sense, research on self-serving biases in judgment suggests that we should be somewhat conceited in our perceptions of our own humility. That is, we should see ourselves as somewhat better than average at not thinking ourselves to be better than average. Ironically, such a tendency would likely work against any prophylactic effects associated with raising people's awareness of the problem. As Myers (1990) noted in concluding his discussion of this literature, "perhaps some readers have by now congratulated themselves on being unusually free of the self-serving bias" (p. 93). The two studies reported here, designed for use as classroom demonstrations, test the hypothesis that even people informed about this bias will see themselves as less frequently self-serving in their judgments than the average person.

Study 1

Method

Participants. Forty-seven upper level undergraduates participated in the study. Thirty-three were enrolled in an Elementary Statistics course, and 14 were enrolled in an Industrial/Organizational (I/O) Psychology course; I taught both courses. Enrollments were non-overlapping, and results of the study were analyzed and discussed with each class as part of the ongoing instructional activities.

Materials and procedure. At the beginning of regular class periods several weeks into the term, students in each class were asked to fill out an anonymous survey. This one page questionnaire began with a quote from Myers (1990, p. 84)—the entire paragraph in which he describes the results of the SAT survey mentioned earlier. Immediately following this attributed quote, students read one of two versions of the following:

> Research such as this has led psychologists to conclude that when people rate themselves in terms of socially desirable qualities or performance, they tend to see themselves as being better than average when they are really nor. This tendency is often referred to as a "self-serving bias" in judgment. How often do you think (you; the average person) make this kind of mistake when judging or evaluating (yourself; him- or herself)?

The self and average person versions were randomized before distribution. Students indicated their answers by circling the appropriate number on a scale ranging from 1 (*almost never*) to 9 (*nearly all the time*).

Results and discussion. A 2 (Statistics vs. I/O students) × 2 (Self vs. Average Person Phrasing) analysis of variance (ANOVA) on these responses produced only the expected main effect for the phrasing of the question (all other $ps > .25$. Students who responded to questions about their own tendency to fall prey to this bias gave significantly lower ratings ($M = 5.13$) than did those who rated the same tendency for the average person ($M = 6.54$), $F(1, 43) = 18.71$, $p < .01$, $\eta^2 = .20$. Note that the quoted research explicitly called attention to the nature and prevalence of self-serving bias effects in a national population of SAT-takers presumably perceived as similar to the respondents themselves. Nevertheless, students tended to see themselves as being significantly less likely than others to distort their self-perceptions in this manner.

Study 2

Method

Participants. Thirty-eight introductory psychology students (one entire section that I taught) participated in the study during a regular class period approximately 2 weeks into the term. Data were analyzed in class, with results and possible interpretations discussed as illustrations of principles covered in lectures.

Materials and procedure. During the last third of a regularly scheduled class period, I lectured on research related to the self-serving bias—material presented in connection with the concurrently assigned chapter on social psychology. At the beginning of the next class period, students were handed a questionnaire and asked to complete it anonymously. This one-page survey read as follows:

> I'm conducting an anonymous survey for my Industrial/Organizational Psychology class. One of the topics for the z course is whether or not people's own self-ratings should be used in the evaluation of their work performance. [The survey results were, in fact, discussed in that course.]

> Some research has suggested that people tend to rate themselves as better than average on most desirable qualities even when they are really nor. How often do you think (you; the average person) makes this kind of mistake when describing (yourself; him- or herself)?

The self and average person versions of the surveys were randomized before distribution. Students indicated their responses on the same 9-point scale used in Study 1.

Results and discussion. As predicted, students who responded to questions about their own tendency to fall prey to this bias gave significantly lower ratings ($M = 4.95$) than did those who rated the same tendency for the average person ($M = 6.62$), $t(36) = 2.78$, $p < .01$, $\eta^2 = .18$. Although the context of the question (SAT example vs. employment example), the type of students surveyed (upper level vs. introductory), and even the institution at which the experiments were conducted differed for Studies 1 and 2, the absolute values of the means for the self and average person groups (and thus their differences) were nearly identical across the two investigations. Students referring to themselves seemed to locate their own tendency at the scale midpoint (5) and the tendency of others somewhat above the midpoint. In this sense, students as a whole did not seem to be denying that they make this mistake. Rather, they simply indicated their belief that others are even more likely than themselves to do so.

General Discussion

The tendency for people to be self-serving in their judgments of self-serving tendencies, documented in both of these studies, is fairly robust. These experiments represent only two of many replications I have conducted with variations of the procedure (e.g., out-of-class surveys, student experimenters, and different courses). Across

224

variations, results have been consistent, and the moderate effect sizes reported in the present studies (roughly equal to point-biserial $rs \geq .4$) are typical. One advantage of this broader replicability is that the demonstration can be adapted to fit the needs and particular instructional goals of different courses. For example, in the studies reported earlier, results were used to discuss the self-serving bias with introductory students reading a chapter on social psychology and to discuss a variety of measurement issues in the use of judgmental ratings of work performance with I/O psychology students. In the Elementary Statistics course, the demonstration was used both as an illustration of significant issues in experimental design (random assignment, equivalent conditions except for the manipulated variable, and use of between subjects designs to control for demand characteristics) and as a quick way to generate an interesting in-class data set for computing statistics (e.g., ANOVAs, t tests, and Pearson or point-biserial correlations).

Some of the best discussions have been in my Social Psychology classes, due in part to the students' greater familiarity with models of self-presentation, self-justification, and information processing that may account for the findings (Myers, 1990). The demonstration also raises an important question about how personal knowledge of particular social psychological processes (e.g., from material taught in the course) affects an individual's behavior. Results obtained in class can serve as a springboard for examining the debate over the historically bound nature of social psychological research (Gergen, 1973) versus the field's claims of identifying trans-historical principles and mechanisms (Schlenker, 1974).

Data reported in this article also point to new empirical work that may further explore this tendency toward self-servingness in estimates of one's self-servingness. For example, no data on sex of participant were collected for the studies. Although past studies on self-serving biases have typically failed to obtain or report significant sex effects (e.g., Allison et al., 1989; Dunning et al., 1989; Van Lange, 1991), the possibility deserves further exploration. For example, when asked to think of an average person, do men and women differ in terms of the sex of the exemplar or prototype they envision? Does the use of gender-neutral pronouns in the stimulus materials influence this process (cf. Hamilton, 1988)? Another methodological question centers on the use of a between-subjects design. Although I typically use such a design in these demonstrations to avoid the demand characteristics associated with explicit self-other comparisons, other researchers (e.g., Allison et al., 1989) have obtained self-serving biases even when the self other comparisons are made directly. Would the effects documented in the present study be obtained with a within-subjects design? If not, would this call into question the claim that people are in fact seeing themselves as being better than others?

The present data also leave open the question of whether the effects are attributable to a tendency to (a) overestimate others' vulnerability to the self-serving bias while judging one's own vulnerability accurately, (b) underestimate one's own vulnerability while judging others' vulnerability accurately, or (c) both underestimate one's own vulnerability and overestimate others'. Research on *false uniqueness* and *false consensus* effects (e.g., Goethals, 1986) has shown that people tend to see their own desirable behaviors as less common than they actually are and their undesirable behaviors as more common than they are, respectively. That is, in an absolute sense, people appear to be meeting self esteem needs by misperceiving typical others. This research paradigm has not, however, tended to examine possible distortions in perceptions of one's own behavior; the participant's own attitude or behavior is specified or taken as a given, and the resulting effect on perceptions of others is then examined. In contrast, research on the better-than average effect has typically been interpreted as revealing objective distortions in perceptions of oneself. Although research findings on the better-than-average effect and the false uniqueness effect have emerged somewhat independently, these phenomena are in several respects variations on a common theme and should be considered jointly in future attempts to explore the relative accuracy of perceptions of self versus others.

In the common debriefing I provide for all my classes, I point out to students that self-serving tendencies like the one illustrated in the demonstration are widespread and that their own responses are not unique. (Students seem to enjoy hearing about the faculty survey noted earlier, for which I was one of the respondents.) I also note that such self-esteem-enhancing perceptions may be adaptive, appearing commonly in people judged to be psychologically healthy by several criteria (Myers, 1990; Taylor & Brown, 1988, 1994). For teachers and students interested in pursuing this last issue more deeply, some researchers have questioned whether such judgments constitute distortions or biases at all and whether true, significant distortions would necessarily be adaptive in mental health terms (Colvin & Block, 1994; Shedler, Mayman, & Manis, 1993). Although the purposes served by the demonstration are different in each of my courses, these in-class studies have been consistently well received, with the irony of their results providing a humorous context for discussing a variety of important issues.

References

Allison, S. T., Messick, D. M., & Goethals, G. R. (1989). On being better but not smarter than others: The Muhammad Ali effect. *Social Cognition, 7,* 275-296.

Colvin, C. R., & Block, J. R. (1994). Do positive illusions foster mental health? An examination of the Taylor and Brown formulation. *Psychological Bulletin, 116,* 3-20.

Dunning, D., Meyerowitz, J. A., & Holzberg, A. D. (1989). Ambiguity and self-evaluation: The role of idiosyncratic trait definitions in self-serving assessments of ability. *Journal of Personality and Social Psychology, 57,* 1082-1090.

Gergen, K. (1973). Social psychology as history. *Journal of Personality and Social Psychology, 26,* 309-320.

Goethals, G. R. (1986). Fabricating and ignoring social reality: Self-serving estimates of consensus. In J. M. Olson, C. P. Herman, & M. P. Zanna (Eds.*), The Ontario symposium on personality and social psychology* (Vol. 4, pp. 135-157). Hillsdale, NJ: Lawrence Erlbaum Associates, Inc.

Hamilton, M. (1988). Using masculine generics: Does generic "he" increase male bias in the user's imagery? *Sex Roles, 19,* 785-799.

Myers, D. G. (1990). *Social psychology* (3rd ed.). New York: McGraw-Hill.

Schlenker, B. (1974). Social psychology and science. *Journal of Personality and Social Psychology, 12,* 564-578.

Shedler, J., Mayman, M., & Manis, M. (1993). The illusion of mental health. *American Psychologist, 48,* 1117-1131.

Taylor, S. E., & Brown, J. D. (1988). Illusion and well-being: A social psychological perspective on mental health. *Psychological Bulletin, 103,* 193-210.

Taylor, S. E., & Brown, J. D. (1994). Positive illusions and well-being revisited: Separating fact from fiction. *Psychological Bulletin, 116,* 21-27.

Van Lange, P. A. M. (1991). Being better but not smarter than others: The Muhammad Ali effect at work in interpersonal situations. *Personality and Social Psychology Bulletin, 17,* 689-693.

Note

I thank students at Hobart and William Smith Colleges (Study 1) and Willamette University (Study 2) for their assistance with this project.

5. TEACHING ABOUT ATTITUDES AND PERSUASION

Bringing Cognitive Dissonance to the Classroom

David M. Carkenord
Joseph Bullington
Georgia Southern University

The concept of cognitive dissonance (Festinger, 1957) is often difficult for instructors to explain and students to understand. Instructors in our department frequently express something akin to dread over an impending "cognitive dissonance" lecture.

Explanation of the concept often begins in a straightforward manner: If a person's thoughts and behaviors are inconsistent, the person is motivated to change attitudes or behaviors to reestablish consistency. After all, we do not want to appear to be hypocritical, either to ourselves or others. Students can generally follow the argument to this point. The problem begins when one then attempts to explain the experimental tests of cognitive dissonance theory, most notably Festinger and Carlsmith's (1959) classic study. In this study, a group of students completed a boring task and were later paid either $1 or $20 to tell a potential "subject" (actually a confederate) that the same task was really interesting. Subjects in each group, then, told the subject that the experiment was very interesting. On a later measure of their attitudes toward the task, subjects in the group that received $1 reported more favorable attitudes toward the boring task than subjects in the group that received $20. The $1 group, according to Festinger and Carlsmith, experienced more dissonance than the $20 group because $1 provided insufficient justification for their attitude-discrepant behavior (telling a person something they themselves did not believe).

In explaining this study to a class, we have noticed that the discussion typically gets bogged down over the notion of how dissonance, a psychological state, provides the motivation for a change in attitude. Many students fail to understand that it is the experience of dissonance that directly motivates the change in Festinger and Carlsmith's (1959) experiment, not the amount of money received (although the amount of money does induce the dissonance). It is as if students forget about the notion of dissonance and focus solely on the money variable. (Our students often state that subjects in the $20 condition should rate the task more favorably because they received more money!) We hypothesized that providing students with an opportunity to experience a state of dissonance resulting from discrepancies between their own attitudes and behaviors might better enable them to understand the concept of cognitive dissonance and, consequently, the subtleties of Festinger and Carlsmith's experimental manipulation. Thus, we developed a simple but effective in-class exercise that induces dissonance by comparing students' personal attitudes and behaviors on a number of social issues. Our findings suggest that a majority of students agree or strongly agree with a series of attitudinal statements, but only a minority perform behavior consistent with their reported attitudes.

Method

Materials

The stimulus material for the exercise consists of one double-sided page. Side 1 is titled "Attitude Survey" and contains four items to be rated on a 5-point scale ranging from *strongly disagree* (1) to *strongly agree* (5). The items are: (a) World hunger is a serious problem that needs attention, (b) Our country needs to address the growing number of homeless, (c) The right to vote is one of the most valuable rights of American citizens, and (d) Our government should spend less money on nuclear weapons and more on helping citizens better their lives. Instructions at the top of the page read, "Please indicate your attitudes on the four statements below."

Side 2 is titled "Behavioral Survey" and is headed with instructions reading, "Please indicate whether or not you perform the stated <u>behavior on a regular basis</u>." Below the instructions are four items corresponding to the attitudinal items on page 1: (a) Do you personally do anything to lessen world hunger (e.g., donate money or food or write your representative)?, (b) Do you personally do anything to help the homeless (e.g., volunteer at homeless shelter or donate money)?, (c) Did you vote in the last election for which you were eligible?, and (d) Do you personally convey your feelings to the government (e.g., write your representatives or participate in protests/marches)? Response options of "yes" and "no" are offered for each item.

Procedure

Prior to any discussion of cognitive dissonance, distribute copies of the handout to students with instructions to complete Side 1 (Attitude Survey) before Side 2 (Behavioral Survey). Then ask the class (by a show of hands) how many agreed or strongly agreed with attitudinal Item 1. Next, ask the students to turn to Side 2 and again raise their hands if they responded "yes" to the corresponding behavioral item. Repeat the process of comparing the attitudinal responses with the corresponding behavioral responses for the remaining three items. Most students will quickly get the point of the exercise.

A subsequent discussion of cognitive dissonance can begin with a simple question like, "How does it make you feel when these inconsistencies are pointed out to you?" Our students responded, "hypocritical," "guilty," or some related remarks. Further discussion can focus on formal definitions of cognitive dissonance and cognitive consonance, research studies on cognitive dissonance (e.g., Aronson & Mills, 1959; Festinger & Carlsmith, 1959), and dissonance reduction strategies.

For purposes of this article, we asked students to return their completed forms, but instructors would typically not need to collect the forms unless they plan to report the specific results to the class later. Table 1 displays the responses of 125 students; 53 were enrolled in two social psychology classes and 72 in two introductory psychology classes. These responses highlight the large discrepancies between students' attitudes and behaviors.

Only one student reported complete attitude-behavior consistency on all items. The remaining 124 students (99.2%) reported attitude-discrepant behavior on at least one of the four items. Twenty-nine students (23%) reported attitude-behavior inconsistencies on all four items. These findings demonstrate that the exercise highlighted inconsistencies in virtually all students in our sample.

Table 1. Attitudinal and Behavioral Responses

Item and Course[a]	Attitudes (% Agree and Strongly Agree)	Behaviors (% Yes)
World hunger a problem		
Social	87	17
Introductory	90	7
Must address homeless problem		
Social	96	32
Introductory	95	33
Right to vote important		
Social	94	47
Introductory	85	40
Government should better people's lives		
Social	91	11
Introductory	88	3

[a]n = 53 for social, n = 72 for introductory.

Student Assessment

After the discussion, students evaluated their experiences on a 5-point scale ranging from *strongly disagree* (1) to *strongly agree* (5). For all four items, students' reactions were quite positive. They reported that (a) the exercise helped in understanding cognitive dissonance ($M = 4.5$), (b) they experienced dissonance ($M = 4.1$), (c) the exercise provided self-insight ($M = 4.0$), and (d) the exercise was a useful learning experience ($M = 4.3$).

Eight students also wrote comments, all of which were positive. One response was particularly interesting: "[The exercise] works well, even to the point where I 'fudged' on the second sheet [Behavioral Survey] to try to relieve some cognitive dissonance." Not surprisingly, this response was from the lone student who reported complete attitude-behavior consistency. Evidently, the exercise was especially effective for this individual.

Discussion

We believe the exercise is very useful for introducing and explaining the concept of cognitive dissonance, because virtually all students actually experience cognitive dissonance. Thus, students learn and understand the concept in direct relation to their own attitudes and behaviors. Later discussions of research on cognitive dissonance take on more meaning because students have recently experienced such a psychological state. Nevertheless, a number of related issues must be addressed.

First, some instructors may be concerned about the ethical nature of our exercise. Asking students to publicly admit to certain attitudes and behaviors may be considered too intrusive for a classroom demonstration. One strategy to avoid this problem would be to collect the completed surveys, shuffle them, and redistribute them to the class. At this point, proceed through the item-by-item comparisons, again by a show of hands. In this situation, students would be expressing the attitudes and opinions of anonymous fellow students. Although our data were not obtained in this manner, we believe such an approach would alleviate any ethical concerns while maintaining the overall usefulness of the exercise .

A second and related issue is whether the public admission of attitude-behavior inconsistencies may have induced the reported dissonance rather than (or in addition to) the inconsistencies themselves. Although this situation is possible, we believe students experienced dissonance before the public admission. We have no empirical data to support our belief, but our subjective appraisal of student responses during the exercise provides some evidence. As students completed Side 2 of the survey, extensive murmuring and mild laughter occurred. We interpret such activities as the behavioral manifestation of the students'

230

dissonance resulting solely from completing the exercise instrument.

A final concern is whether the dissonance induced by our exercise ultimately results in any attitude or behavior changes, as predicted by cognitive dissonance theory. Such evidence, although interesting, would be difficult to obtain and is beyond the intended scope and purpose of our exercise. The goal of our procedure is to induce dissonance so that students can directly experience such a psychological state. The exercise is not intended as a test of cognitive dissonance theory or dissonance reduction strategies. Those topics could be addressed in the discussion following the exercise. Thus, although possible attitude or behavior changes resulting from our exercise would be an intriguing topic, lack of such information does not detract from the usefulness of the procedure. Future users of the exercise may want to devise a means to deal more extensively with this issue.

References

Aronson, E., & Mills, J. (1959). The effects of severity of initiation on liking for a group. *Journal of Abnormal and Social Psychology, 59,* 177-181.

Festinger, L. (1957). *A theory of cognitive dissonance.* Stanford, CA: Stanford University Press.

Festinger, L., & Carlsmith, J. M. (1959). Cognitive consequences of forced compliance. *Journal of Abnormal and Social Psychology, 58,* 203-210.

Note

We thank Bill McIntosh, Michael Zuschlag, and three anonymous reviewers for their helpful comments and suggestions on earlier drafts of this article.

Identifying Major Techniques of Persuasion

Vivian Parker Makosky
St. Lawrence University

Exposure to advertisements is a fact of everyday life. Vast amounts of money are spent on these attempts to control behavior, and there is at least some evidence that the persuasion techniques employed are successful. Surveys conducted by a market research firm indicate that we not only remember what advertisers tell us, we also believe it a lot of the time. In one survey, 82% could correctly name the product for "Please don't squeeze the . . ." (Charmin); 79% knew that "Plop, plop, fizz, fizz, oh what a relief it is" means AlkaSeltzer; 59% identified Coke for "It's the real thing"; 57% knew that Morton Salt goes with "When it rains, it pours"; and 55% knew that you should "Give your cold to . . ." Contac (Feinsilber & Mead, 1980). These same authors report that in a second survey, the percentage of people who consider advertising claims to be "completely true" is surprisingly high.

Most discussions of persuasion in social and introductory psychology textbooks (e.g., Crider, Goethals, Kavanaugh, & Solomon, 1983) focus on such issues as: how credible, attractive, and similar to the target the communicator is; whether or not the communication is one-sided or two sided; whether or not the target person is paying attention to the message, or has agreed to a similar request in the past. Advertising uses additional techniques of persuasion, which are seldom presented, providing an opportunity for the instructor to present useful and interesting information without duplicating the text.

The purpose of this class exercise is to increase student awareness of common persuasion techniques used in advertising such as: (a) the appeal to or creation of needs, (b) social and prestige suggestion, (c) the use of emotionally loaded words and images. The instructor's presentation of these techniques draws on television commercials for illustrations, but the assignments to students use magazine advertisements because they can be brought to class more easily or attached to written reports.

The Appeal To or Creation of Needs

In this technique, the advertiser evokes a need and then represents the product (or recommends action) as a means of satisfying that need. The discussion of needs is structured with a modified version of the Maslow (1954) hierarchy of needs, including the following levels: physiological needs, safety and security needs, needs for belonging and love, self-esteem and status needs, cognitive needs, aesthetic needs, and self-actualization needs. It is easy to find TV commercials to illustrate appeals to physiological needs ("Aren't you hungry for Burger King now?"), safety and security ("Get a piece of the rock"), belongingness and love ("Brush your breath with Dentyne"), and self-esteem and status ("When E. F. Hutton speaks . . .").

Appeals to cognitive, aesthetic, and self-actualization needs are much less common. It would seem that those with advertising dollars to spend believe that some needs really are more basic than others, and are trying to reach as many people as possible. Information on targeting populations by advertising products on particular types of shows can be found in discussions of psycho-graphics (Wells, 1975).

Social and Prestige Suggestion

The main point of this technique is that you should buy or do X because someone else does. With *social suggestion*, that someone else is everyone else. The Pepsi generation, Wrigley's Spearmint Gum, and virtually every other product that features lots of people, in different types of clothes and/or settings, often of different ages and races, is relying on social suggestion. With *prestige suggestion*, on the other hand, you should do or buy X because some famous or prestigious person says to do so. James Garner for Polaroid, Bill Cosby for Jello, Evonne Goolagong for Geritol, and all those famous names with unknown faces for American Express are examples of prestige suggestion.

Loaded Words and Images

This technique is the most subtle because it is not what is said so much as how it is said, or what you are seeing while it is being said. One example is the use of athletic, attractive people in the advertisements for snacks (e.g., jockeys, skiers, etc., who eat Snickers). Certain "buzzwords" fall into this category, including "natural" for beauty products and "light" for anything they want to sound dietetic. Often the best way to illustrate this technique is to talk about the product "image." For example, Anheuser-Busch has created completely different images for Michelob and Budweiser beers. Michelob has had a long series of advertisements emphasizing social situations, often with couples, and using such phrases as "weekends were made for Michelob" and, subsequently,

"put a little weekend in your week" when the people were meeting after work. Budweiser, on the other hand, emphasizes achievement ("For all you do, this Bud's for you"), featuring Clydesdale horses and targeting an almost exclusively male population. Loaded words and images are used to enhance the impact of the message (as when beautiful people are associated with beauty products) and/or to suspend reason (as when cigarette advertisements feature the outdoor scenes and "fresh" taste).

Variations on this activity work well in introductory, social, personality, or motivation classes, or in discussions of the applications of psychology. The background discussion of the techniques is largely the same, regardless of the level of the class or the complexity of the rest of the assignment. Examination of actual advertisements makes it clear that they use more than one technique simultaneously, and the instructor may wish to modify the four variations suggested next in light of that fact.

Variation 1

Students bring to class the first five ads from an expensive magazine (e.g., *Vogue*), and the first five ads from a cheap magazine (e.g., *Family Circle*). Each collection of ads is referenced. Students are grouped in fives to analyze. the ads, the needs appealed to in the two types of ads, which type of suggestion was used, what words and images stood out, assumptions about the target populations of these magazines.

Variation 2

Students bring in the first five ads from a women's magazine and the first five ads from a men's magazine. The in-class activity proceeds as above.

Variation 3

Students bring in ads that appeal to them personally and ads that they think are a "turn off." In this case, the ads should be brought in before the lecture on techniques. In order to avoid potential embarrassment to individual students, the men's ads are pooled and the women's ads are pooled. The class discussion can then focus on the implied needs of college students, and whether the students believe the implications to be accurate. As always, the discussion should bring out the similarities/differences in the persuasion techniques in the two groups of ads.

Variation 4

Students bring in one ad appealing to each level in the needs hierarchy. The source of each ad is referenced. The small in-class groups discuss and then summarize the types of magazines the ads came from, and the products and images associated with each need level.

Students are very enthusiastic about this assignment and it is a good way to get discussion going. You should allow an entire class period for the discussion of ads, approximately half of the time for the small groups to reach their conclusions and half for each small group to report to the class at large.

If you want to make the same points, but do not wish to spend so much in-class time on it, each of these variations can be modified as out-of-class discussion assignments, with a brief report to the class at large. Alternatively, these can be writing assignments. In upper-level classes, frequency distributions in the various categories can be tabulated along with calculations of reliability in coding ads, statistical significance of differences between two groups of ads, and so on. One of the advantages of this assignment is that it can be varied from term to term.

References

Crider, A. B., Goethals, R. D., Kavanaugh, R. D., & Solomon, P. R. (1983). *Psychology*. Glenview, IL: Scott, Foresman.

Feinsilber, M., & Mead, W. B. (1980). *American averages*. Garden City, NY: Doubleday.

Maslow, A. H. (1954). *Motivation and personality*. New York: Harper and Row.

Wells, W. D. (1975). Psychographics: A critical review. *Journal of Marketing Research, 12,* 196-213.

Note

For background material on advertising and persuasion, consult author for bibliographical list.

From Acceptance to Rejection: Food Contamination in the Classroom

D. W. Rajecki
Indiana University-Purdue University at Indianapolis

This article describes an effective and efficient classroom demonstration of induced food rejection. The exercise is recommended for methodology and statistics courses in which students are required to generate and process data. It produces meaningful data sets that appeal to students because they are directly involved. The exercise could be advantageous in certain content courses. For example, in social psychology it could be used for an elaboration of attitude expression and change, and in learning or motivation courses it could provide insight into the formation of associations. Even introductory psychology students can gain from its demonstration of design and measurement principles .

The approach derives from the literature on contamination sensitivity to disgusting substances (Rozin & Fallon, 1987). Psychological contamination of otherwise acceptable food occurs in two ways: (a) trace contamination by contact with a disgusting substance (e.g.,

soup containing a human hair) and (b) associational contamination by contact with material associated with a disgusting substance (e.g., soup stirred with a clean fly swatter). My approach takes advantage of the power of trace contamination.

Materials

Relatively inexpensive materials proved sufficient to demonstrate trace contamination in class. First, I prepared a number of color slides of delectable foodstuffs, including several kinds of popular meats, finger foods, and pastries. The pictures were culled from direct mail catalogs and magazine ads. Other kinds of visual presentations would serve; the point of showing the pictures is to focus peoples' attention on food. Second, I made up color-coded decks of four index cards for the repeated measures to be taken.

Three additional items completed the materials list: (a) my coffee cup that was associated with and frequently used by me in prior meetings with the class, (b) my pocket comb, and (c) a small can (177 ml) of V8 tomato juice cocktail. I picked V8 because I like it as a snack.

Rationale

The point of the tomato juice was to provide a vehicle for trace contamination; the cup and comb served as agents of pollution. Human residues—such as feces, urine, saliva, and mucus—are potent food contaminants. But even much subtler human traces can also be disgusting. For example, Rozin and Fallon (1981, p. 42) mentioned "the unpleasantness experienced by many on feeling the warmth of a seat used by another person." Based on this sort of insight, I expected that my cup would be a contaminant, and my comb even more so.

Procedure

To be effective, the contamination demonstration should be conducted without prior notification or warning. In the middle of a lecture, the decks of index cards were distributed. Scale responses and points used in the project were listed on the blackboard as follows: *like extremely much* (6), *like very much* (5), *like fairly much* (4), *like and dislike equally* (3), *dislike fairly much* (2), *dislike very much* (1), and *dislike extremely much* (0). Dawes and Smith (1985) described this instrument as a general rating scale. The scale and its potential applications were discussed until all students indicated that they understood how to use it. A color code was also drawn on the board to ensure that students would use the colored index cards in the proper sequence.

Apropos of nothing, I stated that it certainly would be agreeable if snacks were available during class. But what would we have? To help make a decision, the tantalizing food slides were shown. After the display, I explained that the idea was to rate one's desire to have a snack. I reminded the students of the food slides and asked them to refer to the scale points and values on the board. Using the designated first card, they were to express their desire for any snack they happened to have in mind by choosing a scale point that matched their desire. The students then recorded that scale point by writing down its particular scale value as an integer. (This first rating serves primarily as a warm-up or practice trial, and it is also useful as a manipulation check, as seen next.) When completed, the first cards were turned face down on the students' desks.

Next, the small, unopened can of V8 was removed from hiding and was held aloft. The students then rated (on the second card) their desire to have the juice as a snack at the moment.

When the second rating was completed, I remarked that it is not very refined to drink out of a can. Looking around for an acceptable serving vessel, I spotted my own coffee mug, dumped out the liquid content (water), opened the can of V8, and poured the juice into the cup. This act presumably tainted the juice because of trace (and possibly associational) contamination with the residues in and on the cup. Holding the cup aloft, I inquired as to how much students desired that particular juice in that particular cup as a snack right now. The third card was used for this rating in the usual fashion.

When the third rating was completed, I said that I forgot to shake up the can of V8 to prepare it for drinking, but this oversight could be corrected. A small plastic comb was taken out of my pocket, and I ran it through my hair once or twice, inserted it into the juice in the cup, and stirred the liquid. With the soiled and contaminating comb jutting out, the cup was held aloft again. The students were asked how much they desired that particular juice in that particular cup containing that particular comb as a snack at the moment. The fourth card was used for this last measure. Each student then collected her or his cards in a package and bound them with a rubber band. The demonstration required less than 20 min.

Results

In a recent semester, I ran a class of 124 undergraduates (75 women and 49 men), through the demonstration. The impact of the slides was as expected; the average rating for "any snack" was 4.82 and 4.59 for men and women, respectively, which is a positive manipulation check. These means are not significantly different, $t < 1.00$, and gender did not affect any of the other tests reported here. Henceforth, gender, although taken into account in the appropriate analyses, will be dismissed from consideration.

The original plan was to use the whole class as a data base to test the effects of contaminating the V8. But, 77% of the men rated V8 per se between 3 and 0 on the scale and 70% of the women also rated it in this low range. Overall, 60% of the students initially rated the juice at 0 on the scale. This finding indicates that the scaling technique was sensitive to some students' aversion to V8, but people who are already at the lower levels—or at the floor—of a rating scale can hardly be expected to show much of a contamination effect. Accordingly, for this report, the data from individuals with initial V8 ratings of 3 or less were set aside. (This post hoc elimination of some subjects and retention of others may have biased the sample toward a certain kind of regression effect, but these concerns were relieved to an extent in a replication, as noted next.) To test the contamination hypothesis with this first class, I was left with a subsample of 33 people who had rated V8 per se at the 4-, 5-, or 6-point levels, and I cast their juice ratings in an analysis of variance (ANOVA). The average ratings by these students over the three V8 evaluations were: V8 alone = 4.67, V8 + cup = 2.30, and V8 + cup + comb = 0.21. The predicted contamination effect was very clear, and the repeated-measures statistical effect over the three ratings was significant, $F(2, 62) = 126.21, p < .01$.

Replication and Evaluation

The demonstration was replicated with refinements. In a meeting of 57 students from another class, I pretested—using the scale already described—a list of beverages that included apple juice, Coke, grape juice, milk, orange juice, Pepsi, R.C. Cola, 7-Up, V8, and water. Orange juice was the most popular beverage with an average pretest rating of 4.98. (Not surprisingly, by now, V8 had the lowest overall rating of 2.75.) It is noteworthy that 54 of the 57 students (95%) rated orange juice at the 4-, 5-, or 6-point levels.

At a subsequent meeting, I ran this second class through the contamination demonstration as described, this time using a small can of Donald Duck orange juice as the target. Based on data from all the students, the replication was a success. The average rating from the "any snack" manipulation check was 4.81. The mean ratings from the demonstration were: orange juice alone = 3.90, orange juice + cup = 1.27, and orange juice + cup + comb = 0.00, $F(2, 122) = 216.05, p < .01$. Of the 63 students who saw this demonstration, 62 (98%) showed some contamination shift over the three juice measures.

I obtained a short evaluation of the demonstration from this second section. After the purpose of the exercise was explained, a one-page questionnaire was distributed that stated: "As a teaching aid, the food slide and orange juice demonstration was . . . ." Judgments were expressed on four bipolar rating scales: dull-interesting, clear-unclear, unconvincing-convincing, and good-bad. Utilizing 10point scales, the students' marks were scored from a low of 1 (negative pole) to a high of 10 (positive pole). The demonstration was fairly well received by the class; it was seen as interesting ($M = 8.84$), clear ($M = 9.71$), convincing ($M = 9.33$), and good ($M = 9.35$).

Discussion

To the extent that personal involvement is motivating in the mastery of subject matter, this trace contamination exercise has value. Students can be given the direct experience of feeling and expressing fairly strong evaluative reactions. The demonstration shows them that the scale can pick up the shift from acceptance to rejection of food, and that the ANOVA detects the effect. The technique has the advantage that large amounts of data from fairly complex designs can be generated quickly and inexpensively. The idea, of course, is that the students would be responsible for the data analysis.

This realistic exercise demonstrates some of the problems and anomalies that emerge in "real life" research. For example, the unexpected, partial floor effect for V8 ratings reported in the first demonstration illustrates the pitfalls of simply trusting one's assumptions in psychological research. The data from the replication also raise some questions. The orange juice mean of 3.90 was substantially lower than the overall pretest mean of 4.98. One explanation for this finding is that during the pretest, the students may have had their own, favorite type of orange juice in mind when they expressed their judgments, whereas in the demonstration itself, they had no choice but to rate a single commercial canned brand. So the two ratings differed. A more interesting possibility is that the instructor's contact with the unopened can was seen as a form of contamination of the juice. These propositions can be tested in the classroom with the technique described here.

References

Dawes, R. M., & Smith, T. L. (1985). Attitude and opinion measurement. In G. Lindzey & E. Aronson (Eds.), *Handbook of social psychology* (3rd ed., Vol. 1, pp. 509-566). New York: Random House.

Rozin, P., & Fallon, A. E. (1981). The acquisition of likes and dislikes for food. In J. Solms & R. L. Hall (Eds.), *Criteria of food acceptance: How man chooses what he eats* (pp. 35-48). Zurich, Switzerland: Foster-Verlag AG.

Rozin, P., & Fallon, A. E. (1987). A perspective on disgust. *Psychological Review, 94,* 23-41.

Note

I thank the students in my introductory psychology classes for their cooperation and assistance and the Methods and Techniques Editor and three anonymous reviewers for their helpful comments on earlier versions of this article.

6. EXPLORING ABOUT AGGRESSION

Defining Aggression: An Exercise for Classroom Discussion

Ludy T. Benjamin, Jr.
Texas A&M University

Aggression is a topic included in virtually every textbook on introductory psychology. Some books place aggression in the section on motivation and emotion while others cover it as part of social psychology. Most include it in reference to research on humans but discussion of some animal studies of aggression is also common. Treatment of related concepts such as violence, anger, frustration, and assertiveness are also common topics.

Whereas textbook coverage of aggression is almost guaranteed, a definition of the term is not. In a nonrandom sample of 10 introductory psychology books (selected from the author's bookcase), 5 provided an explicit definition of aggression but the others left the meaning embedded in a series of paragraphs and so required the reader to serve as lexicographer. Considering the complexity of the term aggression, it is not surprising that these authors might choose to avoid espousing a particular definition.

The exercise described in this paper uses aggression as an example of a typical construct in psychology, permeated with a host of subtle meanings and not so subtle disagreements that make it difficult to reach a consensual definition. One could use other constructs such as intelligence or self-esteem, but aggression was chosen because it generates considerable discussion among students. Anecdotal evidence for the fascination with this topic can be drawn from the prevalence of aggression as a theme in movies and television, the popularity of sports, and the interest many people show in reports of violent crime.

The activity described here can be used in a number of classes, including the course in introductory psychology and, in fact, anywhere you treat the topic of aggression. It should be used prior to any lecture on aggression and benefit the students have read their textbook coverage of the subject. This exercise works best in a class of 50 students or less, but by altering the data reporting procedures it can be used in much larger classes, although discussion obviously will suffer in large classes. The activity requires about 50 minutes but could be made shorter or longer depending on the preferences of the instructor. The instructor's role in this exercise is to serve as a tabulator of the data and as moderator of the discussion.

Procedure

At the beginning of the class, give each student a copy of a questionnaire containing the 25 numbered statements shown in Table 1. Instruct the students to "read each statement and decide whether or not you believe the situation described is one of aggression." Wording of this instruction is critical so as not to bias the responses. Avoid using phrases like "aggressive act" or "aggressive behavior" because one of the issues to be discussed is whether some overt behavior needs to occur in aggression. Ask the students to circle the number of each statement that describes aggression. Tell them they should respond according to their own beliefs and not how they think they should respond or how they think most people would respond. Compliance with this request can be enhanced by telling the students not to put their names on the questionnaires. Indeed, there is no reason in this exercise to know how a particular person responded. You may want to have the students indicate their sex on the questionnaire if you would be interested in looking at potential sex differences in the definition of aggression. Such differences, if obtained, would undoubtedly add to the interest in the discussion.

Allow the students about 5 minutes to complete the questionnaire. Most, if not all, of the students will finish before that time, so you should be ready to proceed when the last person has finished. Collect the questionnaires, shuffle, and redistribute them to the class so that each student gets a copy. Most students will be given a questionnaire other than their own, but it is unimportant if they get their own copy back. This procedure allows students to report on the responses that may or may not be their own, thus eliminating a potential source of embarrassment.

Record the data on the board by asking students for a show of hands on each numbered item, with hands being raised if the item is circled on the questionnaire they are holding. It is important to know the exact size of the class in this exercise to know when you have unanimity. For example, with a class size of 34, total agreement would

Table 1. Aggression Questionnaire

1. A spider eats a fly.
2. Two wolves fight for the leadership of the pack.
3. A soldier shoots an enemy at the front line.
4. The warden of a prison executes a convicted criminal.
5. A juvenile gang attacks members of another gang.
6. Two men fight for a piece of bread.
7. A man viciously kicks a cat.
8. A man, while cleaning a window, knocks over a flowerpot, which, in falling, injures a pedestrian.
9. A girl kicks a wastebasket.
10. Mr. X, a notorious gossip, speaks disparagingly of many people of his acquaintance.
11. A man mentally rehearses a murder he is about to commit.
12. An angry son purposely fails to write to his mother, who is expecting a letter and will be hurt if none arrives.
13. An enraged boy tries with all his might to inflict injury on his antagonist, a bigger boy, but is not successful in doing so. His efforts simply amuse the bigger boy.
14. A man daydreams of harming his antagonist, but has no hope of doing so.
15. A senator does not protest the escalation of bombing to which he is morally opposed.
16. A farmer beheads a chicken and prepares it for supper.
17. A hunter kills an animal and mounts it as a trophy.
18. A dog snarls at a mail carrier, but does not bite.
19. A physician gives a flu shot to a screaming child.
20. A boxer gives his opponent a bloody nose.
21. A Girl Scout tries to assist an elderly woman, but trips her by accident.
22. A bank robber is shot in the back while trying to escape.
23. A tennis player smashes his racket after missing a volley.
24. A person commits suicide.
25. A cat kills a mouse, parades around with it, and then discards it.

come from a score of 34, in which case every student agreed that the item described aggression. A score of zero would mean that no one thought the item described aggression. Such unanimity is rare and typically occurs only on those items in which there seems to be no intent to harm. Tabulating the data on the chalkboard can be accomplished quickly, usually in less than 5 minutes, so that the bulk of the class time can be devoted to discussion.

Class Discussion

Use the questionnaire results to get the students talking about how aggression is defined. You might begin with those items for which there is greatest agreement and proceed to those on which the class is evenly divided. Note that the 25 statements are quite diverse and are intended to span the gamut of issues relevant to consideration of aggression: harm to living versus nonliving things (9 and 23), accident versus intention (8 and 21), actual damage versus no physical damage (10, 13, and 18), self-defense (3, 13, and 14), duty or job responsibility (3, 4, 19, 20, and 22), predation and instinctual behavior (1, 2, and 25), survival (1, 6, and 16), acts involving animals other than humans (7, 16, 17, and 18), covert acts (11 and 14), inaction (12 and 15), self-injury (24), and killing for sport (17 and 25).

Attempt to get students to make these points by grouping the related items in the discussion. For example, items 16 and 17 make an interesting comparison. The latter

is more often viewed as aggressive, and a similar pattern emerges in items 1 and 25. In both pairs, students distinguish between killing for food and killing for sport. Many will argue that food-seeking justifies the act and would not label it aggression. Debate on these items and many others is typically lively and opposing viewpoints are common. Should alternate views not be forthcoming on some issues, the instructor may wish to play the role of devil's advocate.

If there is time, or in a separate lecture in the next class period, you can present some of the definitions of aggression proposed by psychologists. Consider the following examples:

1. "Behavior intended to hurt another person" (Freedman, 1982, p. 259).
2. "Any behavior whose intent is to inflict harm or injury on another living being" (McGee & Wilson, 1984, p. 503).
3. "Hostile or forceful action intended to dominate or violate" (Lefrancois, 1982, p. 596).
4. "Behavior that is intended to injure another person (physically or verbally) or to destroy property" (Atkinson, Atkinson, & Hilgard, 1983, p. 321).
5. "A response that delivers noxious stimuli to another organism" (Buss, 1961, p. 3).

The first four definitions require intent, but the last one does not. The first one limits aggression to humans, while the second and fifth broaden it to include all living organisms. But what about kicking wastebaskets and smashing tennis rackets? That could be considered aggressive under the fourth definition. All definitions talk about behaviors, actions, or responses but leave one unclear as to whether inaction can be aggressive or not. Providing these definitions to students helps them to understand that, like them, psychologists also have some difficulty in-agreeing on what does or does not constitute aggression.

Students in my class consistently have rated this activity high in terms of satisfaction and as an exercise in learning. Written comments indicate that a number of them believe that it serves to sharpen their critical thinking skills. A few miss the point and want to be told the "real" definition of aggression after the exercise is over, but that kind of reaction is quite rare.

Additional Suggestions

You can use this exercise as a basis for discussion or as a lecture on the causes of aggression: Is aggression instinctual?; Is aggression a natural reaction to conditions such as frustration, conflict, and pain?; Is aggression learned, and if so, how and from what sources? This last question presents a good opportunity to discuss aggression in the media, particularly television, and what effect it may have on the behavior of viewers (see Liebert, Sprafkin, & Davidson, 1982).

Other topics of interest include: aggression in athletics, competitiveness versus aggressiveness, assertiveness versus aggressiveness, the positive role of aggression, violet crime, the relation of prejudice to aggression, and methods for the control of aggression.

References

Atkinson, R. L., Atkinson, R. C., & Hilgard, E. R. (1983). *Introduction to psychology* (8th ed.). New York: Harcourt, Brace, Jovanovich.

Buss, A. (1961). *The psychology of aggression*. New York: John Wiley.

Freedman, J. L. (1982*). Introductory psychology* (2nd ed.). Reading, MA: Addison-Wesley.

Johnson, R. N. (1972). *Aggression in man and animals.* Philadelphia: W. B. Saunders.

Kaufmann, H. (1970). *Aggression and altruism.* New York: Holt Rinehart and Winston.

Krech, D., Crutchfield, R. S., Livson, N., Wilson, W. A., & Parducci, A. (1982). *Elements of psychology* (4th ed.). New York: Alfred A. Knopf.

Lefrancois, G. R. (1982). *Psychology* (2nd ed.). Belmont, CA: Wadsworth.

Liebert, R. M., Sprafkin, J. N ., & Davidson, E. S. (1982). *The early window: Effects of television on children and youth* (2nd ed.). New York: Pergamon.

McGee, M. G., & Wilson, D. W. (1984). *Psychology: Science and application.* St. Paul, MN: West Publishing.

Note

The items in Table 1 were taken from Johnson (1972), Kaufmann (1970), and Krech, Crutchfield, Livson, Wilson, & Parducci (1982). Some of their items were modified for use in this questionnaire.

Perspectives on Human Aggression: Writing to Einstein and Freud on "Why War?"

Dana S. Dunn
Moravian College

Referring to the only meeting he ever had with Albert Einstein, Sigmund Freud wrote to his disciple Ferenczi: "He understands as much about psychology as I do about physics, so we had a very pleasant talk" (Jones, 1957, p. 131). Freud later had much to say to Einstein about psychology, however, when they exchanged public letters on the origins of war and human aggression (Einstein & Freud, 1932/1964). The "Why War?" letters, organized by Einstein, were written at the behest of the Intentional Institute of Intellectual Cooperation, a committee of the League of Nations. The letters are an ideal starting point for a discussion of aggression because they focus on the nature of large-scale conflicts among humans. In order to prompt a careful and critical examination of the arguments presented in these historic letters, I ask students to write a letter of response to Einstein and Freud.

The writing assignment serves three goals. First, the correspondence between Einstein and Freud contains an unusual mix of history, psychology, and personal opinion, allowing students to consider aggression in a broader scope than usual. Second, letter writing requires students to analyze and respond to arguments in a concise format. Finally, through writing letters, students can react to aggression as a psychological topic in a personal way. Before presenting the exercise, a brief overview of the letters' contents is appropriate.

Why War?

The first letter was Einstein's. It focused on whether humanity can be free from the threat of war. Early in the letter, he suggested that his usual objective approach to solving problems was limited when dealing with aggressive, human characteristics such as will, feelings, and instinct. Yet he had little difficulty in pinpointing the causes of armed conflicts. Toward the end of the letter, Einstein faulted both "the political power-hunger" of governments and humanity's "lust for hatred and destruction" (Einstein & Freud 1932/1964, p. 201). He closed with an appeal to Freud for insights about how to eliminate armed conflicts.

Freud's reply was longer and more detailed, and it emphasized culture and instinct. He traced the origin of aggression to a general principle "that conflicts of interest between men are settled by the use of violence" (Einstein & Freud, 1932/1964, p. 204). In Freud's view, violence evolved from conflict among individuals and could only be thwarted by laws created by communities. But why do organized communities use violence to settle internal and external disputes? Freud held humanity's self-preserving (erotic) and destructive (death) instincts responsible and suggested that urges toward aggression were not easily eliminated. Freud closed by asking Einstein an important question: "Why do you and I and so many other people rebel so violently against war?" (p. 213). In answering for himself, Freud pointed to the process of civilization, both its benefits (e.g., intellect) and constraints (e.g., repression), as leading to pacifism. Freud neither recommended specific ways to promote pacifism nor commented on the likelihood that this philosophy would be successful.

Writing to Einstein and Freud

Instructions for the exercise are simple and straightforward. Students read the correspondence between Einstein and Freud (1932/1964) and then write a two-page letter responding to either or both of the authors. (It may seem unusual to write to both authors at once, but several students asked to do so because they felt that each letter merited comment.) Students are encouraged to agree or disagree with the authors and to comment on the perspectives on human aggression that each man offers. They may consider whether the content of either author's letter could be accurately described as optimistic or pessimistic about humanity's destiny. Are humans destined, for example, to wage war against one another due to avarice (nurture), to some unfortunate disposition (nature), or a combination of both?

Because students are encouraged to use their own creative ideas, strict guidelines (e.g., reliance on Freudian theory) are not required. I encourage students to be prepared to read their letters to the class so that they can discuss their responses in more detail. If students prefer not to read their letters aloud, they are not required to do so.

I used the exercise in two different classes. The first was an intensive January term course devoted to reading a variety of papers spanning Freud's long career (see Gay, 1989). Students wrote their letters toward the end of the term, which permitted them to incorporate as well as critique material gleaned from their in-depth experience with Freud's ideas. Poignantly, the exercise coincided with Operation Desert Storm. My students were quite upset by the war in the Middle East. They found the letter writing to be cathartic because it provided an opportunity to search for meaning in that conflict. The letters were very moving. They ranged from a portrayal of human aggression as innate but controllable to an acceptance of its inevitability.

I also used the exercise in a freshman core course that explored the theme of community in Western culture. In this context, an overview of Freud's ideas on dreams and the development of civilization served as background for the letters. Less familiarity with Freud's ideas did not decrease the exercise's impact on students. The exercise seems equally suitable for personality courses that cover Freud and for social psychology courses that include general theories of aggression.

Variations

One variation of the exercise I intend to try relies on freewriting (e.g., Belanoff, Elbow, & Fontaine, 1990). *Freewriting* involves writing continuously for a short time (usually 10 min or so) on any topic that comes to the writer's mind. For this variation of the exercise, I will use focused freewriting (Hinkle & Hinkle, 1990), in which uncensored comments are directed toward a chosen topic, such as the arguments found in the letters. Before attending class, students will read the Einstein and Freud (1932/1964) correspondence. When class starts, students will listen to a brief review of the letters' main ideas and then freewrite for 10 min. Discussion of their letters will then proceed as usual. This approach to writing should encourage students to integrate the themes found in the letters with their own experience.

Another variation might have students extend the existing correspondence. After reading the two original letters, for example, students could impersonate Einstein by composing a third letter responding to Freud's views on culture and instinct. An additional letter written from Freud's point of view might consider his theories of aggression in light of historical events that have occurred in the last 60 years.

Although Freud was characteristically negative about the letters, at one point referring to them as "the tedious and sterile so-called discussion with Einstein" (Jones, 1957, p. 175), he was mistaken. The letters not only present the views of two intellectual giants, they can also serve as a fruitful starting point for discussing the nature of human conflict.

References

Belanoff, P., Elbow, P., & Fontaine, S. I. (Eds.). (1990). *Nothing begins with n: New investigations of freewriting.* Carbondale and Edwardsville, IL: Southern Illinois University Press.

Einstein, A., & Freud, S. (1964). Why war? In J. Strachey (Ed. and Trans.), *The standard edition of the complete psychological works of Sigmund Freud (Vol. 22,* pp. 197-215). London: Hogarth. (Original work published 1932)

Gay, P. (Ed.). (1989). *The Freud reader* New York: Norton.

Hinkle, S., & Hinkle, A. (1990). An experimental comparison of the effects of focused freewriting and other study strategies on lecture comprehension. *Teaching of Psychology, 17,* 31-35.

Jones, E. (1957). *The life and work of Sigmund Freud* (Vol. 3). New York: Basic Books.

Note

I thank Steve Gordy, Stacey Zaremba, and three anonymous reviewers for their comments on an earlier draft of this article.

The Dirty Dozen: Classroom Demonstration of Twelve Instigators of Aggression

William B. Davidson
University of South Carolina-Aiken

In my junior-level undergraduate social psychology class, I customarily require that students write a case study of a historical event, analyzing human behavior using the principles found in research on conformity, persuasion, self-justification, aggression, and attraction. Over several years, students have reported that this assignment is a very difficult one. Therefore, I developed several preparatory exercises to get them accustomed to seeing life through the "looking glass" of social-psychological principles. This article briefly describes one particularly effective exercise that trains students to identify 12 instigators of aggression in scenes from movies. Because the topic of aggression is covered in most undergraduate courses in social psychology, this "dirty dozen" exercise may be useful for other courses.

I spend about 2 weeks teaching aggression. On the first class day spent teaching this topic, I distribute a handout of the dirty dozen instigators of aggression (see Table 1) and discuss the meaning of each one. Then I announce the rules of a contest in which students are to find and submit scenes of violence in movies that have the largest number of instigators of aggression from the list of the dirty dozen. Students are limited to entering only one

scene of no more than 5-min duration, and no student is required to enter the contest. Entering the contest is optional because some students do not have access to a VCR and rented movies. The incentive for entering the contest is that the student whose scene is judged to have the largest number of instigators receives one letter grade improvement on the test covering aggression, which counts 10% toward the course grade.

The contest is held during the first class period after the test on aggression, so students generally have about 2 weeks to rent movies in quest of an ideal scene. The contest is held after the test on aggression so that the judges, who are fellow students in the class, have sufficient expertise in the topic.

Students who enter the contest bring to class a videotape of their movie, wound to the selected scene ahead of time. I then show the scenes to all class members, who report the number of instigators they see in each scene by filling out a checklist of the dirty dozen. Contestants are allowed to introduce their scene to the class by providing the title of the movie and a brief background of the circumstances that led up to the scene; they are not allowed to discuss the dirty dozen or rate their own scene

Table 1. Dirty Dozen Instigators of Aggression

1. Insult
2. Attack
3. Bad intentions of frustrator[a]
4. Unexpected interruption in progress toward goal[a]
5. Goal is near when progress toward it is thwarted[a]
6. Illegitimate or arbitrary blocking of progress toward goal[a]
7. Relative deprivation
8. Aggressive cues
9. Aggressive models
10. Deindividuation in aggressor
11. Dehumanization of victim(s)
12. Environmental factors
    a. Heat
    b. Noise
    c. Crowding

[a]Items 3–6 are types of frustration.

in the contest. The winning scene is determined by summing the instigators seen by the student-judges. Interestingly, the winning scene tends not to be the most violent one.

To provide an incentive for good judging during the classroom viewing of the scenes, I award the best judge a half letter grade increment on the aggression test. The judging award is slightly less than the award for the winning scene because entering the contest takes more work than judging. The best judge is the one whose ratings are closest to the class norm for each scene, which is determined by majority vote for each instigator. By using the class norm as an ideal profile against which to rate the judges, I assume that the norm is accurate. If consensus is any indication of accuracy, then my assumption is justified because the judges' ratings are very similar.

Pedagogical Benefits

The primary purpose of the dirty dozen exercise is to sharpen students' ability to identify the social instigators of aggression. The exercise gives them instruction and practice in developing this ability. In the three semesters that I have used this assignment, the sections on aggression in the case study papers have been decisively better, indicating the salutary effect of the exercise. A secondary purpose of the exercise is to improve students' general ability to identify social psychological determinants of attitudes, affects, and actions other than aggression. In other words, the abilities developed in the study of aggression should generalize to the study of other topics in the course, such as conformity, persuasion, self-justification, and attraction. This purpose cannot be directly evaluated because other training exercises are used in the course. However, many students have mentioned that the dirty dozen exercise helps them see the role of social influence in behaviors other than aggression.

In addition to its pedagocial benefits, the dirty dozen exercise generates a lot of interest. About one third of the students generally choose to enter a scene in the contest, and attendance on the contest day is typically very high, even in the classes before I introduce the incentive for judges to win an award. Instructors may adjust the exercise to fit their own needs and goals, but its pedagogical benefits should endure.

A Gender Difference in Acceptance of Sport Aggression: A Classroom Activity

David W. Rainey
John Carroll University

Sport psychology is a growing professional specialty and the focus of increasing scholarly interest. A number of professional journals, including the *International Journal of Sport Psychology*, the *Journal of Sport Psychology*, and the *Journal of Sport Behavior*, are devoted to research in this discipline. College and university courses in sport psychology are becoming more common. The current level of activity was demonstrated by a pre-conference workshop of the North American Society for Psychology of Sport and Physical Activity, entitled "The Teaching of Sport Psychology: Contemporary Course Options" (Landers, Singer, & Williams, 1985). Speakers described a

Table 1. Sport Situations

1. A defensive back on the local football team has been repeatedly criticized by his father for not "punishing" receivers in his zone. He vows to satisfy his father. In the next game, he delivers as hard a "hit" as he can to a receiver who is in mid-air, flipping him, knocking him unconscious and out of the game. Is the defensive back's behavior acceptable or unacceptable?

2. A young woman tennis player has been beaten badly in the singles final. She is also in the doubles final and again facing her singles opponent, whom she thoroughly dislikes. She gets a weak and high return of serve at the net and smashes it at her opponent with obvious delight. Is this young woman's behavior acceptable or unacceptable?

3. An 8-year-old hockey player has been told by his coach that if he does not play more "physically," he will be benched. He is checked hard by an opposing defensive man and retaliates by "spearing" him with his hockey stick. Though he is penalized by the referee, he is cheered by his coach. Is this boy's behavior acceptable or unacceptable?

4. Two high school girls basketball teams meet in the regional finals. The only black player on the court is the star of one team. She is constantly heckled when she has the ball. This includes the organized use of racial slurs by the opposing team's cheering section. Is the behavior of these fans acceptable or unacceptable?

5. The Dodgers are playing the Giants. In the second inning the Dodgers' pitcher hits the Giants' first baseman because "the plate belongs to me." When the Dodgers' pitcher comes to bat the next inning, the Giants' pitcher purposefully hits him on his throwing arm. Is the behavior of the Giants' pitcher acceptable or unacceptable?

6. The coach of a women's volleyball team knows that the star of the opposing team has a very sore back. She instructs her players to "spike" every shot they can at the injured opponent, in an attempt to aggravate her injury and knock her out of the game. Is the coach's behavior acceptable or unacceptable?

---

wide variety of courses. Some are designed primarily for athletes and coaches, some are general elective courses for undergraduates, and others are seminars for graduate students.

A common topic in these courses is aggression in sport. Textbooks on sport psychology also reflect this interest (e.g., Silva & Weinberg, 1984; Cox, 1985, devote chapters to this issue). These authors define aggression, investigate its incidence in sport, examine the causes, development, and impact of aggression in sport, and review the emerging research.

The topic of aggression in sport generates considerable interest among students. Most students can recall incidents of aggression in their own competitive experience and infamous incidents in the history of collegiate and professional sport. However, students hold widely different views about what constitutes aggression, and about what is acceptable and unacceptable behavior in sport. Husman and Silva (1984) proposed some guidelines for dealing with these issues. They define aggression as acting with the intent to physically or psychologically injure someone. They also do not distinguish between aggressive behavior and assertive behavior, with the latter defined as forceful, goal-directed behavior that neither violates the rules of the game nor intends harm to participants. Although they recognize the difficulty in establishing the intent of behavior, Husman and Silva concluded that aggressive behavior, so defined, has no place in sport (with the exceptions of boxing and karate).

The class activity presented here is a partial replication of a study that investigated students' attitudes about aggression in sport. Silva (1983) presented eight slides to 203 male and female athletes and non-athletes. Seven of the slides presented scenes of aggressive, rule-violating behavior, such as fighting in ice hockey, tripping in basketball, and spearing in football. Subjects were asked to rate the acceptability of the depicted behaviors on a 4-point scale ranging from *totally acceptable* (1) to *totally unacceptable* (4). Results indicated that males, on the average, rated the aggressive behaviors as acceptable and as significantly more acceptable than did females, who rated those behaviors as unacceptable on the average. Further, the acceptability ratings of male athletes increased as a function of the amount of contact in their sports, the number of years they played organized sports, and the level of organized sport attained. Conversely, female non-athletes were slightly more accepting of aggression in sport than female athletes who had participated in either contact or non-contact sports, at either the youth sport or high school level, or over a period of 1 to 10 years. Silva concluded that socialization in sport appears to legitimize aggressive behavior for males, but not for females. In fact, the sport socialization process may cause females to become less accepting of such behavior.

Teaching Technique

The following activity is based on Silva's (1983) study. It has been used with Four classes, and data have been collected from three of those classes. It has been most effective when presented as an introduction to the unit on aggression in sport, without prior comment. In beginning the activity, the following instructions were read to each class: "You are going to receive descriptions of six situations or scenes involving sport competition. I want you to label the behavior in these situations as *acceptable* or *unacceptable*, based on your own ethical standards. Do not write your name on the paper, but do mark your paper M if you are male or F if you are female. Do you have any questions?" The six competition scenes are reproduced in Table 1.

Students are typically eager to discuss the six scenes when they hand in their responses, and athletes in each class have provided vivid descriptions of similar personal experiences. The ensuing discussion provides ample opportunity to introduce Husman and Silva's (1984) definitions of assertive behavior and aggression and to present their position against aggression in sport. This position usually generates considerable dissent, especially from male athletes. They often suggest that aggression, even as defined by Husman and Silva, is appropriate in sport. This debate has led regularly to discussion of such topics as the cathartic benefits of aggression in sport or, conversely, the negative effects of modeling such behavior for children. Further, male and female students frequently have marked differences of opinion, which provides the opportunity to present Silva's (1983) study and relate it to the class activity.

At this point in the activity, each class has analyzed its own data to compare them to Silva's (1983) results. First, the number of acceptable judgments by males and females was tabulated, and then the mean was calculated for each group and for the total sample. A t test was then conducted for these independent means. This analysis provided an opportunity for students in two of my advanced classes to apply their statistical skills. In each of the three classes where I have collected data, the results have confirmed Silva's findings that males are more accepting of aggression in sport, $t(63) = 6.05$, $p < .01$. Males have endorsed a mean of 2.8 aggressive behaviors, and females have endorsed a mean of 1.6 aggressive behaviors.

Following these calculations, discussion is focused on why males are so much more accepting of aggression in sports. A common student response has been that this gender difference occurs because males engage in more aggression, both in sport and other settings. Other students have suggested that, in adhering to socially acceptable stereotypes, males may over-report and/or females underreport the number of behaviors they actually find acceptable. A question that has proved to be very productive at this point in the activity is "What do you predict will happen to women's attitudes about aggression in sport as women become increasingly involved in sport?" Some female athletes have argued strongly that they will not succumb to what they perceive as inappropriate male attitudes.

Even if the results for a particular class should fail to reveal a gender difference, there are options for discussion. First, the class could consider why its results failed to replicate earlier findings, possibly by focusing on sample differences. A second point of departure is that all six of the sport situations in the activity contain behaviors that are unacceptable by Husman and Silva's (1984) definition. Thus, the discussion might consider why students in our culture consistently find about one third of the behaviors acceptable.

This activity does not exactly replicate Silva's (1983) study; however, it is a simplification that effectively represents the previous research and it promotes student inquiry. The activity is an effective stimulus for student involvement and generates discussion of such concepts as catharsis, social learning, limitations of self-report data, and the relationship between attitude and behavior. The three classes from which data were collected had an average of about 20 students, but the activity can be adequately presented to classes of 20 to 50 students in a 50-min class period. Further, though it was originally designed for a sport psychology course, it can be modified for use in other courses. It has already been presented to classes studying sex roles and violence and aggression, and it could be readily adapted for social psychology and even introductory psychology courses.

References

Cox, R. H. (1985). *Sport psychology: Concepts and applications.* Dubuque, IA: W. C. Brown.

Husman, B. F., & Silva, J. M. (1984). Aggression in sport: Definitional and theoretical considerations. In J. M. Silva & R. S. Weinberg (Eds.), *Psychological foundations of sport* (pp. 246-260). Champaign, IL: Human Kinetics Publishers.

Landers, D. M., Singer, R. N., & Williams, J. M. (Chairs). (1985, May). *The teaching of sport psychology: Contemporary course options.* Pre-conference workshop at the meeting of the North American Society for Psychology of Sport and Physical Activity, Gulf Park, MS.

Silva, J. M., (1983). The perceived legitimacy of role violating behavior in sport. *Journal of Sport Psychology, 5,* 438-448.

Silva, J. M., & Weinberg, R. S. (Eds.). (1984). *Psychological foundation of sport.* Champaign, IL: Human Kinetics Publishers.

7. EXAMINING GROUP PROCESSES

Learning About Individual and Collective Decisions: All for One and None for All

Blaine F. Peden
Allen H. Keniston
David T. Burke
University of Wisconsin-Eau Claire

Teachers believe that classroom demonstrations promote students' awareness and understanding of psychological concepts and principles. Although students apparently enjoy and learn from these activities, they routinely deny the results and implications of demonstrations in which they (a) make predictable risk-averse and risk-prone choices, and (b) compete rather than cooperate. In both cases, students contend that they would behave differently in a "real" situation (Lutsky, 1987).

To enhance introductory psychology students' understanding of the principles governing individual and collective decisions, we combine two hypothetical decisions into an ecologically valid and personally meaningful demonstration. In this activity, students may earn bonus points by making "tough choices" after each of eight exams. *Tough Choice 1* provides an analogue for the psychology of preferences (modeled after Problem. 3 in Tversky & Kahneman, 1981) in which we expect students to make risk-averse choices. *Tough Choice 2* provides an analogue for cooperation and competition (modeled after the *Science84* Cooperation Experiment in Allman, 1984, 1985) in which we expect students to make risk-prone or uncooperative choices and to underestimate the number of classmates making uncooperative choices. Unlike participants in hypothetical one-trial choice studies, our students repeatedly make the two tough choices with full knowledge about the consequences of their previous decisions (Silberberg, Murray, Christensen, & Asano, 1988).

Method

Subjects

This activity involved three classes of introductory psychology students from three different terms: summer 1988 ($n = 36$), spring 1989 ($n = 117$), and summer 1989 ($n = 35$).

Apparatus

A detachable questionnaire comprised the final page of a test. On *Tough Choice 1*, students selected either a certain outcome (1 bonus point) or an uncertain outcome (0 or 8 bonus points) and then explained their choice in a paragraph. A random number generator determined whether an uncertain choice yielded 8, $p = .125$, or 0 bonus points, $p = .875$.

On *Tough Choice 2*, students requested either a smaller or a larger number of bonus points, wrote a paragraph that explained their choices, and estimated the percentage of their classmates asking for the larger number of points. The instructions clearly stated that: (a) if more than 20% of the class asked for the larger number, then no one would receive any bonus points; and (b) if no more than 20% of the class asked for the larger number of bonus points, then an individual would receive the requested number of points. In summer 1988 and spring 1989, the smaller number was 4 bonus points and the larger number was 20 bonus points, whereas in summer 1989 the numbers were 1 and 5 bonus points, respectively.

Procedure

Students completed the Tough Choices questionnaire after each of eight exams. We reported and discussed the results during the next class meeting.

Students' grades depended on a fixed percentage of the 500 to 600 points from tests and writing assignments. Bonus points from this and other activities contributed to an individual's point total.

We evaluated student opinion about this activity in the 1989 courses by distributing a 10-item debriefing questionnaire after the eighth exam. Students earned 1 bonus point by returning a completed form on the final day.

Results

Scores for the three classes were qualitatively similar in all cases and quantitatively similar in most cases. We computed grand means for quantitatively similar scores.

Some students forfeited bonus points by withholding the questionnaire or by missing an exam. The high questionnaire return rates (95.5%), detailed explanations for choices, comments during discussions, and responses on the debriefing questionnaire confirmed that this activity was ecologically valid and personally meaningful to students.

Tough Choice 1

All three classes tended to make more frequent selections of 1 certain point over successive trials. The grand mean was 73.2%, and outcome somewhat lower than the one obtained for hypothetical choices (see Problem 3 in Tversky & Kahneman, 1981). Selections of the uncertain outcome produced 8 bonus points 11.8% of the time, a payoff ratio somewhat lower than the expected 12.5%. Although students earned from 0 to 21 bonus points on this problem, the grand mean was only 7.6 bonus points.

Tough Choice 2

Despite eight opportunities, all three classes failed to obtain any points on this problem. Over all trials, the percentage of students making the uncooperative choice averaged 49.2%, 36.9%, and 42.7% in the three courses, respectively. The grand mean of 40.4% was somewhat greater than the 34.9% of the participants who uncooperatively chose the larger of two sums of money in a hypothetical one-trial situation (Allman, 1984, 1985). The choices by students who selected either 4 or 20 points did not vary systematically from those made by students who selected either 1 or 5 points. Finally, students who earned a low grade in the course were more likely to select the uncertain outcome than were students who earned a high grade.

The choices by the summer 1988 class deserve special comment. A dramatic decrease in the percentage of students making the uncooperative choice on Trial 4 occurred after a discussion about the tragedy of the commons (Hardin, 1968) and social traps (Platt, 1973). After this discussion and before the fourth exam, a self-appointed and energetic champion of cooperation convinced fellow classmates to make their selections on the basis of a lottery. Seven lucky students were to ask for 20 points; all others were to request 4 bonus points.

Despite warnings that complete cooperation was necessary for success, the endeavor failed because two students either deliberately "defected" or misunderstood the instructions. No similar effort to organize a cooperative venture occurred in the other two courses.

Students also estimated the percentage of classmates who would ask for the larger number of points. The estimate generally was less than the obtained percentage, especially on the initial trials. According to Allman (1985), two thirds of his 33,511 participants predicted that fewer than one fifth of them would choose the larger monetary sum. Moreover, this prediction was the same for those choosing either the smaller or larger monetary sum. Our results replicated this finding in that students' estimate of the number of students who ask for the larger number of bonus points was not related to their own choices. Allman's and our results contradict Dawes, McTavish, and Shaklee's (1977) finding that individuals making uncooperative choices in a commons dilemma situation expected more uncooperative choices than those making cooperative choices.

Debriefing Questionnaire

Sixty-eight of the 101 students completing the course in spring 1989 and all 35 students in the summer 1989 course returned the debriefing questionnaire. Table 1 presents the question, the average rating, and the number of students strongly disagreeing, disagreeing, agreeing, strongly agreeing, or neither disagreeing nor agreeing with each statement. A score of 1.0 indicates strong disagreement; a score of 5.0 indicates strong agreement.

Approximately three fourths of the students gladly participated in this activity and did not feel coerced. Students indicating coercion commonly explained that they were always reminded to answer all the questions, detach the form, and submit it. This response suggests a misunderstanding about the meaning of coercion, an interpretation supported by the same students' comments that allowing these points to influence their course grade was fair.

Approximately two thirds of the students said that the discussions clarified the purpose of the activity, however, some indicated that the class never discussed the activity, and others asserted that the only purpose of the activity was to provide bonus points. Although some students said that this activity had nothing to do with psychology, the majority indicated that it promotes three course objectives. For example, over half indicated that making and discussing these tough choices enhanced their understanding of psychology. Approximately 70% agreed that making and discussing these choices promoted their development of scientific values and skills and stimulated their personal development. Finally, almost 80% of the students endorsed future use of this activity.

Table 1. Relative Frequency and Average for Student Responses

SD	Da	Ne	Ag	SA	M	Questionnaire Statements
1	7	27	46	22	3.8	I am very glad to have been involved in this activity.
9	29	42	20	3	2.8	This activity increased my interest in psychology.
34	38	11	17	3	2.2	I felt coerced or forced to participate in this activity.
23	48	23	8	1	2.2	It was not fair for our grade to be influenced by the points that we received for participating in this activity.
5	18	13	52	15	3.5	The purpose of this activity became clearer to me during our class discussions.
1	6	16	36	44	4.1	The offer of the instructors was genuine, and we really would have gotten the points on Tough Choice 2 if fewer than 20% of the class asked for 20 points.
4	21	21	50	7	3.3	Making and discussing these tough choices promoted my knowledge of psychology.
3	11	14	65	10	3.7	Making and discussing these tough choices promoted my development of scientific values and skills.
2	14	13	61	13	3.7	Making and discussing these tough choices promoted my personal development.
5	4	15	46	33	4.0	I recommend using this activity as part of this class in the future.

Note. SD = strongly disagree; Da = disagree; Ne = neither disagree nor agree; Ag = agree; SA = strongly agree.

Discussion

Our "tale of two tough choices" is interesting; more important, the activity is easy to use and offers many instructional benefits. One or both questions can be included on multiple-choice tests. Evaluations by the instructors and students indicate that this activity promotes knowledge of psychology, develops scientific values and skills, and stimulates personal development.

Knowledge of Psychology

Unlike many easily performed and little remembered activities, this demonstration promotes knowledge of psychology. An instructor and students can analyze and interpret the choices and the outcomes within different domains of psychology, as the following examples illustrate.

Tough Choice 1 data plotted over trials resemble a learning curve and prompt a discussion about the role of experience in making decisions. Tough Choice 2 data raise questions about the control of behavior and an obvious failure of consequences to modify behavior. To the end of the course and sometimes beyond, students lament their inability to obtain points on Tough Choice 2, despite many discussions about the problem.

In a unit on social psychology, this activity illustrates the dilemma of cooperation and competition (Allman, 1984). We encourage students to cooperate on Tough Choice 2, but do not suggest techniques, such as publicly disclosing one's choice, having another complete and submit one's form, or forming cooperative subgroups (Dawes, 1980). Our experience indicates that several students in each class undermine these suggestions by saying that if they cannot have the larger number of points, then they do not care if anyone gets points. This assertion outrages others and produces lively discussion about issues of equity. Alternatively, G. D. Steinhauer (personal communication, November 7, 1989) modified the problem by requiring students to choose to protect or publicly disclose their individual choices. Under these conditions, 75% chose to publicly disclose their selections and only 8% asked for the larger number of bonus points.

Tenacious individuals who argue vehemently for one choice encourage discussion about how personality traits influence choices. Tough Choice 2 illustrates how difficult it is to predict behavior, a prominent concern in clinical psychology

This activity shows how to plot data and helps students learn the distinction between observations and inferences It challenges students' understanding about the concepts of probability. Paragraphs explaining choices typically reveal pathologies of statistical reasoning, such as the gambler's fallacy.

Finally, teachers can use this activity to illustrate that different sciences confront the same problem. The free-rider problem in economics, the irrationality of voting in political science, and the prisoner's dilemma in psychology all oppose group benefits with individual interests. In fact, a similar exercise produces comparable results in a shorter period of time, but involves a monetary cost to instructors (Bishop, 1986).

Scientific Values and Skills

This activity develops scientific values and skills. Students' inability to cooperate for mutual benefit forces them to evaluate their implicit personality theories, stimulates curiosity about behavior, and demonstrates the relation between theory and data: Theory guides observation, and results disconfirm or support theory.

Students use analytical and interpretive skills in their attempt to understand the results of Tough Choice 2. For example, some students note a correlation between trends toward cooperation and class optimism about possible bonus points. Many appear to extrapolate the trend, subsequently choose the larger number of bonus points, and guarantee another payoff of 0 points.

As the bonus point opportunities fall by the wayside, students better appreciate psychological theories about preference and cooperation in a meaningful situation. To further illustrate the value of theory and scientific skill inherent in accurate prediction, we frequently and confidently predict that the students will not obtain points on Tough Choice 2, even though our offer is genuine.

Scientific values include a concern for ethical teaching practices. Chute (1974) asked: How can we protect students as subjects when we develop and explore new instructional techniques? Our answer is three-fold: (a) Our students give implied informed consent by completing and submitting the questionnaire. The majority of students bolster this argument by indicating that they are not coerced to participate. (b) The potential harm from submitting the questionnaire and discussing the results in class is minimal or nonexistent. Students confirm this belief in two ways. They welcome participation in this activity (as did subjects in Milgram's, 1969, research A, and they overwhelmingly endorse its use in the future. (c) The discussion section of this article illustrates that there is a favorable balance of risks to benefits for students. Moreover, the benefits accrue to present students rather than future students, which is an important concern for instructional innovations (Chute, 1974).

Another ethical question is whether grades should be influenced by bonus points from this activity (see Norcross, Horrocks, & Stevenson, 1989). Our defense is three-fold: (a) Our students (like Leak's, 1981) do not believe that it is unfair to obtain bonus points from this activity. (b) This activity is as legitimate a source of bonus points as any other because students learn much in their pursuit of them. (c) The few bonus points from this activity minimally influence students' grades. Perhaps a more pertinent concern is whether students obtain too few points for their efforts.

Personal Development

This activity promotes personal development because students confront their own troublesome and distasteful behavior (Lutsky, 1987). Our students demonstrate something akin to the Pollyanna effect in that the expected level greatly exceeds the observed level of cooperation. Some students eventually recognize and later publicly admit that their own selfishness only hurts themselves and everyone else. Others indicate that the discussions help them understand and better accept opinions different from their own.

The results of Tough Choice 2 dramatically illustrate the tragedy of the commons (Hardin, 1968) and how difficult it is to overcome social fences despite an energetic superordinate authority's championing cooperation (Platt, 1973). In sum, this activity produces a compelling lesson against faith in the saving grace of attempts to induce individual sacrifices for the benefit of all. Our students find new wisdom in Pogo's moral that we have met the enemy and he is us (Kelly, 1972).

References

Allman, W. F. (1984, October). Nice guys finish first. *Science84*, pp. 24-32.

Allman, W. F. (1985, February). *The Science84* cooperation experiment: The results. Science85, p. 20.

Bishop, J. E. (1986, December 4). 'All for one . . . one for all'? Don't bet on it. *The Wall Street Journal*, p. 1.

Chute, D. L. (1974). Innovations in teaching: An ethical paradox. *Teaching of Psychology, 1*, 85.

Dawes, R. M. (1980). Social dilemmas. *Annual Review of Psychology/ 31*, 169-193

Dawes, R. M., McTavish, J., & Shaklee, H. (1977). Behavior, communication, and assumptions about other people's behavior in a commons dilemma situation. *Journal of Personality and Social Psychology, 35*, 1-11.

Hardin, G. (1968). The tragedy of the commons. *Science, 162*, 1243-1248.

Kelly, W. (1972). *Pogo: We have met the enemy and he is us.* New York: Simon & Schuster.

Leak, G. K. (1981). Student perception of coercion and value from participation in psychological research. *Teaching of Psychology 8*, 147-149.

Lutsky, N. (1987). Inducing academic suicide: A demonstration of social influence. In V. P. Makosky, L. G. Whittemore, & A. M. Rogers (Eds.), *Activities handbook for the teaching of psychology* (Vol. 2, pp. 123-126). Washington, DC: American Psychological Association.

Milgram, S. (1969). *Obedience to authority.* New York: Harper & Row.

Norcross, J. C., Horrocks, L. J., & Stevenson, J. F. (1989). On barfights and gadflies: Attitudes and practices concerning extra credit in college courses. *Teaching of Psychology, 16*, 199-203.

Platt, J. (1973). Social traps. *American Psychologist, 28*, 641 -651.

Silberberg, A., Murray, P., Christensen, J., & Asano, T. (1988). Choice in the repeated-gambles experiment. *Journal of the Experimental Analysis of Behavior, 50*, 187-195.

Tversky, A., & Kahneman, D. (1981). The framing of decisions and the psychology of choice. *Science, 211*, 453-458.

Notes

1. We thank Bernard Frank and Ken McIntire for helpful comments on this article. We also appreciate the comments and suggestions of editors Charles Brewer and Joseph Palladino and the anonymous reviewers, especially the one who called our attention to the Bishop (1986) article.

2. The graphics were produced by the University of Wisconsin-Eau Claire Media Development Center with support from the School of Graduate Studies and Office of University Research.

3. A preliminary report of these results was presented at the meeting of the Midwestern Psychological Association, Chicago, IL, May 4-6, 1989.

4. Requests for related materials should be sent to Blaine F. Peden, Department of Psychology, University of Wisconsin-Eau Claire, Eau Claire, WI 54702-4004.

Prisoner's Dilemma as a Model for Understanding Decisions

Janet D. Larsen
John Carroll University

When will people cooperate, and when will they decide to take advantage of others? Introductory and social psychology textbooks present the prisoner's dilemma (PD) as a framework for understanding the decisions people make when they have the choice of taking advantage of others or cooperating with them. It has been used to explain panic behavior in crowds (Gleitman, 1987) and the choices people make in labor union negotiations (Worchel & Cooper, 1983).

PD is best explained by a story about two men who are arrested on a minor charge and placed in separate rooms. Although the authorities believe that both men are guilty of a more serious crime, there is no proof of their guilt. The following options are explained to each man. He can continue to claim his innocence and, if his friend also continues to maintain his own innocence, they will both receive short sentences. The man can turn state's evidence and give the authorities the information they want. If he does, his friend will receive the maximum sentence but he will go free. However, the same options are offered to his friend. If his friend also confesses, both men will receive intermediate sentences. What will the men do?

It would be to the prisoners' mutual advantage for both to remain silent, but each takes a risk in doing so. Choosing to remain silent requires that the man be confident that his friend will not turn state's evidence. If he thinks his friend will confess, it is to his advantage to confess. Then, if his friend confesses, he assures himself of a lighter sentence; if his friend does not confess, the man will get off with no penalty.

This same analysis can be applied to the behavior of people when there is a fire in a theater. Common sense suggests that everyone has the best chance of escaping if people file out, taking turns to get through the door. However, we do not trust others to take turns. Like the prisoner, we make the exploitive choice and look out for ourselves first, because we expect others to act the same way. Rather than taking the chance of being pushed out of the way and burned to death, most people push ahead and many are hurt.

The following class activity allows students to experience the dilemma. If PD is discussed in your textbook, you may want to conduct this activity before students read that assignment; however, the demonstration is effective even if students have already read about PD.

Dollars, Dimes, or Doughnut Holes

Tell your class that you would like to give away some money, but only under certain conditions. Each student may ask for $1.00 or 10¢. You will give all of the students what they ask for if fewer than 20% of the students ask for $1.00. Ask students to write their choices on a slip of paper, along with their name or some identification code if they ask for $1.00. In addition, ask them to indicate the percentage of the class they expect to ask for $1.00. These choices should be made without consulting other members of the class, just as the prisoners made their decisions to confess or not confess without talking to each other.

Collect the slips, and read the choices. Sort the slips into $1.00 or 10¢ requests and, within each category, whether the person expects over or under 20% of the class to ask for $1.00. About half the students usually ask for $1.00. Some of the students in this group expect 20% or less of the class to make the same request (corresponding to the prisoner who decides to confess in the hope of going free). Most of those who ask for $1.00 expect a large proportion of the class to do the same. (These students correspond to the prisoner who confesses because he expects his friend to confess.) After students have had a real experience of choosing to exploit others or to trust that others will not take advantage of them, similar situations are easier to understand. The PD model can be applied to diverse situations such as: driving, where you must decide whether to get in line or stay in the lane that is about to end; infant inoculation, where parents must decide whether their child will receive a shot for diphtheria, pertussis, and tetanus and risk the rare but deadly reaction, and cheating on a test where, if everyone cheats, the curve will be raised and no one will benefit.

This activity can also be used to introduce the ideas in Hardin's (1968) article, "The Tragedy of the Commons." He argued that people behave selfishly in group situations because they expect others to make selfish choices. This analysis can be applied to problems such as trying to get manufacturers to stop polluting the environment or trying to get countries to limit fishing in international waters.

The Matching Game

PD can also provide the basis for understanding how people behave when they know they will relate to one another in the future. The iterated version of PD, or playing the game over and over with the same person, can serve as a model for understanding some of the features of labor union bargaining and international treaty negotiations.

Each student needs a coin for this game. Pairs of students play PD 20 times, indicating their choices by placing a coin on the desk heads up or tails up. If Player A and Player B choose heads, each gets 6 points. If both choose tails, both lose 6 points. However, if one chooses heads and the other chooses tails, the player choosing heads loses 8 points and the player choosing tails gets 8 points. Have students keep track of the number of points each person earns and report to the class the number of points earned by each player. When the pairs play cooperatively, both players have high scores. If one player chooses tails frequently, the other player usually does the same, and both end the game with low or even negative scores.

One of the factors that determines how people will play this game is how they define the goal. One way of viewing the goal of the game is to obtain the most points possible. In this case, players consistently make the cooperative play. As the 20th trial approaches, however, a player may succumb to the temptation to "defect" and earn a few more points than the other player. You should be aware of such defections because they may cause an emotional reaction on the part of the person who has been exploited. Many people define the goal as earning more points than their partner. In this case, both players will often choose tails and will have low scores, compared to people who have played cooperatively.

In the iterated version of PD, the way to get the highest score possible is to be consistently cooperative, but not a fool. Computer simulations have been used to test the success of various strategies for playing this version of the game (Campbell, 1985). The strategy that consistently led to the highest scores was a Tit for Tat strategy in which the player began by making a cooperative choice and continued to be cooperative as long as the other player did not make the exploitive move. If the other player failed to cooperate, the Tit for Tat program began to follow the play

of the opponent, continuing to copy what the opponent did on the last move. In this way, as soon as the other player signaled a willingness to cooperate by making the cooperative move, Tit for Tat responded by returning to cooperative play.

This iterated version of PD is similar to what occurs in labor union bargaining and in the negotiations of treaties between nations. One issue is whether the other party can be trusted to play the game cooperatively. The other issue is how the parties define the goal. For example, if labor and management define the situation as one in which there will be a winner and a loser, they will follow the equivalent of the "all tails" strategy. If they see the situation as one in which both parties can benefit, more cooperative strategies may be used. This model can also be applied to arms limitation talks, school rivalries, and dealing with unfriendly neighbors. By playing the game and discussing their strategies, students get a better view of the kinds of thinking that lead to different behaviors in situations where people have to deal with one another repeatedly.

Student reactions to these demonstrations are almost universally positive. A typical comment written by a student is, "At first I thought it was just a game, but I saw that it applied to many serious subjects in life." Students recognize different implications of the demonstration. For example, "If each would cooperate with each other, everyone would be better off. But because some wish to get ahead of others, we all get hurt"; "Being cooperative, one can get ahead"; and "People always want to get ahead, regardless of the other person." Both activities lead to lively discussions; they provide a model for helping students to understand some human behaviors that seem, at first glance, to be irrational.

References

Campbell, R. (1985). Background for the uninitiated. In R. Campbell & L. Sowden (Eds.), *Paradoxes of rationality and cooperation: Prisoner's dilemma and Newcomb's problem* (pp. 3-41). Vancouver, British Columbia, Canada: University of British Columbia Press.

Gleitman, H. (1987). *Basic psychology* (2nd ed.). New York: Norton.

Hardin, G. (1968). The tragedy of the commons. *Science, 162,* 1243-1248.

Worchel, S., & Cooper, J. (1983). *Understanding social psychology* (3rd ed.). Homewood, IL: Dorsey.

Demonstrating Dynamic Social Impact: Consolidation, Clustering, Correlation, and (Sometimes) the Correct Answer

Helen C. Harton
Laura R. Green
Craig Jackson
Bibb Latané
Florida Atlantic University

Dynamic social impact theory (Latané, 1981, 1996a, 1997) predicts the emergence of four group-level phenomena whenever people in spatially distributed groups, such as residents of an apartment complex or people at a banquet table, influence one another. *Consolidation* represents a reduction in the number and diversity of minority positions; *clustering*, the formation of regional subgroups; and *correlation*, the association of originally unrelated opinions. Finally, *continuing diversity* results from the fact that clustering prevents consolidation from wiping out minorities. These phenomena, which together represent the emergence of subcultures in groups, are predicted by computer simulation (Latané & Nowak, 1997; Nowak,

Szamrej, & Latané,1990), have been confirmed in electronic discussion groups (Latané & L'Herrou, 1996), and can be demonstrated in an easily administered classroom exercise.

In this demonstration, suitable for large or small classes in social psychology or group dynamics, students discuss their answers to multiple-choice questions with their nearest neighbors, then answer the questions again.

Method

Assemble some multiple-choice items. We chose 10 questions from the test bank for the next week's chapter, but the effects are robust for any type of multiple-choice question, as long as there is sufficient diversity in the initial answers. Choose questions labeled *difficult* from the test bank or items that you know from previous experience have at least one or two good distracters.

Before starting, ask students to move to the middle of their rows so that everyone except those on the ends has a neighbor on either side. For adequate power, each row should include at least 15 students. In a small class, you can "snake" the rows, allowing people at the ends of adjacent rows to talk to each other as well as to their neighbors.

Present questions as a handout, with an overhead projector, or by reading them aloud. Randomly determine which questions, if any, to use as non-discussion controls. If you use a before-after design, allow the students about 1 min per question to mark their pre-discussion answers. We used scantron sheets to simplify data entry and analysis.

Give students 1 to 2 min to discuss each question, having them mark their answer as soon as you ask them to stop talking. Encourage students to consult with their neighbors on both sides, but only about the assigned topics, discussing which answer they chose and why.

Lead a discussion of the concepts illustrated. You can demonstrate consolidation, clustering, correlation, and continuing diversity in four ways: (a) using simple in-class methods, (b) showing our sample results as typical of what occurs, (c) receiving a printout of our computer program for analyzing the data, or (d) having us analyze your data.[1]

---

[1]Although you can show the concepts illustrated using this demonstration in class, you may also be interested in presenting more exact statistical results in a later class. We have developed a computer program, DSIT demo, that calculates the indexes described in our results section. We would be happy to analyze and return the data to you or send you a printout of the program. If interested, send an IBM-compatible computer file listing each of the student's row and seat number along with their pre- and postdiscussion responses via electronic mail to harton@uni.edu or through regular mail to DSIT demo, Helen C. Harton, Department of Psychology, University of Northern Iowa, Cedar Falls, IA 50614-0505. We will usually be able to return analyses by electronic mail within 2 days if given advance notice as to when the data may arrive.

Question	Individual responses	D	z	V	%C
1 Before	1211412+212411+1+224++11+22++1	.95	-.28	.43	27
After	111411222221++++22++++11+22+++	.91	4.00	.52	37
2 Before	11++±1±4++1111313+413413411+++	.92	.81	.35	33
After	11++311±+++±133343+±++413411+++	.92	2.29	.41	43
3 Before	++2234+4222±+2+23223+++++2+++2	.84	.82	.39	47
After	++±±3±+22222+±+3322±++++++±++++	.65	4.00	.50	67
4 Before	+1+++11131111111±13++111±11+4+	.75	.79	.37	33
After	+1+++11111111111113++111111+11	.54	2.10	.33	23
5 Before	+++++++++++++++++++++++++++++	.00	0	0	100
After	+++++++++++++++++++++++++++++	.00	0	0	100
	Prediscussion Average	.69	.52	.38	.48
	Postdiscussion Average	.60	3.10	.44	.54

Figure 1. Individual responses and group indexes of diversity (D), clustering (z), association (V), and percentage correct (%C) for a typical group. Individual responses appear in seat-number order, with a "+" indicating the correct response; a "1," the most popular pretest choice for that group; a "2," the second most popular choice; and so forth. Underlines indicate people who changed choices.

Table 1. Average Initial and Final Diversity, Clustering, Association With Other Questions, and Percent Correct for All Eight Groups Across Three Discussed Questions

Group	N	D_0	D_1	z_0	z_1	V_0	V_1	$\%C_0$	$\%C_1$
1	30	.90	.83	.45	3.43	.40	.55	36	49
2	28	.91	.87	-.08	2.76	.29	.33	36	36
3	27	.89	.84	.42	2.73	.38	.41	43	47
4	22	.81	.66	.55	3.28	.31	.44	29	33
5	21	.92	.96	-30	4.00	.36	.53	32	32
6	19	.90	.84	-.65	2.00	.44	.47	35	39
7	18	.82	.78	-.15	2.45	.40	.47	28	30
8	15	.85	.76	.73	2.00	.42	.58	33	34
Average	23	.88	.82	.12	2.83	.38	.47	34	38

Note. 0 = average initial; 1 = final; D = diversity; z = clustering; V = association; %C = percent correct.

Some Typical Results

We conducted this demonstration in one large ($N = 126$) and two small ($N = 27, 28$) introductory psychology classes. The large class consisted of six rows of 15 to 30 people, and we snaked each of the smaller classes to form one group per class, resulting in eight groups of students who answered 10 questions each. Students discussed 5 of the questions for 1 min each. There was little initial diversity on 2 of the discussed questions: One was too easy, with almost everyone having the correct answer, and another was too hard, with 71% (although only 57% in our example) agreeing on a single wrong answer. Such strong initial majorities leave little opportunity for clustering and correlation, so we restricted the analyses to the remaining 3 discussion items, with moderate to high initial diversity across all the groups. The results were clear, strong, and consistent.

Figure 1 shows the pre- and posttest responses for a typical group on all five questions discussed, with the sequence of symbols corresponding to the seating positions of the discussants. This group illustrates each of the predicted phenomena.

Consolidation

Consolidation is a reduction in diversity or the degree to which people choose different answers. To illustrate consolidation, count the students who chose each alternative before and after discussion. The answers that are most popular initially should win converts, whereas the number of students getting the answer right will not necessarily increase after discussion.

To create an index of diversity (D), calculate $k(N^2 - \Sigma R_i^2)/(k-1)N^2$, where R_i is the number of people in each of

256

k categories from a total of N people. A diversity score of 1 indicates an equal number of people adopted each possible response, whereas a diversity score of 0 indicates unanimity. Diversity decreased for three of the five discussion questions shown in Figure 1, with one showing no initial diversity and one, no change. Overall, discussion-induced consolidation was characteristic of seven of the eight independent groups, $F(1, 7) = 238$, $p < .001$ (see Table 1). This finding shows that social influence leads to a decrease in minority viewpoints, as the majority tends to convert those minority members without local support.

Clustering

You can show clustering, or agreement with one's neighbors, in class by having students raise their hands or stand to indicate which answers they gave. Students will notice that those raising their hands for each answer tend to be sitting near others whose hands are also raised.

Following the logic of a standard-runs test, we measured clustering by determining what proportion of a random set of all possible permutations of the group would have as many or more cases of agreement with neighbors. This p value is then converted to a z score, indicating the degree to which the answers in a group have developed a nonrandom spatial organization, with a z greater than 1.96 being statistically significant.

Pre-discussion responses for four of the questions discussed by the group in Figure 1 were randomly distributed before discussion, with one question having no diversity. After discussion, the group exhibited a significant degree of spatial clustering on each of these four questions, as neighbors influenced each other to become more similar. We also found significant ($p < .05$) post-discussion clustering in each of the other seven groups that participated in the demonstration. This finding demonstrates that social influence will lead to regional or local differences on issues, comparable to the development of subcultures in groups.

Correlation

To illustrate correlation, you may write students' responses to two questions in seat-number order on the board. The tendency for answers on one question to become associated with answers on another shows the emergence of correlation. Answers that have no rational reason to be related (for example, "2" on Question 1 and "+" on Question 2, in Figure 1) become associated as a simple consequence of the loss of independence due to clustering (Latane, 1996b). In general, the larger the clusters on different questions, the greater the chance they will overlap, causing correlation to emerge.

Cramer's coefficient of association (V) measures correlation, which increased after discussion for each of the eight groups that participated in the demonstration, $F(1, 7) = 18.36$, $p < .01$. This result may be analogous to the emergence of ideologies and stereotypes, not from higher order rational associations, but from bottom-up processes of influence. This finding may lead into an interesting discussion of how, for example, beliefs such as being pro-death penalty and antiabortion can become related.

Continuing Diversity

Continuing diversity is shown simply by the fact that groups typically fail to reach unanimity. None of the eight groups reached unanimity on any of our three questions with good initial diversity. Even though students were motivated to learn the correct answer, they were unable to reach it unanimously, or even to agree on any other answer. The problem is not that people do not influence each other, but that people in a local majority do not realize they are in the global minority.

Percentage Correct

Although many people change to the correct answer after discussion, many others change to an incorrect answer, and whether there is overall improvement depends on whether the most popular initial answer is correct. When it was (as in Question 3), 69% of our groups improved with discussion. When it was not (as in Questions 1, 2, and 4), only 24% of the groups improved, and in none did even half the individuals give the correct response after discussion. This result demonstrates that truth does not always win and that the social reality of the group is more important than objective reality.

Evaluation

The demonstration was consistently successful in showing the emergence of consolidation, clustering, correlation, and continuing diversity from discussion. Thus, this exercise meets the primary requirement of a good demonstration—it works.

Students seem to enjoy this approved opportunity to discuss test questions with their neighbors, engaging in often animated discussions with the people on either side of them. Objective evidence confirms this impression: A group of 18 social psychology students who participated in this demonstration gave the activity positive ratings ($M = +2.20$) on a series of seven scales ranging from -3 (*hated it / loss of insight / definitely no*) to +3 (*loved it / gain in insight / definitely yes*).[2] They also learned something from the exercise, earning an average of 74% correct answers on

---

[2]The specific items were enjoyed the demonstration, gained in insight, good demonstration to use in classes, worthwhile use of class time, learned something from the demonstration, helped to understand dynamic social impact theory, and learned more from doing the demonstration than would have from the lecture alone.

a short quiz on dynamic social impact theory taken after the demonstration.

As part of a conference presentation, a group of 25 professors from universities and colleges in the United States and Europe also rated this activity on similar -3 to + 3 scales with the same anchors after participation. This group of academic psychologists, who teach over 7,000 students annually, reported that they personally gained in insight ($M = + 1.29$), enjoyed this exercise ($M = + 1.36$), and thought it a good demonstration to use in classes ($M = + 1.58$).

Finally, a beneficial side effect may come in enhanced academic motivation. In a separate project, students in four classes using small, focused discussions such as that used in this demonstration reported that the discussions positively influenced their participation in the class and their interest and learning of the subject matter (Barreras, Harton, & Richardson, 1996). Students also showed this increased learning on their tests, performing not only better on discussed items than on non-discussed items, but better on the chapters from which they discussed items than on chapters with no discussion. Therefore, not only does this demonstration consistently work, but students and instructors believe that it is enjoyable, valuable, and worth doing, and students seem to learn from the experience.

Discussion

This demonstration clearly shows that even a minute of social interaction can have powerful effects, illustrating to students the pervasiveness of social influence and the need for studying this process. It can also be used to initiate a discussion of group process and group decision making. In disjunctive tasks such as this one, individuals should be able to do better in groups than alone but only if they listen to those who know the correct answer. Otherwise, individuals may do worse than if discussion had not exposed them to social influence.

This demonstration can be discussed along with the distinction between informational and normative social influence (both are consistent with dynamic social impact theory). Do students believe that they changed their answers due to new information they learned about the items from their discussions, or did they change to "go along with the crowd"?

Finally, this demonstration provides clear evidence for dynamic social impact theory's predictions that consolidation, clustering, correlation, and continuing diversity will result from interaction in spatially distributed groups. Regional variations in attitudes and food preferences, accents and languages, and even religious values and national character, may have been formed in much the same way (Harton & Latané, 1997). Unfortunately, as the demonstration also shows, such forms of local group consensus are not necessarily more correct just because they become more popular.

References

Barreras, R. E., Harton, H. C., & Richardson, D. R. (1996, June). *Distributed classroom discussions: Focused interactive learning*. Poster session presented at the annual meeting of the American Psychological Society Institute on the Teaching of Psychology, San Francisco, CA.

Harton, H. C., & Latané, B. (1997). The social self-organization of culture. In F. Schweitzer (Ed.), *Self-organization of complex structures: From individual to collective dynamics* (pp. 355-366). London: Gordon & Breach.

Latané, B. (1981). The psychology of social impact. *American Psychologist, 36*, 343-356.

Latané, B. (1996a) . Dynamic social impact: The creation of culture by communication. *Journal of Communication, 46*, 13-25.

Latané, B. (1996b). The emergence of clustering and correlation from social interaction. In R. Hegselmann & H. O. Peitgen (Eds.*), Order and chaos in nature and society* (pp. 79-104). Vienna: Hölder-Pichler-Tempsky.

Latané, B. (1997). Dynamic social impact: The societal consequences of human interaction. In C. McGarty & A. Haslam (Eds.), *The message of social psychology: Perspectives on mind and society* (pp. 75-87). Oxford, England: Blackwell.

Latané, B., & L'Herrou, T. (1996) . Social clustering in the conformity game: Dynamic social impact in electronic groups. *Journal of Personality and Social Psychology, 70*, 1218-1230.

Latané, B., & Nowak, A. (1997). Self-organizing social systems: Necessary and sufficient conditions for the emergence of consolidation and clustering. In G. Barnett & F. Boster (Eds.), *Progress m communication sciences: Persuasion* (pp. 123-145). Norwood, NJ: Ablex.

Nowak, A., Szamrej, J., & Latané, B. (1990). From private attitude to public opinion: A dynamic theory of social impact. *Psychological Review, 97*, 362-376.

Notes

1. The project was supported by National Science Foundation Grants BNS9009198 and SBR9411603.
2. This demonstration was one product of a graduate class in dynamic social impact theory.
3. We thank Ricardo Barreras, Martin Bourgeois, Wendy Chambers, Susan Egan, Kris Kogan, and Elizabeth Martin for their help in the demonstration's design and administration. We thank Deborah Richardson and Elizabeth Schatten for allowing us access to their classes, Vickie Williams and Xiaojing Yuan for helping to administer the demonstration, and Martin Bourgeois and Scott Tindale for their comments and suggestions.

4. Requests for help in analysis should be sent to Helen C. Harton, Department of Psychology, University of Northern Iowa, Cedar Falls, IA 506144505; e-mail: harton@uni.edu. Requests for help in analysis may also be sent to Bibb Latané, Department of Psychology, Florida Atlantic University, Boca Raton, FL 33431; e-mail: latane@fau.edu.

Studying a Social Norm

Marianne Miserandino
University of Rochester

Group norms, the set of implicit or explicit rules established by a group to regulate the behavior of its members (Baron & Byrne, 1987), are studied in many psychology classes. The group's approval or disapproval of certain behaviors is implicit in the idea of norms. Groups may exert considerable pressure on members by making their approval or disapproval known to the deviant and thereby enforce a norm. In the activity described herein, students identify a group norm, take a survey of members' attitudes, graphically represent the group norm, and interpret the results. This project illustrates group norms and involves even beginning psychology students in doing and thinking about research.

This project is based on the returned potential model that has been used to study a variety of norms, including authoritative behavior; job-related attitudes; behavior of mental patients; and the dancing, drinking, smoking, swearing, and church attendance of college students (Jackson, 1965). The group's opinion is graphed along the y-axis for each of the possible behaviors graphed on the x-axis. The curve drawn through these points is called the *return potential curve* and represents the group's opinion of what is accepted as normative behavior.

Class Activity

Survey

After a lecture on research methods, including experimental and quasi-experimental designs, my introduction to social psychology class investigated the amount of time undergraduates at Hobart and William Smith Colleges spend studying in a typical week. Students were instructed to take a survey on study behavior by interviewing five subjects:

Find a volunteer stranger. Tell him or her this is a class project on people's attitudes toward studying and that it takes about five minutes of their time. Have the respondent answer to you privately. Do not have two respondents answer in front of each other. Be sure they haven't already done this for someone else in the class. Ask them the following questions and record their answers:

1. What year in school are you?
2. How many hours a week do you typically study?
3. What do you think about someone at this school who spends 1 hr per week doing classwork in a typical week? For each amount of studying time subjects are to indicate their attitude on a scale ranging from *highly disapprove* (-4) to *highly approve* (4), with 0 labeled *indifferent*.
4. What do you think about someone at this school who spends 3 hr per week doing classwork in a typical week?
5. What do you think about someone at this school who spends 5 hr per week doing classwork in a typical week?

Continue asking the subjects the same question but increase the target behavior by 2 hr. Stop after you reach 51 hr per week. When you have finished the questioning, thank the subject for his or her time. Repeat this procedure for all five subjects. Record subjects' responses on graph paper or coding paper. Remain neutral at all times. Do not act surprised or shocked at the answers people give you.

You do not want your reaction to inadvertently influence the responses of your subjects. Respect your subjects' rights to confidentiality and anonymity.

Calculations

After data collection, students were instructed to calculate the average response to each question. (Remind students that a response of 0 is meaningful and should be included in the average.) Students then plot the return potential curve for their own data by graphing the average responses from the scale (on the y-axis) for each of the hours of study time asked in the questions (along the x-axis).

Interpretation

Finally, while studying their own samples and graphs, students answer the following questions and write a report on their findings:

1. The *ideal behavior* is that behavior for which the group expresses the highest approval. What is the ideal behavior of your sample?
2. The *range of tolerable behavior* includes those behaviors for which the group expresses approval, as illustrated by positive averages. What is the range of tolerable studying behavior in your sample? What is the range of intolerable behavior?
3. The *intensity of the norm* is how strongly people feel about the behavior—either positively or negatively. How intense does your sample feel about studying? On serious issues, people generally feel very strongly and the result is a steep curve peaking at either or both of the extremes (-4 or 4). On matters of personal taste, people

often do not feel so strongly, as evidenced by a relatively flat curve with the highest and lowest points occurring at less than +2 or -2, respectively. What were the highest and the lowest averages in your sample? Did subjects feel more intensely positive or more intensely negative? What can you say about the intensity of the study norm in your sample?
4. How does the ideal behavior, according to your sample, compare to the average amount of time your sample reports studying? Are they the same? Why or why not? Why do you think this occurs?
5. Do you see anything unusual on the graph? Are there any unusual or outliner subjects in your sample?
6. Recall that this survey was about the norm of studying on this campus. Based on the graph, comments your subjects may have made, and your knowledge of this school, how would you explain these results?
7. Describe one problem with this study, and discuss what you could do to solve, or to at least minimize, it.

These questions are challenging because each student's graph is different as a result of the small number of subjects in each sample. Therefore, students must make an interpretation that best fits their own results (see Figure 1 for examples of different student curves). Each student turns in a report, graph, and raw data for grading.

Class Discussion

In discussing these results, students are amazed by variations in reported study behavior and attitudes and by variations in the curves. They quickly realize that they cannot make accurate judgments based on only five

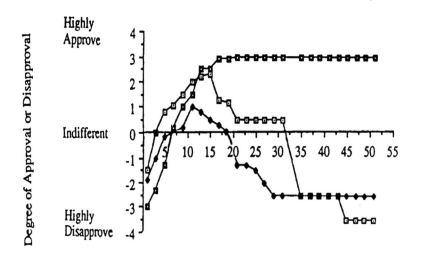

Figure 1. Sample curves from individual students' data collection. Each curve is based on the average responses of five subjects.

260

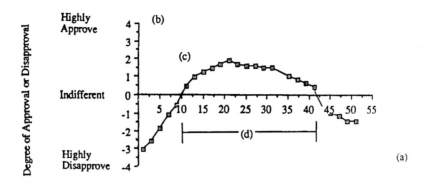

Figure 2. The return potential model of studying at Hobart and William Smith Colleges. (a) = the behavioral dimension—number of hours spent studying in a typical week; (b) = the evaluation dimension—approval or disapproval for each amount of time; (c) = the return potential curve; (d) = the range of tolerable studying behavior. Averages are based on the responses of 146 subjects collated from the data collected by 30 students.

subjects. (Depending on students' level and course content, you could discuss proper sample selection and size.) Suggest to them that combining all of the individual data can increase sample size and allow them to draw more accurate conclusions, but that this procedure would add a possible mediating factor by increasing the number of experimenters. Then display—on the chalkboard, overhead or a prepared handout—what their combined data look like. To do this, I have students turn in the assignment on one day, and I grade their reports, collate their data, and present the results for the next class. To illustrate interpretation of the results, the return potential curves of the collated social psychology class's data are presented in Figure 2.

As the graph illustrates, these students ($N = 146$) disapproved of studying 1 to 5 or 43 to 51 hr per week. Indifference was indicated toward those who study 7 to 13 hr or 33 to 43 hr, whereas approval was indicated toward those who study 15 to 31 hr. Although subjects were not asked their opinions for studying beyond 51 hr, the curve indicates that the group would continue to disapprove of studying this much, though not very strongly. Students reported that subjects were unwilling to indicate strong disapproval of a socially desirable behavior, such as studying. The average number of hours spent studying by this sample in a typical week was 17.86 ($SD = 9.86$) with a range of 2 to 60.

The range of tolerable behavior for hours spent studying in a typical week was 9 to 3 7 hr. In varying degrees, the group approved of all behavior within this range. The ideal behavior—the point at which the group expressed the highest approval—occurred for studying 21 hr per week, with a mean approval rating of 1.80. Surprisingly, this "ideal" behavior is viewed by the sample with only slight approval and is not generally put into practice; the mean studying time of this sample is less than the ideal (see Table 1 for reported studying times).

The intensity of the norm is indicated by the height of the curve above and below the point of indifference.

Norms about matters of personal taste, such as dress, usually have low intensity and will show a relatively flat curve when graphed. When people are more concerned about the issue in question, the norms are generally more intense, as shown by higher peaks and lower valleys (Jackson, 1965). When it comes to studying, students on this campus do not have very strong feelings about the acceptability of various amounts of study time, as indicated by the wide range of tolerable behavior and by the strongest approval being only 1.80 for studying 21 hr per week. The subjects felt more strongly about a person studying too little; they expressed the greatest disapproval of -2.93 for studying 1 hr per week. Similarly, the sample did not feel very strongly about the point at which a person studies too much. Indeed, the class reported that their subjects said it was people's prerogative to study as much as they wanted to or felt they needed to. Furthermore, many students reported that although subjects said that they personally would not spend so much time on their studies, many felt it was acceptable for others to do so.

Students spontaneously mentioned several sources of bias and mediating variables that could affect the results. Sources of bias include the location of the survey, time of the survey, subject selection, and attractiveness of the experimenter to the subject. Among the mediating variables mentioned by the class were a subject's major, year in school, gender, GPA, reasons for being in school, who pays tuition, and intellectual ability. Statistical analyses could be done to test some of these ideas.

Variations

Many variations of this demonstration are possible. One student suggested asking the questions in a random order so that subjects would not anticipate the questions or get bored. Another variation would be to compare the same norm in different groups (family vs. friends, fraternity/sorority members vs. nonmembers, friends vs.

strangers) and discuss how the social pressures toward conformity change depending on the cohesiveness of the group. Other campus norms may elicit stronger approval or disapproval (e.g., drinking, dating, late-night noise, tuition increases, class length, TV viewing, and clothing). Depending on the norm under investigation, smaller or larger increments of behavior may be more appropriate and would help reduce subjects' fatigue and/or boredom. Hence, the assignment can be de signed to study whatever issue is most relevant to the class.

Evaluation and Conclusion

After collecting data, interpreting the results, and discussing the project as a class, students came to appreciate the need for experimentation and the problems of social desirability response bias, biased sampling, and limits in generalizing the results.

Overall, this demonstration effectively illustrates survey research methods and group norms in an enjoyable and engaging way. On a scale ranging from *not at all* (1) to *very much* (7), 29 students in the introductory social psychology class gave this demonstration a median rating of 6 for being "helpful in making me understand the group norm of studying at Hobart and William Smith Colleges," "helpful in making me understand group norms in general," and "helpful in making me understand survey research methods." For "enjoyable, fun" and "overall usefulness," the median rating was 5. Students' comments, however, were the most revealing: "It was really interesting to do this study. I enjoyed listening to people's comments and seeing their reactions on [sic] studying," "It'll make me think a little more about surveys when I take them and when I give them," and "Active participation such as this exercise is more interesting and more significant to learning than simply reading about it."

This research experience enriches students' understanding, interpretation, and critiques of the experiments they learn about later in the course. This approach enables students to learn research skills, experience research, and gain insights about the power of a norm held by their own peer group.

References

Baron, R. A., & Byrne, D. (1987). *Social psychology: Understanding human interaction*. Boston: Allyn & Bacon.

Jackson, J. (1965). Structural characteristics of norms. In I. V. Steiner & M. Fishbein (Eds.), *Current studies in social psychology* (pp. 301-309). New York: Holt, Rinehart & Winston.

8. TEACHING ABOUT SPACE AND NONVERBAL BEHAVIOR

Intimacy and Personal Space: A Classroom Demonstration

Bryan Gibson
Carleton College

Paul Harris
Carol Werner
University of Utah

Research and theory on personal space has stressed the importance of personal space norms in regulating the intimacy of interpersonal interaction (Aiello & Thompson, 1980). In this regard, personal space norms can be seen as one of a number of interdependent nonverbal intimacy cues, including eye contact (Argyle & Dean, 1965), body orientation (Aiello, 1972), and topic intimacy (Baker & Shaw, 1980). This intimacy regulating function can be demonstrated to students through a straightforward activity that allows students to see how their personal space needs vary depending on the relative level of intricacy of other components of the interaction.

Procedure

Before any discussion of personal space, all students are asked to stand and choose a partner (preferably a person they do not know very well). Then they are asked to find space in the aisles or at the front of the classroom so that they can stand facing each other at a distance of about 8 ft. One student in each pair is then told to remain in a stationary position, and the other student is told to approach the partner. Students are asked to look toward the floor, and the approacher must then walk toward the stationary student until the approacher feels comfortable. Students are next instructed to look at each other; then the students who were stationary are asked to readjust their position by moving forward or backward until they feel comfortable. Finally, the students who were approached are asked to describe to their partners the appropriate steps necessary to use a condom properly. (Any intimate topic of conversation may be substituted here.) Other topics that have been used successfully include describing their first kiss, describing their most embarrassing experience, or imagining themselves in their underwear. At this point, there is typically a pause, and then students begin to look away from their partner, move back, turn their body, and/or laugh. After a few seconds, the instructor tells the class that they need not describe how to use a condom and that they can return to their seats.

Discussion

This activity demonstrates the important principle that personal space is one of several nonverbal mechanisms used to regulate intimacy. When students are instructed to look each other in the eye after one approaches the other, the most typical adjustment made by the person who was approached is to move back slightly. This movement shows that once eye contact is made, the interaction becomes more intimate, and adjustments in personal space are necessary to regain a comfortable state of interaction. Similarly, when students are asked to describe the proper use of a condom, a number of adjustments are made in the nonverbal cues used by students. They look away, reorient their body so as not to face their partner, or they move back even more. Each of these adjustments is designed to reduce the intimacy of the interaction once the topic of conversation increases in intimacy.

While discussing the variety of behaviors students used to regulate intimacy, the instructor can also have students report their subjective experiences during the exercise. Most students will report that they felt uncomfortable or nervous when eye contact was established and when the topic of conversation became more personal; in fact, it is common to hear nervous giggling or laughter from students when these shifts in intimacy take place. Discussing these subjective experiences may help students relate at a personal level to the "discomfort" of intimacy shifts discussed in equilibrium models of intimacy (Argyle & Dean, 1965) and the increases in arousal postulated by arousal models of interpersonal intimacy (Patterson, 1976).

Discussion of these issues leads to a greater understanding of one of the purposes of personal space norms (i.e., intimacy regulation), the behaviors associated with regulation, and the psychological processes that have been proposed as mediating this phenomenon. In addition, knowledge of the intimacy regulating function of personal space norms elicits discussion of interesting misunderstandings that may arise due to different personal space norms held by people of different cultures and by men and women. Hall (1966) first noted cultural differences in personal space use between what he called contact cultures (Latin American, Arab, and Mediterranean) and non-contact cultures (Northern European and North American). When people from contact cultures interact with people from non-contact cultures each may misinterpret the other on the basis of personal space use. The individual from the contact culture may view his or her non-contact culture acquaintance as distant and aloof, whereas the individual from the non-contact culture may see his other opposite as overly assertive or intimate.

Similarly, men typically have greater personal space needs than do women (Patterson, 1977; Tennis & Dabbs, 1975). Thus, interactions between men and women also have the potential for misunderstanding on the basis of personal space use. A woman may feel that a man is uninterested in her because of his larger personal space needs, whereas a man may misinterpret the closer interaction distance of a woman to mean that she is attempting to increase intimacy when in fact she is simply interacting at a distance that is more comfortable for her. Discussions of these gender differences may lead to insights regarding misunderstandings that could occur between men and women in dating situations.

Evaluation

This demonstration has been received enthusiastically in courses from introductory psychology to social psychology and environmental psychology. Evaluations were collected in an introductory psychology class. Students were asked to rate the demonstration on a scale ranging from *not very useful* (1) to *very useful* (5). The class mean was 3.8 ($N = 35$), indicating a generally positive response to the demonstration. In addition, students were asked to make a recommendation regarding the use of this demonstration in future classes. Eighty percent thought that the demonstration should be used in the future, 20% responded "maybe," and no one suggested that the demonstration not be used in the future.

Results of this evaluation are particularly important, given the potentially embarrassing nature of this demonstration. To encourage a natural response from students, little information is given before the demonstration. This fact ensures that when the intimate topic is raised, students will respond with genuine surprise and without a measured consideration of their nonverbal behavior. Thus, it is encouraging to note that students rate this demonstration positively and support its continued use in the classroom.

Conclusion

Other teaching activities using personal space have successfully focused students on data collection and ethics in personal space research (Burzynski, 1990; Ferraro, 1990). However, these activities have focused on retreat as the only response to an invasion of personal space. In contrast, the demonstration described in this article makes students aware of the communicative nature of personal space and enhances discussion of how personal space differences may lead to misunderstandings across culture and gender. In addition, students gain insight into their own use of personal space—a process that is typically so highly ingrained that students have not recognized its communicative function.

References

Aiello, J. R. (1972). A test of equilibrium theory: Visual interaction in relation to orientation, and sex of partner. *Perceptual and Motor Skills, 49*, 85-86.

Aiello, J. R., & Thompson, D. E (1980). When comparison fails: Mediating effects of sex and locus of control at extended interpersonal distances. *Basic and Applied Social Psychology, 1*, 65-82.

Argyle, M., & Dean, J. (1965). Eye-contact, distance and affiliation. *Sociometry, 28*, 289-304.

Baker, E., & Shaw, M. E. (1980). Reactions to interpersonal distance and topic intimacy: A comparison of strangers and friends. *Journal of Nonverbal Behavior, 5*, 80-91.

Burzynski, P. R. (1990). The personal space violation demonstration. In V. P. Makosky, C. C. Sileo, L. G. Whittemore, C. P. Landry, & M. L. Skutley (Eds.), *Activities handbook for the teaching of psychology* (Vol. 3, pp. 136-137). Washington DC American Psychological Association.

Ferraro, F. R. (1990). Field experiments in personal space invasion for introductory psychology. *Teaching of Psychology, 17*, 124-126.

Hall, E. T. (1966). *The hidden dimension.* New York: Doubleday.

Patterson, M. L. (1976). An arousal model of interpersonal intimacy. *Psychological Review, 83*, 235-245.

Patterson, M. L. (1977). Interpersonal distance, affect, and equilibrium theory. *Journal of Social Psychology, 101*, 205-214.

Tennis, G. H., & Dabbs, J. M. (1975). Sex, setting and personal space: First grade through college. *Sociometry, 38*, 385-394.

Note

We thank Sharon Akimoto and Neil Lutsky for their helpful comments on a draft of this article.

Field Experiments in Personal Space Invasion for Introductory Psychology

F. Richard Ferraro
University of Kansas

To supplement the typical introductory psychology lectures on personal space invasion, my students experienced this interesting topic firsthand. I had used class projects in previous semesters, but this effort was my first use of personal space invasion experiments.

This project coincided with the social psychology section of my course. My lecture discussed how behavior is influenced by other people (or groups of people) and what responses are elicited by others in certain situations (e.g., riding an elevator with a group of friends vs. riding the same elevator with a group of strangers). Because I emphasized the empirical aspect of psychology, a discussion arose in class concerning how experiments in personal space invasion could be conducted and what their practical value would be. This discussion led to my suggestion that the class members ($N = 80$), in groups of four to six, design and conduct their own personal space experiments, with a later class period being devoted to group presentations and discussion. In addition, each group was required to prepare an APA-style manuscript. During the next period, groups proposed their experiments to the class. This procedure helped to avoid overlap and to ensure that the research was feasible and ethical. All groups were encouraged to consult with me during the course of their projects, but few did so. I periodically inquired about each group's progress to be sure that all would finish in the allotted 2 weeks.

Locations for data collection included a library, an elevator, a cafeteria, a bus stop, and a dormitory lounge. The more ambitious groups performed experiments in several locations, although the majority remained at one site. The experiments were diverse. Some groups observed subjects unobtrusively (e.g., group members would sit in a parked car while taking notes). Other groups used confederates with one member recording subject reactions from a safe distance.

The popular choice for a dependent variable was the time taken by subjects to respond to the invasion of their *personal space*, operationally defined as the time from initial subject contact with an experimenter (or vice versa) until the subject left the testing area. One group used a questionnaire to inquire about personal space. This group diagrammed a variety of personal space situations (e.g., a schematic of an elevator floor plan, varying the number of people in it) and asked subjects to place an X where they would stand if confronted with these situations.

Following data collection and analysis, groups made their presentations and submitted their manuscripts. Because no student had prior experience with formal statistics or APA style, great leniency was allowed in these areas (e.g., most groups used simple frequency tabulations). Results generally conformed to previous findings (see Felipe & Sommer, 1966; Fisher & Byrne, 1975), but there were a few exceptions. Some students noted that people being observed often became interested in what the group members were doing. Such unexpected outcomes did not deter group enthusiasm, however, and added to class discussions concerning improved procedures for future experiments. Most group members were enthusiastic during all phases of their projects, with many expressing interest in future research opportunities in the psychology department, such as independent study and research assistantships.

All groups reported that the field experience was more valuable than lectures on the same topic. This information came from two sources. First, during data collection, many students said that their understanding was greatly increased by being the experimenter. Unfortunately, I was unable to compare performance on relevant examination questions between this semester and an earlier semester. Second, student evaluations at the end of the semester frequently noted that the non lecture activities complemented a lecture or assignment on the same topic.

The hands-on experience highlighted problems associated with conducting research (e.g., time and effort expenditure) and reinforced the notion that research is not as easy as it is often portrayed to be in introductory texts. The students enjoyed their research experience, which provided opportunities for problem solving, critical thinking, cooperation, and collaborative learning. Such opportunities rarely occur in a large introductory psychology class.

References

Felipe, N. J., & Sommer, R. (1966). Invasion of personal space. *Social Problems, 14,* 206-214.

Fisher, J. D., & Byrne, D. (1975). Too close for comfort: Sex differences in response to invasions of personal space. *Journal of Personality and Social Psychology, 32,* 15-21.

Detecting Deception: A Classroom Demonstration

James W. Grosch
Colgate University

John E. Sparrow
State University of New York
College at Geneseo

The attempt by behavioral scientists to detect when a person is lying has a long and varied history (see Ekman, 1985; Ekman & O'Sullivan, 1991). One of the most widely used instruments in lie detection is the polygraph, a device that simultaneously measures several physiological responses, including heart rate, respiration, and galvanic skin response (GSR). The GSR measures electrical resistance of the skin, which is affected by slight changes in moisture content. The polygraph's accuracy in detecting lies is controversial (e.g., Lykken, 1984; Raskin & Podlesny, 1979). Students can better appreciate this controversy when they view a classroom demonstration of lie detection and judge the process for themselves. Unfortunately, polygraphs are expensive and bulky, making it difficult, if not impractical, to bring them into the classroom.

The lie detection demonstration we developed uses an inexpensive GSR monitor. This technique can be carried out quickly and used in connection with many different topics, including physiological psychology, emotion, perception, and industrial/organizational psychology.

The GSR Monitor

We use an inexpensive, reliable GSR monitor described as a "biofeedback stress monitor" by its manufacturer, Micronta. This particular model has been updated to an electronically similar, although cosmetically different, model. The newer version works in the same fashion as the older model, although we have limited our review to the older prototype.

The device employs two metal finger electrodes held in place by Velcro fasteners. These electrodes plug into the lightweight (185 g), palm-sized main unit that houses the electronic circuitry necessary for monitoring changes in the GSR. The electronics used on the main circuit board are modest, consisting of three capacitors, a potentiometer, four resistors, three transistors, and a small transformer. Mounted in the case's front is a 5-cm speaker that emits a tone whose pitch changes as skin resistance changes. The case also provides an earphone jack that bypasses the speaker for private listening. This jack can also be used to route the monitor's auditory output to an external amplifier for use with large audiences. We have tested this feature in large sections of introductory psychology and found it produced a tone easily audible throughout the classroom. The device is powered by a single 9-V battery; hence, the unit is completely self-contained, including the power source, and is easily transported.

Demonstrating Lie Detection

Our classroom demonstration involves a number-selection procedure analogous to the Guilty Knowledge Technique (Lykken, 1981) used by professional polygraphers. We begin with a brief introduction of the polygraph and its use in lie detection, emphasizing that the GSR is only one of several measures that comprise the polygraph. After we describe the GSR monitor, the two electrodes of the GSR are attached to the middle and forefinger of a volunteer from the class. (We recommend cleaning the fingers with alcohol before attaching the electrodes to ensure a proper electrical contact.) To ensure a reliable reading, the subject's hand must be kept in a comfortable, stable position; the two electrodes should not touch.

While the instructor's back is turned, the subject selects one of five index cards, each of which has a number from 1 to 5 written on it; shows its number to the class; returns it to the deck; and shuffles the cards. At this point, the instructor turns around and adjusts the GSR so that its tone can be clearly heard by the class. The instructor then holds up each card so that the class and the subject can see it and asks, "Is this the number you chose?" The subject is told to say "no" each time, resulting in a lie being told when the correct card is held up.

We recommend going through the deck at least twice, giving the class a chance to contrast the change in the GSR tone with each answer given. The instructor identifies the card that produces the largest GSR response as the target. This procedure takes approximately 10 min per subject and can be repeated several times with the same or new subjects.

We have used the GSR monitor in various sections of introductory psychology, research methodology, and industrial/organizational psychology. Across 16 occasions, the GSR monitor has produced accurate results 88% of the time.

Relevant Areas of Psychology

This demonstration can be used in many courses. For example, when discussing physiological psychology in the introductory course, we have used the GSR monitor to illustrate how the autonomic nervous system reacts to a situation involving arousal, such as that produced by telling a lie. In the area of emotion, changes in the GSR represent one of many sources of information that can be used to infer an emotional state (presumably guilt when one is telling a lie). The GSR can be compared with other sources (e.g., facial expressions) for accuracy and

reliability. Sensation and perception students could profit from the demonstration if it is couched in terms of signal detection theory (Green & Swets, 1966). Here, hits, misses, correct rejections and false alarms could be described as plausible outcomes in a lie detection task. An important criticism of the polygraph is that although the percentage of hits may be high, so too are the number of false alarms, and innocent subjects may be falsely accused of lying (Lykken, 1984). Finally, lie detection is relevant to the field of industrial/organizational psychology because it has often served as a personnel screening device. A demonstration of the GSR monitor could be followed by a discussion of the problems that arise when a technique used in employment testing is not 100% accurate (see Sackett & Decker, 1979).

Ethical Issues Concerning Lie Detection

Whatever the context, students should understand that both the polygraph and the GSR monitor are far from foolproof and measure only physiological responses, not whether the subject is actually telling a lie. Indeed, it is this inference from a physiological response that makes the use of the GSR and the polygraph so controversial in detecting deception and so interesting in class.

In lecture, we stress that research on the polygraph presents a mixed picture of its overall accuracy. Some researchers (e.g., Raskin & Podlesny, 1979) have found polygraph accuracy as high as 90%, others (e.g., Lykken, 1979) have reported false alarms as often as 50% of the time. Factors that affect the accuracy of a polygraph test include the examiner's questioning technique, the subject's expectations, the severity of the lie being told, and the base rate of deception within the population (Ekman, 1985). Because the polygraph is less than perfectly accurate, ethical objections have been raised concerning its widespread use (e.g., Abeles, 1985; Alpher & Blanton, 1985), and about 25 states have banned its use in detecting deception. We present this information in class to emphasize that the GSR results must be interpreted cautiously. We want students to appreciate the complexity involved in lie detection and to realize that the accuracy of the device may vary with the situation and the subject.

An Experimental Assessment of the GSR Monitor

Although accuracy of the GSR monitor is fairly impressive (Raskin & Podlesny, 1979), a classroom setting may not be a fair test because the instructor may use cues other than the monitor's tone to detect deception. These cues, although often subtle, include the subject's facial expressions, the audience's reactions to the demonstration, and the subject's reactions to the monitor's auditory feedback. How accurate is the GSR monitor in light of these and other extraneous cues?

To address this question, we designed two laboratory experiments using the number-selection procedure mentioned earlier but with no audience present. In the first experiment, we tested the role played by facial cues in the context of auditory feedback. Twenty-eight introductory psychology students at Colgate University were randomly assigned to either a GSR/no facial cues condition in which they were seated behind a barrier, not visible to the experimenter, or a GSR/facial cues condition in which they were visible. In both conditions, the experimenter used the GSR monitor to help detect deception. Each subject also went through a no GSR/facial cues (or control) condition that consisted of the experimenter guessing the subject's selected number while the GSR monitor was turned off and while the subject was in full view of the experimenter. All three conditions consisted of three trials; a *trial* was defined as the experimenter guessing the selected number.

In the second experiment, we again looked at the role of facial cues but without the auditory feedback. We did this to make the GSR monitor more analogous to a standard polygraph that typically does not provide auditory feedback. To eliminate feedback to the subject, we routed the monitor's audio signal to an oscilloscope rather than the audio speaker. The experimenter made decisions based on changes in the waveform's pattern. Twenty-seven introductory psychology students at the State University of New York-College at Geneseo were randomly assigned to the same three conditions as in the first study.

We analyzed the data using a modified Bonferroni test (Keppel, 1991) to control the familywise error rate for eight planned nondirectional comparisons. We determined the adjusted alpha level to be .044. As Figure 1 indicates, the auditory feedback was much more helpful than the visual feedback in detecting deception for both the GSR/facial cues and GSR/no facial cues conditions. Independent t tests revealed that these differences were statistically significant, $t(29) = 3.49$ for GSR/facial cues and $t(22) = 3.13$ for GSR/no facial cues, $ps < .01$. Thus, auditory feedback appears to make an important contribution to the device's overall accuracy. Although the GSR/facial cues condition produced slightly greater accuracy than the GSR/no facial cues condition for both auditory and visual feedback, these differences were not statistically significant ($p > .044$), as determined by independent t tests. Furthermore, for the control condition, in which only facial cues were available, accuracy was below chance performance for three of the four groups. This result suggests that facial cues alone contributed little, if anything, to accurate detection.

The GSR monitor itself provided fairly accurate information concerning deception. This was especially true for auditory feedback, in which both the GSR/facial cues and GSR/no facial cues conditions produced significantly greater accuracy than the control condition, $t(14) = 8.09$ for GSR/facial cues and $t(12) = 3.09$ for GSR/no facial cues, $ps < .01$, in paired observation tests. For visual feedback, however, only the GSR/facial cues condition was significantly greater than the control, $t(15) = 3.22$, $p <$

.01, in a paired observation test. Finally, note that the highest accuracy in any condition was 71%, which is substantially less than the 88% we found for the class. This difference suggests that other variables, such as the social influence produced by an audience watching a subject, are at work in a classroom setting and contribute to the accurate detection of deception.

Although many factors contribute to the GSR monitor's accuracy, our data show that, with auditory feedback, the device works well in classroom and laboratory settings. Even when the instructor fails to detect deception, the results can lead to a useful discussion of issues surrounding lie detection and the complexity of using physiological measures for inferring a psychological state.

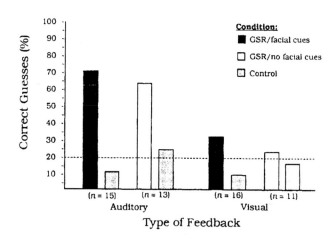

Figure 1. Percentage of correct experimenter guesses as a function of the type of feedback (auditory or visual) and the three different experimental conditions (GSR/facial cues, GSR/no facial cues, and control). The broken line indicates chance performance.

References

Abeles, N. (1985). Proceedings of the American Psychological Association, 1985. *American Psychologist, 41*, 633-663.

Alpher, V. S., & Blanton, R. L. (1985). The accuracy of lie detection: Why lie tests based on the polygraph should not be admitted into evidence today. *Law and Psychology Review, 9*, 67-75.

Ekman, P. (1985). *Telling lies: Clues to deceit in the marketplace, politics, and marriage.* New York: Norton.

Ekman, P., & O'Sullivan, M. (1991). Who can catch a liar? *American Psychologist, 46*, 913-920.

Green, D. M., & Swets, J. A. (1966). *Signal detection theory and psychyphysics.* New York: Wiley.

Keppel, G. (1991). *Design and analysis: A researcher's handbook (2nd ed.).* Englewood Cliffs, NJ: Prentice Hall.

Lykken, D. T. (1979). The detection of deception. *Psychological Bulletin, 86*, 47-53.

Lykken, D. T. (1981). *Tremor in the blood.* New York: McGraw-Hill.

Lykken, D. T. (1984). Detecting deception in 1984. *American Behavioral Scientist, 27*, 481-499.

Raskin, D. C., & Podlesny, J. A. (1979). Truth and deception: A reply to Lykken. *Psychological Bulletin, 86*, 54-59.

Sackett, P. R., & Decker, P. J. (1979). Detection of deception in the employment context: A review and critical analysis. *Personnel Psychology, 32*, 487-504.

Note

We thank Rachel Andrews, Judith Brown, Sarah Duggan, and Sharon Feeney for assisting with data collection. We also thank Kathy Barsz and Ganie DeHart for their valuable comments on a draft of this article

Detecting Deception Is Not as Easy as It Looks

Donna M. Desforges
Thomas C. Lee
University of Wisconsin-Stevens Point

Deception and its detection are topics that readily capture the attention of students in introductory and social psychology classes. Students easily recognize the importance of deception detection and its implications for interpersonal relationships. Consistent with research on the topic (e.g., DePaulo, Stone, & Lassiter,1985), students typically believe that they are fairly accurate in detecting deception. This fallacy stems from students' lack of knowledge of the difference between cues for perceived deception and cues for actual deception. Cues associated with perceived deception, but not with actual deception, are those that violate perceivers' expectations (Bond et al., 1992). For example, cues for perceived deception include things such as eye contact, smiling, and posture shifts, whereas cues for actual deception include speech hesitation, increased vocal pitch, blinking, and pupil dilation (DePaulo et al., 1985; Ekman, 1985; Zuckerman, DePaulo, & Rosenthal, 1981). This article presents an exercise that helps students distinguish cues associated with perceived deception from cues associated with actual deception.

Before introducing the topic of nonverbal communication, deception, and detection of deception in a social psychology class, I solicited volunteers from the class to participate in a project. Five students (three women and two men) agreed to participate and were sworn to secrecy about the nature of the project. The project entailed videotaping the student volunteers while they told the truth and lied about different acquaintances. The videotape procedure was modeled after Bond et al. (1992). Students took turns of approximately 2 min each describing an acquaintance as though they liked the person very much. Six of the descriptions were truthful, and four were false. The order of truths and lies was randomly determined. For half of the truths, students displayed poses that violated normative expectations: ear to shoulder, hand on top of head, and eyes to the ground. All but one of the lies were told unopposed. In the one posed lie, the student stared directly and continuously at the camera, a pose that is consistent with perceived deception detection. In all cases, students were told to be as credible as possible without being absurd.

All students reported feeling uncomfortable talking to a blank wall and, therefore, requested that the instructor sit across from them during videotaping. This procedure seemed to put the students at ease and facilitate the acquaintance descriptions.

The class viewed the videotape and indicated on a simple binary scale whether they believed the person was lying or telling the truth. After all deception judgments were made, students were given feedback about who was lying and when. The feedback led to a lively discussion of

Table 1. Judgments of Honesty and Dishonesty

Behavior	Judgments Percentage Correct	Judgments Percentage Incorrect
Truths—posed		
Hand on head	18	82
Ear to shoulder	18	82
Eyes to ground	11	89
Lies—not posed		
Description 1	18	82
Description 2	11	89
Description 3	11	89
Lie—posed	86	14
Truths—not posed		
Description 1	36	64
Description 2	68	32
Description 3	82	18

students' decision-making processes concerning who was telling the truth and who was lying. Students discovered that, consistent with prior research (e.g., Zuckerman et al., 1981), they had tuned into the wrong aspects of communication. This discussion led naturally to a consideration of the cues that indicate actual deception. For example, research was discussed that demonstrates that the body is more revealing of actual deception (e.g., Ekman & Friesen, 1974) and that smiles can often mask unpleasant emotions (Ekman, Friesen, & O'Sullivan, 1988). After the exercise and discussion students completed two 11-point scales ranging from *did not enjoy/help very much* (-5) to *enjoyed/helped very much* (+5) that measured the extent to which they enjoyed the exercise and the extent to which they felt that it helped them understand deception and detection of deception.

Students were fairly poor at correctly identifying when their classmates were telling the truth and lying. Table 1 presents the percentage of correct and incorrect deception judgments for each acquaintance description. The table reveals that when classmates were seen telling the truth while posed (truths—posed), students thought the classmates were lying. The opposite phenomenon occurred when the classmates were lying in a natural, unposed manner (lies—not posed). When a lie was seen in combination with a pose that is consistent with perceived deception (lie—posed), judgment accuracy improved. Students indicated that they enjoyed the exercise ($M =$ 4.12, $SD = .99$) and that the exercise enhanced their understanding ($M = 3.85$, $SD = 1.29$).

Before this exercise was incorporated into lectures on deception and its detection, students found it difficult to believe that cues such as eye contact were unrelated to actual deception. The exercise allowed students to experience firsthand that the manner in which they typically assess truth in others was seriously flawed. Students realized that cues commonly believed to be associated with deception are unrelated to actual deception. Discussion of the distinction between cues for perceived deception and actual deception was facilitated by this exercise in a way that was enjoyable and meaningful to students. This exercise could also be used to illustrate the tendency to associate eye contact with deception as a way of introducing the concept of illusory correlation's and their importance in person perception (e.g., Hamilton & Gifford, 1976).

References

Bond, C. F., Jr., Omar, A., Pitre, U., Lashley, B. R., Skaggs, L. M., & Kirk, C. T. (1992). Fishy-looking liars: Deception judgment from expectancy-violation. *Journal of Personality and Social Psychology, 63*, 969-977.

DePaulo, B. M., Stone, J., & Lassiter, G. D. (1985). Deceiving and detecting deceit. In B. R. Schlenker (Ed.), *The self and social life* (pp. 323-370). New York: McGraw-Hill.

Ekman, P. (1985). *Telling lies.* New York: Norton.

Ekman, P., & Friesen, W. V. (1974). Detecting deception from the body or face. *Journal of Personality and Social Psychology, 29*, 288-298.

Ekman, P., Friesen, W. V., & O'Sullivan, M. (1988). Smiles when lying. *Journal of Personality and Social Psychology, 54*, 414-420.

Hamilton, D. L., & Gifford, R. K. (1976). Illusory correlation in interpersonal perception: A cognitive basis of stereotypic judgments. *Journal of Experimental Social Psychology, 12*, 392-407.

Zuckerman, M., DePaulo, B. M., & Rosenthal, R. (1981). Verbal and nonverbal communication of deception. In L. Berkowitz (Ed.), *Advances in experimental social psychology* (Vol. 14, pp. 1-59). New York: Academic.

Note

We thank Charles L. Brewer and three anonymous reviewers for their thoughtful advice and comments on an earlier version of this article.

A Method for Teaching About Verbal and Nonverbal Communication

Mark Costanzo
Claremont McKenna College

Dane Archer
University of California, Santa Cruz

The study of verbal and nonverbal communication has assumed a prominent role in psychology during the past 20 years (Knapp, 1978; Patterson, 1983). Nonverbal behavior discloses critical information about emotions and relationships (Hickson & Stacks, 1985). Even barely perceptible nonverbal behaviors can have interpretable meaning—for example, we can recognize a person's facial expressions of emotion from as little as a 1/24th-s exposure (Rosenthal, Hall, DiMatteo, Rogers, & Archer, 1979). Research on social intelligence shows that it is possible to interpret people's behavior, feelings, and relationships from something as simple as a photograph (Archer, 1980). Nonverbal cues are often more powerful and reliable than verbal cues (Archer & Akert, 1984).

Researchers are also investigating the process of interpretation—how we use nonverbal cues to form impressions and conclusions about others. Correct interpretation is a remarkable feat because, in any interaction, hundreds or thousands of verbal and nonverbal cues stream by us, vanishing in milliseconds. How do we discard most of these cues, seizing the few (e.g., a momentary facial expression, a vocal inflection) that tell us what another person means or is feeling? The process of interpretation is one of the most impressive and least understood of human abilities.

Research attests to the importance of subtle expressive behaviors in how we communicate with others and in how we interpret their behavior. However, teaching about verbal and nonverbal behavior is a difficult challenge because the subtlety and complexity of verbal and nonverbal behavior are difficult to convey in lectures and readings. Students often come away with the impression that there is a simple codebook of nonverbal cues—that specific cues have invariant and unambiguous meanings.

This article describes instructional techniques that make use of the Interpersonal Perception Task (IPT). These techniques sensitize students to the variety and complexity of verbal and nonverbal cues, facilitate classroom discussion and help students understand the process of interpreting these cues.

The IPT

The IPT consists of a videotape of 30 brief (20 s to 60 s) scenes. Every scene is paired with a multiple-choice question that has two or three options. The questions appear on the screen before each scene. Viewers are asked to reach a conclusion about the people who appear in the scene that follows. A 6-s blank interval on the videotape enables viewers to enter their responses on an answer sheet after each scene.

The design of the IPT is best conveyed by describing a few scenes. The first scene shows a woman and a man having a conversation with two 7-year-old children. The question corresponding to this scene is "Who is the child of the two adults?" A second scene shows a man first telling his true life story and then, after a pause, telling a completely fabricated version of his life story. The question posed is "Which is the lie, and which is the truth?"

In the IPT, accuracy can always be verified against an external standard. In the examples just mentioned, one of the children is the child of the two adults, and one of the two versions of the man's life story is a lie. For every scene, there is an objectively correct answer, which is verifiable and unambiguous.

The IPT has four other important design features:

1. Every scene contains a full communications repertoire, with information presented naturalistically in all channels (verbal, vocal paralanguage, and nonverbal behavior). Because natural streams of behavior are used, clues to correct interpretation can be found in a variety of channels.

2. All scenes contain spontaneous behavior and unscripted conversation. The 30 brief scenes were extracted from longer videotaped interactions.

3. A total of 54 different encoders (28 females and 26 males ranging in age from 18 months old to 67 years old) appear in the videotape. Each scene shows one to four people.

4. There is a coherent content focus. Viewers are asked to reach conclusions about five types of social interaction: status, kinship, intimacy, competition, and deception. There are six scenes for each of these areas.

The IPT challenges viewers to identify the right answer to each question by using the broad range of communication present in each scene (e.g., facial expressions, words, tones of voice, hesitations, eye movements, gestures, personal space, posture, and touching). The cues occur simultaneously in the scenes, just as they do in everyday life. The IPT has been shown to be both valid and reliable, and previous research indicates that performance on the task relates to social skills that are important in everyday life (Costanzo & Archer, 1989).

Instructional Uses of the IPT

Are People Just Guessing?

The simplest use focuses on audience accuracy for specific scenes or for the whole videotape. In making interpretations like those involved in the IPT, people may feel that they are choosing an answer at random. However, even when people feel they are guessing, they almost always reach correct conclusions at well above chance levels of accuracy. A quick test of whether people are "just guessing" is whether or not performance exceeds chance.

The multiple-choice format makes it possible to determine whether viewers are more accurate than chance would predict. After a portion of the IPT has been shown, the instructor can read aloud the correct answers while students score their own tests for accuracy. The instructor can ask for a show of hands of those who chose each answer. This show of hands illustrates dramatically that people are not choosing answers randomly but, instead, are systematically decoding the informative cues present in the scenes. Accuracy rates can also be used to identify scenes that are relatively easy or difficult.

Comparing Verbal and Nonverbal Cues

The IPT can be used to sensitize students to the varieties and importance of different communication channels. One way to approach this issue is to ask, "What cues found in nonverbal communication are unavailable in words alone?" A simple demonstration involves contrasting the usefulness of purely verbal information with the richer cues available in full-channel (verbal + nonverbal) communication. One way to do this is to compare the accuracy of students given only verbal transcripts of IPT scenes (written transcripts are included)

with the accuracy of students shown the IPT videotape. Research indicates that the interpretability of words is overshadowed by the power of nonverbal cues (Archer & Akert, 1984). The group using verbal transcripts will be less accurate than the group with access to both verbal and nonverbal cues.

Alternatively, an entire class can be asked to determine the answers for several scenes using the transcript alone. Then, the same scenes can be shown using the full-channel videotape to see whether (and why) people would revise their original judgments.

Student Interpretations of Specific Cues

Another instructional technique involves focusing on viewer perceptions of potentially important cues. A good way to do this is to invite comments about why people chose a specific answer. The video can be stopped after a given scene to ask members of the audience two questions: "What do you think the correct answer is?," and "What specific cues led you to choose this answer?" This process is valuable and informative, because viewers will cite quite different cues, even if they agreed on the answer.

There is usually a high level of consistency across channels, and many different cues can lead a viewer to the correct interpretation (Archer, 1980). This tendency toward consistency usually produces a high level of redundancy across channels. The varied cues cited by viewers demonstrate that cues to correct interpretation are available in many channels simultaneously and that there are several paths to the correct answer.

Viewer perceptions provide a lively source of classroom participation because different people do not decode scenes in precisely the same way. The perceptions of people who chose an incorrect answer are also important because the cues that lead people astray will become apparent. Viewers who reach the correct judgment may have noticed these misleading cues, but assigned them less weight in their interpretation process. The IPT includes some illustrative viewer perceptions for each of the five scene types.

Silent Cues

Facial expressions, gestures, and other nonverbal behaviors usually occur along with words and act to change the perceived meaning of words. In many cases, however, nonverbal acts have independent meaning. It is easy to use the IPT to demonstrate the power of this "silent language." Scenes can be shown with the audio level on the TV monitor turned off. Students can use the cues they have available (e.g., facial behavior, gestures, eye contact, touching) to answer the questions.

This approach encourages viewers to focus exclusively on nonverbal behavior—for example, to determine if people are lying merely by watching (but not hearing) them. After students have tried answering the IPT questions using only visual cues, the scenes can be replayed with the audio. Do they change their answers? If so, what reasons do they give? Remind students that playing the videotape silently not only removes verbal cues, but also the important cues found in vocal paralanguage (e.g., pauses, tone of voice, and interruptions). This exercise also illustrates that verbal cues and vocal paralanguage are especially important for decoding some types of scenes (e.g., deception).

Subjective and Objective Accuracy

The process of interpreting verbal and nonverbal cues is only partly understood. However, it is clear that the processing of cues is not entirely conscious and that people have imperfect awareness of the cues they use (Smith, Archer, & Costanzo, in press). One way to encourage students to focus on process is to ask them to provide a confidence rating for each answer (e.g., a value between 0% to 100%). Students can also be asked to estimate the total number of items they answered correctly for some portion of the IPT. These subjective estimates can be compared to accuracy scores.

After a segment of the IPT has been shown, the instructor can announce the correct answers. If viewers are more accurate on the scenes they felt more confident about, it indicates that they were able to identify (and were consciously aware of) specific cues. If viewers were unexpectedly right (or unexpectedly wrong) on specific scenes, it may be that they were reaching interpretations without full awareness. Because the process of interpretation seems to rely on different types of cues (those we can articulate and those that we are not conscious of), both outcomes are possible.

This exercise sensitizes students to the tenuous relation between confidence and accuracy. Frequently, there is an overconfidence effect: People believe they scored higher than they actually scored, and most people think that they scored significantly better than average.

Using the IPT to Introduce Research Findings

The IPT is also useful for introducing important findings and current issues in the field of nonverbal behavior. For example, a substantial body of research indicates that women are somewhat more accurate than men at decoding nonverbal behavior (Hall, 1985). Research using the IPT supports this conclusion. Women may be better decoders because they detect more nonverbal cues or, perhaps, because they interpret what they detect differently. Before telling students about this gender difference, it is useful to ask them to indicate (by a show of hands) if they think men or women do better on tasks like the TPT. The introduction of this issue leads quite naturally to a discussion of differences in male and female socialization that may produce females' decoding advantage.

The IPT can also be used to prompt discussions of unresolved issues in the study of communication. An example is the question of whether there are "special" decoding abilities: Would police detectives be unusually skilled at decoding deception scenes? Would parents be more accurate than nonparents at identifying parent-child relationships in the kinship scenes? Would athletes be better able to spot winners and losers in the competition scenes? The answers are not yet clear, although research on the issue of special abilities is in progress.

Another set of unresolved issues concerns the role of cultural factors in verbal and nonverbal communication. For example, would interactions between status unequals be more formal (and, therefore, more easily decoded) if filmed in Japan? Would parent-child interactions be recognizable across cultural boundaries, or is there something uniquely American about the interactions depicted in the IPT? Assuming that the problem of verbal translation could be solved, would there still be a problem of nonverbal translation? Would a college student in China, Zaire, or Brazil have trouble decoding some scenes? The expressive behaviors present in the scenes are more complex than simple smiles or frowns (which may be universally recognizable), and it may help to be a cultural "insider" when trying to answer questions like those on the IPT.

Evaluation of the IPT as a Teaching Method

The pedagogical effectiveness of these exercises was evaluated in two social psychology classes. Theories and research findings on communication processes were summarized in both classes. One class ($n = 34$) received this information in traditional lecture format. The other class ($n = 30$) received the same information, but most of the material was presented via the exercises just described. Presentations to both groups included an outline of communication channels, examples of how different channels complement, reinforce, or contradict each other; and discussions of the readability of verbal and nonverbal cues.

Two weeks after the presentations, students in both groups took a midterm exam, which included the communication material. The exam contained three multiple choice questions and one essay question on communication processes. Although the lecture group and the IPT group did not differ in the number of multiple-choice questions answered correctly (lecture group $M = 2.03$; IPT group $M = 2.33$), $t(62) = 1.48$, $p < .072$, one-tailed, the IPT group performed significantly better on the essay question (lecture group $M = 10.68$; IPT group M = 12.07), $t(62) = 2.83$, $p < .01$, one-tailed. The essay was scored using a grading scale on which 15 was equal to an A+ and 1 was equal to F- . The grader was blind to group membership. Finally, a global index of student interest and enjoyment was obtained by asking students to grade the overall quality of the presentations using the 15-point grading scale. The IPT group rated the presentation significantly higher than did the lecture group (lecture group $M = 12.35$; IPT group $M = 13.60$), $t(62) = 2.93$, $p < .01$.

These findings appear to indicate that use of the IPT offers advantages over the traditional lecture. Students gained a more sophisticated understanding of communication processes and rated the approach as preferable to a standard lecture. We also note a more qualitative, impressionistic finding: Use of the IPT produced greater student involvement and fuller, more wide-ranging discussions. The pattern of findings suggests that the IPT is an effective means of presenting complex material and promoting student involvement and participation.

A Cautionary Note: Feedback on Individual Performance

The IPT is designed for research and instructional uses. Although researchers sometimes communicate their findings to research participants, information about individual performance is usually not provided. In instructional settings, however, students are accustomed to being told how they scored on a particular task. We have found that students are usually eager to learn their IPT scores. A problem may arise if students interpret their score as an infallible indication of interpersonal sensitivity. It would be a disservice to allow students who obtain low scores to feel that they are poor judges of behavior. This negative feedback could outweigh the learning benefits of the IPT.

If people are told their overall scores, they should also be told that performance is probably influenced by several factors: motivation, practice, viewing conditions, fatigue, attention, and experience with similar tasks. It should also be pointed out that the IPT focuses on interpreting the behavior of unfamiliar others—it does not directly address the perception of one's intimates and acquaintances or other dimensions of social intelligence, such as judging motives or personality characteristics. Providing this information suggests alternative explanations for poor performance and cautions students against drawing sweeping conclusions on the basis of their score.

The classroom exercises described here do not require giving students information about their total score. These exercises are designed to focus attention on the process of interpretation and the nature of verbal and nonverbal behavior, not the issue of individual accuracy. As a teaching device, the IPT highlights the subtlety and complexity of expressive behavior and promotes active learning by presenting social interaction in a vivid and involving manner.

References

Archer, D. (1980). *How to expand your social intelligence quotient*. New York: Evans & Co. (Dutton-Elsevier).

Archer, D., & Akert, R. M. (1984). Nonverbal factors in person perception. In M. Cook (Ed.), *Issues in person perception* (pp. 114-144). New York: Methuen.

Costanzo, M., & Archer, D. (1989). Interpreting the expressive behavior of others: The Interpersonal Perception Task. *Journal of Non verbal Behavior, 13,* 225-245.

Hall, J. A. (1985). *Nonverbal sex differences: Communication accuracy and expressive style.* Baltimore: Johns Hopkins University Press.

Hickson, M. L., & Stacks, D. W. (1985). *Nonverbal communication: Studies and applications.* Dubuque, IA: Brown.

Knapp, M. L. (1978). *Nonverbal communication in human interaction.* New York: Holt, Rinehart & Winston.

Patterson, M. L. (1983). *Nonverbal behavior: A functional perspective.* New York: Springer-Verlag.

Rosenthal, R., Hall, J. A., DiMatteo, M. R., Rogers, P., & Archer, D. (1979). *Sensitivity to nonverbal communication: A profile approach to the measurement of differential abilities.* Baltimore: Johns Hopkins University Press.

Smith, H. J., Archer, D., & Costanzo, M. (in press). Just a hunch Accuracy and awareness in person perception. *Journal of Nonverbal Behavior.*

Notes

1. The IPT is available from the University of California Media Extension Center, 2176 Shattuck Avenue, Berkeley, CA 94704. Telephone: (415) 642-0460. Rental price is $36.
2. Preparation of this article was supported by a Faculty Research Grant from Claremont McKenna College to Mark Costanzo.
3. We thank Joseph J. Palladino and three anonymous reviewers for their helpful comments on an earlier draft of this article.

9. EXAMINING STEREOTYPES OF GENDER AND RACE

Stereotype Measurement and the "Kernel of Truth" Hypothesis

Randall A. Gordon
Western Carolina University

Katz and Braly's (1933) work is usually cited as one of the earliest examples of stereotype measurement. Replications of this classic study by Gilbert (1951) and Karlins, Coffman, and Walters (1969) revealed changes in the uniformity of racial stereotypes across time and a tendency for Americans to attribute more negative characteristics to themselves. However, the technique used to quantify social stereotypes in these studies has been criticized (Brown, 1986).

In the three studies just cited, Princeton University undergraduates were instructed to select from a large list of traits all descriptors that were typical of various ethnic groups (e.g., Germans, Japanese, and Jews). One problem with this technique is an incomplete understanding of how subjects interpreted the word *typical*. For example, was *typical* interpreted to mean that a trait could be found in all members of a specific group, 75% of the group, or at least 50% of the group? More recent research by Brigham (1971, 1973) and McCauley and Stitt (1978) used different methods that shed light on how subjects from the Princeton studies may have interpreted "typical" traits.

This demonstration can be used to introduce stereotypes and to lead into a discussion on how they are formed and their relative degree of accuracy. Data from the demonstration illustrate advances in measurement, which can help students understand the cognitive basis of social stereotypes. The technique is appropriate for courses in general psychology, social psychology, attitude and survey research, or any other class that covers measurement. The demonstration, based on Experiment 3 from McCauley and Stitt (1978), also allows for an assessment of stereotype validity and the "kernel of truth" hypothesis (LeVine & Campbell, 1972). This hypothesis suggests that there is a kernel of truth in most stereotypes when they are obtained from people who have firsthand knowledge of the stereotyped group.

Method

This demonstration provides data on the validity of social stereotypes by comparing diagnostic ratios based on students' estimates of various measurable characteristics with criterion ratios (i.e., ratios calculated from objective data). According to McCauley and Stitt (1978), a diagnostic ratio is a quantitative measure of stereotyping "based on defining stereotypes as probabilistic predictions that distinguish the stereotyped group from others" (p. 929). The ratio is computed by obtaining estimates of the probability of a trait occurring among members of a specific group (e.g., the percentage of Germans who are efficient) and dividing this by the probability that the trait occurs among all people (e.g., the percentage of all people who are efficient).

Before conducting the demonstration, it is necessary to obtain data regarding the actual prevalence of various characteristics (e.g., having four or more children or completing high school) within specific populations (e. g., Black Americans, White Americans, or all Americans). With one exception, the data for the demonstration discussed herein were gathered from the *Statistical Abstract of the United States: 1986* (U.S. Bureau of the Census, 1986). The following reports of percentages of characteristics were collected for Black Americans, White (non-Hispanic) Americans, Hispanic Americans, and for all Americans: who completed high school, who received food stamps, who had four or more children, who had a female head of household, and who were unemployed in the last month. The unemployment information was based on data from September 1988 (Bureau of Labor Statistics, 1988).

Forty-seven students (42 White, 5 Black) from two undergraduate social psychology courses were asked to respond to the following instructions: "In the spaces provided, indicate the percentage of American people who have the traits or characteristics listed below." The five

279

Table 1. Criterion and Mean Diagnostic Ratios for White, Black, and Hispanic Americans

Characteristic	White Americans		Black Americans		Hispanic Americans	
	Criterion Ratio	Diagnostic Ratio	Criterion Ratio	Diagnostic Ratio	Criterion Ratio	Diagnostic Ratio
Completed high school (1986)	1.02	1.06*	.83	.81*	.65	.70*
Unemployed (Sept. 1988)	.90	.89	2.03	1.87*	—ᵃ	1.92*
Received food stamps (1986)	.81	.68**	1.89	1.35**	1.47	1.11**
Had 4 or more children (1986)	.89	.93	2.19	1.94*	2.63	1.77**
Female head of household (1986)	.83	.89	1.43	1.45*	.89	.92

ᵃUnemployment data were not available for this group.
*Significantly different from 1.00, $p < .05$, two-tailed; $df = 46$. **Significantly different from 1.00 and from criterion ratio, for both tests, $p < .05$, two-tailed; $df = 46$.

items on each page of the questionnaire appeared as follows:

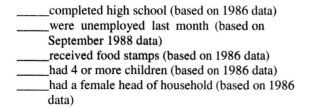

_____completed high school (based on 1986 data)
_____were unemployed last month (based on September 1988 data)
_____received food stamps (based on 1986 data)
_____had 4 or more children (based on 1986 data)
_____had a female head of household (based on 1986 data)

Each student responded to the page regarding all American people and then responded to similar pages with the words *Black*, *White*, and *Hispanic* substituted for the word *all* at the top of the sheet. The order of completing the last three pages of the questionnaire was counterbalanced. Before they complete the questionnaire, it is important to inform students that the purpose of the demonstration is to examine the accuracy of their perceptions and that they should give their best estimates.

Results and Discussion

Results of the demonstration provide a method for assessing the accuracy of various stereotypes. To accomplish this, first calculate the diagnostic ratios (i.e., divide each subject's percentage estimate of a characteristic occurring within a specific group by the estimate for that same characteristic occurring among all Americans) and list the mean diagnostic ratios with the corresponding objective criterion ratios. The criterion and mean diagnostic ratios are listed in Table 1.

Consistent with results obtained by McCauley and Stitt (1978), the relative accuracy of the mean diagnostic ratios was striking. Ten of the 15 diagnostic ratios were significantly different from 1.0, all ts (46) > 2.04 and all ps < .05, two-tailed. However, of the 14 possible comparisons between criterion and mean diagnostic ratios, only 4 revealed significant differences, all ts (46) > 2.92 and all ps < .05, two-tailed. These results suggest that stereotypical perceptions should not automatically be characterized as gross overgeneralizations. In each case,

the minority group diagnostic ratios were less extreme than the corresponding criterion ratios.

Presenting students' mean diagnostic ratios can start a discussion of techniques for measuring stereotypes. A good beginning point is Lippmann's (1922) discussion of stereotypes, their origins, and maintenance. The techniques used by Katz and Braly (1933), Brigham (1971), and McCauley and Stitt (1978) to measure stereotypes can be compared.

Students who have participated in this demonstration are usually surprised at the high level of accuracy among the group. An informal assessment showed that most students believed their participation in the demonstration and the classroom discussion helped them to understand the diagnostic ratio measure. Students also reported that comparing the three techniques helped them to understand the concept of stereotypes. Most students reacted favorably to the demonstration and felt that it should be included in future classes.

Although the data usually support, in part, the "kernel of truth" hypothesis, responses typically indicate less extreme stereotypes than the objective criterion ratio. A discussion of research pertaining to the "contact hypothesis" and its relation to stereotyping and intergroup conflict can be introduced at this point. Amir (1969) provided a good review of this literature. If the class is racially heterogeneous, a breakdown of the data by race of student can be used to make comparisons based on degree of familiarity and contact with members of a given race.

This type of outcome can also be used to introduce the topic of response biases (e.g., social desirability) that might influence stereotypes in general. It is important to remind students, however, that the instructions they received presented the task as one that focused on prediction and accuracy, not on attitudes or stereotype measurement. Data collected using this technique should be less likely to suffer from these response set problems (McCauley & Stitt, 1978).

Finally, the prescribed use of diagnostic ratios as individual measures of stereotypes should be mentioned. McCauley and Stitt (1978) introduced the diagnostic ratio as an individual and quantitative measure of stereotypes, not as a means of examining a stereotype held by a group of people. Unfortunately, they did not caution readers about the interpretation of mean diagnostic ratios.

Although most students will be impressed by how accurate their mean diagnostic ratios are, part of this accuracy is due to the "statisticized" nature of the group task. A statisticized group task involves averaging the products (estimates) of independent, noninteracting individuals. It is important to conclude the discussion of the demonstration with a description of "statisticized groups" (Stroop, 1932). One way to accomplish this is to select one of the classes' mean diagnostic ratios that was relatively accurate and list the corresponding distribution of individual diagnostic ratios. For example, the mean diagnostic ratio for Hispanic Americans having four or more children was 1.92. However, the distribution of these ratios ranged from .25 to 10. Students will see that what accounts for much of the accuracy is that overestimates and underestimates cancel each other out. Providing additional examples (e. g., guessing the temperature of the classroom or the number of jelly beans in a jar) should help students further understand the concepts of statisticized group tasks and random error.

I leave you with one final word of caution. Although the data collected in the demonstration are related to racial and ethnic stereotypes, they differ fundamentally from more traditional assessments of stereotypes that involve rating groups on personality characteristics (e.g., materialistic, industrious, or lazy). Accuracy found in the demonstration may be due, in part, to the transmission of relevant statistical information (e.g., unemployment figures) through the mass media. This type of transmission does not occur in quite the same manner for personality traits related to stereotypes.

References

Amir, Y. (1969). Contact hypothesis in ethnic relations. *Psychological Bulletin, 71*, 319-341.

Brigham, J. C. (1971). Ethnic stereotypes. *Psychological Bulletin, 76*, 15-38.

Brigham, J. C. (1973). Ethnic stereotypes and attitudes: A different mode of analysis. *Journal of Personality, 41*, 206-233.

Brown, R. (1986). *Social psychology the second edition.* New York: Free Press.

Bureau of Labor Statistics. (1988). *Employment and Earnings, 35*, 20.

Gilbert, G. M. (1951). Stereotype persistence and change among college students. *Journal of Abnormal and Social Psychology, 46*, 245-254.

Karlins, M., Coffman, T. L., & Walters, G. (1969) . On the fading of social stereotypes: Studies in three generations of college students. *Journal of Personality and Social Psychology, 13*, 1-16.

Katz, D., & Braly, K. W. (1933). Racial stereotypes of one hundred college students. *Journal of Abnormal and Social Psychology, 28*, 280-290.

LeVine, R. A., & Campbell, D. T. (1972*). Ethnocentrism.* New York: Wiley.

Lippmann, W. (1922). *Public opinion.* New York: Harcourt, Brace.

McCauley, C., & Stitt, C. L. (1978). An individual and quantitative measure of stereotypes. *Journal of Personality and Social Psychology, 36*, 929-940.

Stroop, J. R. (1932). Is the judgment of the group better than that of the average member of the group? *Journal of Experimental Psychology, 15*, 550-562.

U. S. Bureau of the Census. (1986). *Statistical abstract of the United States: 1986* (98th ed.). Washington, DC: U.S. Government Printing Office.

Note

I thank Bruce Henderson, Hal Herzog, and three anonymous reviewers for their helpful comments on an earlier draft of this article.

The Power of Stereotypes: A Labeling Exercise

Susan B. Goldstein
University of Redlands

The purpose of this exercise is to convey to participants the powerful cognitive, affective, and behavioral impact of stereotypes on the perceiver as well as the target. Research indicates that once strong stereotypes are activated, people are likely to attend to (Bodenhausen, 1988; Major, Cozarelli, Testa, & McFarlin, 1988) and recall (Stangor & McMillan, 1992; von Hippel, Sekaquaptewa, & Vargas, 1995) expectancy-confirming information. They are also likely to make stereotype-consistent attributions for the behavior of others (Hewstone, 1990) . As targets of stereotypes, people may alter their behavior in anticipation of being perceived in a stereotypical manner (Steele & Aronson, 1995) or may even fulfill the stereotypical expectancies of others (Hilton & Darley, 1991; Jussim & Fleming, 1996). Both the outgroup members (Stephan & Stephan, 1993) and the ingroup members (e.g., Fichten, Robillard, Tagalakis, & Amsel, 1991) of stigmatized groups are likely to link particular affective reactions to group labels.

This exercise provides a set of stereotypes that guide the selective attention, recall, and attributions of participants as they interact with each other. It also demonstrates the impact of being stereotyped on the self-perception and behavior of the targeted individual.

The Labeling Exercise

Preparation

The labeling exercise takes approximately 1 hr to conduct. I have found it to be successful with classes as small as 10 and as large as 60. With some assistance it may be feasible to conduct the exercise with numbers larger than 60. The setting should be a room large enough to allow participants to move about easily. A circular arrangement of chairs works well because participants can interact easily as they move within the circle and then can return to their chairs during the debriefing and discussion phases.

The only material needed is adhesive (e.g., file folder) labels for each participant; each label indicates a different stereotypic trait descriptor. Examples include *good at math, childlike, violent, materialistic, musical, frail, artistic, uneducated, lazy, overemotional, athletic, dishonest, forgetful, unclean, cute, helpless, exotic, jovial,* and *quick tempered.* I find that using trait descriptors is preferable to using the names of specific target groups (e.g., Puerto Rican, disabled, African American). Asking participants to treat others according to group labels requires that they generate the accompanying stereotype, which they may be unable or unwilling to do. Further, the use of trait descriptors allows participants to focus on the stereotyping process rather than the accuracy of specific trait-group associations.

Procedure

Introduce the exercise. For participants without academic background on the psychology of stereotyping, a brief (10-15 min) explanation of theoretical perspectives may be useful. Duckitt (1992) and Hilton and von Hippel (1996) are helpful instructor resources. The former provides a comprehensive overview of major theoretical approaches, whereas the latter presents a review of the stereotyping literature with particular attention to cognitive and motivational aspects of stereotype formation and maintenance.

The instructor should tell participants that to learn more about how stereotypes work, they will be labeled. It is also important to explain that participation is voluntary, and that students who wish not to be labeled can play a useful role as observers. The facilitator may also wish to acknowledge that although some participants have had a great deal of experience being the target of stereotypes, this may still be a useful exploration of the process of stereotyping.

Distribute labels. Attach adhesive labels (to participants' forehead or back) so that they are not visible to the wearer. I deliberately emphasize the act of randomly distributing labels to minimize the effect of the specific assigned trait on the participant.

Assign the task. Tell participants to converse with one or two others on the topic of "future goals." Although other topics may be used, I have found that the discussion of future goals easily elicits reactions based on the trait descriptors and is appropriate for a variety of participant populations. As time allows, participants may shift conversation partners and hold brief discussions with several different people (cocktail party style). Instruct participants that throughout this process they are to treat others according to their label. For example, someone engaged in conversation with a participant labeled *uneducated* may intentionally use very simple words, or one may frequently remind the person labeled *forgetful* about the requirements of the task. This phase lasts approximately 15 min.

Debrief. I begin the debriefing session by reiterating that I distributed labels randomly and that the way participants were treated does not in any way reflect their actual characteristics. Although participants are generally anxious to see and remove their labels, I encourage them to keep their labels on initially as we debrief. Otherwise, participants tend to tailor their descriptions of their experiences to fit the label. With smaller groups, all participants can talk about their own behavior and the treatment they received during the exercise. With larger groups, some volunteers can discuss their experiences. Ask any observers to comment on their observations. Participants may then view their labels and debrief further if desired. This debriefing phase often focuses on the degree to which it is uncomfortable to knowingly stereotype others and the frustration experienced in being stereotyped oneself.

Discussion. This exercise raises several topics for discussion. First, participants usually notice the ease with which one can find stereotype-confirming information. When asked, they will generally say that it was easy for them to respond to others in a manner consistent with the trait descriptors. In exploring the nature of these stereotype-consistent responses, participants can be guided to recognize the role of selective attention and attribution.

Second, possible reactions to being labeled may be discussed. Participants tend to either expend a great deal of energy attempting to disprove the label or they behave in a manner that confirms the stereotype-based expectation. They may also acknowledge the difficulty of ignoring stereotypical treatment. Students can often provide vivid examples of the way they have altered their own behavior in anticipation of being stereotyped. A third topic for discussion focuses on positive stereotypes. Participants labeled with positive traits, such as *jovial* or *good at math* can be asked to reflect on their experiences. These reports generally indicate that positive stereotypes can be just as limiting and frustrating as negative ones.

A fourth issue deals with the social interaction of participants. If participants can describe a rough sociogram of the group as it occurred during the exercise, they may find that similarly labeled individuals (e.g., *childlike, frail,* and *slow*) clustered together. Participants can then speculate on the reasons for such groupings and on implications for intergroup relations. A fifth topic for discussion is the significance of this exercise for prejudice reduction. Participants can be asked to think about what would have led them to reject the trait descriptors. This generally results in a discussion of efforts to attend to stereotype-disconfirming information.

Finally, it is counterproductive to leave students concerned about stereotyping to the extent that subsequent classroom discussion of group differences closes down. Participants can be asked to suggest ways to discuss issues of diversity without stereotyping. Some ideas include distinguishing between rigid stereotypes and generalizations, focusing on diversity within groups and the multiple group identities of each individual, emphasizing similarities across groups, and maintaining an awareness of stereotyping processes.

Participant Evaluations

A total of 75 participants evaluated this exercise immediately following its completion. These participants were enrolled in three separate Psychology of Prejudice classes of approximately 25 students each. None of these students elected to observe rather than participate in the exercise. Participants responded to five items on a 7-point scale ranging from 1 (*strongly disagree*) to 7 (*strongly agree*), with 4 (*not sure*) as the midpoint. Several students also responded to a request for written comments following the rating scales. Responses were quite positive, with participants indicating that they found the instructions clear ($M = 6.5$, $SD = 0.8$) and the activity interesting ($M = 6.4$, $SD = 0.9$). Participants also believed that the activity taught them something useful about prejudice ($M = 6.4$, $SD = 0.7$) and that it should be used in future classes ($M = 6.7$, $SD = 0.6$). Finally, participants generally felt comfortable

participating in this activity ($M = 6.0$, $SD = 1.3$) although the rating for this item was somewhat lower and more variable than the other items. In each of the cases where students' scores indicated that they were uncomfortable participating, they also indicated that they felt the exercise should be used in future classes. I believe that the lower mean on this last item is indicative of the degree to which it is uncomfortable to become aware of one's stereotypes or to knowingly stereotype others. The participants' written comments support this interpretation. For example, typical comments were "It was uncomfortable to learn about my biases," and "It was difficult to treat people stereotypically, but [the exercise] was extremely helpful in learning about prejudice." I have found that former students refer to this exercise as a meaningful experience that provided them with a clearer understanding of the power of stereotypes in guiding their self-perceptions and their view and treatment of others.

References

Bodenhausen, G. V. (1988). Stereotypic biases in social decision making and memory: Testing process models for stereotypic use. *Journal of Personality and Social Psychology, 55,* 726-737.

Duckitt, J. (1992). Psychology and prejudice: A historical analysis and integrative framework. *American Psychologist, 47,* 1182-1193.

Fichten, C. S., Robillard, K., Tagalakis, V., & Amsel, R. (1991). Casual interaction between college students with various disabilities and their nondisabled peers—The internal dialog. *Rehabilitation Psychology, 36,* 3-20.

Hewstone, M. (1990). The "ultimate attribution error"? A review of the literature on intergroup causal attribution. *European Journal of Social Psychology, 20,* 311-335.

Hilton, J. L., & Darley, J. M. (1991). The effects of interaction goals on person perception. *Advances in Experimental Social Psychology, 24,* 235-267.

Hilton, J. L., & von Hippel, W. (1996). Stereotypes. *Annual Review of Psychology, 47,* 237-271.

Jussim, L., & Fleming, C. (1996). Self-fulfilling prophecies and the maintenance of social stereotypes. In N. Macrae, M. Hewstone, & C. Stangor (Eds.), *The foundations of stereotypes and stereotyping* (pp. 161-192). New York: Guilford.

Major, B., Cozarelli, C., Testa, M., & McFarlin, D. B. (1988). Self-verification versus expectancy-confirmation in social interaction: The impact of self focus. *Personality and Social Psychology Bulletin, 14,* 346-359.

Stangor, C., & McMillan, D. (1992). Memory for expectancy-congruent and expectancy-incongruent information: A review of the social and social developmental literatures. *Psychological Bulletin, 111,* 42-61.

Steele, C. M., & Aronson, J. (1995). Stereotype threat and the intellectual test performance of African-Americans. *Journal of Personality and Social Psychology, 69,* 797-811.

Stephan, W. G., & Stephan, C. W. (1993). Cognition and affect in stereotyping: Parallel interactive networks. In D. M. Mackie & D. L. Hamilton (Eds.), *Affect, cognition, and stereotyping: Interactive processes in group perception* (pp. 111-136). Orlando, FL: Academic.

von Hippel, W., Sekaquaptewa, D., & Vargas, P. (1995). On the role of encoding processes in stereotype maintenance. *Advances in Experimental Social Psychology, 27,* 177-254.

Notes

1. Portions of this article were presented at the Western Psychological Association Convention, April 1996, San Jose, CA.
2. I thank Ruth L. Ault and the anonymous reviewers for their helpful comments on a draft of this article.

Using Science Fiction to Teach the Psychology of Sex and Gender

Hilary M. Lips
University of Winnipeg

We are seldom aware of how our own gender and the very concept of gender shape our lives. It is difficult to take issue with Bem and Bem's (1970) argument that gender is in many ways a "nonconscious ideology" (p. 89): We are like the fish that are too surrounded by water to understand what it means to be wet. When teaching about the psychology of sex and gender, I use science fiction to increase students' awareness of this nonconscious ideology. In recent years, a host of feminist writers of science fiction have elaborated worlds in which new possibilities for gender and/or sex are explored (see Rose, 1988, for an overview). I use the worlds two of these writers have created to jolt my students into thinking about how much they take gender for granted and to help them imagine how things could be different.

The first world to which I introduce them is the one created by Ursula Le Guin (1969) in *The Left Hand of Darkness.* On the planet described by her narrator, people do not come in two sexes and there are no all-inclusive gender roles. Every individual is simply an individual, not a woman or a man. Individual's status changes only for a few days every month when they go into a period of sexual desire labeled *kemmer.* During that time, the individual "becomes" either a woman or a man in terms of sex organs and reproductive capacity and tries to connect sexually with another individual who is also in kemmer. If approached in an early stage of kemmer, an individual may respond by "becoming" a man if the first individual is a woman or a woman if the first individual is a man. An interesting aspect of the process is that, each month, individuals do not know whether they will become a man or a woman and have no control over this outcome. There are some fascinating implications to this potential to become, at random, either a woman or a man: A sexual liaison may result either in becoming pregnant, if the individual turns into a woman, or in inseminating the sexual partner, if the individual turns into a man. In Le Guin's world, a person who is the mother of several children may also be the father of several others!

Once my students have become familiar with the world fantasized in *The Left Hand of Darkness,* I ask the class of 50 to 60 students to meet in small groups (5 or 6 students) to discuss its implications for society. For the first 10 min, I provide no structure for the discussion except the question, "How would daily life be different in the world described by Le Guin?" After giving the groups this initial opportunity to define for themselves what aspects of life might be most affected by the absence of gender except in a limited sexual context, I feed some specific questions to the discussion groups: What would such an arrangement mean for the definition of family? Monogamy? Social attitudes toward contraception, abortion, day care ? Rape ? What about homosexuality? In non-kemmer situations, what would be the implications for ordinary social interaction of not having gender roles as cues to behavior? One person in each group serves as notetaker. After 30 min, each group reports its conclusions to the class and a general class discussion follows.

Two major themes emerge regularly from the group discussions: (a) the pervasiveness with which gender is used in our society to frame expectations about individuals and their behavior, and (b) the extent to which family structure affects social life and the intergroup relationships between women and men. Students comment frequently on the near impossibility of imagining what social interactions would be like without gender cues. The exercise helps even those who think they are already "liberated" from the constricting notions of femininity and masculinity to see how these concepts still affect their own assumptions and behavior. Students' comments also often reveal an increased awareness that women's and men's biological contributions to reproduction need not necessarily lead to a particular type of family structure or power relationship between women and men. They speculate in their discussions about how "things might be different" if men could become pregnant; they often come to the conclusion that "things could be different," even with our current biological arrangement.

I use this exercise at the beginning of my undergraduate course in sex and gender, but it would be equally appropriate for units on gender in other courses. My students appear to enjoy the exercise, and it reminds all of us just how much our society is structured by sex- and gender-related expectations.

Another world from science fiction that I introduce in my course is the utopian portrait of a future society created by Marge Piercy (1976) in *Woman at the Edge of Time*. In Piercy's world, there are women and men, but their lives are structured in ways that minimize the impact of sex and gender on social relationships. Women do not go through pregnancy: Babies are grown in tenderly managed test-tube nurseries, each cared for by three chosen female and male "co-mothers," who nurture them until puberty. Male as well as female co-mothers breastfeed the babies. Rather than individual parents, society has major responsibility for the care of children, and at adolescence, children make a ritual break from their parents and gain a set of specially selected advisers. The picture she paints is idyllic; my students have an interesting time articulating their reactions to it. Many of them are not at all convinced of the desirability of her solutions to social problems.

My favorite aspect of Piercy's novel, however, is the language. In the world fantasized by Piercy, there are no masculine and feminine pronouns—there is only *per* (for

person), as in "I want to talk to per, but per won't listen." I introduce the language aspect to the course when we discuss the role played by language in shaping children's attitudes about gender. We talk about the evidence that children are exposed to a constant stream of language using the masculine gender as normative and so learn to think of the typical person as being a man—a step toward adopting the cultural assumption that the man is normative and the woman atypical or deviant. Then I ask them to imagine whether we could have a workable language that did not include gendered words, such as *he*, *she*, *policeman*, *chairman*, and *waitress*, that are already being replaced by more neutral ones. Usually they feel it would be awkward and unworkable, but when they are exposed to Piercy's approach, they are often surprised at how quickly it becomes easy and natural to read language that is not filled with references to gender. Sometimes, as an exercise, we hold small-group discussions in which all personal pronouns must be replaced by *per*. As the exercise begins, l hear bursts of laughter from the groups as they struggle with the unfamiliar forms, but after a few minutes most of the groups settle into the new linguistic requirements with only occasional lapses. Student comments after the exercise often reflect, first, their surprise at their ability to adapt to a genderless language, and second, their observation that when using the neutral pronoun per they often forgot to think of the gender of the person being discussed.

Piercy's novel alters language in a number of ways, highlighting how language is shaped by cultural assumptions and by power relationships. The inhabitants of her utopia have no "family" names, and their first names are chosen or discovered rather than bestowed. She creates new words for new possibilities in relationships and renames familiar concepts and processes in order to make the reader think about them in a new way. This is typical of many writers of the new feminist science fiction (Wiemer, 1987) who, convinced that women's self-expression is constrained by a language that is shaped by and reflects traditional male-female power relationships, are struggling to create new forms of language. This whole enterprise presents psychology students with some interesting possibilities to consider and may ultimately motivate them to delve more deeply into not only the psychology of gender, but also the social psychology of language. Her approach enables me, for example, to ask my students to consider how a particular social relationship is legitimized by being assigned a universally recognized label: wife, husband, mother, father, stepfather. Are there, for instance, roles analogous to Piercy's "co-mothers" that go unrecognized in our society because of the lack of a label?

Because much science fiction now being produced is actually "social science" fiction, its usefulness in teaching psychology extends beyond the examples given here. Some other interesting examples of different visions of equality in male-female relationships can be found in Le Guin's (1974) *The Dispossessed* and Bryant's (1976) *The*

Kin of Ata Are Waiting for You. A more detailed exploration of the relation between language and power is central to Elgin's (1984) *Native Tongue* and Staton's (1975) *From the Legend of Biel.* Gotlieb's (1976) *O Master Caliban* delves into the relation between humans and ever more sophisticated computers. Sargent's (1976, 1978) *More Women of Wonder and The New Women of Wonder* contain many discussion-provoking short stories that challenge conventional notions about gender, including the work of James Tiptree, Jr., who is, in reality, psychologist Alice Sheldon. As stimuli for helping students notice and perhaps break free of their unacknowledged assumptions about people and behavior, these and other works of science fiction can be extremely useful.

References

Bem, S. L., & Bem, D. J. (1970). Case study of a nonconscious ideology: Training the woman to know her place. In D. J. Bem (Ed.), *Beliefs, attitudes, and human affairs* (pp. 89-99). Monterey, CA: Brooks/Cole.

Bryant, D. (1976). *The kin of Ata are waiting for you.* New York: Random House.

Elgin, S. H. (1984). *Native tongue.* New York: DAW Books.

Gotlieb, P. (1976). *O Master Caliban!* New York: Harper & Row.

Le Guin, U. (1969). *The left hand of darkness.* New York: Ace Books.

Le Guin, U. (1974). *The dispossessed.* New York: Harper & Row.

Piercy, M. (1976). *Woman at the edge of time.* New York: Fawcett Crest.

Rose, H. (1988). Dreaming the future. *Hypatia, 3*(1), 119-137.

Sargent, P. (1976). *More women of wonder.* New York: Vintage.

Sargent, P. (1978). *The new women of wonder.* New York: Vintage.

Staton, M. (1975). *From the legend of Biel.* New York: Ace Books.

Wiemer, A. J. (1987). Foreign l(anguish), mother tongue: Concepts of language in contemporary feminist science fiction. *Women's Studies, 14,* 163-173.

Gender Stereotyping in Advertisements

Melinda Jones
University of Pittsburgh at Bradford

Students are seldom aware of how gender stereotypes and expectations develop and are maintained. Messages about appropriate gender roles and behaviors permeate our language, school curriculum, working life, religion, and media (Basow, 1986). The effects of gender stereotypes can be seen on individuals and on society in general. On a personal level evidence suggests that gender stereotypes affect peoples' self-esteem (Whitley, 1983) and psychological well-being (Whitley, 1984). On a societal level, gender stereotypes have contributed to gender bias in hiring decisions (Glick, Zion, & Nelson, 1988). Given these consequences, instructors may want to increase students' awareness of gender stereotypes and how cultural institutions foster gender distinctions. One effective technique to demonstrate the pervasiveness of gender stereotypes is to expose students to mass media, a ubiquitous source of gender stereotypes that both reflects and shapes society.

In an analysis of "gender advertisements," Goffman (1976) found numerous examples of subtle stereotyping in the portrayal of women and men. Five of these are: (a) function ranking (the tendency to depict men in executive roles and as more functional when collaborating with women), (b) relative size (the tendency to depict men as taller and larger than women, except when women are clearly superior in social status), (c) ritualization of subordination (an overabundance of images of women lying on floors and beds or as objects of men's mock assaults), (d) the feminine touch (the tendency to show women cradling and caressing the surface of objects with their fingers), and (e) family (fathers depicted as physically distant from their families or as relating primarily to sons, and mothers depicted as relating primarily to daughters).

This article describes a demonstration that helps students realize that advertisements can communicate messages about gender roles. Using Goffman's framework to analyze selected advertisements leads students to think about advertisements in a novel way and to realize that advertisements not only sell products but also develop and maintain gender stereotypes.

Method

This demonstration requires the instructor to assemble a set of stimulus materials. My preference for stimulus materials is magazine advertisements displayed on slides because slides can be easily presented to large and small classes and the time of their exposure can be controlled. Finding advertisements that illustrate each of the five "genderisms" is not a difficult task. I have used advertisements taken from popular magazines (e.g., *Cosmopolitan*, *Glamour*, *Newsweek*, and *Vogue*), which promote a wide variety of products, including cigarettes, clothes, cologne, liquor, and soft drinks. Some of the selected advertisements depict more than one gender theme. Although not a requirement for the success of the demonstration, I intersperse the recent advertisements with some from the 1950s. This technique allows students to compare the portrayal of the sexes across different decades. To ensure that students do not perceive gender stereotypes when none are present, I also include advertisements that do not fit into Goffman's categories.

First, I introduce students to Goffman's work on advertisements by describing the five gender themes and displaying ads depicting each of these themes. Next, I inform students that they are to view a series of advertisements (20 slides) and instruct them to classify each ad according to Goffman's framework. Then, l remind students that some of the ads may not fit any of the gender themes and that some ads may depict more than one gender theme.

To assist with students' analyses of the advertisements, I provide an answer sheet numbered from 1 to 20, corresponding to each ad to be analyzed, with the names of the five gender themes placed beside each number. Students view each ad for approximately 15 s and respond by circling the "genderisms" they believe are depicted in the ad. After the slide presentation, students review the advertisements and contribute their perceptions of them. Then, I encourage students to use their imaginations to change the sex of the models and see whether the pictures still seem "natural." Usually the students' imaginary advertisements appear unnatural and somewhat silly to them, indicating that advertisements display men and women in roles consistent with our

cultural beliefs. Class discussion focuses on the similarities and differences in the portrayal of men and women in today's advertisements and those of the 1950s. After reviewing the ads, I ask for a show of hands from those who correctly identified all the gender themes. Approximately 40% of the students successfully recognize the gender themes.

Results

Students are often amazed that they have not previously noticed the gender themes. Typical statements made during the discussion include: "It gave me a new and unique outlook into advertising"; "It made me realize some of the gender stereotyping I never considered before"; "I enjoyed looking at advertisements that I usually just take for granted"; "It was interesting to see how advertisers use gender."

Students ($N = 67$) in my recent introductory psychology course evaluated the slide presentation and ensuing discussion of gender stereotyping on several dimensions using scales ranging from *not at all* (1) to *extremely* (7). Students indicated that the demonstration was interesting ($M = 5.92$, $SD = .65$), informative ($M = 5.74$, $SD = .88$), and effective ($M = 5.86$, $SD = .93$) and recommended the use of the demonstration in future classes ($M = 6.35$, $SD = .85$). Students also judged the overall quality of the demonstration on a scale ranging from *poor* (1) to *excellent* (5), and the outcome was very favorable ($M = 4.36$, $SD = .65$).

Discussion

This classroom exercise has many advantages for instructors. First, it is appropriate for use in a variety of courses, including introductory psychology, psychology of women, social psychology, and consumer psychology. Second, it introduces the topic of gender roles and gender stereotyping in a non-threatening manner by using advertisements, a medium that is virtually impossible to ignore (Snyder & DeBono, 1985). Third, this demonstration facilitates discussion on a number of follow-up topics, such as how advertisements influence the viewer and whether advertisers are becoming more sensitive to the portrayal of women in advertisements (Ford, LaTour, & Lundstrom, 1991; Soley & Reid, 1988). Fourth, this discussion gives instructors an opportunity to address the role of imitation learning in acquiring sex-typed behavior in children (Bussey & Bandura, 1984) and to review research indicating that adults may be similarly affected by the content of advertisements (Geis, Brown, Jennings, & Porter, 1984). Finally, instructors may discuss other sources of gender role socialization, such as the educational curriculum and language.

From the students' perspective, this demonstration increases their knowledge of how advertisements communicate messages about gender roles. Student comments after the demonstration often reflect their surprise at the pervasiveness of gender stereotyping in the media and their observation that the media are powerful agents of sexist socialization. The issues surrounding gender stereotypes, particularly the personal implications, are often not carefully considered by college students. This demonstration provides an excellent vehicle for introducing the topic of gender and exploring students' beliefs about the sexes.

References

Basow, S. A. (1986). *Gender stereotypes: Traditions and alternatives* Monterey, CA: Brooks/Cole.

Bussey, K., & Bandura, A. (1984). Influence of gender constancy and social power on sex-linked modeling. *Journal of Personality and Social Psychology, 47*, 1292-1302.

Ford, J. B., LaTour, M. S., & Lundstrom, W. J. (1991). Contemporary women's evaluation of female role portrayals in advertising. *Journal of Consumer Marketing, 8*, 15-28.

Geis, F., Brown, V., Jennings, J., & Porter, N. (1984). TV commercials as achievement scripts for women. *Sex Roles, 10*, 513-525.

Glick, P., Zion, C., & Nelson, C. (1988). What mediates sex discrimination in hiring decisions? *Journal of Personality and Social Psychology, 55*, 178- 186.

Goffman, E. (1976*). Gender advertisements* New York: Harper & Row.

Snyder, M., & DeBono, K. G. (1985). Appeals to image and claims about quality: Understanding the psychology of advertising. *Journal of Personality and Social Psychology, 49*, 586-597.

Soley, L., & Reid, L. (1988). Taking it off: Are models in magazine ads wearing less? *Journalism Quarterly, 65*, 960-966.

Whitley, B. E., Jr. (1983). Sex role orientation and self-esteem: A critical meta-analytic review. *Journal of Personality and Social Psychology, 44*, 765-778.

Whitley, B. E., Jr. (1984). Sex role orientation and psychological well-being: Two meta-analyses. *Sex Roles, 12*, 207-225.

Note

I gratefully acknowledge the helpful comments of Joseph J. Palladino, Jeff S. Topping, and three anonymous reviewers on a draft of this article.

Rethinking the Romance: Teaching the Content and Function of Gender Stereotypes in the Psychology of Women Course

Mary Crawford
University of South Carolina

Gender stereotyping is a core topic in courses on the psychology of women and gender. It is important for students to learn the content of gender stereotypes (i.e., the characteristics that are ascribed to women and men) and their function as social demands. Although gender stereotyping is widespread in the mass media, students have rarely learned to think critically about what they read and see in entertainment media, such as television, comic strips, magazines, and popular fiction. Moreover, many students mistakenly believe that the women's liberation movement of the 1970s freed women from sexism and discrimination, so that today's woman can be and do anything she wants. They are surprised to learn that gender stereotypes show considerable cross-cultural consistency (Williams & Best, 1990), have changed little over the past 30 years (Ruble, 1983; Werner & LaRussa, 1985), and are held by both women and men (Wallston & O'Leary, 1981).

If it is difficult to convince students that gender stereotyping is alive and well in the 1990s, it is even more difficult to convince them that gender stereotypes function not just as static images but as guiding models by which women and men are judged as worthy members of their sex. Because gender stereotypes consist of a network of associations involving personality traits, social roles, behaviors, and psychological characteristics, they have a prescriptive and a descriptive function. They inform people about what behavior ought to be as much as they tell them what it is, providing compelling "scripts" for behavior. Thus, stereotypes operate as mechanisms of social control.

Most textbooks on the psychology of women cover images and stereotypes of women, sexuality, love and relationships, and issues of status and power (Hyde, 1990; Lott, 1994; Unger & Crawford, 1992). As a supplement to the textbook material, for the past 10 years I have used a two-part writing and group discussion project that has been enduringly popular with students and very successful in helping them discover for themselves the content and functions of stereotypical images of women and men. The project is to read a romance novel critically and discuss a set of questions about it with others who have read similar novels. By providing concrete examples of human behavior, books make gender stereotypes more salient to students (Boyatzis, 1992). In addition, novels increase students' motivation to learn and their awareness of how abstract concepts such as gender stereotypes could be reflected in human behavior (Fernald, 1987; Levine, 1983). Whichever textbook or novels are chosen, for maximum educational value in connecting the romance novel's contents to psychological research, it is best to set a due date that follows reading and class discussion of these topics.

Method

The Reading Assignment

Paperback romance novels are ubiquitous. Most students are familiar with the genre and will have no trouble obtaining an example at low cost. Any mass-market bookstore will have several racks devoted to popular series; used copies are readily available for about 25¢ at secondhand bookstores. Many students report borrowing one from a sister, roommate, or friend. I also keep a stock on hand, which I obtain by the bagful at yard sales, to lend to students.

Students are instructed that novels published by Harlequin and Silhouette are eligible. These include the Second Chance at Love series that feature older heroines (a favorite with nontraditional students) and the Candlelight Ecstasy series that are somewhat more sexually explicit than the norm for this genre. Not eligible are historical romances (a.k.a. "bodice-rippers") or those involving supernatural events.

Instructions to students are as follows:

Read a Harlequin romance. In a 5-page paper, analyze its plot and characters for the message it gives about femininity, masculinity, love, and relationships. Connect your analysis to research and theory in (relevant chapters of text). Address the following questions: Why are these books so popular among women, and why do women choose to write them?

Criteria for grading include the extent to which the student has recognized the gender stereotypes in the attributes of the heroine and hero and analyzed the assumptions about women's and men's proper roles and priorities inherent in the plot. Moreover, I look for insights into why these novels are so popular with women. These should go beyond the superficial (e.g., escape) and avoid blaming women for their social position. Useful analyses for instructors to read on this point (which could also be assigned as related reading for more advanced students) are those by Radway (1984) Rose (1985), and Modleski (1980). While grading the papers, I note particularly compelling examples of images of women and men and the social prescriptions for the experience of love and romance. I jot the student's name next to the relevant question for the subsequent class discussion.

Class Discussion

This part of the assignment is essential. Because each student has read a different romance novel, each has arrived independently at an original analysis of similar but not identical instances of stereotyping. Through group discussion and analysis, the solitary reading and writing assignment becomes an opportunity for shared and expanded learning.

I ask one or two students to read aloud the relevant passages in their papers as we discuss responses to such questions as the following: What are the personality traits of the heroine and hero? What are their material resources

Table 1. Project Evaluations From the University of South Carolina and Swarthmore College

Project Evaluations	USC[a]		Swarthmore[b]	
	M	SD	M	SD
In doing this project, I gained in my understanding of how women, men, and gender relations are represented in the mass media.	4.63	.48	4.60	.80
Doing this project added to my understanding of the cultural impact of gender.	4.75	.43	4.80	.40
Doing this project contributed to my interest in the study of women and gender.	4.14	.64	4.80	.40
I would recommend using the Harlequin romance project again in a course of this type.	4.88	.31	4.80	.40

Note. Scores range from strongly disagree (1) to strongly agree (5).
[a]n = 8. [b]n = 5.

and social status? How is falling in love experienced by each? What is the relative importance of love versus work? How are women's multiple identities as daughter, sister, friend, worker, and romantic partner portrayed as integrated or separate?

Students discuss the sexual backgrounds and experience of the female and male characters, the occurrence of sexual coercion in the novels, the absence of recognition of sexually transmitted diseases, and the need for contraception. Finally, I raise the question of the possible effects of repeated exposure to romantic fiction: How do romantic stereotypes and scripts shape the way we interpret our experiences?

The exercise coincides with discussion of the phenomenal popularity of romance novels. Simply by obtaining a book for the assignment, students will have noticed their ready availability. Romance novels account for 25% of all paperback sales in the United States, forming a $250 million industry each year. Each month, 120 new titles are published, and most sell out (Brown, 1989). This information can provoke thought and discussion about the effects of exposure to the genre on the self-perceptions and aspirations of its readers.

Evaluation

I have used the romance novel project in undergraduate and graduate psychology of women courses at four institutions, including a very selective undergraduate liberal arts college, a selective public institution, and two public universities. The schools ranged in size from 1,600 to 25,000 students, and three of the four enrolled more women than men. In all four, the majority of psychology majors and psychology of women students were women.

Evaluations of the romance novel project in a Psychology of Women course at the University of South Carolina and at Swarthmore College revealed strong positive reactions to the assignment (see Table 1). Students rated the assignment on its effectiveness at exposing representations of women and men in mass media and increasing knowledge and interest in the cultural impact of gender. Students were nearly unanimous in recommending that future students read romance novels for the course.

Their comments about the romance project were as follows: (a) "Doing this assignment . . . made me realize just how much my consciousness has, and continues to be, raised. Now everything I read or see is held to much more scrutiny," (b) "Saw how insidious [mass media representations of women and men] can be"; (c) "Came away from [the assignment] with new understanding and renewed anger"; (d) "This project has raised my awareness of . . . the troubling issue of romance as the ultimate goal for women."

At various times I have experimented with giving students a choice of two out of three short writing assignments. Typical options included the romance project, a personal essay on "Gender in My Family," and an analysis of sexism in a print advertisement. Although the romance novel project is the only option that requires extra reading, it has been chosen at least as often as the other options. For example, at West Chester University, 80% of students chose the romance novel project, compared with 70% for the family essay and 47% for the advertisement essay. When the assignment is optional, those who did not do it can still learn from the class discussion.

Discussion

Reading a romance novel takes little time. Most are only about 200 pages, and all constitute a quick read. Most students approach the assignment eagerly and in a spirit of adventure. They often report completing the reading in one sitting, although one male student noted that he took his romance novel along on spring break—in a plain brown wrapper!

Students receive positive feedback on their analysis of the novel by being asked to share portions of it with their classmates. They learn more about the concept of a literary genre when they directly compare the formulaic plots and the stereotypic attributes of heroines and heroes. Most important, they come to see aspects of gender that were previously unexamined, and this can be a powerful experience. The cumulative effect of 12 or more romance novels, all with naive, malleable heroines and experienced, dynamic heroes engaged in a predictable game of domination and submission, can teach students more about the content and function of gender stereotypes than any other single assignment.

References

Boyatzis, C. J. (1992). Let the caged bird sing: Using literature to teach developmental psychology. *Teaching of Psychology, 19,* 221-222.

Brown, E. A. (1989, June 9). Happily ever after. *Christian Science Monitor,* p. 13.

Fernald, L. D. (1987). Of windmills and rope dancing: The instructional value of narrative structures. *Teaching of Psychology, 14,* 214-216.

Hyde, J. S. (1990). *Understanding human sexuality* (4th ed.). New York: McGraw-Hill.

Levine, R. V. (1983). An interdisciplinary course studying psychological issues through literature. *Teaching of Psychology, 10,* 214-216.

Lott, B. (1994). *Women's lives: Themes and variations in gender learning* (2nd ed.). Pacific Grove, CA: Brooks/Cole.

Modleski, T. (1980). The disappearing act: A study of Harlequin romances. *Signs, 5,* 435-448.

Radway, J. (1984). *Reading the romance: Women, patriarchy, and popular literature*. Chapel Hill, NC: University of North Carolina Press.

Rose, S. (1985). Is romance dysfunctional? *International Journal of Women's Studies, 8*, 250-265.

Ruble, T. L. (1983). Sex stereotypes: Issues of change in the 1970s. *Sex Roles, 9*, 397-402.

Unger, R., & Crawford, M. (1992). *Women and gender: A feminist psychology*. New York: McGraw-Hill.

Wallston, B., & O'Leary, V. (1981). Sex makes a difference: Differential perceptions of women and men. In L. Wheeler (Ed.), *Review of personality and social psychology* (Vol. 2, pp. 9-41). Beverly Hills: Sage.

Werner, P. D., & LaRussa, G. W. (1985). Persistence and change in sex-role stereotypes. *Sex Roles, 12*, 1089-1100.

Williams, J. E., & Best, D. L. (1990). *Measuring sex stereotypes: A multination study*. Newbury Park, CA: Sage.

Note

I thank Ruth L. Ault and three anonymous reviewers for their helpful comments on a draft of this article, Lori Fitton for assistance in manuscript preparation, and Jeanne Marecek for collecting evaluation data from her Swarthmore College class.

Gender Bias in Leader Selection

Michelle R. Hebl
Texas A&M University

The pervasiveness of stereotypes and how they affect behavior are often not evident to students. Helping students see this relation is also not easily illustrated through textbooks or class discussions. The present exercise is designed to show the possible behavioral ramifications of gender stereotyping. Specifically, students experience firsthand gender stereotyping when they select leaders of small, mixed-sex groups.

Past research has indicated that men are significantly more likely to be chosen as leaders than women in initially leaderless, mixed-sex groups (Eagly & Karau, 1991). Gender stereotypes about leadership may have influenced these findings. For example, subjects endorsed the abilities to "separate feelings from ideas," "act as leaders," and "make decisions" as being much more descriptive of men than women (Broverman, Vogel, Broverman, Clarkson, & Rosenkrantz, 1972, p. 63). These and other stereotypically masculine items have been positively correlated with college students' perceptions of leaders (Lord, De Vader, & Alliger, 1986). Eagly and Mladinic (1989) proposed that gender stereotypes also are comprised of beliefs that men occupy advantaged social positions of power and status relative to women. Such views lead people to perceive men as more in control and more powerful than women,

even when they are not. Indeed, research by Porter, Geis, and Jennings (1983) revealed that, given an ambiguous setting involving both men and women, independent raters perceive men to be in charge much more often than women.

Stereotypes about women may also enhance biases in leader selection (Geis, Brown, Jennings, & Corrado-Taylor, 1984; Nye & Forsyth, 1991). Geis, Brown, Jennings, and Porter (1984) suggested the most general stereotype about women is that they are not autonomous and are unqualified to assume achievement-oriented responsibilities in the world. However, women, relative to men, are believed to be more "talkative," "tactful," and "aware of others' feelings" (Broverman et al., 1972, p. 63), as well as more expressive and communal (Eagly & Mladinic, 1989). Thus, gender stereotyping may have a differential impact on leader selection when type of leadership is manipulated (Eagly & Karau 1991). Whereas task-oriented competitive leaders focus on task contributions and productivity, social cooperative leaders focus on social contributions, prosocial behavior, and social climate. Male group members make more task-oriented contributions than do females (Wood,1987), so group members may choose male leaders in task-oriented competitive situations. However, social leaders may focus on prosocial behaviors, so men may be selected as social leaders less often than they are selected as task-oriented competitive leaders.

The present demonstration illustrates the gender bias in leader selection. The type of group leadership (task-oriented competitive or social cooperative) is manipulated across groups.[1] Men were expected to emerge as leaders more often than women in task-oriented competitive groups but not in social cooperative groups.

Procedure

Students are divided into groups of four or six, each comprised of an equal number of men and women. Any students left over can be grouped together and their data later discarded or analyzed separately. If possible, students should not know other members of their group because previous direct experience may override the heuristics of gender stereotyping and weaken the effects of the demonstration.

The demonstration should be used before students read about gender stereotypes and group dynamics. The activity can be introduced as a psychology game. Distribute written instructions describing the group task to each member of each group; otherwise, the person receiving or reading the instructions may be chosen or accepted as the leader. The two sets of instructions are as follows:

Task-Oriented Competitive
You will be playing a board game with your group. The board game involves competition against another group, and you will focus on specific tasks. You should try your hardest to win the game. To do

this, you should focus on the game's objectives as much as possible. To start, your group should first select a person who will be in charge of the group. After this leader is selected, specific instructions about the game will be given and you will start playing.

Social Cooperative
You will be playing a board game with your group. The board game does not involve winning but, instead, involves agreeing with each other, supporting one another, and setting aside differences in order to get along maximally with each other. To start, your group should first select a person who will be in

charge of the group. After this leader is selected, specific instructions about the game will be given and you will start playing.

Students take 2 min to read their instructions and select group leaders. Groups are not specifically instructed about how to select leaders. Any method of nomination and selection is acceptable as long as all group members ultimately agree on the leader.

After verifying that leaders for each group have been chosen, the instructor informs the groups that they will not play a game after all. Instead, the actual purpose of the activity was to examine leader selection and processes. The gender of each student chosen as task-oriented and social leaders is compiled. The instructor or a student volunteer can tally both the gender of the leader selected as well as the technique each group used in selecting its leader.

Results

This study examined leader selection in 103 groups of introductory psychology students, with two men and two women comprising each group. Students participated in one of eight sessions that varied from 30 to 250 members each. Fifty-one of the groups received the task-oriented competitive instructions, and 52 groups received the social cooperative instructions. The results, by gender and type of instruction, are displayed in Table 1.

A binomial test revealed that, as predicted, significantly more men than women were selected as leaders, $z = 2.66$, $p < .01$. Also as predicted, a chi-square test using the Yates correction revealed that, as the type of instruction differed, the gender of the leader selected also differed, $\chi^2(1, N = 103) = 8.93$, $p < .01$. This significant effect is largely attributable to the underselection of women for task-oriented group activities (11 observed and 18.8 expected) coupled with the overselection of women as leaders of social activity groups (27 observed and 19.2 expected).

[1]It may be possible to differentiate a social orientation from cooperation and a task orientation from competition. Future research may address this issue by including social competitive instructions and task-oriented cooperative instructions in addition to the social cooperative and task-oriented competitive instructions described herein.

Table 1. Number of Leaders Selected by Gender and Instructions

Type of Instruction	Gender		Total
	Men	Women	
Task-oriented			
Observed	40	11	
Expected	32.2	18.8	
			51
Social			
Observed	25	27	
Expected	32.8	19.2	
			52
Total	65	38	103

Evaluation

To evaluate the impact of the demonstration, 71 students completed a questionnaire about the activity. They responded on a 7-point scale ranging from *not at all* (1) *to very much* (7). Items on the scale and mean ratings were as follows: (a) This activity would be a valuable addition to a class discussion on stereotypes ($M = 6.24$). (b) This activity gave me a clear understanding of the influence of stereotypes on behavior ($M = 5.97$). (c) How aware of stereotypes' influence on leadership behavior are you as a result of this demonstration ($M = 6.38$)? (d) This activity would benefit other students in psychology ($M = 6.06$).

Students were also asked for additional comments about the activity. Only positive aspects of the exercise were mentioned, such as the following: (a) "This activity was a good way of meeting others and loosening up the classroom." (b) "Very interesting . . . surprising . . . opens many questions." (c) "It's interesting how gender subconsciously affects our decisions." (d) "After you explained it, it really made sense. I never thought about stereotypes in that way." (e) "Most people already realize that there are stereotypes, but this graphically demonstrates how prevalent they are." (f) "I was fooled. I really thought we were going to play a game and nominated our leader because he was the tallest and biggest member of the group, and he looked like he already had authority."

Discussion

Results revealed that, overall, leadership positions were most likely to be filled by men, but this finding was evident only under task-oriented competitive conditions in which the ratio of male to female leaders was nearly four to one. Eagly and Karau (1991) suggested that, as leadership goals change from a position that requires task-oriented behaviors to one requiring socially complex tasks or the maintenance of good interpersonal relationships and group harmony, slightly more women than men emerge as leaders. Although a comparable finding was not statistically significant in the present study, data from the social cooperative instructions were in that direction. The classroom activity produces reliable and provocative effects that should make students more cognizant of gender stereotypes and their effects on leader selection.

Class discussion after the activity could be stimulated by the following questions:

1. Discuss the selection procedure. Did men or women more commonly nominate themselves? Which gender was more commonly nominated by other group members? What were the common procedures used in selecting leaders? In the present study, students' descriptions of their selection process included (a) "He was chosen because he was the tallest . . . he looked like he should be in charge,"

(b) "I knew from the beginning he would be the leader-he just looked the part," and (c) "The two women in our group asked him to be the leader."

2. Discuss the stereotypes students use in selecting leaders. When and why are stereotypes about men and women likely to influence leader selection? Are these stereotypes used when the groups meet for longer periods of time?

3. Discuss possible causes for the bias against female leaders. In everyday life, we witness more men than women as leaders; how may that affect leader selection? Do women avoid leadership positions? When women become leaders, how are they typically viewed in comparison with men?

4. Examine the gender differences that result when the task becomes one in which a social leader is required. Why does the gender bias disappear?

One possible variation of this demonstration is to assign groups to either feminine or masculine sex-typed activities. For instance, one group may be told to choose a leader for their discussion of the use of cloth versus disposable diapers for babies. The other group's discussion topic may be the choice of repairing cars at home with the guidance of manuals and friends versus taking the car to a repair shop. The visibility of stereotypes should be demonstrated as women are selected more often when the task is feminine sex-typed and men when the task is masculine sex-typed. In both cases, gender stereotypes guide individuals in their selection of leaders.

References

Broverman, I. K., Vogel, S. R., Broverman, D. M., Clarkson, F. E., & Rosenkrantz, P. S. (1972). Sex-role stereotypes: A current appraisal. *Journal of Social Issues, 28(2)*, 59-78.

Eagly, A. H., & Karau, S. J. (1991). Gender and the emergence of leaders. *Journal of Personality and Social Psychology, 60*, 685-710.

Eagly, A. H., & Mladinic, A. (1989). Gender stereotypes and attitudes coward women and men. *Personality and Social Psychology Bulletin, 15*, 543-558.

Geis, F. L., Brown, V., Jennings, S., & Corrado-Taylor, D. (1984). Sex versus status in sex-associated stereotypes. *Sex Roles, 11*, 771-785.

Geis, F. L, Brown, V., Jennings, J., & Porter, N. (1984). TV commercials as achievement scripts for women. *Sex Roles, 10*, 513-524.

Lord, R. G., De Vader, D. I., & Alliger, G. M. (1986). A meta-analysis of the relation between personality traits and leadership perceptions: An application of validity generalization procedures. *Journal of Applied Psychology, 71*, 402 410.

Nye, J. L., & Forsyth, D. R. (1991). The effects of prototype-based biases on leadership appraisals: A test of leadership categorization theory. *Small Group Research, 22*, 360-379.

Porter, N., Geis, F. L., & Jennings, J. W. (1983). Are women invisible as leaders? *Sex Roles, 9,* 1035-1049.

Wood, W. (1987). Meta-analytic review of sex differences in group performance. *Psychological Bulletin, 102,* 53-71.

Notes

1. An earlier version of this article was presented at the 16th annual National Institute on the Teaching of Psychology, St. Petersburg Beach, FL, January 1993.
2. I thank Ludy Benjamin, Jr., Deborah Kashy, and Wendy Wood for their assistance in preparing this article and Ruth Ault and three anonymous reviewers for their helpful comments on an earlier version.

Filmed in Black and White: Teaching the Concept of Racial Identity at a Predominantly White University

Harriette W. Richard
Northern Kentucky University

In answer to calls for diversity, many institutions have included in either their general studies requirement or elective selection a course on race, gender, or both. Youngstrom (1992) cited Guzman's warning that psychology departments cannot have quality and excellence if their programs lack diversity. Exposure to perspectives on race enhance college students' experiences even when contact with minority groups is limited (Whitten, 1993). The American Psychological Association's Division Two (Teaching of Psychology) created a task force on diversity to investigate how instructors incorporate issues of diversity into their classrooms. Preliminary findings indicate that, for survey respondents (adjunct to full professor), issues of diversity involve ethnicity and social class (86.3%) and racial identification (43.4%). Heightening sensitivity and

Table 1. Definition of Black and White Racial Identity Stages

Stage	Definition
Black racial identity	
1. Preencounter	Person denigrates Black culture, idealizes White culture, and denies personal significance of race or racism.
2. Encounter	Person questions self and others about racial issues. Stage terminates with a decision to restructure one's racial identity.
3. Immersion/emersion	Phase 1—Person shows extreme anger, idealizes everything Black, and denigrates and avoids everything White.
	Phase 2—Person actively redefines *self* according to Black and African historical perspectives.
4. Internalization	Person adopts positive realistic Black identity, interacts with others from a humanistic orientation, and fights oppression.
White racial identity	
1. Contact	Person is oblivious to own racial characteristics ("color-blind") and pretends others have none, is naive, and shows "accidental" insensitivity.
2. Disintegration	Person consciously acknowledges own White identity and experiences race-related moral dilemmas from the perspective of an unfairly advantaged group.
3. Reintegration	Person resolves racial moral dilemmas by trying to reestablish a status quo in which Whites are superior and entitled to privilege and Blacks are inferior and entitled to disadvantage.
4. Pseudoindependence	Person has an intellectualized awareness of own race and societal racial issues. "Intelligent non-Whites" are the best ones to understand and explain racism.
5. Immersion/emersion	Person honestly appraises what it means to be White in this society.
6. Autonomy	Person adopts a positive realistic White identity, interacts with others from a humanistic orientation, and fights oppression.

Note. From *Training Manual for Diagnosing Racial Identity in Social Interactions* (pp. 7–12), by J. E. Helms, 1990b, Topeka, KS: Content Communications. Copyright 1990 by Janet E. Helms. Adapted with permission.

awareness (86.3 %) was the highest ranking goal (Sexton-Radek et al., 1995).

Assignments that highlight issues of race and gender are valuable when placed in the context of theories of racial identity. The two most prominent theories are by Cross and Thomas (Cross, 1978) for Black individuals and by Helms (1990a) for White individuals. Cross and Thomas proposed that Black individuals move through four racial identity stages, starting with preencounter (Eurocentric viewing of the world and devaluing their Afrocentric self) and ending with internalization (integrating full understanding of cultural self into their identity; Mosley-Howard & Harris, 1993). Helms's (1990a) theory described five stages in White individuals' movement from contact (naiveté and color blindness) to autonomy (nonracist and activist). Table 1 outlines the stages in more detail.

Outside activities, especially self-directed projects, can enhance students' learning (Rickabaugh, 1993) . Many authors have written about the merits of having psychology students analyze films (e.g., Anderson, 1992; Bolt, 1976, Boyatzis, 1994). None of these authors, however, has dealt with controversial issues. A film analysis can be effective when the topic is controversial and, as in this case, personal. Presenting evidence for placing a character in a particular stage is not threatening or self-incriminating. Because students are not determining or justifying their own stage of racial identity development but analyzing a character's statements and motives, they can be more critical in their analyses.

In addition, this assignment is a way for students and faculty to understand the role race plays in our psychological makeup. Just as our culture defines us by gender, height, and looks, race functions in most situations to portray us to others and dictate our own attitudes and behavior. This assignment helps us see that not only racial minority status but also White racial identity affects our view of the world and ourselves.

Assignment

On the first day of class, students were told of the assignment—to trace the development of a character from a movie or a book using two stages of either the Black racial identity or White racial identity model. During the first 2 weeks, the instructor defined such terms as *race* and *ethnicity* and led students in interactive activities and exercises designed to break down barriers of race, gender, and class. The activities, drawn from Chan and Disch (1994), included student pairs telling each other the first time they were aware of racial and gender differences and what those differences meant for them. Thus, the backdrop for the assignment was an open dialogue about course topics.

To prepare for the next four 50-min class meetings, students read the nigrescence or Black racial identity model (Cross, 1978; Parham, 1989; see Santrock, 1993, for

Table 2. Movies and Characters Exemplifying Black and White Racial Identity Stages

Stage	Movie	Character
Black racial identity		
Preencounter	*Imitation of Life*	Sara Jane
Encounter	*Do the Right Thing*	Buggin Out
	Super Fly	Priest
Immersion/emersion	*Malcolm X*	Malcolm X
Internalization	*The Ernest Green Story*	Ernest Green
White racial identity		
Contact	*Forrest Gump*	Forrest Gump
Disintegration	*Guess Who's Coming to Dinner*	Matt
Reintegration	*Do the Right Thing*	Pino
Pseudoindependence	*Driving Miss Daisy*	Miss Daisy
Immersion/emersion	*To Kill a Mockingbird*	Scout
Autonomy	*Cadence*	Bean

a simplified explanation) and *A Race is a Nice Thing to Have* (Helms, 1992), which outlines Helms's (1990a) White racial identity model. The instructor reviewed the stages in each theory and gave illustrations of statements indicative of each stage (see Parham, 1989, for examples pertaining to nigrescence). The unit ended with a discussion of the details of the assignment. Students could select any movie or book character that illustrated their comprehension of two stages of Black or White racial identity. They had about 2 weeks to write a four- to five-page paper that defined two stages of either model and illustrated those stages with statements about the character's actions. Beginning the day the written papers were due, students also made 5- to 10-min oral, illustrated presentations on one of the stages for their movie or book character (see Table 2 for selected examples). Three class sessions later, students took an examination on the theories.

The grade for the written paper, worth 70% of the assignment points, was based on comprehensiveness, analysis, quality of presentation, and grammar. The oral presentation was worth 30% of the total assignment, and the grade was based on organization, clarity, and style of presentation. If students selected the same film but analyzed different characters, they could combine their oral presentations in a panel discussion. In my class, only two or three groups of students reviewed the same film.

Evaluation

Of the 38 students (37 White and 1 Black) in two sections of The Psychology of Race and Gender, 34 chose a film character and 4 selected a book character. Twenty-one students (55%) used the Black racial identity model, 17 (45%) used the White. The examination was multiple choice, in which students were required to identify the stage of each speaker after reading various statements under the sections Black racial identity and White racial identity. The examination grades ($M = 84$, $SD = 6.7$) for the complex issues of identity illustrated that students learned the stages and could identify them in various contexts. The average test grade for the previous test in The Psychology of Race and Gender class was lower ($M = 81$, $SD = 13.6$).

Students anonymously completed an evaluation form assessing the assignment 1 week after oral presentations. Because the same instructor taught both sections in the same semester, evaluation data from all students were pooled. Students responded to four questions on a scale ranging from 1 (*not at all*) to 5 (*very much*). The means (and *SD*s) for understanding Black and White racial identity were 3.9 ($SD = .85$) and 3.6 ($SD = 1.0$), respectively. The means for understanding another ethnic group and your own were 3.5 ($SD = 1.0$) and 3.0 ($SD = 1.2$), respectively. These seemingly mediocre ratings for understanding the theories may be due to students' lack of exposure to any racial identity theory. The test data indicate that students learned the material, even though their self-reported ratings do not show much confidence in what they learned. Identifying themselves as part of a racial or ethnic group may not be a new experience for most of the students. However, analyzing what each test or movie character's statement and stage imply about where he or she is in racial identity development is a new experience.

Three other questions called for yes-no responses. All students circled yes indicating that the assignment should be continued, 87% wanted the written assignment continued, but only 66% wanted the oral assignment continued. The last two questions on the evaluation were open ended: "What did you like most about the assignment?" and "How would you improve the assignment ?" Typically, students said "This gave me an excuse to see a movie that had value and that was eye opening," "I really liked listening to the total presentations," and "I liked watching a movie for homework." Overwhelmingly, students found the analysis of the character, seeing him or her move from one stage to another, most intriguing. To improve the assignment, students suggested (a) introducing the racial identity theories earlier in the semester, (b) completing the oral assignment before the test on the stages, (c) allowing more time for the oral report, (d) having students turn in a rough draft before the final paper, and (e) giving students a suggested list of movies and books. (Such a list is available from the author.)

Discussion

Students were enthusiastic about examining a theoretical model of racial identity. They were also excited about sharing their understanding of the characters' stages of racial identity. Unfortunately, in the oral presentation many students wanted to tell the entire story, then identify the character's movements through the stages. A few students sought help with identifying their characters'

stages. The handout given them with examples and definitions was invaluable (Helms, 1990b).

Some students indicated the need to view five or six videotapes before finding an appropriate one. Four students chose a book because they had difficulty selecting a videotape or preferred written material. A suggested listing of movies and books would solve this problem. Some students chose a film they had already watched or one that involved a character's search to find himself or herself. Few students selected a film simply because it featured a particular actor or actress. Students were encouraged to find appropriate material available at local video stores.

A few students wanted to apply the Black racial identity model to groups other than Blacks. This provided an excellent opportunity to help students understand that research gathered and designed for use with specific populations should not be generalized to other populations. The topic of overgeneralizations can be extended to other course issues, such as health insurance, gender, and heart disease. For example, research on heart disease, usually gathered on men, is not generalizable to women. This set breaking helps students see racial issues as connected to issues of oppression as opposed to being fragmented special interests.

After the assignment, students became more comfortable discussing issues of race and ethnicity. One asked, for example, "Why is there a Miss Black America pageant?" I guide the subsequent class discussion by suggesting other pertinent factors to consider: "What has been the history of the Miss America pageant?," "Who has watched both pageants?," and "Are there different standards of beauty for the two pageants?" Using racial identity models, students can see the issue from various theoretical perspectives. For instance, if one does not see color, as in the first stage of White racial identity, then the question of a Miss Black America is valid. However, if one uses Stage 4 of Black racial identity, then the question may be absurd.

This assignment provided students with a lively, memorable, and objective way to study racial identity. It allowed students to view and discuss movies they might not have seen. Students may or may not agree with a character's statements, but each student could examine the statements objectively. Students could discuss issues of race or ethnicity without being defensive about their own personal statements or attitudes. The assignment can stand on its own merits in a race and gender class, but I found the addition of the Chan and Disch (1994) activities handout helpful. In addition, the assignment to analyze characters is not limited to a race and gender course; it can be used in other courses to create an open dialogue. The exercise was enjoyable for faculty and students and assisted students in beginning to understand subtle messages and examine complex racial issues.

References

Anderson, D. D. (1992). Using feature films as tools for analysis in a psychology and law course. *Teaching of Psychology, 19*, 155-158.

Bolt, M. (1976). Using films based on literature in teaching psychology. *Teaching of Psychology, 3*, 189-190.

Boyatzis, C. J. (1994). Using feature films to teach social development. *Teaching of Psychology, 21*, 99-101.

Chan, C., & Disch, E. (1994, June). *Diversity awareness exercises.* Paper presented at the Seventh Annual National Conference on Race and Ethnicity in American Higher Education, Atlanta, GA.

Cross, W. E., Jr. (1978). The Thomas and Cross models of psychological nigrescence: A review. *Journal of Black Psychology, 5*, 13-31.

Helms, J. E. (Ed.). (1990a). *Black and White racial identity: Theory, research and practice.* Westport, CT: Greenwood.

Helms, J. E. (1990b). *Training manual for diagnosing racial identity in social interactions.* Topeka, KS: Content Communications.

Helms, J. E. (1992). *A race is a nice thing to have.* Topeka, KS: Content Communications.

Mosley-Howard, G. S., & Harris, Y. R. (1993). Teaching a course in African-American Psychology. *Teaching of Psychology, 20*, 234-235.

Parham, T. A. (1989). Cycles of psychological nigrescence. *The Counseling Psychologist, 17*, 187-226.

Rickabaugh, C. A. (1993). The psychology portfolio: Promoting writing and critical thinking about psychology. *Teaching of Psychology, 20*, 170-172.

Santrock, J. W. (Ed.). (1993*). Adolescence.* Madison, WI: Brown & Benchmark.

Sexton-Radek, K., Lundquist, A., Richard, H., Simoni, J., Yescavage, K., & Behling, C. (1995, August). *Embraced by the light of diversity.* Poster presented at the annual meeting of the American Psychological Association, New York.

Whitten, L. A. (1993). Infusing Black psychology into the introductory psychology course. *Teaching of Psychology, 20*, 13-21.

Youngstrom, N. (1992, February). Adapt to diversity or risk irrelevance, field warned. *APA Monitor, p. 44.*

Note

A list of suggested films and books and a detailed explanation of the stages will he mailed upon request.

Unveiling Positions of Privilege: A Hands-On Approach to Understanding Racism

Sandra M. Lawrence
Mount Holyoke College

Teaching courses involving racism and other forms of oppression to White, middle-class undergraduates can be difficult for a host of reasons (Adams & Zhou-Govern, 1994; Sleeter, 1994; Tatum, 1992, 1994). For one, White undergraduates tend to view racism as synonymous with personal prejudice (Wellman, 1993) and are less likely to consider racism as deeply rooted in systems of advantage. Teaching White, middle-class students about racism is further complicated because race- and class-privileged positions are often invisible to them, therefore White students do not see themselves as race privileged. They have been educated, both formally and informally, not to see color or, when they do, to minimize its importance (Helms, 1990, 1995; Katz, 1978). Making race more visible for students holding onto this "colorblind orientation" (Frankenberg, 1993) is an important step in helping students understand how racism functions in this society.

One successful classroom exercise that enables students to see the privileged positions of the White, middle class involves a collaborative activity of making mobiles. Schniedewind and Davidson (1983) designed this activity for elementary and middle school teachers who wanted to help their students understand how institutional racism, sexism, classism, and other forms of oppression lead to inequalities in resources. The creators also expected this activity to provide school-aged children with an opportunity to witness how individuals or groups who are targets of oppression are often blamed for the inequalities imposed on them.

As I read the description of this exercise, it was evident to me that this exercise could be a powerful means for revealing to White college students their "White privilege" (McIntosh, 1988), an abundance of advantages that they often have trouble seeing. The capacity to make the invisible visible is the primary reason I incorporated this exercise into my curriculum and have used it successfully for 4 years with sophomore, junior, and senior students in a Race, Class, Culture, and Gender course.

Method

For the mobile activity, 21 White, female students from predominantly middle-class backgrounds sat in groups of 4 (one group of 5) at five tables separated from one another. I began the class by asking students in each group to work collaboratively to compose a working definition of an abstract concept related to the course. One term that I often used is *multiculturalism* (others such as *social justice*, *equity*, and *tolerance* could also be used). While the group members exchanged ideas and took notes on their discussion, I placed a packet of materials for making a mobile on each table.

All five packets contained basic construction elements for making mobiles, but three of the packets contained more elaborate materials. For example, the packet with the least materials contained a 12-in. wooden dowel, one coat hanger, two pieces of construction paper, and a spool of thread. The packet with the most materials contained three dowels, two coat hangers, string, fishing line, precut wire, 10 pieces of colored paper, felt tip markers, crayons, pipe cleaners, streamers, scissors, ribbon, pom-poms, glue, and tape.[1]

I gave students 15 min to reach consensus on their definitions (even though they could have continued for longer); thereafter, I instructed them to work with their group men1bers for 30 min to create a mobile representative of their definition using only the materials provided. At the conclusion of the mobile construction period, I asked students to demonstrate their finished products to the class. I asked the group with the most

resources to present first, followed by the group with the least materials. Once students displayed their mobiles, I asked one open-ended question: "What was it like for you to participate in this exercise?" During the discussion, students remarked about the feelings and ideas that occurred to them during the exercise. As a follow-up assignment, I asked students to reflect in writing either about their experience during the class session or about their thoughts concerning one of the required readings dealing with racism.

Results and Discussion

From the beginning of the mobile task, groups with minimal materials were hampered and frustrated by limited resources. As they noticed the lavish materials of more privileged groups, they muttered about the "unfairness" of the exercise. In reflection papers, students wrote about their feelings trying to make do with their inadequate supplies although others had abundant materials. They also commented on their reluctance to display their projects knowing they could have created more artistic mobiles if they had received better resources. In describing their feelings, students in these disadvantaged groups remarked about being angry and "feeling robbed and cheated."

Once out of their "less privileged" roles, students learned more about the real privilege they do have. They had an opportunity to "stand in someone else's shoes" if only for a brief period and gain a new perspective. One student described in writing the impact the exercise had on her thinking about power and privilege:

> I came out of today's class thinking that it was, very possibly, the best class I have had so far at the college. I realized many things during this class. . . . Most important, I felt "underprivileged" for probably the first time in my life. . . . It showed me that American's underprivileged children DO feel cheated and DO notice that others have what they don't have. I can see why what you are given DOES make a difference. . . . It was an immediate feeling like something had clicked in my head and I now had a new understanding.

This student, like others, realized that groups who get less are aware of the differential treatment they receive even if those in more privileged positions are oblivious to those differences. They also learned that power and privilege have a direct bearing on chances for academic success and social mobility.

Although all of the students in the less privileged groups recognized the inequality of materials during mobile construction, not one student in the privileged groups noticed that some groups had fewer materials. These students began to recognize that some groups were advantaged (and others were not) only during the discussion following the demonstration when less privileged groups shared their feelings. Only then did the

---

[1]For those making these packets, be sure to prepare packets two and three with increasing amounts of "meager" materials. Packet four should contain scissors plus an assortment of "lavish" materials bur not as many as packet five.

students privileged with a colorful array of construction elements come to understand what had occurred, and they were shocked that they did not notice sooner. One privileged student wrote about how unaware she and her group members were to the unequal conditions in the room:

> It never occurred to me that there were differences in the materials that were distributed. . . . I was in the upper middle class group, completely unaware of my position or privilege, just because I was content with what I had. I had no desire to be interested in the other groups. I kept my blinders on to the inequalities.

Another member of a privileged group, "amazed at her obviousness" to the differential treatment during the exercise, remarked about the shame she felt at the thoughts she entertained about her classmates' abilities. When the second group demonstrated their rather drab mobile, she found herself questioning the group's creativity:

> It actually occurred to me, "what was wrong with them that they didn't make a colorful collage?" I imagined that perhaps they weren't as creative as our group was, or they spent too much time planning what they were going to do, instead of actually doing it. . . . I was so ashamed that I thought that.

Other students in privileged groups found themselves thinking similar negative thoughts about their classmates' motivation, organizational skills, and ability to focus. Once out of their roles, they realized how their privileged status had kept them from seeing the reasons for their classmates' poor performance. They also recognized similarities in their assumptions and those commonly made in reference to the poor academic performance of some students of low income or of color, attributing differences in performance to deficiencies within students rather than to systems of inequality in operation (Darling-Hammond, 1995; Nieto, 1992).

By reflecting on their obliviousness and the invalid assumptions they were quick to make, students were able to understand their own race and class privilege. In fact, 15 of the 21 students who participated in the mobile exercise reported in their writings that the activity had a profound effect on their views of themselves and others. Students related in writing how the class session "surprised," "rattled," or "jolted" them into a greater understanding of the advantages they receive because of their positions in society. From this experience, students also learned that they needed to look beyond their assumptions and stereotypes to understand the differences in performance that many people targeted by race and class oppression display. Because race and class stratification are not often visible to those in privileged positions, they acknowledged their need to be more vigilant and ask questions of the institutional policies and practices in place, instead focusing on those targeted by oppression and asking "what's wrong with them?"

Conclusions

Because attitudes and beliefs about race are deeply rooted and often long-standing, I would be remiss to claim that any single class activity, no matter how carefully designed or implemented, could change those attitudes. Research has demonstrated, however, that semester-long courses in the psychology of racism and antiracist education can be successful in both altering belief systems and changing racist behaviors (Lawrence & Bunche, 1996; Lawrence & Tatum, 1997; Tatum, 1992, 1994). Such courses combine readings, films, reflective writing, and experiential activities in ways that create dissonance (often painful) in students' knowledge and perceptions about themselves and society. Establishing trusting classroom environments that invite risk taking and provide ample opportunities to process emotional reactions that often accompany new ways of viewing the self and the world are essential.

Although one activity cannot effect change, it can initiate that process. Through this brief exercise, White, middle-class undergraduates had the opportunity to try on a new pair of spectacles, lenses that enabled them to see their privileged positions, while at the same time bringing their assumptions about those less privileged into clearer view, a requisite step in unlearning racism.

References

Adams, M., & Zhou-McGovern, Y. (1994, April). *The sociomoral development of undergraduates in a "social diversity" course: Theory, research, and instructional applications.* Paper presented at the meeting of the American Educational Research Association, New Orleans, LA.

Darling-Hammond, L. (1995). Inequality and access to knowledge. In J. A. Banks & C. A. McGee-Banks (Eds.), *Handbook of research on multicultural education (pp. 465-483).* New York: Macmillan.

Frankenberg, R. (1993). *White women, race matters: The social construction of whiteness.* Minneapolis: University of Minnesota Press.

Helms, J. E. (Ed.). (1990). *Black and White racial identity: Theory, research and practice.* Westport, CT: Greenwood.

Helms, J. E. (1995). An update of Helms's White and people of color racial identity models. In J. G. Ponterotto, J. M. Casas, L. P. Suzuki, & C. M. Alexander (Eds.), *Handbook of multicultural counseling* (pp. 181-197). Thousand Oaks, CA: Sage.

Katz, J. H. (1978). *White awareness: Handbooks for anti-racism training.* Norman: University of Oklahoma Press.

Lawrence, S. M., & Bunche, T. (1996). Feeling and dealing: Teaching White students about racial privilege. *Teaching and Teacher Education, 12*, 531-542.

Lawrence, S. M., & Tatum, B. D. (1997). White educator as allies: Moving from awareness to action. In M. Fine, L. Weiss, L. Powell, & M. Wong (Eds.), *Off White: Readings on race, power, and society* (pp. 333-342). New York: Routledge.

Mclntosh, P. (1988). *White privilege and male privilege: A personal account of coming to see correspondences through work in women's studies* (Working Paper No. 189). Wellesley, MA: Wellesley College Center for Research on Women.

Nieto, S. (1992). *Affirming diversity: The sociopolitical context of multicultural education*. New York: Longman.

Schniedewind, N., & Davidson, E. (1983). *Open minds to equality: A sourcebook of learning activities to promote race, sex, class, and age equity*. Englewood Cliffs, NJ: Prentice Hall.

Sleeter, C. A. (1994, Spring) . White racism. *Multicultural Education, 5-8*.

Tatum, B. D. (1992). Talking about race, learning about racism: The application of racial identity development theory in the classroom. *Harvard Educational Review, 62*, 1-24.

Tatum, B. D. (1994). Teaching White students about racism: The search for White allies and the restoration of hope. *Teachers College Record, 95*, 462-476.

Wellman, D. (1993). *Portraits of White racism* (2nd ed.). New York: Cambridge University Press.

Teaching About Unintentional Racism in Introductory Psychology

Thomas E. Ford
Western Michigan University

Robert W. Grossman
Elizabeth A. Jordan
Kalamazoo College

After the director of multicultural affairs at Kalamazoo College suggested that teaching about racism would foster appreciation of cultural diversity (J. Baraka-Love, personal communication, August 16, 1992), we developed a unit on unintentional racism for the introductory psychology course. A 50-min group discussion of a case study preceded a 50-min lecture on unintentional racism and a second 50-min group discussion of the case study. The goal of this unit was to help White faculty teach classes of mainly White students about subtle forms of racism.

Case Study

In discussion groups (*n* = 20), students read a case study describing a White professor's behavior toward Tim, the only African American student in the class. Tim attended class sporadically and performed poorly on assignments. The professor made generous offers to help, but Tim continually missed appointments. Students wrote and then discussed reasons for Tim's behavior and how they would have reacted if they were the professor. Next, students learned that Tim had failed the class and that the professor attributed Tim's failure to lack of academic skills and motivation. However, Tim enrolled in the professor's course the next semester and earned an A. When the professor asked what had changed, Tim replied that he now owned a car. Em explained that he missed classes and appointments the previous semester because White bus drivers often would not stop for him. Students wrote and discussed their reactions before reading that the professor concluded he was a racist because his attributions for Tim's poor performance were unfair. Again, students

300

wrote and discussed their reactions to the professor's conclusion.

From discussion of the conclusion, students learned that they did not share the same definition of racism. Conflicting definitions centered around two issues. First, does racism imply differential treatment of minority group members? Some students argued that the professor was not racist because he treated Tim in a color-blind manner—as he would any other student. Others claimed that the professor's color-blind perspective is precisely why he was racist. The professor failed to consider Tim as an individual who faced unique social constraints and barriers that impeded academic achievement (e.g., encounters with racist bus drivers who refused to pick him up for school). Second, does racism imply malicious intentions? Some students believed that the professor should not be considered racist because he did not intentionally discriminate against Tim. Other students, however, argued that although the professor did not intentionally discriminate, his behavior and thoughts contributed to Tim's difficulties and thus were racist.

Unintentional Racism

During the next class, we presented a lecture on unintentional racism based on Gaertner and Dovidio's (1986) dichotomy of old-fashioned racism characterized by overt hatred for African Americans or other minorities and aversive (unintentional) racism characterized by a more complex, ambivalent racial attitude of White Americans. Aversive racists typically avoid acting in a racist manner and regard themselves as nonprejudiced. However, they almost unavoidably feel discomfort, uneasiness, or fear in the presence of African Americans, and this negative affect is frequently unacknowledged because it conflicts with one's egalitarian self-concept (Gaertner & Dovidio, 1986). Aversive racists do not intentionally discriminate against African Americans. Rather, they are likely to discriminate only when their behavior can be easily rationalized as nondiscriminatory (i.e., Gaertner,1973; Gaertner & Dovidio, 1977).

In this lecture we also introduced the concept of fundamental attribution error (FAE; e.g., Fiske & Taylor, 1991). The FAE can have racist implications because Whites are more likely to make derogatory dispositional attributions (e.g., the student who fails an exam is dumb) for an African American's behavior relative to a White's behavior (Frey & Gaertner, 1986) Pettigrew, 1979).

In the discussion after the lecture on unintentional racism, students readily comprehended the FAE's racist implications in the professor's attributions for Tim's academic difficulties. Many students also admitted to making the FAE themselves when explaining Tim's behavior. Some of the more popular attributions presented Tim as disliking the class and being shy, lazy, *responsible, or embarrassed by his poor performance.

Strategies for Dealing With the Emotional Intensity of Discussions

Consistent with Weinstein and Obear (1992), the case study and lecture prompted strong emotional reactions. Five strategies permitted civil but full expression of the strong emotions. First, introducing the concepts of aversive racism and FAE allowed students to use those concepts to understand the case and thus, respond on an intellectual as well as an emotional level. Second, using three class periods to complete the unit helped temper initial emotional reactions, permitting "cooler" consideration of "hot" topics in latter discussions. Third, having students write their reactions before voicing them helped balance the expression of feelings and ideas. Fourth, having the instructor write comments on the chalkboard encouraged students to critique those comments rather than the individuals presenting them. Finally, labeling emotions expressed by students (e.g., "You sound really angry about this.") helped to keep those emotions directed toward an individual's opinion and not the individual. In sum, each of these strategies contributed to directing emotional reactions toward ideas and away from other students.

Student Responses to the Unit

Students ($N = 77$) rated the extent to which they agreed with the following statements designed to assess the effectiveness of the unit: "This unit helped me understand unintentional racism," and "This unit was an interesting learning experience." Ratings were made on a 5-point scale ranging from 1 (*strongly disagree*) to 5 (*strongly agree*) . Responses to the first item suggest that the unit helped students better understand unintentional racism ($M = 4.08$, $SD = .76$). Supporting this conclusion, many White students noted in "minute papers" their susceptibility to behaving and thinking in ways that may have racist implications. In addition, 2 African American students commented that the lecture on aversive racism helped them understand certain experiences they had had with White people. Students also reported that the unit was interesting ($M = 3.96$, $SD = .87$).

For extra credit, students ($N = 64$) also completed a questionnaire (Katz & Hass, 1988) to assess Whites' attitudes toward African Americans. One 10-item subscale of the questionnaire measured positive attitudes toward African Americans; a second 10-item subscale measured negative attitudes. In one class, students ($n = 21$) responded to the questionnaire 1 day before completing the unintentional racism unit, and in a second class students ($n = 43$) responded 4 days after completing the unit.

Responses to each subscale were averaged to form aggregate measures of positive and negative attitudes. Each of these aggregate measures was subjected to a one-way analysis of variance with questionnaire administration (preunit, postunit) serving as the between-subject factor. Results on the positive-attitude measure indicate that students who completed the unit did not report more favorable attitudes toward African Americans ($M = 4.16$, $SD = .76$) than students who had not completed the unit ($M = 4.07$, $SD = .64$), $F(1, 62)$ $p < 1.0$. However, results on the negative-attitude measure show that students who completed the unit reported significantly less negativity ($M = 2.81$, $SD = .87$) than students who had not yet completed the unit ($M = 3.35$, $SD = .76$), $F(1, 62) = 6.27$, $p = .015$. This finding provides some encouraging, albeit preliminary, evidence that our unit may temper negative racial attitudes. Of course, to draw unequivocal conclusions about the effectiveness of the unit, more systematic research in which students are randomly assigned to conditions (e.g., completing the questionnaire before vs. after participating in the unit) is necessary.

Although the data reflected positive responses to the unit, almost 25% of the students criticized it. For instance, some students said the case was biased (e.g., "Too one-sided—there are many other types of racism than mere Whites being racist toward Blacks"; "He [the lecturer] was trying to place guilt on the White majority, and this made me a little uncomfortable").

Summary and Conclusions

Teaching about unintentional racism can promote awareness of how our behavior and thought processes may subtly and unconsciously discriminate. Through the concepts of aversive racism and FAE, students considered the possibility that racism can be the product of normal cognitive processes of educated, sensitive people like themselves. This unit is a valuable contribution to the introductory psychology curriculum, but we have used it successfully in other courses as well (e.g., Social Psychology, Psychology of Prejudice). Finally, the unit can be modified to fit one extended class period (e.g., a 1 hr and 20 min session) by limiting discussion of the case to the first half of the period and presenting a shortened lecture on aversive racism and the FAE during the second half of the period.

References

Fiske, S. T., & Taylor, S. E. (1991). *Social cognition* (2nd ed). New York: Random House.

Frey, D., & Gaertner, S. L. (1986). Helping and the avoidance of inappropriate interracial behavior: A strategy that perpetuates a nonprejudiced self-image. *Journal of Personality and Social Psychology, 50,* 1083-1090.

Gaertner, S. L. (1973). Helping behavior and racial discrimination among liberals and conservatives. *Journal of Personality and Social Psychology, 25,* 335-341.

Gaertner, S. L., & Dovidio, J. F. (1977) . The subtlety of white racism, arousal, and helping behavior. *Journal of Personality and Social Psychology, 35,* 691-707.

Gaertner, S. L., & Dovidio, J. F. (1986).The aversive form of racism. In J. F. Dovidio & S. L. Gaertner (Eds.), *Prejudice, discrimination, and racism: Theory and research* (pp. 61-89). Orlando, FL: Academic.

Katz, I., & Hass, R. G. (1988). Racial ambivalence and American value conflict: Correlational and priming studies of dual cognitive structures. *Journal of Personality and Social Psychology, 55,* 893-905.

Pettigrew, T. F. (1979). The ultimate attribution error: Extending Allport's cognitive analysis of prejudice. *Personality and Social Psychology Bulletin, 5,* 461 476.

Weinstein, G., & Obear, K. (1992). Bias issues in the classroom: Encounters with the teaching self. In M. Adams (Ed.), *Promoting diversity in college classrooms: Innovative responses for the curriculum, faculty, and institutions* (pp. 39-50). San Francisco: Jossey-Bass.

Notes

1. Authors are listed alphabetically; all authors made equal contributions to this article.
2. The case study described herein was developed by Robert W. Grossman in a White awareness workshop sponsored by a grant from the Upjohn Company.
3. We thank reviewers for their helpful comments.
4. Requests for copies of the White awareness workshop should8;e sent to Robert W. Grossman, Department of Psychology, Kalamazoo College, 1200 Academy Street, Kalamazoo, Ml 49007; e-mail: grossman@kzoo.edu.

10. INTEGRATING SOCIAL PSYCHOLOGY AND PERSONALITY

Linking Dispositions and Social Behavior: Self-Monitoring and Advertising Preferences

Melinda Jones
University of Pittsburgh at Bradford

Social psychologists have devoted considerable attention to understanding the effects of personality and the self on specific social behaviors (Snyder & Ickes, 1985). Despite this attention to the integration of personality and social psychology, students may underestimate the extent to which dispositions influence everyday social behavior. One effective way to demonstrate the link between personality and social behavior is to show students how a disposition they possess (self-monitoring propensity) is related to interesting differences in consumer behavior.

Self-monitoring refers to how individuals control and regulate their self presentation in social situations (see Snyder, 1987, for a review). High self-monitoring individuals (as identified by their relatively high scores on the Self-Monitoring Scale; Snyder, 1974; Snyder & Gangestad, 1986) typically act in accordance with the demands of their social setting. They are attuned to the image they project to others, and they are particularly adept at regulating their self-presentation to fit these situational demands. As a result, their behavior may change from situation to situation. In contrast, low self-monitoring individuals rely on their attitudes, beliefs, and values to guide their behavior. Consequently, they are more likely than high self-monitoring individuals to show greater consistency in their behaviors from one situation to the next.

Research suggests that these differences in self-monitoring propensity may be reflected in differing preferences for advertising strategies (DeBono & Packer, 1991; Snyder & DeBono, 1985). Because high self-monitoring individuals tend to be acutely sensitive to the image they project to others, they tend to be more responsive to image-oriented ads that emphasize the extrinsic rewards associated with a product (e.g., prestige). Low self-monitoring individuals are less concerned with situational and interpersonal considerations, and they accord greater weight to inner states (e.g., attitudes and dispositions). Thus, these individuals are more responsive to quality-based advertising that emphasizes the intrinsic rewards associated with the product.

In this article, I describe a demonstration, based on Snyder and DeBono (1985), linking self-monitoring tendencies and reactions to advertising strategies. In addition to getting students to think about advertising in a novel way, this demonstration relates an individual difference variable to an important everyday behavior.

Method

The instructor needs to collect magazine advertisements to be displayed on slides. Fortunately, finding ads that represent image-oriented and quality-oriented advertisements is easy. To create the stimulus materials, randomly select 30 to 35 advertisements from popular magazines (e.g., *Cosmopolitan, Newsweek,* and *Time*). Ask a small group (about 15) of undergraduates who are not taking the course to rate each ad on two 7-point scales: an image orientation scale ranging from *not at all image oriented* (1) to *very image oriented* (7) and a quality orientation scale ranging from *not at all quality oriented* (1) to *very quality oriented* (7). Subtract the average quality score from the average image score for each item to determine the five ads that are most predominantly image oriented and the five ads that are most predominantly quality oriented. Slides of these ads serve as the stimuli.

To introduce this exercise, describe how individual difference variables may affect social behavior. However, avoid specifically discussing self-monitoring orientation in order to reduce potential demand characteristics.

First, students complete the 18-item Self-Monitoring Scale (Snyder & Gangestad, 1986). Next, tell students that they will see 10 slides for 15 s each. Then, tell students they are to answer these questions—"Overall, how effective do you think this ad is?," and "Overall, how appealing do you think this ad is?"—using a 7-point scale ranging from *not at all* (1) to *very* (7). To assist with students' ratings, provide an answer sheet listing the rating scales for each slide.

After students rate the slides, provide an answer key to the Self-Monitoring Scale (keyed in the high self-monitoring direction) so students can score their own Self-Monitoring Scale. A simple median split yields high and low self-monitoring groups. (In my class, the median was 9.5.) Then, identify the image-oriented and quality-oriented advertisements and have students find their total appeal rating and total effectiveness rating for each of the five image-oriented and each of the five quality-oriented advertisements. Students then pass all materials to the front of the room.

Data analysis can be geared to the students' degree of statistical sophistication If students are generally unfamiliar with statistical analysis, the instructor may analyze the data outside of class and present the results in a sense of graphs at the next class meeting. For statistically sophisticated students, the class can compute descriptive statistics and conduct t tests or analyses of variance, testing for differences in high and low self-monitoring individual's' ratings of the appeal and effectiveness of the image-oriented ads and of the quality-oriented ads. These tests should indicate that high self-monitoring individuals rated the image-oriented ads as more appealing and more effective than did low self-monitoring individuals. Conversely, low self-monitoring individuals should rate the quality-oriented ads as more appealing and more effective than do high self-monitoring individuals.

Although the link between self-monitoring orientation and preferences for advertisements is a fairly robust finding in the social psychological literature, the tests from this demonstration may fail to reach statistical significance in small classes. Instructors may use this opportunity to discuss issues relating to sample size and sampling variability.

Evaluation

Using 7-point scales ranging from *not at all* (1) to *extremely* (7), students ($N = 67$) in my recent social psychology course evaluated this demonstration on four dimensions. Students indicated that the demonstration was interesting ($M = 5.40$, $SD = 1.06$), informative ($M = 5.64$, $SD = 1.16$), and effective ($M = 5.55$, $SD = 1.10$). They recommended its use in future classes ($M = 6.19$, $SD = .86$). Students also rated very favorably the overall quality of the demonstration ($M = 4.28$, $SD = .69$) on a 5-point scale ranging from *poor* (1) to *excellent* (5) .

Students' open-ended comments on the survey were overwhelmingly positive as well: "This activity used data from us and applied it to what we are currently learning. And it did so in an interesting way." "This demonstration will probably make the concept of self-monitoring more memorable." "It brought a bit of reality into the classroom." "I never really thought much about image-based and quality-based ads. Now I know what to look for in advertisements." Judging from both the quantitative and qualitative sections of the survey, students found the demonstration to be a useful learning experience.

Discussion

This classroom demonstration has many advantages for instructors. First, it can be used in a number of courses, including introductory psychology, personality, social psychology, and consumer psychology. Second, students are interested and involved in the demonstration because they have seen many of the advertisements selected for the demonstration. Finally, this demonstration facilitates discussion on a number of follow-up topics, such as how advertisements influence the viewer and how image-oriented and quality oriented ads may reflect the soft-sell and hard-sell strategies used in the advertising industry (Fox, 1984). In addition, instructors could discuss how self-monitoring is related to other aspects of social behavior, such as friendship formation (Jamieson, Lydon, & Zanna, 1987; Snyder, Gangestad, & Simpson, 1983), motivations for forming dating relationships (Jones,1993), and commitment in dating relationships (Snyder, Simpson, & Gangestad, 1986).

Overall, this demonstration effectively increases students' knowledge of the strategies advertisers use to sell products. More important, it reveals the impact that an individual difference variable may have on consumer preferences.

References

DeBono, K. G., & Packer, M. (1991). The effects of advertising appeal on perceptions of product quality. *Personality and Social Psychology Bulletin, 17,* 194-200.

Fox, S. (1984). *The mirror makers.* New York: Morrow.

Jamieson, D. W., Lydon, J. E., & Zanna, M. P. (1987). Attitude and activity preference similarity: Differential bases of interpersonal attraction for low and high self-monitors. *Journal of Personality and Social Psychology, 53,* 1052-1060.

Jones, M. (1993). Influence of self-monitoring on dating motivations. *Journal of Research in Personality, 27,* 197-206.

Snyder, M. (1974). The self-monitoring of expressive behavior. *Journal of Personality and Social Psychology, 30,* 526-537.

Snyder, M. (1987). *Public appearances/private realities: The psychology of self-monitoring.* New York: Freeman.

Snyder, M., & DeBono, K. G. (1985). Appeals to image and claims about quality: Understanding the psychology of advertising. *Journal of Personality and Social Psychology, 49,* 586-597.

Snyder, M., & Gangestad, S. (1986). On the nature of self-monitoring: Matters of assessment, matters of validity. *Journal of Personality and Social Psychology, 51,* 125-139.

Snyder, M., Gangestad, S., & Simpson, J. A. (1983). Choosing friends and activity partners: The role of self-monitoring. *Journal of Personality and Social Psychology, 45*, 1061-1072.

Snyder, M., & Ickes, W. (1985). Personality and social behavior. In G. Lindzey & E. Aronson (Eds.), *Handbook of social psychology* (3rd ed., pp. 883-947). New York: Random House.

Snyder, M., Simpson, J. A., & Gangestad, S. (1986). Personality and sexual relations. *Journal of Personality and Social Psychology, 51*, 181-190.

Notes

1. An earlier version of this article was presented at the 15th Annual National Institute on the Teaching of Psychology, St. Petersburg Beach, FL, January 1993.

2. I thank Melissa Ford and James Little for their assistance in preparing the stimulus materials and analyzing the student evaluations and Ruth L. Ault and the anonymous reviewers for their helpful comments on a draft of this article.

Forming and Testing Implicit Personality Theories in Cyberspace

Miri D. Goldstein
Gustavus Adolphus College

Through its rising popularity, the Internet is leading to a notable change in the nature of human interactions. In 1995, the number of people using the Internet was between 20 and 40 million, with the number of users growing rapidly (Lewis, 1995). Indeed, International Data Corporation (1996), a provider of market research, predicted that the total number of Internet users by the end of the decade will reach 163 million. The growing interest in the Internet is understandable: It offers instant and engaging access to information, resources, databases, and electronic bulletins. More important, the Internet also offers instant access to fellow Internet users.

In the past, first encounters with others occurred at places such as the town market or a coffee shop. The Internet allows one to "meet" others in chat rooms, "talk" via e-mail, and to make introductions with a personal web page. The Internet thus offers a unique and convenient platform for examining various aspects of social behavior, specifically social perception (e.g., impression formation, interpersonal attraction, impression management).

The study of social or person perception examines how individuals form impressions and make judgments of others. Simply stated, social perception researchers address the question "how do we think about other people?" (for reviews, see Anderson & Sedikides, 1991; Fiske, 1993;

Hamilton & Sherman, 1996). Some theorists suggest that processes of social perception follow a rational, almost scientific script (e.g., Kelley, 1955). However, others posit that when forming impressions, people operate more like "cognitive misers" than scientists (Taylor, 1981). In other words, we take mental shortcuts whenever we can. An example of such a shortcut is the formulation of implicit personality theories (IPT's; see Schneider, 1973).

IPT's are sets of assumptions about what personality traits are associated with one another. In other words, people are perceived in terms of trait covariations. For example, on learning that a certain individual is physically attractive, one might also assume that he or she is smart, savvy, and self-confident. In this example of an IPT, the traits of physical attractiveness, intelligence, and social composure are assumed to co-occur. Therefore, individuals make inferences about other people's personalities on the basis of little information. Such theories are implicit because they are often unconscious and are not formally stated. Moreover, they often are not tested.

Because IPT's are often not subjected to objective tests, an important question addressed by researchers is "where do IPT's come from?" One possibility is that such theories reflect the actual distribution of traits among stimulus persons. Using my previous example, perhaps physically attractive people are smart, savvy, and self-confident. Research, however, has demonstrated that IPT's are biased by a variety of situational, cognitive, cultural, and linguistic factors (e.g., Alloy & Tabachnik, 1984; Anderson, 1995; Crocker, 1981; Schneider, 1973; Trolier & Hamilton, 1986).

To assess IPT's, psychologists provide individuals with a series of personality traits and instruct them to rate the degree to which each trait is characteristic of a target person (e.g., Rosenberg & Olshan, 1970). To interpret the data, researchers subject the resulting matrix of intercorrelations to statistical methods of reduction, typically factor analysis, multidimensional scaling, or cluster analysis. Alternatively, researchers apply the concurrence likelihood method (e.g., Warr & Sims, 1965). Using this method, individuals indicate the likelihood that target persons have Trait A, given that they have Trait B.

Traditional social perception research presents the target person in a written description, a videotaped vignette, or in a face-to-face interaction (e.g., Chiu, Hong, & Dweck, 1997 Gilbert, Pelham, & Krull,1988; Sherman & Klein,1994) . The Internet presents an novel and exciting platform for examining impression formation processes.

Information on the Internet is posted as a page of text and visual images. Many individuals maintain personal home pages that function as electronic presentations of the self (or certain aspects thereof). For students and researchers of social perception, the emergence of personal home pages is of specific interest because home pages represent a new form of both self-presentation and attempts at impression management. In the following sections, I describe an exercise that allows students to formulate IPT's by accessing personal home pages on the World Wide Web (Web). Moreover, students further test their theories by "directly" approaching the target of their theory via e-mail.

Exercise Objectives

The exercise's principal objective is to complement and augment discussion of IPT's within a more general discussion of the field of person perception. Students view a personal home page of a psychologist and apply the methods traditionally used in IPT research to form an impression of their target. This exercise thus illustrates what IPT's are and how psychologists scientifically assess IPT's. Furthermore, students examine the degree of agreement across their theories, potentially illustrating the subjective nature of IPT's. By contacting the target of their IPT, students can test their IPT and examine whether conflicting data result in a change from their preliminary IPT. The exercise thus demonstrates the stability or malleability of IPT's. This hands-on exercise should facilitate discussion and scrutiny of IPT's as a form of social perception.

Exercise Description

Forming IPTs

This exercise is most appropriate for students in introductory level psychology classes (e.g., Social Psychology, Personality Psychology, General Psychology). Direct your students to a web site authored by Scott Plous (1997) that lists social psychologists' home pages. They will use this list to identify the Uniform Resource Locator (the web page address) of the home page of a psychologist that provides them with enough material from which to form an IPT. Because students will later contact their target to test their theory, I recommend that students conduct this exercise in small groups. This will reduce the volume of contacts to the psychologists listed on Plous's home page.

Data collection. First, remind your students that the amount or content of information needed to form IPT's is subjective. Thus, the students should determine and justify the criteria they use to choose a certain web page. Once each group has identified a web page, ask them to individually complete a trait rating of their target (for sample forms, see Anderson & Sedikides, 1991; Rosenberg & Olshan, 1970). In addition, ask students to provide a written description of their theory, supported by quotes and printouts from the web site. Students should use the following questions to guide their reports:

1. Who is this person?
2. What is this person like?
3. What information from the web page allowed you to form your IPT?
4. Would you like to get to know this person?

To further illustrate the capacity of the Web for the formation of IPT's, instruct your students to write a web page for themselves. Due to equipment, time, and programming knowledge constraints, you might not want to require students to post their page on the Internet. Remind students that they are providing other people with information about themselves in designing their web page. Ask students to consider what they want people to know about them and which aspects of their personality they would like to share with others. Instruct them to discuss the tone their page would take (e.g., humorous or serious). Once they have completed designing their pages, ask them to describe the IPT that a stranger might derive by viewing their page and identify information from the page that a viewer would use in such a theory. Students should also reflect on how this IPT might differ from a theory as the result of a real-life interaction.

Data reduction. To simply yet effectively illustrate the scientific examination of IPTs, instructors need not include any statistical analyses in the exercise. Some instructors, however, might want to demonstrate how psychologists use statistical analyses to evaluate IPTs. The following guidelines will assist these instructors.

The level of analysis you use to evaluate the IPTs formed by your students should depend on your students' statistical background and your own course objectives. Factor analysis and other multivariate forms of data analysis are beyond the scope of most introductory level courses. If you would like to illustrate some of the statistical analyses researchers use to study IPTs, instruct each group of students to aggregate their trait ratings (forming a Trait × Perceiver matrix). If you have not already done so, this would be a good time to provide students with a brief overview of means and correlation's. You might also clarify the limitations of the current analyses (e.g., small sample size, use of descriptive statistics only). Instruct your students to calculate the mean rating for each trait and the correlation matrix for the traits. Following a brief explanation of how researchers might use cluster analysis and factor analysis to examine IPTs (Everitt & Dunn, 1992), ask the students to visually assess which trait ratings appear to be most characteristic of the target and whether certain traits appear to cluster together, as indicated by their correlations.

Additional analyses. To examine the degree of agreement in IPT's across students, instructors might require students to calculate an index of interrater reliability. For example, the value of an intraclass correlation for two raters is based in part on the correlations between their ratings, but also on the differences between the means and standard deviations of the two sets of scores (see Cronbach, Gleser, Nanda, & Rajaratnam, 1972; Hays, 1994).

Time permitting, you might require that students rate the web pages generated by the other students. Students will thus be able to assess whether perceivers did in fact arrive at the IPT they desired to produce.

Testing IPTs

To further explore their IPTs and test their accuracy, instruct each group of students to contact the target of their IPT by e-mail. The purpose of this contact is to establish a personal interaction with each target, thus providing another source of information about the target's personality. All targeted home pages on Plous's (1997) web site include e-mail addresses, and many encourage correspondence. As a professional courtesy, please e-mail the targets identified by the students alerting them in advance of the potential for student correspondence. Advise them of the upcoming message, and identify a particular subject title that students will use on the e-mail (e.g., "IPT Class Exercise") . This will allow targets to easily ignore the message if they are unable or unwilling to respond.

Instruct students to politely identify themselves and to explain that the reason for the contact was a classroom exercise on the nature of IPTs on the Internet. In their e-

mail messages, they should briefly share their specific IPT's (omitting any negative impressions) and ask for comments on the following issues: How did the targets decide what information to present in their web pages? Did they feel that their web page was a true reflection of their personality? Were they trying to project a certain image with their page? Encourage your students to ask other specific questions that are of interest to them. However, remind them to keep their messages brief, professional, and polite. As a precautionary measure, ask students to forward all communications to you. You will thus be able to monitor the professional tone of your students' messages. I recommend that you contact the targeted social psychologists following the exercise and thank them for their participation.

Inform your students that you will ask them to reevaluate their IPT based on their target's response (or lack of response). Ask them to, once again, complete a trait rating of their target and submit a written report, based on their current IPT. You could ask students to assess their trait ratings for postcontact changes in ratings.

Exercise Integration

Once students have completed the various stages of the exercise, you can discuss its implications. Use the following questions in a classroom discussion of this exercise:

1. How easy was it for you to form an impression of your target?
2. Did you find that certain traits appeared to be more characteristic of your target than other traits?
3. If so, did the presence of these traits lead you to assume the presence of other traits?
4. Are there certain characteristics of home pages that led to a specific impressions (e.g., use of color, animation, nature of material included) ?
5. In what ways is impression formation based on a web page similar or different from that based on other types of interaction?

Students might note that they found the process of assigning trait ratings artificial. Such comments (or eliciting such comments) provide an elegant transition to discussion of theories of social perception that are not based on simple associations between traits (see Anderson & Sedikides, 1991). For example, the dimensional view suggests that people think about others in terms of a small number of global dimensions, rather than as a series of trait covariations (e.g., McCrae & Costa, 1987). On the other hand, typological views suggest that we think about others in terms of person types, which may be described as exemplars (e.g., Smith, 1992), multiple feature sets (Hayes-Roth & Hayes-Roth, 1977) or prototypes (e.g., Andersen & Klatzky, 1987).

Student Evaluation of the Exercise

I conducted this exercise in an introductory Social Psychology class. For many students, this exercise resulted in their first exposure to the Internet. In fact, many of the students were surprised by the abundance of information available on the Internet. Moreover, students were excited about the opportunity to interact with prominent social psychologists who, up to that point, had been reduced to a reference in a text book. As one student pointed out: "With a click of the mouse and a twist of the wrist, I just met Dr. X, labeled her personality, and formed an opinion of her. All without ever talking with her." Students unanimously reported being amazed at how well they believed they knew their targets after the exercise. Indeed, students noted being somewhat uncomfortable at the ease with which they labeled another individual's personality. One student noted: "I would like to think that I don't make such quick personality attributions about people because they aren't fair . . . this exercise was hard for me because I had to admit that I do."

Other students reported being less comfortable with the validity of their impressions. One student commented: "What I saw was what he wanted seen. Also, I did not see anything too in depth. I don't know who he really is—I can't!" In the context of such comments, I encourage students to discuss the differences between impressions formed in cyberspace and those formed face to face or through other forms of interaction. For example, I ask students to characterize the ease of implementing impression management strategies (e.g., Goffman, 1959; Schlenker, 1980) in various types of interactions.

Students were excited about contacting the target of their theory to, as one student put it, "take [the exercise] a step further and find out if we were right." These interactions most often served to further confirm student-generated IPTs and resulted in pleasant interactions. As indicated by the following comment, some students were inspired to learn more about their targets: "It was really exciting to hear from a 'famous psychologist.' . . . I have since read some of her work, and I feel cool because I had one-on-one contact with her." However, sometimes these interactions resulted in information that conflicted with

Table 1. Mean Student Ratings for Questions Assessing the Value of the Internet Exercise

Question	M	SD
The exercise clarified my understanding of IPTs.	4.1	0.67
I enjoyed this exercise.	4.8	0.39
I enjoyed the opportunity to contact the target of my theory.	4.5	0.71
My general understanding of social perception was enhanced by this exercise.	4.3	0.65
I recommend using this exercise in future classes.	4.8	0.45

Note. N = 27. Ratings were based using a 5-point scale ranging from 1 (*strongly disagree*) to 5 (*strongly agree*). IPTs = implicit personality theories.

students' theories. For example, some students who formed negative impressions of their targets were surprised by friendly and warm responses. On the other hand, some students were forced to incorporate somewhat negative information (such as might result from a dry, formal response or the lack of any response whatsoever) into an otherwise rosy personality description. One student noted that:

> From the simple fact that Dr. Y included personal information about himself, I concluded that he was a very open, friendly, and approachable person. But after receiving his very impersonal message, I learned that, quite to the contrary, he was not at all enthusiastic about a contact from an interested students.

Such instances easily lead to lively discussions of the stability or malleability of IPTs in light of inconsistent information (e.g., Hastie & Kumar, 1979) and the validity of IPTs. They also lead to a more general discussion of accuracy in interpersonal perception (e.g., Kenny & Albright, 1987).

Students formally evaluated the value of this exercise as a teaching tool, using a 5-point scale ranging from 1 (*strongly disagree*) to 5 (*strongly agree*) . As indicated in Table 1, students viewed the exercise as positive and enjoyable. Most important, they reported that the exercise enhanced and clarified their understanding of the topic in question.

Discussion

The web exercise allows students to experience the powerful impact that IPTs have on impression formation. Moreover, students learn firsthand about prominent figures in the field of social psychology. More important, much of the information students obtain from web pages would not be included in a traditional review class. Indeed, aside from serving the pedagogical purpose of enhancing students' understanding of IPTs, this exercise augments the traditional lecture and textbook classroom by personalizing the individuals behind the research discussed in class. Thus, students can learn about a certain psychologist's hobbies, sense of humor, family, and even current research. I have found that encouraging students to access such information increases students' engagement and excitement regarding the topic at hand. This exercise demonstrates to students that the field of social psychology includes active researchers who are excited about their research and their lives. Thus this exercise emphasizes that social psychology as a discipline is not limited to historical figures and classic research but rather is alive and current.

References

Alloy, L. B., & Tabachnik, N. (1984). Assessment of covariation by humans and animals: The joint influence of prior expectations and current situational information. *Psychological Review, 91*, 112-149.

Andersen, S. M., & Klatzky, R. L. (1987). Traits and social stereotypes: Levels of categorization in person perception. *Journal of Personality and Social Psychology, 53*, 235-246.

Anderson, C. A. (1995). Implicit personality theories and empirical data: Biased assimilation, belief perseverance and change, and covariation detection sensitivity. *Social Cognition, 13*, 25-48.

Anderson, C. A., & Sedikides, C. (1991). Thinking about people: Contributions of a typological alternative to associationistic and dimensional models of person perception. *Journal of Personality and Social Psychology, 60*, 203-217.

Chiu, C., Hong, Y., & Dweck, C. S. (1997). Lay dispositionism and implicit theories of personality. *Journal of Personality and Social Psychology, 73*, 19-30.

Crocker, J. (1981). Judgment of covariation by social perceivers. *Psychological Bulletin, 90*, 272-292.

Cronbach, L. J., Gleser, G., Nanda, H., & Rajaratnam, N. (1972). *The dependability of behavioral measurements: Theory of generalizability for scores and profiles.* New York: Wiley.

Everitt, B. S., & Dunn, G. (1992). *Applied multivariate data analysis.* New York: Oxford University Press.

Fiske, S. T. (1993). Social cognition and social perception. *Annual Review of Psychology, 44*, 155-194.

Gilbert, D. T., Pelham, B. W., & Krull, D. S. (1988). On cognitive busyness: When person perceivers meet persons perceived. *Journal of Personality and Social Psychology, 54*, 733-739.

Goffman, E. (1959). *Presentation of self in everyday life.* Garden City, NY: Doubleday.

Hamilton, D. L., & Sherman, S. J. (1996). Perceiving persons and groups. *Psychological Review, 103*, 336-355.

Hastie, R., & Kumar, P. A. (1979). Person memory: Personality traits as organizing principles in memory for behavior. *Journal of Personality and Social Psychology, 37*, 25-38.

Hayes-Roth, B., & Hayes-Roth, B. (1977). Concept learning and the recognition and classification of exemplars. *Journal of Verbal Learning and Verbal Behavior, 16*, 321-338.

Hays, W. L. (1994). *Statistics* (5th ed.). Fort Worth, TX: Harcourt Brace.

International Data Corporation. (1996, November). *Unprecedented growth in global usage of the Internet and the World Wide Web* [Report Abstract]. Retrieved January 8, 1997 from the World Wide Web: http://www.idcresearch.com/HNR/cpr4ic.htm

Kelley, H. H. (1955). *The psychology of personal constructs.* New York: Norton.

Kenny, D. A., & Albright, L. (1987). Accuracy in interpersonal perception: A social relations analysis. *Psychological Bulletin, 102*, 390-402.

Lewis, P. H. (1995, May 29). The Internet and gender. *The New York Times, p. 39.*

McCrae, R. R., & Costa, P. T. (1987). Validation of the five-factor model of personality across instruments and observers. *Journal of Personality and Social Psychology, 52*, 81-90.

Plous, S. (1997). *Home pages of social psychologists* [Electronic listing of social psychologists on the World Wide Web]. Retrieved October 7, 1997 from the World Wide Web: http://www.wesleyan.edu/spn/profs.htm

Rosenberg, S., & Olshan, K. (1970). Evaluative and descriptive aspects in personality perception. *Journal of Personality and Social Psychology, 16*, 619-626.

Schlenker, B. R. (1980). *Impression management: The self-concept, social identity, and interpersonal relations.* Monterey, CA: Brooks/Cole.

Schneider, D. J. (1973). Implicit personality theory: A review. *Psychological Bulletin, 79*, 294-309.

Sherman, J. W., & Klein, S. B. (1994). Development and representation of personality impressions. *Journal of Personality and Social Psychology, 67*, 972-983.

Smith, E. R. (1992). The role of exemplars in social judgment. In L. L. Martin & A. Tesser (Eds.), *The construction of social judgments* (pp. 107-132). Hillsdale, NJ: Lawrence Erlbaum Associates, Inc.

Taylor, S. E. (1981). The interface of cognitive and social psychology. In J. Harvey (Ed.), *Cognition, social behavior, and the environment* (pp. 189-211). Hillsdale, NJ: Lawrence Erlbaum Associates, Inc.

Trolier, T. K., & Hamilton, D. L. (1986). Variables influencing judgments of correlation relations. *Journal of Personality and Social Psychology, 50*, 879-888.

Warr, P. B., & Sims, A. A. (1965). A study of cojudgment processes. *Journal of Personality, 33*, 598-604.

Note

I thank David Pittenger, David Simpson, Randolph Smith, Saera Khan, Kim Davis, and two anonymous reviewers for their thoughtful and helpful comments on an earlier version of this article

Self-Monitoring and Commitment to Dating Relationships: A Classroom Demonstration

Jeffry A. Simpson
Texas A&M University

Individual differences can be strongly and systematically related to important aspects of social behavior. However, students are not always aware of and may underestimate the extent to which dispositions are associated with significant areas of their lives. One way to highlight the impact of dispositions on social behavior is to show students how a specific disposition they possess relates to an important aspect of their own social behavior. To introduce students to this topic, I use a classroom demonstration that reveals how a widely studied individual difference dimension (self monitoring orientation) is meaningfully related to an important social behavior (commitment in dating relationships).

Self-monitoring orientation is assessed by an 18-item true/false inventory known as the Self-Monitoring Scale (Snyder, 1974; Snyder & Gangestad, 1986). The scale identifies persons whose behavior tends to be guided by what is socially appropriate in a given situation (high self-monitors) and persons whose behavior tends to be guided by their own attitudes, beliefs, and feelings, regardless of the situation at hand (low self-monitors). High self-monitors tend to endorse items such as, "In different situations and with different people, I often act like very different persons" and "I'm not always the person that I appear to be." Conversely, low self-monitors tend to endorse items such as, "I have trouble changing my behavior to suit different people and different situations" and "I can only argue for ideas that I already believe."

Because their social behavior tends to be guided by relatively stable factors, such as personal attitudes and feelings, low self-monitoring individuals should have stable relationships with persons toward whom they have strong, positive attitudes and feelings (e.g., dating partners). On the other hand, because their social behavior typically is guided by less stable, more transient external factors, such as concerns about social and situational appropriateness, high self-monitoring individuals should have less durable and rather short-term relationships with others. Relationship stability and permanence serve as indicators of commitment to relationships (Kelley, 1983); therefore, self monitoring should be strongly associated with orientations individuals adopt toward commitment in dating relationships. In fact, high self-monitors typically do adopt an uncommitted orientation to dating relationships, whereas low self-monitors tend to adopt a committed one (Snyder & Simpson, 1984). To demonstrate this association, two studies reported by Snyder and Simpson can be replicated as part of the following classroom demonstration.

Method

Students first complete the Self-Monitoring Scale. (The scale and its scoring instructions can be found in Synder & Gangestad, 1986.) Students then respond to a Dating Survey attached to the Self-Monitoring Scale. The Dating Survey is presented in Table 1.

The survey assesses past dating behavior and willingness to change dating partners, both of which are components of commitment to relationships (Kelley, 1983). Students who answer "yes" to the first question on the survey (i.e., those who are dating one person exclusively) are referred to as *exclusive daters*. Students who answer "no" to the first question but "yes" to the third one (i.e., those who are not dating one person exclusively but who have dated at least two people in the past year) are referred to as *multiple daters*. Those who respond "no" to both questions because they are married or do not date cannot provide data for classroom analysis. However, only about 15% to 20% of undergraduates enrolled in daytime courses typically fall into this category. Although these students cannot provide data themselves, they find the exercise just as interesting, educational, and valuable as do students who can.

Once students have completed the survey, they score their own Self-Monitoring Scale as the high self-monitoring response to each of the items is read out. The scale is keyed in a high self-monitoring direction. Students scoring above the median are classified as high self-monitors, and those scoring below the median are classified as low self-monitors. Students turn to Questions 6 through 8 on the Dating Survey to record the total number of items they selected a friend over the current partner as a preferred dating partner. They then pass all materials to the front of the room.

Table 1. Dating Survey

1. Are you currently dating someone *exclusively* (that is, one person and no one else)? (Check one.)

    Yes _____   No _____

2. If yes, how many *months* have you dated this person?

    _____

    (If you answer question No. 2, go to Question No. 5. If you did not, go to Question No. 3.)

3. If you are *not* dating one person exclusively at the present time, have you dated at least two different people in the past year? (Check one.)

    Yes _____   No _____

4. If yes, how many different persons have you dated in the past year? _____

5. If you are currently dating someone (whether exclusively or not), please write your current (or most steady) dating partner's initials on the first line below. Then write the initials of 3 opposite-sex friends on the lines that follow.

    Current partner _____   .

    Friend No. 1 _____

    Friend No. 2 _____

    Friend No. 3 _____

6. If you could *ideally* form a close, intimate dating relationship with either your current dating partner or Friend No. 1, whom would you choose? _____

7. If you could *ideally* form a close, intimate dating relationship with either your current dating partner or Friend No. 2, whom would you choose? _____

8. If you could *ideally* form a close, intimate dating relationship with either your current dating partner or Friend No. 3, whom would you choose? _____

Results

One of the most desirable features of this exercise is that it allows students to see data generated and analyzed. I first focus on students' responses to Questions 2 and 4 on the Dating Survey, both of which deal with past dating behavior. I create four columns on the chalkboard, one for each of the four groups on which dating history data have been collected. They are: high self-monitoring—exclusive daters, high self-monitoring—multiple daters, low self-monitoring—exclusive daters, and low self-monitoring—multiple daters. The raw data are then written on the chalkboard.

Once the data have been reproduced, a student calculates the mean and variance for each of the four groups. I then compute two *t* statistics, one to test for differences in the number of months high and low self-monitoring—exclusive daters have dated the current partner, and one to test for differences in the number of different partners high and low self-monitoring—multiple daters have dated in the past year. Among exclusive daters, low self-monitoring students should report that they have dated their current partner for a significantly longer time than should high self-monitoring students. Among multiple daters, high self monitoring students should indicate that

they have dated a significantly larger number of different persons in the past year than should low self-monitoring students. These outcomes provide support for individual differences in commitment as revealed in past dating behavior.

Occasionally, these *t* tests may not reach significance because of small class sizes or the presence of extreme scores. Under these circumstances, the proportion of high and low self-monitoring students who classified themselves as exclusive and multiple daters can be calculated. I then compute two *z* statistics, one to test for differences in the proportion of high and low self-monitors who are dating someone exclusively, and one to test for differences in the proportion of high and low self-monitors who have dated multiple partners. A larger proportion of students classified as exclusive daters should be low, rather than high, self monitors. Conversely, a larger proportion of students classified as multiple daters should be high, rather than low, self-monitors. These outcomes provide additional evidence for individual differences in commitment to dating relationships.

I next focus on the total number of friends students chose instead of the current partner as the preferred dating partner. I create two columns on the chalkboard, one for high and one for low self-monitoring students, and list the total number of friends chosen by each respondent. A student then calculates the mean and variance for each of the two groups and I compute a *t* statistic to test for differences in the number of friends chosen in place of the current dating partner by high and low self-monitoring students. High self-monitors should choose a significantly larger number of friends as preferred dating partners than should low self-monitors. This result provides support for individual differences in commitment as revealed in willingness to change dating partners.

When class sizes are small and/or extreme scores exist, I compute a *z* statistic to test for differences in the proportion of high and low self-monitors who express a preference for dating someone other than their current partner. A larger proportion of high, rather than low, self-monitors should express such a preference. This result provides further evidence for individual differences in commitment to dating relationships.

If time does not permit the instructor to analyze the data in class, the data can be analyzed outside of class and the results presented during the next class meeting. Depending on students' familiarity with statistical issues and the content of the course, the instructor may want to present the results in a series of graphs and/or use alternative test statistics (e.g., chi-squares) to analyze the data.

Discussion

This demonstration has several desirable features. First, it tends to replicate well. Second, it is suitable for use in a variety of courses, including personality, social,

313

interpersonal relations, motivation, and human sexuality. Third, men and women do not differ in their responses to the Dating Survey. Fourth, it can be used in classes of 30 or more students. And fifth, students find the exercise interesting and educational.

Students ($N = 60$) in one of my recent courses evaluated the demonstration on several dimensions. Using 7-point Likert-type scales ranging from *not at all* (1) to *extremely* (7), students indicated that the demonstration was interesting ($M = 5.83$, $SD = .86$), educational ($M = 5.33$, $SD = .91$), and effective relative to other classroom demonstrations they had participated in ($M = 5.70$, $SD = .69$). Moreover, 58 out of 60 students (96.67%) recommended that the demonstration should be used in future courses.

This exercise provides the instructor with a number of follow-up discussion topics. First, it can be used to introduce and discuss additional theory and research on selfmonitoring (see Snyder, 1979, 1987, for reviews of selfmonitoring research). For example, to clarify why high and low self-monitoring students might adopt different orientations to commitment, the instructor can discuss how selfmonitoring is systematically related to other important areas of behavior that might influence commitment (e.g., attitude-behavior consistency). Second, because the demonstration replicates previous work, it gives the instructor an opportunity to discuss the importance of replication in research. When the demonstration does not replicate, the instructor can discuss how sampling variability and extreme responses affect the replication process. Finally, the demonstration can result in a discussion of whether individual differences in

commitment are likely to be stable over time and across the life span of whether they are likely to be transient states associated with only one stage of life (the college years).

References

Kelley, H. H. (1983). Love and commitment. In H. H. Kelley, E. Berscheid, A. Christensen, J. H. Harvey, T. L. Huston, G. Levinger, E. McClintock, L. A. Peplau, & D. R. Peterson (Eds.), *Close Relationships* (pp. 265-314). San Francisco: Freeman.

Snyder, M. (1974). The self-monitoring of expressive behavior. *Journal of Personality and Social Psychology, 30*, 526-537.

Snyder, M. (1979). Self-monitoring processes. In L. Berkowitz (Ed.), *Advances in experimental social psychology* (Vol. 12, pp. 85-128). New York: Academic.

Snyder, M. (1987). *Public appearances/private realities: The psychology of self-monitoring*. New York: Freeman.

Snyder, M., & Gangestad, S. (1986). On the nature of selfmonitoring: Matters of assessment, matters of validity. *Journal of Personality and Social Psychology, 51*, 125-139.

Snyder, M., & Simpson, J. A. (1984). Self-monitoring and dating relationships. *Journal of Personality and Social Psychology, 47*, 1281-1291.

11. EXAMINING MISCELLANEOUS ISSUES

Using the World Wide Web to Teach Everyday Applications of Social Psychology

Richard. C. Sherman
Miami University

The World Wide Web (Web) is an exciting new tool for teaching college courses in psychology. The potential benefits of the Web stem from the wealth of information it makes available to instructors and students, the ease of access to that information, and the "hypermedia" richness of Web documents. However, instructors must take care in evaluating educational claims for the Web. Proponents of many technological innovations, including those who promote educational uses of the Web, often do not consider the possible practical difficulties and pitfalls of implementation, and they make recommendations without adequate assessment of the impact of new technologies. Indeed, some recent reports indicate that negative outcomes may occur if teachers do not pay careful attention to designing student experiences in web-oriented courses (Locatis & Weisberg, 1997; Rothenberg, 1997). In this article, I describe my experiences in introducing the Web into an advanced course in social psychology, and I attempt to evaluate the strengths and weaknesses of using the Web in this context.

Course Background and Context

Social psychology is a popular undergraduate topic at most institutions, and it is often a core element in the psychology curriculum. My department's course offerings are typical in this content area and consist of an introductory survey course, an advanced course that builds on the introductory content, and a collection of courses that focus on specific topics. Enrollments in the introductory course are typically 60 to 70 students, usually with multiple sections in a given term. Enrollments in the advanced and topically focused courses are smaller, ranging from 10 to 30 students. Given the experimental nature of the Advanced Social Psychology (ASP) course described here, the size of the class was at the low end of the range (10 students). However, there is nothing inherent in the principles employed that would prevent their use with larger classes.

The exact content and emphasis in the ASP course are left to the instructor and vary from term to term. For example, one offering of the course might emphasize cognitive approaches to social phenomena. Another might stress group interaction. A third might focus on cross-cultural comparisons. In the section of ASP I describe, the emphasis was on translating theoretical principles and empirical research findings into useful analytic tools for understanding everyday social events from a social psychological perspective. Although the applicability of social psychology to problems of living in a social world might seem obvious, my observation is that students often do not connect their academic or classroom knowledge to extracurricular life experiences (see also Duch, 1996; Wilson, 1994). My motivation was to explore ways of getting them to do so.

The common pedagogical approach in the ASP course is to emphasize reading and discussion of original source material, often accompanied by short reaction or analysis papers. Other typical elements include one or two topical presentations to the class, a major term paper that involves analysis and synthesis of literature research on a topic of the student's choosing, and two or three essay examinations.

Amplifying and Transforming Effects of Instructional Technology

In planning changes to the ASP course, it became immediately apparent that there were a number of ways to incorporate the Web, each with alternative implementations that seemed to have different possible effects on the structure and focus of the course. In discussing these changes, it is useful to consider two broad categories of potential impact that technological innovations can have (Kiesler, 1997) . First, technology can *amplify* certain capabilities, functions, or processes that are already in place. For example, using the Web as an electronic bulletin board to post the course syllabus, reading assignments, copies of old exams, and other materials makes information more easily available to students than conventional means (handouts or library reserve materials).

However, technological innovations may also transform the way people function and interact, thus producing fundamental changes in their roles and relationships. In educational settings transformation may occur when computer-based learning technologies alter the traditional roles of student and teacher by shifting the focus from instructor-centered to student-centered activities (Collins, 1991; Locatis & Weisberg, 1997; Menges, 1994; Reinhardt, 1995). For example, in a traditional classroom setting the instructor controls the flow of information though lectures, selection of assigned readings, or other means. In a computer-mediated learning environment students are more likely to confront information directly, through activities involving electronic databases and interactive courseware. The role of the student in these activities shifts from recipient—consumer to producer—participant. Students "transform information from one medium to another, and they create new knowledge as a result of their interactions with teachers and other students" (Menges, 1994, p. 183). The role of the instructor is changed from controller of information to guide or coach—one who facilitates or assists students in sampling and interpreting material.

Amplifying Components in the ASP Course

I used the Web in ways that had both amplifying and transforming effects. Amplification followed from using the Web as a course organizational tool. I created a class web site (http://miavx1.muohio.edu/~shermarc/p324.htmlx) that served as a repository of relevant course information that students could consult at any time. The site included the course syllabus and schedule, team assignments for various projects, exam questions, project instructions, and the class roster with e-mail addresses. It also included information that was unique to the Web aspect of the course, such as a collection of Web tools (links to search engines, online news sources, and several compendia of Internet resources relevant to psychology). Also unique were links relevant to the topics of the off-line assigned readings. For example, links to the campaign pages of the 1996 presidential candidates and to political analyses of campaign developments accompanied the assigned reading on attitudes and persuasion (Petty, 1995).

There were two noteworthy aspects of using the Web in these ways. First, the centralization and electronic format of course information made it easy for students to access materials at any time and from many locations both on and off campus. Although the traditional method of placing materials on library reserve centralizes information, availability is restricted in time and place. Second, it was easy to add new information or to change existing material, and I could do both at any time and from a variety of locations. The medium gave me greater flexibility as an instructor because I did not have to distribute materials or make announcements during class meetings. For example, even though the class met on Tuesdays and Thursdays, I frequently posted information at other times, announcing during a preceding class meeting that I was going to do so. An unintended effect of these changes was that important course events frequently took place out side of the designated meeting time. Given students' tendency to isolate classroom experiences from other aspects of their lives, I regard the occurrence of class activities outside the regular meeting times as a positive move toward reducing that isolation.

Tranformational Components in the ASP Course

Beyond using the Web as an organizational tool, several features of my experimental introduction of the Web into the ASP course had more transformational effects and are therefore perhaps more interesting from a pedagogical point of view. These features involved Web activities that entailed, to varying degrees, collaboration and knowledge sharing, direct experience with information in various formats, and manipulation of information into new forms. The activities included Web Assignments associated with assigned readings, a Social Psychology and Humor project, a Social Psychology in the News project, and the development of a Web Tutorial on a social psychological topic.

Web Assignments

The Web Assignments directed students to explore Internet links relevant to social psychological principles contained in the assigned readings and then to answer online questionnaires about their experiences and observations. The starting point for each exploration was the collection of links for each reading assignment that I provided on the course website, and each questionnaire asked students to assess how the links illustrated specific principles. For example, in considering the topic of attitudes and persuasion, I asked students to compare the campaign web pages of then-Presidential candidates Dole and Clinton and evaluate the relative effectiveness of the pages in terms of persuasion principles discussed in the assigned readings. Another part of the same assignment directed students to the websites of political parties in other countries and asked them to interpret platform similarities and differences relative to current U.S. political campaign issues. The same assignment also included a more open-ended component in which I directed students to explore links that were not in the existing collection and to locate a website that they believed illustrated a particular persuasion principle. They specified the location of the site on their questionnaire and described their reasons for selecting it.

I compiled the questionnaire responses for each assignment and posted them on the course website. In the following class meeting, I gave a verbal summary of the responses and occasionally asked a student to amplify or clarify a response that I regarded as particularly interesting or insightful. Posting questionnaire responses to the Web allowed students to share their observations with each other and gave the assignments a social importance they would not have otherwise had—students knew that their observations would be public and would potentially impact the thinking of other students. Thus, although students worked on the Web independently, the assignment contained an implicit collaborative component.

Social Psychology and Humor

Many instructors, including myself, frequently attempt to illustrate principles and concepts by showing cartoons drawn by professional artists. This technique can provide an interesting and entertaining introduction to a topic and can also serve as a convenient and memorable reference for subsequent discussions. I find, however, that cartoons that seem humorous to me do not necessarily produce the same reaction among undergraduates. To counter this problem, I randomly assigned students to teams and gave them the task of selecting a cartoon that they found humorous and relevant to social psychological principles, leading a class discussion of the cartoon, and producing a written analysis of the cartoon that I then published on the course website. The relevance of a selected cartoon could be in terms of how it illustrated some concept, theory, or line of inquiry or in terms of how certain concepts or principles were useful in understanding the emotional or intellectual impact of the cartoon.

Team members met at least three times outside class to complete their assignment. The first meeting was organizational, focusing on possible topics and sources of cartoons. At the second meeting students shared and discussed the cartoons they found, made a final selection, and planned their class presentation. I linked the cartoon to the course website, along with the team's suggestions to the rest of the class regarding ways to prepare for the upcoming discussion. At the final meeting the team produced their written analysis, which often included insights contributed by other class members during the general discussion.

Social Psychology in the News

A second team project involved selecting a current news event and analyzing it from a social psychological perspective. I again assigned students to teams randomly, with the constraint that the teams did not have students who were previously teammates on the humor project. As with the humor project, the team members met outside of class to evaluate possible topics, led an in-class discussion of their selection, and produced a written analysis that I posted on the course website. Prior to the class discussion, I posted the team's preliminary analysis of the topic for others in the class to examine. I exploited the availability of online news sources and other reference material in this project by encouraging the teams to include hypertext links in their preliminary and final analyses to give them depth and substance. This activity brought students into direct contact with information sources and provided opportunities for collaboratively evaluating and transforming the information they encountered. Deciding on which links to include and how to incorporate the links into the narrative required team members to think carefully about how their topic related to other events and concepts and required them to evaluate the usefulness and appropriateness of information sources on the Internet.

Another positive aspect of the Web component of the news project was that nonteam members who examined the preliminary analyses seemed motivated and informed by them and consequently contributed actively and effectively to the class discussions. For example, one team's analysis of the TWA Flight 800 crash of 1996 included links to personal backgrounds of the victims and to online causal theories that illustrated various aspects of counterfactual thinking and biased processing. Class members who examined these links saw an intimate connection between an emotion-charged event and specific social psychological principles that helped them understand the intensity of emotional reactions and the distortions in the ways observers and participants interpreted the event.

Development of Web Tutorials

By far the most challenging and rewarding aspect of incorporating the Web into the ASP course was the web tutorial project. I gave teams of students the task of developing a web-oriented tutorial on a social psychological topic of their choosing. Members of each team were not teammates for the other projects. The tutorial project was an ongoing activity for most of the semester and students completed it in stages, with each team providing progress reports for the rest of the class and receiving interim reactions and suggestions from other class members. I published the final versions of the tutorials on the course website with students identified as the authors.

My motivation for developing the tutorial project came from the fact that when I was planning the course I could find few examples of web tutorials in social psychology, whereas demonstrations and tutorials were available for other psychological topics, such as visual and auditory perception, learning and memory, and biopsychology.[1] It seemed to me that having students create social psychological tutorials would have a dual benefit of adding to the range of Internet resources in psychology

---

[1]The following are examples of collections of tutorials and demonstrations in psychology http://server.bmod.athabascau.ca/html/aupr/demos.htm; http://psych.hanover.edu/Krantz/tutor.html; http://psych.hanover.edu/APS/exponnet.html. Collections that contain material pertaining more to personality and social psychology include the following: http://sticky.usu.edu/~psychol01/cyb_social.html; http//www.wesleyan.edu:80/psyc/psyc260/; http://Miavxl.MUOhio. edu/~psy2cwis/webinfo. html.

and simultaneously challenging class members to apply their knowledge of social psychological principles in a way that would provide a positive educational experience for others.

One of the most challenging aspects of the tutorial project for me was providing students with enough structure and guidance to keep them focused and on track, while still maintaining the student-oriented nature of the project. A decision that I had to make early in the project, for example, was how much of the technical features of producing web documents students would have to learn. My assessment was that the focus of the project should be on the content of the topic, not on computer programming skills. Most students in the class had little prior experience with creating web documents, and although the language for producing web materials is not complex, learning it would have detracted from the substantive focus of the course. My solution was to act as the students' technical consultant—the teams provided me with the content and layout of their project, instructed me how they wished it to appear in web form, and I applied the necessary technical manipulations to produce the final result. This arrangement was certainly a transformation of the usual student and instructor roles in the sense that students directed my activities rather than the other way around. It also provided students experience with a common type of collaborative work arrangement in which conceptualization and production are separate yet interdependent roles.

A second challenge was how to give the student teams structural parameters for the tutorial when there were no examples to show them. My solution was somewhat arbitrary and based only on my intuitive grasp of pedagogical theory, although it seemed to provide reasonable guidance for the students. The minimal requirements for the tutorial included an opening document with hypertext links to three subtopic pages. The opening document and each subtopic page were two to three manuscript pages long. Students wrote this material based on their research of the topic. The tutorial included a minimum of five references to original source material and at least four links to "external" Web sites, with the links distributed across at least two of the tutorial pages. Finally, the opening page and each subtopic page contained at least one graphical element (picture, diagram, chart, etc.) that students chose to illustrate, amplify, or clarify the text.

Evaluation

The amplifying and transforming aspects of using the Web had both positive and negative impacts on the course. On the negative side, the amount of time I spent in preparation for the ASP class was greater than for other courses. In part this increased time was due to the technological demands of the web components, particularly in preparing and maintaining web documents. In addition, some of the increase in time demand involved interacting with students outside of class as part of the

"guide" and "coach" instructor role that the various individual and team projects entailed. Of course, it is likely that additional interaction would also occur with nonweb-oriented innovations that are student centered in other ways, and one could argue that additional time spent interacting with students outside of class is beneficial to both students and the instructor.

Another shortcoming of the Web orientation of the course was a tendency for the technology to overshadow content. As one student commented on the course evaluation, "I think that there might have been a little too much emphasis on using the Internet at the expense of information about social psychology." Another student gave a specific example of this problem when evaluating the educational benefit of the web tutorial project: "We spent more time looking for URLs [uniform resource locators—Web addresses] than learning about the concepts." These comments converge on my own assessment that at times I felt there was too much focus on procedure relative to substance. I note also that these comments provide retrospective support for my decision to serve as students' technical consultant for producing web documents, rather than having them learn the coding language to produce their own, because that would have devoted even more class time to technical matters.

These shortcomings may stem from the newness of the technology for most of the students, as revealed by a survey of the class taken during the first week of the semester. Forty-four percent of the class members indicated they had never used the Web in a college course, and another 33% reported using it in just one other course. Learning the basics of using web software and techniques for searching the Internet required going over computer procedures during class time and this necessarily reduced time available for discussing substantive topics related to social psychology. However, student familiarity with the Web is likely to grow quickly over the next few years, and the amount of technical instruction required will diminish. If so, future offerings of the course may avoid the problem of overemphasis of technology relative to substantive content.

Despite the limitations, I believe that the overall impact of incorporating the Web into the course was positive. My assessment is based on my own observations as well as the comments of students collected as part of the course evaluation and student responses to a questionnaire administered at the beginning of the semester and again at the end. Students seemed particularly motivated by the facts that their work was available for others to examine and that their projects might assist other students to learn about social psychology. For example, regarding the web tutorial project one student commented: "I felt I gained the most from this project because it can help others to learn." Other students focused on the accountability and authorship aspect of the web projects: "I think it's really cool to see my name on the Web—to know that my work exists there" and "by posting our answers to things on the

Web, I found myself checking my answers because I knew the potential existed for others to see them."

These quotes illustrate that students perceived that the Web activities had changed the nature of their role from passive and private receivers of information to active and identifiable producers of material with potential impact on the educational experiences of other people. This awareness of the "transforming" quality of technology (Kiesler, 1997) may allow students to evaluate other technological innovations and educational experiences more critically.

There was also evidence that the web activities helped students develop skills in applying social psychological principles to everyday life experiences. A student whose web tutorial focused on persuasion principles in advertising commented: "I found this to be a positive experience because every time I see an advertisement I start to analyze it." To varying degrees the other projects also heightened students' awareness of links between social psychological concepts and everyday events. For example, several students emphasized the positive contribution of the news analysis project: "I learned about a lot of psychological principles behind many events taking place around the world." "I found it very educational in learning how to evaluate everyday things in a social psychological perspective." "The news analysis was very positive. The election year made it especially interesting" and "this was helpful in applying social psychology to everyday occurrences."

A final bit of relevant evidence comes from student responses to a question about the quality of their experiences in working with computers. Students expressed how positive or negative it was for them generally to work with computers on a scale ranging from 1 (*very negative*) to 6 (*very positive*). Although fairly positive at the beginning of the term ($M = 4.3$, $SD = 1.6$), the average sentiment was even more so at the end of the course ($M = 5.0$, $SD = .9$). An examination of the individual responses revealed that none of the students changed in the negative direction, and 50% changed one or more points in the positive direction. It is perhaps worth emphasizing that the question was quite general and not explicitly restricted to the ASP course. Thus, the encouraging implication is that students may be willing to extend their positive experience with computer technology to other situations. As one student put it,

> On the first day of class I was scared after hearing about the extensive computer use, but now I realize how much better off I am with the knowledge. . . . I know more about the Web than I ever thought I would. . . . I think it will help a great deal m the future.

In summary, the experimental introduction of web components into the ASP course seems to have had three major outcomes. First, the web components engendered an overall positive response from students, as evidenced by their comments and questionnaire ratings. Second, the transforming aspects of the web activities were successful in heightening student motivation and involvement in the course. Third, the web projects were effective in achieving the course goal of increasing students' application of social psychological principles to everyday life experiences. Anyone contemplating similar kinds of activities should note the two primary shortcomings of using the Web in this context—increased demands on instructor time and an emphasis on procedural matters at the expense of substantive content. However, in this case these shortcomings were far outweighed by the positive aspects of using the Web as an educational tool.

References

Collins, A. (1991). The role of computer technology in restructuring schools. *Phi Delta Kappan, 73*, 28-36.

Duch, B. (1996, Spring). Problem based learning: A note from the editor. *About Teaching, 50.* Retrieved October 8, 1997 from the World Wide Web: http://www.udel.edu/pbl/cte/spr96-edit.html

Kiesler, S. (1997). Preface. In S. Kiesler (Ed.), *Culture of the internet* (pp. ix-xvi). Mahwah, NJ: Lawrence Erlbaum Associates, Inc.

Locatis, C., & Weisberg, M. (1997). Distributed learning and the internet. *Contemporary Education, 68*, 100-103.

Menges, R. J. (1994). Teaching in the age of electronic information. In W. J. McKeachie (Ed.), *Teaching tips: Strategies, research, and theory for college and university teachers* (9th ed., pp. 183-193). Lexington, MA: Heath.

Petty, R. E. (1995). Attitude change. In A. Tesser (Ed.), *Advanced social psychology* (pp. 195-256). New York: McGraw-Hill.

Reinhardt, A. (1995, March). New ways to learn. *Byte, 50-72.*

Rothenberg. D, (1997, August 15). How the Web destroys the quality of students' research papers. *The Chronicle of Higher Education, p 44*

Wilson, J. (1994). The CUPLE Physics Studio. *The Physics Teacher, 32(9)*, 518-523. Retrieved October 8, 1997 from the World Wide Web: http://www.educom.edu/program/nlii/articles/wilson.html

Notes

1. The course revision described here was supported by a summer fellowship awarded by the Miami University Office for the Advancement of Scholarship and Teaching.

2. Portions of this work were presented to the 27 the Annual Meeting of the Society for Computers in Psychology, November 20, 1997, in Philadelphia.

3. The author gratefully acknowledges the skillful assistance of Undergraduate Teaching Fellow Maria Durante in the implementation of the World Wide Web activities and projects.

Robbers in the Classroom: A Deindividuation Exercise

David K. Dodd
Saint Mary College

A deindividuation demonstration, which I have developed and evaluated over the past 5 years, has yielded excellent results. The objective of the exercise is to illustrate deindividuation by asking students to imagine and anonymously report those behaviors in which they might engage if they were actually in such a deindividuated state. The idea for this demonstration is taken directly from Zimbardo (1979a), and is based more generally on Zimbardo's (1970) theory of deindividuation. Zimbardo defined deindividuation as "a complex process in which a series of social conditions lead to changes in perception of self and of other people," consequently "behavior that is normally restrained and inhibited is 'released' in violation of established norms of appropriateness" (1979b, p. 702). A major contributing factor to deindividuation, according to Zimbardo (1979b), is perceived anonymity, which psychologically protects individuals from being held responsible for their actions.

The primary purpose of this classroom demonstration is to illustrate the concept of deindividuation, and to reveal that even "normal, well-adjusted" college students are capable of highly inappropriate, antisocial behavior, given certain social and situational conditions. In the present study, 312 responses were generated from 229 undergraduate psychology students. Because 26 of the respondents were students in prison college programs, a secondary objective was to compare the responses of prisoners to nonprisoners in terms of the proportion and kinds of antisocial responses.

Method and Results

The deindividuation demonstration was used with 13 undergraduate psychology classes, including 11 general and 2 social psychology classes. Three classes (hereafter "prison") were conducted in maximum security prison settings: one of these classes was exclusively female and consisted of five respondents; the other two were exclusively male and consisted of 10 and 11 respondents. These students, all convicted of felonies, generally fell in the age range of 24-32, came from lower socioeconomic backgrounds, and were evenly divided between Caucasians and non-Caucasians. The remaining 203 respondents

(hereafter "campus") were enrolled in on-campus programs and were predominantly female, Caucasian, middle-class, and traditional college age (17-24).

The stimulus question for the demonstration was "If you could be totally invisible for 24 hours and were completely assured that you would not be detected, what would you do?" Because this instruction tended to yield many responses that were not humanly possible, such as "walk on the ocean" and "fly around at a party pinching people," the instruction was modified to, "If you could do anything humanly possible with complete assurance that you would not be detected or held responsible, what would you do?"

Students quickly recorded their responses and were asked to turn them in to the instructor, with no identifying information included. After receiving all the responses, the instructor outlined the basic premises of deindividuation theory and read the responses aloud to the class. The entire demonstration was usually completed in about 15 minutes.

In order to examine the deindividuation hypothesis, it was necessary to categorize and rate each response according to content and social desirability. After examining the data, the author established to content categories of responses: aggression, charity, academic dishonesty, crime, escapism, political activities, sexual behavior, social disruption, interpersonal spying and eavesdropping, travel, and a catch-all "other" category. To rate the social desirability of responses, the following terms and definitions were employed. *Prosocial* behavior was defined as intending to benefit others; *antisocial* behavior as injuring others or depriving them of their rights; *nonnormative* behavior as clearly violating social norms and practices, but without specifically helping or hurting others; and *neutral* behavior as meeting none of the above three definitions.

Three raters, blind to the specific deindividuation hypothesis and to the backgrounds of the individual respondents, independently categorized each response according to its content and rated its social desirability. A criterion of at least two-thirds agreement among the trio of raters was established, and this criterion was met for 97% of the responses for content and 98% for social desirability. Responses for which the criterion was not met were excluded from the relevant analyses.

322

Results revealed that 36% of the responses were antisocial, 19% nonnormative, 36% neutral, and only 9% prosocial. There was no significant difference between the social desirability of the responses of prison versus campus students, $\chi^2 (3) = 3.67$, *ns*. Regarding response content, the most frequent responses were criminal acts (26%), sexual acts (11%), and spying behaviors (11%); here again, the prison and campus students did not differ significantly, $\chi^2 (5) = 6.22$, *ns*. The most common single response was "rob a bank," which accounted for 15% of all responses, and jewel theft and counterfeiting were also popular responses under the "crime" category. Responses categorized as "sexual" were evenly divided among: sex with a famous person, stranger or casual acquaintance; sex with a lover; exhibitionism and public nudity; and voyeurism. Infrequent but notable responses from campus students included murder, rape, and political assassination.

Discussion and Evaluation

This is a highly educational and entertaining demonstration. When the instructions for this demonstration are given, there is invariably an immediate reaction of excitement and anticipation of the results. Indeed, the results provoke much laughter and surprise at such "murderous thoughts," as one student put it.

Evaluation data were collected from 53 subjects representing three different campus classes. On a 7-point scale (7 = *high value*, 1 = *little or no value*), the demonstrations received mean ratings of 5.5 and 5.8 for educational and entertainment value, respectively. These high ratings are corroborated by written and spontaneous comments from students, who frequently describe the demonstration as "fascinating," "funny," and "hard to believe!"

In addition to illustrating the concept of deindividuation, this exercise can also be used to demonstrate the strengths and weaknesses of statistical prediction. After collecting the responses from a class, but before examining them, I can boldly predict the kinds of responses that have just been turned in based on analyses of previous data. For example, it is safe to predict that responses involving bank robbery, spying, and sexual behavior will be quite frequent. Academic cheating and vandalism, although infrequent, will usually draw at least one or two responses from even a small class. Likewise, charitable responses, also infrequent, appear to be reliable in content, and usually include freeing hostages or solving international conflicts, alleviating social inequities such as poverty and hunger, and being kind to one's enemies.

Of course, I point out to my classes that my statistical predictions are based entirely on data obtained from previous demonstrations, and the issue of generalizing from one sample to another naturally arises. Furthermore, I emphasize that the data do not permit me (nor is it my intention) to predict the responses of individual students, and it is explained that this inability to predict the behavior of individuals is true of most social psychological research at this time.

Students are also impressed by the fact that no significant differences were found between my prison and campus students, regarding either the kinds of responses or the extent of their antisocial content. In this respect, the deindividuation demonstration emphasizes the important role of situational conditions, such as perceived anonymity, rather than personal traits or characteristics, in antisocial behavior. Therefore, the demonstration can be effectively used in conjunction with lecture or discussion of such social psychological studies as Milgram's (1974) obedience studies or Zimbardo's Stanford prison study (Haney, Banks, & Zimbardo, 1973), both of which also emphasize the crucial role of situational determinants of antisocial behavior. Finally, whether or not my students fully appreciate the "moral of the story," that is, the educational value of the exercise, they quite obviously delight in observing the antisocial and nonnormative responses that are elicited from their own classmates!

References

Haney, C., Banks, C., & Zimbardo, P. (1973). Interpersonal dynamics in a simulated prison. *International Journal of Criminology and Penology, 1*, 69-97.

Milgram, S. (1974). *Obedience to authority*. New York: Harper & Row.

Zimbardo, P. G. (1970). The human choice: Individuation, reason and order versus deindividuation, impulse, and chaos. In W. J. Arnold & D. Levine (Eds.), *Nebraska symposium on motivation, 1969* (pp. 237-307). Lincoln, NE: University of Nebraska Press.

Zimbardo, P. G. (1979a). *Instructor's resource book to accompany Psychology and Life* (l0th ed.). Glenview, IL: Scott, Foresman.

Zimbardo, P. G. (1979b). *Psychology and life* (l0th ed.). Glenview, IL: Scott, Foresman.

Table - Volume 3

Articles	Topics												
	1	2	3	4	5	6	7	8	9	10	11	12	13
Section I: Personality													
1. Discovering Students' Perspectives													
Wang, A. Y.	S									P			
Anderson, D. D., Rosenfeld, P., & Cruikshank, L.	S									P			
Embree, M. C.	S									P			
Dunn, D. S.	S									P			
Einhorn, J.	S									P			
2. Exploring Theories													
Miserandino, M.	S									P			
Bear, G.	S									P			
Carlson, J. F.	S								S	P			S
Handelsman, M. M.										P			
Polyson, J.										P			
Logan, R. D.										P	S	S	
3. Emphasizing Writing													
Mueller, S. C.										P			
Carlson, J. F.	S									P			
Beers, S. E.										P			
Section II: Abnormal													
1. Teaching with Simulations													
Lambert, M. E., & Lenthall, G.											P	S	
Rabinowitz, F. E.											P		
Osberg, T. M.	S										P		
2. Teaching with Case-Studies													
Procidano, M. E.										S	P	S	
Perkins, D. V.											P	S	
3. Teaching Abnormal Psychology Through the Arts and Literature													
Chrisler, J. C.											P	S	
Anderson, D. D.											P		
Chrisler, J. C.											P	S	
Fleming, M. Z., Piedmont, R. L., & Hiam, C. M.											P		
4. Examining Miscellaneous Issues													
Scogin, F., & Rickard, H. C.											P		
Hubbard, R. W., & McIntosh, L. J.											P	S	
Keutzer, C. S.	S	S	S	S	S	S	S	S	S	S	P	S	S
Wurst, S. A., & Wolford, K.						S			S		P	S	
Keeley, S. M., Ali, R., & Gebing, T.											P		

Articles	Topics												
	1	2	3	4	5	6	7	8	9	10	11	12	13
Section III: Clinical-Counseling													
1. Learning Concepts and Principles													
Bibace, R., Marcus, D., Thomason, D., & Litt, E. A.	S									S		P	
Parrott, L.	S									S		P	
2. Acquiring Skills--Undergraduate Students													
Lane, K.												P	
Balleweg, B. J.												P	
Suler, J. R.												P	
Fernald, P. S.										S		P	
Goldstein, G. S.			S	S	S	S	S	S	S	S	S	P	S
3. Acquiring Skills--Graduate Students													
Rickard, K. M., & Titley, R. W.												P	
Sommers-Flanaga, J., & Means, J. R.												P	
Anderson, D. D., Gundersen, C. B., Banken, D. M., Halvorson, J. V., & Schmutte, D.												P	
Weiss, A. R.												P	
4. Treating Fears													
Hughes, D.	S									S		P	
Lawson, T. J., & Reardon, M.	S									S		P	
5. Advocating a Research Perspective													
Osberg, T. M.			S									P	
Viken, R. J.			S									P	
Section IV: Social													
1. Focusing on Experimentation													
Carpenter, S.			S										P
Lutsky, N.			S										P
Wann, D. L.			S										P
Symbaluk, D. G., & Cameron, J.			S										P
Sattler, D. N., Back, S., & Pollitt, H.			S										P
2. Emphasizing Writing in Social Psychology													
Snodgrass, S. E.									S	S	S	S	P
Miller, S.										S	S	S	P
Osborn, D. R.													P
3. Illustrating Concepts in Social Perception and Social Cognition													
Eflin, J. T., & Kite, M. E.			S										P
McAndrew, F. T.													P
White, M. J., & Lilly, D. L.													P
Forsyth, D. R., & Wibberly, K. H.													P
Boatright-Horowitz, S. L.													P
Hom, H. L., Jr.													P
Berrenberg, J. L.	S												P
Lashley, R. L.	S												P

Articles	\multicolumn{13}{c}{Topics}

Articles	1	2	3	4	5	6	7	8	9	10	11	12	13
4. Demonstrating Bias in Social Perception and Social Cognition													
Kite, M. E.	S												P
Gordon, R. A.													P
Demakis, G. J.	S												P
Snyder, C. R.													P
Dunn, D. S.													P
Friedrich, J.													P
5. Teaching about Attitudes and Persuasion													
Carkenord, D. M., & Bullington, J.													P
Makosky, V. P.													P
Rajecki, D. W.													P
6. Exploring about Aggression													
Benjamin, L. T., Jr.	S		S										P
Dunn, D. S.										S			P
Davidson, W. B.													P
Rainey, D. W.	S												P
7. Examining Group Processes													
Peden, B. F., Keniston, A. H., & Burke, D. T.													P
Larsen, J. D.													P
Harton, H. C., Green, L. R., Jackson, C., & Latané, B.													P
Miserandino, M.													P
8. Teaching about Spatial and Nonverbal Behavior													
Gibson, B., Harris, P., & Werner, C.	S												P
Ferraro, F. R.	S												P
Grosch, J. W., & Sparrow, J. E.													P
Desforges, D. M., & Lee, T. C.													P
Costanzo, M., & Archer, D.													P
9. Examining Stereotypes of Gender and Race													
Gordon, R. A.													P
Goldstein, S. B.	S												P
Lips, H. M.													P
Jones, M.	S												P
Crawford, M.													P
Hebl, M. R.													P
Richard, H. W.													P
Lawrence, S. M.	S												P
Ford, T. E., Grossman, R. W., & Jordan, E. A.													P
10. Integrating Social Psychology and Personality													
Jones, M.										S			P
Goldstein, M. D.										S			P
Simpson, J. A.	S									S			P

Articles	Topics												
	1	2	3	4	5	6	7	8	9	10	11	12	13
11. Examining Miscellaneous Issues													
Sherman, R. C.													P
Dodd, D. K.	S												P

1	Introductory	8	Cognition
2	Statistics	9	Developmental
3	Research Methods	10	Personality
4	History	11	Abnormal
5	Physiological-Comparative	12	Clinical-Counseling
6	Perception	13	Social
7	Learning		

P = Primary   S = Secondary

Appendix-Volume 3

Forsyth, D. R., & Wibberly, K. H. (1993). *20*, 237-238.

Boatright-Horowitz, S. L. (1995). *22*, 131-133.

Hom, H. L., Jr. (1994). *21*, 36-37.

Berrenberg, J. L. (1987). *14*, 169-170.

Lashley, R. L. (1987). *14*, 179-180.

Demonstrating Bias in Social Perception and Social Cognition

Kite, M. E. (1991). *18*, 161-164.

Gordon, R. A. (1987). *14*, 40-42.

Demakis, G. J. (1997). *24*, 190-191.

Snyder, C. R. (1997). *24*, 197-199.

Dunn, D. S. (1989). *16*, 21-22.

Friedrich, J. (1996). *23*, 107-109.

Teaching about Attitudes and Persuasion

Carkenord, D. M., & Bullington, J. (1993). *20*, 41-43.

Makosky, V. P. (1985). *12*, 42-43.

Rajecki, D. W. (1989). *16*, 16-18.

Exploring about Aggression

Benjamin, L. T., Jr. (1985). *12*, 40-42.

Dunn, D. S. (1992). *19*, 112-114.

Davidson, W. B. (1990). *17*, 252-253.

Rainey, D. W. (1986). *13*, 138-140.

Examining Group Processes

Peden, B. F., Keniston, A. H., & Burke, D. T. (1990). *17*, 235-238.

Larsen, J. D. (1987). *14*, 230-231.

Harton, H. C., Green, L. R., Jackson, C., &

Latané, B. (1998). *25*, 31-35.

Miserandino, M. (1992). *19*, 103-106.

Teaching about Spatial and Nonverbal Behavior

Gibson, B., Harris, P., & Werner, C. (1993). *20*, 180-181.

Ferraro, F. R. (1990). *17*, 124-125.

Grosch, J. W., & Sparrow, J. E. (1992). *19*, 166-168.

Desforges, D. M., & Lee, T. C. (1995). *22*, 128-130.

Costanzo, M., & Archer, D. (1991). *18*, 223-226.

Examining Stereotypes of Gender and Race

Gordon, R. A. (1989). *16*, 209-211.

Goldstein, S. B. (1997). *24*, 256-258.

Lips, H. M. (1990). *17*, 197-198.

Jones, M. (1991). *18*, 231-233.

Crawford, M. (1994). *21*, 151-153.

Hebl, M. R. (1995). *22*, 186-188.

Richard, H. W. (1996). *23*, 159-161.

Lawrence, S. M. (1998). *25*, 198-200.

Ford, T. E., Grossman, R. W., & Jordan, E. A. (1997). *24*, 186-188.

Integrating Social Psychology and Personality

Jones, M. (1994). *21*, 160-161.

Goldstein, M. D. (1998). *25*, 216-220.

Simpson, J. A. (1988). *15*, 31-33.

Examining Miscellaneous Issues

Sherman, R. C. (1998). *25*, 212-216.

Dodd, D. K. (1985). *12*, 89-91.

Subject Index